JUSTICE ADMINISTRATION LEGAL SERIES

John C. Klotter, B.A., J.D.

Professor Emeritus and Former Dean
School of Justice Administration
University of Louisville

CRIMINAL EVIDENCE

Fifth Edition

anderson publishing co.
2035 reading road
cincinnati, ohio 45202
(513) 421-4142

Criminal Evidence, Fifth Edition

ISBN 0-87084-505-5

Library of Congress Catalog Number 91-70556

Kelly Humble *Managing Editor*   *Project Editor* Elisabeth Roszmann

PREFACE

Although the rules of evidence are most often directed to the courts and concern the admissibility of evidence at trial, in most criminal cases criminal justice personnel are as much concerned as the courts are with the rules. Whether the evidence is testimonial, documentary or real, much of it is discovered, prepared for trial and evaluated by police and corrections personnel. Failure to comply with the rules of evidence can so contaminate the evidence that it becomes worthless for purposes of prosecution and of less value in considering disposition of the cases.

This book is prepared primarily as a textbook for those involved in the administration of justice and those who are preparing for a career in criminal justice. No effort has been made to use local laws of any particular jurisdiction. However, as at least 26 states have adopted rules of evidence patterned after the Federal Rules of Evidence, and the states have looked to federal decisions for interpretation, much emphasis has been placed on the Federal Rules as interpreted by federal and state courts.

A study of criminal evidence necessarily involves legal principles discussed in such subjects as criminal law and constitutional law.[1] For example, the requirements for proving the elements of murder discussed in criminal law are related to evidence, and the search and seizure provisions of the Constitution limit the use of evidence in criminal cases. To keep this book within reasonable limits, only the traditional evidence rules are discussed in detail.

The cases used in this book are primarily criminal cases. However, in some instances civil or quasi-criminal cases are included in order to have a more comprehensive coverage of the subject matter.

In Part One of the book, the rules of evidence are stated, defined and discussed, with emphasis on those rules which are of most importance to justice personnel. In Part Two, leading decisions rendered by state and federal courts are included to give the reader an understanding of the rules

---

1 For a detailed discussion of substantive criminal law, *see* Klotter, CRIMINAL LAW (3d ed. 1990), Anderson Publishing Co., Justice Administration Legal Series. For a discussion of constitutional law principles, *see* Klotter & Kanovitz, CONSTITUTIONAL LAW (6th ed. 1991), Anderson Publishing Co., Justice Administration Legal Series.

and the reasoning of the courts in framing and explaining the rules. These decisions should be studied carefully by the student or reader.

When this book is used as a text, it is recommended that the student be required to brief the cases included in Part Two as well as additional cases which the instructor feels are of current importance. To make it possible for the reader to study cases relating to specific principles and rules, and to substantiate the conclusions reached, footnotes are included throughout the book.

CONTENTS

B. PROOF BY EVIDENCE AND SUBSTITUTES

CHAPTER 6
PRESUMPTIONS, INFERENCES AND STIPULATIONS   **91**

Section

C. GENERAL ADMISSIBILITY TESTS

D. EVIDENCE VIA WITNESS TESTIMONY

F. EXCLUSION OF EVIDENCE ON CONSTITUTIONAL GROUNDS

PART II

PART I
TEXT

A. HISTORY AND APPROACH TO STUDY

CHAPTER 1
HISTORY AND DEVELOPMENT
OF RULES OF EVIDENCE

The fundamental basis upon which all rules of evidence must rest—if they are to rest upon reason—is their adaptation to the successful development of the truth.
Funk v. United States, 290 U.S. 371 (1933)

§ 1.1   Introduction

The observer of the trial of a criminal case is often confused by the procedures he witnesses. Logically assuming that the purpose of the trial is to seek the truth, the lay observer is likely to be bewildered by objections to the introduction of apparently relevant evidence. Some evidence which could have a direct bearing on the case is in fact excluded at the trial in a criminal case. To understand why certain evidence is admitted and other evidence is rejected, it is necessary to study the long history of the rules of evidence.

§ 1.2   Early attempts to determine guilt or innocence

Through the ages, man has sought fair methods of reaching the truth in criminal cases. Each culture arrived at a method which was congenial to that culture. Some of these systems of determining guilt or innocence were ridiculous and often barbarous. However, a study of history has helped succeeding generations to develop systems that are more workable.

This study leads to the conclusion that every tribe and every people

1

devised a system for protecting the lives and property of its citizens. According to the authorities, however, there were only a few who developed a well-defined, organized, continuous body of legal ideas and methods which could be called a legal system. According to Wigmore, sixteen legal systems developed to a stage at which they could be recognized as such: Egyptian, Mesopotamian, Chinese, Hindu, Hebrew, Greek, Maritime, Roman, Keltic, Germanic, Church, Japanese, Mohammedan, Slavic, Romanesque, and Anglican.[1] Although all of these systems had some effect on modern evidence rules, only a few of the older systems have been selected for discussion, as these represent systems that were adopted in part by other cultures and eventually led to our judge-jury system, which in turn was responsible for our rules of evidence. Some of the procedures that developed under these systems are gone, and some remain.

To demonstrate that our system of evidence was adopted only after empirical investigation over many centuries, some of the methods used to determine guilt or innocence are described briefly.

a. Egyptian legal system

In the Egyptian system (the oldest of the systems listed above) the court was made up of thirty judges chosen from the states that constituted Egypt. The defendant was advised in writing of the charges against him, and he was authorized to answer each charge in writing by either (1) asserting that he did not do it; (2) that if he did it, it was not wrongful or (3) if it was wrongful, it should bear a lesser penalty than that advocated by his accusers. It is interesting to note that at this time (beginning at approximately 4,000 B.C.) all formal proceedings of the court were conducted without speeches from advocates. It was believed that speeches of advocates would cloud the legal issues, and that such speeches, combined with the cleverness of the speakers, the spell of their delivery, and the tears of the accused, would influence many persons to ignore the strict rules of law and the standards of truth.[2]

The Greek historian Diodorus describes the procedure developed by the Egyptians as follows:

> After the parties had thus twice presented their case in writing, then it was the task of the thirty judges to discuss among themselves their judgment and of the chief justice to hand the image of truth to one or the other of the parties.[3]

---

1   For a complete, interesting and informative study of the world's legal systems, see Wigmore, A Panorama of the World's Legal Systems (1928).

2   Wigmore, A Panorama of the World's Legal Systems (1928).

3   Kocourek & Wigmore, Sources of Ancient and Primitive Law, Evolution of Law Series (1915).

b. Mesopotamian legal system

Under the early Mesopotamian system, the king was the fountain of justice, receiving the law from divine guidance. But under King Hammurabi, approximately 2100 B.C., the administration of justice passed from the hands of the royal priests to a body of royal secular judges sitting at the great gate and marketplace of the city. A record of the trials of this period indicates that the judges called upon the accusers to "produce witnesses or instruments to show guilt." The judges then examined the facts and reached a conclusion as to guilt or innocence. This perhaps was the origin of the modern use of testimony and real evidence.[4]

c. Hebrew legal system

Under the Hebrew legal system, the rabbis developed the law in the early periods. However, the law was tied closely with religion, and the judges were considered to act with divine authority. Even after the Jewish people came under the control of the Persian, Greek and Roman rulers, they continued to have their own court system. Decisions were made by individual jurists. There appears to be no record of the use of a jury, or of counsel to represent the defendant.[5]

d. Chinese legal system

One of the earliest recorded legal systems in the world is the Chinese legal system, beginning before 2500 B.C. It is unique in that it is the only one that survived for approximately 4,500 years, until the country was taken over by the communists during this century. Under the ancient Chinese system, there was little difference between civil law and criminal law because the Chinese believed in the existence of the natural order of things, or the law of nature, and considered the written law good only if it was a correct translation of the law of nature. The decision as to guilt or innocence was made by one man—from emperor down to magistrate. Under the Chinese system, there was little distinction between morality and law, and in determining guilt or innocence there were no lawyers, as we know them now. There were notaries and brokers, but no licensed professional class. Decisions were made only by judges and these decisions could be reviewed by higher courts.[6]

e. Greek legal system

Unlike the systems previously discussed, under the early Greek legal system a jury determined if a person charged with a crime was guilty.

---

4   Wigmore, *supra* n. 2.
5   *Ibid.*
6   *Ibid.*

According to the records, in Athens in approximately 500 B.C., a jury list of about 6,000 or more names was drawn up. Ordinarily a panel of 201 names was drawn by lot, but for special cases a panel might consist of as many as 1,000 or 1,500 people. In the trial of Socrates, in about 400 B.C., 501 jurors voted and found a verdict of guilty by a majority of only 60. In one period in Greek history the decision of guilt or innocence was entirely in the hands of nonprofessionals. The presiding magistrate was selected by lot and the jurors were drafted from the whole citizen body. Under this system the defendant conducted his own defense and presented his own evidence. There was no presiding judge to declare the law, and there was no appeal.[7]

f.   Roman legal system

The Roman instinct for constitutional and legal ideas produced the best and most well-developed system of law. As this system had the greatest influence on modern evidence law, it is discussed in greater detail.

The Roman law system can be divided into three periods: the Period of the Republic, the Period of the Early Empire, and the Period of the Later Empire. During the Period of the Republic, the Romans began a code which was chiefly procedural. Even this early period, approximately 400 B.C., has influenced the law of the present day. During this period the lay courts were made up of judges both of law and fact, there was little judicial discretion of law, and there was no appeal. Under this early system the decision of the tribunal that first tried the case was final.

During the Early Empire Period, professional judges and jurors came to the forefront, while the culmination of Roman judicial science was reached in the second and third centuries A.D. By this time, the Roman legal system had developed far beyond that of any earlier civilization. The administration of justice was separated from general political administration, and schools of law were started for the training of lawyers. Also during this period, records of cases were kept, and according to Wigmore, these court records were of a type strikingly similar to those later kept in England.

During the Period of the Later Empire (about A.D. 550), Justinian undertook to reduce the enormous bulk of laws to manageable form. The results were the famous Pandects (or Digest), the Code, and the Institute.[8]

Jurisprudence had been one of the most advanced of Roman sciences, and it perished with the Roman government. But as other civilizations developed, the legal concepts developed by the Romans, including the use and admissibility of evidence, strongly influenced the later legal procedures. As a matter of fact, Quintilian's teachings, recorded about A.D. 68 to 88, contained legal precepts which are pertinent today and reveal how little the

---

7   *Ibid.*

8   *Ibid.*

nature of law practice has changed in 2,000 years. Some of the evidence rules, such as those relating to the testimony of witnesses and preparation of real and documentary evidence, are still valid today.

Thus we have examples of ancient systems in which guilt or innocence was determined by professional judges without the assistance of a jury, and examples of procedures in which the determination was made entirely by laypersons who were not instructed in the law. In some civilizations, the legal systems were well developed, while in others the administration of justice was a farce, with the person or group in power making decisions concerning life and liberty without guidelines or precedent.

Not only have the experiences of other cultures affected our own evidence rules today, but they have served as guides for other modern systems and surely will be considered during future attempts to reach a just and fair method of administering justice.

§ 1.3   Modern legal systems—Romanesque system

From the world's sixteen systems as described by Wigmore, three primary world systems exist today. These systems have spread beyond the country and race of their origin. These are the Romanesque, the Anglican and the Mohammedan. The two which are most dominant in modern times and of most importance in Western civilization are the Romanesque and Anglican.

Some five centuries after the Roman Empire fell, the law texts that were prepared by Roman scholars were resurrected and became the basis of the legal system, first in Italy, then in many other countries in Europe, and finally far beyond Europe. The city of Bologna in Italy became the center of the study of the Roman law, and legal scholars arrived from all over Europe. During the 1200s, 1300s and 1400s, thousands of foreign students carried the new advanced ideas of the Roman law to the countries of Europe. Faculties of law sprang up in Spain, France, Germany and the Netherlands. Roman law, or a modification of it, was codified and nationalized.

In the early 1800s, after three centuries of effort, France completed civil, criminal and commercial codes developed rules of civil and criminal procedure. Napoleon himself presided at many of the debates and his wishes shaped the code.9 This so-called Code Napoleon was soon translated into almost every language and set the fashion in the other countries of Europe. It was adopted in Austria in 1811, the Netherlands in 1838, Italy in 1865, Spain in 1888, Germany in 1898 and Switzerland in 1907. The Code had taken eight centuries from the resurrection of the Roman law in the 1100s

---

9   *Ibid.* at 1031.

to the final formation of the Romanesque law in the 1800s.

When the Romanesque system was first developed, the judges established the rules for gathering and admitting evidence and were the finders of fact as well as of the law. At first there were few rules of evidence, but eventually a complex set of rules for obtaining and weighing evidence evolved. As often happens, these rules began to be merely restrictive, that is, they were not guides but self-sufficient formulas.

The restrictive rules of evidence became so overdeveloped that by the end of the 1700s the system had been abolished in France and in other countries. To replace this system, the continental nations of France, Germany and Italy adopted a system that allowed a judge to hear and weigh any evidence, without limitations. Although certain rules have developed in recent times to limit the type and amount of evidence to be considered in this judge-directed system, there are no elaborate controlling rules, such as have been developed in the Anglo-American system. A main reason for this is that the judge's discretion, even when a jury is used, largely determines what evidence is to be admitted.

The Romanesque system is now used in many countries throughout the world, from Quebec to Cairo and from Budapest to Buenos Aires. At least 300 million people now live under this system, and of the three world systems today, the Romanesque system is the most extensive. In 1928 it governed almost one-sixth of the world's inhabitants.[10]

§ 1.4   —Anglican system

Unlike the other countries of Europe, England rejected the Romanesque legal system. Like other systems, the Anglican legal system developed in several phases. The first of these was "The Period of Building a Common Law," the second was "The Period of Rejection of the Romanesque Law," and the third was "The Period of Cosmopolitanization and Expansion."

The early methods of determining guilt or innocence in England were crude by our modern standards. For example, one kind of trial known as "trial by battle" was brought to the British isles by William the Conqueror in 1066. Instead of a formal trial before a judge, the accused was required to fight his victim or the victim's representative. This method of trial continued until the 1800s, when Parliament finally passed an act abolishing it.[11] The case which finally brought trial by battle to the attention of Parliament involved a man who was accused of murdering his sweetheart. He claimed the right of trial by battle. The judges, after considering the law

---

10   *Ibid.* at Chapter XV.
11   Tracy, Handbook of the Law of Evidence (1952).

in the matter, agreed that this type of trial had never been abolished. They therefore allowed the accused to select this type of trial. The brother of the deceased refused to fight the accused, and the accused went free.

Following the Norman Conquest, the Norman judges organized the jury to assist in their investigation. However, jurors were not selected as unbiased triers of fact, as is the practice today, but were selected because they had knowledge of the case. An ordinance of Henry II in the twelfth century provided that a certain number of jurors should be selected in criminal cases; it specified that jurors be knights.[12] In contrast to modern procedure, the prospective juror was excused if he was ignorant of the facts of the case. The jurors were first left to their own discretion in the use of evidence and were allowed to go among the people in the community and ask for information outside of court. During this period the jurors were forbidden to call in outside witnesses. However, starting about 1500, witnesses were used more frequently, and gradually the requirement that the triers of the facts possess knowledge of the crime came to be less important. By the end of the 1600s, the jury was allowed to receive no information except that which was offered in court. Thus, in a period of three or four hundred years, there was a complete reversal of the juror's role.

Given the development of the jury system and the English tradition of protecting the rights of the individual, the need for guidance was obvious. Both the judges and the laymen who participated in the trial recognized that the jurors must have guidance to prevent them from being misled by false testimony or by evidence that was not relevant to the issue. Accordingly, in the 1600s and 1700s, numerous exclusionary rules were developed which kept certain kinds of evidence from the jurors unless the evidence met various tests, as determined by the judge. These rules of admissibility were based upon long judicial experience with parties, witnesses and jurors. The purpose of these rules was to allow the jury to consider only evidence that was as free as possible from the risks of irrelevancy, confusion and fraud.[13]

The Anglican system is now followed in Scotland, Ireland, Sri Lanka, Hong Kong, and some other countries in Asia, to a great extent in India and some African countries, in Canada, and of course, in the United States. From the very beginning, the American colonies followed the English law. For example, part of Virginia's plan in 1606 was that "the disposing of all causes happening within the colonies should be done as near to the common law of England and the equity thereof as may be."[14]

---

12 *Ibid.*
13 Wigmore on Evidence, p. 5 (1935).
14 *Ibid.*

§ 1.5   Development of the rules of evidence in the United States

During the past two centuries, a system of rules for the presentation of evidence has been established in the United States. In some instances the rules are the result of centuries of deep thought and experience. In other instances the rules have been established in a haphazard manner and often without much thought. Although this country adopted the English system, the rules concerning the admissibility of evidence are not the same in the two countries. Due to legislation and court decisions, some of which interpret constitutional provisions, the rules for obtaining and weighing evidence are now more restrictive in this country than in England.

Certainly the rules are not perfect and are always subject to change—either by the courts or by statute. As stated in *Funk v. United States:*

> The fundamental basis upon which all rules of evidence must rest if they are to rest upon reason is their adaptation to the successful development of the truth. And, since experience is of all teachers the most dependable, and since experience also is a continuous process, it follows that a rule of evidence at one time thought necessary to the ascertainment of the truth should yield to the experience of a succeeding generation whenever that experience has clearly demonstrated the fallacy or unwisdom of the old rule.[15]

The rules of evidence are changed not only by court decisions, but also by congressional or legislative enactments. For example, in 1878 Congress allowed the defendant in a criminal case to be a witness when he so requested.[16] In Illinois the legislature provided, under the Sexually Dangerous Persons Act, that it shall be competent to introduce evidence of the commission of any number of crimes by the respondent, together with whatever punishment, if any, was inflicted.[17] More recently, Congress has enacted specific legislation relating to the admissibility of confessions, wiretap evidence and eyewitness testimony.[18]

a.   Adoption of the Federal Rules of Evidence

In an effort to obtain more uniformity in court procedures, in 1972 the United States Supreme Court adopted the "Rules of Evidence for United States Courts and Magistrates." In 1987, the scope of these rules was

---

15 290 U.S. 371, 54 S. Ct. 212, 78 L. Ed. 369 (1933). *See* case in Part II, *infra.*
16 28 U.S.C. § 632.
17 Ch. 38, § 105-5.
18 Title 18, § 2518 as amended.

extended to include proceedings before a United States bankruptcy judge.[19]

A study of the development and application of this set of rules demonstrates how rules of evidence are changed by legislative action. The Supreme Court order of November 20, 1972 directed the federal district courts and United States magistrates to follow these rules after July 1, 1973. However, in accordance with federal laws, the proposed rules were required to be transmitted to Congress for approval. The House Judiciary Committee wrestled with the provisions for nearly a year, and finally approved a modified version in early 1974 by a vote of 377 to 130. Before approving the Supreme Court draft of the rules of evidence, the House Judiciary Committee changed provisions concerning privileged communications.

It is interesting to note that Justice Douglas did not agree with the other members of the Court concerning the proposed Federal Rules of Evidence, arguing that the Supreme Court did not have authority to promulgate such rules and that the rules should be "channeled through the Judicial Conference whose members are more qualified than we to appraise their merits when applied in actual practice."[20]

In explaining the purpose and construction of the Federal Rules of Evidence, the drafters included this comment:

> These rules shall be construed to secure fairness in administration, elimination of unjustifiable expense and delay, and promotion of growth and development of a law of evidence to the end that the truth may be ascertained and proceedings justly determined.[21]

The adoption of the Federal Rules of Evidence has contributed to establishing a uniform body of law. However, there is some doubt that the adoption of the rules has achieved the goal of simplicity as its drafters envisioned.[22]

b. Uniform Rules of Evidence

In 1974 the National Conference of Commissioners on Uniform State Laws approved a revised Rules of Evidence, which was recommended for adoption by state legislatures. This codification of evidence laws was purposely patterned after the Federal Rules of Evidence in order to encourage

---

19 Federal Rules of Evidence prescribed pursuant to §§ 3402, 3771 and 3772, Title 18 U.S.C. §§ 2072 and 2075, Title 18 U.S.C., Nov. 20, 1972. These rules are included herein as Appendix and are referred to throughout this text.

20 Moore, Federal Practice Rule Pamphlet (1975).

21 Fed. R. Evid. 102.

22 Wigmore on Evidence, § 6.5 (1988).

uniformity in the application of evidence rules in both state and federal courts.

As the evidence rules followed in the United States today are a product of a combination of legislative acts (as discussed in previous paragraphs) and court decisions, a study of evidence requires an examination of federal and state legislation and cases.

§ 1.6   Application of the rules of evidence in state and federal courts

The history of this country and the separation of powers concept have influenced the legislative bodies and courts in establishing evidence rules. As a general rule, questions of evidence are governed by the laws of the forum, i.e., the state rules of evidence apply in state courts, and the federal rules apply in federal courts. If the state has jurisdiction over the parties and the cause of action, the rules of evidence and the laws of that state generally will apply.

The United States Constitution gives Congress the power to make regulations guiding the Supreme Court and to constitute tribunals inferior to the Supreme Court. The rules of evidence as established by Congress are to be followed in federal courts. However, no codification of rules can be applied without court interpretation. Therefore, one must carefully examine federal cases, especially Supreme Court cases, in applying the law governing the admissibility of evidence in federal courts.

While the legislation of each jurisdiction is supreme, and state rules of evidence provide general guides in state courts, legislation is subject to such limitations as may be prescribed in federal constitutional provisions applicable to the state. For example, the United States Supreme Court has determined that a state rule requiring that a defendant desiring to testify in a criminal case must do so before any other testimony for the defense is heard violates the Fifth Amendment to the Constitution and the due process clause of the Fourteenth Amendment.[23] Also, Congress may establish rules relating to the admissibility of evidence in state courts, such as the Omnibus Crime Control and Safe Streets Act of 1968, Title 18 of the United States Code, which provides that evidence relating to wire or oral communications that has been intercepted in violation of that section shall not be used "in or before any court, grand jury, department . . . or other authority of the United States, state or political subdivision thereof."[24]

---

23   Brooks v. Tennessee, 406 U.S. 605, 92 S. Ct. 1891, 32 L. Ed. 2d 358 (1972).
24   For a more thorough discussion of the powers of the federal and state governments, *see* Klotter & Kanovitz, CONSTITUTIONAL LAW, ch. 1 (6th ed. 1991).

While state legislative bodies and state courts have the authority to establish the rules of evidence for the respective states, there is no doubt that the adoption of the Federal Rules of Evidence has influenced the states. It is significant that at least 26 states have adopted rules of evidence patterned after the Federal Rules, although some of these states have made significant changes—either before adoption or after their rules were in existence for some time.25 Some of the states have patterned their legislation after the Revised Uniform Rules of Evidence rather than the Federal Rules of Evidence. According to the directory of Uniform Acts and Codes, which includes the Uniform Rules of Evidence, 35 jurisdictions have adopted Uniform Rules of Evidence, some with modifications.26 A note accompanying the Uniform Rules of Evidence as compiled by the National Conference of Commissioners on Uniform state laws notes that "the Uniform Rules of Evidence are almost identical to the Federal Rules of Evidence."

Because the Federal Rules of Evidence have had a major impact on state laws and evidence rules, and because the states have increasingly

---

25 The states that have adopted the rules of evidence patterned after the Federal Rules of 1988 are *Alaska:* ALASKA R. EVID. (1979); *Arizona:* ARIZ. REV. STAT. ANN., ARIZ. R. EVID. (1977); *Arkansas:* ARK. STAT. ANN. § 28-1001, et seq. (1976), modeled after the Rev. Uniform Rules of Evidence; *Colorado:* COLO. R. EVID. (1980); *Delaware:* DEL. UNIF. R. EVID. (1980); *Florida:* FLA. STAT. ANN. EVID. CODE § 90.101, et seq. (1977); *Hawaii:* HAWAII REV. STAT. Tit. 33, ch. 626 (1981); *Idaho:* IDAHO R. EVID. (1985); *Iowa:* IOWA R. EVID. (1983); *Maine:* ME. REV. STAT. ANN. (1976); *Michigan:* MICH. R. EVID. (1978); *Minnesota:* MINN. R. EVID. (1977); *Montana:* MONT. R. EVID. (1977); *Nebraska:* NEB. REV. STAT. § 27-101 (1975); *Nevada:* NEV. REV. STAT. § 47.020, et seq. (1973); *New Hampshire:* N.H. R. EVID. (1985); *New Mexico:* N.M. STAT. ANN. § 20-4-101, et seq. (1976); *North Carolina:* N.C. R. EVID. (1984); *North Dakota:* N.D. R. EVID. (1977); *Ohio:* OHIO R. EVID. (1980); *Oklahoma:* OKLA. STAT. ANN. Tit. 12, § 2101, et seq. (1979); *Oregon:* OR. REV. STAT. §§ 40.010-40.585 (1984); *Puerto Rico:* P.R. LAWS ANN. Tit. 32 (1980); *South Dakota:* S.D. R. EVID. (1979); *Texas:* TEX. R. EVID. (1986); *Vermont:* VT. R. EVID. (1983); *Washington:* WASH. R. EVID. (1979); *Wisconsin:* WIS. STAT. ANN. § 901.01, et seq. (1975); *Wyoming:* WYO. R. EVID. (1978). The Board of Governors of the Kentucky Bar ha supported legislation which would schematically pattern Kentucky Rules Evidence after the Federal Rules.

26 Vol. 13A, UNIF. RULES OF EVIDENCE, U.L.A. (1974) with 1986 amendments West Publishing Co.; The appendix to this book contains a list of states th have adopted the Uniform Rules of Evidence with the effective date an statutory citation.

looked to federal decisions for interpretations, federal cases interpreting the Federal Rules of Evidence are included throughout the text. Nevertheless, in order to be fully acquainted with the specific rules of criminal evidence, it is necessary to consult the individual state codes and court decisions on the subject.

§ 1.7   Future development of the rules of evidence

In studying rules of criminal evidence, then, it must be recognized that our rules are a product of progressive growth and adaptation to new circumstances. The rules of evidence will continue to change and, in fact, probably will change more rapidly in the next decade as judicial officials and members of the legislature attempt to fashion a more effective system to meet the modern needs of society. Some changes may be made to meet some attractive current theory and then later may be rejected, while other changes will be made based on good reasoning and will have lasting effect.

The application of the rules of evidence to the administration of the law is and should be within the sound discretion of the judiciary. However, contrary to statements made in some cases, recent decisions of reviewing courts appear to require more strict application of the rules of evidence, thus leaving lower courts with less discretion concerning the administration of the business of the court and the admissibility of evidence.

In 1967, the President's Commission on Law Enforcement and the Administration of Justice, seeking to describe the criminal justice system in the United States, pointed out some shortcomings. The report stated that court proceedings are the subject of continual, careful study by lawyers and are now receiving intensive scrutiny from other groups.[27] Certainly there is sufficient justification to warrant such a degree of study. As stated in the Commission report, "An inquiry into the performance of America's criminal courts, therefore, must of necessity examine both their effectiveness and their fairness, and proposals for improving their operations must aim at maintaining or redressing the essential equilibrium between these two qualities."[28]

Have the restrictive rules of evidence become overdeveloped? Perhaps we have reached the point where exclusionary rules no longer rest on reason. However, it would be unwise to abolish our system entirely, as was done in France in the 1700s. Appropriate changes should be made by the courts and legislatures after careful study and with regard to the objectives

---

[27] The President's Commission on Law Enforcement and the Administration of Justice, *Task Force Report: The Courts*, p. 1 (1967).

[28] Advisory Committee on Rules of Evidence, Revised Draft, 51 F.R.D. 315 (1971).

to be achieved. Therefore, not only is it necessary that all who are involved in the criminal justice system be aware of the rules of evidence as they exist today, but everyone must also be familiar with the history of the rules, keep up with changes as they occur, and take an active part in recommending improvements when experience has demonstrated that the old rules are no longer workable.

§ 1.8   Summary

In every society, efforts have been made to determine the guilt or innocence of a person charged with violation of the rules of that society. Some of the world's legal systems were built on sound foundations and have continued for many centuries. However, other legal systems disappeared when the governments responsible for developing them were overthrown, or when governments developed other methods for determining guilt or innocence. Fortunately, history has preserved descriptions of some of the methods of earlier systems for consideration by later generations.

In England, after centuries of experimentation, a system for determining guilt or innocence developed by utilizing parts of earlier systems. With the development of the jury system, a complex set of rules for determining the admissibility of evidence gradually developed. Although a jury system patterned after that of England was adopted by the United States, the rules for admitting the evidence have been changed by our courts and legislative bodies. Today, the rules of exclusion are more strict in the United States than in England.

The rules for determining the admissibility of evidence have changed and will continue to change. In this country, judges, legislators and other criminal justice personnel must work together to seek better methods for determining guilt and protecting society, while at the same time protecting the rights of the individual.

CHAPTER 2
APPROACH TO THE STUDY
OF CRIMINAL EVIDENCE

The word "evidence" is applied to that which renders evident; and is defined to be any matter of fact, the effect, tendency, or design of which is to produce in the mind a persuasion, affirmative or disaffirmative, of the existence of some other matter of fact.
State v. Ward, 61 Vt. 153, 17 A. 483 (1889)

§ 2.1   Introduction

Before searching the cases and statutes for evidence guidelines on specific issues such as the admissibility of hearsay evidence, one must comprehend the general concepts. There are good reasons for the rules of evidence and logical justifications for excluding pertinent evidence. A knowledge of these rules and the rationale used by the courts in framing the rules which exclude some evidence assists immeasurably in understanding the specific rules of evidence. Under the Anglican system (with the jury deciding the facts), evidence is not admitted when it would be *unduly prejudicial* to the accused.

Although the rules of evidence generally apply in both civil and criminal cases, there are some important differences that are of special interest to those involved in criminal justice. These differences are discussed in this chapter. In addition, the flow and use of evidence from the time it is located and packaged by the investigator to the time it is considered by the parole board are discussed. In Chapter 4 the use of evidence at the trial is more particularly considered.

§ 2.2   Definitions

In order to comprehend fully the discussion of the rules of evidence, it is necessary to define some of the words and phrases used. Other words or phrases are defined in future chapters as they are discussed.

a.   Evidence

Evidence has been defined as the means employed for the purpose of proving an unknown or disputed fact, and it is either judicial or extrajudicial. Every determination of the judgment, whatever may be its subject, is the result of evidence.[1] Evidence is any information upon which a person can make a decision. For example, before a used car is purchased, the car dealer is questioned as to the condition of the car or perhaps the former owner is called, and in some instances, the car is taken to another garage for an inspection. All of this information or evidence is then considered before a decision is reached as to whether the purchase will be made.

b.   Legal evidence

Legal evidence is defined in *Black's Law Dictionary* as "a broad general term meaning all admissible evidence, including both oral and documentary, but with a further implication that it must be of such a character as tends reasonably and substantially to prove the point, not to raise a mere suspicion or conjecture."[2] Legal evidence is that which is used or is intended to be used at the trial or at inquiries before courts, judges, commissioners, referees, etc. To state this more succinctly, evidence as used in law means "that which demonstrates or makes clear or ascertains the truth of the very fact or point in issue, either on the one side or the other."[3]

c.   Direct evidence

Direct evidence is that means of proof which tends to show the existence of a fact in question without the intervention of the proof of any other fact.[4] Direct evidence has also been defined as that which immediately

---

1   Rice, Law of Evidence (1893).
2   Black's Law Dictionary (5th ed. 1979).
3   Leonard v. State, 100 Ohio St. 456, 127 N.E. 464 (1919).
4   Black's Law Dictionary (5th ed. 1979).

points to a question at issue. For example, a witness testifies that he saw the acts which constituted the precise fact to be proved. If in a homicide case the witness testifies that he saw the accused stab the victim, this would be direct evidence.

d.   Circumstantial evidence

Circumstantial evidence, sometimes called indirect evidence, is so called because the truth is arrived at through inferences of probabilities arising from an association of facts. Circumstantial evidence means that the existence of a principal fact is only inferred from the circumstances.5 One judge stated that the only difference between direct and circumstantial evidence is that direct evidence is more immediate and has fewer links in the chain of connection between the premise and the conclusion. An example of circumstantial evidence is the testimony of a witness in an adultery case that he saw the accused and a woman who was not his wife together in a hotel room and both were undressed. It should be noted that circumstantial evidence is not necessarily of less value than direct evidence.

e.   Testimony

Testimony is evidence which comes to the court through witnesses speaking under oath or affirmation. In some instances the word "testimony" is used synonymously with the word "evidence." It is obvious when considering the two words, however, that testimony is limited to that which is oral, while the word "evidence" includes writing and other forms. The word "evidence" is the broader term and includes "testimony," which is only one type of evidence.6

f.   Documentary evidence

Documentary evidence includes all kinds of documents, records and writings which are not objectionable under some of the various exclusionary rules of evidence. It is such evidence as is furnished by written instruments, inscriptions and documents of all kinds.7 An extortion note in a kidnapping case is an example of documentary evidence.

g.   Real evidence

Real evidence, or "physical" evidence, has been defined as meaning a fact, the existence of which is perceptible to the senses. A clearer definition is "evidence furnished by things themselves, on view or inspection, as distinguished from a description of them by the mouth of a witness; e.g., the

---

5   Twin City Fire Ins. Co. v. Lonas, 255 Ky. 717, 75 S.W.2d 348 (1934).

6   31 C.J.S. *Evidence* § 3 (1964).

7   BLACK'S LAW DICTIONARY (5th ed. 1979).

physical appearance of the person when exhibited to the jury (marks, scars, wounds, fingerprints, etc.)."8 Real evidence also includes weapons or implements used in the commission of a crime and evidence of the physical appearance of a place (as obtained by a jury when they are taken to view it).

h. Prima facie evidence

Prima facie evidence is evidence which, if unexplained or uncontradicted, is sufficient to carry a case to the jury and to sustain a verdict in favor of the issue which it supports. This type of evidence, however, may be contradicted by other evidence. The word prima facie means "at first sight" or "on the first appearance" or "on the face of it." It is evidence which suffices for the proof of a particular fact until contradicted and overcome by other evidence.9 An example is the certificate of a recording officer in a proceeding for which a document is part of the record. The evidence may be afterward rejected upon proof that there is no such record.

i. Proof

Proof is the effect of evidence; that is, it is the establishment of fact by evidence. Even though the terms *proof* and *evidence* are sometimes used synonymously, they are different. Properly speaking, evidence is only the medium of proof; proof is the effect of evidence. Proof is defined as "the conviction or persuasion of the mind of a judge or a jury, by the exhibition of evidence, of the reality of a fact alleged."10

j. Cumulative evidence

Cumulative evidence is that which goes to prove what has already been established by other evidence. In legal phraseology it means evidence from the same or a new witness that simply repeats, in substance and effect, or adds to what has already been testified.

k. Corroborative evidence

Corroborative evidence is evidence supplementary to that already given. It tends to strengthen or confirm previously admitted evidence. It is additional evidence of a different character, but it seeks to prove the same point as the earlier evidence. For example, a conviction cannot stand on a confession without corroborating evidence. Such corroborating evidence may be the testimony of a witness who saw the accused at the scene of the crime.

---

8 *Ibid.*
9 Dotson v. Watson, 110 Tex. 355, 220 S.W. 771 (1920).
10 Ellis v. Wolfe-Shoemaker Motor Co., 227 Mo. 508, 55 S.W.2d 309 (1932).

l.   Relevant evidence

Relevant evidence is evidence having any tendency to make the existence of any fact that is of consequence to the determination of the action more probable or less probable than it would be without the evidence.[11]

m. Material evidence

Material evidence is that which goes to the *substantial* matters in dispute or has a legitimate and effective influence or bearing on the decision of the case.

n. Competent evidence

Although the terms "relevancy," "competency" and "materiality" are frequently used conjunctively, a matter may be relevant and material to an issue but still be incompetent, and inadmissible under the established rules of evidence. Competent evidence is evidence which, in legal proceedings, is admissible for the purpose of proving a relevant fact. The competency of evidence depends on whether it is of the sort or type which may be accepted on any issue to which it is relevant.[12] Evidence may be made competent (or incompetent) by legislation or by judicial construction.[13]

o. Hearsay evidence

Hearsay is a statement, other than one made by the declarant while testifying at the trial or hearing, that offered to prove the truth of the matter asserted.[14] A witness' statement based upon what someone else has told him, and not upon personal observation or knowledge, is hearsay.

§ 2.3   Reasons for the rules of evidence

By the seventeenth century the evolution of the jury function was well advanced, and the jury depended on the testimony of witnesses for facts on which to base a verdict. Members of juries were generally ordinary lay people, impressionable and unacquainted with the laws; it was therefore recognized that specific rules for sifting the evidence were necessary. To protect the accused, rules were gradually developed to help assure that evidence was dependable, credible and trustworthy before it could be considered.

---

11 FED. R. EVID. 401. For further discussion concerning relevant evidence, see *infra* Chapter 7.

12 Maddox v. News Syndicate Co., 176 F.2d 897 (2d Cir. 1949).

13 Funk v. United States, 290 U.S. 371, 64 S. Ct. 212, 78 L. Ed. 2d 369 (1933).

14 FED. R. EVID. 801(c). For further definitions of hearsay and terms related to hearsay evidence, see *infra* Chapter 12.

Evidentiary rules, then, were developed in part to keep out evidence that was not trustworthy or was unduly prejudicial to the accused. Also, it was obviously necessary for the court to establish rules to carry on the proceedings in an orderly and efficient manner. To achieve these and other lesser objectives, our present-day evidentiary rules have been formulated by the courts and by legislative action.

Efforts have been made to state in more specific terms the reasons for the rules of evidence and to account for the many varied rules which must be interpreted by the courts. As these rules have been developed by gradual evolution and in fact are still developing, it is difficult to categorize them and to explain why each rule exists. However, some progress has been made toward this goal. Although it appears that in some instances there is an effort to rationalize or justify an outmoded or outdated rule, there is some logic to the explanations given for most of the specific rules of evidence.

§ 2.4   Reasons for excluding evidence

Much evidence is excluded even though it would help the jury or the court in determining the true facts concerning the matters at issue. The reasons for excluding the evidence have been numerous and phrased in many ways. An effort is made here to categorize these reasons in order to make them more meaningful and more comprehensible. The general reasons for excluding otherwise pertinent evidence are listed below.

a.   Protection of interests and relationships

A court weighs the value of having all of the facts before the court against the protection of certain interests and relationships, and it may decide to exclude relevant evidence. Such interests and relationships are regarded, rightly or wrongly, as of sufficient social importance to justify some incidental sacrifice of sources of fact needed in the administration of justice.[15] Examples of evidence excluded on the basis of this public policy of protection of relationships are:

1. Evidence protected by the husband and wife privilege.
2. Evidence protected by the attorney-client privilege.
3. Evidence protected by the penitent-confessor privilege.[16]

b.   Avoidance of undue prejudice to the accused

Some evidence which would be relevant to the issue is not admitted

---

15 McCormick, Evidence § 72.
16 Testimonial privileges are discussed in Chapter 10, *infra.*

because it may be unduly prejudicial to the accused. For example, the criminal record of the accused generally is not admitted, except to impeach the testimony of the accused, because to admit this evidence would unduly prejudice the accused in the minds of the jurors. Sometimes photographs are not admitted into evidence, even though relevant, because to do so would unduly prejudice the accused.

c. Prohibition of consideration of unreliable evidence

Other evidence is not permitted, even though it might have a bearing on the case, if it is considered unreliable. In this category are hearsay evidence and opinion evidence.[17] To illustrate, the testimony of a police officer that a bystander told him that the accused was driving the car involved in an accident is not admissible. Such evidence is relevant but not reliable enough for use in court.

d. Reduction of violations of constitutional safeguards

A more recently developed reason for the exclusion of evidence is that evidence obtained in violation of the Constitution will not be admitted into evidence. Until the beginning of the present century, it was almost universally accepted that evidence was admissible even though it was illegally obtained. However, the courts now reason that such evidence as that secured by illegal search, in violation of the self-incrimination provisions, or in violation of the right-to-counsel provisions, is often not admissible, even though pertinent to the issue. In fact, such evidence often the only basis for a conviction.[18] The rationale for excluding such evidence has not been consistent, but generally, exclusion has been justified on the ground that by rejecting such evidence, public officials will be less likely to violate constitutional rights.

e. Avoidance of waste of time

Cumulative evidence is unnecessary and repetitive, and thus is inadmissible because of the interest in conserving the court's time. This follows the principle of judicial economy.

There have been arguments that some of the historical reasons for excluding relevant evidence have long since disappeared, leaving the technical rules without a logical basis. In some instances so many exceptions have developed that the rules are no longer meaningful. However, most of the justification for the rules is still valid and should be carefully considered, as the reasons behind the rules can help one to understand their application.

---

17 These rules are discussed in Chapters 11 and 12, *infra.*
18 Discussed more thoroughly in Chapter 16, *infra.*

§ 2.5 Rules of evidence in criminal cases compared to rules in civil cases

An early English court stated that there is no distinction between the rules of evidence in criminal and civil cases. The court continued:

> What may be received in the one case, may be received in the other; and what is rejected in the one ought to be rejected in the other. A fact must be established by the same evidence, whether it is to be followed by a criminal or civil consequence.[19]

In some states the civil rules of evidence have been made applicable in criminal cases by case law or by statute unless otherwise provided.[20] There are, however, some differences in the current rules and in the application of the rules of evidence which arise solely, or more frequently, in criminal cases.

In civil cases the two parties approach the contention indicated by the pleadings upon terms of approximate equality, with no legal presumption favoring the plaintiff or defendant. In criminal cases the law seeks to protect the person accused of crime, and a presumption accompanies him from the time of apprehension to the moment of conviction: the presumption that he is innocent until proven guilty. Throughout the trial the burden of proof is on the state, and the state must prove guilt beyond a reasonable doubt, rather than by a preponderance of the evidence. Because of this presumption of innocence, special rules for overcoming the presumption have been developed. One writer spells out the difference in these terms:

> The chief distinction which prevails will be found to originate in that caution which is always observed when life or liberty is in question, and in those benign presumptions with which the law meets every accusation involving moral turpitude.[21]

In addition to requiring the state to meet a higher (or greater) standard of proof in a criminal prosecution, the rules differ in a few other instances. For example, the rule concerning admission of a dying declaration is different in a criminal case.[22]

The degree of proof must be stronger in a criminal case because, with few exceptions,[23] the accused must be found guilty by all twelve members

---

19 Rex v. Watson, 2 Stark. 116; Lord Melville's Case, 29 How. St. Tr. 763.
20 Mich. Comp. Laws Ann. § 768.22 (1). *See also* Rev. Code Wash. Ann. § 10.58.010.
21 *Ibid.*
22 29 Am. Jur. 2d *Evidence* § 74. See also *infra* Chapter 12.
23 *See* Johnson v. Louisiana, 406 U.S. 356, 92 S. Ct. 1620 (1972), which upheld

of the jury, while in a civil case an unanimous decision is not required. Therefore, it is much easier to obtain a money judgment against a person in a civil case than it is to find him guilty under the penal laws. A good example is assault and battery; in many instances a money judgment is obtained even after an attempt to convict has failed.

Although the distinction between criminal evidence and civil evidence may be slight when defining the rules, from a practical standpoint there is a great deal of difference. While a jury may accept weak evidence in determining the rights of parties in a civil case, the members of the jury are more hesitant to accept such evidence when life or liberty is in issue. To the prosecutor this means that evidence must be presented which will be given great weight by the jury, and sufficient evidence must be presented in court to overcome any "reasonable doubt" on the part of the jury or judge. Any act or conduct by the judge which indicates the slightest bias or unfairness is grounds for reversal in a criminal case.[24]

§ 2.6   Pretrial flow of evidence

Although much valuable evidence is made available in court by lay persons who are not connected with the criminal justice process, in most instances the police officer is responsible for discovering, evaluating, protecting, analyzing and presenting evidence. If he does not present the evidence himself, he is still primarily responsible for guiding the flow of evidence, at least until the indictment or information stage.

The officer must develop and preserve the evidence in such a way so as to maximize its usefulness in subsequent proceedings. For example, at the beginning of an investigation, if names and addresses of witnesses to a crime are not recorded by the officer, this information may be forever lost. The techniques of sound criminal investigation are outside the scope of this work, but it bears repeating that failure to gather the available evidence in a workmanlike manner affects all subsequent proceedings.

The Federal Rules of Criminal Procedure and the rules of criminal procedure of all states require an officer making an arrest to take the arrestee before the nearest available magistrate without unnecessary delay. The offi-

---

a conviction in a criminal case where the state statute provided that 9 of 12 jurors may find the defendant guilty. *See also* Burch v. Louisiana, 441 U.S. 130, 99 S. Ct. 1623 (1979), which held that a defendant who is on trial for a nonpetty offense and is subsequently convicted by a nonunanimous six-person jury has been denied his right to a trial by jury.

24 State v. Perkins, 130 W. Va. 708, 45 S.E.2d 17 (1947). *See* case in Part II, *infra.*

cer at this first appearance is not required to present the evidence to convict, but at the preliminary hearing he must produce sufficient evidence for
the magistrate to determine whether there is probable cause to believe that an
offense has been committed and that the accused committed the offense.[25]

If the magistrate determines that there is probable cause to "bind" the
defendant over to the grand jury in a felony case, the officer must make
available all of the evidence that he has collected, together with names and
pertinent information, to the prosecutor. Although the prosecutor may and
should enter into the case at an earlier time, this is usually the step where
the prosecutor takes charge, at least temporarily.

The next step in the procedure is the indictment or information. The
prosecution must have sufficient evidence available for the indictment or
information. One might argue—and with justification—that the process is
redundant. Evidence that a crime has been committed and evidence that the
accused committed the crime has already been presented to a magistrate
and will be presented at the trial. In most states, however, evidence must be
presented again to the grand jury before an indictment is returned.

The grand jury proceeding is usually guided by the prosecutor, but here
again, he must, in almost every case, call on the officer-investigator to give
evidence before the grand jury. Generally, formal evidence rules are not followed when presenting evidence to the grand jury, but sufficient admissible
evidence must be presented to convince the jury (usually twelve persons)
that an offense against the state has been committed by the person accused.

In some states, process by way of information is substituted for the
grand jury hearing. Here, the prosecutor, still using the evidence presented
by officers and other witnesses, makes the decisions and prepares the information which notifies the accused of the specific charge.

Is the case now ready for trial? Not quite. Following the return of the
indictment or the preparation of the information, the defendant appears personally before the judge. Here he is arraigned (informed of the charges
against him) and enters his plea. Evidence is not presented at the arraignment, but often a date is set to hear pretrial motions.

At the pretrial hearing, some evidence is often required, especially if a
motion to suppress is made by the defense attorney. Evidence of the facts
surrounding the seizure or taking of evidence by the officer is presented so
that the judge can determine the legality of the procedure. Often the outcome of the suppression hearing determines the fate of the accused. If, for
example, the judge determines that a confession was obtained illegally, the
prosecutor may decide to drop the charge. Conversely, if the judge rules
against the defendant at the suppression hearing, the defendant's attorney

---

25 See *infra* Chapter 16 for a discussion of evidence needed to determine probable cause for the issuance of a search warrant.

may advise the defendant to enter a guilty plea. If there are no more delaying motions, the case is ready for trial.

§ 2.7   Use of evidence at the trial

Even before the trial the evidence acquired by the police officer, by the prosecutor or by other means has been already considered several times. Assuming that there has been sufficient evidence to indict the defendant, the case eventually comes before the court and the jury at the trial. By this time, there is a good possibility that some evidence has been found inadmissible by the court. If so, the prosecutor must determine if there is still enough admissible, relevant evidence to continue with the case.

In addition to the parties on each side, the court is made up of the judge, jury, the witnesses, the prosecutor and the defense attorney.26 In early English proceedings, the jurors were the only witnesses and were called upon by the judge to give information concerning the case because they had knowledge of the facts. This is no longer true, however. The jury now hears the evidence presented by the witnesses and, based upon that evidence, and the facts judicially noticed by the court, and using presumptions and inferences as instructed by the court, it makes a determination as to those facts.

The trial judge's duty is to instruct the jury concerning the law applicable to the case and to determine, sometimes with the later approval of the jury, if the evidence is relevant, material and competent. In a trial without a jury, the judge takes on the role of the trier of fact.

The prosecutor has the responsibility to evaluate all evidence presented to him, to determine the legality of the evidence, to arrange the evidence in sequence so that it is best suited to achieve the objective, to identify the witnesses for the prosecution, to examine the witnesses and to cross-examine witnesses for the defense.

Finally, the defense attorney is responsible for seeking evidence with which to present a defense for the accused. The defense attorney also arranges the evidence in the sequence most likely (in his opinion) to convey his message to the finders of fact. He can also introduce, examine and cross-examine witnesses.

---

26 State v. Perkins, *supra* note 24. *See* case in Part II, *infra.* In Chapter 4, *infra,* the procedure for introducing and considering evidence at the trial is presented in more detail.

§ 2.8   Consideration of evidence on appeal

If the defendant is acquitted at the trial level, the state has no right to appeal the acquittal. The prohibition against double jeopardy mandates this result. If, however, the defendant is convicted, he may appeal the conviction, and the appellate court may examine what occurred in the trial court and reverse the conviction, with or without granting the state the option of retrying the defendant. Ordinarily an appellate court will not overturn a verdict of guilty if there was sufficient evidence upon which the defendant could reasonably have been found guilty beyond a reasonable doubt. Where a defendant succeeds in having a conviction overturned on appeal, the state may appeal to a higher appellate court.

§ 2.9   Use of evidence at the probation hearing

Even after the determination of guilt or innocence, the judge may make additional use of evidence in determining whether the person who has been found guilty will be placed on probation or incarcerated. The probation officer now enters the picture. The general rules of evidence which limit the use of evidence at the trial do not apply to the use of the presentence report by the judge. Although this presentence report should be as factual as possible, evidence such as hearsay evidence is not excluded from the report. However, it is obvious that this evidence is available only for determining the disposition of the person who has been convicted of a crime and that it cannot be used in determining guilt or innocence.

While in most states the probation report is confidential and available only to the judge, some jurisdictions require that the presentence report be made available for inspection by the offender or his attorney.27

§ 2.10   Use of evidence when considering parole

Evidence is also used by the parole board in determining if the person who has served time in an institution is to be released under the supervision of a parole officer. A report is prepared by the parole officer after making a complete investigation in the field and, although the report may contain information that cannot be admitted into court, the information is important as evidence. This report should be carefully prepared, and all facts pertinent to the case should be included. As is the case with probation

---

27 *See* Carlson, Criminal Justice Procedure (4th ed. 1991).

reports and presentence reports, parole reports are not subject to the same evidentiary limitations as are trials that determine guilt or innocence.

§ 2.11 Summary

In a criminal case the objective is to gather all of the evidence, whether favorable or unfavorable to the prosecution, that will help the trial court and the reviewing courts in reaching the truth and disposing of the case according to law. Although it would appear that all of the relevant evidence should be admitted, after long empirical investigation, the courts have determined that certain evidence should be excluded. These rules for excluding evidence are generally justified on the grounds that they avoid waste of time and confusion, protect certain interests and relationships, avoid undue prejudice to the accused, prevent the jury from considering unreliable evidence, and enforce the constitutional safeguards.

Generally there is little distinction between the rules of criminal evidence and rules of civil evidence. However, because the prosecution must prove the accused guilty beyond a reasonable doubt and because the jury verdict usually must be unanimous, a higher degree of evidence is required in a criminal case.

The importance of recognizing, protecting, preserving and evaluating evidence begins at the time that the crime is committed. Even prior to trial the evidence plays a very important part in determining whether there are sufficient grounds for the magistrate to bind the defendant over to the grand jury and for the grand jury to determine whether there is sufficient evidence for an indictment. (In some cases an *information* may be filed by the prosecutor and substituted for the indictment.)

The evidence has been sifted, challenged and evaluated prior to the time that the trial begins, but it is at the trial that evidence is of greatest importance. In a criminal case, the prosecution must introduce sufficient evidence which, together with facts judicially noticed and legal presumptions and inferences, will justify the factfinders in finding the defendant guilty beyond a reasonable doubt. At the trial, the judge, the jury, the witnesses, the prosecutor and the defense attorney are all concerned with the admissibility and weight of evidence.

Even after the trial the reviewing courts often consider the record of evidence presented at the court in order to determine if the conviction should be set aside for one reason or another.

Evidence of a different type, as well as legally acquired evidence, is used by the judge in determining whether a defendant who has been convicted should be placed on probation. Although the strict rules of evidence do not apply to the probation officer obtaining information for the judge, evidence should be acquired that will help the judge in determining the truth and that will assist in making the decision.

Finally, evidence again is considered by the parole board before a determination is made as to whether the person who has served time in the institution should be paroled.

In the chapters that follow, the many general admissibility tests and special tests for the use of evidence are discussed more comprehensively.

B. PROOF BY EVIDENCE AND SUBSTITUTES

CHAPTER 3
BURDEN OF PROOF

The term "burden of proof" imports the duty of ultimately establishing any given proposition. This phrase marks the peculiar duty of him who has the risk of any given proposition on which the parties are at issue, who will lose the case if he does not make this proposition out, when all has been said and done.

Thayer, PRELIMINARY TREATISE ON EVIDENCE AT THE COMMON LAW, Ch. 9, p. 353

§ 3.1 Introduction

In approaching the study of evidence logically and progressively, one starting point is to consider the task of producing evidence with which to prove the truth of a given proposition. One does not take a criminal or civil case to court unless there is a good chance that the proposition can be proved. In a criminal case, the state has the burden of proving the guilt of the accused beyond a reasonable doubt. Therefore, the "burden of proof" is on the prosecution throughout the trial. The term denotes the duty of establishing the truth of the charge against the accused. Ascertaining the truth then becomes an important, if not the most important, objective of the court and jury.

In the criminal justice process, it is necessary that those involved understand the considerations and obligations of the parties in presenting sufficient evidence and the consequences of failing to do so. Failure on the part of the prosecution to introduce sufficient evidence, or failure properly to explain the evidence, will make it impossible for the jury (or judge where the case is tried without a jury) to determine the truth and will therefore result in a miscarriage of justice. Therefore, a thorough knowledge of the concept of burden of proof is an essential starting point on which to build an understanding of the rules of evidence.

In a civil case, the party who has the burden of establishing the truth of a given proposition is a private individual, corporation or, in some instances, a governmental unit. In a criminal case, however, the prosecution has the responsibility of establishing the truth of the charges stated in the indictment or information. The rule in criminal cases imposing upon the state the burden of proving guilt of the accused beyond a reasonable doubt does not apply in civil actions. Therefore, the burden of proof becomes even more important when considering criminal cases than when considering civil cases.

In a criminal case, the investigator must compile evidence sufficient to convince the jury not only by a "preponderance of the evidence" but that the accused is guilty "beyond a reasonable doubt;" that is, the prosecution or the state has the burden of proving the existence of every element necessary to constitute the crime charged.

Recognizing this requirement, the defense can be expected to deliver an attack against the weak links in the chain, as the defense knows that if even one of the elements is not proved beyond a reasonable doubt, there can be no conviction on that specific charge.

Because there has been some confusion concerning the term "burden of proof," the pertinent terms are comprehensively defined and explained in the following sections of this chapter. In other sections of the chapter, the obligation of the prosecution to prove guilt, and the obligation of the accused to produce evidence in a criminal trial are discussed.

In Chapters 4, 5 and 6, rules relating to the process for establishing or ascertaining truth at the trial are defined, explained and considered.

§ 3.2   Definitions and distinctions

A statement of what the burden of proof *isn't* makes it easier to frame a positive definition. First, the burden of proof does not relate to the number of witnesses, but to the merit and weight of the evidence produced— whether by one or many witnesses. Secondly, the fact that evidence is admissible in conformity with the general principles concerning admissibility, relevancy, materiality and competency does not necessarily mean that it will be given such weight as to sustain the burden of proof. The testimony of one well-prepared, reliable witness or evidence of a documentary or real nature may result in better proof than testimony from a large number of witnesses whose credibility is inherently suspect.

Generally the phrase "burden of proof" denotes the duty of establishing the truth of a given proposition or issue. Because the term has been used somewhat loosely by some courts, the definition of burden of proof as used in law requires further explanation. To avoid confusion, the phrases "burden of going forward" and "burden of persuasion" are also defined.

a. Burden of proof

This term is properly defined as the burden which rests upon a party to establish the ultimate truth of a given proposition or issue by the quantum of proof demanded by law. In a criminal case, this means that the prosecution has the burden of proving the guilt of the accused. This burden never shifts during the course of the trial, but it remains with the prosecution throughout the trial. Here the emphasis is on the final outcome rather than on individual questions within the case.

b. Burden of going forward

This refers to the obligation resting upon a party to produce prima facie evidence on a particular issue. For example, in a criminal case, if the accused claims alibi or insanity, the accused has the responsibility of going forward with some credible evidence supporting that defense. This is often expressed by the term "burden of evidence."[1]

c. Burden of persuasion

This definition does not cause as much difficulty. The burden of persuasion refers only to the burden of persuading the factfinder of the truth of evidence produced by one side or the other. This refers to the burden of the trial lawyer, often in the closing arguments to the jury, to prove that his client's version of the truth is correct.

When the term burden of proof is used in the following sections, the definition as stated in subsection (a), *supra,* is applied.

In meeting the burden of proof, the amount of evidence varies depending on whether the case is criminal or civil and depending sometimes on other factors. Generally, in a civil case, the party who has the duty of establishing the truth of a specific proposition must do so by a preponderance of the evidence. However, there are some issues in a civil case which must be proved by a higher degree of proof—by *clear and convincing* evidence. In a criminal case, the state has the burden of proving its proposition—the guilt

---

1 McCloskey v. Koplar, 329 Mo. 527, 46 S.W.2d 557 (1932). *See* United States v. Fatico, 458 F. Supp. 388 (E.D.N.Y. 1978), for a discussion of degrees of proof.

of the accused—beyond a reasonable doubt.2 These three degrees of proof are discussed and distinguished in the following sections.

§ 3.3   Preponderance of the evidence

In a civil case, the burden of proof rests on the plaintiff. This means that the truth of the plaintiff's claim must be established by a fair preponderance of the credible evidence. A preponderance means the greater weight of evidence. It does not mean the greater number of witnesses or the greater length of time taken by either side. The phrase "preponderance of the evidence" refers to the quality of the evidence, i.e., its ability to convince and the weight and the effect that it has on the jurors' minds.

The law requires that, in order for the plaintiff to prevail, the evidence that supports his claim must appeal to the jurors as more nearly representing what took place than the evidence that is opposed to his claim. If plaintiff's evidence is not convincing, or if the evidence from both sides weighs so evenly that the jurors are unable to say that there is a preponderance on either side, then the jury must resolve the question in favor of the defendant. It is only when the evidence favoring the plaintiff's claim outweighs the evidence opposed to it that the jury can find in favor of the plaintiff.

§ 3.4   Clear and convincing evidence

Ordinarily, in civil matters, the burden of proof is carried by a preponderance (greater weight) of the evidence. In some civil cases, however, the evidence must be clear and convincing. "Clear and convincing evidence" is that measure or degree of proof which will produce in the mind of the trier of fact a firm belief or conviction as to the facts sought to be established. Such evidence is intermediate, being more than a mere preponderance, but being less than certainty beyond a reasonable doubt (as is required in criminal cases). Clear and convincing does not mean clear and unequivocal. For example, in order to maintain an action to rescind a contract on the ground that it was procured by fraudulent representations, it must be proved by clear and convincing evidence that (1) there were actual or implied representations of material matters of fact, (2) such representations were false, (3) such representations were made by one party to the other with knowledge of their falsity, (4) representations were made with intent to mislead a party to rely thereon, and (5) such party relied on such representations with a right to rely thereon.

---

2   Kohlsaat v. Parkersburg & Marietta Sand Co., 266 F. 283 (4th Cir. 1920).

According to a law review article written in 1946, the "clear and convincing" standard of proof was first applied to actions for fraud or deceit.[3] In the case of *Addington v. Texas*, Chief Justice Warren Burger wrote that "the intermediate standard, which usually employs some combination of the words "clear," "cogent," "unequivocal," and "convincing," is less commonly used, but nonetheless is no stranger to civil law."[4]

In distinguishing between the levels of proof, the Oregon Supreme Court explained that there are three standards of proof: "a preponderance," "clear and convincing," and "beyond a reasonable doubt." Quoting from a previous decision, the court commented that:

> Proof by a "preponderance of the evidence" means that the jury must believe that the facts asserted are more probably true than false. To be "clear and convincing," evidence must establish that the truth of the facts asserted is "highly probable." "Beyond a reasonable doubt" means that the facts asserted are almost certainly true.[5]

Clear and convincing evidence usually is required in suits to correct a mistake in a deed or other writing, on oral contracts to make a will, to establish the terms of a lost will, and for the specific performance of an oral contract. The 1984 amendment to the United States Code requires the defendant to prove the defense of insanity by clear and convincing evidence.[6]

§ 3.5　Beyond a reasonable doubt

This degree of proof is only required in criminal cases, where the accused is presumed to be innocent until his guilt is established beyond a reasonable doubt. This means that every element of the offense charged in the indictment must be proved beyond a reasonable doubt. Otherwise, the accused must be acquitted of the charge.

In 1970, the United States Supreme Court traced the history of the "beyond a reasonable doubt" requirement and concluded that this standard of proof is indispensable to command the respect and confidence of the community in applications of criminal law. In making this constitutional requirement, the Court emphasized:

3　*Appellate Review in the Federal Courts of Findings Requiring More Than a Preponderance of the Evidence*, 60 HARV. L. REV. 119 (1946).

4　Addington v. Texas, 441 U.S. 418, 99 S. Ct. 1804, 60 L. Ed. 2d 323 (1979).

5　Riley Hill General Contractor v. Tandey Corp., 757 P.2d 595 (Or. 1987).

6　*See* § 3.11, this chapter.

Lest there remain any doubt about the constitutional stature of the reasonable-doubt standard, we explicitly hold that the Due Process Clause protects the accused against conviction except upon proof beyond a reasonable doubt of every fact necessary to constitute the crime with which he is charged.7

In some states, the exact wording of the charge to the jury dealing with this standard of proof is stated by statute. In other states, there is no such requirement, and in fact, the judge does not have to explain the term at all.8 However, where a statute specifically includes the charge that a judge makes to the jury, this charge must be read as stated in the statute. For example, one California statute provides that:

It is not a mere possible doubt; because everything relating to human affairs, and depending on moral evidence, is open to some possible or imaginary doubt. It is that state of the case, which, after the entire comparison and consideration of all the evidence, leaves the minds of jurors in that condition that they can not say they feel an abiding conviction, to a moral certainty, of the truth of the charge.9

One court-approved definition describes reasonable doubt as "an honest, substantial doubt of the defendant's guilt, reasonably arising from the evidence or want of evidence, as opposed to a captious or possible doubt."10 If the judge does define what is meant by reasonable doubt, the wording must be exact because the substitution of one word could lead to error which could be grounds for reversal. As an example, the instruction by a district judge that "proof beyond a reasonable doubt is established if the evidence is such that you would be willing to rely and act upon it in the most important of your own personal affairs" was challenged on appeal when the defendant contended that the judge should have used the phrase "you would not hesitate" instead of "you would be willing." Although the case was not reversed by the Fifth Circuit Court of Appeals, a majority of that court concluded that the phrase "you would not hesitate" was a fairer—thus bet-

---

7   In re Winship, 397 U.S. 358, 90 S. Ct. 1068, 25 L. Ed. 2d 368 (1970). *See* case in Part II, *infra. See also* United States v. Johnson, 718 F.2d 1317 (5th Cir. 1983). In the case of *State v. Stevenson,* 504 A.2d 1029 (Conn. 1986), the Supreme Court of Connecticut noted that "due process requires that the state establish beyond a reasonable doubt every essential fact necessary to establish the crime charged . . . including intent, where intent is one of those elements."

8   State v. Sauer, 38 Minn. 438, 38 N.W. 355 (1888).

9   Cal. Penal Code § 1096 (1985).

10   Lane v. State, 222 A.2d 263 (Del. 1960).

ter—statement of the proposition, and that the phrase should henceforth be used by district courts in the Fifth Circuit.11

The proposition that the degree of proof necessary to find a person guilty beyond a reasonable doubt applies throughout the trial of a case. It not only applies at the trial, but also influences the case from the time of investigation to the release of the defendant from parole or by termination of sentence. It is one of the fundamental differences between a criminal and civil case, and it must be thoroughly comprehended by all who are involved in the criminal justice system.12

§ 3.6   Burden on the prosecution

Throughout the trial the prosecution has the burden of proof and the obligation to convince the jury or the court of the accused's guilt beyond a reasonable doubt. This includes the responsibility of the prosecution to prove criminal intent when a specific intent is an element of the crime charged. The burden of proof as understood in criminal law is never on the accused to establish his innocence or to disprove the facts necessary to establish a crime charged. Nor is the burden ever upon the defendant to show that he did not commit the crime. The defendant does have some responsibility in the trial, which will be discussed in future sections.

If the defense generally denies the crime charged, this necessarily imposes upon the government the burden of showing affirmatively the existence of every material fact or ingredient which the law requires.13 In addition to proving each element of the crime, the prosecution must prove: (1) that the act itself was committed (corpus delicti); (2) the identity of the person who committed the crime;14 and (3) that the crime violated the penal laws of the community where it was committed.

Before the case can progress further, the burden is on the prosecution to establish that a crime has actually been perpetrated.15 The accused is not required in any case to answer a charge against him in absence of evidence on the part of the prosecution sufficient to establish the corpus delicti; if the prosecution fails to establish the corpus delicti, there is no point in authorizing the introduction of further evidence. This generally means that the prosecution has the burden of showing that the specific offense charged has

11 United States v. Richardson, 504 F.2d 357 (5th Cir. 1974).
12 Jackson v. Virginia, 443 U.S. 307, 99 S. Ct. 2781, 61 L. Ed. 2d 560 (1979).
13 State v. Sullivan, 34 Idaho 68, 199 P. 647 (1921). *See also* UNIF. R. EVID. 303 (b).
14 State v. Marcy, 189 Wash. 620, 66 P.2d 846 (1937).
15 *Ibid.*

actually been committed by a named defendant. The commission of the crime includes two elements: (1) the production of a certain result, such as the death of a person, and (2) evidence to show criminal responsibility for such result on the part of a specific human agency.[16]

§ 3.7   Burden to prove all elements of the crime

Part of the prosecution's responsibility to prove guilt beyond a reasonable doubt is the requirement that each of the elements of the offense for which the accused is charged be proved.[17] For example, in the common law crime of burglary, there are six elements: (a) breaking, (b) entering, (c) the dwelling, (d) of another, (e) at night, and (f) with intent to commit a felony therein. Each of these elements must be proved in accordance with the definition of the element as decided by the court. To explain further, "breaking" requires that the prosecution show that there is a trespass. Therefore, where a lodger, who had lawful access to the premises, entered to commit a felony, there was no burglary.

In referring to the burden of proof and the requirement that the prosecution prove every element of the crime, the Supreme Court of Massachusetts made it clear that the prosecution must prove each of the elements.[18] In this case, the defendant was convicted of unauthorized possession of a controlled substance and operating an uninsured motor vehicle. The defendant on appeal asserted that the trial judge's instructions to the jury on the uninsured motor vehicle charge were improper because they shifted the burden of proof to the defendant on an essential element of the crime. After explaining to the jury that the Commonwealth had the burden to show beyond a reasonable doubt that the defendant was guilty of the crime, the trial court had continued with this instruction:

> Under this special circumstance, our law requires, one, the Commonwealth has made out these two elements and alleges there was no insurance on the vehicle. It is up to the defendant to show there was insurance.

In reversing the conviction, the reviewing court determined that the Commonwealth must prove as an element of the crime the charge that the motor vehicle was in fact uninsured. The court admonished that the defen-

---

16 *Ibid.*

17 Connecticut v. Johnson, 460 U.S. 74, 103 S. Ct. 969, 74 L. Ed. 2d 823 (1983).

18 Commonwealth v. Munoz, 426 N.E.2d 1161 (Mass. 1981). *See* case in Part II, *infra.*

dant cannot be under any obligation to aid the Commonwealth in its proof of this central element of the case against him. The court went on to explain that "if the Commonwealth fails to carry its burden of proof on this element, its entire case must fail."

If the prosecution fails to prove one element of the crime beyond a reasonable doubt, the accused may sometimes be found guilty of a lesser degree of that crime or a lesser-included offense. For example, under some statutes a person may be found guilty of burglary in the second degree if the prosecution does not prove that the breaking and entering occurred at night rather than in the daytime. In such instances, of course, the penalty for the offense is less severe.

§ 3.8   Burden on the accused

A criminal trial would be a cumbersome proceeding if the prosecution had to include, in its case in chief, evidence disproving every fact that could conceivably create a defense. Therefore, the prosecution does not have to show beyond a reasonable doubt, for instance, that the defendant was sane at the time of the crime until the defendant first produces evidence tending to show his insanity. However, in some states, once the defendant has introduced evidence sufficient to raise the issue of insanity or other affirmative defenses, the prosecution will generally be required to introduce evidence to counteract the defendant's claim.

When claiming affirmative defenses, such as coercion, self defense, entrapment or mistake, all of which could absolve him from liability, the defendant has the burden of proving the defenses, usually by a preponderance of the evidence. Thus, it is sometimes stated that the defendant has the responsibility of "going forward" with the evidence. For example, the defendant has the burden of introducing evidence to prove self-defense when he raises this plea in his defense.[19] Some jurisdictions go further, placing the burden of persuasion as well as the burden of producing evidence upon the defendant with respect to such affirmative defenses. For example, a former Oregon statute permitted acquittal on the grounds of insanity only when the defendant proved his insanity beyond a reasonable doubt. This statute was held to be constitutional even though it required a higher degree of proof than is generally required.[20]

Because the prosecution must prove each and every element of the crime, the burden cannot be shifted to the defendant to show that one element of the crime is not present. For example, when specific intent is an

---

19 Commonwealth v. Palmer, 222 Pa. 299, 71 A. 100 (1908).

20 Leland v. Oregon, 343 U.S. 790, 72 S. Ct. 1002, 96 L. Ed. 1302 (1952).

element of the crime, instructions which would shift the burden onto the defense to produce evidence demonstrating lack of intent are improper. In 1963, in *Mann v. United States*,[21] the Fifth Circuit Court of Appeals held that the trial judge's instructions, which shifted the responsibility of proving lack of intent, were plain error. The Court of Appeals then reversed the conviction.

Despite that decision, some judges continued to give instructions to the jury which were challengeable as possibly shifting the burden to the defendant. For example, in *United States v. Garrett*,[22] a mail fraud case in which intent was an element, the trial court charged:

> As a general rule it is reasonable to infer that a person intends all the natural and probable consequences of an act knowingly done or knowingly omitted. So unless the evidence of a case leads you to a contrary conclusion you may draw the inference and find that the accused intended all the natural and probable consequences which one standing in like circumstances and possessing like knowledge should reasonably have been expected to result from an act knowingly done or knowingly omitted by the accused.

Counsel for the defendant objected, claiming that instructing the members of the jury that they may infer from acts committed by the accused the specific intent to defraud as an element of the crime, "unless the evidence leads the jury to a contrary conclusion," shifted the burden onto defendants to introduce evidence of lack of intent to defraud. The objection was overruled by the trial court. On appeal, the Fifth Circuit approved the trial court's finding of guilty because the other instructions as a whole fully informed the jury of the government's burden of proof on the question of intent. However, the court said that in future cases, the district courts in that circuit would not use language and instruction that reasonably could be interpreted as shifting the burden to the accused to produce the proof of innocence.[23]

Similar wording was used in other circuits, and the matter came to the Supreme Court in 1979 in *Sandstrom v. Montana*.[24] In this murder case, the defendant was charged with deliberate homicide, and the question of intent was an important element of the crime. At the trial, the defendant's attorney informed the jury that, although his client admitted to killing the victim, he did not do so "purposely or knowingly," and he was, therefore, not guilty of

---

21 319 F.2d 404 (5th Cir. 1963), *cert. denied*, 375 U.S. 986, 84 S. Ct. 520, 11 L. Ed. 2d 474 (1964).

22 574 F.2d 778 (3d Cir. 1978). This case included eight instructions to the jury regarding burden of proof and presumption of innocence.

23 *Ibid.*

24 Sandstrom v. Montana, 442 U.S. 510, 99 S. Ct. 2450, 61 L. Ed. 2d 39 (1979).

a deliberate crime but guilty, rather, of a lesser crime. The defendant's counsel objected to the instruction that "the law presumes that a person intends the ordinary consequences of his voluntary act." He argued that this instruction had the effect of shifting the burden of proof on the issue of purpose or knowledge to the defendant, and it was therefore impermissible because it was in violation of the constitutional guarantee of due process of law. The Supreme Court, in reversing the decision, reasoned that:

> A reasonable jury could have interpreted the presumptions as "conclusive," i.e., not technically as a presumption at all, but rather an irrebuttable direction by the court to find intent once convinced of the facts triggering the assumption. Alternatively, the jury may have interpreted the instruction as a direction to find intent upon proof of the defendant's voluntary actions, unless the defendant proved the contrary.

Under either interpretation, according to the Court, the burden of persuasion on the element of intent effectively shifted to the defendant. The Court then stated:

> We conclude that under either of the two possible interpretations of the instruction set out above, precisely that effect (relieving the state of the burden of proof) would result, and that the instruction therefore represents constitutional error.

To summarize, the defendant has the burden of going forward with the evidence to show an affirmative defense such as alibi or insanity; however, instruction that tends to require the defendant to prove his innocence, or any instruction which relieves the prosecution of proving an element of the crime, violates the due process requirement that the prosecution must prove every element of the offense beyond a reasonable doubt.

§ 3.9   Burden of proving affirmative defenses—general

If the defendant in a criminal case relies upon distinct substantive matters which exempt him from punishment and absolve him from liability, he has the burden of proving his defenses, usually by a preponderance of the evidence. The defendant has only to raise in the minds of the jury a reasonable doubt of his guilt, arising out of the evidence of the case, to be entitled to acquittal. When the defendant claims extenuation or justification, the burden of proof is on him to establish such a fact by a preponderance of the evidence.[25]

---

25 Commonwealth v. Dietrick, 218 Pa. 236, 66 A. 1007 (1907).

In the sections that follow, some of the more common instances of justification, excuse and other affirmative defenses are discussed (with the burden of proof question emphasized).

§ 3.10 —Alibi

In some jurisdictions, courts have held that the issue of alibi is an affirmative defense, and that when it is asserted, the burden of proof by a preponderance of the evidence rests upon the defendant.26 Others hold that it is incorrect to classify an alibi as an affirmative defense because the defendant merely offers evidence to rebut the evidence introduced by the state. As an alibi is a denial of any connection with the crime, the defendant must be acquitted if his proof raises a reasonable doubt of his guilt—either by itself or in conjunction with other facts in the case.27

Some states require by statute that the defense must give notice in advance to the prosecution that alibi witnesses are to be used at the trial. The defense must also furnish the names of the witnesses. If prior notice is not given and names are not furnished, the witnesses normally are not allowed to testify. The reason for this, as expressed in *Williams v. Florida,* is that alibi evidence is particularly susceptible to fabrication; therefore, the state has a legitimate interest in not being surprised at trial with a parade of witnesses avowing that the defendant was not at the scene of the crime.28

Such a statute cannot be used however, to prohibit a defendant from testifying in his own behalf even if he has not given the notice to the prosecution. In *State v. Hibbard,* the court pointed out that the state already has the burden of proving beyond a reasonable doubt that the defendant was at the scene of the crime during the time in question. Accordingly, the court held that the trial court erred in denying the appellant the opportunity to testify concerning his whereabouts at the time that the crime occurred.29

---

26 State v. Stump, 254 Iowa 1181, 119 N.W.2d 210 (1963).

27 Halko v. State, 54 Del. 180, 175 A.2d 42 (1961).

28 Williams v. Florida, 399 U.S. 78, 90 S. Ct. 1893, 26 L. Ed. 2d 446 (1970). *See also* State v. Lewis, 391 N.W.2d 726 (Iowa 1986), which held that a trial court's exclusion of the defendant's alibi witness was an abuse of discretion when the defense counsel filed a notice of alibi one day after he heard of the existence of witnesses, witnesses were made available for all informal interviews or depositions before the trial, and the state had one week before the trial to investigate the alibi defense, but chose to do nothing, even declining interviews with witnesses.

29 State v. Hibbard, 273 N.W.2d 172 (S.D. 1978).

In the case of *People v. O'Neill,* a New York court determined that the state has the burden of disproving the alibi defense beyond a reasonable doubt after the defendant had raised the issue.[30] The court in that case also held that the alibi defense, when considered with other evidence, may raise a reasonable doubt as to guilt.

§ 3.11 —Insanity

There are two distinct and divergent rules respecting the degree of evidence necessary to rebut the presumption of sanity normally prevailing in a criminal case. Under the first rule, the ultimate burden of proof of sanity is, like any other element of the crime, upon the prosecution, and sanity must be shown beyond a reasonable doubt. However, the matter of the defendant's insanity must be put in issue by the defendant before the duty of the prosecution to prove sanity beyond a reasonable doubt will arise. Under this approach, some evidence of insanity will suffice to dissipate the presumption of sanity and put the burden of proof on the prosecution. To raise the issue of sanity, the defendant has the burden of introducing evidence sufficient to evoke the possibility that, as a result of mental disease or defect, he lacked a substantial capacity to appreciate the wrongfulness of his conduct or to conform his conduct to the requirements of the law.

The rule followed by most state courts (and federal courts until 1984) requires that when the defendant introduces substantial evidence of his insanity, the issue of his capacity to commit the offense becomes a question of proof, and the prosecution's burden of going forward with the evidence requires it to introduce sufficient evidence on the issue of sanity to preclude a verdict of acquittal for the defendant.[31]

A considerable number of courts take a different approach and hold that insanity is an affirmative defense which must be shown by the defendant by a preponderance of the evidence. The statutes in a number of states provide that the defendant has the burden of proving his legal insanity by a preponderance of the evidence.[32] The United States Supreme Court in several instances has determined that placing this burden on the defendant does not violate the Constitution of the United States.[33]

In 1984, as part of the Comprehensive Crime Control Act, Congress enacted legislation entitled "Insanity Defense Reform Act of 1984." New

---

30 People v. O'Neill, 79 A.D.2d 429, 437 N.Y.S.2d 202 (1981).

31 United States v. Westerhausen, 283 F.2d 844 (7th Cir. 1960).

32 CAL. EVID. CODE § 522.

33 Patterson v. New York, 432 U.S. 197, 97 S. Ct. 2319, 53 L. Ed. 2d 281 (1977); Leland v. Oregon, 343 U.S. 790, 72 S. Ct. 1002, 96 L. Ed. 1302 (1952).

Section 402 of Title 18 of the United States Code defines the scope of the insanity defense for federal offenses and shifts the burden of proof to the defendant. This section provides:

(a) Affirmative Defense—It is an affirmative defense to a prosecution under any Federal statute that, at the time of the commission of the acts constituting the offense, a defendant as a result of a severe mental disease or defect, was unable to appreciate the nature and quality or the wrongfulness of his acts. Mental disease or defect does not otherwise constitute a defense.

(b) Burden of Proof—The defendant has the burden of proving the defense of insanity by clear and convincing evidence.[34]

The standard of proof—clear and convincing evidence—is a higher standard than a mere preponderance of the evidence. However, it is less than beyond a reasonable doubt. The committee discussing this defense believed that a more rigorous requirement than proof by a preponderance of the evidence was necessary to insure that only those defendants who plainly satisfy the requirements of the defense are exonerated from what is otherwise criminal behavior.[35] The purpose of this amendment is to eliminate the confusing spectacle of competing expert witnesses testifying to directly contradictory conclusions as to the ultimate legal issue to be found by the trier of fact. According to the new law, expert psychiatric testimony is limited to presenting and explaining the diagnosis of the psychiatrist. The expert witness may not state an opinion as to whether the defendant did or did not have the mental conditions constituting an element of the crime charged. Such ultimate issues are matters for the trier of fact alone.

Another provision of the Crime Control Act relates to the disposition of a person found not guilty by reason of insanity.[36] This section of the Act provides:

If a person is found not guilty only by reason of insanity at the time of the offense charged, he shall be committed to a suitable facility until such time as he is eligible for release pursuant to subsection (e).

Subsection (d) of the Act relates to burden of proof. It provides that:

In a hearing pursuant to subsection (c) of this section, a person found not guilty only by reason of insanity of an offense involving

---

34 Pub. L. No. 98-473, ch. IV, § 402 (amending 18 U.S.C. § 20).

35 Senate Comm. on Judiciary, 98th Cong. 2d Sess. (1982), *reprinted in* 1984 U.S. Code Cong. & Admin. News 232.

36 Pub. L. No. 98-473, § 403.

bodily injury to, or serious damage to property of, another person, or involving a substantial risk of such injury or damage, has the burden of proving by clear and convincing evidence that his release would not create a substantial risk of bodily injury to another person or serious damage of property of another due to present mental disease or defect. With respect to any other offense, the person has the burden of proof by the preponderance of the evidence.

Placing the burden of proof on the accused person is the procedure in effect in the District of Columbia. It was upheld by the Supreme Court in *Jones v. United States*.[37] In the *Jones* case, the defendant was acquitted of attempted shoplifting by reason of insanity. The court upheld the District of Columbia Code provision which required the defendant to demonstrate at the commitment hearing by a preponderance of the evidence that he was no longer mentally ill or dangerous. Although a recent provision of Congress placed the burden of proof on the defendant, the issue has not reached the Supreme Court. In view of previous decisions, in all likelihood the provision will be approved.

In 1984, when Congress was considering the amendments to the United States Code relating to the insanity defense, the committee considering the modifications found that more than half the states placed the burden of proving insanity on the defendant. Most of the states that place the burden on the defendant require that the defendant must prove severe mental disease or defect by a preponderance of the evidence, while the federal law now places the burden on the defendant to prove this by clear and convincing evidence.

To summarize, Title IV—Offenders with Mental Disease or Defect—as enacted in 1984, clearly establishes the burden of proof in federal cases. However, the law is not uniform in the various states. In some states, the issue of a defendant's capacity to commit the offense becomes a question of proof and the prosecution must introduce evidence sufficient to preclude a verdict of acquittal for the defendant. In other states, the burden is on the accused to prove insanity by a preponderance of the evidence while, in a third group of states and in the federal courts, the burden of proof is on the defendant under a standard of clear and convincing evidence. In any event, however, the defendant who claims insanity as a defense has at least some burden to go forward with evidence to overcome the presumption of sanity.

---

37 463 U.S. 354, 103 S. Ct. 3043, 77 L. Ed. 2d 694 (1983).

§ 3.12 —Self-defense

In criminal prosecutions involving violence to the "victim," justifiable self-defense may be set up as a complete defense to, or exoneration from, liability for the act charged. As a general rule, the prosecution throughout a homicide case has the burden of establishing the killing, but after it has shown the fact of the killing under circumstances where it does not appear that the defendant acted in self-defense, the defendant must go forward with proof that he did so act.[38]

Specifically stating that the United States Supreme Court will follow the *Patterson* case and other such decisions, which allow states to follow their own affirmative defense and burden of proof rules, the Supreme Court in 1987 agreed that placing on the defendant the burden of proving that he was acting in self-defense when he committed the alleged homicide did not violate due process.[39] Ohio's definition of aggravated murder requires the prosecution to prove that the defendant both purposely and with prior calculation and design caused another's death. On the other hand, Ohio requires the defendant to prove self-defense by a preponderance of the evidence. The United States Supreme Court agreed that neither Ohio law nor the instructions concerning self-defense violate the due process clause of the Fourteenth Amendment by shifting to the petitioner the state's burden of proving the elements of the crime. The court went on to note that the "mere fact that all but two States have abandoned the common-law rule that affirmative defenses, including self-defense, must be proved by the defendant does not render the rule unconstitutional."

While a state statute requiring the defendant to prove self-defense does not have an improper burden-shifting result so as to be unconstitutional, some states require only that the defendant raise some evidence tending to prove the affirmative defense of self-defense. In these states the state has the burden of establishing beyond a reasonable doubt that the defendant did not act in self-defense—after the defendant has presented evidence of self-defense.[40] In the Illinois case of *People v. Harris,* the Appellate Court of Illinois, after first noting that at least some evidence of self-defense must be introduced at trial in order for an affirmative defense or self-defense to be properly raised, continued by making it clear that "the state must prove beyond a reasonable doubt that the defendant did not act in self defense, once the defense is raised," in addition to proving beyond a reasonable

---

38 40 AM. JUR. 2D *Homicide* § 246.

39 Martin v. Ohio, 480 U.S. 228, 107 S. Ct. 1098, 94 L. Ed. 2d 267 (1987). *See* case in Part II.

40 People v. Florey, 153 Ill. App. 3d 530, 505 N.E.2d 1096 (1987); People v. Harris, 153 Ill. App. 3d 308, 506 N.E.2d (1987).

doubt the other elements of the offense with which the defendant is charged. In the case of *Lilly v. State,* the Supreme Court of Indiana, after making reference to a previous case, made this finding:

> When the defendant claims self-defense, he must prove three facts: that he was in a place where he had a right to be; that he acted without fault; and that he had a reasonable fear or apprehension of death or great bodily harm . . . .

> Once self-defense has been asserted, the State carries the burden of showing the absence of one of these elements beyond a reasonable doubt.[41]

The court went on to explain that the state may carry its burden by rebutting the defense directly, by affirmatively showing that the defendant did not act in self-defense, or by simply relying upon the sufficiency of its evidence in chief. Finally, the court admonished that a defendant's conviction in spite of a claim of self-defense would be reversed only if no reasonable person could say that self-defense was negated by the state beyond a reasonable doubt.

To summarize, in some states when the accused offers the affirmative defense of self-defense and produces some evidence thereof, the burden is on the prosecutor to prove beyond a reasonable doubt that the accused did not act in self-defense. In other states the accused has not only the burden of producing evidence of self-defense, but must prove by a preponderance of the evidence that he acted in self-defense. A state statute requiring that this burden be placed upon the defense does not violate the Constitution.

§ 3.13   Sufficiency of evidence

In determining the sufficiency of the evidence to sustain a conviction, the reviewing court must determine whether the evidence, construed most favorably for the prosecution, is such that a jury could logically have found that the defendant was guilty beyond a reasonable doubt.[42] Even if the jury, after hearing all of the evidence, finds the defendant guilty, a reviewing court, on appeal or in a habeas corpus action, may find that the evidence was not sufficient to support the finding of guilty. In *Jackson v. Virginia,* the United States Supreme Court, in confirming the authority of a federal court to review a state court decision on the sufficiency of the evidence, made this comment:

---

41   Lilly v. State, 506 N.E.2d 23 (Ind. 1987).
42   Wallace v. United States, 281 F.2d 656 (4th Cir. 1960).

Yet a properly instructed jury may occasionally convict even when it can be said that no rational trier of fact could find guilt beyond a reasonable doubt, and the same may be said of a trial judge sitting as a jury.43

Once it is recognized that a reviewing court can look behind the decision of the jury to determine if there was sufficient evidence to justify a finding of guilt beyond a reasonable doubt, the question then becomes: What is the test of sufficiency?

In *Jackson,* the United States Court of Appeals for the Fourth Circuit had applied the so-called *Thompson v. Louisville*44 sufficiency-of-the-evidence rule and refused to reverse the state court's conviction. Under the *Thompson* rule, a state court conviction must be affirmed by a reviewing court if there is any evidence in the record to support it. Under *Thompson,* if there is absolutely no evidence to justify the jury in finding guilt, then the court will reverse the conviction. But if there is any evidence to support the intent, as there was in *Jackson,* the case will be affirmed.

The defendant in *Jackson* appealed to the United States Supreme Court, claiming that the "any evidence rule" was inadequate to protect against misapplication of the constitutional standards of reasonable doubt. The United States Supreme Court agreed, stating that the rule that should have been applied was not the "any evidence rule," but rather the rule that was stated in *In re Winship,*45 which held that a federal habeas corpus court must consider not whether there was any evidence to support a state conviction, but whether there was sufficient evidence to justify a rational trier of facts to find guilt beyond a reasonable doubt. The Supreme Court in *Jackson* first held that the *Thompson* "no evidence rule" is simply inadequate to protect against misapplications of the constitutional standard of reasonable doubt. That Court then insisted:

> Instead the relevant question is whether after reviewing the evidence in the light most favorable to the prosecution, any rational trier of fact could have found the essential elements of the crime beyond a reasonable doubt.

In affirming that a federal court can and will apply the *Winship* sufficiency rule, the Court in *Jackson* made this conclusion as to the rules to be followed:

---

43 Jackson v. Virginia, 443 U.S. 307, 99 S. Ct. 2781, 61 L. Ed. 2d (1979).

44 Thompson v. Louisville, 362 U.S. 199, 80 S. Ct. 624, 4 L. Ed. 2d 654 (1960).

45 In re Winship, 397 U.S. 358, 90 S. Ct. 1068, 25 L. Ed. 2d 368 (1970). *See* case in Part II, *infra.*

> We hold that in a challenge to a state criminal conviction . . . the appellant is entitled to habeas corpus relief if it is found that upon the record evidence adduced at the trial no rational trier of fact could have found proof of guilt beyond a reasonable doubt.

After asserting that the Supreme Court has this authority and after stating the rule, the Court then found that when applying the rule to the facts of this case, Jackson still had no cause of action. The Court said that from the evidence in the record it was clear that the judge could reasonably have found beyond a reasonable doubt that the petitioner did possess the necessary intent at or before the time of the killing to justify the first degree murder conviction.

To summarize the sufficiency-of-the-evidence rule, in a criminal case the prosecutor must introduce relevant and otherwise admissible evidence sufficient for the triers of fact to find the defendant guilty beyond a reasonable doubt. The reviewing court may set aside a conviction even after the triers of fact have rendered a guilty verdict if that court finds that no rational trier of fact could logically have found the defendant guilty beyond a reasonable doubt.

§ 3.14 Summary

The burden to prove the accused guilty beyond a reasonable doubt is always on the prosecution and never shifts to the defense in a criminal case. This is one of the primary differences between civil and criminal cases, as in civil cases the plaintiff has only the burden of proving the claim by the greater weight of the evidence.

Depending upon the nature of the case, there are three degrees of proof required. These are a preponderance of the evidence, clear and convincing evidence, and beyond a reasonable doubt. While in a civil case the plaintiff is usually only required to establish his claim by a preponderance of the evidence, in some instances—even in civil cases—it is necessary to go beyond this standard and require proof by clear and convincing evidence. In a criminal case, however, there is no doubt that the accused is assumed to be innocent until his guilt is established beyond a reasonable doubt.

The burden is on the prosecution in a criminal case to show affirmatively the existence of every material fact, including each element of the crime, the identity of the person committing the crime and that the crime was perpetrated in violation of the penal laws of the place where it was committed.

Even though the primary burden in a criminal case is on the prosecution, the accused has some responsibility to introduce evidence. For example, when claiming an affirmative defense such as coercion, self-defense, entrapment or mistake, the defendant may have the burden of proving the defense, usually by a preponderance of the evidence. But any instruction by the court that tends to require the defendant to prove his innocence, or which relieves the prosecution of the duty of proving an element of the crime, violates the due process clause of the Fourteenth Amendment.

Even though alibi, strictly speaking, is not an affirmative defense, as the defendant merely offers evidence to rebut the evidence introduced by the prosecution that he was at the scene of the crime, the defendant must introduce evidence to substantiate this alibi claim. If the defense is insanity, the law in some jurisdictions requires that the defendant prove his legal insanity by preponderance of the evidence. Some jurisdictions require proof by clear and convincing evidence. Also, when evidence is introduced to show self-defense to justify an otherwise criminal act, the defendant may be constitutionally required to offer proof by a preponderance of the evidence that he did act in self-defense.

All criminal justice personnel, starting with the law enforcement investigator, must recognize the additional burden on the prosecution and must be aware that sufficient evidence must be gathered to convince the jury or the judge not only that the accused is probably guilty of the offense charged but that he is guilty beyond a reasonable doubt. Those involved in the criminal justice process should also recognize the fact that the defense will make every effort to create a doubt in the minds of the jury.

A study of the burden of proof accentuates the necessity of becoming familiar with other evidence rules which bear upon the admissibility of evidence. Much of the remainder of the book is devoted to a discussion of such rules.

CHAPTER 4
PROOF VIA EVIDENCE

At the trial of a person charged with murder, the fact of death is provable by circumstantial evidence, notwithstanding that neither the body nor any trace of the body has been found and that the accused has made no confession of any participation in the crime. Before he can be convicted, the fact of death should be proved by such circumstances as render the commission of the crime morally certain and leave no ground for possible doubt; the circumstantial evidence should be so cogent and compelling as to convince a jury that upon no rational hypothesis other than murder can the facts be accounted for.
Rex. v. Horry, 1952 N.Z.L.R. 111

§ 4.1   Introduction

In the previous chapter, cases were cited and discussed which leave no doubt that the burden of proving guilt in a criminal case is on the prosecution. How does the prosecutor go about meeting this burden? Must each fact or each bit of knowledge used by the jury or other factfinder in determining guilt or innocence be placed before the jury in the form of direct evidence?

Although the parties have the responsibility of introducing evidence to verify the claims presented, it is not necessary that all facts before the court be in the form of direct evidence. To save time and to avoid placing an unnecessary burden on the parties, the judge may take judicial notice of certain facts and may advise the jury that they may make certain presumptions and inferences. The factfinders may also consider facts stipulated by the parties. Therefore, the jury or other factfinders may make a decision from (1) facts presented in the form of evidence; (2) information judicially noticed by the judge; (3) legal presumptions; (4) judicially approved inferences; and (5) accepted stipulations. In this chapter, emphasis is on the first of these, facts presented in the form of evidence.

After considering the procedure relating to pretrial motions to exclude evidence, this chapter discusses general admissibility tests. This is followed by a section describing the order of presenting evidence at the trial. Also, the role of the judge, jury, witness, prosecuting attorney and legal counsel for the defense in relation to the introduction and evaluation of evidence is explained. Finally, the rules relating to the admissibility and weight of direct and circumstantial evidence are comprehensively considered.

In Chapters 5 and 6, "substitutes for evidence"—judicial notice, presumptions, inferences and stipulations—are defined and examples of each are offered.

§ 4.2 Pretrial motions pertaining to evidence

Rule 104

PRELIMINARY QUESTIONS

(a) Questions of admissibility generally

Preliminary questions concerning the qualification of a person to be a witness, the existence of a privilege, or the admissibility of evidence shall be determined by the court, subject to the provisions of subdivision (b). In making its determination it is not bound by the rules of evidence except those with respect to privileges.

(b) Relevancy conditioned on fact

When the relevancy of evidence depends upon the fulfillment of a condition of fact, the court shall admit it upon, or subject to, the introduction of evidence sufficient to support a finding of the fulfillment of the condition.[1]

* * *

Even before the trial begins, the parties may challenge the evidence that has been made ready for introduction at the trial. Any defense or objection which is capable of a determination without a trial of the general issue may be raised by motion before trial. These pretrial motions include

---

1 Fed. R. Evid. 104 (a) & (b).

challenges to the competence or fairness of the tribunal, the statement of the charges, the competency of the defendant to stand trial, the legality of the evidence, and constitutional challenges such as multiple prosecutions or failure to grant a speedy trial.

As a general rule, the motion to suppress evidence must be made before the plea is entered or within a reasonable time after entry of the plea, by leave of the court, but the failure to challenge the evidence in a timely manner may be excused by the court for good cause. If a motion is made to suppress evidence, and the judge grants this motion, the evidence, even though relevant to the issues, will not be admitted at the trial.

The most common pretrial motion to exclude evidence is that which challenges the use of illegally seized evidence in violation of either the Fourth Amendment to the United States Constitution or the search and seizure provisions of state constitutions. For example, if the defendant claims that evidence has been obtained illegally, a motion will be made to exclude that evidence. This motion is heard at a pretrial hearing. If, upon motion to suppress, the accused can show in fact that evidence was secured by unlawful search and seizure, and such evidence does not come within an exception recognized by the courts, the evidence will be suppressed.2 But if the prosecutor can show that the evidence was obtained without violating the Constitution, or is within an exception to the exclusionary rule, the motion to suppress will be denied, and the evidence will be admitted unless excluded for some other reason.

Evidence may also be challenged as having been secured in violation of other constitutional provisions. For example, if the self-incrimination provisions of the Fifth Amendment, the right-to-counsel provisions of the Sixth Amendment, or the due process clause of the Fifth or Fourteenth Amendments have been violated by enforcement personnel in obtaining evidence, the evidence may be inadmissible.3

§ 4.3   General approach to admissibility

The rules of evidence for all practical purposes are rules of exclusion. Therefore, all evidence offered is admissible unless, upon objection, it is subject to exclusion. When one party asks a question of the witness and his adversary has an objection to it, it will be found that the adversary's objection is based either upon the form of the question that was asked or upon

---

2   Mapp v. Ohio, 367 U.S. 643, 16 Ohio Op. 2d 384, 81 S. Ct. 1684, 6 L. Ed. 2d 1081 (1961).

3   *See* Chapter 16, *infra,* for more comprehensive coverage of the exclusion of evidence which has been illegally obtained.

the substance of the answer solicited. One way to approach the rules of evidence is to keep these simple tests of form and substance in mind as each rule is discussed.

a.   Objections as to form

In order to avoid confusing the witness, the court will require that a question be clear and intelligent. Questions which are confusing, improperly phrased, misleading or argumentative will not be allowed if an objection is raised by opposing counsel. In fact, often the judge himself will ask that such questions be rephrased. The question which is phrased in such a way that there can be no definite answer will, of course, mislead the witness as well as the jury.

Also, a question which has two parts is sometimes objectionable as to form because it is impossible to answer both parts with one answer. Other questions which are sometimes objectionable as to form are classified as leading questions.[4]

b.   Objections as to substance

If there is no objection as to form or if an objection is made and settled, the test of substance is then applied. One easy way to understand the test of substance is to imagine three hurdles erected between the evidence and the court. Before the evidence can be admitted into court all three hurdles must be cleared. They are: relevancy, materiality and competency.

The *relevancy* test is: does the information have a tendency to prove or disprove one or more of the facts and issues of the case? To be relevant, the information must have a tendency to establish or disprove the matter in issue in the case.[5] *Materiality* concerns the importance of evidence. Evidence is material only when it affects a fact or issue of the case in a significant way. The definition of *competency* is more elusive. Competent evidence is that which is legally adequate and sufficient. The competency test is a catch-all for the exclusionary rules. For example, evidence obtained by illegal search in violation of the Constitution is inadmissible not because it is immaterial or irrelevant but because of its legal inadequacy or incompetency.

If the proposed evidence meets the tests of form and substance, it is admitted into court. The weight or the importance of the evidence depends on many other factors.

4   Leading questions are discussed in Chapter 9, *infra*.
5   The relevancy and materiality rules and examples are comprehensively discussed in Chapter 7, *infra*.

§ 4.4   Order of presenting evidence at the trial[6]

The judge has much discretion in establishing court procedures, but he generally follows the procedures which have been developed over a period of years and which have become standard. The usual order of procedure in presenting the case is as follows:[7]

1. State's (prosecution's) evidence in chief.
2. Defense's evidence in chief.
3. Prosecution's evidence in rebuttal.
4. Defense's evidence in rejoinder.

Each of these steps is discussed to point out its scope and limitations.

a.   State's evidence in chief

As the prosecution has the burden of proof, it first introduces evidence on behalf of the state. The prosecutor may call as many witnesses as he feels are necessary and may introduce exhibits, photographs, documents or other types of evidence which may help the jury in determining the guilt or innocence of the accused—provided that these meet the admissibility tests. During this phase of the procedure, the prosecutor is "carrying the ball" and "calling the plays." He selects the witnesses for the prosecution and guides the flow of evidence. Each prosecution witness is questioned by the prosecutor first.[8] Although the defense has an opportunity to cross-examine the prosecution witnesses, the defense at this stage cannot introduce its own witnesses and—according to the majority view—must limit cross-examination to matters testified to on direct examination.

When the prosecuting attorney has introduced his evidence in chief or what he feels is sufficient evidence to make a case against the defendant, he signifies the completion of his case in chief by announcing, "The prosecution rests."

b.   Defense's evidence in chief

After the prosecution rests, the defense has the opportunity to present its evidence in chief. The defense may present evidence in denial of the prosecution's claim; the defendant may attempt to establish an alibi or attempt to establish one of the other affirmative defenses. The defendant does not have to take the stand in his own behalf, but he may do so. If he

---

6 For a more comprehensive explanation of criminal procedure from arrest to final release, *see* Carlson, CRIMINAL JUSTICE PROCEDURE (4th ed. 1991).

7 McCormick, EVIDENCE, p. 7.

8 The procedure to be followed in the examination of witnesses is discussed in Chapter 9, *infra*.

does, the defendant is usually the first witness to take the stand at this stage of the procedure.9 As in the case of the prosecution, each defense witness is questioned first by defense counsel and then may be cross-examined by the prosecution. When the defense counsel has completed the presentation of his evidence, the defendant's attorney announces, "The defense rests."

c. Prosecution's rebuttal

The prosecution now has the opportunity to rebut the evidence presented by the defense. The prosecution at this stage may not present witnesses that merely support the allegations of the indictment. That should have been done when the prosecution presented its evidence in chief. At this point, the prosecution is limited to the introduction of testimony or other evidence which is directed to refuting the evidence of the defense. New witnesses may be called at this time, but only if they can rebut the evidence presented by the defendant. For example, if the defense raises the question of insanity, the prosecution may offer evidence to show that the defendant was not insane as defined by law. In this stage, as in other stages, the witness may not only be examined on direct but may also be cross-examined by opposing counsel.

d. Defense rejoinder

The defense also has the opportunity to introduce evidence contrary to that introduced by the prosecution during the rebuttal. That is called the rejoinder. Again, the evidence here is limited to refuting the evidence presented by the prosecution on rebuttal.

There are instances when the case may continue with the prosecution and the defense having the opportunity to refute the evidence presented by the other. However, it is obvious that this becomes more and more limited and, in the usual case, both parties will have presented all the evidence that they intend to present by the end of the defendant's rejoinder.

When both parties have announced that they have rested their cases, the hearing on the facts comes to an end, and the trial proceeds with the arguments of counsel and the court's instructions to the jury.

---

9   In 1972 the United States Supreme Court held that requiring the defendant to testify before other defense witnesses violates the self-incrimination provisions of the Constitution. Brooks v. Tennessee, 406 U.S. 605, 92 S. Ct. 1891, 32 L. Ed. 2d 358 (1972).

§ 4.5   Procedure for offering and challenging evidence

Rule 103

RULINGS ON EVIDENCE

(a) **Effect of erroneous ruling.** Error may not be predicated upon a ruling which admits or excludes evidence unless a substantial right of the party is affected, and

    (1) **Objection.** In case the ruling is one admitting evidence, a timely objection or motion to strike appears of record, stating the specific ground of objection, if the specific ground was not apparent from the context; or

    (2) **Offer of proof.** In case the ruling is one excluding evidence, the substance of the evidence was made known to the court by offer or was apparent from the context within which questions were asked.

(b) **Record of offer and ruling.** The court may add any other or further statement which shows the character of the evidence, the form in which it was offered, the objection made, and the ruling thereon. It may direct the making of an offer in question and answer form.10

* * *

It is obvious that not all evidence is admitted into court. The courts follow a complex set of rules in determining what evidence should be admitted and what evidence should be excluded. Much of the rest of this book will be devoted to the rules which have been developed for the judge in determining the admissibility of evidence. It is safe to say that most of these rules are rules of exclusion.

The usual way of offering and eliciting oral testimony is to place the witness on the stand and ask him a question or series of questions. If either the prosecution or the defense believes a question is improper, an objection is made and the court then decides if the answer should be allowed. If an objection is made, the party who elicited the information may be required to state the purpose of the proof offered, and the objector may be required to state the specific grounds for his request that an answer be excluded.

---

10 FED. R. EVID. 103. The Federal Rules of Evidence, as effective Jan. 2, 1975 (Pub. L. No. 93-595) and as amended Nov., 1988, are applicable to United States Courts, Magistrates, and Bankruptcy Courts. Portions of these Rules, as well as the Committee Comments thereto, are inserted where relevant to the text discussion. The complete Rules appear in the Appendix, *infra.*

In the case of real evidence such as bullets, guns, articles of clothing, or the like, the party offering the evidence, after having it identified or authenticated by a witness, submits it to the opposing counsel for inspection. When this has been done, it is presented to the judge and, depending upon the type of evidence, to each juror individually or to the jury as a whole.

If the judge makes what one party considers an erroneous ruling, this can be challenged on appeal. In general, however, error will not be predicated upon a ruling unless a substantial right of the party—especially the defendant in a criminal case—is affected.

In some states it is still necessary to "except." That is, after the judge's adverse ruling excluding the evidence or overruling the objection, the counsel comments, "We except." That, in effect, is a protest against the correctness of the ruling of the judge and saves the matter for review. To avoid the waste of time, the rules in many states provide that the formal exception procedure is not necessary.

In emphasizing the requirement of Rule 103 that the opposing party must make a timely objection, federal courts have indicated that objections to the admission of evidence are preserved only if they are timely and state the specific grounds for the objection.[11]

§ 4.6   Role of trial judge in evidence matters

In the English and American systems, the trial judge is responsible for insuring that the trial is administered in an orderly way and that it progresses efficiently and smoothly. In a criminal case with a jury, the jury decides which facts have been established beyond a reasonable doubt by the evidence and makes a decision on the facts; however, the judge still plays a very important role in relation to the evidence. Some of these duties are enumerated and explained. The judge:

---

[11] Wilson v. Attaway, 727 F. 2d 1227 (11th Cir. 1985); for further analysis of the harmless error rule, see Rose v. Clark, 54 U.S.L.W. 5023 (1986), and discussion in § 6.7 of this book; *see also* United States v. Yamin, 868 F. 2d 130 (5th Cir. 1989), where the court, in interpreting Federal Rule 103 (a) (1), held that in a prosecution for trafficking in counterfeit designer watches, the defendant did not preserve for appeal his argument that the best evidence rule barred the admission of testimony about the marks on the watches. As the defendants did not object to the admission of any testimony or evidence on the basis of the best evidence rule, the court held that the objection was not sufficient to preserve the contention that the evidence should not have been admitted.

Determines before trial if evidence is admissible at the trial—In the first instance, the judge determines, after listening to arguments from both sides, what evidence will be admitted during the trial and what evidence will be suppressed. If a motion to suppress is made before the trial starts, the parties may appeal the ruling on that motion to a higher court, but the trial judge does make the initial decision.

Acts on motions regarding evidence during the trial—During the trial, if a party challenges evidence as being irrelevant, immaterial or incompetent, the judge makes the decision and announces that decision in court.

Makes decisions concerning the constitutionality of law enforcement activities—A motion to exclude evidence obtained in violation of the Constitution may be made at a pretrial hearing on a motion to suppress or may be made during the trial if the point arises then. To decide this challenge properly, the judge must be familiar with the decisions regarding such matters as search and seizure, confessions, right to counsel, self-incrimination and due process. If a motion is made to exclude evidence because these provisions are violated and the judge admits the evidence that has been obtained in violation of the Constitution, the reviewing court on appeal can and probably will reverse the decision unless the error is harmless.

Protects the witnesses from overzealous examination and cross-examination by counsel—Overzealous counsel sometimes browbeats a witness by continuing to ask questions or by unnecessarily cross-examining a witness. The judge in his discretion has control over this process.

Takes judicial notice—The judge plays a very important role in judicially noticing facts which may be considered by the jury in making the decision.[12]

Determines competency of the witness to testify—The judge determines if the witness is competent to testify.[13]

In addition, the judge makes the decisions as to the law in the case, advises the jury as to what facts may be considered, and gives them alternatives in returning their verdict.

Finally, when a trial is without a jury, such as when the defendant waives his right to a jury, the judge also acts as the factfinder. In this instance, the judge acts in a dual capacity; he acts in his normal capacity as a judge, and he also performs the function of the jury in determining the facts of the case.

While the trial judge in the criminal case has a wide latitude in making decisions regarding the admissibility of evidence, he is limited in the quality

---

12 Judicial notice is discussed in Chapter 5, *infra.*
13 The competency of the witness is discussed in Chapter 9, *infra.*

of comments that he may make to the members of the jury while they are making their decision. For example, in *Commonwealth v. Jones,* the reviewing court held that the trial court erred in instructing the jury that the testimony of an accomplice which tended to exonerate the defendant "comes from a corrupt and polluted source" and that the jury "should examine it closely and accept it only with caution and with care."[14] The reviewing court believed that this instruction invaded the province of the jury.

In another case, the reviewing court affirmed that the judge has the discretion to review the evidence presented at the trial. The court cautioned, however, that the statements made to the jury must have a reasonable basis and that the jury must decide the facts, regardless of any opinion expressed by the judge.[15]

§ 4.7   Function of the jury

In a jury trial in a criminal case, the function of the jury is to determine the facts. This is not an easy task. In almost every case, contradictory evidence is introduced by the parties, and the jurors have the almost impossible task of determining which witnesses to believe and what evidence should be given the most weight. The ultimate goal is to ascertain whether the defendant is guilty of the crime with which he has been charged and for which he is being tried. The decision is made after all of the evidence has been introduced by the prosecution and the defense and after the opposing counsel have made their arguments.

In determining what actually happened, the jurors must have the opportunity to see and hear the accuser and to ask questions to clarify matters. From the questions asked by counsel, from the answers by the witnesses, from the documentary and real evidence, from the demeanor of the witnesses on trial, and from their own knowledge of people, the jurors must reach a decision based on the evidence and substitutes for evidence that have been made available at the trial. The jurors cannot—or at least should not—make a decision from the facts that they have obtained outside the court, *i.e.,* from newspaper articles or from stories broadcast by the media.

For example, in a 1982 New York case, the Supreme Court, Appellate Division, pointed out that a verdict may be overturned on grounds of improper influence where even well-intentioned conduct by the jury tends to put before the jury evidence not introduced at the trial.[16] The court concluded that if a jury makes use of information not contained in the record,

---

14 Commonwealth v. Jones, 490 Pa. 599, 417 A.2d 201 (1980).

15 Commonwealth v. Rough, 275 Pa. Super. 50, 418 A.2d 605 (1980).

16 People v. Smith, 451 N.Y.S.2d 429 (1982).

such as the defendant's address (which a deadlocked jury might learn from newspaper accounts of a case), or if the jurors make unauthorized visits to locations described in the trial testimony, a jury verdict may be overturned. The court cautioned, however, that if the juror's conduct constituted nothing more than application of everyday perceptions and common sense to issues brought out at trial, the subsequent verdict is not tainted.

The Sixth Amendment to the Constitution guarantees a trial by jury, and when a jury trial is not waived, it is the jury's exclusive province to apply the law to the facts and make a decision.[17] Also, it is clear that a judge may not direct a verdict of guilty—no matter how conclusive the evidence.

The jurors' job is not an easy one, but the jury system is one factor that distinguishes the Anglican system from other legal systems in existence today.

§ 4.8   Role of witnesses

In many instances, criminal justice personnel act as witnesses in criminal cases. This is especially true of police investigators, but corrections officers and probation and parole officers often serve as witnesses also. The witness plays a very important part; in fact, if there were no witnesses, there could be no trial. The witnesses are the eyes and ears of the court. The jury must evaluate the testimony of the witness, and it is therefore important to recognize that it is not only *what* is said by the witness, but also *how* it is said, that is evaluated. For this reason the witness must be aware not only of what evidence he is to present, but also of his demeanor, the method of presenting the facts, his voice and even his dress. In addition to giving oral testimony, the witness is called upon to introduce real evidence or documentary evidence. This evidence is of little value if the witness does not properly explain each piece of evidence so that the jury can understand its significance.[18]

§ 4.9   Prosecuting attorney's responsibility

In a criminal case, the prosecuting attorney represents the state and has the burden of introducing evidence to prove guilt beyond a reasonable doubt. By the time the case is ready for trial, he will have collected physical evidence, interviewed the witnesses, discussed the case with the investigator, and prepared the case for trial.

---

17   United States v. Johnson, 718 F.2d 1317 (5th Cir. 1983).

18   *See* Chapter 9 for a discussion of the examination of witnesses.

Even prior to the time the trial starts, the prosecutor must decide which criminal charges should be prosecuted and which should be dismissed in the interests of justice. If he decides to prosecute, he then must decide which witnesses will be used and what evidence will be presented.

In relation to evidence, the prosecutor must decide not only what evidence is to be introduced, but how that evidence is to be introduced and the sequence of introduction. He must have supporting cases ready to present to the court in the event that the opposing counsel challenges a piece of evidence as violating one of the many exclusionary rules.

The prosecutor guides the case for the state by putting prosecution witnesses on the stand and proving the state's case in chief. After asking the preliminary questions, the prosecutor then must be so familiar with the evidence that he can ask the proper questions of the witness and can ask follow-up questions to clear up any possible misconceptions.

It is not enough for the prosecutor to be familiar with the state's case; he should be aware of the defense of the accused. He should have questions prepared for cross-examination of the defendant's witnesses and be prepared to offer evidence in rebuttal.

Finally, the prosecutor has the right to give opening remarks and closing remarks. In the opening remarks to the jury, the prosecutor explains what the state intends to prove and how the state will go about proving this. In the final closing argument, the prosecutor summarizes the evidence that has been presented in such a way as to cast it in the light most favorable to the prosecution.

Before leaving the responsibilities of the prosecutor, it should be mentioned that the prosecutor also has the responsibility to protect the innocent by making exculpatory evidence available to the defense. Also, it is reversible error for the prosecutor to use evidence that he knows—or should know—is untrue, to use evidence that was acquired in violation of the law, or to withhold evidence favorable to the defense.[19]

In the 1963 case of *Brady v. Maryland,* the U.S. Supreme Court held that suppression by the prosecution of evidence favorable to the accused upon request violates due process where evidence is material either to guilt or to punishment, irrespective of good faith or bad faith on the part of the prosecution. In interpreting the *Brady* decision, the U.S. Court of Appeals for the Eighth Circuit enumerated four types of situations in which the *Brady* doctrine applies. These are: (1) the prosecutor has not disclosed information despite a specific defense request; (2) the prosecutor has not disclosed information despite a general defense request for all exculpatory information or

---

[19] Maddox v. Montgomery, 718 F.2d 1033 (1983). *See* case in Part II, *infra;* Brady v. Maryland, 373 U.S. 83, 83 S. Ct. 1194, 10 L. Ed. 2d 215 (1963).

without any defense request at all; (3) the prosecution knows or should know that a conviction was based on false evidence; and (4) the prosecutor fails to disclose purely impeaching evidence not concerning the substantive issue, in absence of specific defense requests.[20] The court pointed out that in order to prevail on a claim under *Brady,* it must be shown that the prosecution suppressed evidence requested by the defendant, which is favorable to the defendant. One must also establish materiality of the exculpatory information suppressed by the prosecutor. In the *Maddox* case, the court reasoned that the defendant's due process rights were not violated when the prosecution suppressed evidence which was not material and which would not have any effect on the determination of guilt or innocence.

In another United States Court of Appeals case, the circuit judge indicated that it is misconduct on the part of the prosecutor to engage in trial tactics calculated to consume practically all available time, leaving the defense with the alternative of incurring the wrath of the jury or presenting a skimpy case. If the tactic is detected by this court, it will not hesitate to reverse a conviction thus obtained.[21] However, the court, after reviewing the record in that case, did not find grounds for a new trial.

In 1985, the Supreme Court of the United States, in a very comprehensive opinion, discussed the responsibility of the prosecution and that of the defense counsel.[22] In this case, the defendant was charged with defrauding a refinery by submitting false certifications that oil purchased by the refinery from the defendant's company was crude oil when it was, in fact, a less valuable fuel oil. At the trial, the defense counsel first challenged the integrity of the prosecutor and then charged that the prosecutor did not believe in the government's case. His exact words were, "I submit to you that there's not a person in this courtroom, including those sitting at this table, who thinks that Billy Young intended to defraud Apco." In response, the prosecutor said that the defendant's action was fraudulent, and that the defendant did not act with honor and integrity.

The defendant was found guilty on several counts of mail fraud, and of falsifying testimony. When the defendant appealed, the Court of Appeals reversed the conviction and remanded for retrial. The court held that the prosecutor's statements constituted misconduct and were sufficiently egregious to constitute plain error. The Court of Appeals rejected the government's contention that the statements were invited by the defense counsel's own closing arguments.[23] The prosecution then appealed to the United

---

20 *Ibid.*
21 United States v. Russell, 717 F.2d 518 (11th Cir. 1983).
22 United States v. Young, 470 U.S. 1, 105 S. Ct. 1038, 84 L. Ed. 2d 1 (1985). *See also* United States v. Skarda, 845 F.2d 1508 (8th Cir. 1988).
23 *Ibid.*

States Supreme Court. The Supreme Court, quoting from other cases, discussed the standard of conduct for prosecutors with these words:

> Nearly a half century ago, this Court counselled prosecutors to "refrain from improper methods calculated to produce a wrongful conviction. . . ." The Court made clear, however, that the adversary system permits the prosecutor to "prosecute with earnestness and vigor." In other words, "while he may strike hard blows, he is not at liberty to strike foul ones."

The Court continued by asserting that counsel on both sides of the table share a duty to confine arguments to the jury within proper bounds. Just as the conduct of the prosecutor is circumscribed, "the interest of society and the preservation of courtroom control by the judges are no more to be frustrated through unchecked improprieties by defenders."[24]

In referring to the defense counsel's conduct, the Court explained that the defense counsel, like the prosecutor, must refrain from interjecting personal beliefs into the presentation of the case, warning that defense counsel, like his adversary, must not be permitted to make unfounded and inflammatory attacks on the opposing advocate.

In this same case, *United States v. Young*, the Supreme Court even mentioned the responsibility of the judges in a criminal case. The Court declared:

> We emphasize that the trial judge has the responsibility to maintain the quorum in keeping with the nature of the proceedings; "the judge is not a mere moderator, but is the governor of the trial for the purpose of assuring its proper conduct." The judge "must meet situations as they arise and be able to cope with the contingencies inherent in the adversary process."[25]

While determining that the prosecutor's remarks in the *Young* case might be considered improper, the Supreme Court held that they could not be said to rise to the level of plain error. The Court concluded, therefore, that the remarks made by the prosecutor were not of such character as to undermine the fundamental fairness of the trial and contribute to the miscarriage of justice. The Supreme Court accordingly reversed the judgment of the Court of Appeals and upheld the conviction.

In a more recent case, the United States Supreme Court reversed the conviction of a defendant charged with murder, on the ground that the prosecutor had improperly led the jury to believe that the responsibility for determining the appropriateness of the death penalty rests with someone

---

24 Sacher v. United States, 343 U.S. 1, 72 S. Ct. 451, 96 L. Ed. 717 (1952).
25 Quercia v. United States, 289 U.S. 466, 53 S. Ct. 698, 77 L. Ed. 1321 (1933).

other than the jury.26 After evaluating the remark made to the jury by the prosecutor, the majority concluded:

> It is constitutionally impermissible to rest a death sentence on a determination made by a sentencer who has been led to believe that the responsibility for determining the appropriateness of the defendant's death rests elsewhere.

§ 4.10 Defense attorney's responsibility

When the Bill of Rights was first considered by Congress in 1791, the right to counsel was included in the draft as part of the Sixth Amendment. This amendment reads in part:

> In all criminal prosecutions the accused shall enjoy the right to have the assistance of counsel for his defense.

In addition to the federal Constitution, all of the states require by their respective constitutions that the accused shall have the right to appear and defend in person and by counsel.

This right to counsel includes the right to have effective assistance of counsel, *i.e.,* counsel that is qualified and that has "the normal customary skills and knowledge" to represent the accused.27 The primary function of the defense attorney at the trial is to make certain that all of the rights of the defendant are properly protected. As in the case of the prosecutor, the defense attorney should have the case ready for trial. This includes a pre-trial conference with the defendant and the key witnesses.

Although the defense attorney should not tell the defendant what to say in his testimony before the jury, he can advise the defendant concerning the statements that he may or may not make. The defense attorney, if he fulfills his obligation, will have investigated the case, will be prepared to ask questions of the defendant and other witnesses, and will introduce the witnesses in such a way as to present the best case for the defense. He has a responsibility to cross-examine the prosecution's witnesses and to introduce evidence to rebut the testimony of such witnesses.

Failure on the part of defense counsel to effectively assist the defendant can result in a new trial. For example, in the case of *Dufresne v. Moran,* a federal court found that a prisoner did not receive reasonable competent assistance from his counsel in the pretrial preparation and investigation of his case.28 The court also found in that case that the defendant received

---

26 Caldwell v. Mississippi, 472 U.S. 320, 105 S. Ct. 2633, 86 L. Ed. 2d 231 (1985).

27 Cardarella v. United States, 375 F.2d 222 (8th Cir. 1967).

28 Dufresne v. Moran, 572 F. Supp. 334 (D.R.I. 1983).

inadequate assistance because the defendant's counsel failed to recognize or appreciate that his client's intoxication either could have served as a potential defense to murder in the first degree, or that such state of intoxication was material to the issue of voluntariness of the petitioner's confession. Because of this failure to prepare properly for the case and to recognize the legal implications of intoxication as a defense, a writ of habeas corpus was granted to the defendant.

Even though the law requires that defense counsel effectively represent the defendant in a criminal case, the fact that the attorney used strong measures to dissuade his client from giving perjured testimony at the criminal trial does not render the assistance of counsel ineffective and unconstitutional.29 In the *Nix v. Whiteside*, the defendant had told his lawyer that he would testify that, just before the stabbing, he had seen something metallic in the victim's hand. Believing that such testimony would be perjury, the lawyer told the defendant that the existence of a gun was not necessary to establish a claim of self-defense, and that if the defendant so testified, the lawyer would inform the court and seek to withdraw from representation. After the defendant was convicted, he convinced the Eighth Circuit Court of Appeals that he had been denied effective assistance of counsel by his lawyer's refusal to allow him to testify as he proposed. Noting that a defendant who claims deprivation of the right to effective assistance of counsel must show both serious attorney error and prejudice, the Supreme Court refused to hold that the attorney's conduct was error, the Court explained that an attorney's first duty when confronted with perjury in the making is to attempt to dissuade the client from that course. The attorney is not required to breach ethical standards in order to be effective counsel.

Finally, the defense attorney has the right to make opening statements following the prosecution's statements or after the prosecution has presented its case in chief. The defense attorney also has the right to give a closing statement immediately prior to the statement given by the prosecutor. In the closing statement, the defense attorney summarizes the evidence presented by defense witnesses, plays down the evidence presented by the prosecution's witnesses, and explains the evidence in such a way as to be most favorable to the defendant.

§ 4.11 Admissibility and weight of direct and circumstantial evidence

When discussing the responsibilities of the prosecutor and the defense attorney in the preceding sections, it was made clear that the purpose of

---

29 Nix v. Whiteside, 475 U.S. 157, 106 S. Ct. 988, 89 L. Ed. 2d 123 (1986).

introducing evidence at the trial is to cause the factfinders to be convinced that certain acts took place or did not take place. In a criminal case, the responsibility of the prosecutor is to prove beyond a reasonable doubt that the defendant committed the acts charged, and that these acts were in violation of the law.

In meeting this objective, is the prosecutor limited to the use of direct evidence? Or is it possible to prove this guilt beyond a reasonable doubt by circumstantial evidence?

Historically, the question has been debated by both state and federal courts. Although today the matter seems to be more settled, there is still some doubt in the minds of students of law as to the admissibility, weight and sufficiency of circumstantial evidence. In any event, the education of a student in the law of evidence would be incomplete if he could not distinguish between direct and circumstantial evidence and give some examples.

The mere fact that evidence is characterized as either direct or circumstantial may indicate that circumstantial evidence is not as reliable as direct evidence. Although it is true that, all things being equal, direct evidence probably carries more weight, circumstantial evidence has a definite place in the trial of criminal cases. History is replete with examples of convictions based exclusively on circumstantial evidence.

The value of circumstantial evidence is obvious when one considers that crimes are generally not committed in the open. An investigator would be very pleased if every crime were witnessed by someone who could testify that he saw the acts which made up the crime. In crimes such as burglary, however, it would be very difficult to convict without the use of circumstantial evidence.

There is often the mistaken belief that direct evidence always carries more weight than circumstantial evidence. For example, if an unbiased witness testified that he saw the accused near the scene at the approximate time of the crime, such evidence would be considered circumstantial, but it would probably carry more weight in the eyes of the jury than would the testimony of an obviously biased witness who stated that he saw the crime committed by someone other than the accused.

Before continuing with the discussion of admissibility, weight and sufficiency of direct and circumstantial evidence, some definitions are in order.

a. Direct evidence

Direct evidence proves a fact without inference. It is evidence which is applied immediately and directly to the fact to be proved—without the aid of any intervening fact or process. For example, in a trial for murder, a witness positively testifies he saw the accused inflict the mortal wound. Evidence is declared to be direct and positive when the very acts in dispute are communicated by persons who have actual knowledge of the facts by means of their senses. When direct evidence is introduced, it is not necessary that the factfinders make any inference or that there be any presumptions flowing from the evidence to connect it with the crime. The sole determination which the trier of fact must make is whether the evidence is true.30

b. Circumstantial evidence

Circumstantial evidence is evidence from which a fact is reasonably inferred but not directly proven. Another definition is "circumstantial evidence is evidence which, without going directly to prove the existence of a fact, gives rise to logical inference that such fact does exist."31

Circumstantial evidence is testimony based not on actual personal knowledge or observation of the facts in controversy, but rather on knowledge of other facts from which deductions are drawn, showing indirectly the facts in controversy to be true.32

After making this distinction between direct evidence and circumstantial evidence, it must be quickly pointed out that all that is required of the jury is that it weigh all of the evidence—direct or circumstantial—against a standard of reasonable doubt.33 This was made clear in a 1969 circuit court case which held:

> Thus the trial court properly instructed the jury that "the law makes no distinction between direct and circumstantial evidence but simply requires that the jury be satisfied of the defendant's guilt beyond a reasonable doubt from all of the evidence in the case," including "such reasonable inferences as seem justified, in the light of your own experiences."34

There is no doubt that, under the existing decisions, some circumstantial evidence may be equally reliable—or more reliable—than direct evidence. And as the court in the above-mentioned case stated, it would be wholly irrational to impose an absolute bar upon the use of circumstantial evidence to prove any fact, including a fact from which another fact is to be

---

30 State v. Frantzel, 717 S.W.2d 863 (Mo. App. 1986).

31 Bland v. Fox, 172 Neb. 662, 111 N.W.2d 537 (1961).

32 People v. Goldstein, 139 Cal. App. 2d 146, 293 P.2d 495 (1956); State v. Famber, 358 Mo. 288, 214 S.W.2d 40 (1948); People v. Christiansen, 118 Ill. App. 2d 51, 254 N.E.2d 156 (1969).

33 Holland v. United States, 348 U.S. 121, 75 S. Ct. 127, 99 L. Ed. 150 (1954). United States v. Williams, 798 F.2d 1024 (7th Cir. 1986); People v. Bryant, 499 N.E.2d 413 (Ill. 1986).

34 United States v. Nelson, 419 F.2d 1237 (9th Cir. 1969). *See* case in Part II, *infra.*

inferred. Therefore, either direct evidence or circumstantial evidence may be used to prove the fact in issue, and likewise, either direct or circumstantial evidence may fail to prove the fact in issue.

As to the weight and sufficiency of circumstantial evidence to justify a finding of guilty, the United States Supreme Court has made it clear that circumstantial evidence will justify a conviction. In *United States v. Nelson*,[35] the Ninth Circuit held that when the jury is properly instructed on the standard of reasonable doubt, but in addition is given an instruction that, if the evidence is circumstantial, it must be such as to exclude every reasonable hypothesis other than that of guilt, such instruction is confusing and incorrect. The *Nelson* court emphasized that the Supreme Court in *Holland v. United States*[36] did more than reject the particular instruction; it clearly stated that no instruction is to be given distinguishing the manner in which direct evidence and circumstantial evidence are to be weighed.

In 1978, the Indiana Court of Appeals set out two principles which should guide the reviewing court in determining the sufficiency of the evidence in circumstantial evidence cases.[37] In that case, a police officer testified that he walked into a public restroom and saw the defendant kneeling in front of another man's groin area. A few seconds later, the defendant's companion spotted the police officer and pulled away from the kneeling defendant, thus exposing the first man's open pants and erect penis. The jury found the defendant guilty of having committed an act of fellatio on the basis of this circumstantial evidence.

When the case was appealed to the Indiana Court of Appeals, that court established two principles which control the review of the sufficiency of evidence in circumstantial evidence cases. These are:

1. Convictions should not be overruled or overturned simply because this court determined that the circumstances do not exclude every reasonable hypothesis of innocence.

2. Convictions should not be sustained when the inference of guilt is based on "mere suspicion, conjecture, conclusion, guess, opportunity, or scintilla."

In the concluding paragraph, the court stated: "We hold that eyewitness testimony of such circumstantial evidence is . . . sufficient to support a charge of sodomy fellatio."

This view was reiterated in a Texas case in 1982.[38] The defendant was convicted of murder in a non-jury trial, and he was sentenced to life impris-

---

35 *Ibid.*
36 Holland v. United States, *supra,* n. 33.
37 Knowlton v. State, 382 N.E.2d 1004 (Ind. App. 1978).
38 Longoria v. State, 636 S.W.2d 521 (Tex. 1982).

onment. Although the conviction rested solely on circumstantial evidence, the Texas Court of Appeals affirmed the conviction. In explaining the use of circumstantial evidence, the court expounded: "In such a case, the circumstance must exclude to a moral certainty every other reasonable hypothesis except the defendant's guilt." After reviewing all the evidence introduced, the court concluded that the evidence was "sufficient to support the trial judge's reasonable conclusion that it excluded to a moral certainty every hypothesis except the appellant's guilt."

The same reasoning was applied in a robbery case, in which the court made this comment: "Every circumstantial evidence case must necessarily be tested by its own facts to determine the sufficiency of the evidence to support the conviction."39 Here the court agreed that:

> The evidence does not exclude the reasonable hypothesis that the defendant's proximity to the scene of the crime was mere coincidence. The evidence does not exclude all other reasonable hypotheses except the defendant's guilt. The evidence presented by the state amounts to nothing more than a strong suspicion of probability that the defendant committed the crime for which he was convicted.

Based on this finding that the circumstantial evidence was not sufficient to sustain the conviction in the case, the judgement of the lower court was reversed, and the defendant was acquitted.

From these cases, one can conclude that, while circumstantial evidence is certainly admissible in determining guilt or innocence, the conviction will not be justified on circumstantial evidence alone unless the jurors could reasonably have concluded that every reasonable hypothesis except the defendant's guilt should be excluded from their conclusion.

§ 4.12 Summary

The prosecutor in a criminal case has the responsibility of proving guilt beyond a reasonable doubt. The defense attorney has the responsibility of introducing evidence to substantiate the defendant's claims. Over the years, courts and legislatures have established rules for the admissibility of evidence and for the procedure to be followed in presenting evidence in court.

Before the trial begins, motions may be made by the parties to exclude or suppress certain types of evidence. When such a motion is presented, the burden is upon the person who makes the motion to show that there is some legal reason that the evidence should not be admitted.

---

39 Spencer v. State, 628 S.W.2d 220 (Tex. 1982).

The rules of evidence, for all practical purposes, are rules of exclusion. All evidence is admissible unless it is excluded upon objection. Objections may be as to form. For example if the questions of counsel are confusing, improperly phrased, misleading or argumentative, the opposing counsel may object as to form. There also may be objections as to substance. If the objection is made because the evidence is irrelevant, immaterial or incompetent, the complaining party will usually be requested to state why such a claim is made.

The usual order for presenting evidence is for the state to present its evidence in chief, followed by the defendant's evidence in chief. The prosecution then has the opportunity to introduce evidence to rebut evidence presented by the defense. The defense may, if it deems necessary, follow with evidence contrary to that introduced by the prosecution during the rebuttal. When both parties have rested their cases, the hearing on the facts comes to an end, and the trial proceeds with the arguments of counsel and the court's instructions to the jury.

The normal way of offering evidence is to place the witness on the stand and ask a question, or a series of questions. The opposing party through counsel may challenge the question before an answer is given and then present an objection. The court then decides if the answer should be allowed and makes a ruling. If either party feels that the ruling is improper, exception is taken and the point is recorded for review following the trial.

In English and American courts, the trial judge, jury, witnesses, prosecuting attorney and defense attorney all play specific roles. The judge determines whether evidence is admissible and gives instructions to the jury. The jury determines the facts from the evidence and from the instructions given by the judge. The witnesses are the eyes and ears of the court. The prosecuting attorney guides the case for the state by producing witnesses on behalf of the state, and the defense attorney represents the accused.

Although there is still some disagreement concerning the admissibility, weight and sufficiency of circumstantial evidence as compared to direct evidence, circumstantial evidence may be introduced if it meets the other requirements. Modern reasoning is that the law makes no distinction in determining the sufficiency of direct and circumstantial evidence but simply requires that the jury be satisfied of the defendant's guilt beyond a reasonable doubt from all evidence—direct or circumstantial.

All who are involved in the criminal justice process, whether they are actively involved in collecting, presenting or evaluating the evidence, or only concerned indirectly, should be aware of the process by which evidence is introduced, challenged and evaluated for trial purposes. Inadmissible evidence is no evidence.

CHAPTER 5
JUDICIAL NOTICE

Judicial notice takes the place of proof, and is of equal force. As a means of establishing facts, it is therefore superior to evidence. In its appropriate field, it displaces evidence, since, as it stands for proof, it fulfills the object which evidence is designed to fulfill, and makes evidence unnecessary.
State v. Maine, 69 Conn. 123, 36 L.R.A. 623, 61 Am.St.Rep. 30, 37 A. 80 (1897)

§ 5.1 Introduction

At the close of a criminal trial, the jury members are instructed that they are to determine, from the facts presented at the trial and from the instructions given by the judge, the guilt or innocence of the accused. Generally the prosecution and the defense have the burden of establishing facts by producing sworn witnesses, authenticated documents or real evidence. However, the courts, recognizing that it would be unreasonable to require the opposing parties to introduce evidence for every fact considered by the jury or other factfinding body, have made some exceptions. Criminal trials are drawn out enough under our present system, and it would be ridiculous to require the parties to prove, for example, that the state of Kentucky is located in the United States, or that the force of gravity causes an object to fall to earth.

To save the time of the court and for procedural convenience, substitutes for evidence have found their way into the procedure. The first substitute for evidence is judicial notice. The principle of judicial notice authorizes the court to take notice of certain facts without the necessity of introducing evidence to show these facts.

The second substitute for evidence is the presumption, which is sometimes referred to as presumptions and inferences. By court decisions and statutory enactments, certain facts are presumed, therefore relieving the parties of the burden of presenting evidence to prove the particular fact.

The third substitute for evidence is the stipulation. This substitute is also designed to save the time of the court and to allow the court to continue about its business without being bogged down with the introduction of evidence concerning every possible question. The stipulation renders proof unnecessary as to the matters stipulated. The remainder of this chapter is devoted to a discussion of specific examples of judicial notice of facts and judicial notice of laws. In the following chapter, the other substitutes for evidence—presumptions, inferences and stipulations—are explained.

§ 5.2 Judicial notice defined   JUDICIAL NOTICE IS EVIDENCE.

Judicial notice may be defined as the cognizance of certain facts which a judge, under the rules of legal procedure or otherwise, may properly take or act upon without proof—either because these facts are already known to him or because of the knowledge which the judge has, or is assumed to have, by virtue of his office.[1] To say that a court will take judicial notice of a fact is merely another way of saying that the usual forms of evidence will be dispensed with if the fact is one of public concern or is of sufficient notoriety to be known generally by all well-informed persons.

Judicial notice is taking cognizance of certain facts and laws without the necessity of introducing evidence. To say this another way, judges will not shut their minds to truths that all others can see and understand. When a fact is judicially noticed by the court as true, the party who ordinarily would be required to offer evidence need not do so.

The judge is not limited to taking judicial notice of facts that he has within his own personal knowledge but may make reference to books, articles and other sources of information. Although the judge has great discre-

---

1 Riley v. Wallace, 188 Ky. 471, 222 S.W. 1085 (1920).

tion in taking judicial notice, the power of judicial notice must be exercised with great caution. Generally speaking, matters of judicial notice have at least two material requisites: (1) the matter must be of common and general knowledge, and (2) it must be authoritatively settled and not uncertain.2

The judge may take judicial notice upon the request of either party, or on his option, even if a request is not made. The judge may seek sources of information to assist him in making a decision regarding judicial notice. He is entitled to aid himself in reaching the decision by consulting any sources of information that serve the purpose. He may use official records, encyclopedias, any books or articles, or any source which suffices to satisfy his mind in making a decision. For example, in one case, the court held that the judge may examine historical data, maps, public papers and records, and that he may take judicial notice concerning whether a gambling ship was within the state boundaries.3 Also, in taking judicial notice, the judge may request assistance from counsel and, for lack of such assistance, he may decline to notice the desired fact.4 In the case of *People v. Maxwell*, the court asserted that a court is not required to seek indisputable sources of information on its own initiative when a request for judicial notice is made. The court explained further that in some cases the original source document may be required to provide the court with sufficient information, but if the information supplied is not sufficient, the trial judge is entitled to refuse to take judicial notice of the matter.

For convenience, the rules concerning judicial notice are often categorized as judicial notice of facts and judicial notice of laws. In the following sections, the two categories are discussed and distinguished.

---

2   Mutual Life Ins. Co. v. McGraw, 188 U.S. 291, 23 S. Ct. 375, 47 L. Ed. 480 (1903).
3   People v. Stralla, 14 Cal. 2d 617, 96 P.2d 941 (1939).
4   People v. Maxwell, 78 Cal. App. 2d 124, 144 Cal. Rptr. 95 (1978).

§ 5.3   Judicial notice of facts

RULE 201

JUDICIAL NOTICE OF ADJUDICATIVE FACTS

(a) Scope of rule. This rule governs only judicial notice of adjudicative facts.

(b) Kinds of facts. A judicially noticed fact must be one not subject to reasonable dispute in that it is either (1) generally known within the territorial jurisdiction of the trial court or (2) capable of accurate and ready determination by resort to sources whose accuracy cannot reasonably be questioned.

(c) When discretionary. A court may take judicial notice, whether requested or not.

(d) When mandatory. A court shall take judicial notice if requested by a party and supplied with the necessary information.[5]

* * *

In federal courts and generally in state courts, the trial court may take judicial notice without motion of counsel for a party, or a party may request the court to take judicial notice of specific facts. The party so requesting must furnish the judge with sufficient information to enable him to comply with the request, and the party must give notice to counsel for the adverse party to enable the opposition to prepare to challenge the request. For example, in a suit by a state prisoner for relief under the Civil Rights Act for alleged discrimination, the attorney general for the state of Illinois asked the federal court to take judicial notice of certain social studies which show that the Black Muslim movement, in addition to being a religious movement, is an organization that, outside of prison walls, has for its object the overthrow of the white race, and inside prison walls, has an impressive history of inciting riots and violence. The court decided to take judicial notice of official or otherwise accredited social studies of the Black Muslim movement.[6] Also, a federal court took judicial notice of the fact that there had been major hijacking gangs preying on interstate and international commerce at Kennedy Airport.[7] In both of the cited examples, the court took judicial notice only after one party brought forth evidence to show that facts could

---

5   Fed. R. Evid. 201.

6   Cooper v. Pate, 324 F.2d 165 (7th Cir. 1963), *reversed for other reasons,* 378 U.S. 546, 12 L. Ed. 2d 1030.

7   United States v. Fatico, 458 F. Supp. 388 (E.D.N.Y. 1978).

be reasonably and accurately determined by reference to trustworthy source material.

In most states, the code or statute pertaining to evidence provides the rules that must be followed by the court relating to judicial notice of fact. For example, the Alaska statute provides:

Judicial Notice of Fact

(a) *Scope of the Rule.* This rule governs only judicial notices of fact. Judicial notice of a fact as used in this rule means a court's on-the-record declaration of the existence of a fact normally decided by the trier of fact, without requiring proof of that fact.

(b) *General Rule.* A judicially noticed fact must be one not subject to reasonable dispute in that it is either (1) generally known within the state, or (2) capable of accurate and ready determination by resort to sources whose accuracy cannot reasonably be questioned.

(c) *When Discretionary.* A court may take judicial notice as specified in subsection (b) whether requested or not.

(d) *Upon Request of a Party.* The court shall take judicial notice of each matter specified in subdivision (b) if the requesting party furnishes sufficient information and has given each party notice adequate to enable the party to meet the request.[8]

Judicial notice of facts is not the same as extrajudicial or personal knowledge of the judge; what the judge knows and what facts the jury may judicially notice are not identical, and private knowledge of the judge is not a sufficient basis for taking judicial notice of facts.[9] In *State v. Vejvoda*, the reviewing court, after explaining the limits on the use of judicial notice, decided that the trial court improperly took judicial notice of the fact that the defendant was driving in a city within the county of prosecution when the arresting officer's testimony referred only to street names but not to their location. The fact that the judge was aware that the streets were probably in the county of prosecution did not cure the failure to introduce evidence.

Although the courts are not in complete agreement as to what facts must be judicially noticed and what facts may be judicially noticed on request, some matters are traditionally considered as being proper for consideration. These are discussed in the sections that follow. The examples given are not, however, meant to be exhaustive.

---

8   ALASKA STAT. § 201 (1979). *See* Appendix 2 for list of states which follow the Model Code of Evidence.

9   State v. Vejvoda, 231 Neb. 668, 438 N.W.2d 461 (1989). *See* case in Part II, *infra.*

§ 5.4   —Matters of general knowledge

While it is accepted practice to take judicial notice of facts of common knowledge, and such facts need not be proved by the opposing party, this question arises: What facts are common knowledge? A fact is said to be generally recognized or known when its existence or operation is accepted by the public without qualification or contention.[10] This does not mean that everyone must be aware of the fact; scarcely any fact is known by everyone. All that is necessary is that a matter be familiar to the majority of mankind or to those persons familiar with a particular matter in question. When the matter depends upon uncertain testimony and becomes a disputable item in court, it ceases to fall under the heading of common knowledge and will not be judicially recognized.

Facts judicially noticed may be of purely local knowledge, such as the character of the location where an accident occurred, the name of a street or the location of a business area. For example, a federal court in South Carolina, in an action under the Federal Tort Claims Act, decided that it is common knowledge that livestock in general and mules in particular are easily frightened by sudden loud noises such as helicopters propelling directly over their heads.[11]

Facts generally known throughout the nation may also be judicially noticed. For example, the fact that one of the vital roles of Nike missile sites is national defense is an appropriate subject for judicial notice.[12] However, one court would not take judicial notice of the wealth of defendant Charles Chaplin from so-called common knowledge derived from newspapers and magazines.[13]

Other examples of instances when the court has taken judicial notice of matters of general knowledge are these: a pistol is a deadly weapon;[14] a full-choke shotgun scatters less than a modified-choke shotgun, and an open-bore shotgun splatters more than either of them, provided that the distance is not extremely short;[15] every day, automobiles cause tremendous injury and loss of life;[16] witnesses are often unable to accurately remember dates;[17] and a defendant nearly always wants his trial to be postponed.[18]

---

[10] Byrd v. State, 212 Ala. 266, 102 So. 223 (1924). *See also* State v. Lawrence, 120 Utah 323, 234 P.2d 600 (1951).

[11] Long v. United States, 241 F. Supp. 286 (W.D.S.C. 1965).

[12] United States v. National Surety Corp., 179 F. Supp. 598 (E.D. Pa. 1959).

[13] Berry v. Chaplin, 74 Cal. App. 2d 669, 169 P.2d 453 (1946).

[14] State v. Taylor, 182 S.W. 159 (Mo. 1916).

[15] Sanders v. Allen, 65 U.S. 220, 56 S. Ct. 69 (1911).

[16] State v. Przybyl, 6 N.E.2d 848 (Ill. 1937).

[17] People v. Berne, 51 N.E.2d 578 (1943).

[18] Sam v. State, 265 P. 609 (Ariz. 1928).

More recently, the courts have held that a prevailing rate of interest is a proper subject for judicial notice, and that a court may take judicial notice of the fact that telephone lines carry interstate calls.[19] In state cases the courts have held that the judge may take judicial notice of mortality tables as proof of life expectancy, and that judicial notice may be taken of the fact that there are many qualified corporate bonds and public utility stocks that provide a rate of return between 10 and 15 percent.[20]

On the other hand, the courts have, from time to time, held that certain facts are not presumed to be known by the court. Courts have refused to take judicial notice of a pardon;[21] of the death of an appellant's counsel subsequent to the trial and prior to the hearing;[22] that all strikers desire to commit murder;[23] and that a non-law-abiding citizen is always a perjurer.[24] One court refused to take judicial notice of the presumed fact that no one would drive six miles for a drink of whiskey.[25]

Common knowledge can also relate to current events. For instance, it is common knowledge that there has been an increase in the number of serious crimes committed by persons under eighteen years of age. The judge may take judicial notice of economic facts, such as the constant increase in the cost of living and the decrease in the purchasing power of the dollar. In such instances the facts are noticed judicially without proof by either side.

§ 5.5   —History and historical facts

Courts may take judicial notice of events which make up the history of the state or country. The financial history of the United States, including events such as the 1929 stock market collapse and the depression of the 1930s, is a matter of common knowledge. The day of the week on which a particular date fell, the date on which war was declared or ended, the destructive character of a flood or other disaster—all can be matters of judicial notice. The court, in an action to declare life insurance policies in force, judicially noticed the flight of refugees from Castro's Cuba to

---

19 Havens Steel Co. v. Randolph Eng. Co., 813 F.2d 186 (9th Cir. 1987); United States v. Deckard, 816 F.2d 428 (8th Cir. 1987).

20 Stewart v. State, 394 So. 2d 1337 (Miss. 1981); Svetenko v. Svetenko, 306 N.W. 2d 607 (N.D. 1981).

21 State v. Garrett, 188 S.W. 58 (Tenn. 1916).

22 People v. Gow, 175 P. 917 (Cal. App. 1918).

23 State v. Jones, 155 S.W. 33 (Mo. 1913).

24 State v. Baird, 195 S.W. 1010 (Mo. 1917).

25 Colbaugh v. United States, 15 F.2d 929 (8th Cir. 1926).

Miami, Florida, and their acceptance, encouragement and support by the United States.26

In criminal cases as well as civil cases, the court may take judicial notice of historical facts of a national character, such as the fact that a state of war existed in Korea in 1950,27 that an intense hatred against Hitler existed during World War II,28 and that the national economic and commercial condition of the country changes.29

Although the court may take judicial notice of local as well as national history that is not of general or public interest, it cannot generally take judicial knowledge of local unrecorded history. For example, the court could not take judicial notice that: (1) a certain schoolhouse and church, and (2) an old meetinghouse formerly existed at certain separate locations.30

The judge does not have to be personally aware of historical facts to take judicial notice of them. It would be asking too much for the judge to be aware of all the details of history. He may refer to properly authenticated public official documents, encyclopedias, history books, periodicals or even newspaper articles. However, such judicial knowledge is generally limited to what a judge may properly know in a judicial capacity, and he cannot take judicial notice of an historical fact of which only he is aware.

§ 5.6 —Geography and geographical facts

Although the prosecutor must introduce evidence to show that the court has jurisdiction in the case in the initial stages, he does not have to introduce evidence to show, for example, that Chicago is in Cook County, Illinois. Courts take judicial notice of: (1) the prominent geographical and natural features of the country, such as large lakes, rivers and mountains; (2) the division of the country into states; (3) the existence, location and population of cities within states; and (4) distances between well-known points and general routes of travel.31

In some instances, it is very easy to show geographical facts, but in other cases the geographical fact is not clear. For example, in a criminal

---

26 Blanco v. Pan-American Life Ins. Co., 221 F. Supp. 219 (S.D. Fla. 1963); Perez v. Department of Revenue, 778 P.2d 326 (Colo. App. 1989).

27 Gagliormella v. Metropolitan Life Ins. Co., 122 F. Supp. 246 (D.C. Mass. 1954).

28 Tidmore v. Mills, 33 Ala. App. 243, 32 So. 2d 769, *cert. denied,* 249 Ala. 648, 32 So. 2d 782 (1947).

29 Young v. Phillips, 170 Tenn. 169, 93 S.W.2d 634 (1936).

30 Burch v. Amity, 92 Or. 152, 180 P. 312 (1919).

31 31 C.J.S. *Evidence* § 32.

case, a state court properly took judicial notice that the distance between two cities was such as to permit the accused to be both at the scene of the crime and at the alibi location on the same day. Another court, however, determined that a court cannot take judicial notice of the exact length of time it takes to travel from one point to another. Such evidence must be introduced to allow a jury to make this determination.[32]

While some courts have decided that the judge should not take judicial notice of the exact length of time it takes to travel from one point to another, the court may take judicial notice of the fact that a trip between the island of Rota (in the Trust Territory of the Pacific Islands) and Guam must have involved travel through international waters.[33]

§ 5.7   —Facts relating to nature and science

The court may take judicial notice of facts which, although not specifically known by the general public, can be readily determined by reference to sources, the accuracy of which cannot reasonably be disputed. Of special significance in criminal cases is the fact that the courts may take judicial notice of scientific facts which have a bearing on the case, and scientific facts which have been well established by authoritative scientists and are generally accepted as irrefutable. Under this theory, courts frequently take judicial notice of the elementary principles of physics, such as the force of gravity. Also, facts relating to the climate of the state and the climate elsewhere may be judicially noticed.

The scope of judicial notice in scientific areas changes as man's knowledge expands. A number of these scientific areas are of special interest in the criminal justice process. For example, at one time, firearms identification evidence was considered worthless. Today, its reliability is a fact that is subject to judicial notice. Likewise, courts now may take judicial notice of the scientific validity of blood grouping tests resulting in exclusion of paternity.[34] Judicial notice may be taken of the validity of techniques for identifying questioned handwriting and typewriting.[35] So far, however, courts have generally been unwilling to take judicial notice of the scientific validity of the polygraph (or lie detector) test on the ground that the results of the test depend more on the operator's skill than on the inherent reliability of the device.[36]

---

32 29 AM. JUR. 2D *Evidence* § 69.

33 United States v. Perez, 769 F.2d 1336 (9th Cir. 1985).

34 Jordan v. Mace, 144 Me. 351, 69 A.2d 670 (1949); Commissioner of Welfare of City of New York v. Costonie, 277 A.D. 90, 97 N.Y.S.2d 804 (1950).

35 Fenelon v. State, 195 Wis. 416, 217 N.W. 711 (1928); United States v. Hiss, 107 F. Supp. 128 (S.D.N.Y. 1952).

36 State v. Brown, 177 So. 2d 532 (Fla. 1965).

§ 5.8   —Language, abbreviations and symbols

To avoid confusion, some statutes mandate that judicial notice be taken of words defined in the dictionary. For example, a Utah statute requires that courts take judicial notice of the "true signification of English words and phrases and of all legal expressions." The statute further provides that "in all cases the court may resort for its aid to appropriate books or documents of reference."[37] Even without a statute, judicial notice may be taken of the usual meanings of words and phrases, and a judge may take judicial notice of the meaning of words as defined in standard dictionaries.

Ordinarily the court may not take judicial notice of the meaning of slang words or expressions. However, if the word has come into such frequent use as to convey a particular meaning, and it no longer can be considered as simply the language of slang that is understood only by a certain segment of the population, the court can take judicial notice of the word. For example, the court may take judicial notice of the meanings of such terms as "cold check" and "hot check" as they are in common use, at least in Texas.[38] Idioms which have acquired a special meaning may be judicially noticed. The term "Democrat" may be judicially noticed as meaning the members and candidates of the Democratic party, and the court may take judicial notice that "pig" has come to be used as a derogatory name for the police.[39]

The courts may take judicial notice of the meaning of abbreviations generally known and in common use, such as abbreviations for days and months. But judicial notice may not be taken of the meaning of abbreviations, symbols or initials when such meaning is not generally known or when they have no meaning without explanation. The court, for example, may take judicial notice that the initials "M.D." refer to a physician,[40] and that "Chas." is an abbreviation for "Charles."[41]

§ 5.9   Judicial notice of laws

In addition to taking judicial notice of facts, courts take judicial notice of most laws. The basic justification for authorizing the court to take judicial notice of laws is the same as justifies the court in taking judicial notice of facts. It would be time-consuming and useless to require the opposing parties to introduce evidence to prove that laws which are known or ought

---

37 UTAH CODE ANN. § 78-25-1 (1953).
38 Elder v. Evatt, 154 S.W.2d 684 (Tex. 1941).
39 St. Petersburg v. Waller, 261 So. 2d 151 (Fla. 1972).
40 State v. Brady, 223 Or. 433, 354 P.2d 811 (1960).
41 Cumbol v. State, 205 Tenn. 260, 326 S.W.2d 454 (1959).

to be generally known are in fact laws of the jurisdiction. The normal method of finding the applicable law, common as well as statutory, is by informal investigation. Counsel usually bring to the judge's attention statutes or citations in references to decisions applicable to the case being tried. Occasionally the judge will make his own independent investigation of the law.

State trial courts judicially notice federal law, and a federal court will judicially notice the law of every state. When, however, the United States Supreme Court reviews a decision of a state court, it will not take judicial notice of a law of another state unless the state court below could have done so.[42]

In the following sections (§§ 5.10-5.16), the extent to which courts take judicial notice of laws prevailing within the forum and the laws of other states and counties are discussed specifically.

§ 5.10 —Law of the forum

It is axiomatic that all courts must take judicial notice of the law prevailing within the forum, *i.e.,* the law that exists within the state (when the trial is in state court). The purpose of the existence of the laws of the state is that they be used by the courts. It would be foolish to permit courts to take judicial notice of federal laws and laws of other states and counties without taking judicial notice of their own laws. It is immaterial whether the forum law is statutory law or case law. The only limitation to judicial recognition of the law of the forum is that it be public law.[43] Generally speaking, a strictly private act is not judicially noticed.

§ 5.11 —Federal law

Article VI of the United States Constitution provides that the Constitution, and the laws of the United States which shall be made in pursuance thereof, and all treaties made, or which shall be made, under the authority of the United States, shall be the supreme law of the land; the judges in every state shall be bound thereby. Accordingly, all federal and state courts must take judicial notice of the provisions of the federal Constitution, the amendments thereto, and the laws of the United States made pursuant to the Constitution. In regard to congressional enactments,

---

42 Hanley v. Donoghue, 116 U.S. 1, 6 S. Ct. 242, 29 L. Ed. 535 (1885).
43 State v. Miller, 778 S.W.2d 292 (Mo. 1989) (court took judicial notice that driving while intoxicated was an offense under state law).

judicial notice is not limited to their existence, wording and interpretation, but extends to all matters connected therewith.44

§ 5.12 —Law of sister states

Many states have adopted the Uniform Judicial Notice of Foreign Law Act, which provides that every court in the state must take judicial notice of the common law and statutes of every state, territory and other jurisdiction of the United States. The court may inform itself of such laws in such manner as it may deem proper, and it may call upon counsel to aid it in obtaining such information. To enable counsel for a party to ask that judicial notice may be taken of the law in another jurisdiction, reasonable notice must be given to counsel for the adverse party in the pleadings or otherwise. The reasonable notice requirement is to assure fairness to the opponent when a party plans to rely on laws of other jurisdictions.

Public laws of general application are clearly included within the term "statutes." This term also fairly includes other states' constitutions and rules of procedure having force of law throughout each such state, although such rules were adopted by the highest court of the state rather than its legislature. These materials are usually accessible through state codes, and being that they are of the general nature of public laws, these laws should be judicially noticed.45

§ 5.13 —Law of foreign countries

The federal courts and most state courts will not take judicial notice of the law of a foreign country.46 As a result, the rules of law for a foreign country must be pleaded and proved as facts along with the other elements of a cause of action.

§ 5.14 —Municipal ordinances

Generally, judicial notice may be taken of municipal ordinances only when the case is being tried in a municipal court. In all other courts, municipal ordinances must be pleaded and proved. Recent statutory amendments

---

44 Gardner v. Barney, 73 U.S. (6 Wall.) 499, 18 L. Ed. 890 (1868).
45 Litsinger Sign Co. v. American Sign Co., 11 Ohio St. 2d 1, 40 Ohio Op. 2d 30, 227 N.E.2d 609 (1967).
46 Kearney v. Savannah Foods, 350 F. Supp. 85 (S.D. Ga. 1972).

in a few states now allow every court to take judicial notice of ordinances.

The Tenth Circuit Court of Appeals in 1982 held that municipal ordinances may not be judicially noticed by courts of general jurisdiction but must be pleaded and proved as any other fact except when a statute specifically provides otherwise.[47] Such a statute exists in Alaska. It provides that "duly enacted ordinances of municipalities or other governmental subdivisions, and emergency orders or unpublished regulations adopted by agency of this state, may be judicially noticed."[48]

A municipal court which has exclusive jurisdiction of cases involving the violation of traffic ordinances of a city situated within its territorial jurisdiction may take judicial notice of those ordinances.[49]

§ 5.15 —Administrative regulations

The Uniform Rules of Evidence provide that judicial notice may be taken of the published regulations of governmental subdivisions or agencies of the state. The federal administrative regulations published in the FEDERAL REGISTER must be judicially noticed by all federal courts, and many state courts also notice such regulations. A federal court may judicially notice a state administrative regulation.[50] For example, in one case, a federal district court took judicial notice of the Interstate Commerce Commission's orders which had been entered in related proceedings.[51]

In 1988 a federal court held that OSHA regulations were subject to judicial notice.[52] A state court properly took judicial notice of the regulations of the Department of Corrections.[53] In California, the court was required to take judicial notice of the contents of regulations printed or incorporated by appropriate references to the California Code of Regulations.[54] Also, an Alabama court agreed that the trial court may take judicial notice of regulations promulgated by the State Board of Health as part of the predicate for admitting the results of a driver's Breathalyzer test.[55]

---

47 Ruhs v. Pacific Power and Light, 671 F.2d 1268 (10th Cir. 1982).

48 ALASKA STAT. § 202 (1979).

49 People v. Cowles, 142 Cal. App. 2d 865, 298 P.2d 732 (1956); Cook v. Superior Court, 261 Cal. Rptr. 706 (1989).

50 Milwaukee Mechanics Ins. Co. v. Oliver, 139 F.2d 405 (5th Cir. 1943).

51 Missouri Pacific Railroad Co. v. United Transportation Union, General Committee of Adjustment, 580 F. Supp. 1490 (D.C. Mo. 1984).

52 Northern Heel Corp. v. Compo Industries, Inc., 851 F.2d 456 (1st Cir. 1988).

53 Rogers v. State, 413 So. 2d 1270 (Fla. 1982); see also Mitchell v. State, 769 S.W.2d 18 (Ark. 1989).

54 Auchmody v. 911 Emergency Service, 263 Cal. Rptr. 278 (1989).

55 Terry v. City of Montgomery, 549 So. 2d 566 (Ala. 1989).

§ 5.16 —Jurisdiction of courts

A court will take judicial notice of the limits of its jurisdiction and the extent of the territory included therein. In a criminal case, the state or municipality is required to prove that the offense was committed within the territorial jurisdiction of the court; however, a court may take judicial notice of the fact that a particular milepost or interchange of an interstate highway is within the court's territorial jurisdiction.56

In a 1989 murder case that was appealed to the United States Supreme Court, the trial court refused to take judicial notice of the future actions of other courts. In this case the defendant had requested that the trial court take judicial notice of the fact that a writ of habeas corpus would be granted in the future. The Supreme Court agreed that the trial court was permitted to take judicial notice of the fact that writs of habeas corpus are granted in some cases, but that it is not possible to prove in advance that the judicial system would lead to any particular result.57

§ 5.17 Judicial notice process

RULE 201

JUDICIAL NOTICE OF ADJUDICATIVE FACTS

* * *

(e) Opportunity to be heard. A party is entitled upon timely request to an opportunity to be heard as to the propriety of taking judicial notice and the tenor of the matter noticed. In the absence of prior notification, the request may be made after judicial notice has been taken.

(f) Time of taking notice. Judicial notice may be taken at any stage of the proceeding.

(g) Instructing jury. In a civil action or proceeding, the court shall instruct the jury to accept as conclusive any fact judicially noticed. In a criminal case, the court shall instruct the jury that it may, but is not required to, accept as conclusive any fact judically noticed.58

---

56 State v. Scott, 3 Ohio App. 2d 239, 32 Ohio Op. 2d 360, 210 N.E.2d 289 (1965). *See* case in Part II, *infra.*

57 Whitmore v. Arkansas, ___ U.S. ___, 110 S. Ct. 1717, ___ L. Ed. 2d ___ (1990).

58 Fed. R. Evid. 201.

One court explained that judicial notice of facts takes the place of proof and is of equal force. It displaces evidence, as it stands for the same thing as evidence.59 How does the jury become aware that it may consider facts judicially noticed by the court? When the judge makes a decision that a certain fact or a certain law will be judicially noticed, he states in open court that such fact is noticed. If a party requests that a fact be judicially noticed and the judge agrees with the party, the jury will be so advised. Also, the court may of its own volition determine that the fact will be judicially noticed and so advise the jury.

Once a matter is judicially noticed, evidence generally will not be admitted to dispute the fact noticed. To allow evidence to contradict the facts judicially noticed would be contrary to the rationale for the rule in the first place. A fact should not be judicially noticed if it is doubtful or uncertain. However, in a criminal case, the jury is not required to accept the fact as conclusive.

Prior to the decision, the party is entitled, on timely request, to have a chance to be heard—outside the hearing of the jury—on the propriety of taking judicial notice and on the nature of the matter proposed to be judicially noticed.

In some states, the rules relating to the procedure followed in judicial notice situations are spelled out by rule or statute. For example, in Alaska, the procedures for taking judicial notice are stated as follows:

Alaska R. Evid. 203 (1979) "Procedure for Taking Judicial Notice. *(a) Determining Propriety of Judicial Notice.* Upon timely request, a party is entitled to be heard as to the propriety of taking judicial notice and the tenor of the matter noticed. In the absence of proper notification, the request may be made after judicial notice has been taken. In determining the propriety of taking judicial notice on a matter or the tenor thereof, the judge may consult and use any source of pertinent information, whether or not furnished by a party. *(b) Time of Taking Notice.* Judicial notice may be taken at any stage of the proceeding. *(c) Instructing the Jury.* In a civil action or proceeding, the court shall instruct the jury to accept as conclusive any fact judicially noticed. In a criminal case, the court shall instruct the jury that it may, but it is not required to, accept as conclusive any fact judicially noticed. Judicial notice of any matter of law falling within the scope of Rule 202 shall be a matter for the court and not the jury."60

---

59 Ricaud v. American Metal Co., 246 U.S. 304, 38 S. Ct. 312, 62 L. Ed. 733 (1918).

60 ALASKA STAT. § 203 (1979).

In Texas, a rule provides that the court shall instruct the jury to accept as conclusive any fact judicially noticed; however, this rule does not apply in criminal cases.61

§ 5.18 Judicial notice in criminal cases

Some courts are more reluctant to permit the use of judicial notice in a criminal case than in a civil case. In a Utah case in 1951, in which the defendant was charged with theft of property worth $50 or more (a felony under the statute of that state), the prosecution failed to introduce evidence to prove that the value of the automobile was more than $50. Instead of reopening the case so that new evidence could be introduced concerning the car's value, the trial judge took notice that its value exceeded $50. On appeal, the conviction was reversed, as the appellate court determined that evidence concerning the value of the car should have been admitted so that the jury could make the decision.62

This is not to say that the judge in a criminal case will not take judicial notice of facts and laws. Judicial notice has been taken of the fact that the fingerprint method of identification is reliable and accurate and that no two sets of fingerprints are exactly alike,63 and of the scientific reliability and accuracy of radar.64 Also, as the preceding paragraphs indicate, there are numerous instances in which the courts will take judicial notice of other well-established facts.

However, it is pointed out that Rule 201(g) of the Federal Rules of Evidence and the rules of most states, while providing that the court shall instruct the jury to accept as conclusive any fact judicially noticed in civil cases, require that the court instruct the jury that it may, but is not required, to accept as conclusive any fact judicially noticed in a criminal case. Recognizing that judges are hesitant to take judicial notice of facts and laws in criminal cases, especially in borderline situations, and recognizing that the jury is instructed that it is not required to accept as conclusive any fact judicially noticed in criminal cases, justice personnel are cautioned not to place too much reliance on the judicial notice concept. Rather than taking a chance that judicial notice will not be taken, traditional evidence should be prepared and made ready to introduce in the event that the judge fails to take judicial notice of facts.

---

61 Tex. Stat. § 201 (1982).
62 State v. Lawrence, 120 Utah 323, 234 P.2d 600 (1951). *See* case in Part II, *infra.*
63 State v. State, 292 P. 885 (Okla. 1930).
64 Everight v. Little Rock, 326 S.W.2d 796 (Ark. 1959).

§ 5.19 Summary

Although the usual procedure is for the parties to introduce evidence to prove a fact in dispute, in some instances such evidence is not necessary because the court will take judicial notice of certain facts. This procedure is obviously necessary and reasonable in order to save the time of the court.

Judicial notice is the court recognizing certain facts and laws without requiring the parties to introduce proof. For convenience, the rules concerning judicial notice are often categorized as judicial notice of facts and judicial notice of laws. Rule 201 of the Federal Rules of Evidence relates only to the taking of judicial notice of adjudicative facts.

The general rule is that the trial judge may take judicial notice without motion of counsel, or he may take judicial notice of certain facts on the request of counsel. The judge, in fact, is given much discretion concerning judicial notice, and he is not second-guessed by a higher court unless there is a clear abuse of discretion.

It is obvious that there are many facts and laws which are commonly known and need not be proved in court. Examples of these are historical facts, geographical facts, scientific facts and other facts that are generally known to the ordinary person.

In addition to facts, the judge may take judicial notice of certain laws such as the Constitution of the United States, laws of the various states and in some instances, municipal ordinances.

All of the persons involved in the criminal justice process must be aware of the fact that the judge may take notice of certain facts and certain laws, but it is a grave mistake to assume that the judge will always take judicial notice of even well-known facts. If there is any doubt as to the character of the fact to be introduced or proved in court, evidence should be acquired and made ready for presentation in court. Also, the good investigator must recognize that even though the judge may judicially notice certain matters, the opposing party may challenge the propriety of such actions, and failure to prepare documented information to enable the court to take judicial notice of certain facts can weaken a case.

CHAPTER 6
PRESUMPTIONS, INFERENCES
AND STIPULATIONS

The use of presumptions and inferences to prove an element of the crime is indeed treacherous, for it allows men to go to jail without any evidence on one essential ingredient of the offense. It thus implicates the integrity of the judicial system.

Barnes v. United States, 412 U.S. 837, 93 S. Ct. 2357 (1973) (Douglas, J., dissenting)

§ 6.1   Introduction

In Chapter 4 the process followed in introducing evidence in a criminal case was considered. There it was explained that, in the usual situation, the parties have the burden of introducing evidence to establish facts from which a decision is made. However, in some instances the jury may consider information other than that derived from evidence specifically introduced by the parties. One way of distinguishing this information source is to designate it as "substitutes for evidence."

In Chapter 5 one of those substitutes for evidence—judicial notice—was explained. Included were the reasons for authorizing the judge to take notice of certain facts and laws. In addition, case decisions and statutes placing limitations on the use of judicial notice were noted. In this chapter, emphasis is on other substitutes for evidence—presumptions, inferences and stipulations.

In some instances, facts are presumed, thereby relieving the parties from the burden of presenting evidence to prove them. And under traditional common law principles, some facts can be inferred from other facts presented in court.

In this chapter, presumptions, inferences and stipulations are defined and distinguished. In addition, the reasons for the presumptions and inferences as well as the types of presumptions recognized by the courts are discussed. Also, some specific examples of situations where presumptions and inferences play an important role in the trial process are considered in more detail. Finally, the remaining substitute for evidence—the stipulation—is defined and explained with important, specific examples.

§ 6.2 Definitions and distinctions

a. Presumptions

RULE 301

**PRESUMPTIONS IN GENERAL IN
CIVIL ACTIONS PROCEEDINGS**

In all civil actions and proceedings not otherwise provided by Acts of Congress or by these rules, a presumption imposes on the party against whom it is directed the burden of going forward with evidence to rebut or meet the presumption, but does not shift to such party the burden of proof in the sense of the risk of nonpersuasion, which remains throughout the trial upon the party on whom it was originally cast.[1]

* * *

The committee which considered Rule 301 limited the scope of the rule to civil actions and proceedings to effectuate the decision not to deal with the questions of presumptions in criminal cases. In criminal cases the par-

---

1 FED. R. EVID. 301.

ties must look to federal court decisions or state statutes and decisions for answers to questions relating to presumptions.

The term "presumption" has been used by courts and legal writers to describe several different consequences which flow from the introduction of evidence in a trial. A general definition is that a presumption is a rule of law that attaches definite probative value to specific facts or draws a particular inference as to the evidence of one fact, not actually known, arising from its usual connection with other particular facts which are known or proved. It is a legal principle whereby the court accepts the existence of one fact from other facts already proved.

Another definition is that a presumption is an inference which common sense, enlightened by human knowledge and experience, draws from the connection, relation and coincidence of facts and circumstances with each other.2 Some courts argue that a true legal presumption is in the nature of evidence and is to be weighed as such. Others hold (probably more properly) that a presumption is not evidence but is a substitute for evidence.3

b. Inferences

An inference has been defined as a logical deduction from circumstances known to exist.4 It also has been defined as a deduction which the jurors may make from facts shown without the law directing them to make such a deduction.

Although the terms "presumptions" and "inferences" are sometimes used synonymously, the courts have attempted to distinguish between them as to both their origin and effect. According to some courts, an inference should be recorded as a permissible deduction from the evidence before the court, which the jury may accept or reject. "Presumption," on the other hand, is a rule of law, relatively fixed or relatively definite in scope and effect, which attaches to certain evidentiary facts and is productive of a specific procedural consequence. To state this more simply, in these courts a presumption is a mandatory deduction that the law expressly requires, while an inference is no more than a permissible deduction which the trier of fact may adopt.

In the case of *Commonwealth v. DiFrancesco*, the court held that an "inference is merely a logical tool which permits the trier of fact to proceed from one fact to another, whereas a 'presumption' is a procedural device which not only permits an inference of the 'presumed' fact, but also shifts to the opposing party the burden of producing evidence to disprove the pre-

---

2 Commercial Credit Co. v. Maxey, 289 Ill. App. 209, 7 N.E.2d 155 (1937).
3 Siler v. Siler, 152 Tenn. 379, 277 S.W. 886 (1925); Amend v. Bell, 89 Wash. 2d 124, 570 P.2d 138 (1978).
4 Works v. Krausse, 162 Va. 107, 173 S.E. 497 (1934).

sumed fact."5 In a criminal case, an Iowa court explained the difference by noting that a true "presumption" is a conclusion which the law makes mandatory upon proof of the required preliminary facts, while an "inference" is a permissible finding based on the existence of other facts.6 In another case the court made this distinction:

> Presumptions are one thing; inferences another. Presumptions are assumptions of fact which the law requires to be made from another fact or group of facts; inferences are logical deductions or conclusions from an established fact. Presumptions deal with legal processes, whereas inferences deal with mental processes.7

The court went on to explain that an inference is simply a logical deduction or conclusion which the law allows, but does not require, following the establishment of the basic facts.

For a trier of fact to draw inferences from proven circumstances, the inferences must be "rationally related" to the proven facts. That is, a rational connection must exist between the initial fact proven and the further fact inferred. For example, the jury is permitted to infer from one fact the existence of another that is essential to guilt, if reason and experience support the inference.8

While a court may give instructions regarding inferences that can be drawn from proven facts, an instruction which permits the jurors to infer an element of the crime charged is constitutional only if the presumed fact follows beyond a reasonable doubt from the proven fact. In the case of *State v. Jackson,* the Supreme Court of Washington held that, when the charge is attempted burglary, a trial court cannot instruct the jury that it may infer that the defendant acted with intent to commit a crime within a building when the evidence is that the defendant may have attempted entrance into a building, but there exist other equally reasonable conclusions which follow from the circumstances.9 In this case an officer saw the defendant kicking the front door of a shop. When the defendant spotted the officer, he proceeded to walk away briskly. When the door was examined, it was found that about ten inches of plexiglass had been pushed inward and that part of the wood stock around the plexiglass was broken out of its frame. The defendant was charged with second degree burglary. In the instruction to the jury, the judge instructed that the jury may infer that the defendant acted

---

5   Commonwealth v. DiFrancesco, 329 A.2d 204 (Pa. 1974).

6   States v. Hansen, 203 N.W.2d (Iowa 1974).

7   State v. Jackson, 112 Wash. 867, 774 P.2d 1211 (1989). *See* case in Part II, *infra.*

8   Tot v. United States, 319 U.S. 463, 63 S. Ct. 1241, 87 L. Ed. 2d 1519 (1943).

9   State v. Jackson, *supra* n. 7.

with intent to commit a crime within the building. In reversing the conviction, the court noted that an inference shall not arise when there exist other reasonable conclusions that could follow from the circumstances. Applying this reasoning, the court determined that the instruction that the jury may infer that the defendant intended to commit a crime within the building merely because he had repeatedly kicked the door prior to the officer's approach was improper.

c. Stipulations

A stipulation is less difficult to define than presumptions and inferences. A stipulation merely means that both parties concede the existence or nonexistence of a fact, the contents of a document, or the testimony of a witness. A stipulation may be written or oral and is generally encouraged in order to expedite the trial.

A stipulation as to a fact authorizes the court to find the existence of such a fact and to consider that fact without any further proof. The triers of fact are not, however, bound to accept the fact as true and may find to the contrary if persuaded by other evidence.

§ 6.3   Reasons for presumptions and inferences

Although there is still some confusion concerning the use of presumptions, presumptions play an important part in the judicial process. Some of the reasons or explanations for using presumptions are discussed below.

a. Procedural technique

One court stated that a presumption is no more than a procedural technique designed for trial convenience to facilitate the production of proof by requiring the party with easier means of access to come forward with the evidence.10 Without a presumption, it would be difficult for the trial to go forward in some instances. One purpose of the presumption is to place the burden on the person who alone is in possession of the facts with respect thereto. To make it possible to go forward with the trial, the presumption assumes a certain condition to exist until the contrary is shown.

Presumptions affect the burden of offering evidence. Normally when a presumption is met by evidence to the contrary, the presumption vanishes from the case. Therefore, despite some reasoning to the contrary, a better conclusion is that a presumption is not evidence but stands in the place of evidence and makes it possible to proceed with the trial of a case.11

---

10 Waugh v. Commonwealth, 394 Pa. 166, 146 A.2d 297 (1958).
11 *Ibid; See also* Amend v. Bell, 89 Wash. 2d 124, 570 P.2d 138 (1977).

b. Public policy

Some presumptions of law are sanctioned by the courts and legislatures for public policy purposes. One such presumption is that a child born in wedlock is legitimate. The California Code, Section 621, provides that "except as provided in subsection (b) the issue of a wife cohabiting with her husband, who is not impotent or sterile, is conclusively presumed to be a child of the marriage."12 The code provides, however, that, notwithstanding the provisions of subsection (a), if the court finds at the conclusions of all the experts that the husband is not the father of the child, the question of paternity of the father shall be resolved accordingly. In the case of *McKenzie v. Harris,* the Third Circuit, applying Pennsylvania law, held that only "overwhelming" evidence of nonaccess, lack of intercourse, or impotency may prove that a child born during a marriage is not a child of the marriage.13

Another example of a presumption of law that was determined by the courts and legislatures for public policy purposes is that all persons are presumed to know the law.

c. Allowance of normal governmental activities

Presumptions such as honest and proper conduct by public officials allow normal governmental activities to be accepted at face value. Without this presumption, it would be burdensome for all concerned to prove affirmatively each and every routine record that is material to the case. It would be virtually impossible to prove a record when, for example, the clerk who made the entry has died, or due to the heavy caseload of police court, no one in the court or clerk's office can personally remember anything about the case in question.

§ 6.4   Presumptions of law

A presumption of law is an inference or deduction which, in the absence of direct evidence on the subject, the law requires to be drawn from the existence of certain established facts.14 Examples of presumptions of law are the presumption of innocence, the presumption of sanity, and the presumption that all men are free.

A presumption of law is a rule announcing that a definite probative weight is attached by jurisprudence to a proposition of logic. When such a pronouncement is made, it is considered prima facie correct and will sustain the burden of evidence until conflicting facts on the point are shown.15

---

12 Cal. Evid. Code § 621 (West Supp. 1984).

13 679 F.2d 8 (3d Cir. 1982).

14 Waugh v. Commonwealth, 394 Pa. 166, 146 A.2d 297 (1958).

15 In re Wood's Estate, 374 Mich. 278, 132 N.W.2d 35 (1965).

In distinguishing between a presumption of law and a presumption of fact, a federal court noted that a "presumption of law," i.e., the procedural rule dictating the factual conclusion in the absence of contrary evidence, is to be distinguished from a "presumption of fact," which in reality is not a presumption at all, and from a "conclusive presumption," which is actually a substantive rule of law.16

§ 6.5 Presumptions of fact

Presumptions of fact are not the subject of fixed rule but are merely natural presumptions, such as appear from common experience, that arise from the particular circumstances of any case. In one case, the court said that a presumption of fact is the mental process by which the existence of one fact is inferred from proof of some other fact or facts which experience show are usually associated by succession or coexistence.17

Some argue that a presumption of fact is really not a presumption because it amounts to no more than an inference.18 In any event, the presumption or inference of fact must not be drawn from premises which are uncertain, but it must be founded on facts established by direct evidence. Presumptions may not be founded on other presumptions. To say this another way, presumptions do not create their own foundations. Presumptions of fact are derived from circumstances of a particular case, by means of the common experience of mankind.

Presumptions of fact can be rebutted when evidence is introduced which is contrary to the presumption.

§ 6.6 Classes of presumptions

For purposes of discussion, presumptions are further divided into conclusive (irrebuttable) presumptions and rebuttable presumptions. A conclusive presumption *(presumption juris et de jure)* is a rule of substantive law, rather than a rule of evidence. A disputable or rebuttable presumption is a species of evidence which may be accepted and acted on when there is no other evidence to refute the contention for which it stands.

A statute may make a presumption conclusive, in which case the presumption cannot be destroyed or overcome by evidence. For example, a

---

16 Legille v. Dann, 544 F.2d 1 (D.C. Cir. 1976).
17 Cox v. Nance, 24 Tenn. App. 304, 143 S.W.2d 897 (1940).
18 Hoge v. George, 27 Wyo. 423, 200 P. 96 (1921).

child born in wedlock is conclusively presumed to be a legitimate child.[19] The rationale for having conclusive presumptions is that the public policy expediency overrides the general fundamental requirement that fact questions should be resolved according to proof. Over the years, the courts have concluded that certain kinds of facts should be excluded because their admission would injure some other cause more than they would help the cause of truth.

A rebuttable presumption *(presumption juris tantum)* is one which requires the trier of fact to consider the deduction as true until disproved by contrary evidence. An example of a rebuttable presumption—when evidence may be offered to overcome the presumption—is the presumption which states that an accused is presumed to be innocent.

Rebuttable presumptions cannot override facts which the trier of fact believes to be established by evidence, but the province of rebuttable presumption is meant to resolve doubt concerning ultimate fact, that is, when evidence is not convincing either way.[20]

§ 6.7   Specific presumption situations

A clearer understanding of the presumption is gained when one studies the specific presumptions that are most often encountered in the trial of cases. In studying the specific presumptions, one should also keep in mind the reasons for presumptions and the origin of presumptions. Some are created by statute, and some are the result of decisions. Where presumptions are a matter of public policy promulgated by the legislature, some presumptions may be rebutted when substantial evidence of contrary facts is introduced, while others cannot be brushed aside by contradictory evidence.

Although the better rule is that a presumption is not evidence and may stand in lieu of evidence to support a finding or decision unless or until rebutted, some courts have held that a presumption has the effect of evidence and must be weighed against conflicting evidence.[21]

Presumptions are used sparingly in criminal cases and are looked at very carefully by reviewing courts if they put an unreasonable burden on

---

19 *See* G____ M____ H____ v. J____ L____ H____, 700 S.W.2d 506 (Mo. App. 1985), which reaffirmed that at common law the presumption that a child born in wedlock is conclusively presumed to be legitimate, but indicated that today the presumption is rebuttable, is an evidentiary presumption, and is overcome by a showing of substantial evidence to the contrary.

20 Hartford-Empire Co. v. Obear-Nester Glass Co., 71 F.2d 539 (8th Cir. 1934), *cert. denied,* 293 U.S. 625, 55 S. Ct. 345, 79 L. Ed. 712 (1934).

21 Palmer v. Palmer, 101 Cal. App. 2d 819, 226 P.2d 613 (1951).

the accused. Moreover, statutory presumptions must not, under the guise of regulating the presentation of evidence, operate to preclude the accused from presenting his defense.[22]

The number of statutory presumptions and judicial presumptions is voluminous. A high percentage of these do not find their way into criminal cases, and therefore, they will not be discussed in detail. Some examples of presumptions that are not given further attention are: (1) a private transaction has been fair and regular; (2) the ordinary course of business has been followed; (3) a promissory note or a bill of exchange was given or endorsed for a sufficient consideration; and (4) a writing is accurately dated.

In the following sections, some of the more well-known presumptions are discussed, with special emphasis placed upon the presumptions that are important in criminal cases.

§ 6.8   —Innocence

The defendant in a criminal case is presumed to be innocent. This presumption exists until evidence is introduced to prove that he is guilty of the crime charged beyond a reasonable doubt. This rebuttable presumption of innocence places upon the prosecution the burden of proving the defendant guilty beyond a reasonable doubt.

The so-called presumption of innocence is not, strictly speaking, a presumption in the sense of a deduction from a given premise. It is more accurately an assumption which, as a procedural aid, compels the state to maintain the burden of proving guilt.[23] A federal court has pointed out that the presumption of innocence:

> is not a mere belief at the beginning of the trial that the accused is probably innocent. It is not a will-o'-the-wisp, which appears and disappears as the trial progresses. It is a legal presumption which the jurors must consider along with the evidence and the inferences arising from the evidence, when they come finally to pass upon the case. In this sense, the presumption of innocence does accompany the accused through every stage of the trial.[24]

---

22 State v. Kelly, 218 Minn. 247, 15 N.W.2d 554 (1944).

23 Carr v. State, 192 Miss. 152, 4 So. 2d 887 (1941); Wells v. State, 288 So. 2d 860 (Miss. 1974).

24 Dodson v. United States, 23 F.2d 401 (4th Cir. 1928); United States v. Thaxton, 483 F.2d 1071 (5th Cir. 1973); United States v. Friday, 404 F. Supp. 1343 (Mich. 1975).

In the 1989 case of *United States v. Castro,* the United States Court of Appeals for the Fifth Circuit considered an instruction regarding the presumption of innocence in a case in which the defendant was convicted of a narcotics violation. The defendant argued on appeal that the instruction to the jury did not explain the presumption of innocence in clear enough terms.[25] The instructions challenged were:

> I remind you that the indictment is merely the formal charge against the defendants; it is not evidence of guilt. Indeed, the defendants are presumed to be innocent. The law does not require a defendant to prove innocence or produce any evidence at all, and no inference whatever may be drawn from the election of a defendant not to testify.

> The government has the burden of proving a defendant's guilt beyond a reasonable doubt, and if it fails to do that, you must acquit the defendant.

In making reference to its earlier decision in *United States v. Walker,*[26] the Fifth Circuit affirmed that the instruction was sufficient to comply with the "presumption of innocence." The court in the *Castro* case pointed out that not only did the trial court instruct the jury on the presumption of innocence at the close of the trial, but it also stressed the presumption of innocence on numerous occasions at other phases of the proceedings.[27] Apparently this repetition by the judge during the proceedings was persuasive when the case was considered on review.

Generally, in a criminal case, the judge instructs the jury on the presumption of innocence. Until recently, some courts had held that failure to give a specific instruction on the presumption of innocence was reversible error. However, in 1979, the United States Supreme Court in *Kentucky v. Whorton* held that failure to give a requested instruction on the presumption of innocence does not in and of itself violate the Constitution.[28] In this case, the defendant was charged, in three separate indictments, with committing several armed robberies. At the conclusion of all the evidence, the defendant's counsel requested that the jury be instructed on the presumption of innocence. The instruction requested was:

> The law presumes an accused to be innocent of crime. He begins a trial with a clean slate, with no evidence against him. And the law

---

25 United States v. Castro, 874 F.2d 230 (5th Cir. 1989).
26 United States v. Walker, 861 F.2d 810 (5th Cir. 1988).
27 United States v. Castro, *supra,* n. 25.
28 Kentucky v. Whorton, 441 U.S. 786, 99 S. Ct. 2088, 60 L. Ed. 2d 640 (1979). *See* case in Part II, *infra.*

permits nothing but legal evidence presented before the jury to be considered in support of any charge against the accused. So the presumption of innocence alone is sufficient to acquit an accused unless the jury members are satisfied beyond a reasonable doubt of the accused's guilt from all of the evidence in the case.

The judge refused this instruction, but gave one to the effect that the jury could return a verdict of guilty only if they found beyond a reasonable doubt that the respondent with the requisite criminal intent had committed the acts charged in the indictment.

The jury found the defendant guilty of ten counts of first degree robbery, two counts of first degree wanton endangerment, and two counts of first degree attempted robbery. He was sentenced to consecutive terms of imprisonment totaling 230 years. The defendant appealed. The Kentucky Supreme Court determined that failure to give the instruction concerning the presumption of innocence was reversible error. The state appealed to the United States Supreme Court.

Reversing the Kentucky Supreme Court, and finding that a presumption of innocence is not required in all cases, the United States Supreme Court held that:

> In short, the failure to give a requested instruction on the presumption of innocence does not in and of itself violate the Constitution.29

The Court went on to explain that failure to give a specific instruction of innocence should be evaluated in light of the totality of the circumstances, including: all of the instructions to the jury, the arguments of counsel, whether the weight of evidence was overwhelming, and other relevant factors. A dissenting opinion expressed the view that the due process clause of the Fourteenth Amendment mandates that an instruction on the presumption of innocence be given if it is requested, unless there is clearly presented evidence that failure to give the instruction constitutes harmless error.30

While agreeing with the Court's decision in the *Kentucky v. Whorton* case, the Fifth Circuit warned that it is preferable to give an instruction which clearly describes the juror's task in those cases requiring an instruction on the presumption of innocence.31 The instruction suggested by that court—and which the Court said was widely followed—is:

> The defendant has been charged by the Government with _____.
> The indictment is simply the description of the charge made by the

---

29 *Ibid.,* at p. 789.

30 *Ibid.,* at p. 791.

31 United States v. Walker, 861 F.2d 810 (5th Cir. 1988).

Government against the defendant; it is not evidence of his guilt. The law presumes the defendant innocent. The presumption of innocence means that the defendant starts the trial with a clear slate. In other words, I instruct you that the defendant is presumed by you to be innocent throughout your deliberations until such time, if ever, you as a jury are satisfied that the Government has proven him guilty beyond a reasonable doubt. Unless you are satisfied beyond a reasonable doubt that the defendant is guilty, the presumption alone is sufficient to find the defendant not guilty.

While recommending this instruction, the court nevertheless declared that, when the charge, taken as a whole, adequately instructs the jury on the presumption of innocence and the government's burden of proof, the case should not be reversed.[32]

§ 6.9 —Sanity

Every person is presumed to be sane, in the absence of evidence to the contrary. Without evidence of insanity, therefore, it is not incumbent upon the prosecution to prove the defendant's legal sanity. The presumption of sanity is a rule of law which stands in the place of evidence. However, in some jurisdictions, when evidence of insanity is produced, from whatever source, the presumption of sanity disappears, and the mental capacity of the accused to commit the crime becomes an essential element that must be proven by competent evidence beyond a reasonable doubt.[33]

This rule was succinctly stated in the case of *United States v. Lyons.*[34] In that case the defendant was convicted of knowingly and intentionally securing controlled narcotics by misrepresentation, fraud, deception and subterfuge. At the trial, he was not allowed to present an insanity defense based on involuntary drug addiction. In summarizing the rule regarding the presumption of sanity, the court made this comment:

> It is equally well established that the defendant is presumed sane, and where no evidence to the contrary is presented, that presumption is wholly sufficient to satisfy the required proof that the defendant is sane, and hence responsible for his actions . . . however, should the defendant produce even slight evidence tending to

---

32 *Ibid.*

33 Davis v. United States, 160 U.S. 469, 16 S. Ct. 353, 40 L. Ed. 499 (1895); Hartford v. United States, 362 F.2d 63 (9th Cir. 1966); United States v. Bohle, 445 F.2d 54 (7th Cir. 1971).

34 United States v. Lyons, 704 F.2d 743 (5th Cir. 1983).

prove his insanity at the time of the alleged offense, the government has the burden of proving the defendant's sanity beyond a reasonable doubt.

Although the 1984 Comprehensive Crime Control Act dealt with offenders with mental disease or defect, it did not change the rule that a defendant is presumed sane.[35] Under the provisions of the Act, mental disease or defect does not constitute a defense unless the defendant proves by clear and convincing evidence that, at the time of the commission of the acts and, as a result of severe mental disease or defect, he was unable to appreciate the nature and quality or the wrongfulness of his acts. As indicated in previous chapters, in federal court, the burden of proving the defense of insanity by clear and convincing evidence is now on the accused. If he does not meet this burden, then, in effect, the presumption of sanity prevails.

While the federal law now requires that a defendant has the burden of proving the defense of insanity by clear and convincing evidence, the law is not uniform in the various states. In some states, the issue of the defendant's capacity to commit the offense becomes a question of proof, and the prosecution has the burden of proving sanity after the defendant, who claims insanity as a defense, has come forward with evidence to overcome the presumption of sanity. In those states, if the evidence is legally sufficient to raise the issue of insanity and the prosecution offers no evidence of sanity, there is no factual issue for the jury, and the defendant is entitled to a directed verdict of acquittal.

The nature and quantum of evidence which the prosecution must produce to meet the burden of proof of sanity in such cases, in order to justify an instruction on the issue of sanity to the jury, varies with the nature and quantum of evidence indicating mental illness. Lay testimony may be sufficient to satisfy the prosecution's burden of proving sanity, even though there is expert testimony to the contrary.[36] While expert testimony of insanity, particularly the testimony of psychiatrists, may be adequately rebutted by personal opinions of laymen, the opinions of experts may not be arbitrarily ignored.[37]

Since Congress adopted the Insanity Defense Reform Act, which provides that the defendant has the burden of proving the defense of insanity by clear and convincing evidence, the Act has been challenged on several occasions as violating the due process clauses of the Fifth and Fourteenth Amendments.[38] In a case heard before the United States Court of Appeals

---

35 Insanity Defense Reform Act of 1984, Pub. L. No. 98-473, 18 U.S.C. § 17.
36 Mims v. United States, 375 F.2d 135 (5th Cir. 1967).
37 Brock v. United States, 387 F.2d 254 (5th Cir. 1967).
38 United States v. Freeman, 804 F.2d 1574 (11th Cir. 1986); United States v. Amos, 803 F.2d 419 (8th Cir. 1986).

for the Eighth Circuit, the defendant asserted that the statute, by placing upon him the burden of proving insanity, deprived him of due process of law as guaranteed by the Fifth Amendment. His attorney claimed that shifting the burden of proving insanity to the defendant in a robbery case effectively requires the defendant to disprove an element of the crime. Upholding the constitutionality of the Act, the court agreed with the prosecution that insanity is an affirmative defense and not an element of the government's case, and that it is not unconstitutional to require the defendant to prove insanity by clear and convincing evidence.[39]

§ 6.10 —Suicide

The presumption against suicide stems from and is raised by our common knowledge and experience that most sane persons possess a natural love of life and an instinct for self-protection which effectively deter them from suicide or the self-infliction of serious bodily injury. It is commonly recognized that there is an affirmative presumption of death by accidental means which arises under appropriate circumstances from the negative presumption against suicide.[40]

When it was shown that an insured under a double indemnity life insurance policy met his death by external and violent means, and there was no ground for an inference that his death was brought about through suicide, intentional self-infliction of injury, criminal assault by a third person or other nonaccidental means, there was a presumption that death was caused by accidental rather than nonaccidental means. This legal presumption arises and operates only when the means of causing death—as distinguished from the cause of death—are unknown. The presumption is a procedural device which will, on the proof of basic facts that bring the presumption into operation, stand in lieu of any evidence of the accidental nature of the means causing death. The presumption thus makes a prima facie case for the plaintiff. But the presumption cannot prevail against any substantial evidence of the nonaccidental nature of the means.[41]

The presumption against suicide and in favor of accidental or other means of causing death is not evidence and should not be weighed as evi-

---

39 United States v. Byrd, 834 F.2d 145 (8th Cir. 1987).

40 Hinds v. John Hancock Mut. Life Ins. Co., 155 Me. 349, 155 A.2d 721 (1959); Melville v. American Home Assurance Co. 443 F. Supp. 1064 (E.D. Pa. 1977).

41 Shepherd v. Midland Mut. Life Ins. Co., 152 Ohio St. 6, 39 Ohio Op. 352, 87 N.E.2d 156 (1949).

dence. However, courts in several states follow the minority view that the presumption is itself evidence or has evidentiary weight.[42] This presumption against suicide and in favor of accident or natural cause operates procedurally once the insurance company has set up the defense of suicide. The presumption serves to place the burden of coming forward with evidence of suicide upon the insurer.[43]

When the party against whom the presumption against suicide operates produces substantial credible contrary evidence regarding the means of causing death, the presumption disappears as a rule of law. The case must be disposed of, regarding the issue of means of causing death, on the facts produced, independently, without reference to any presumption. The issue must be decided under the burden of proof and on the weight of the evidence, as though no presumption had ever existed.[44]

§ 6.11 —Possession of fruits of crime

When the evidence establishes that the accused possesses recently stolen property, and there is no plausible explanation for such possession consistent with innocence, the jury may be instructed that inferences of guilty knowledge may be drawn from the fact of unexplained possession of the stolen goods.[45] In *Barnes v. United States*, part of the instruction to the jury was as follows:

> Possession of recently stolen property, if not satisfactorily explained, is ordinarily a circumstance from which you may reasonably draw the inference and find, in the light of the surrounding circumstances shown by the evidence in the case, that the person in possession knew the property had been stolen.[46]

In this case, the judge pointed out that the jury is not required to make the inference and has the exclusive province to determine whether the facts and circumstances shown by the evidence in the case warrant an inference which the law permits the jury to draw.

---

42 Under North Dakota law, the presumption that death was accidental has the weight of affirmative evidence. Dick v. New York Life Ins. Co., 359 U.S. 437, 79 S. Ct. 921, 3 L. Ed. 2d 935 (1959).

43 Hines v. Prudential Ins. Co., 235 F. Supp. 695 (E.D. Tenn. 1964).

44 Carson v. Metropolitan Life Ins. Co., 165 Ohio St. 238, 59 Ohio Op. 310, 135 N.E.2d 259 (1956); Kettlewell v. Prudential Ins. Co., 4 Ill. 2d 383, 122 N.E.2d 817 (1954); Ziegler v. Equitable Life Assur. Soc., 284 F.2d 661 (7th Cir. 1960).

45 Barnes v. United States, 412 U.S. 837, 93 S. Ct. 2357 (1973).

46 *Ibid.*, at pp. 839-40.

The strength of such a presumption, which the possession of stolen property raises, depends upon the circumstances surrounding the case. The defendant's possession must be exclusive, and it must have occurred within a relatively short time after commission of the crime.

Although some researchers believe that the presumption of an accused party's guilt arising from the doctrine of recent possession does not hold the validity that it once held,[47] this presumption is still accepted in the courtroom. For example, in the 1984 case of *State v. Fields,* the doctrine of recent possession and the presumption arising therefrom was approved by the Court of Appeals of North Carolina.[48] In *State v. Fields,* the defendant was convicted of credit card theft and larceny of personal property. On appeal, the defendant argued that the state erred in indicating that his possession of the credit card constituted proof of theft of the card. The appellate court, in denying reversal of the conviction by the lower court, made this comment:

> This evidence gives rise to the logical deduction that defendant, possessing the card so soon after it was stolen and under such circumstances, is unlikely to have obtained possession of the card honestly. Consequently, the state was entitled to the benefit of the doctrine of "recent possession" and the presumption arising therefrom, that the defendant took the credit card and twenty dollars from Ms. Winston's pocketbook.

Based on these circumstances, the trial court properly denied the defendant's motion to dismiss.

In *State v. McAllister,* the Ohio Appeals Court held that "it has long been established in Ohio that the unexplained possession by a defendant of recently stolen property may give rise to a permissive inference from which a jury may conclude, beyond a reasonable doubt, that the accused is guilty of the theft.[49] If the presumption rule is applied, these conditions must be met: (a) the possession must be unexplained by any innocent origin; (b) the possession must be fairly recent; and (c) the possession must be exclusive.[50]

§ 6.12 —That person intends the ordinary consequences of his voluntary acts

For some years, both federal and state courts have considered the effect of an instruction to the jury in a criminal case that "the law presumes that a

---

47 Wigmore, Evidence § 2513 (Cladbourn Rev. 1981).
48 State v. Fields, 321 S.E.2d 915 (N.C. App. 1984).
49 State v. McAllister, 53 Ohio App. 2d 176, 372 N.E.2d 1341 (1977).
50 Wigmore, Evidence § 2513 (Cladbourn Rev. 1981).

person intends the ordinary consequences of his voluntary acts."51 This issue was again before the United States Supreme Court in the case of *Sandstrom v. Montana* in 1979.52 Sandstrom was charged with deliberate homicide: that he purposely or knowingly caused the victim's death. At the trial, the defendant argued that although he killed the victim, he did not do so purposely or knowingly, and therefore was not guilty of deliberate homicide.

The trial court instructed the jury that "the law presumes that a person intends the ordinary consequences of his voluntary acts." The jury was not told that the presumption could be rebutted. The defendant's attorney argued that the instruction had the effect of shifting the burden of proof on the issue of purpose or knowledge to the defense and that the instruction was impermissible under the federal Constitution as a violation of due process of law.

Nevertheless, the defendant was found guilty and appealed to the Supreme Court of Montana. That court upheld the conviction, conceding that cases cited by the defense did prohibit shifting the burden of proof to the defendant by means of the presumption, but held that the cited cases "do not prohibit allocation of some burden of proof to the defendant under certain circumstances." The court also found that, as the defendant had only the burden to produce some evidence that he did not intend the ordinary consequences of his voluntary act but not to disprove that he acted purposely or knowingly, the burden of proof had not shifted.

The Supreme Court of the United States, after a consideration of the previous decisions on the question, reasoned that the jury could interpret this instruction as conclusive on the issue of intent. The Court agreed that the instruction violated the Fourteenth Amendment's requirement that the state prove every element of a criminal offense beyond a reasonable doubt. The Court therefore found that the instruction "that the law presumes a person intends the ordinary consequences of his voluntary acts" was—in this case, at least—improper and unconstitutional.

In the *Sandstrom v. Montana* case, the United States Supreme Court held that the due process clause of the Fourteenth Amendment was violated by a jury instruction "that the law presumes that a person intends the ordinary consequences of his voluntary acts." The Court expressly left open the question whether, if a jury is so instructed, the error can be held harmless. Following *Sandstrom,* courts took different approaches to the harmless error problem, and the Supreme Court considered the matter again in 1983 in the case of *Connecticut v. Johnson.*53 In the *Johnson* case, the defendant was convicted of attempted murder, kidnapping in the second degree, robbery in the

---

51 United States v. Wharton, 433 F.2d 451 (D.C. Cir. 1970), and cases cited.
52 Sandstrom v. Montana, 442 U.S. 510, 99 S. Ct. 2450, 61 L. Ed. 2d 39 (1979).
53 Connecticut v. Johnson, 468 U.S. 73, 103 S. Ct. 969, 74 L. Ed. 2d 823 (1983).

first degree, and sexual assault in the first degree. The defendant appealed to the Supreme Court of Connecticut on the ground that the charge to the jury was improper.

The trial court's charge to the jury, which was challenged, began with the general instructions regarding the presumption of innocence and the state's burden of proving beyond a reasonable doubt the existence of every element of the crime charged. The jury was then advised on the issue of intent: "a person's intention may be inferred from his conduct and every person is conclusively presumed to intend the natural and necessary consequences of his act." The court then gave specific instructions on the elements of each crime. With respect to attempted murder, the court again spoke of a conclusive presumption. Also, on the charge of kidnapping in the second degree, the instructions of the court referred to the intent as "very largely a matter of inference."

The respondent argued on appeal that the conclusive presumption language in the jury instructions on intent rendered the instructions unconstitutional under *Sandstrom*. The state argued on appeal that the error, if any, was harmless. The Supreme Court of Connecticut affirmed the conviction for kidnapping and sexual assault, but reversed the convictions for attempted murder and robbery on the ground that the instructions concerning the conclusive presumption shifted the burden of proof as to intent. The Court concluded that the "unconstitutional conclusive presumption language in the general instruction was not cured by the specific instructions on attempted murder and robbery." In upholding the conviction for sexual assault, the Supreme Court of Connecticut ruled that sexual assault was a "specific intent" crime and that, consequently, the jury was not influenced by the erroneous general instructions concerning the presumption of intent.

When the defendant appealed to the United States Supreme Court, that Court agreed with the lower court that the proposition that "every person is conclusively presumed to intend the natural and necessary consequences of his act" was erroneous conjecture, and thus violated the due process clauses of the Constitution. The Supreme Court further explained that "an erroneous presumption on a disputed element of the crime renders irrelevant the evidence on the issue because the jury may have relied upon presumptions rather than upon that evidence." If the instruction is given on the presumption, especially the conclusive presumption, the concern is that the jury will look no further in determining the intent, which is an element of the crime.

As to the harmless error issue, the Court indicated that "there may be rare situations in which the reviewing court can be confident that a *Sandstrom* error did not play any part in the jury's verdict. For example, if the instruction had no bearing on the offense for which the defendant . . . was convicted, it would be appropriate to find the error harmless." However, the Court explained that, in this case, the conclusive presumption instruction permitted the jury to convict the respondent without ever examining the evidence concerning an element of the crime charged. Such an error deprived the respondent of "constitutional rights so basic to a fair trial that their infraction can never be treated as harmless error."

In the 1986 case of *Francis v. Franklin,* the United States Supreme Court again considered the constitutionality of the instruction to the jury concerning presumptions about a defendant's intent.54 In this case the Court, by a 5 to 4 decision, found reversible error in an instruction, given in a murder trial, for which intent was a central issue, that "the acts of a person of sound mind and discretion are presumed to be the product of the person's will, but the presumption may be rebutted." The lower court had also given an instruction that "a person of sound mind and discretion is presumed to intend the natural and probable consequences of his acts, but the presumption may be rebutted." According to the Supreme Court, these charges created a mandatory rebuttable presumption, which violates the principles outlined in the *Sandstrom v. Montana* case.

The Court noted that the *Sandstrom* case and related cases held that the due process clause bars the state from using evidentiary presumptions that effectively relieve the state of its burden of persuasion beyond a reasonable doubt as to every essential element of the crime. The Court explained that a permissive presumption, which suggests a possible conclusion but does not require it to be drawn, does not shift the burden of persuasion and is permissible so long as the conclusion follows logically from the predicate. But a mandatory presumption, even a rebuttal one, is prohibited if it relieves the state of the burden of persuasion as to an element of the offense.

The fact that the jury in the *Francis* case, unlike the jury in the *Sandstrom* case, was informed that the presumption may be rebutted did not cure the constitutional infirmity. The court emphasized that the very statement that the presumption may be rebutted could have indicated to a reasonable juror that the defendant bore an affirmative burden of persuasion once the state proved the underlying act giving rise to the presumption.

The issue of whether the *Sandstrom* error can ever be held harmless, left undecided in *Connecticut v. Johnson,* went unanswered again in this case. Again, the judgment of the United States Supreme Court does not say once and for all that such an instruction would violate constitutional protections in all situations. In both the *Johnson* and the *Francis* cases, the Court refused to find harmless error but did not close the door to a finding of harmless error if other evidence of intent was overwhelming.

---

54 Francis v. Franklin, 471 U.S. 307, 105 S. Ct. 1965, 85 L. Ed. 2d 344 (1986).

§ 6.13 —Knowledge of the law

All persons are presumed to know the general public laws of the state and country where they reside, and the legal effects of their acts. This is founded on public policy and necessity. The rationale for the rule is that one's acts must be considered as having been done with knowledge of the law, otherwise the evasion of the law would be facilitated and the courts would be burdened with collateral inquiries into the content of men's minds.[55] For example, a federal court held that the defendant was presumed to know that money posted for bail was subject to liens in favor of the government.[56]

While a number of decisions have held that the presumption that one knows the law is a conclusive presumption, it is recognized that few, if any, persons in fact do know the law. The rule exists because it is necessary for the administration of justice, and because it merely expresses the proposition that ignorance of the law will not relieve one from the legal consequences of wrongful acts.[57]

While the presumption extends to judicial holdings, persons are not presumed to know how the courts will construe the law or what laws will be held to be unconstitutional.[58]

A person is not presumed to know the laws of a sister state or foreign country, but he is presumed to know that laws are subject to change, and he is presumed to know of the changes.[59]

§ 6.14 —Flight or concealment

Some enforcement officers assume that flight or concealment raises a presumption of guilt. However, this evidence rule should be studied carefully. Although there are some cases in certain jurisdictions indicating that flight before arrest raises a presumption of guilt, the better—and majority—rule is that the flight of the accused or his concealment does not raise a legal presumption or inference of guilt, although flight or concealment may constitute evidence thereof.[60] Evidence may be admitted to show that the defendant, after the commission of a crime, fled from the vicinity. This evidence may be presented as a circumstance tending to indicate guilt. When, however, the state introduces evidence to show flight or concealment,

---

55 Atlas Realty Corp. v. House, 123 Conn. 74, 192 A. 564 (1937).
56 United States v. Cannistraro, 694 F. Supp. 62 (D.N.J. 1988).
57 State v. Moreland, 152 Okla. 37, 3 P.2d 803 (1931).
58 Screws v. United States, 32 U.S. 91, 65 S. Ct. 103, 89 L. Ed. 1495 (1945).
59 *See* 31A C.J.S. *Evidence* § 132.
60 State v. Rodriguez, 23 N.M. 156, 167 P. 426 (1918).

the defendant is entitled to introduce evidence to explain why he fled or concealed himself.61

The question as to whether "flight" instructions are proper depends upon the facts of the case. In one case the court noted that the government is entitled to a flight instruction when the evidence in the case supports the following inferences: (1) from defendant's behavior to flight; (2) from flight to consciousness of guilt; (3) from consciousness of guilt to consequences of guilt concerning the crimes charged; and (4) from consciousness of guilt concerning the crime charged to actual guilt of the crime charged.62

Another court, in making reference to flight instructions, noted that flight instructions point out to jurors that they may consider the defendant's behavior at or near the scene of the crime as bearing on guilt or innocence; thus, such instructions necessarily refer in a very general manner to the defendant's post-crime behavior.63 In this case the court suggested that instructions providing that running away after the crime did not in itself prove guilt, but that evidence of running away or concealment or destruction of evidence could be considered by the jury with other evidence.

In a federal case the evidence indicated that the defendants, upon observing an FBI agent in an unmarked car drive out of an apartment complex, ran a stoplight, ran two additional stoplights without making any effort to slow down, passed three cars while going uphill in a no passing zone, and drove at speeds of 50-60 miles per hour.64 The reviewing court upheld an instruction that flight can be considered as evidence of guilt. In another case the court indicated that evidence that the defendant ran from the scene of the crime, ducked into his girlfriend's apartment when police spotted him and quickly exited out the back, entered two other apartments, and changed his clothes, was sufficient to warrant a flight instruction.65 Evidence that the defendant, while in another state six weeks after the crime, gave a fictitious name and address to a detective, coupled with testimony of the defendant's employer that on the date of the crime the defendant called to tell him that he would not be returning to work, was also sufficient to support a jury instruction on flight as consciousness of guilt.66

---

61 Hines v. Commonwealth, 136 Va. 728, 117 S.E. 843 (1923).
62 United States v. Cook, 580 F. Supp. 948 (N.D.W. Va. 1983), aff'd, 782 F.2d 1037 (4th Cir. 1983); see also State v. Woodal, 385 S.E.2d 253 (W. Va. 1989). See case in Part II, infra.
63 State v. Weible, 142 Ariz. 113, 688 P.2d 1005 (1984).
64 United States v. Beard, 775 F.2d 1577 (11th Cir. 1985), cert. denied, 475 U.S. 1030, 106 S. Ct. 1235, 89 L. Ed. 2d 343 (1985).
65 State v. Weible, 142 Ariz. 113, 688 P.2d 1005 (1984).
66 Garrett v. State, 59 Md. App. 97, 474 A.2d 931 (1984).

While a flight instruction is proper when there is evidence of flight or concealment and the evidence reasonably supports an inference that the defendant fled because of a consciousness of guilt and a desire to avoid an accusation based thereon, there must be some meaningful evidence of actual flight before the instruction can be given.67 Also, the court must fully apprise the jury that flight may be prompted by a variety of motives, and it must admonish the jury to consider all evidence before making an inference of guilt from the fact of flight.

§ 6.15 —Death after unexplained absence

At common law, where a person leaves his home or usual place of residence for parts unknown, and is not heard of or known to be living for a period of seven years, the legal presumption arises that he is dead. Some states have enacted "presumed decedents laws," under which the presumption of death in the case of an unexplained absence of a specified number of years arises as of the date of the court decree finding of a legal presumption of death.

The cases are not in agreement with respect to the presumed death of a fugitive from justice. In an action on a life insurance policy, an Illinois court held that the fact that the absent person was a fugitive from justice did not preclude the application of the presumption.68 A surety on a defendant's bail bond attempted to avoid forfeiture of bail and introduced evidence that the defendant had disappeared, after leaving his car at an airport, and that an intensive search failed to locate him. Other evidence indicated that the defendant had been indicted, was a member of a group on whom a murderous assault had been made, and had a good reason for flight. The court upheld the forfeiture on the ground that, where a motive or where doubt about the reason for the absence exists, the presumption of continued life remains.69

The presumption of death is not conclusive and may be rebutted by proof of facts which tend to show the contrary, or which raise a conflicting presumption.

---

67 Logan v. United States, 489 A.2d 485 (D.C. App. 1985).
68 Blodgett v. State Mutual Life Assurance Co., 32 Ill. App. 2d 155, 177 N.E.2d 1 (1961).
69 People v. Niccoli, 102 Cal. App. 2d 814, 228 P.2d 827 (1951).

§ 6.16 —Regularity of official acts

A presumption of regularity supports the official acts of public officials, and courts presume that public officials have properly discharged their official duties.[70] The presumption that public officials will in good faith discharge their duties and observe the law is a very strong presumption, and will prevail until overcome by clear and convincing evidence to the contrary.

The proceedings of grand juries are covered by the presumption that official acts are regular. For example, in *Costello v. United States*,[71] the United States Supreme Court refused to dismiss the indictment even though the defense alleged that there were some irregularities in it. In doing so, the Court stated:

> An indictment returned by a legally constituted and unbiased grand jury, like an information drawn by a prosecutor, if valid on its face, is enough to call for a trial of the charges on the merits.

§ 6.17 Tests for constitutionality

The Fifth and Fourteenth Amendments set limits upon the legislature to make proof of one fact (or group of facts) proof of the ultimate fact upon which guilt is predicated. Early decisions of the United States Supreme Court set forth a number of different standards to measure the validity of statutory presumptions. One test was whether there was a "rational connection" between the basic fact and the presumed fact. A second was whether the legislature might have made it a crime to do the thing from which the presumption authorized an inference. A third was whether it would be more convenient for the defendant or for the prosecution to adduce evidence of the presumed fact.

However, in *Tot v. United States*,[72] the Court singled out one of these tests as controlling, and the *Tot* rule has been followed in the two subsequent cases in which the issue has been presented. The *Tot* Court had before it a federal statute which, as construed, made it a crime for a person previously convicted of a crime of violence to receive any firearm or ammunition in an interstate transaction. The statute further provided that "the possession of a firearm or ammunition by any such person shall be

---

70 United States v. Chemical Foundation, Inc. 272 U.S. 1, 47 S. Ct. 1, 71 L. Ed. 131 (1926); Charleston Television, Inc. v. South Carolina Budget and Control Bd., 373 S.E.2d 890 (S.C. 1988).

71 Costello v. United States, 350 U.S. 359, 76 S. Ct. 406, 100 L. Ed. 397 (1956).

72 Tot v. United States, 319 U.S. 463, 63 S. Ct. 1241, 87 L. Ed. 1519 (1943).

presumptive evidence that such firearm or ammunition was shipped or transported or received, as the case may be, by such person in violation of this Act."

The Court held the presumption unconstitutional and decided that the controlling test for determining the validity of a statutory presumption was that there be a rational connection between the fact proved and the fact presumed. The Court stated:

Under our decisions a statutory presumption cannot be sustained if there be no rational connection between the fact proved and the ultimate fact presumed, if the inference of the one from proof of the other is arbitrary because of lack of connection between the two in common experience. This is not to say that a valid presumption may not be created upon a view of relation broader than that a jury might take in a specific case. But where the inference is so strained as not to have a reasonable relation to the circumstances of life as we know them, it is not competent for the legislature to create it as a rule governing the procedure of courts.[73]

Two subsequent cases in which the Supreme Court ruled upon the constitutionality of criminal presumptions, *United States v. Gainey*[74] and *United States v. Romano*,[75] involved companion sections of the Internal Revenue Code dealing with illegal stills. The presumption in *Gainey* permitted, but did not require, a jury to infer from a defendant's presence at an illegal still that he was "carrying on" the business of a distiller, unless the defendant explained his presence to the satisfaction of the jury. The Court held that the *Gainey* presumption should be tested by the "rational connection" standard announced in the *Tot* case, and the Court sustained the statutory presumption.

The presumption under attack in the *Romano* case was identical to that in *Gainey*, except that the former authorized the jury to infer from the defendant's presence at an illegal still that he had possession, custody or control of the still. The Court held this presumption invalid, on the ground that "absent some showing of the defendant's function at the still, its connection with possession is too tenuous to permit a reasonable inference of guilt; the inference of the one from proof of the other is arbitrary."

As indicated in a previous section of this chapter, in the case of *Sandstrom v. Montana* the United States Supreme Court determined that the due process clause of the Fourteenth Amendment was violated by jury instructions that "the law presumes that a person intends the ordinary consequences of his voluntary acts." As this instruction could have been viewed

73 *Ibid.*, at 467-468.
74 United States v. Gainey, 380 U.S. 63, 85 S. Ct. 754, 13 L. Ed. 2d 658 (1965).
75 United States v. Romano, 382 U.S. 136, 86 S. Ct. 279, 15 L. Ed. 2d 210 (1965).

by the jury members as requiring them to draw conclusions about the defendant's intent, the instructions shifted the burden of proof to the defendant. The Court in its decision included the statement that:

> Because David Sandstrom's jury may have interpreted the judges's instruction as construing either a burden-shifting presumption . . . or a conclusive presumption . . . and because either interpretation would have deprived the defendant of his right to the due process of law, we hold the instruction given in this case unconstitutional.

A statutory presumption for criminal cases must be regarded as "irrational" or "arbitrary"—hence unconstitutional, unless it can at least be said with substantial assurance that the presumed fact is more likely than not to follow from the proved fact on which it is made to depend. This was spelled out by the Supreme Court in *Leary v. United States,* when the Court held that, in the absence of demonstrating that the majority of marijuana possessors either were cognizant of the high rate of importation or otherwise were aware that their marijuana was grown abroad, a federal statute authorizing the jury to infer from the defendant's possession of marijuana that the defendant knew that the marijuana was illegally brought into the United States, was invalid under the due process clause.[76]

In the year following the *Leary* decision, the Supreme Court considered the constitutionality of instructing the jury that it may infer from the defendant's possession of heroin and cocaine that the defendant knew that the drugs had been illegally imported.[77] The Court held that the inference with regard to heroin was valid, judged by either of the two tests stated in the *Tot* decision.

To summarize, when determining the constitutionality of statutory presumptions, the court must find a rational connection between the basic fact and the presumed fact, and it must find that there is a reasonable possibility in the ordinary course of events that the conclusion required by the presumption is in accord with human experience. Secondly, a presumption which has the effect of shifting the burden to the defense to prove an element of the crime is unconstitutional.

A question raised in a number of cases is the constitutionality of a state statute making the fact that a defendant was armed with a pistol, for which he had no license, prima facie evidence of his intent to commit a crime of violence. A Washington court held such a statute constitutional, as the court found a rational connection between carrying pistols without a license and

---

76 Leary v. United States, 395 U.S. 6, 89 S. Ct. 1532, 23 L. Ed. 2d 57 (1969).
77 Turner v. United States, 396 U.S. 398, 90 S. Ct. 642, 24 L. Ed. 2d 386 (1970).

intending crimes of violence.[78] On the other hand, an Indiana court concluded that the fact that a person was armed with an unlicensed gun was irrelevant to the question of whether that person intended to commit a crime of violence.[79]

In a California case the trial court had instructed the jury that a defendant charged with grand theft "shall be presumed to have embezzled the vehicle if it was not returned within five days of expiration of the rental agreement," and that "intent to commit theft by fraud is presumed" for failure to return the rental property within 20 days of demand. The United States Supreme Court held that these instructions constituted a mandatory presumption relieving the state of proving the elements of the crime, in violation of the defendant's due process rights.[80]

However, an instruction that the jury "may presume" that the defendant was under the influence of intoxicating liquors if the defendant's blood-alcohol level was 0.10 percent or more but that the presumption was "not binding" created a permissive presumption that did not violate the defendant's due process rights, although the instruction did not contain the words "beyond a reasonable doubt."[81]

§ 6.18 Stipulations

Another substitute for evidence is the stipulation. A stipulation is a concession by both parties to the existence or nonexistence of a fact, to the contents of a document, or to the testimony of a witness. It may be written or oral and is generally encouraged in order to expedite the trial.

In 1984, the United States Court of Appeals for the Fifth Circuit commented on the right of the adverse party to refuse acceptance of a stipulation. According to that court, as a general rule, a party may not preclude his adversary's offer of proof by admission or stipulation, provided, however, that the offer is qualified by the rule that requires evidence to be excluded if its potential for unfair prejudice substantially outweighs its probative value.[82]

A stipulation regarding a fact authorizes the court to find the existence of such a fact and to consider that fact without any further proof. The triers of fact are not, however, bound to accept the fact as true; they may find to the contrary if persuaded by other evidence.

---

[78] State v. Thomas, 58 Wash. 2d 746, 364 P.2d 930 (1961).

[79] Everett v. State, 208 Ind. 145, 195 N.E. 77 (1935).

[80] Carella v. California, ___ U.S. ___, 109 S. Ct. 2419 (1989).

[81] People v. Hester, 181 Ill. 2d 91, 544 N.E.2d 797 (1989).

[82] United States v. Oshea, 724 F.2d 1514 (5th Cir. 1984).

Stipulated testimony merely amounts to a mutual agreement by both parties that if a certain person were present, he would testify under oath to the facts stated. In the case of *Barnes v. State*, a Maryland court held that when evidence is offered by way of "stipulation," the parties do not necessarily agree to the facts that the evidence seeks to establish, but that the stipulation goes only to the content of the testimony of a particular witness if he were to appear and testify.[83] However, once a stipulation is agreed upon, as a general rule, the stipulation may not be withdrawn without the consent of both parties or for cause, such as fraud, mistake or undue influence.[84]

While the courts have indicated that stipulations should be encouraged, it is error for the trial court to require one of the parties to a litigation to stipulate with his adversary.[85] In the Tennessee case of *State v. Ford*, the reviewing court decided that the trial court had erred in requiring a motorist to stipulate to the use of the court's summary of a defense witness' testimony rather than allowing the witness' live testimony, when both the motorist and the state objected to the stipulation. In this case, the court noted that a stipulation is an agreement between counsel with respect to business before the court and should be encouraged and enforced by the court, as stipulations expedite the business of the court. The reviewing court continued, however, by cautioning that it is not the duty or function of the trial court to require one of the parties to a litigation to stipulate with his adversary.

A stipulation is also used as a means of determining whether certain evidence will be admitted into court. In criminal cases where the parties have stipulated to the admissibility of certain evidence, that evidence is admissible to corroborate other evidence of the defendant's participation in the crime charged. In the absence of any claim that the stipulation was entered into by mistake, inadvertence, fraud or misrepresentation, counsel may stipulate regarding that evidence which may be received.

There are limitations upon the use of stipulations. It is clear that a stipulation amounting to a complete concession by the defense to the prosecutor's case would be inconsistent with a plea of not guilty and should not be permitted. A stipulation that is clearly erroneous should not be accepted, and its acceptance probably would be justification for reversal on constitutional grounds. Also, the court is not required to admit a stipulation as a substitute for evidence which may be detrimental to the defendant's case.[86]

As a general rule, a stipulation may be withdrawn, and if withdrawn, it ceases to be effective for any purpose. The withdrawal of a stipulation,

---

83 Barnes v. State, 354 A.2d 499 (Md. 1976).
84 Harlan v. Harlan, 544 N.E.2d 553 (Ind. 1989).
85 State v. Ford, 725 S.W.2d 689 (Tenn. 1986). *See* case in Part II, *infra*.
86 United States v. Grassi, 602 F.2d 1192 (5th Cir. 1979).

however, would be a reasonable basis for a continuance in order for the opposing party to prepare evidence concerning matters formerly embraced by the stipulation.

§ 6.19 —Polygraph tests

An example of the use of a stipulation is the admission of results of a polygraph examination. Although it is generally held that polygraph tests are not judicially acceptable because of their unreliability, there is a distinction drawn when there is a stipulation; then the results of the test may be admitted. Courts from many jurisdictions have found a valid exception for the admissibility of polygraph tests taken on stipulation.[87]

In a Washington state case, the state supreme court held that the admission of the results of a polygraph test pursuant to a stipulation entered into by the defendant, his counsel, and the prosecuting attorney (and providing for the defendant's submission to the test, the admission of the graphs, and the examiner's opinion at the trial) was not error.[88]

In the case of *State v. Ross*, the defendant was charged with two counts of second-degree assault with a knife. After the defendant submitted to a polygraph test, which was given pursuant to a stipulation that the results, favorable or not, would be admissible into evidence, the results of the test were admitted. However, when at trial the examiner testified that Ross was not telling the complete truth in answering certain questions which were prejudicial to the defendant, the defendant's attorney objected. The court agreed that, notwithstanding these stipulations, the admissibility of results of polygraph tests is subject to the discretion of the trial judge. However, the court found that all of the safeguards were followed, and therefore, it admitted the evidence over the objection of the defendant.

There are some cases to the contrary,[89] but the trend would allow the examiner's opinion after a polygraph examination is conducted and the parties stipulate to its admissibility. The courts, however, have laid down some conditions which must be met. If the polygraph and polygraph examiner's opinion are offered in evidence, the opposing party must have the right to cross-examine the examiner regarding (a) the examiner's qualifications and training; (b) the conditions under which the tests were administered; (c) the

---

87 State v. Chambers, 451 P.2d 27 (Ariz. 1969); State v. McNamara, 252 Iowa 19, 104 N.W.2d 568 (1960); Herman v. Eagle Star Ins. Co., 283 F. Supp. 33 (C.D. Cal. 1966).

88 State v. Ross, 497 P.2d 1343 (Wash. 1972).

89 State v. McNamara, 252 Iowa 19, 104 N.W.2d 568 (1960). *See* § 15.5 *infra* for a discussion of the use of the results of polygraph examinations.

technique of polygraph interrogation and the possibilities for errors; and (d) at the discretion of the trial judge, other matters deemed pertinent to the inquiry.

Also, when such evidence is admitted, the trial judge should instruct the jury that the examiner's testimony does not tend to prove or disprove any element of the crime, but tends only to indicate that, at the time of the examination, the defendant was or was not telling the truth.

§ 6.20 Summary

To save the time of the court and to achieve results which the courts and legislatures have determined to be necessary in the administration of justice, presumptions and inferences are utilized. The presumption takes the place of evidence in certain instances, and until facts in lieu of which a presumption operates are shown, the presumptive facts are accepted as true.

Presumptions are classified as rebuttable presumptions and conclusive presumptions. A rebuttable presumption may be overcome by evidence to the contrary; the conclusive presumption cannot be rebutted.

There are many specific examples of both rebuttable and conclusive presumptions. Presumptions are used sparingly in criminal cases and are looked at very carefully by reviewing courts if they put an unreasonable burden on the accused. Some of the specific presumptions that are prevalent in criminal cases are: the presumption that a person is innocent until proven guilty beyond a reasonable doubt; the presumption that a person is sane; the presumption that a person in possession of recently stolen property knows that the property was stolen; and the presumption that all persons are presumed to know the general public laws of the state and country in which they reside.

Legislative bodies are not without controls when determining what presumptions are effective in law. The due process clauses of the Fifth and Fourteenth Amendments set limits upon the legislature when making proof of one fact or group of facts proof of the ultimate fact upon which guilt is predicated. Especially in recent years, statutory presumptions have been subject to review on the grounds that they are unconstitutional. Obviously a presumption that is arbitrary or irrational would be in violation of the due process clauses of the Constitution.

Another means of relieving the parties of the necessity of introducing evidence is the use of the stipulation. The stipulation, which should be used more often by the courts, indicates that the parties are willing to agree to the truth of certain allegations, leaving only the truly disputed facts to be determined by the jury or court.

It is a mistake for those involved in the criminal justice process to rely heavily on presumptions. Countervailing evidence may be offered when the presumption is in favor of the prosecution, and the prosecution must be prepared to reinforce the presumption. Also, the prosecution must be prepared to rebut presumptions in favor of the defense.

Although stipulations are excellent ways of saving the time of the court and concerned parties, their improper use can lead to acquittal of guilty persons. Many prosecutors have gone to trial unprepared because of misinterpretation of the stipulation. To avoid this pitfall, the investigator and prosecutor should be prepared in the event that the opposing party disputes the fact that a stipulation was made, or if mistake or fraud is claimed.

C. GENERAL ADMISSIBILITY TESTS

CHAPTER 7
RELEVANCY AND MATERIALITY

There is a principle—not so much a rule of evidence as a presupposition involved in the very conception of a rational system, as contrasted with the old formal and mechanical systems—which forbids receiving anything irrelevant, not logically probative. . . .

The two leading principles should be brought into conspicuous relief, (1) that nothing is to be received which is not logically probative of some matter requiring to be proved; and (2) that everything which is thus probative should come in, unless a clear ground of policy or law excludes it.
Thayer, EVIDENCE (1898)

§ 7.1   Introduction

In this chapter and the next, emphasis is on the general admissibility tests (relevancy, materiality and competency) that are applied by the courts when considering the admissibility of evidence. This chapter deals with the general relevancy and materiality tests, while Chapter 8 explains competency of evidence and witnesses.

Because the primary objective and purpose in a criminal trial is to determine the truth regarding the issues presented, all evidence is admissible unless upon objection it is subject to exclusion under the established evidence rules. The usual procedure followed in making a general challenge to

123

the evidence is for the attorney to object on the grounds that the evidence is irrelevant, immaterial and incompetent. Unless the reason for the objection is obvious, however, the judge will often require a more detailed explanation concerning the challenge. He may request that the challenger explain what the reasoning is for complaining that the evidence is irrelevant or immaterial.

For those involved in the criminal justice process it is important to understand these relevancy and materiality rules. In many instances, evidence which has been laboriously obtained and prepared for introduction is excluded because it does not meet the relevancy and materiality tests as determined by the trial judge.

§ 7.2   Relevancy and materiality defined

Rule 401

DEFINITION OF "RELEVANT EVIDENCE"

"Relevant evidence" means evidence having any tendency to make the existence of any fact that is of consequence to the determination of the action more probable or less probable than it would be without the evidence.[1]

Lawyers and judges frequently treat the terms *relevant* and *material*—and particularly their opposites *irrelevant* and *immaterial*—as interchangeable and synonymous. Although *relevant* is a broad term that is often used to mean both relevant and material, the distinction between the two concepts is significant.

a.   Relevant evidence

Black's Law Dictionary states that evidence is relevant if reasonable inferences can be drawn therefrom regarding, or if any light is shed upon, a contested matter.[2]

One author describes relevant evidence as "evidence that in some degree advances the inquiry, and thus has probative value and is *prima facie* admissible."[3]

In *Corpus Juris Secundum* logical relevancy is defined as "the existence of such a relationship in logic between the fact of which evidence is offered

---

1   Fed. R. Evid. 401.

2   Black's Law Dictionary (5th ed. 1979).

3   McCormick, Law of Evidence, p. 319.

and a fact in issue that the existence of the former renders probable or improbable the existence of the latter."4

A more simple definition from a Georgia case is: "Relevancy is a logical relationship between evidence and a fact in issue or to be established."5

Other definitions include:

- The basic test for admissibility of evidence is "relevancy," and testimony is "relevant" if a reasonable inference can be drawn therefrom regarding or, if any light is shed upon, a contested matter.6

- Real evidence is "relevant" if it sheds any light on the circumstances.7

- "Evidence is relevant when it throws or tends to throw light on guilt or innocence of the accused even though its tendency to do so is slight."8

b. Material evidence

*Black's Law Dictionary*9 defines material evidence as evidence that is material to the question in controversy, that must necessarily enter into the consideration of the controversy, and that by itself or in connection with other evidence is determinative of the case.

Materiality concerns the importance of evidence. Evidence is material only when it significantly affects the matter or issue in a case. The concept boils down to this: Would the evidence offer a substantially material fact in this particular case to prove or disprove a charge against the defendant?

Some definitions of material evidence—as framed by courts in criminal cases—are:

- "Material evidence" is that which is relevant and goes to substantial matters in dispute, or has legitimate and effective influence or bearing on the decision of the case.10

- For purposes of a motion for a new trial based upon newly discovered evidence, "material evidence" is evidence that is relevant and goes to the substantial matters in dispute or has a legitimate and effective influence or bearing on the decision of the case.11

---

4   31A C.J.S. *Evidence* § 58.
5   Continental Trust Co. v. Bank of Harrison, 36 Ga. App. 149, 136 S.E. 319 (1926).
6   State v. Smith, 5 Wash. App. 237, 487 P.2d 277 (1971).
7   State v. Jones, 56 N.C. App. 259, 289 S.E.2d 383 (1982).
8   BLACK'S LAW DICTIONARY (5th ed. 1979).
9   Beighler v. State, 481 N.E.2d 78 (Ind. 1985).
10 Hill v. State, 159 Ga. App. 489, 283 S.E.2d 703 (1981).
11 United States v. Riggs, 495 F. Supp. 1085 (M.D. Fla. 1980).

c. Materiality and relevancy distinguished

In one case, the court distinguished between materiality and relevancy by stating, "As used with respect to evidence, 'material' has wholly different meaning from 'relevant.' To be relevant means to relate to the issue. To be material means to have probative weight, that is, reasonably likely to influence the tribunal in making the determination required to be made."12

Although evidence may be relevant, it is not necessarily material. Whether facts are material to an inquiry depends upon the particular circumstances involved. Thus, although evidence may be relevant, in that it relates to or has some bearing on the case, it may have such slight relevancy as to be immaterial.

In making these fine distinctions between relevancy and materiality, the discussion would not be complete if the point were not made that in actual practice the distinction is blurry at best and that in most cases whether evidence is characterized as irrelevant or immaterial makes little difference in effect.13

§ 7.3   Admissibility of relevant evidence

RULE 402

RELEVANT EVIDENCE GENERALLY ADMISSIBLE; IRRELEVANT EVIDENCE INADMISSIBLE

All relevant evidence is admissible, except as otherwise provided by the Constitution of the United States, by Act of Congress, by these rules, or by other rules prescribed by the Supreme Court pursuant to statutory authority. Evidence which is not relevant is not admissible.14

The general rule is that all relevant evidence is admissible subject to exceptions. If the evidence logically bears upon any point in issue, it should be admitted to help the triers of fact determine what took place. If the evidentiary proposition advanced by either party tends to prove a proposition in issue, then the evidence is normally relevant and should be admitted. On the other hand, if the offered evidence does not logically contribute to the determination of a material proposition, to introduce that evidence would only confuse the triers of fact, especially if the factfinders are laypersons.

---

12 Weinstock v. United States, 231 F.2d 699 (D.C. Cir. 1956).
13 Holmes v. State, 40 Ala. App. 251, 112 So. 2d 511 (1959).
14 FED. R. EVID. 402.

The trial court has great latitude in passing on the admissibility of evidence, and its determination of legal relevancy must be considered an act of discretion not to be disturbed absent a clear showing of abuse.[15] Thus, guns seized in the search of an automobile of a defendant charged with conspiracy to break and enter a post office were relevant to prove conspiracy and were properly admitted into evidence even though there was no direct evidence that the guns were actually used by the defendant.[16] A federal court held that where there is proof that the weapon has been employed in a bank robbery, the district court may permit introduction of that weapon or weapons of similar kind to show identity or to corroborate testimony linking the defendant to the crime charged. The court noted that such evidence is relevant to establish opportunity or preparation to commit the offense charged and thus would tend to prove identity of the robbers.[17] However, in a jury trial for armed robbery of a bank where there was a discussion of guns which police officers had taken from defendant's dresser at the time of his arrest, the court determined that there was no testimony that the guns had been used in the robbery, that they were not relevant to the issues in the case, and that therefore the jury was not to consider the testimony about the guns in any way whatsoever.[18]

Once the trial judge makes a decision as to relevancy, an appellate court should not quickly substitute its judgment for that of the trial judge.[19] In a Texas case, the reviewing court cautioned that the trial judge is in a superior position to weigh the true potency of proffered evidence, and as his decision is made in the rapid-fire tempo of trial, it ought not to be judged too harshly with the advantage of hindsight. The reviewing court agreed that a decision as to relevancy should stand unless there was clear evidence of abuse.

The Federal Rules of Evidence make it clear that evidence should be admitted unless some specific rule forbids the admission of the evidence. The wording of section 402 of the Federal Rules has been copied by many states in formulating their own rules. Some states have adopted the rule as written, with some modifications. For example, the Iowa Code provides that "all relevant evidence is admissible, except as otherwise provided by the Constitution of the United States or the State of Iowa, by statute, by these rules, or other rules of the Iowa Supreme Court. Evidence which is not rel-

---

15   Holmes v. State, 40 Ala. App. 251, 112 So. 2d 511 (1959). United States v. Leamous, 754 F.2d 795 (8th Cir. 1985), *cert. denied,* 471 U.S. 1139, 105 S. Ct. 2684, 86 L. Ed. 2d 701 (1985).

16   Wangrow v. United States, 399 F.2d 106 (8th Cir. 1968).

17   United States v. Ferreira, 821 F.2d 1 (1st Cir. 1987).

18   United States v. Peacock, 400 F.2d 992 (6th Cir. 1968).

19   United States v. Johnson, 585 F.2d 119 (5th Cir. 1978).

evant is not admissible."20 Other states that have adopted the wording of the Federal Rules are North Carolina,21 Texas,22 and Vermont.23

Recent decisions of the federal courts have applied the reasoning that all evidence should be admissible unless it comes within one of the specific exceptions. For example, in a prosecution for income tax evasion in which the government alleged that the defendant's increases in net worth were attributable to drug smuggling activities, the prosecution provided evidence that in 1980, the defendant's plane was found loaded with over 4,000 pounds of marijuana. Such evidence was admissible to substantiate the government's net worth claims for 1978 and 1979.24 However, evidence of the defendant's financial transactions and general financial status were not relevant in a federal case where the defendant was charged with possession of, attempting to manufacture, and intending to distribute marijuana, and the district court properly excluded such evidence.25

§ 7.4   Reasons for exclusion of relevant and material evidence

---

Rule 403

EXCLUSION OF RELEVANT EVIDENCE ON GROUNDS OF PREJUDICE, CONFUSION, OR WASTE OF TIME

Although relevant, evidence may be excluded if its probative value is substantially outweighed by the danger of unfair prejudice, confusion of the issues, or misleading the jury, or by considerations of undue delay, waste of time, or needless presentation of cumulative evidence.26

Although relevant evidence is generally admissible, there are some rules of exclusion. The Federal Rules of Evidence, a portion of which have been included herein, enumerate and codify some of these exclusions, but one must look to the cases for an explanation. Some of the reasons for excluding relevant evidence are indicated here.

---

20 Iowa Rules of Evidence 402 (1983).
21 North Carolina Rules of Evidence 402 (1983).
22 Texas Rules of Evidence 402 (1984).
23 Vermont Rules of Evidence 402 (1983).
24 United States v. Heyward, 729 F.2d 297 (4th Cir. 1984).
25 United States v. Fuesting, 845 F.2d 564 (7th Cir. 1988).
26 Fed. R. Evid. 403.

a. The probative value is substantially outweighed by the danger of unfair prejudice

If the probative value of the evidence is slight and the danger of unfair prejudice is great, the judge should direct that the evidence not be introduced. For example, gruesome photographs were improperly introduced at a trial in a homicide case in which the cause of death was not in controversy, and the purpose of such introduction was meant to influence the jurors.[27]

In interpreting the unfair prejudice portion of Rule 403 of the Federal Rules of Evidence, the Eleventh Circuit Court of Appeals cautioned that this rule should be relied upon very sparingly but that the trial court should have wide discretion whether to exclude evidence under this provision.[28] In another case the Third Circuit Court of Appeals held that, even if the evidence regarding the defendant's prior cocaine sales was relevant, the evidence was inadmissible in light of the prejudice to the defendant arising from the fact that the generalized nature of the evidence precluded any meaningful refutation.[29]

b. Introduction of the evidence would confuse the issues

If the evidence to be introduced would normally be relevant but would detract from the main issue and emphasize side issues, it may be excluded at the discretion of the court. For example, evidence of prior crimes by the accused is usually inadmissible even though relevant because such evidence would tend to confuse the issues. In our system of trial by jury, the courts have gone far in making sure that the evidence introduced does not distract the jury from the case being tried. For this reason, some evidence, although relevant at least peripherally, is excluded.

In making reference to the "confusion of the issues" provision of Rule 403, the Seventh Circuit reasoned that in the prosecution of a judge arising out of the acceptance of bribes for quashing parking tickets, the trial court did not err in refusing admission of evidence showing that the defendant dismissed cases for other reasons, on the ground that the probative value of that evidence would be clearly outweighed by its effect and would confuse the jury by extending an already very long trial.[30]

---

27 State v. Makal, 104 Ariz. App. 476, 455 P.2d 450 (1969). Some writers criticize this rule, stating that the concept is a nuisance, as "probative value" defies definition. *See Relevancy, Probability, and the Law,* 29 CAL. L. REV. 689 (1941).

28 Wilson v. Attaway, 757 F.2d 1227 (11th Cir. 1985).

29 United States v. Swartz, 790 F.2d 1059 (3d Cir. 1986).

30 United States v. LeFevour, 798 F.2d 977 (7th Cir. 1986).

c. The evidence would mislead the jury

If evidence is such that it would tend to lead the jury to an incorrect conclusion, it should not be admitted. As an example, a federal court in 1984 properly refused the introduction of evidence which might have been misleading to the jury.[31] In that case, the defendant was accused of crimes arising from fraudulent cattle transactions. The defendant attempted to introduce evidence that was meant to characterize a certain transaction as a debt collection made legitimately and in good faith. The court reasoned, however, that because this evidence would be misleading and would divert attention from the crimes for which the defendant was charged, the evidence should not be admitted.[32]

d. The evidence would unduly delay the trial of the case, waste time or needlessly accumulate evidence

The judge, at his discretion, may exclude relevant evidence if it unnecessarily delays the case or only accumulates evidence which has already been covered sufficiently by other evidence.[33] For example, a federal court in 1984 held that a lower court did not abuse its discretion in excluding evidence that would be duplicative.[34] In this case, the defendant was accused of tax evasion and falsifying a tax return. The court agreed that the testimony of the taxpayer's expert, while having some probative value, was properly excluded when the expert's testimony essentially would duplicate prior testimony by another witness.[35]

In considering the "needless presentation of cumulative evidence" provision of Rule 403, evidence from the defendant's wife that she feared the Internal Revenue Service officers and agents was properly excluded when the defendant's wife had already testified on cross-examination concerning her apprehension of agents and that she thought the agents were strange people that were going to kill her or rob her.[36] In an income tax evasion case, it was not an abuse of discretion to exclude documents on which the taxpayer allegedly relied in concluding that he did not have to file a federal income tax return. Here, the court deteremined that the documents were cumulative of the taxpayer's testimony and presented a danger of confusing the jury by suggesting that the law was unsettled.[37]

---

31 United States v. Miller, 725 F.2d 462 (8th Cir. 1984).

32 *Ibid.*

33 Thompson v. American Steel & Wire Co., 317 Pa. 7, 175 A. 541 (1934).

34 United States v. Marabelles, 724 F.2d 1374 (9th Cir. 1984).

35 *Ibid.*

36 United States v. Streich, 759 F.2d 579 (7th Cir. 1985).

37 United States v. Flitcraft, 903 F.2d 184 (5th Cir. 1986).

e. The evidence would unfairly and harmfully surprise a party who has not had reasonable opportunity to anticipate that such evidence would be offered

Some courts advocate the exclusion of evidence if the opposing party is caught by surprise. The reasoning is that if the opponent is caught by surprise and has had no warning or could not have logically anticipated that such evidence would be offered, then the evidence should be excluded, even though relevant. Because this rule has brought about some confusion, many writers feel that the situation would be handled better by instructions to the jury at the trial stage or by a continuance in order for the adverse party to become better prepared.

As indicated in the previous section, the trial judge must have a great degree of latitude in making decisions concerning the admissibility of relevant evidence. If the evidence is relevant, it should be admitted unless there is a clear-cut reason for the exclusion. In the final analysis, the factfinders should have the opportunity to give weight to the evidence, keeping in mind that the mere fact that evidence is admissible because it is relevant does not mean that the evidence probably establishes the case. If the sum total of the evidence received falls short of satisfying the burden of persuasion, then the jury has a responsibility of finding against the party who bears the burden. On the other hand, the jury should have the benefit of hearing as much of the evidence as possible in determining whether the sum total of the evidence received justifies finding for the party who has the burden of proof or burden of persuasion.

§ 7.5   Relevancy of particular matters

In previous sections of this chapter, the general concepts relating to relevancy and materiality have been examined. These rules apply in all instances when evidence is proposed for introduction. However, there are some particular instances in which not only the general rules apply but also some specific rules relating to peculiar situations have been developed.

It is obvious that evidence is necessary to prove the essential elements of a case as well as the preliminary facts such as identity, jurisdiction of the court, and the mental condition of the accused. Because challenges have been frequent in certain areas, such as the admissibility of character evidence and the use of real evidence (especially in criminal cases), these and other particular matters are discussed in detail in the sections that follow.

§ 7.6 —Identity of persons

Because it is essential that persons who are being prosecuted in a criminal case be positively identified, evidence to prove identity is allowed with much latitude. Any fact, however slight, which tends to satisfy a person of ordinary judgment regarding identity is admissible if other rules are met.[38]

Evidence of a suspect's past activities is often admitted to show identity, even though this may include evidence of other crimes. For example, in one federal case in which the defendant was accused of making sawed-off shotguns, evidence that the defendant stole the shotguns before they were sawed off was admissible to prove that he also sawed them off.[39]

In another case, a state court held that evidence of one crime need not be excluded as evidence of another crime in identifying the defendant as the perpetrator of the crime in question, even though the prosecution has other means of proving identity.[40] The court said that the test for admissibility of such evidence is relevancy, not necessity.[41] In one homicide case, evidence of attacks by the defendant on two other young women was admissible to prove the identity of the assailant in the case being tried, and to reveal a plan or scheme and the modus operandi.[42]

However, such evidence of prior acts is not admissible to prove identity when "the characteristics of the prior crime, although resembling those of the crime charged, do not show a modus operandi common to the charged offense and the previously uncharged offense which would tend to identify the defendant as the perpetrator of the offense charged."[43]

Even though the identity of a person, especially the accused in a criminal case, is important and the evidence thereof is usually relevant, courts have formulated guidelines for the use of evidence of identity obtained from a lineup or with the use of photographs.[44] If the lineup or other pretrial confrontation for identification is so suggestive as to contaminate the in-court identification, the evidence will not be admitted even though it would normally be relevant.[45]

The same reasoning applies to photographs used to aid prospective wit-

---

38 United States v. Zeiler, 296 F. Supp. 224 (W.D. Pa. 1969); Commonwealth v. Rivera, 397 Mass. 244, 490 N.E.2d 1160 (1986).

39 United States v. Day, 591 F.2d 861 (D.C. Cir. 1978).

40 Ruffin v. State, 397 So. 2d 277 (Fla. 1981), *cert. denied,* 454 U.S. 882 (1981).

41 *Ibid.*

42 State v. Ellis, 208 Neb. 379, 303 N.W.2d 741 (1981).

43 Coty v. State, 627 P.2d 407 (Nev. 1981).

44 Neil v. Biggers, 409 U.S. 188, 93 S. Ct. 375, 34 L. Ed. 2d 401 (1972).

45 For a more thorough discussion, *see* Klotter & Kanovitz, Constitutional Law (6th ed. 1991).

nesses or victims in the identification process. If these are so suggestive that the in-court identification is prejudiced, the evidence will be inadmissible.[46]

These challenges to identifying evidence are constitutional challenges, rather than challenges based on irrelevancy or immateriality.

§ 7.7 —Identity of things

Although there are some exceptions, evidence which concerns the identity of things connected with the crime is also considered relevant. For example, for the purpose of identifying the accused as the guilty party, evidence that the accused's tracks are identical to the tracks found near the scene of the crime is admissible. This is similar to fingerprint evidence, which is usually admissible for the purpose of identifying the accused as the offender and to connect him with the offense.[47] When a clothing company's merchandise tag, found on the floor of a savings and loan association after a robbery, led officers to the defendant, who was identified by the victims as wearing a dark business suit, two dark suits of clothing identified by the defendant's wife as belonging to the defendant were relevant and material as evidence.[48] In another case, trousers belonging to the defendant and found abandoned in a dressing room at the scene of a robbery were admissible in evidence. Police officers were also permitted to testify that they found at the scene of the crime a paper identifying the defendant by name and address, and that such information led to his arrest.[49]

Other examples of relevant, tangible evidence against a defendant are found in the following cases: In *People v. Young,* the court approved the comparison of the defendant's blood with blood found at the scene of the crime.[50] In three other cases, evidence was authorized to show that bite marks were made by the defendant.[51] The court in the case of *People v. Middleton* found that the reliability of a bite mark as a means of identification is sufficiently established in the scientific community to make such evidence admissible in a criminal case without separately establishing the scientific reliability in each case.

---

[46] Simmons v. United States, 390 U.S. 377, 88 S. Ct. 967, 19 L. Ed. 2d 1247 (1968).

[47] McClard v. United States, 386 F.2d 495 (8th Cir. 1967). See Chapter 15, *infra,* for a discussion of the rules relating to the use of fingerprints.

[48] United States v. Alloway, 397 F.2d 105 (6th Cir. 1968).

[49] United States v. Dorman, 294 F. Supp. 1221 (D.D.C. 1967).

[50] People v. Young, 105 Mich. App. 323, 308 N.W.2d 194 (1981).

[51] State v. Sager, 600 S.W. 2d 541 (Mo. Ct. App. 1980); People v. Middleton, 54 N.E.2d 42, 429 N.E.2d 100 (1981); State v. Jones, 273 S.C. 723, 259 S.E.2d 120 (1979).

In *United States v. Lopez,* the Ninth Circuit found that the district court did not abuse its discretion in admitting into evidence at the defendant's trial for robberies and extortions, a mask, a wig and a pair of rubber gloves found in the van pursuant to a search warrant. The court found that the evidence seized was relevant to show the defendant's plan, preparation and identity with respect to the crimes charged in the indictment.52 In another Ninth Circuit case, the danger of unfair prejudice as a result of the admission of scales and firearms found in the defendant's residence did not outweigh the probative value to show intent to distribute in a prosecution for possession of cocaine with intent to distribute and attempted distribution.53

§ 7.8   —Circumstances preceding the crime

It is obvious that evidence which relates to circumstances and events preceding the crime would reasonably be relevant to the issue. The best test of relevancy of testimony concerning antecedent circumstances that may shed light upon the alleged crime is whether a particular fact tends to render probable a material proposition in issue.54 Generally, evidence of conduct of the accused shortly before the offense, which is inconsistent with his innocence, is relevant and admissible. For example, the trial judge admitted as evidence a witness's testimony that he had discussed with the defendant the selling of lewd films and had been engaged by the defendant to go to another city to pick up films but later changed his mind. This same witness was also allowed to testify that he was told by the defendant that he was not needed any more, as the defendant had obtained his sales list and was able to make the purchase contact himself. This evidence was relevant as related to the charges of interstate transportation of lewd, lascivious and filthy films for the purpose of sale and distribution, and to charges of conspiracy to commit such act.55

Citing a previous case, the Missouri Court of Appeals reiterated the rule that conduct before and after the commission of the charged crime is relevant, when it relates to the elements of the crime charged.56 The defendant in the case of *State v. Hemphill* appealed his conviction, claiming that

---

52 United States v. Lopez, 803 F.2d 969 (9th Cir. 1986), *cert. denied,* 481 U.S. 1030, 107 S. Ct. 1958, 95 L. Ed. 2d 530 (1986).

53 United States v. Savinovich, 845 F.2d 834, (9th Cir. 1988).

54 State v. Hymore, 9 Ohio St. 2d 122, 38 Ohio Op. 2d 298, 224 N.E.2d 126 (1967); United States v. Gipson, 385 F.2d 341 (7th Cir. 1967). *See also* State v. Hemphill, 699 S.W.2d 83 (Mo. App. 1985). *See* case in Part II, *infra.*

55 Kirschbaum v. United States, 407 F.2d 562 (8th Cir. 1969).

56 State v. Hemphill, 699 S.W.2d 83 (Mo. App. 1985).

(1) evidence of uncharged crimes which occurred on the day after the killing could not have been admitted; and (2) evidence of an episode involving the defendant and the victim occurring approximately one month prior to the killing of the victim should not have been admitted. In this case, the defendant was seen carrying a rifle and running from a vacant building by detectives who were investigating the case. The detectives gave chase, stopped the fleeing vehicle and later located a 30-30 Winchester rifle on the street a short distance from the end of the chase. It was determined that the bullet found in the murder victim's body had been fired from the rifle. The murder had been committed a day earlier. In upholding the use of this evidence, the court stated that the rule which prohibits evidence of an uncharged crime is inapplicable when, as here, the evidence has a legitimate tendency to establish the identity of the killer.

The next objection concerned an episode involving the defendant and the victim which took place approximately one month prior to the killing. The evidence established that the defendant and the victim's sister discontinued their relationship and that the defendant physically prevented the sister's daughter from leaving a store that she was visiting. The evidence also indicated that a jack was thrown through the window of the front door of the house by the defendant. The court agreed that this evidence was admissible under the motive and intent exceptions to the general rule. The court explained that "this evidence combined with the defendant's actions the day after the killing establish a continuing vendetta by the defendant against the family of his former girlfriend and thus establishes 'hatred motive' in the inexplicable shooting of Hamilton."

Is it a violation of the rules of evidence to introduce evidence that the defendants used aliases at the time that the alleged crime occurred? In the case of *People v. Derello,* the court held that evidence of the defendants' use of aliases, their tagging of their luggage with aliases, and the peculiar manner of their movement through the concourse was admissible in a drug prosecution to prove the material fact of knowledge and intent.[57]

Evidence of prior difficulties between one of the defendants and a property owner was admissible in a prosecution for burglary and criminal damage to property. The prosecution's evidence of events occurring prior to the crime was admissible to show motive and intent.[58]

The defendant, too, may introduce evidence of events preceding the crime. For example, a defendant in a murder case may offer evidence of prior attacks upon him by the deceased in order to prove his belief that the deceased was reaching for a firearm.[59] In another case, the court agreed

---

[57] People v. Derello, 259 Cal. Rptr. 265 (1989).
[58] Watkins v. State, 190 Ga. App. 429, 379 S.E.2d 227 (1989).
[59] Milton v. State, 245 Ga. 20, 262 S.E.2d 789 (1980).

that the defendant in a murder trial may introduce evidence of a victim's prior acts of violence. Such evidence is admissible to prove that the victim was the aggressor.[60]

§ 7.9 —Subsequent incriminating or exculpatory circumstances

Equally important and relevant is evidence of conduct subsequent to the act. For example, evidence of flight, resistance to arrest, concealment, assumption of a false name and of criminal conduct during flight for the purpose of financing and accomplishing further flight is admissible in a criminal prosecution. While such conduct does not raise a presumption of guilt, the jury may consider circumstances thereof, together with other facts in evidence, to determine whether there was a guilty connection with the crime charged.[61]

In a Texas case, the court clearly stated the rule concerning the admissibility of a pistol taken from the defendant, who was arrested while in possession of the weapon within hours after the crime. The court not only found the weapon admissible under the general flight doctrine, but it also found that the weapon need not be the same one used in the crime for which the defendant was arrested. The state court justices explained that the weight given to the evidence on the question of identity should be resolved by the jury and does not affect the weapon's admissibility as evidence.[62]

There are limitations on the weight of such evidence. The United States Supreme Court in *Hickory v. United States*[63] set aside a conviction because the trial judge had charged the jury that flight created a presumption of guilt. The Court concluded that flight and concealment "are mere circumstances to be considered and weighed in connection with other proof with that caution and circumspection which their inconclusiveness when standing alone require." The assumption that one who flees shortly after a criminal act is committed, or when he is accused of committing it, does so because he feels some guilt concerning that act has been subjected to considerable judicial criticism on the ground that, in fact, common experience does not support the assumption.

In *Miller v. United States*,[64] a federal court decided that when evidence

---

60 Commonwealth v. Stewart, 483 Pa. 176, 394 A.2d 968 (1978).
61 State v. Ross, 92 Ohio App. 29, 49 Ohio Op. 196, 108 N.E.2d 77 (1952).
62 Hicks v. State, 508 S.W.2d 400 (Tex. Crim. App. 1974), and cases cited therein.
63 160 U.S. 408, 40 L. Ed. 474, 16 S. Ct. 327 (1896).
64 320 F.2d 767 (D.C. Cir. 1963). *See* cases discussed in the previous chapter relating to presumptions concerning flight after the alleged crime.

of flight has been introduced into a case, the trial court should explain to the jury that flight does not necessarily reflect feelings of guilt, and that feelings of guilt, which are present in many innocent people, do not necessarily reflect actual guilt. This explanation may help the jurors to understand and follow the instruction which should then be given: (1) that they are not to presume guilt from flight, (2) that they may, but need not, consider flight as one circumstance tending to show feelings of guilt, and (3) that they may, but need not, consider feelings of guilt as evidence tending to show actual guilt.65 Evidence of attempts or threats to commit suicide is admissible, on the same theory, as a form of flight.66

The courts generally have held that evidence of flight is admissible to prove consciousness of guilt.67 Although proof that the suspect had actual knowledge of being wanted by authorities for committing a criminal offense is generally not required for the admission of evidence of flight, at least one federal court has taken a contrary view. In the case of *United States v. Howze,* the reviewing court declared that the trial court had erred in admitting evidence of flight. The court said that where there is no immediacy between the flight and the crime, the trial court must be certain that there is evidence that the defendant knew that he was being sought for the crime, and not for some other crime or event.68

The law permits the jurors to infer that a person fleeing from crime does so out of a consciousness of guilt, and jurors are likewise permitted to infer that a person refusing to flee from crime, though opportunity offers, does so because of no consciousness of guilt.69

In some instances comments made by the defendant subsequent to the charged crime are admissible. For example, evidence presented by the prosecution that the defendant, several hours after an incident, laughed after describing his flight and stated that he "beat the hell out of someone" was admissible as it was relevant in identifying the defendant as an assailant in an assault case.70

Other instances where the court has considered the activities of the suspect following the crime concern (1) the use of a false name after the commission of a crime; (2) the suspect's refusal to consent to the entry of his home; and (3) the growth of a beard to change appearance. In the case of

---

65 *Ibid,* at p. 773.
66 People v. Duncan, 261 Ill. 339, 103 N.E. 1043 (1914).
67 State v. Ferrara, 176 Conn. 508, 408 A.2d 265 (1979); State v. Nemeth, 182 Conn. 403, 438 A.2d 120 (1980).
68 United States v. Howze, 668 F.2d 322 (7th Cir. 1982).
69 Wigmore, EVIDENCE (3d Ed.) § 276, p. 111; State v. Milam, 108 Ohio App. 254, 9 Ohio Op. 2d 252, 156 N.E.2d 840 (1959).
70 State v. Taylor, 770 S.W.2d 531 (Mo. 1989).

United States v. Boyle, the use of a false name and a false I.D. card after the commission of a crime was, as stated by the court, commonly accepted as being relevant on the issue of consciousness of guilt.[71] In another case, however, the court reasoned that evidence of the defendant's refusal to consent to a warrantless entry into his home by the police is not admissible as evidence of consciousness of guilt. Here the suspect is merely claiming a constitutional right.[72] In at least one case, the reviewing court has determined that evidence introduced by the prosecution that the accused had grown a beard during the period that police were actively looking for him was admissible to support an inference of consciousness of guilt.[73]

§ 7.10 —Defenses

In a criminal case, evidence is not only relevant to show the guilt of the accused, but the accused must have the opportunity to introduce evidence in his defense. Such evidence is usually admissible if it meets the other admissibility tests. Some of these defenses are discussed here.

a. Insanity

The test of sanity applicable in a criminal prosecution is directed toward mental responsibility at the time of the alleged criminal act. Therefore, temporary insanity is recognized as a defense. Evidence concerning an accused's mental condition before or after the offense, if not unreasonably far removed in time, is usually admissible because it is relevant to the question of mental condition at the time of the offense.[74]

b. Voluntary intoxication

Intoxication and insanity are not unalike. Drunkenness is a voluntary insanity, but it will not excuse one from crime. It is a generally accepted truism that voluntary intoxication is neither an excuse for the commission of crime, nor a defense to a prosecution for it. This general rule is the settled view of the common law and is articulated in the statutes of some twenty states. It also is the rule by judicial decision in the federal courts.

It is well settled that an exception to the general rule exists when one is accused of a crime, the definition of which involves some specific intent or the operation of some mental process such as deliberation or premeditation.

---

71 United States v. Boyle, 675 F.2d 430 (1st Cir. 1982).
72 People v. Keener, 148 Cal. App. 3d 73, 195 Cal. Rptr. 733 (1983).
73 Commonwealth v. Berrios, 495 Pa. 444, 434 A.2d 1173 (1981).
74 Beardslee v. United States, 387 F.2d 280 (8th Cir. 1967). *See* § 3.11 of this book for a discussion of the burden of proving sanity.

Under the so-called exculpatory rule, drunkenness may be taken into account to show that a particular state of mind, or specific intent, regarded as a necessary ingredient of some crimes, was not present.

Where intoxication is established as a defense to a. specific intent crime, the result may not be acquittal, but rather conviction of a lesser degree of the offense for which no proof of specific intent is necessary. Evidence that the defendant was so drunk that he could not have committed the physical acts constituting the offense is relevant to the issue of guilt.[75]

c. Other defenses

Evidence may also be introduced as relevant to show other defenses claimed by the accused. However, these must meet the other tests of admissibility in addition to the relevancy and materiality tests.

§ 7.11 —Character evidence

Rule 404

Character Evidence Not Admissible To
Prove Conduct; Exceptions; Other Crimes

(a) Character evidence generally. Evidence of a person's character or a trait of character is not admissible for the purpose of proving action in conformity therewith on a particular occasion, except:

    (1) Character of accused. Evidence of a pertinent trait of character offered by an accused, or by the prosecution to rebut the same;

    (2) Character of victim. Evidence of a pertinent trait of character of the victim of the crime offered by an accused, or by the prosecution to rebut the same, or evidence of a character trait of peacefulness of the victim offered by the prosecution in a homicide case to rebut evidence that the victim was the first agressor;

    (3) Character of witness. Evidence of the character of a witness, as provided in rules 607, 608, and 609.[76]

* * *

---

75 Murphy v. Commonwealth, 279 S.W.2d 767 (Ky. 1955).
76 FED. R. EVID. 404.

It would seem that the character of the accused would be relevant in any criminal case. If the state could prove that a person's character is not sterling, one could argue that this would have some probative value in determining whether that person actually committed the offense. However, to protect the accused, the rule has evolved that evidence showing the bad character of the accused is usually not admitted because of the possibility of overriding dangers.

The general rule is that evidence of a person's character or of a particular character trait is not relevant to prove that on a particular occasion the person acted in a certain way. However, the rule excluding this evidence has quite a few exceptions.

The accused in a criminal case is afforded the opportunity to introduce evidence of his good character to show that it was improbable that he committed the crime for which he was charged. When the accused has introduced such evidence, the prosecution may rebut it with the same type of evidence. In this situation, the defendant is said to have opened the "reputation and character door," and the prosecution may then go into the matter by using the same type of evidence.[77]

The prosecution cannot offer evidence of bad character unless the defendant offers as relevant evidence his good character. In a Georgia case, in which the defendant was convicted of murdering his infant daughter, the court proclaimed:

> We hold that unless a defendant has placed his character in issue or has raised some defense which the battering parent syndrome is relevant to rebut, the state may not introduce evidence of that syndrome, nor may the state introduce character evidence showing the defendant's personality traits and personal history as its foundation for demonstrating the defendant has the characteristics of a typical battering parent.[78]

To support a defense, the accused in a criminal case is also sometimes permitted to introduce evidence of his alleged victim's character. For example, to support a claim of self-defense, the accused may introduce evidence that the accuser had a violent temper.[79]

The character of the ordinary witness—one who is not accused, including the victim—can also be shown by evidence if it bears upon the case. As in the case of other character evidence, once the door is opened, the other side may introduce evidence to challenge that introduced by the first party.

---

[77] 1 Wigmore, EVIDENCE § 58.

[78] Sanders v. State, 251 Ga. 70, 303 S.E.2d 13 (1983).

[79] Robertson v. State, 91 Okla. Crim. 217, 218 P.2d 414 (1950).

§ 7.12 —Proof of other crimes, wrongs or acts

Rule 404

CHARACTER EVIDENCE NOT ADMISSIBLE TO PROVE CONDUCT; EXCEPTIONS; OTHER CRIMES

* * *

(b) Other crimes, wrongs, or acts. Evidence of other crimes, wrongs, or acts is not admissible to prove the character of a person in order to show action in conformity therewith. It may, however, be admissible for other purposes, such as proof of motive, opportunity, intent, preparation, plan, knowledge, identity, or absence of mistake or accident.[80]

* * *

The general rule in criminal cases is that evidence of other crimes or misconduct by the defendant is admitted when used to establish an element of the crime charged, as opposed to showing that the defendant had a criminal propensity.[81] Evidence of prior crimes committed by the accused is admissible to show the existence of a larger continuing plan, scheme or conspiracy of which the present crime is a part. This is relevant to show motive—hence commission—of the criminal act or the identity of the actor and his intention (when these are in dispute).

While evidence of other crimes, wrongs or acts committed by the defendant may sometimes be introduced by the prosecution, the government

---

80 FED. R. EVID. 404. In March 1990 the Committee on Rules of Practice and Procedure of the Judicial Conference of the United States submitted a draft of a proposed amendment to Federal Rules of Evidence, Rule 404(b). In making this recommendation, the committee noted that Rule 404(b) has emerged as one of the most cited rules in the rules of evidence. The committee also found that in many criminal cases evidence of "uncharged misconduct" is viewed as an important asset in the prosecution's case against an accused. The proposal would add this paragraph to Rule 404(b). Provided that upon request by the accused, the prosecution in a criminal case shall provide reasonable notice in advance of trial, or during trial if the court excuses pretrial notice on good cause shown, of the general nature of any such evidence it intends to introduce at trial." *See* Supreme Court Reporter, proposed rules, p. CXLVII (1990).

81 People v. Zackowitz, 245 N.Y. 192, 172 N.E. 466 (1930); State v. Meek, 584 S.W.2d 188 (Mo. 1979).

has the burden of demonstrating how such evidence is relevant to the issue in the case by articulating precisely the evidentiary hypothesis by which the fact of the consequences may be inferred from the evidence of other acts. That is, there must be some clear and logical connection between the alleged earlier offense or misconduct and the case being tried.[82]

An example of the admissibility of evidence indicating past criminal acts is the exception which allows the prosecution to show that the act for which the defendant is on trial was not inadvertent, accidental, unintentional or without knowledge. For example, in *People v. Williams,* the defendant, who was charged with larceny of a coin purse, claimed that he picked up the purse from the floor, thinking it was lost. The court allowed evidence that the detective had seen the defendant take another purse from another woman's bag in the same manner.[83]

Since the Federal Rules of Evidence were approved in 1975, several cases have been decided on the basis of Rule 404(b). In one case, the reviewing court held that the trial court judge's allowance of evidence of a prior conviction to show knowledge, intent, and the absence of mistake or accident was not an abuse of discretion.[84] Here the circumstances indicated that the alleged interstate transportation of forged securities, for which the defendant was on trial, occurred only a few months after the defendant was released from a sentence imposed upon prior conviction for the same statutory offense.

In a more recent case, the United States Court of Appeals for the Eleventh Circuit established a two-step test to be applied in determining the admissibility of evidence of other crimes. Here, the court declared that the trial judge must employ a two-step test in determining the admissibility of extrinsic evidence, in that it must first be determined that such evidence is relevant to an issue other than the defendant's character, and then it must be determined that the evidence possesses probative value not substantially outweighed by undue prejudice, and that other requirements of Rule 403 of the Federal Rules of Evidence are met.[85] In applying this rule, another court held that, in a prosecution for kidnapping and transporting women in interstate commerce for immoral purposes, testimony showing that before committing the offenses alleged in the indictment, the defendant had similarly beaten, raped and forced other young women into prostitution was admissible to establish the defendant's modus operandi, motive and intent.[86]

---

82 United States v. Hogue, 827 F.2d 660 (10th Cir. 1987).
83 People v. Williams, 58 P.2d 917 (Cal. 1936).
84 United States v. Askew, 584 F.2d 960 (10th Cir. 1978).
85 United States v. Gray, 730 F.2d 733 (11th Cir. 1984).
86 United States v. Winters, 729 F.2d 602 (9th Cir. 1984).

In 1988 the Supreme Court was requested to clarify the application of Rule 404(b).[87] In this case the petitioner was charged under federal law with knowing possession and sale of stolen video tapes. At the trial, the district court allowed the government to introduce, as evidence of "similar acts" under Rule 404(b), evidence of the petitioner's involvement in a series of sales of allegedly stolen televisions and appliances from the same suspicious source as the tapes. On appeal, the defendant conceded that similar acts evidence was admissible to show his knowledge that the tapes had been stolen, but he argued that the grave potential of similar acts evidence for causing undue prejudice calls for a preliminary determination by the court that the defendant committed such acts before the jury is allowed to hear that evidence. In a footnote to that case, the Supreme Court noted that there was inconsistency in the circuit courts, as six circuits apparently required a preliminary finding of the trial court that the government has proven commission of the similar act.

The United States Supreme Court then decided that there is no need for a preliminary finding by the trial court that the government has proven the commission of the similar acts and that such a requirement is inconsistent with the legislative history behind Rule 404(b). In making reference to the relevancy issue, the court included this paragraph:

> Evidence is admissible under Rule 404(b) only if it is relevant. "Relevancy is not an inherent characteristic of any item of evidence but exists only as a relation between an item of evidence and a matter properly provable in the case." In Rule 404(b) context, similar act evidence is relevant only if the jury can reasonably conclude that the act occurred and that the defendant was the actor.[88]

While evidence of other crimes is admissible under the Federal Rules and the rules of most states for the purposes of showing motive, opportunity, intent, preparation, plan, knowledge or absence of mistake, the court in its discretion may exclude the evidence if the prejudicial impact outweighs the probative value of the evidence. However, in a kidnapping case, the Eighth Circuit determined that the probative value of allowing the evidence outweighed the prejudicial impact, and it subsequently authorized testimony of a witness who had been attacked by the defendant nine months earlier. This evidence of other crimes was admissible to prove intent, as the defendant placed in issue his intent by attempting to establish during cross-examination of the victim that the victim had voluntarily gotten into the defendant's car and consented to sexual intercourse.[89]

---

[87] Huddleston v. United States, 485 U.S. 681, 108 S. Ct. 1496, 96 L. Ed. 2d 771 (1988). *See* case in Part II.

[88] *Ibid.*

[89] United States v. Link, 728 F.2d 1170 (8th Cir. 1984).

In another intent case, the North Carolina Supreme Court approved the introduction of evidence from the defendant's accomplice. The accomplice testified that the defendant had told him of a robbery that the defendant had committed in another state.[90] In this case, the defendant was convicted of first degree murder, attempted robbery and kidnapping. The testimony in the case disclosed that the defendant and an accomplice had entered a drug store and handed the owner a note, demanding certain drugs. The defendant's accomplice had testified that the defendant told him of another robbery of a drug store in Ohio where a similar modus operandi was followed. The defendant on appeal objected to the use of this evidence, contending that the evidence of the prior commission of similar crimes should have been excluded.

The North Carolina Supreme Court rejected this argument, explaining that, as a general rule, evidence of other crimes committed by the defendant is inadmissible if its only purpose is to show the defendant's disposition to commit such crimes. The court observed that the testimony in this instance was properly admitted under two exceptions to that rule. First, when the defendant has been charged with a crime for which specific intent must be shown, evidence of other crimes is admissible if it will aid the jury in determining whether the defendant had the requisite intent to perpetrate the crime for which he is being tried. Second, evidence of other crimes will be admitted if it tends to show the defendant's motive for committing the crime charged. The court continued by explaining that, as the defendant was known to be a heavy drug user who had developed a pattern for robbing Ohio drug stores to supply his narcotic habit, both the evidence of the previous crime and that of the modus operandi were relevant and admissible. The court then upheld the defendant's conviction.[91]

On the other hand, in a prosecution for conspiracy to possess marijuana and the actual possession of marijuana with intent to distribute it, the Ninth Circuit determined that the defendant's prior marijuana convictions were not relevant to prove any common scheme, plan, system or design, absent any evidence which tended to connect the defendant's prior criminal conduct with the marijuana found in the alleged co-conspirator's garage.[92]

But in a prosecution for distribution of cocaine, the Eighth Circuit held that the testimony concerning a prior unrelated cocaine transaction was inadmissible to rebut the defendant's denial of the present transaction as there was no connection between the prior transactions and the present transaction, and the testimony did not contradict the defendant's claim of innocent dealing.[93]

---

90 State v. Irwin, 304 N.C. 93, 282 S.E.2d 439 (1981).
91 *Ibid.*
92 United States v. Powell, 587 F.2d 443 (9th Cir. 1978).
93 United States v. Nichols, 808 F.2d 660 (8th Cir. 1987), *cert. denied,* 481 U.S. 1938, 107 S. Ct. 1976, 95 L. Ed. 2d 816 (1987).

For evidence of past acts to be admitted, the party introducing the evidence must clearly show that there is a connection between the acts and the crime charged. For example, in a kidnapping and criminal sexual misconduct case, the state offered testimony of the defendant's wife regarding sexual acts during their marriage, not only to identify the defendant as a man who attacked and committed bizarre sexual acts on the prosecutrix, but also to show a common scheme. The reviewing court, in setting aside the conviction, held that the wife's testimony had only slight probative value and should have been excluded. The court pointed out that, although both the wife and the prosecutrix described similar unusual conduct, this was not enough to authorize the evidence to show a common scheme.[94]

In Alaska, where the state has adopted a rule of evidence which is identical to Federal Rule 404(b), the court of appeals admonished that evidence of other crimes, wrongs or acts of the defendant is admissible only if it has relevance apart from the defendant's propensity to commit crime and only if that relevance outweighs the presumed highly prejudicial impact of that evidence. The court went on to say that "other crimes" evidence must be excluded if there is sufficient other evidence that will be introduced for the same purpose.[95]

In deciding whether evidence of other crimes or acts is relevant and admissible, the trial court must balance the probative value of such evidence against the possibility that the jury would be unduly prejudiced against the defendant because of his participation in the other criminal conduct or other questionable acts.[96]

§ 7.13 —Experimental and scientific evidence

Of particular importance to those in the criminal justice field are the rules concerning the admissibility of scientific evidence and evidence resulting from experiments. This includes such evidence as weapons, bullets, photographs, motion pictures, x-rays, tape recordings, maps and drawings. This type of evidence will be discussed more thoroughly in other chapters under specific headings, especially in Chapter 14, titled *Real Evidence*.

One could logically argue that the introduction of all scientific evidence (e.g., the testing of firearms to show patterns of powder and shot made upon the object at different distances, tests of speed of motor vehicles,

---

94 State v. Rivers, 254 S.E.2d 299 (S.C. 1979).

95 Moore v. State, 709 P.2d 498 (Alaska 1985).

96 United States v. Sangrey, 586 F.2d 1312 (9th Cir. 1978); United States v. Schwartz, 790 F.2d 1059 (3d Cir. 1986).

blood tests, etc.) should be admissible as relevant in criminal cases. Such evidence often does come within the relevancy and materiality scope. However, as was pointed out earlier, in some instances the trial judge in his discretion may exclude the evidence to avoid possible undue prejudice to the accused. Moreover, the court may impose a limit on the prosecution's demonstrations to avoid procedures that may unduly arouse the jury. Usually the discretionary decision concerning the admissibility of such evidence is sustained by the reviewing court unless there is a clear abuse of discretion.

Although evidence of scientific tests is considered relevant in many instances, the burden of proof that the test is reliable is on the proponent; that is, in a criminal case, the prosecution has the burden of proving that the evidence is reliable if the prosecution is introducing the scientific evidence.[97] Before the evidence is admitted, the party seeking to introduce the results must lay the proper foundation by connecting the specimen with its source; that is, the party must show that the specimen was properly labeled and preserved, properly transported for analysis, properly taken by an authorized person, and properly tested.[98]

An example of a situation in which scientific evidence was admitted in a criminal case as being relevant and having probative value was the use of genetic fingerprint evidence which matched the defendant's DNA configuration with the DNA configuration of semen recovered from the victim's clothing.[99] Other examples of the admissibility of relevant scientific evidence include intoxication tests, blood grouping tests, fingerprint comparisons, ballistic test results and speed detection readings.[100]

It is a mistake to conclude that such evidence should or will be admitted in all cases. Other principles of exclusion must be considered along with the relevancy and materiality tests.

§ 7.14 Summary

In a criminal trial, the primary objective is to determine the truth as to the issues presented. However, over the years the courts have developed rules of exclusion, including rules concerning relevancy and materiality. If

---

97 State v. Woodall, 385 S.E.2d 253 (W. Va. 1989).

98 Lawless v. New Orleans Police Department, 550 So. 2d 252 (La. 1989).

99 Martinez v. State, 549 So. 2d 694 (Fla. 1989); *see also* State v. Swartz, 447 N.W.2d 422 (Minn. 1989), in which the court held that DNA test results are admissible if performed in accordance with appropriate laboratory standards and controls to insure reliability.

100 *See* Chapter 15 of this text for rules relating to the admissibility of various test results.

the evidence does not meet the tests of relevancy and materiality, it will not be admitted. Generally, evidence which has a tendency to prove or disprove a pertinent fact in issue is relevant. That which goes to substantial matters in dispute and has an effective influence or bearing on the decision of the case is material.

The trial court has great latitude in passing on the admissibility of the evidence and in determining whether it has legal relevancy or materiality. The court's interpretation as to what evidence is relevant and material is usually given great weight, and its determination will be final unless there is a clear abuse of discretion.

Both court decisions and statutes must be considered in determining what evidence meets the relevancy and materiality tests. The following general rules have been developed through this procedure.

- Evidence which tends to establish the identity of persons involved is admissible as being relevant and material. This, of course, is subject to the other rules of admissibility.
- Evidence which concerns the identity of things connected with the crime is considered relevant, although there are some exceptions.
- Generally, evidence which relates to the circumstances and events which precede or follow the crime is admissible as relevant to the issues.
- Evidence relating to the defenses claimed by the defendant, such as mental disease, coercion, self-defense, and alibi, is generally admissible if it meets the other admissibility tests in addition to the relevancy and materiality tests.
- Although evidence concerning the character and reputation of the accused as well as other evidence concerning the commission of other crimes is sometimes recognized as relevant and material, it is often excluded because of overriding dangers. For this reason only certain evidence of this type is admissible.
- Evidence of other crimes, wrongs or acts, while not admissible to show criminal propensity, is sometimes admissible to show the existence of a continuing plan, scheme or conspiracy of which the crime charged is a part.
- Evidence concerning experimental and scientific evidence is also usually considered relevant, but it must pass other tests before it can be admitted into court.

From the discussion it is obvious that, even though the parties may succeed in excluding evidence that is not relevant and material, there is certainly no reciprocal assurance that evidence which is relevant and material necessarily will be admitted. In future chapters some of the other requirements will be discussed, and relevancy and materiality as they relate to specific types of evidence will be explored in more detail.

CHAPTER 8
COMPETENCY OF EVIDENCE
AND WITNESSES

The terms "relevancy," "competency," and "materiality" are frequently used conjunctively in such manner as to suggest that they are synonymous, yet it is obvious upon second thought that a matter which may be relevant to an issue of the case may be rendered incompetent and inadmissible as to the established rules of evidence, such as the rule which excludes hearsay evidence or requires the production of the best evidence. . . . In other words evidence must be not only logically relevant, but of such a character as to be receivable in courts of justice.
20 AM. JUR. *Evidence* 253

§ 8.1 Introduction

In the preceding chapters, some of the rules concerning relevancy and materiality were discussed. The third hurdle which must be cleared before evidence is admissible is the competency hurdle. Evidence is inadmissible if it is incompetent, but, on the other hand, evidence is admissible if it is competent, provided it is also relevant and material.1

Simply stated, evidence which is competent, relevant and material is admissible evidence. The application of this rule, however, is not so simple. As a matter of fact, many writers and even some of the legal encyclopedias fail to explain adequately the competency restrictions. In some legal writings, the authors seem to take it for granted that the definition and explanation of competency as it relates to evidence is known by the reader.

This chapter will consider the rules relating not only to the competency of witnesses but also to the competency of evidence. The fact that a witness is competent to testify does not necessarily mean that the proof which may be offered by that witness is competent.

§ 8.2 Definitions

In *Black's Law Dictionary*,2 competent evidence is defined as that which the very nature of the thing to be proven requires, for example, the production of a writing when its contents are the subject of inquiry. Competent evidence is also defined as evidence which tends to establish the fact in issue and that does not rest on mere surmise or guess.3

Perhaps a better understanding can be had of the definition of competent evidence if *incompetent* evidence is defined. In *Black's Law Dictionary*,4 incompetent evidence is defined as evidence which is not admissible under the established rules and evidence which the law does not permit to be presented at all, or, in relation to the particular matter, on account of lack of originality or of some defect in the witness, the document, or the nature of the evidence itself. One court defines incompetent evidence as that which is not proper to be received, as distinguished from that which the court should admit for the consideration of the jury, though the jury may not find it worthy of credence. If evidence is not found to be incompetent due to one of the many rules, it should be admitted if it meets the other tests.5

In seeking answers as to what evidence is held to be incompetent and therefore not admissible, many avenues are open, and volumes of material are available. Much of this book is devoted to determining what evidence is considered to be incompetent and therefore inadmissible in court.

---

1   Egger v. Egger, 225 Mo. 116, 123 S.W. 928 (1909).
2   Black's Law Dictionary (5th ed. 1979).
3   31 C.J.S. *Evidence* § 2.
4   Black's Law Dictionary (5th ed. 1979).
5   International Brotherhood of Electrical Workers v. Commission on Civil Rights, 140 Conn. 537, 102 A.2d 366 (1953).

§ 8.3   General categories of incompetent evidence

If evidence is found to be incompetent, it is usually because the courts have found that it comes within one of the three general categories discussed herein.

a.   Evidence wrongfully obtained

Evidence which has been obtained in violation of the Constitution, such as that obtained by an illegal search, often will not be admitted because the courts have reasoned that to admit such evidence would encourage the state to disregard the constitutional rights of citizens. This evidence is inadmissible not because it is not relevant and material, but because it is incompetent as determined by the courts. Evidence obtained directly or indirectly as a result of an involuntary confession usually will not be admitted because the process used in obtaining the evidence violates the due process clauses of the Constitution.6

b.   Statutory incompetency

Some evidence is admissible as competent evidence because a statute says it is, and similarly, some evidence is not admissible because a state or federal statute prohibits the admissibility of the evidence. For example, section 2515 of the Omnibus Crime Control and Safe Streets Act of 1968 provides that evidence obtained by wiretapping or eavesdropping in violation of the statute is not admissible. Again, this is not because the evidence is not relevant or material, but because the statute specifically provides that the evidence is not admissible or usable in court.

c.   Evidence excluded because of a court-established rule

Although many of the rules of evidence have now been codified, most evidence is excluded because the courts over a period of years have established certain rules concerning the admissibility of evidence. Some excellent examples which will be discussed more thoroughly in forthcoming chapters are those rules which prohibit the use of certain opinion testimony, hearsay evidence and privileged communications.

§ 8.4   Competency of evidence—documentary evidence

Legal evidence includes not only oral testimony given under oath by witnesses in open court but also all kinds of documents, records and writings, which are roughly classified as documentary evidence. Documentary

---

6   The exclusion of evidence illegally obtained is discussed in Chapter 16, *infra.*
   See also Klotter & Kanovitz, CONSTITUTIONAL LAW, 6th Ed. (1991).

evidence is subject to the same rules of relevancy, materiality and competency as is oral testimony, *i.e.,* the subject matter must pass all of the competency tests, such as the hearsay test, the opinion evidence test and the constitutional tests. In addition, documentary evidence must meet other qualifications before it is admissible as being competent.

Documentary evidence is not admissible until it has been authenticated; i.e., it must be shown to be genuine and that it is what it purports to be. Documentary evidence must also pass the "best evidence" test and comply with requirements that are peculiar to "questioned documents."7

§ 8.5 —Tests and experiments

Evidence relating to tests and experiments made in or out of court is challenged for many reasons, among them the competency of such tests. Generally, where it is necessary to show the condition or quality of a certain article or substance, the item itself may be introduced in evidence as supplementing the testimony of the witness or as direct evidence when properly identified. Evidence showing the outcome of an experiment or test is admissible to aid in determining the issues in a case where it is shown that the conditions under which the experiment or test was made is similar to the circumstances prevailing at the time of the occurrence.

Examples of this type of evidence that have been found to be competent and admissible are blood tests, ballistics tests and evidence showing that a piece of cloth found at the scene of the crime was from a garment worn by a suspect.

§ 8.6 —Conduct of trained dogs

Evidence of the conduct of a dog in tracking a suspect (sometimes referred to as "bloodhound evidence") has been held to be competent and admissible in both civil and criminal cases, provided the proper foundation has been laid.8

Evidence of the conduct of a dog in tracking the accused from the scene of the crime to the place where the accused was found, is competent and admissible merely as circumstantial or corroborative evidence against a defendant toward whom other circumstances point as being guilty of the

---

7 The rules relating to the admissibility of documentary evidence are discussed fully in Chapter 13, *infra.*
8 Crosby v. Moriarity, 181 N.W. 199 (Minn. 1921).

commission of the crime charged. The Kentucky Court of Appeals set forth the basic rule in 1898 in *Pedigo v. Commonwealth*,9 in which the court stated:

> In order to make such testimony competent, even when it is shown that the dog is of pure blood, and of a stock characterized by acuteness of scent and power of discrimination, it must also be established that the dog in question is possessed of these qualities, and has been trained or tested in their exercise in the tracking of human beings, and these facts must appear from the testimony of some person who has personal knowledge thereof. We think it must also appear that the dog so trained and tested was laid on the trail, whether visible or not, concerning which testimony has been admitted, at a point where the circumstances tend clearly to show that the guilty party had been, or upon a track which such circumstances indicated to have been made by him. When so indicated, testimony as to training by a bloodhound may be permitted to go to the jury for what it is worth as one of the circumstances which may tend to connect the defendant with the crime of which he is accused. When not so indicated, the trial court should exclude the entire testimony in that regard from the jury.

Before any evidence pertaining to the results of the dog's tracking is admitted, the handler of the dog must testify as to his own qualifications and experience and those of the dog, along with an account of the dog's skill and ability to track. Next, the circumstances pertaining to the tracking itself must be shown; for example, it must be established that the trail was fresh and had not been trampled, and that there was no interference with the dog while he was tracking. Once the proper foundation has been laid, the evidence may be used to identify the accused as the perpetrator, or it may be used for some other reason, as long as the evidence is corroborated.

In one case, the trial court properly admitted evidence that a German Shepherd dog had tracked the defendant, as the qualifications and experience of the dog and the trainer were shown, the scene of the robbery had been protected until the dog arrived, the dog had been placed on the apparent trail that the perpetrator of the crime had taken, there were no interruptions in tracking, the dog went to the automobile in which the defendant was hiding, and the defendant was identified by the robbery victim.10

Evidence gathered by an officer and a trained dog was admitted in a case in which the suspect was convicted of attempting to enter a federally insured bank with intent to commit a felony therein.11 The facts of the case indicate that an officer instructed his tracking dog "Damian" to sniff the

---

9   103 Ky. 41, 44 S.W. 143, 42 L.R.A. 432 (1988).
10   Terrell v. State, 239 A.2d 128 (Md. 1968).
11   United States v. Carroll, 710 F.2d 164 (4th Cir. 1983).

night deposit box and to track the individual whose scent the dog detected on the box. The dog first led the officer to a path leading into the woods, and then to the location of two burlap bags and copper tubing. A few yards down the path, the dog indicated that it could smell the suspect nearby. As the suspect was then detained by another officer, the search was halted.

The following morning, after the suspect had been apprehended, the officer and "Damian" went to the bank, where the dog was ordered to sniff the suspect's trousers and was again instructed to track the scent. The dog led the officer into the woods and past the spot where the bag and copper tubing were found. The dog then indicated that the trail turned back to where the deputy sheriff had apprehended the suspect.

On appeal, the attorneys for the defendant argued that the evidence relating to the tracking by the dog should not have been admitted because the prosecution did not establish a proper foundation. However, the prosecution showed that the officer and the dog had successfully completed a 10-day detection and tracking course, that the detective and "Damian" had practiced tracking at least three times a week, that the dog previously had worked on approximately 17 to 25 cases, and that he had successfully tracked objects and people on hundreds of prior occasions in training sessions and actual police work. This showing was sufficient to establish a proper foundation.

The defense argued that it was error for the district court to refuse to "put the dog on the stand," as requested by the defendant. The defendant claimed that he was denied his Sixth Amendment right of confrontation. The court, however, citing another case, determined that the witness is the handler, not the dog.

The Eleventh Circuit agreed that evidence that a trained dog had located and identified Colombian drug smugglers was admissible.[12] In this case a dog named "Jessie" began tracking at the site where four sets of footprints were left on the beach in Florida. After the arrest, "Jessie" sniffed the suspects and the jury was asked to accept the trainer's testimony that this was the dog's way of identifying the subject of the track.

In justifying the admissibility of the evidence, the court noted that the trainer had testified to his own experience and training in using tracking dogs, which extended for nearly ten years. The trainer had also explained the methodology for training and had testified to prior experience with "Jessie" and to her reliability. Citing previous cases, the court agreed that such evidence was admissible for identification purposes in criminal cases.

---

12 United States v. Lavado, 750 F.2d 1527 (11th Cir. 1985).

§ 8.7   —Telephone conversations

Evidence of a telephone conversation is generally competent and admissible as substantive evidence when the identities of the parties to the conversation are established, either by direct evidence or by facts and circumstances.

Before evidence of a telephone conversation may be admitted at trial, it is necessary to have the declarant's voice identified. This identification may be made on the basis of the witness' then-existing familiarity with the declarant's voice, or on the basis of a subsequent conversation with the declarant and a retroactive recognition of the voice used in the antecedent conversation.[13]

The requirement of direct recognition of the voice is not an inexorable or mechanical rule. Circumstantial evidence may be sufficient to identify the speaker. In *Van Riper v. United States,*[14] Judge Learned Hand approved lower court decisions which held that when a witness obtains the correct telephone number of the person whose statements are relevant, calls that number, and gets an answer from one professing to be the person called, it is prima facie proof of identity. However, the mere identification by a person who has placed a telephone call does not suffice to make statements admissible against the person so identified.

In a prosecution for knowingly and intentionally distributing cocaine, the defendant challenged the admissibility of evidence of a telephone conversation, alleging that the government had failed to establish a proper foundation. Explaining that the court had recently set forth the standard of familiarity necessary for a witness to identify the voices of participants in conversations, the court found that the rules of evidence permit voice identification as long as the basic requirement of familiarity with the voice is met, and that lay opinion testimony is an acceptable means for establishing the speaker's identity. The court admitted the evidence, stating that a proper foundation for the admission of the telephone conversations between the informant and the defendant regarding attempts to consummate the second drug transaction was established through the testimony of an undercover officer, even though the officer did not fully participate in the conversation. The court emphasized that the officer was present during every recorded conversation, attached recording devices to the telephone used, and was suf-

---

13 United States v. Lo Bue, 180 F. Supp. 955 (S.D.N.Y. 1960); *see also* FED. R. EVID. 901(b)(6) and United States v. Alessi, 638 F.2d 466 (1980), which interpreted the rule.

14 13 F.2d 961 (2d Cir.), *cert. denied sub. nom.,* Ackerson v. United States, 273 U.S. 702, 47 S. Ct. 102, 71 L. Ed. 848 (1926).

ficiently familiar with the defendant and the informant to identify their voices on the tape.15

§ 8.8 Negative evidence as competent evidence

Negative evidence, that is, evidence that an act did *not* take place or that something was *not* done, is generally held incompetent. However, such evidence, even though it may be weak, is admissible if it tends to contradict positive evidence introduced by the other party. In such circumstances, the testimony of the witness is not confined to what he saw or heard; he may also state what he did not see or did not hear.16

In one case, a federal circuit court authorized the statement of a lay witness that he had never observed an abnormal act on the part of the accused; the issue was one of insanity, and the witness had had a prolonged and intimate contact with the accused.17 In the case of *Williams v. State,* a state court concluded that negative evidence in support of good character is admissible and that automatically refusing to admit it is error.18 Citing numerous other cases, the court summarized that these cases stand for the proposition that the trial court's refusal to allow the defense counsel to elicit such negative testimony requires a reversal unless the error was harmless.

§ 8.9 Evidence competent for some purposes but not for others

The courts have decided that, in the usual situation, evidence which is competent for one purpose may not be excluded merely because it is incompetent for other purposes, even though there is a certain risk of confusing the jury.19 If, on the other hand, that risk is so great as to upset the balance of advantages of receiving the evidence, it will not be admissible.

---

15 United States v. Shukitis, 877 F.2d 1322 (7th Cir. 1989); *see also* Woodson v. State, 777 S.W.2d 525 (Tex. 1989) (the state court held that the defendant's voice was sufficiently identified to support the admissibility of testimony concerning a telephone conversation between a witness and the defendant, whereby the defendant admitted to the commission of the murder and the witness stated that he had previously talked to the defendant and that he believed that he was talking to the defendant).

16 Weber v. Park Auto Transportation Co., 244 P. 718 (Wash. 1926).

17 Carter v. United States, 252 F.2d 608 (D.C. Cir. 1956).

18 Williams v. State, 548 So. 2d 584 (Ala. 1988).

19 City of Phoenix v. Boggs, 403 P.2d 305 (Ariz. App. 1971).

When evidence is competent for one purpose but not competent for others, the court should limit its application by proper instruction.

Before moving to the discussion relative to the competency of witnesses and the rules relating thereto, an additional reminder is in order. As previously mentioned, many of the rules of exclusion—for example, the hearsay rule, the opinion rule, and the rule rejecting proof of bad character as evidence that a defendant committed the offense charged, which in effect hold that such evidence is incompetent—are not discussed here, not because they are not pertinent, but because they are discussed in detail in other chapters.

§ 8.10 Competency of witnesses

Rule 601

General Rule of Competency

Every person is competent to be a witness except as otherwise provided in these rules. However, in civil actions and proceedings, with respect to an element of a claim or defense as to which State law supplies the rule of decision, the competency of a witness shall be determined in accordance with State law.[20]

To avoid any confusion, a distinction should be made between the competency of a witness and the competency of evidence. A witness may meet the tests of competency and yet not be authorized to testify concerning evidence which is incompetent, such as certain hearsay evidence.

The test of the competency of a witness is his capacity to communicate relevant material and his ability to understand that there is an obligation to communicate truthfully. The determination of the competency of a witness is within the sound discretion of the trial judge. Thus, in a prosecution for transportation of a stolen motor vehicle in interstate commerce, when the only evidence relating to a witness' credibility was his previous brief addiction to narcotics, the trial judge properly decided that the witness was competent to testify[21]

In determining the competency of a witness, an "understanding of the proceedings" is clearly not a prerequisite as it would be in the case of a

---

20 FED. R. EVID. 601.
21 Brown v. United States, 222 F.2d 293 (9th Cir. 1955); Gurleski v. United States, 405 F.2d 253 (5th Cir. 1968); *see also* United States v. Odom, 736 F.2d 104 (4th Cir. 1984).

defendant. Such an argument was rejected in *Carter v. United States,*22 in which the difference in the standards to determine competency of witnesses and competency of a defendant to stand trial was clearly delineated.

The tests in determining competency of a witness before the grand jury are: (1) the witness must have a sufficient understanding to comprehend the obligation of an oath and to tell the truth before the grand jury; and (2) the witness must be capable of giving a correct account, or at least a reasonably correct account, of the matters which he or she has seen or heard, and in reference to which the questions at issue are being asked. These two issues must be determined by the court, not only upon the testimony of expert medical witnesses, who may be called by the prosecution or by the witness' counsel, but also upon the court's own examination. This is a duty that the court cannot avoid merely by referring to or quoting from the statements of the medical experts. The court must make its own determination and its own examination. The court must be assured that the physical and mental health of the witness will not be damaged, impaired or harmed in any significant way.23

In the sections immediately following, the specific grounds advanced for challenging the competency of witnesses are discussed.

§ 8.11 —Mental incapacity

The basic standard or rule applied when considering the mental capacity of the witness to testify is the one first announced by the United States Supreme Court in *District of Columbia v. Armes:*24

> The general rule is that a lunatic or a person affected with insanity is admissible as a witness if he has sufficient understanding to apprehend the obligation of an oath, and to be capable of giving a correct account of the matters which he has seen or heard in reference to the questions at issue; and whether he has that understanding is a question to be determined by the court, upon examination of the party himself, and any competent witnesses who can speak to the nature and extent of his insanity.

In *Armes,* the Court upheld the admissibility of the testimony of an acute melancholic who was confined to an asylum and had attempted suicide several times by sticking a fork into his neck. The Court stressed that "the existence of partial insanity does not unfit individuals so affected . . .

---

22 332 F.2d 728 (8th Cir. 1964).
23 In re Loughran, 276 F. Supp. 393 (C.D. Cal. 1967).
24 107 U.S. 519, 522, 2 S. Ct. 840, 27 L. Ed. 618 (1882).

from giving a perfectly accurate and lucid statement of what they have seen or heard."25

The standard of competency established in *Armes* was cited and relied upon by the Ninth Circuit Court of Appeals in *Shibley v. United States,*26 which held that a trial court did not err in admitting the testimony of a witness who had been previously adjudicated insane. The fact that the witness was formerly committed for insanity is not conclusive, and a subsequent adjudication of insanity and confinement in a mental hospital does not render the prior testimony of the witness incompetent.

Even if a trial court accepts abstruse psychiatric concepts of mental ailment or illness as a basis for measuring criminal capacity and responsibility, it will not project such theoretical concepts into the field of competency of witnesses as a substitute for the test of capacity to communicate relevant material and to understand the obligation to do so truthfully. For example, the trial judge was not required to hold incompetent a witness who had been found by the warden and psychiatric staff of a medical center for federal prisoners to be competent to understand the proceedings against him and competent to consult with his attorney.27

The trend, then, is to allow testimony of witnesses even though they have been found to be mentally incompetent for one reason or another. This has been reflected in the Federal Rules of Evidence, as interpreted by the various courts. For example, in one federal case, the court held that, under the Federal Rules of Evidence, it is doubtful that mental incompetence can ever be grounds for disqualifying a prospective witness.28 In the case of *United States v. Lightly,* the trial court erred in ruling that a witness was incompetent to testify "because he had been found to be criminally insane and incompetent to stand trial, and was subject to hallucinations."29 There the Fourth Circuit advised that the trial court should have conducted an *in camera* examination of the witness to determine whether the witness was capable of testifying.

Citing the *Lightly* case referred to in the previous paragraph, the Fourth Circuit stated that the appropriate time to determine whether a witness is mentally qualified to testify is at the trial when the testimony of the challenged witness is to be offered, as the relevant question is whether the witness is presently competent to testify.30 The court went on to point out that,

---

25 *Ibid. See* Juvilier, *Psychiatric Opinions As To The Credibility of Witnesses: A Suggested Approach,* 48 CAL. L. REV. 648 (1960).

26 237 F.2d 327 (9th Cir.), *cert. denied,* 352 U.S. 873, 77 S. Ct. 94, 1 L. Ed. 2d 77 (1956).

27 Carter v. United States, 332 F.2d 728 (8th Cir. 1964).

28 United States v. Roach, 590 F.2d 181 (5th Cir. 1979).

29 United States v. Lightly, 677 F.2d 1027 (4th Cir. 1982). *See* case in Part II, *infra.*

30 United States v. Odom, 736 F.2d 104 (4th Cir. 1984).

under Rule 601 of the Federal Rules of Evidence, every witness is presumed to be competent, and neither feeblemindedness nor insanity renders a witness incompetent or disqualified. The court concluded that the only grounds for disqualifying a party as a witness under Rule 601, based on *Lightly*, are that the witness does not have the capacity to recall or that he does not understand the duty to testify truthfully.

In summary, a witness is competent to testify unless evidence is introduced to show that incompetency exists. The burden of persuasion is on the party alleging that the potential witness is incompetent.[31] To meet that burden, the challenging party must establish either a lack of ability to understand the obligation of the oath and to comprehend the obligation imposed by it, a lack of understanding of the consequences of false swearing, or a lack of the ability to perceive accurate impressions and to retain them.

§ 8.12 —Children

It is the duty of the trial judge to determine the competency of a child to testify. The determination rests largely within his discretion, and his exercise of such discretion will not be disturbed unless the error is plain. The trial judge should consider the child's age, intelligence (or lack of intelligence), and sense of moral and legal responsibility. A child is competent to testify if he possesses the capacity to observe the events, if he can recollect and communicate them, and if he has the ability to understand questions and to answer intelligently with an understanding of the duty to speak the truth. It is not necessary to show that the child witness has religious beliefs or detailed knowledge of the nature of the oath. All that is required is that the child understands that some punishment will follow if he does not tell the truth.

Although some statutes are similar to Ohio's in providing that "children under ten years of age, who appear incapable of receiving just impressions of the facts respecting which they are examined, or of relating them truly" are incompetent as witnesses, there is no fixed age at which a child must have arrived in order to be a competent witness. In *Wheeler v. United States*,[32] the United States Supreme Court said:

> That the boy was not by reason of his youth [five and one-half years], as a matter of law, absolutely disqualified as a witness is clear. While no one would think of calling as a witness an infant only two or three years old, there is no precise age which determines the question of competency. This depends on the capacity

---

31 Logan v. State, 773 S.W.2d 413 (Ark. 1989).
32 159 U.S. 523, 16 S. Ct. 93, 40 L. Ed. 244 (1895).

and intelligence of the child, his appreciation of the difference between truth and falsehood, as well as of his duty to tell the former. The decision of this question rests primarily with the trial judge, who sees the proposed witness, notices his manner, his apparent possession or lack of intelligence, and may resort to any examination which will tend to disclose his capacity and intelligence as well as his understanding of the obligations of an oath. As many of these matters cannot be photographed into the record the decision of the trial judge will not be disturbed on review, unless from that which is preserved, it is clear that it was erroneous.

In numerous cases, children of very tender years are accepted as witnesses. To cite an instance, a five-year-old rape victim and her seven-year-old sister were permitted to testify in a rape case even though they were challenged as incompetent due to youth.33

The child's capability to receive just impressions of the facts relates to the time that the events occurred, while his capacity to state them truly relates to the time of trial. For example, where a proffered witness is over ten years of age when he is called to testify but was only four years old at the time that he witnessed happenings about which he proposes to testify, the capability of such witness to receive just impressions of such happenings must necessarily be determined as of the time of those happenings.34 On the other hand, the child's competency or incompetency to testify must be determined as of the date that the child is offered as a witness and not at the time that the incidents testified to occurred. In a Virginia case, the court held that the fact that a child was held to be incompetent at the time of the first trial is not of itself an adjudication of his continued incompetency to testify concerning events that occurred prior to his becoming competent.35

In a Delaware sodomy case, the supreme court of that state, after stating that age is not the sole criterion for competency, followed some guidelines that had been set forth in a previous case.36 There the court noted that the guidelines for determining the competency of a child witness are: (1) the child's ability to perceive accurate impressions of fact or capacity to observe the acts about which he is to testify, (2) the child's ability or capacity to recollect these impressions or observations, (3) the child's ability to recall and his capacity to communicate what was observed, and (4) the

---

33 Pocatello v. United States, 394 F.2d 115 (9th Cir. 1968) (an eight-year-old witness); Webster v. Peyton, 294 F. Supp. 1359 (E.D. Va. 1968).
34 Huprich v. Paul W. Varga & Sons, Inc., 3 Ohio St.2d 87, 209 N.E.2d 390 (1965).
35 Cross v. Commonwealth, 195 Va. 62, 77 S.E.2d 447 (1953).
36 Kelluem v. State, 396 A.2d 166 (Del. 1978).

child's understanding of truth and falsity and his capacity to appreciate the moral responsibility to be truthful.

A Rhode Island court in 1989 drafted its own guidelines for determining whether a child is competent to testify.37 According to the court, the four testimonial capacities that are required for a child to be found competent to testify are that the child can (1) observe, (2) recollect, (3) communicate and (4) appreciate the necessity of telling the truth. The court indicated that the child need not articulate magic words that he or she knows the difference between a lie and the truth, as long as the child understands the definitions of both and was there to tell the truth.

While the preferable course is apparently to accept a child's testimony if the tests are met, the testimony should not be allowed if evidence indicates that the child is not competent. For example, a reviewing court held that a trial court had properly found that a four-year-old child was not competent to testify at the trial, as she was unresponsive to questions in open court from both prosecution and the court, and she could not state what it meant to tell the truth or a lie.38

An article that appeared in the *Journal of Social Issues* in 1984 indicated that a child's memory is more accurate than previously believed.39 This article, which dealt with studies relating to the subject of the child as a witness, presents some interesting facts concerning the testimony of children. The studies concluded that children do have a tendency to recall less than adults, but there was little evidence to support the assumption that children, when compared to adults, forget faster, are more susceptible to suggestions, and are more likely to confuse imagination and perception in remembering. The article indicated that children are less adept at sorting relevant observations from irrelevant ones as they occur, and therefore, children are less able to recall relevant information. However, the article went on to say that "there is some intriguing evidence that young children sometimes notice potentially interesting things that older children and adults miss."

Summarizing several studies, the article states that "taken together, the results . . . support the conclusion that adults spontaneously recall more about events they have witnessed than do children, but not the simple notion that children are always more suggestible than adults." It was rec-

---

37 State v. Girouard, 561 A.2d 882 (R.I. 1989).

38 People v. District Court of El Paso County, 776 P.2d 1083 (Colo. 1989); *see Unavailability and Admissibility: Are a Child's Out-of-Court Statements About Sexual Abuse Admissible if the Child Does Not Testify at Trial?* 76 KY. L.J. 531 (1987-1988) for a comprehensive discussion regarding the competency of a child to testify in court.

39 JOURNAL OF SOCIAL ISSUES, Vol. 40, No. 2 (1984).

ommended that interrogators try to avoid having preconceived impressions when questioning either children or adults.

The authors of the article offered some suggestions to improve the accuracy of children's testimony while minimizing psychological trauma. Among these were: (1) that children should be allowed to identify suspects and submit testimony to the court by way of closed-circuit television; (2) that if a child must testify in court, the child should be allowed to visit the courtroom in advance to meet the judge and other court officials; (3) that judges should caution attorneys against questions that are too advanced for the child's level of education; and (4) that a tired or traumatized child should be given time to rest and should receive comfort from a trusted person before resuming testimony.

§ 8.13 —Husband and wife

The common law rule was that husband and wife were incompetent as witnesses for or against each other. The rule rested mainly on a desire to foster peace in the family and on a general unwillingness to use testimony of witnesses tempted by strong self-interest to testify falsely. As a defendant was barred as a witness in his own behalf because of interest, it was quite natural to bar his spouse in view of the prevailing legal fiction that husband and wife were one person.[40] This early rule, however, yielded to exceptions in certain types of cases. Thus, in *Stein v. Bowman*,[41] the United States Supreme Court noted that the rule did not apply when the husband commits an offense against the person of his wife.

In 1933, the United States Supreme Court rejected the phrase of the common law rule which excluded testimony by spouses for each other.[42] The Court recognized that the basic reason underlying this exclusion of evidence had been the practice of disqualifying witnesses with a personal interest in the outcome of the case. Widespread disqualifications because of interest, however, had long since been abolished both in this country and in England in accordance with the modern trend, which permitted interested witnesses to testify, leaving the jury to assess the credibility of such witnesses. Certainly, as defendants were uniformly allowed to testify in their own behalf, there was no longer a good reason to prevent them from using their spouses as witnesses.

---

40 1 Coke, COMMENTARY UPON LITTLETON, p. 6b (19th ed. 1832). *See* Chapter 10, *infra,* for a discussion of the husband-wife testimonial privilege.

41 38 U.S. (13 Pet.) 209, 10 L. Ed. 129 (1837).

42 Funk v. United States, 290 U.S. 371, 54 S. Ct. 212, 78 L. Ed. 369 (1933). *See* case in Part II, *infra.*

If there is a scheme to defraud, marriage does not make the spouse incompetent. For example, in a prosecution for conspiracy to defraud the United States by obtaining illegal entry into the country for three aliens who claimed to be spouses of honorably discharged veterans, there was evidence from which the jury might reasonably have believed that the three aliens went through marriage ceremonies with the veterans, that both the aliens and the veterans intended to exploit the marriages solely for the purpose of obtaining admission to the United States, and that none of the parties intended to live in normal marriage relationships. The question confronting the court was whether the so-called wives were competent to testify against their purported husbands in this criminal prosecution. The court held that when it is made to appear that the relationship was entered into by the parties with no intention to live together as husband and wife, but only for the purpose of using the marriage ceremony in a scheme to defraud, the ostensible spouses are competent to testify against each other.[43]

In another case of spousal testimony, the Supreme Court decided that a man prosecuted for transporting a woman in interstate commerce for the purpose of prostitution—a woman whom he thereafter married before trial—was subject to having the compelled testimony of his wife introduced against him.[44] As to the husband's objection, the Court invoked the common law doctrine that in the case of certain kinds of offenses committed by the party against the spouse witness, the party may not bar the spouse's testimony. This exception is applicable in a Mann Act prosecution.

In 1887, Congress enabled either spouse to testify in prosecutions against the other for bigamy, polygamy or unlawful cohabitation. In 1917, and again in 1952, Congress made wives and husbands competent to testify against each other in prosecutions for importing aliens for immoral purposes.[45] Statutes in many states permit spouses to testify against each other in prosecutions for only certain types of crimes. For example, under the Ohio statute relative to the competency of witnesses in criminal cases, a husband and wife are competent to testify on behalf of each other in all criminal prosecutions.[46] However, they are competent witnesses to testify against each other only in (1) prosecutions for personal injury of either by the other; (2) prosecutions for bigamy; and (3) prosecutions for failure to provide for, for neglect of, or for cruelty to their minor children or their physically or mentally handicapped children under 21 years of age.

---

43 Lutwak v. United States, 344 U.S. 604, 73 S. Ct. 481, 97 L. Ed. 593 (1953).
44 Wyatt v. United States, 362 U.S. 525, 80 S. Ct. 901, 4 L. Ed. 2d 931 (1960).
   See chapter 10, *infra,* for a discussion of testimonial privileges.
45 18 U.S.C. § 1328.
46 OHIO REV. CODE ANN. § 2945.42 (Anderson 1986).

The state of Georgia has a statute which provides that one spouse is competent to testify against the other, but the state cannot compel this testimony.47 In interpreting this statute, a Georgia court held that the privilege of refusing to testify belongs to the witness and not the accused. However, if the witness decides to testify, that witness is competent. According to the Court of Appeals of Georgia, when the witness voluntarily takes the stand and testifies, it is presumed that this act is done pursuant to a waiver of the marital privilege. The testimony of the spouse is competent testimony.48 The court also indicated that the lower court did not err in failing to advise the wife of the marital privilege.

The Texas Rules of Criminal Evidence grant a privilege to the spouse of the accused not to testify against the accused.49 However, this rule does not prohibit the spouse from testifying voluntarily for the state—even over the objection of the accused. In the case of *Fuentes v. State*, the wife of the accused, who was charged with assault, stated that she did not want to testify against her husband nor did she want the state to prosecute him.50 Nevertheless, the trial court compelled her to testify against her husband. On review, the reviewing court explained that the wife did have a right to assert the privilege not to testify against her husband. According to Georgia law, as interpreted, the spouse is competent to testify against the accused in a criminal case, but to require such testimony is error.

From the examples it is clear that the competency of a spouse to testify for or against the other spouse depends on the provisions of the federal or state statutes. It is reasonably clear that spouses may testify for each other in all jurisdictions. In some jurisdictions the spouse is not required to testify against the other spouse in any criminal case, while in others the spouse is required by statute to testify against the accused spouse only when the spouse is accused of a specific crime. If the statute makes wives and husbands competent to testify against each other regarding a specific crime, then a spouse may be compelled to testify. Under these circumstances, if the spouse does refuse to testify, the spouse may be found to be in contempt of court.

§ 8.14 —Conviction of crime

More than fifty years ago, the United States Supreme Court decided that "the dead hand of the common law rule" disqualifying a witness who

---

47 OCGA, § 24-9-23.
48 Mapp v. State, 382 S.E.2d 618 (Ga. App. 1989).
49 TEX. R. CRIM. EVID. 504(2).
50 Fuentes v. State, 775 S.W.2d 64 (Tex. App. 1989).

had been convicted of crime should no longer be applied in criminal cases in the federal courts.51 Most states have enacted statutes which expressly remove the disqualification of a witness convicted of a crime to testify, but in some instances, these statutes allow the conviction to be shown for the purpose of impeaching the credibility of the witness.52

In interpreting federal and state statutes, the courts have made it quite clear that a criminal conviction does not render the witness incompetent to testify. For example, in a Connecticut case the court held that the fact that the principal witness had been treated for chronic alcoholism and drug abuse in several mental institutions and had an extensive criminal record did not render the witness incompetent to testify.53 In a federal case the court agreed that "the government cannot be expected to depend exclusively upon the virtuous in enforcing the law, and so long as a reasonable jury could believe an informant's testimony, after hearing relevant impeachment evidence regarding his or her reliability, the government may rely upon such testimony" even though the witness had been previously convicted.54

The general rule is that prior convictions of witnesses affect the weight and credibility of the witness's testimony but do not disqualify the witness.55 There are some exceptions to the rule that a person convicted of a crime is competent to testify in a criminal case. Several cases have held that if the conviction is for perjury the witness may be incompetent as a witness. In the case of *Hourie v. State,* a Maryland court decided that a perjurer is disqualified as a witness in a criminal case and that such disqualification is not considered as an additional penalty imposed upon the perjurer himself.56 However, in another Maryland case, an allegation that the witness was "an admitted perjurer" did not make the witness incompetent when he had never been convicted of the crime of perjury.57

§ 8.15 —Religious belief

In most jurisdictions, the state constitutions or statutes provide that no person shall be rendered incompetent to be a witness on account of his reli-

---

51 Rosen v. United States, 245 U.S. 467, 38 S. Ct. 148, 62 L. Ed. 406 (1918).

52 For the rules regarding impeachment of witness, *see* Chapter 9, *infra.*

53 State v. Valeriano, 468 A.2d 936 (Conn.), *cert. denied,* 466 U. S. 974. 104 S. Ct. 2531, 80 L. Ed. 2d 824 (1983).

54 United States v. Richardson, 764 F.2d 1514 (11th Cir. 1985).

55 Lassiter v. State, 333 S.E.2d 412 (Ga. 1985).

56 Hourie v. State, 452 A.2d 440 (Md. 1982).

57 Erman v. State, 434 A.2d 1030 (Md.), *cert. denied,* 456 U.S. 908, 102 S. Ct. 1756, 72 L. Ed. 2d 165 (1981).

gious opinions or for want of any religious belief.58 This, however, does not prohibit inquiry concerning religious opinions for purposes of impeachment.

The courts also have been consistent in holding that one's religious belief or lack thereof is not a criterion upon which testimonial capacity is to be based. The question is "whether or not the individual has the ability to observe, recollect and communicate and some sort of moral responsibility."59 If the witness is able to understand the obligation of an oath and the consequences of false swearing, the witness is "competent" even if there is no evidence that he has a religious background.60

§ 8.16   Competency of judge as a witness

Rule 605

COMPETENCY OF JUDGE AS WITNESS

The judge presiding at the trial may not testify in that trial as a witness. No objection need be made in order to preserve the point.61

For some years, the matter of whether a judge should be incompetent to testify as a witness in the trial over which he presides has been debated. Some authorities advocate that this matter should be left to the discretion of the judge, and in some states this is the rule that is followed.62 However, 28 U.S.C. § 455 mandates that federal judges disqualify themselves in cases in which they are or have been material witnesses. This requirement is carried over into Rule 605 of the Federal Rules of Evidence, which became effective in 1975 for federal courts and magistrates.

Some states allow the judge to testify only in matters that are not material.63 Critics of this rule reject it on the ground that no one would object

---

58 Gillars v. United States, 182 F.2d 962 (D.C. Cir. 1950). *See* case in Part II, *infra*. **Rule 610. Religious Beliefs or Opinions.** Evidence of the beliefs or opinions of a witness on matters of religion is not admissible for the purpose of showing that by reason of their nature the witness' credibility is impaired or enhanced.

59 State v. Phipps, 318 N.W.2d 128 (S.D. 1982).

60 Chapell v. State, 710 S.W.2d 214 (Ark. 1986).

61 FED. R. EVID. 605.

62 See cases collected in Annotation, *Judge as a Witness in a Case on Trial Before Him,* 157 A.L.R. 315. *See also* Morris, FEDERAL PRACTICE, including the advisory committee's note on Rule 605.

63 Annotation, *supra* note 60.

to the testimony. Also, the critics claim that a judge would not be impeached or cross-examined. To avoid any problems, the rule of general incompetency was adopted for federal courts.

§ 8.17 Competency of juror as witness

Rule 606

Competency of juror as witness

(a) At the trial—A member of the jury may not testify as a witness before that jury in the trial of the case in which the juror is sitting. If the juror is called so to testify, the opposing party shall be afforded an opportunity to object out of the presence of the jury.

(b) Inquiry into validity of verdict or indictment.—Upon an inquiry into the validity of a verdict or indictment, a juror may not testify as to any matter or statement occurring during the course of the jury's deliberations or the effect of anything upon that or any other juror's mind or emotions as influencing the juror to assent to or dissent from the verdict or indictment or concerning the juror's mental processes in connection therewith, except that a juror may testify on the question whether extraneous prejudicial information was improperly brought to the jury's attention or whether any outside influence was improperly brought to bear upon any juror. Nor may a juror's affidavit or evidence of any statement by the juror concerning a matter about which the juror would be precluded from testifying be received for these purposes.64

The general rule is that a juror may not testify as a witness in the trial of a case in which he is sitting. Considerations which bear upon the permissibility of testimony are similar to those invoked when the judge is called as a witness. The chances are too great that the testimony of the juror would have an undue influence on the outcome of the case. This rule was codified in the Federal Rules of Evidence, which without exception prohibit the members of a jury from testifying in the case in which they sit as jurors.

Section (b) of Rule 606 of the Federal Rules of Evidence is more complicated. This makes a juror incompetent to testify not as to facts to prove the case, but concerning activities which took place during the jury's deliberations. The federal courts have long recognized that permitting an indi-

---

64 Fed. R. Evid. 606.

vidual to attack a jury verdict based upon the jury's internal deliberations is unwise. The reasoning is that jurors should not be harassed and beset by the defeated party in an effort to secure from them evidence of facts that may establish misconduct sufficient to set aside a verdict.65 Under the federal decisions, the protection to the jurors extends to each of the components of the deliberation, including arguments, statements, discussions, mental and emotional reactions, and any other feature of the process.66

Rule 606 (b) makes an exception which authorizes the juror to testify on the question of whether extraneous prejudicial information was improperly brought to the jury's attention or whether any outside influence was improperly brought to bear upon any juror. The purpose of this is to allow the courts to determine whether there were irregularities such as the introduction of a prejudicial newspaper account into the jury room or statements by the bailiff concerning the case.

Several cases have been decided which interpret Federal Rule 606(b). In one of these cases, the court provided some guidelines to be followed in determining when a juror may testify regarding extraneous prejudicial information.67 There the court advised that, rather than question the jurors directly in determining whether extrajudicial contact with a juror was prejudicial to the defendant, the district court should make findings of fact at two separate levels. First, the court reasoned that the district court must find basic or subsidiary facts, e.g., nature, content and extent of the extrajudicial contact. Based on its finding, the district court must then make the ultimate factual determination as to whether the contact likely affected the juror's impartiality.68 This procedure carries out the intent of not questioning the juror concerning his decision-making process, but allows the juror to testify in order to determine whether the extrajudicial contact would be likely to affect the juror's impartiality.

In further explaining the application of Rule 606(b), a federal court agreed that evidence that two jurors, after the trial, had stated to the defendant's counsel that the defendant was insane at the time of the murder but that they had reached a guilty verdict because they feared a not guilty by

---

65 McDonald v. Pless, 238 U.S. 264, 35 S. Ct. 785, 59 L. Ed. 1300 (1915).

66 United States v. Crosby, 294 F.2d 928 (2d Cir. 1961).

67 Owen v. Duckworth, 727 F.2d 643 (7th Cir. 1984); *see also* United States ex rel. Buckhaha v. Lane, 787 F.2d 239 (7th Cir., 1986), in which the court explained that the intent of Federal Rule 606(b) is to prohibit questioning of jurors regarding the effect of extraneous information, such as newspapers, television, other media information or personal contact directly concerning guilt or innocence of the defendants on trial, on the deliberations of the jurors.

68 *Ibid.*

insanity verdict would have been less effective in assuring the defendant's removal from society could not be considered in any subsequent challenge to the conviction.[69] The court reasoned that this evidence did not come within the exception as stated in Rule 606(b). However, testimony of a juror that she attended a substantial portion of the trial of other persons involved in the same case was not precluded by Rule 606(b), as this concerns an outside influence which was improperly brought to bear upon a juror.[70]

In a state case, a juror also was authorized to testify concerning improper outside influence. In that case, the court decided that the juror's contact with a third party constituted improper influence resulting in the transmission of extraneous prejudicial information to the jury. During that contact, the juror discussed the merits of the case with the third party, who had a vital interest in the outcome of the prosecution's case. Consequently, the juror's testimony concerning such improper contact was admissible.[71]

The rules relating to the competency of a juror to testify regarding the matters of reaching a verdict were summarized in the case of *United States v. Moten* in 1978.[72] Here the court concluded that the proper functioning of the jury requires courts to protect jurors from being harassed and beset by defeated parties, but when reasonable grounds exist to believe that the jury may have been exposed to outside influence, that influence should be investigated.

§ 8.18 Summary

To be admissible in court at the trial in a criminal case, evidence must pass the competency hurdle. Even though the evidence has passed the relevancy and materiality tests, it will be excluded if the court finds that it is not competent.

Care must be taken to avoid confusion concerning the rules regarding competency of the evidence and competency of the witness. A witness may be competent, and yet the evidence may be incompetent.

In the chapters that follow, many rules are discussed which relate to the competency of evidence. From a general point of view, evidence is incompetent if: (1) it is wrongfully obtained; (2) a statute declares it to be incompetent; or (3) it has been declared incompetent by the courts.

---

69 Fulgham v. Ford, 850 F.2d 1529 (11th Cir. 1988), *cert. denied,* ___ U.S. ___, 109 S. Ct. 802, 102 L. Ed. 2d 793 (1989).

70 Isaacs v. Kemp, 778 F.2d 1482 (11th Cir.), *cert. denied,* 476 U.S. 1164, 106 S. Ct., L. Ed. 2d 730 (1985). *See* case in Part II, *infra.*

71 State v. Blackwell, 664 S.W.2d 686 (Tenn. 1984).

72 582 F.2d 654 (2d Cir. 1978).

Documentary evidence must meet the usual competency tests such as the hearsay test, but it also must comply with special requirements. For example, it must be authenticated. Likewise, real evidence is incompetent if specific requirements are not met.

Negative evidence is generally incompetent, but this rule too has exceptions. Evidence is sometimes admissible for some purposes, although it would be incompetent for others. When such evidence is introduced, the court limits its application by proper jury instructions.

Both the courts and legislative bodies have established rules concerning the competency of persons to testify in court. Although the rules have been liberalized in recent years, there are still certain requirements which, if not met, may make a witness incompetent to testify in court.

Even though a person may not have normal mental capacity, in the discretion of the court, he may be allowed to testify if he can understand the obligation of an oath and can give a correct account of the matters which he has seen or heard. A child is generally competent to testify if he possesses the capacity to observe the events and to recollect and communicate them, and if he has the ability to understand questions and to make intelligent answers with the understanding of the duty to speak the truth.

At common law, neither the husband nor the wife was permitted to testify for or against the other. Most states by statute have made the husband and wife competent to testify for the accused spouse, but it is generally provided that the prosecution may not force the spouse to testify against the accused. This rule too is subject to some exceptions.

The prevailing rule is that a person who has been convicted of a crime is not made incompetent to testify. However, certain convictions may be shown for the purpose of challenging the credibility of the witness.

In some states the competency of the presiding judge to testify as a witness is within the discretion of the judge. But under Rule 605 of the Federal Rules of Evidence, judges in federal courts are incompetent to testify as to any matter. Jurors too are incompetent to act as witnesses at the trial of a case if they are jurors in that case. Under Federal Rule 606, jurors also may not testify about the verdict except when the inquiry relates to prejudicial information that may have been improperly brought to the jurors' attention.

As a practical matter, justice personnel should be fully aware of the rules which make testimony or other evidence inadmissible because of competency rules. In some instances a case may hang on the one piece of real evidence or testimony which an attorney attempts to get the court to exclude.

D. EVIDENCE VIA WITNESS TESTIMONY

CHAPTER 9
EXAMINATION OF WITNESSES

For two centuries past, the policy of the Anglo-American system of Evidence has been to regard the necessity of testimony by cross-examination as a vital feature of the law. The belief that no safeguard for testing the value of human statements is comparable to that furnished by cross-examination, and the conviction that no statement (unless by special exception) should be used as testimony until it has been probed and sublimated by that test, has found increasing strength in lengthening experience. Wigmore, EVIDENCE, Vol. 5, § 1367 (3d ed. 1940)

§ 9.1   Introduction

Without witnesses, there could be no trial in a criminal case. The function of the witness is to present evidence from which the trier of fact can make a determination of what happened. As the purpose of the trial in a criminal case is to determine whether the accused is guilty of the crime charged, it would seem logical to assume that all testimony of witnesses would be admissible. However, for various reasons, the witnesses are limited not only in what they may reveal but also in how they may reveal it.

In conducting the trial in a criminal case, the normal procedure is first, for the prosecution to present evidence which tends to prove the offense charged. In so doing, the prosecution calls a witness and then proceeds to ask questions of the witness. After the prosecution has presented its case, the defense has an opportunity to put witnesses on the stand and to introduce evidence. Before either the prosecution witnesses or the defense witnesses can testify, however, they must meet certain requirements. Even after the witnesses have been qualified, their testimony is subject to many rules which will be discussed in this chapter and in future chapters.

In this chapter, general rules concerning the examination of witnesses are noted and explained. Specifically, the sections in this chapter deal with the qualifications of the witnesses, the giving of the oath or affirmation, oath or affirmation requirements, separation of witnesses, direct examination of witnesses, cross-examination, impeachment and rehabilitation of witnesses. In future chapters, some of the rules which limit the admissibility of testimonial evidence are discussed in more detail, as they are complicated and have many exceptions. In this category are testimonial privileges, opinion testimony and the hearsay rule (with exceptions).

§ 9.2 Essential qualities of a witness

> **Rule 602**
>
> **Lack of Personal Knowledge**
>
> A witness may not testify to a matter unless evidence is introduced sufficient to support a finding that the witness has personal knowledge of the matter. Evidence to prove personal knowledge may, but need not, consist of the witness' own testimony. This rule is subject to the provisions of Rule 703, relating to opinion testimony by expert witnesses.[1]

Generally, to be eligible to testify, a witness must have a personal connection with the relevant occurence, coupled with mental and physical facilities sufficient to be able to observe the events at the time of their occurence and to recollect and relate them to the jury or a court in a manner that ren-

---

1 FED. R. EVID. 602. Rule 703, which is referred to in Rule 602, provides that the expert witness need not have personal knowledge of facts or dates.

ders the testimony relevant. In other words, the witness must be qualified. In order to qualify, the witness himself may be asked questions relating to his personal knowledge of the matter in issue or others may be asked questions relative to the personal knowledge of the witness who is to testify.

If the witness demonstrates on the stand that he is unable to remember, the court may find that the witness is not qualified. For example, when a defense witness, a motorcycle gang leader, had allegedly ordered the murder of his former girlfriend by three female followers of the gang, stated at the trial in answer to a question that "he had trouble remembering the incident," his competency to testify was challenged. In reply to questions, the witness stated that he suffered from recurring blackouts and bouts of memory failure; that he had been in a mental institution the preceding year; that he was in need of medication for headaches; that his nerves were shot; and that in fact he could not remember whether he had just testified in court or not. The court, over defense's objection, held that the witness was not competent to testify and directed the jury to disregard the witness' testimony. On appeal, the reviewing court held that the trial court had not erred in its ruling or in its instruction to the jury to disregard the testimony, and the court then sustained the conviction.[2]

As a general rule, the party offering the testimony must prove that the witness had an opportunity to observe the incident about which he is testifying. This does not necessarily mean that the witness has to say positively that he can without doubt testify as to exactly what happened. Frequently in criminal cases, witnesses are called upon to testify about events which they only casually observed, as when making an identification. It is permissible under the firsthand knowledge requirement for a witness to testify that to the best of the witness' belief, the defendant committed the criminal act, while acknowledging he may be mistaken as to the identity of the defendant.

§ 9.3 Oath or affirmation requirement

Rule 603

Oath or Affirmation

Before testifying, every witness shall be required to declare that the witness will testify truthfully, by oath or affirmation administered in a form calculated to awaken the witness' conscience and impress the witness' mind with the duty to do so.[3]

---

2 Turnbull v. Commonwealth, 216 Va. 328, 218 S.E.2d 541 (1975). *See* case in Part II, *infra.*
3 FED. R. EVID. 603.

Before testifying, every witness is required to state that he will testify truthfully. The purpose of this is to impress upon the witness' mind and conscience the importance of telling the truth and only the truth at the trial. To further impress upon the witness the responsibility of telling the truth, the courts require that the prospective witness take an oath that he will tell the truth or affirm that the statements that he will make are truthful.

It is not proper to require the witness to affirm God in the court's administered oath. In *United States v. Looper,*[4] the United States Court of Appeals for the Fourth Circuit stated that at common law there was neither a requirement of affirming God's name, nor a requirement of raising a hand for a valid oath. In that case, the witness refused to affirm God in making the oath based upon his religious belief in the Church of God. The trial court denied him the right to testify, but the reviewing court set aside the conviction.

Most states have statutes which allow the witness to make an affirmation rather than an oath. This choice is provided for those who lack the requisite belief in God, and for those who are forbidden by conscientious scruples to take an oath. Under these statutes, the witness must explicitly state that the scruple exists.

The use of the affirmation as an alternative to taking the oath is designed to afford the flexibility required when members of religious cults, atheists or conscientious objectors object to taking an oath. In states where a statute requires the witness at an administrative hearing to be sworn, a hearing conducted without the witness being sworn is "fatally flawed," and the results must be set aside.[5] However, in New Jersey, where there exists a statute which requires that a witness, before testifying, take an oath or make an affirmation or declaration to tell the truth, under the penalty provided by the law, a court held that the statute was complied with when a four-year-old was not actually administered the formal oath.[6] The court in that case reasoned that a four-year-old witness need not be given the formal oath when the court conducts a "ceremony," which obtains from the infant a commitment to comply with this obligation. The court explained that this procedure, in lieu of a formal oath under that statute, was proper. In another case, a New York court held that the trial court did not abuse its discretion in allowing children who were victims of sexual molestation to testify unsworn.[7]

Using the affirmation in place of an oath does not itself weaken the weight of the testimony of a witness, but it may have some bearing on the

---

4   419 F.2d 1405 (4th Cir. 1969).
5   Sewell v. Spinney Creek Oyster Co., 421 A.2d 36 (Me. 1980).
6   In the Interest of R.R., 79 N.J. 97, 398 A.2d 76 (1979).
7   People v. St. John, 74 A.D.2d. 85, 426 N.Y.S.2d 863 (1980); *see also* State v. Dixon, 684 P.2d 725 (Wash. App. 1984).

weight given that testimony by some members of the jury.

Rule 603 of the Federal Rules of Evidence requires that every witness shall be required to declare that the witness will testify truthfully by oath or affirmation administered in a form calculated to awaken the witness' conscience and impress the witness' mind with the duty to do so. Most states have adopted this or a similar rule. Generally, this requirement is satisfied by an oath or affirmation given in any manner designed to impress the witness that he must tell the truth.[8] Although the rule states that the oath or affirmation must be administered, failure of the opposing party to object is considered a waiver. A party may not permit the trial to proceed and then raise the question after the verdict.[9]

§ 9.4   Judicial control of testimony

> **Rule 611**
>
> **MODE AND ORDER OF INTERROGATION AND PRESENTATION**
>
> (a) Control by court. The court (JUDGE) shall exercise reasonable control over the mode and order of interrogating witnesses and presenting evidence so as to (1) make the interrogation and presentation effective for the ascertainment of the truth, (2) avoid needless consumption of time, and (3) protect witnesses from harassment or undue embarrassment.[10]
>
> * * *

The ordinary method of introducing evidence in the trial is through witnesses' answers in response to questions asked by the attorney. Whether the testimony takes the form of a free narrative or individual responses to specific questions is a matter to be decided by the trial judge under the particular circumstances. Usually, the judge does not interfere with the attorney's choice unless there is some indication that improper evidence will be admitted. The judge has the authority and, in fact, the responsibility to exercise reasonable control over the mode and order of interrogating witnesses and presenting evidence so as to make the interrogation and presentation effective for the ascertainment of the truth, to avoid needless consumption of time, and to protect witnesses from undue harassment.

---

8   Larson v. State, 686 P.2d 583 (Wyo. 1984).

9   United States v. Perez, 651 F.2d 268 (5th Cir. 1981).

10   FED. R. EVID. 611.

The trial judge has wide discretion in ruling on the forms of questions and the examination of witnesses. He not only may rule upon objections to questions, but he also may instruct a witness to answer the questions as offered. The judge has the ultimate responsibility for the orderly reception of evidence, and his decisions in relation to the control of testimony will usually be upheld by a reviewing court unless there is a clear abuse of discretion.

Rule 611 of the Federal Rules of Evidence makes it clear that the judge exercises control over the examination of witnesses in determining what evidence shall be admitted. In interpreting this section, the Sixth Circuit Court of Appeals made this comment:

> Under Rule 611, a trial judge has considerable discretion, and a judge's ruling will not be the basis for reversal of a criminal conviction unless a defendant's substantial rights are affected.[11]

The trial judge refused to reopen that case after it was discovered that the government witness had come to the courthouse on the day of the trial in the company of a fugitive and in a truck equipped with stolen parts; the judge explained that the witness' testimony had been impeached without this information. The reviewing court's comment was:

> We hold that the trial court's denial of the motions to reopen the case were not in abuse of his discretion.

§ 9.5 Separation of witnesses

Rule 615

Exclusion of Witnesses

At the request of a party the court shall order witnesses excluded so that they cannot hear the testimony of other witnesses, and it may make the order of its own motion. This rule does not authorize exclusion of (1) a party who is a natural person, or (2) an officer or employee of party which is not a natural person designated as its representative by its attorney, or (3) a person whose presence is shown by a party to be essential to the presentation of the party's cause.[12]

Statutes or rules of all courts in all jurisdictions authorize the judge to exclude witnesses from the courtroom except when testifying. The purpose

---

11 United States v. Terry, 729 F.2d 1063 (6th Cir. 1984).
12 Fed. R. Evid. 615.

is to prevent one witness from being influenced deliberately or subconsciously by hearing what another witness says. The procedure is variously called separation, exclusion, sequestration of witnesses or "putting witnesses under the rule." Although the authority of the judge to sequester witnesses has long been recognized as a means of discouraging collusion, there has not been agreement as to whether this is a matter of discretion for the judge or whether the parties have a right to demand that witnesses be placed under the rule. The Federal Rules of Evidence take the position that this is a matter of right; the rule states that the court shall order witnesses excluded at the request of a party.

Several categories of persons are excepted. Those who are parties to the action are not excluded from the courtroom because excluding them would raise serious problems of confrontation and due process. In most instances, police officers who have been in charge of the investigation are allowed to remain in the court despite the fact that they will be witnesses.13

In interpreting Rule 615 of the Federal Rules of Evidence, the Fifth Circuit Court of Appeals determined that police officers and other agents in charge of the investigation are embraced within the scope of exception to the witness exclusion rule because "officers are employees of a party" which is not a natural person, and such officers are designated as that party's representative by its attorney.14 In the case just cited, the court held that a federal agent who was involved in the preparation of the criminal case may not be excluded from the courtroom.

In another case an undercover agent, who was the prosecuting witness during a cocaine distribution conspiracy trial, was permitted to be designated to sit at the government counsel's tables, even though he was also to be a witness in the case.15 And Federal Evidence Rule 615 did not require the exclusion of a testifying government agent from the trial during the testimony of other witnesses, as the agent was an officer for the government.16

In order to come within the exception indicated in Rule 615(3), the party must demonstrate that the presence of a witness is essential to the presentation of the party's cause. In one case, for example, a defendant could not demonstrate to the satisfaction of the court that his girlfriend possessed such specialized expertise or intimate knowledge of the facts of the case that counsel could not effectively function without her presence to the extent that exemption from sequestration was warranted.17

---

13 United States v. Infanzon, 235 F.2d 318 (2d Cir. 1956).
14 In re United States, 584 F.2d 666 (5th Cir. 1978).
15 United States v. Adamo, 882 F.2d 1218 (7th Cir. 1989).
16 United States v. Thomas, 835 F.2d 219 (9th Cir.), cert. denied, 486 U.S. 1010, 108 S. Ct. 1741, 100 L. Ed. 2d 204 (1987).
17 United States v. Agnes, 581 F. Supp. 462 (E.D. Pa. 1984).

The question has arisen in several courts concerning the admissibility of the testimony of a witness when the trial court has failed to follow the rules relating to sequestration of witnesses. In interpreting Rule 615 of the Federal Rules of Evidence, one court explained:

> Although we expect that the trial court will comply with the requirements of the rule, we hold that in the absence of other circumstances showing reversal is appropriate, the failure to sequest[er] a witness is not, in itself, grounds for reversal, unless the defendant can show prejudice resulting from the failure to sequester.18

On the other hand, another reviewing court held that a trial court acted within its discretion in refusing to allow the witness for the defense to testify when the witness had remained in court despite a sequestration order issued under Rule 615 of the Federal Rules of Evidence.19

Generally, the reviewing courts will uphold the decision of a lower court in determining whether a witness who has failed to follow the rules regarding sequestration should be allowed to testify. In criminal cases, the defense witnesses will generally be allowed to testify even if they fail to follow the rules. For example, in one case, the court held that it ordinarily would be an abuse of discretion to disqualify a witness for the accused unless either the accused or his counsel had somehow cooperated in the violation of the order.20

§ 9.6   Direct examination of witnesses

After the court has determined that a witness is qualified to testify, the witnesses have been sequestered, and the witness has been administered the oath or affirmation, the direct examination of the witness begins. Direct examination usually begins by asking the witness his name, address and occupation. Even though this information may be well-known to all in the courtroom, it is necessary for completing the court records of the case. After these preliminary background inquiries are completed, the general questioning of the witness about his knowledge of the case begins.

If the witness cannot understand or speak English or for some other reason is not able to communicate, an interpreter is permitted to assist in

---

18 Government of Virgin Islands v. Edinborough, 625 F.2d 472 (3d Cir. 1980).
19 United States v. Gibson, 675 F.2d 825 (6th Cir.), *cert. denied,* 459 U.S. 972, 103 S. Ct. 305, 74 L. Ed. 2d 285 (1982). *See* case in Part II, *infra. See also* United States v. Lamp, 779 F.2d 1088 (5th Cir.), *cert. denied,* 476 U.S. 1144, 106 S. Ct. 2255, 90 L. Ed. 2d 700 (1986).
20 Commonwealth v. Scott, 496 Pa. 78, 436 A.2d 161 (1981).

the procedure. The interpreter is not permitted to give his individual conclusions with respect to the answers of the witness, but must give a literal interpretation of the language employed by the witness.21

Even after the case has progressed to this stage, there are still rules that are applied during the direct examination of the witness. For example, leading questions are usually not authorized on direct examination, and limiting procedures have evolved concerning the authorization of a witness to refer to records to revive memory or to use memoranda of past recollection as a substitute for memory. These are discussed in the sections that follow.

§ 9.7 —Leading questions

Rule 611

MODE AND ORDER OF INTERROGATION AND PRESENTATION

(c) **Leading questions.** Leading questions should not be used on the direct examination of a witness except as may be necessary to develop the witness' testimony. Ordinarily leading questions should be permitted on cross-examination. When a party calls a hostile witness, an adverse party, or a witness identified with an adverse party, interrogation may be by leading questions.22

The use of leading questions on direct or redirect is, with certain exceptions, forbidden, and the adversary has the right to object to such questions.23 The reason for this rule is that the suggestive powers of leading questions are, as a general proposition, undesirable.

The principal test of a leading question is: "Does it suggest the answer desired?" In order to elicit the facts, a trial lawyer may find it necessary to direct the attention of a witness to the specific matter about which his testimony is desired, and if the question does not suggest the answer, it is not leading. Even though the question may call for a yes or no answer, it is not leading unless it is so worded that, by permitting the witness to answer yes or no, the witness would be testifying in the language of the interrogator rather than in his own.

The alternative form of question: "State whether or not . . . ," or "Did

---

21 FED. R. EVID. 604

22 FED. R. EVID. 611.

23 For reasons which will be explained in later sections, leading questions are permitted on cross-examination.

you or did you not . . . ," is free from this defect of form because both affirmative and negative answers are presented for the witness' choice. Nevertheless, such a question may become leading, insofar as it rehearses lengthy details which the witness may not otherwise have mentioned, and thus supplies him with full suggestions, which he would incorporate—without any effort—by the simple answer, "I did" or "I did not." Such a question may or may not be improper, according to the amount of palpably suggestive detail which it embodies.24

The extent to which the use of leading questions may be indulged or limited is a matter primarily for the discretion of the trial judge. Generally, abuse of discretion is not found in permitting or limiting the use of leading questions, in the absence of prejudice or clear injustice to the defendant.25 Also, most states have statutes relating to the use of leading questions.26 These statutes may limit the authority of the judge in permitting or limiting the use of leading questions.

Although the general rule is that leading questions may not be used on direct examination, there are well-known exceptions to this rule. These exceptions are based upon necessity, and the right to lead is given only to the extent reasonably required to meet the necessity. The best-known exceptions are as follows:

a. Introductory matters

Only questions relating to the name of the witness, his address or other matters which are introductory are authorized. These permissible, introductory leading questions, however, must always stop short of the disputed facts, however.

b. Hostile witnesses

Anyone who has watched the television court battles recognizes the rule that leading questions are authorized when the witness is hostile, even though he is the witness of the party presenting his case. Where the witness has manifested an intention to evade and an unwillingness to testify, the court may authorize the use of leading questions to the extent deemed necessary.

---

24 State v. Scott, 20 Wash. 2d 696, 149 P.2d 152 (1944).

25 United States v. Durham, 319 F.2d 590 (4th Cir. 1963); People v. Fields, 49 Mich. App. 652, 212 N.W.2d 612 (1973). *See* United States v. Greybear, 883 F.2d 1382 (8th Cir. 1989), in which the court held that it was not improper to ask that leading questions during the direct examination of the witness when the record indicated that the questions were used infrequently and judiciously in order to develop testimony given by an unusually soft-spoken and frightened witness.

26 For a list of the states that follow the Federal Rule, see 3 Wigmore, Evidence, § 770 (1989), Pocket Supplement.

The rule permitting leading questions of hostile witnesses is of special significance in criminal matters in which the state must often rely on reluctant or hostile witnesses to prove its case. The trial judge must rule that the witness is hostile or reluctant before leading questions may be asked.

In an Illinois case, an appellate court ruled that the trial court did not err in finding that the states' witnesses were hostile nor in permitting the state to cross-examine and impeach them.[27] In a federal case, the Fourth Circuit found that the trial court did not abuse its discretion in permitting the government to ask two leading questions of the defendant's girlfriend, who was called as a government witness, in that she clearly was a person "identified with an adverse party."[28]

c. Obviously erroneous statements

Where it appears that the witness has inadvertently answered a question incorrectly, or that he did not comprehend the question, a leading question may be used on direct to afford the witness an opportunity to correct the mistake.[29] For example, if a police witness, in answer to a question, inadvertently gave the date as 1964, the prosecutor would be authorized to say, "You mean 1974, don't you?"

Applying this rationale, a North Carolina court determined that the trial judge in his discretion may allow the prosecutor to cross-examine with leading questions an unwilling or hostile witness for the purpose of refreshing his recollection or awakening his conscience, thus enabling him to testify correctly.[30]

d. Child witnesses, mentally retarded witnesses, and witnesses with slight command of the English language

Because of necessity, the court will allow restricted use of leading questions in order to obtain testimony from children or witnesses who have difficulty expressing themselves. Included in this category are witnesses who are mentally retarded but not incompetent to testify. The exception is limited to the leading questions reasonably necessary to overcome the obstacle of securing testimony.[31]

---

[27] People v. Davis, 88 Ill. App. 3d 265, 410 N.E.2d 533 (1980).

[28] United States v. Hicks, 748 F.2d 854 (4th Cir. 1984).

[29] *See* State v. White, 259 S.E.2d 281 (N.C. 1979), which held that a witness may be interrogated with leading questions on direct examination when it appears that the witness has exhausted his memory or has trouble understanding the questions.

[30] State v. Smith, 289 N.C. 143, 221 S.E.2d 247 (1976).

[31] United States v. Nabors, 762 F.2d 642 (8th Cir. 1985).

§ 9.8 —Refreshing memory—present memory revived

Rule 612

Writing Used To Refresh Memory

Except as otherwise provided in criminal proceedings by section 3500 of title 18, United States Code, if a witness uses a writing to refresh memory for the purpose of testifying, either—
(1) while testifying, or
(2) before testifying, if the court in its discretion determines it is necessary in the interests of justice,
an adverse party is entitled to have the writing produced at the hearing, to inspect it, to cross-examine the witness thereon, and to introduce in evidence those portions which relate to the testimony of the witness. If it is claimed that the writing contains matters not related to the subject matter of the testimony the court shall examine the writing in camera, excise any portions not so related, and order delivery of the remainder to the party entitled thereto. Any portion withheld over objections shall be preserved and made available to the appellate court in the event of an appeal. If a writing is not produced or delivered pursuant to order under this rule, the court shall make any order justice requires, except that in criminal cases when the prosecution elects not to comply, the order shall be one striking the testimony or, if the court in its discretion determines that the interests of justice so require, declaring a mistrial.32

It is clear that witnesses do not remember all the facts, especially after a long period of time. It is also apparent that the latent memory of an experience may be revived by referring to a written statement. In other words, by referring to statements or other past experiences, the recollection of the witness may be refreshed. If the witness has absolutely no recollection regarding the matters being contested, he obviously is not competent to testify at all. However, if the witness remembers the transaction in general but not the essential details, or if he remembers that he recorded the transaction, some evidence concerning the transaction is admissible. This process involves two concepts which have become known as "present memory revived" and "past memory recorded." These two concepts are different in theory and therefore the tests for admissibility differ. In the first instance, the testimony of the witness and not the writing is the evidence, while in the second instance (past recollection recorded), the writing and not the testimony is the evidence.

---

32 FED. R EVID. 612.

In this section the first of these two concepts, that is, *present memory revived* or as it is sometimes called, refreshing recollection, will be discussed. In the next section the second concept, *past recollection recorded,* will be discussed.

In many instances the trial court allows a witness to refer to records, accounting sheets or reports while testifying. Generally, doctors, engineers, accountants and other lay witnesses testifying are allowed to refer to data on their reports. It is practically impossible for justice personnel making daily investigations of alleged violations of law to remember the names, dates and what took place without referring to notes made by them at the time or immediately thereafter. However, the court must excercise caution to assure that the memorandum is not a written summary made specifically for use in court.

When a witness has a lapse of memory while testifying, the court allows the witness to refer to some form of memorandum to refresh or revive his recollection of the facts. After the witness' memory is revived and he presently recollects the facts and swears to them, his testimony, and not the writing, is the evidence. When a party uses an earlier statement of his own witness to refresh the witness' memory, the only evidence recognized as such is the testimony so refreshed.

Documents shown to a witness for the purpose of reviving his recollection may not be read or shown to the jury, as the documents themselves are not evidence and have no independent evidentiary value. The fact that such material is sought to be introduced on cross-examination rather than on direct examination is not a difference of significance. The fact that a tape recording is involved, rather than a written document, also does not affect the result.[33]

In one case involving the use of memoranda to refresh the memory, the reviewing court found that the trial court did not abuse its discretion in a prosecution for violation of the antiracketeering statute when it permitted a witness to refresh his recollection with a copy of the statement given by him to an agent of the FBI.[34] Moreover, the Tenth Circuit determined that the use of grand jury testimony for the purpose of refreshing the recollection of a witness is not an abuse of the discretion of the trial judge.[35] However, the United States Supreme Court found that a deposition used in an attempt to refresh the witness' recollection is not itself admissible as evidence.[36]

---

33 United States v. McKeever, 271 F.2d 669 (2d Cir. 1959); *see also* United States v. Booz, 451 F.2d 719 (3d Cir. 1971); People v. Parks, 485 P.2d 257 (Cal. 1971).

34 Esperti v. United States, 406 F.2d 148 (5th Cir. 1969).

35 Collins v. United States, 383 F.2d 296 (10th Cir. 1967).

36 United States v. Socony-Vacuum Oil Co., 310 U.S. 150, 60 S. Ct. 811, 84 L. Ed. 1129 (1940).

In 1982, a Wyoming court was called upon to decide whether a trial court erred in allowing the victim to testify after his memory was refreshed during two sessions of hypnosis.[37] The witness in a burglary case was hypnotized by a city police officer to help the witness recall the events surrounding the burglary. On the day of the trial, the defendant's attorney objected to the identification testimony of the witness because it was enhanced by the use of hypnosis. The court ruled that the state could allow the witness to testify, but that no mention could be made of the hypnosis during the opening statements, and that the state could not present any evidence on hypnosis unless the defendant first introduced the subject of hypnosis.

At the trial, the defendant did, in fact, introduce the subject by inquiring at length into the hypnosis sessions. The witness then testified at the trial that his recollection was refreshed in part by the hypnotic sessions, and subsequently identified the appellant in court as the burglar.

The court, in considering testimony from previously hypnotized witnesses, pointed out that the issue relative to the admissibility of testimony of witnesses who were previously hypnotized is whether hypnosis was meant to refresh or develop the witness' own recollection, or to suggest to the witness additional facts. The court advised that the issue is properly one for the factfinder, as are all issues relative to the credibility of the witness.

In referring to decisions in other states, the reviewing court indicated that the majority of the states agree that such testimony should be allowed, leaving the factfinders to gauge the credibility of such testimony on the basis of the facts presented to them concerning the effect of hypnotism—both generally and in a specific case.

In the case of *State v. Beacham,* a New Mexico court, after noting that hypnosis is now receiving widespread use in criminal investigations to aid witnesses in recalling events or details which have apparently been forgotten or unconsciously absorbed, adopted a six-pronged test for the admissibility of hypnotically induced testimony of a witness.[38] A summary of the six-pronged test is as follows: (1) the session must be conducted by a professional psychiatrist or psychologist experienced in the use of hypnosis; (2) the professional conducting the hypnotic session should be independent of and not regularly employed by the prosecutor, investigator or defense; (3) any information given to the hypnotist by law enforcement personnel or the defense prior to the hypnotic session must be recorded; (4) before inducing hypnosis the hypnotist should obtain from the subject a detailed description of the facts as the subject remembers them; (5) all contacts between the hypnotist and the subject must be recorded; and (6) only the hypnotist and the subject should be present during any phase of the hypnotic session, including the pre-hypnotic testing and the post-hypnotic interview.

---

37 Chapman v. State, 638 P.2d 1280 (Wyo. 1982).
38 State v. Beacham, 97 N.M. 682, 643 P.2d 246 (1982).

Although the court has discretion in determining if hypnotically-refreshed testimony is admitted, a per se rule excluding all hypnotically-refreshed testimony infringes impermissibly on a criminal defendant's right to testify on his or her own behalf.[39]

The trial judge has a duty to prevent a witness from putting into the record the contents of an otherwise inadmissible writing under the guise of refreshing recollection. Counsel should not be permitted to give a witness a written statement, especially prepared for his use in testifying, to obviate the necessity of introducing original records, on the assumption that anything can be used to refresh recollection.[40]

Although the court may allow witnesses to refer to records or reports to refresh memory while testifying, it is preferable to testify without this "crutch." If the witness prepares adequately, he will need to refer to written statements only in rare instances. If the question concerns a situation in which the jury would normally expect the witness to remember the facts without the aid of the writing, use of the "crutch" lessens the weight of the testimony.

Also, in criminal cases, the defendant has the right to compel the production of any document used by a prosecution witness to refresh his memory. If the document is not produced, the judge may order the testimony stricken.

In interpreting Rule 612 of the Federal Rules of Evidence, which provides in general terms that the adverse party is entitled to have the writing produced, a federal district court explained that it is not every time a witness looks at any document in preparation for the trial that such document must be disclosed to the other side. In determining whether the document must be disclosed, the court should consider the extent to which the documents were consulted and relied upon, and the extent to which the opinions and conclusions were reflected therein, as opposed to factual recitations.[41] The judge has much discretion in exercising control over the introduction of such evidence and in interpreting the rules.[42]

Making reference to Federal Evidence Rule 612, the Tenth Circuit determined that the defendant in a perjury prosecution is not entitled to require disclosure of the entire transcript of a perjury prosecution witness' prior testimony before a grand jury, but rather, disclosure of the grand jury transcript is properly confined to those pages actually used by the government in examining the witness.[43]

---

39 Rock v. Arkansas, 483 U.S. 44, 107 S. Ct. 2704, 97 L. Ed. 2d 37 (1987). *See* case in Part II, *infra.*

40 Thompson v. United States, 342 F.2d 137 (5th Cir. 1965).

41 In re Comair Air Disaster Litigation, 100 F.R.D. 350 (1983).

42 United States v. Terry, 729 F.2d 1063 (6th Cir. 1984).

43 United States v. Larranaga, 787 F.2d 489 (10th Cir. 1986); *see also* United States v. Sai Keung Wong, 886 F.2d 252 (9th Cir. 1989).

§ 9.9 —Past recollection recorded

Rule 803

Hearsay Exceptions; Availability of Declarant Immaterial

The following are not excluded by the hearsay rule, even though the declarant is available as a witness:

(5) Recorded recollection.—A memorandum or record concerning a matter about which a witness once had knowledge but now has insufficient recollection to enable the witness to testify fully and accurately, shown to have been made or adopted by the witness when the matter was fresh in the witness' memory and to reflect that knowledge correctly. If admitted, the memorandum or record may be read into evidence but may not itself be received as an exhibit unless offered by an adverse party.[44]

When the witness has no present recollection of the events recorded in the writing, the writing becomes a substitute for his memory and, therefore, substantive proof of the facts that it relates. However, before the writing is admitted, a foundation must be laid.

A memorandum of past recollection recorded is admissible in evidence when the witness who made it, or under whose direction it was made, testifies that he at one time had personal knowledge of the facts, that the writing, when made, was an accurate record of the event, and that after seeing the writing, he does not have sufficient present independent recollection of the facts to testify accurately in regard thereto.[45] To meet the accepted standards of admissibility, the trial judge must be satisfied that the writing was made at a time when the events were fresh in the writer's mind, and the witness must verify the writing's authenticity and truthfulness.

The doctrine of past recollection recorded has long been favored by the federal courts and practically all of the state courts that have had occasion to decide the question.[46] The application of this doctrine does not deprive the accused of the opportunity to cross-examine the witness as guaranteed by the Sixth Amendment.[47] As an example of the application of the rule,

---

44 FED. R. EVID. 803(5).
45 Kinsey v. State, 49 Ariz. 201, 65 P.2d 1141 (1937); Morgan v. Paine, 312 A.2d 178 (Me. 1973); *see also* FED. R. EVID. 803(5).
46 United States v. Riccardi, 174 F.2d 883 (3d Cir.), *cert. denied*, 337 U.S. 941, 69 S. Ct. 1519, 93 L. Ed. 1746 (1949).
47 United States v. Kelly, 349 F.2d 720 (2d Cir. 1965); People v. Banks, 50 Mich. App. 622, 213 N.W.2d 817 (1974); People v. Hobson, 369 Mich. 189, 119 N.W.2d 581 (1963).

the Supreme Court of Oregon held that a checklist used by a police officer in the operation of a breath analysis machine was admissible in a prosecution for drunken driving, although the witness had a present recollection of the subject matter, of which the checklist was a record.48 The witness had identified the checklist, had recalled making it at the time of the event—when his recollection was fresh—and had testified to its accuracy.

This reasoning was followed by the United States Court of Appeals for the Seventh Circuit, which held that a memorandum of a phone conversation between an IRS agent and a tax defendant was properly admitted at trial.49 The court indicated that it "would seem, as the government argues, that the report satisfies the criteria for admissibility as a recorded recollection under F.R. Ev.:803(5)." The agent, in laying a foundation, had testified that the history sheet was prepared immediately after the conversation, but that he no longer recalled the details of the conversation.

§ 9.10   Cross-examination of witnesses

Rule 611

MODE AND ORDER OF INTERROGATION
AND PRESENTATION

* * *

(b) Scope of cross-examination. Cross-examination should be limited to the subject matter of direct examination and matters affecting the credibility of the witness. The court may, in the exercise of discretion, permit inquiry into additional matters as if on direct examination.50

* * *

It was indicated earlier that the purpose of the direct examination is to have the witness relate to the court whatever relevant and competent information that he may possess. It was there stated that leading questions ordinarily may not be asked on direct examination. Leading questions are, however, allowed on cross-examination. Three reasons are given for authorizing leading questions when examining the opposing party's witnesses. These are: (1) to challenge the credibility of the direct examination; (2) to

---

48 State v. Sutton, 450 P.2d 748 (Or. 1969).
49 United States v. Sawyer, 607 F.2d 1191 (7th Cir. 1979); see also United States v. Ray, 768 F.2d 991 (8th Cir. 1985).
50 FED. R. EVID. 611(b).

bring out additional facts relating to those elicited on direct, in addition to the facts which were favorable to the opposing party; and (3) to give the triers of fact an opportunity to observe the witness under stress.

The right of cross-examination is included in the right of an accused in a criminal case to confront the witnesses against him. No one experienced in the trial of lawsuits would deny the value of cross-examination in exposing falsehood and bringing out the truth in a criminal case. The fact that this right appears in the Sixth Amendment of the Constitution reflects the belief of the framers of those liberties and safeguards that confrontation was a fundamental right essential to a fair trial in a criminal prosecution. The decisions of courts throughout the years have constantly emphasized the necessity of cross-examination as a protection for defendants in criminal cases.[51]

A full cross-examination of a witness upon the subjects of his examination in chief is an absolute right, and not the mere privilege of the party against whom the witness is called. The denial of this right is reversible error except in certain limited circumstances. For example, the denial of this right is not reversible error when a witness, having given his direct testimony, dies prior to cross-examination. Here, the judge often allows the direct examination to stand and gives precautionary instructions to the jury.

The extent of cross-examination with respect to an appropriate subject of inquiry is within the sound discretion of the trial judge. He may exercise a reasonable judgment in determining when the subject is exhausted.

A long-established rule has been that cross-examination of a witness is limited to the scope of direct examination. One exception to this rule is that cross-examination may be permitted for the purpose of testing the capacity of the witness to remember, to observe and to recount, and for the purpose of testing the sincerity and truthfulness of the witness. This may be done with respect to subjects not strictly relevant to the testimony given by the witness on direct examination.

Although, under the traditional rules, the prosecution usually may not cross-examine on matters not brought out on direct, he may and should make the opposing witness the prosecution witness at the proper time, and ask additional questions of the witness if necessary to get all the facts before the court. But the prosecution in a criminal proceeding may not seek to establish, either by cross-examination of the defendant himself or by the independent testimony of other witnesses, that it is likely that the accused is guilty of the offense with which he is presently charged because he has committed prior criminal acts.[52]

---

51 Pointer v. Texas, 380 U.S. 400, 85 S. Ct. 1065, 13 L. Ed. 2d 923 (1965); Chambers v. Mississippi., 410 U.S. 287, 93 S. Ct. 1038, 35 L. Ed. 2d 297 (1973).

52 United States v. Hall, 342 F.2d 849 (4th Cir. 1965); Unbaugh v. Hutto, 486 F.2d 904 (8th Cir. 1973).

The extent to which cross-examination upon collateral matters will be permitted is a matter peculiarly within the discretion of the trial judge. His decision will not be reversed by a reviewing court unless there has been a plain abuse of discretion on his part. Although shutting off cross-examination is not a practice that should be encouraged, a trial judge does not abuse his discretion when he shuts off a continuation of extended cross-examination into collateral and immaterial matters.[53]

In a case before the United States Court of Appeals for the Seventh Circuit, the court agreed that the trial court has the discretion to impose reasonable limitations on cross-examination of witnesses in a criminal trial, based upon concerns regarding harassment, confusion of issues, and repetitive or marginally relevant interrogation.[54] The court cautioned that, even though the Sixth Amendment guarantees a defendant the right to cross-examine hostile witnesses and defense counsel should be afforded every opportunity to effectively cross-examine a government witness, this does not mean that the right to cross-examination is unlimited. In this case, after the defense counsel had cross-examined the witness for most of the afternoon and evening, and had exposed facts showing virtually every possible motive or bias which the witness might have for testifying against the defendant, the cross-examination was properly terminated by the court.

The trial court may not preclude all inquiry into a subject appropriate for cross-examination, but it may and should exercise such control over the scope of the examination as is necessary to prevent the parties from unduly burdening the record with cumulative or irrelevant matters.[55] To enable the court to discharge this duty, when a question is objected to as irrelevant, counsel conducting the inquiry should advise the court of the question's purpose. If he fails to do so, and the question is not "inevitably and patently material," the objection may be sustained without error.[56]

One common exception to the rule that cross-examination should be limited to subject matter brought out on direct is the exception that permits cross-examination on matters relating to the name and address of witnesses. The witness' name and address open countless avenues of in-court examination and out-of-court investigation. To forbid this most rudimentary inquiry at the threshold effectively emasculates the right of cross-examination itself.

This principle was well stated in *Alford v. United States*,[57] a case in which the Supreme Court reversed a federal conviction because the trial

---

53   United States v. Mills, 366 F.2d 512 (6th Cir. 1966).
54   United States v. Spivey, 841 F.2d 799 (7th Cir. 1988). *See* case in Part II, *infra*.
55   FED. R. EVID. 611(b).
56   Harris v. United States, 371 F.2d 365 (9th Cir. 1967).
57   282 U.S. 687, 51 S. Ct. 218, 75 L. Ed. 624 (1931).

judge had sustained objections to questions by the defense seeking to elicit
the "place of residence" of a prosecution witness over the insistence of the
defense counsel that "the jury was entitled to know who the witness is,
where he lives and what his business is." The reviewing court said:

> The question, "Where do you live?" was not only an appropriate
> preliminary to the cross-examination of the witness, but on its face,
> without any such declaration of purpose as was made by counsel
> here, was an essential step in identifying the witness with his envi-
> ronment, to which cross-examination may always be directed.

Under almost all circumstances, the true name of the witness must be
disclosed. For example, the defendant in a state narcotics case has the right
guaranteed to him under the Sixth and Fourteenth Amendments to cross-
examine the informer, who is the principal prosecution witness, about that
informer's actual name and address.[58] If the witness is residing in a penal
institution, this too must be disclosed. The purpose of the inquiry as to the
witness' address and present employment is to make known to the jury the
setting in which to judge the character, veracity or bias of the witness, and
it is necessary to show the possibility of the witness' being in custody in
order to make such inquiry.

As is true with many rules of evidence, this rule has an exception.
Where there is a threat to the life of the witness, the right of the defendant
to have the witness' true name, address and place of employment is not
absolute.[59] However, the threat to the witness must be actual and not the
result of conjecture. When threat to the life of a witness is shown, the prosecution must disclose relevant information to the judge in his chambers. The
judge must then determine whether the witness' true name, address and
place of employment must be disclosed in order to protect the right to effective cross-examination. If the trial judge concludes that the defendant does
not have a right to the witness' exact address and place of employment, the
defendant is entitled to ask any other relevant questions which may aid the
jury in weighing the witness' credibility.[60]

The rules relating to cross-examination for purposes of impeachment
are discussed in other sections of this chapter.

---

58 Smith v. Illinois, 390 U.S. 129, 88 S. Ct. 748, 19 L. Ed. 2d 956 (1968).
59 United States v. Varelli, 407 F.2d 735 (7th Cir. 1969); United States v.
   Smaldone, 484 F.2d 311 (10th Cir. 1973).
60 United States v. Palermo, 410 F.2d 468 (7th Cir. 1969).

§ 9.11   Redirect and recross-examination

After a witness has been cross-examined, the party calling him may, by redirect examination, afford the witness the opportunity to make full explanation of the matters made the subject of cross-examination, allowing him to rebut the discrediting effect of his testimony on cross-examination and to correct any wrong impression which may have been created. On redirect examination, a witness may give the reasons for his actions in order to refute unfavorable inferences from matters brought out on cross-examination. He may state the circumstances connected with the matter inquired about, although the facts brought out may be detrimental to the other party.

The scope and extent to which the redirect examination of a witness will be permitted is a matter largely within the discretion of the trial judge, and his ruling will not be disturbed unless an abuse of discretion is clearly shown.

Recross-examination generally is limited to new matters brought out on redirect examination. While a court should not by rule prohibit recross-examination of a witness about new matters brought out on redirect examination, recross-examination should be denied when there is no new matter developed on the redirect examination of the witness.[61]

For example, the First Circuit determined that when the credibility of the prosecution's witness is raised on redirect examination, questions relating to the witness' credibility are outside the permissible scope of recross-examination.[62] In this case, the reviewing court indicated that the admission of evidence lay within the judge's discretion and that the court did not subsequently abuse its discretion in refusing to allow the introduction of evidence on recross-examination.

§ 9.12   Impeachment of witness

> ### Rule 607
>
> #### Who May Impeach
>
> The credibility of a witness may be attacked by any party, including the party calling the witness.[63]

Impeachment is defined as the process of attempting to diminish the credibility of a witness by convincing the jury or court that his testimony is

---

61   State v. McSloy, 127 Mont. 265, 261 P.2d 663 (1953); United States v. Morris, 485 F.2d 1385 (5th Cir. 1973).

62   United States v. Sorrentino, 726 F.2d 876 (1st Cir. 1984).

63   FED. R. EVID. 607.

not truthful or is unreliable. Although one witness' testimony conflicting with testimony given by another witness may not be considered to be impeachment, it may lead to a similar result. There are various methods of impeachment, some of which will be discussed in the following sections.

The prerogative of impeachment in a criminal case is subject to limitation by the trial judge in the exercise of his discretion. In determining whether the trial judge abused his discretion in limiting a defendant's impeachment of the complaining witness, the question is whether the rejection of a defendant's efforts to impeach the credibility of the complaining witness withholds from the jury information necessary to make a discriminating appraisal of the witness' trustworthiness to the prejudice of a defendant's substantial rights. Thus, denying impeachment of the complaining witness in a prosecution for robbery by reference to the complaining witness' prior convictions for assault and rape was not an abuse of discretion affecting substantial rights of the defendant. However, impeachment of the witness with three convictions for the crimes of auto theft, robbery and burglary— each crime having an element of dishonesty—was properly permitted.[64]

A witness may not be impeached by evidence that merely contradicts his testimony on a matter that is collateral—and not material—to any issue in the trial.[65] The rule precluding impeachment of a witness by otherwise admissible evidence directed to collateral issues serves policies such as the prevention of confusion and surprise. Those policies have peculiar force when the attempt to impeach serves to discredit a witness by means of introducing purported misconduct short of a conviction.[66]

A criminal defendant who takes the stand to testify in his own behalf may be cross-examined and impeached as may any other witness unless, under the particular circumstances of the case, specific questions should be excluded because their probative value as to the issue of the defendant's credibility is negligible when compared with their possible prejudicial impact on the jury.[67]

---

[64] Davis v. United States, 409 F.2d 453 (D.C. Cir. 1969); *see also* United States v. Frankenthal, 582 F.2d 1102 (7th Cir. 1978).

[65] Byomin v. Alvis, 169 Ohio St. 395, 8 Ohio Op. 2d 420, 159 N.E.2d 897 (1959); Kilpatrick v. State, 285 So. 2d 516 (Ala. 1973).

[66] Lee v. United States, 368 F.2d 834 (D.C. Cir. 1966).

[67] Raffel v. United States, 271 U.S. 494, 46 S. Ct. 566, 70 L. Ed. 1054 (1926); Sharp v. United States, 410 F.2d 969 (5th Cir. 1969).

§ 9.13 —Own witness

The traditional rule is that a party may not impeach his own witness. Rule 607 of the Federal Rules of Evidence indicates—apparently—that a party may attack the credibility of his own witness without showing any proof of surprise.

The traditional exception to the rule that a party cannot impeach his own witness is that the party may impeach that witness if there is a demonstration of surprise. The reasoning is that if the party is taken by surprise and his witness testifies differently than he has indicated on past occasions, the party so surprised may show the facts to be other than stated.[68] In order for the party to claim surprise, the witness' testimony must be contrary to that which was anticipated and the testimony must be actually injurious to the party's case.[69]

In accordance with the general rule that a party may impeach his own witness if there is a demonstration of surprise, before such proof is admitted the circumstances of the supposed statements sufficient to designate the particular occasion must be mentioned to the witness, and he must be asked whether or not he made the statements and, if so, he must be allowed to explain them.[70]

§ 9.14 —Bias or prejudice

One of the most effective ways to impeach a witness is to show bias on the part of that witness. In criminal cases, great latitude is generally permitted in cross-examination of a witness in order to test his credibility and to develop facts which may tend to show bias, prejudice or any other motive that the witness may have for giving his testimony. If a witness denies facts constituting bias or prejudice, his denial may be rebutted with extrinsic evidence.[71] Although it is error for the trial judge to exclude a defendant's testimony which would reasonably show bias or prejudice, the trial court retains the normal discretion to limit the extent of proof even where bias or prejudicial interests are involved.[72]

---

68 Hickory v. United States, 151 U.S. 303, 14 S. Ct. 334, 38 L. Ed. 170 (1894).

69 United States v. Miles, 413 F.2d 34 (3d Cir. 1969).

70 United States v. Scarbrough, 470 F.2d 166 (9th Cir. 1972). *But see* Eubanks v. State, 516 P.2d 726 (Alaska 1973); D.C. Code §§ 14-102 (1973 ed.); *see also* Fed. R. Evid. 613(b).

71 United States v. Frankenthal, 582 F.2d 1102 (7th Cir. 1978).

72 Wynn v. United States, 397 F.2d 621 (D.C. Cir. 1967); *see also* Austin v. United States, 418 F.2d 456 (D.C. Cir. 1969).

§ 9.15 —Character and conduct

> **Rule 608**
>
> **EVIDENCE OF CHARACTER AND CONDUCT OF WITNESS**
>
> (a) **Opinion and reputation evidence of character.** The credibility of a witness may be attacked or supported by evidence in the form of opinion or reputation, but subject to these limitations: (1) the evidence may refer only to character for truthfulness or untruthfulness, and (2) evidence of truthful character is admissible only after the character of the witness for truthfulness has been attacked by opinion or reputation or otherwise.
>
> (b) **Specific instances of conduct.** Specific instances of the conduct of a witness, for the purpose of attacking or supporting the witness' credibility, other than conviction of crime as provided in Rule 609, may not be proved by extrinsic evidence. They may, however, in the discretion of the court, if probative of truthfulness or untruthfulness, be inquired into on cross-examination of the witness (1) concerning the witness' character for truthfulness or untruthfulness, or (2) concerning the character for truthfulness or untruthfulness of another witness as to which character the witness being cross-examined has testified.
>
> The giving of testimony, whether by an accused or by any other witness, does not operate as a waiver of the accused's or the witness' privilege against self-incrimination when examined with respect to matters which relate only to credibility.[73]

Generally, the state may not introduce evidence of a defendant's character. However, when a defendant places his reputation in issue by introducing what is loosely described as a "character" witness, he "opens the door" for the prosecution to test the credibility of such witness by inquiring on cross-examination if the witness had knowledge of specific facts which, if known generally, would tend to detract from the summary of reputation testified to by the character witness. Allowing the right to test the credibility of character witnesses by such means is fraught with great danger. Unless the right is circumscribed by rules of fairness, and grounded in demonstrated good faith on the part of the prosecution, the result may be most prejudicial to the defendant, thus causing a miscarriage of justice.

When the prosecution attempts to attack the credibility of the defen-

---

[73] FED. R. EVID. 608.

dant's character witnesses, there should be a prior demonstration, out of the hearing of the jury, establishing to the trial judge's satisfaction the truth of the basis for such inquiry. Moreover, cautionary and guiding instructions should be given, preferably at the time of the inquiry and in the closing charge to the jury.

In *Michelson v. United States*,[74] the United States Supreme Court carefully considered the manner and extent of cross-examination of character witnesses in criminal cases. The Court there stated:

> Wide discretion is accompanied by heavy responsibility on trial courts to protect the practice from any misuse. The trial judge was scrupulous to so guard it in the case before us. He took pains to ascertain, out of the presence of the jury, that the target of the question was an actual event, which would probably result in some comment among acquaintances if not injury to defendant's reputation. He satisfied himself that counsel was not merely taking a random shot at a reputation imprudently exposed or asking a groundless question to waft an unwarranted innuendo into the jury box.

Where the defendant's character witnesses have been cross-examined through inquiry concerning whether the witness had knowledge of specific facts which, if known generally, would tend to detract from the character testimony, the jury must be carefully cautioned that the testimony refers solely to reputation and not to the truth of collateral facts.[75] The prosecution may explore the basis and scope of the witness' knowledge of the defendant's reputation by asking the witness if he has heard various reports about the defendant, provided that the questions have a basis, in the sense that arrests or accusations, for example, have been rumored and discussed. The danger lurking in this impeachment process is that in order to frame an intelligible question, the examiner's query often gives details of specific misconduct affecting general reputation, which would not otherwise be admissible.[76]

The prosecutor may in some instances inquire on cross-examination whether a defendant's character witness "has heard" of the defendant's prior arrests or convictions. Such cross-examination is not admitted to establish that such events took place, but only to test the foundations and reliability of the witness' testimony. It is, in general, inadmissible to establish the defendant's bad character or his propensity to commit the crime charged. The oft-stated purpose for permitting such questions, even when they refer

---

74 335 U.S. 469, 69 S. Ct. 213, 93 L. Ed. 168 (1948).

75 Gross v. United States, 394 F.2d 216 (8th Cir. 1968); United States v. Lewis, 482 F.2d 632 (D.C. Cir. 1973).

76 Shimon v. United States, 352 F.2d 449 (D.C. Cir. 1965).

to a defendant's prior arrests, is that they enable the jury to better evaluate the character testimony which has been profferred. If a witness has heard these damaging rumors and adheres to his statement that the defendant's reputation is good, some light will have been shed upon the standards which the witness has employed; alternatively, if he has not heard of these rumors, some doubt will have been cast upon his ability to speak on behalf of the community.

In one case in which the defendant's character witness was cross-examined, the court found no prejudicial error in permitting questions concerning whether the witness ever discussed the fact of the defendant's association with a convicted felon and gambler.[77] On the other hand, when a defendant was on trial for willfully making false entries in bank records, for embezzlement and for misapplication of bank funds, the court in that case determined that direct examination of his character witness was properly limited to areas involving the question of his honesty and fair dealing; rumors of an illicit affair with a woman, even if true, were wholly immaterial to the character traits involved.[78]

Recognizing some of the problems in using character evidence, the United States Supreme Court, in interpreting the Federal Rules, attempted to answer some questions. Under these rules, the credibility of a witness may be attacked or supported by evidence in the form of reputation or opinion, but this is subject to several limitations. Under Rule 608(a), the evidence may refer only to character for truthfulness or untruthfulness, and evidence of truthful character is admissible only after the truthfulness of the witness has been attacked by opinion or reputation evidence or otherwise. Specific instances of conduct of the witness may not be proved by extrinsic evidence unless there is conviction of a crime as provided in Rule 609 of the Federal Rules.[79]

In interpreting Rule 608 of the Federal Rules, the United States Court of Appeals for the Second Circuit agreed with the lower court in allowing cross-examination of the witness concerning the truthfulness of his character.[80] In this prosecution for possession and distribution of heroin, the court ruled that the government was entitled to use the defendant's otherwise unexplained or unexplainable sources of income to prove illegal dealings and to cross-examine the defendant regarding his lavish expenditures; the government could further cross-examine the defendant regarding his false credit card application to show general lack of credibility.

---

[77] United States v. Gosser, 339 F.2d 102 (6th Cir. 1964).

[78] Aaron v. United States, 397 F.2d 584 (5th Cir. 1968).

[79] Fed. R. Evid. 608.

[80] United States v. Sperling, 726 F.2d 69 (2d Cir. N.Y. 1984).

§ 9.16 —Conviction of crime

Rule 609

IMPEACHMENT BY EVIDENCE OF CONVICTION OF CRIME

(a) General rule. For the purpose of attacking the credibility of a witness, evidence that the witness has been convicted of a crime shall be admitted if elicited from the witness or established by public record during cross-examination but only if the crime (1) was punishable by death or imprisonment in excess of one year under the law under which the witness was convicted, and the court determines that the probative value of admitting this evidence outweighs its prejudicial effect to the defendant, or (2) involved dishonesty or false statement, regardless of the punishment.

(b) Time limit. Evidence of a conviction under this rule is not admissible if a period of more than ten years has elapsed since the date of the conviction or of the release of the witness from the confinement imposed for that conviction, whichever is the later date, unless the court determines, in the interests of justice, that the probative value of the conviction supported by specific facts and circumstances substantially outweighs its prejudicial effect. However, evidence of a conviction more than 10 years old as calculated herein, is not admissible unless the proponent gives to the adverse party sufficient advance written notice of intent to use such evidence to provide the adverse party with a fair opportunity to contest the use of such evidence.

(c) Effect of pardon, annulment, or certificate of rehabilitation. Evidence of a conviction is not admissible under this rule if (1) the conviction has been the subject of a pardon, annulment, certificate of rehabilitation, or other equivalent procedures based on a finding of the rehabilitation of the person convicted, and that person has not been convicted of a subsequent crime which was punishable by death or imprisonment in excess of one year, or (2) the conviction has been the subject of a pardon, annulment, or other equivalent procedure based on a finding of innocence.

(d) Juvenile adjudications. Evidence of juvenile adjudications is generally not admissible under this rule. The court may, however, in a criminal case allow evidence of a juvenile adjudication of a witness other than the accused if conviction of the offense would be admissible to attack the credibility of an adult and the court is satisfied that admission in evidence is necessary for a fair determination of the issue of guilt or innocence.

(e) Pendency of appeal. The pendency of an appeal therefrom does not render evidence of a conviction inadmissible. Evidence of the pendency of an appeal is admissible.[81]

---

[81] FED. R. EVID. 609.

As a general rule, it would be unfair to introduce evidence to show that a suspect in a criminal case committed other crimes. On the other hand, if the defendant takes the stand and testifies, his credibility, just as that of any other witness, may be challenged. Evidence that certain other crimes were committed may be admitted, not to prove that the defendant committed the crime for which he is being tried, but to reflect upon his credibility as a witness.82 The reason for exposing a criminal record is to call into question the reliability of the witness for telling the truth.

The ordinary witness may usually be asked, for purposes of impeachment, whether he has been convicted of a felony, infamous crime or crime involving moral turpitude. For purposes of attacking the credibility of the witness, some courts have limited the evidence to certain types of crime. The California Supreme Court left no doubt about this issue. That court wrote:

> The case law is clear. The only relevant consideration is whether the prior conviction contains as a necessary element the intent to deceive, defraud, lie, cheat, steal, etc.83

In applying this rule to the offense of possession of heroin for sale, the court indicated that one who posseses heroin, intending to sell it illegally to another, may fairly and properly be deemed a dishonest person and may reasonably be deemed "unworthy of belief." Evidence of a previous conviction for possession of heroin intended for sale was properly admitted for impeachment purposes.

As a general rule, a witness may not be impeached by inquiry into prior misdemeanors unless those misdemeanors involve moral turpitude. For example, shoplifting, whether it is labeled a felony or a misdemeanor, involves moral turpitude, and accordingly, a shoplifting conviction may be used as a basis for impeaching a witness.84

A witness may not be impeached by the introduction of evidence regarding a pending charge that has not been tried.85 When the prosecutor asked a defense witness questions concerning the fact that he was about to stand trial for murder, kidnapping and robbery, the question was not only erroneous but also unduly prejudicial to the defendant. His constitutional right to a fair trial was violated.

A Washington court authorized the use of evidence of a crime not amounting to a felony under a statute similar to Rule 609(a)(2) of the Federal Rules of Evidence. There the court indicated that some crimes of

---

82 State v. Meek, 584 S.W.2d 168 (Mo. 1979). *See* case in Part II, *infra*.

83 People v. Spearman, 157 Cal. 883 (1979).

84 United States v. Lloyd, 400 F.2d 414 (6th Cir. 1968).

85 Moore v. Commonwealth, 634 S.W.2d 426 (Ky. 1982).

theft, such as embezzlement, involve an element of deceit or untruthfulness; thus, they are admissible under subdivision (a)(2) of Rule 609 for the purpose of attacking the credibility of a witness.[86]

The trial judge has quite a bit of discretion in determining the admissibility of evidence relating to prior convictions. Courts are especially hesitant to approve the admissibility of evidence relating to convictions that occur long before the crime on the ground of remoteness. As expressed by the Second Circuit, the decision whether ancient or even middle-aged convictions should be used to impeach calls for careful consideration by the trial judge.[87] The Federal Rules of Evidence provide that such evidence is not admissible if more than ten years have elapsed since the date of conviction or from the confinement imposed for that conviction unless the court determines that the probative value substantially outweighs its prejudicial effect. By relying upon the provisions of Rule 609, the Seventh Circuit Court of Appeals held that, in a prosecution for conspiracy to extort for the purpose of collecting a gambling debt, the trial court did not abuse its discretion in excluding evidence of the prior criminal record of a government witness.[88] In that case, the prior criminal record was comprised only of misdemeanors and juvenile convictions over ten years old.

In interpreting Rule 609, one federal reviewing court agreed that the prosecutor was not in error to secure from the defendant an admission that he had physically assaulted a tow truck driver, when the defendant, who was charged with violation of the Hobbs Act, had stated on direct examination that he had "never threatened anyone in my life, including my drivers who were my friends."[89]

In addition, Rule 609 prohibits the use of evidence of conviction where the person has been pardoned or the conviction is the subject of annulment or certificate of rehabilitation.

The examiner, in his inquiries about conviction, generally may not go beyond the name of the crime, the time and place of conviction, and the punishment. Further details, such as the name of the victim and aggravating circumstances, may not be included in the inquiry. A substantial number of states, while not opening the door to a retrial of the previous conviction, do permit the witness to make a brief and general statement of explanation, mitigation or denial of guilt, and other states recognize the discretion of the trial judge to permit the witness to do so.[90]

---

86   State v. Burton, 676 P.2d 975 (Wash. 1984).
87   United States v. Zubkoff, 416 F.2d 141 (2d Cir. 1969).
88   United States v. Muscarella, 585 F.2d 242 (7th Cir. 1978).
89   United States v. Cusmano, 729 F.2d 380 (6th Cir. 1984).
90   Wittenberg v. United States, 304 F. Supp. 744 (D. Minn. 1969); United States v. Bray, 445 F.2d 178 (5th Cir. 1971).

§ 9.17 —Prior inconsistent statements

> ### Rule 613
>
> ### PRIOR STATEMENTS OF WITNESSES
>
> **(a) Examining witness concerning prior statement.** In examining a witness concerning a prior statement made by the witness, whether written or not, the statement need not be shown nor its contents disclosed to the witness at that time, but on request the same shall be shown or disclosed to opposing counsel.
>
> **(b) Extrinsic evidence of prior inconsistent statement of witness.** Extrinsic evidence of a prior inconsistent statement by a witness is not admissible unless the witness is afforded an opportunity to explain or deny the same and the opposite party is afforded an opportunity to interrogate the witness thereon, or the interests of justice otherwise require. This provision does not apply to admissions of a party-opponent as defined in Rule 801(d)(2).[91]

The testimony of a witness may be impeached by showing former declarations, statements or testimony which are contradictory or inconsistent with the answers given at trial. Under the Federal Rules, the statement need not be shown to the defendant, but on request the same shall be shown or disclosed to opposing counsel. The witness should be informed about what the statements were, and about the conditions and circumstances under which they were made. In a 1978 federal case, the court held that the witness must be afforded an opportunity to explain or deny the statements and that the opposing party must be afforded an opportunity to interrogate the witness concerning the statement.[92]

In interpreting Rule 613, a federal reviewing court agreed that a statement made by the government's alibi rebuttal witness to a government agent was inconsistent with the testimony that she could not remember any conversation with the agent or conversation concerning what her husband had told her, and thus the agent's testimony as to the prior conversation with the witness was proper impeachment evidence.[93]

Former contradictory statements introduced for the purpose of impeachment are not admissible as substantive evidence. However, contradictory

---

[91] Fed. R. Evid. 613.

[92] United States v. Martoramo, 457 F. Supp. 803 (D.C. Mass. 1978).

[93] United States v. Causey, 834 F.2d 1277 (6th Cir.), *cert denied,* 486 U.S. 1034, 108 S. Ct. 2019, 100 L. Ed. 2d 606 (1987).

statements may become substantive evidence when the witness recants the testimony that he gave at trial and admits that his prior statements correctly reflect the true facts. The effect of so doing makes those prior statements a part of the witness' present testimony.[94]

While evidence of prior inconsistent statements is generally admissible only for impeachment purposes, in one federal case the court noted that failure to instruct the jury that a letter implicating the defendant was admissible only to impeach the witness, and not as proof of the defendant's guilt, at the time that the letter was offered, was not erroneous when the court gave a limiting instruction at the end of the evidence.[95]

§ 9.18 —Defects of recollection or perception

Another method of impeaching a witness is to demonstrate to the judge or jury that a witness has a defective capacity to observe, remember or recount matters about which he testified. For example, a witness whose hearing or eyesight is impaired may be impeached by calling the impairment to the attention of the jury or judge or by demonstrating it in court. Also, the witness' testimony may be impeached by showing that he has poor memory and is unable to recall like events. Here, as in other matters involving impeachment of the witness, the trial judge has much discretion in determining whether to admit or exclude such evidence.[96]

In determining that the witness' ability to perceive what took place was impaired, evidence may be introduced to show that the witness was under the influence of drugs or alcohol at the time that he perceived the events, or when testifying. However, evidence to show that the witness is a chronic alcoholic, without more evidence than that needed to show influence at a specific time, is not admissible on the issue of the witness' credibility.[97]

In order for a witness to be competent to testify it is not necessary that the witness have perfect recall. The defects in the witness' recollection are proper subjects for cross-examination and impeachment but do not render the testimony inadmissible.[98] The witness may testify to facts within his knowledge, although his recollection thereof is vague or imperfect.[99]

---

94 Tripp v. United States, 295 F.2d 418 (10th Cir. 1961).
95 United States v. Livingston, 816 F.2d 184 (6th Cir. 1987).
96 State v. Vigliano, 232 A.2d 129 (N.J. 1969).
97 Wilson v. United States, 232 U.S. 563 (1914).
98 United States v. Lema, 497 F. Supp. 1352 (W.D. Pa.), aff'd, 649 F.2d 861 (1st Cir. 1980).
99 Staton v. State, 397 So. 2d 227 (Ala. 1981).

§ 9.19 —Use of confession for impeachment purposes

In recent years, a body of law has developed concerning the use of a confession for impeachment purposes. First, in the case of *Miranda v. Arizona* in 1966, the United States Supreme Court concluded that when an individual is taken into custody or otherwise deprived of his freedom by the authorities and is subject to questioning, he must be advised of certain rights.100 In that decision, the Court indicated that until such warnings and waiver are demonstrated by the prosecution at trial, no evidence obtained as a result of interrogation may be used against the defendant. However, in 1971 in *Harris v. United States,* the Supreme Court determined that an extrajudicial confession obtained without administering the *Miranda* warning could be used for impeachment purposes.101 The Court reasoned that the defendant, having voluntarily taken the stand, is under an obligation to speak truthfully and accurately, and the prosecution may make use of the *Miranda*-less confession in utilizing the traditional truth-testing devices of the adversary processes.

If the confession is not free and voluntary, it may not be used for impeachment purposes. In 1978 in *Mincey v. Arizona,* the Supreme Court refused to extend the *Harris* reasoning to a confession obtained in violation of the free and voluntary rule.102 To state this more succinctly, the rule is that if a confession is obtained without administering the *Miranda* warning, it may be used for impeachment purposes, but not by the prosecution for its case in chief. If the statement is obtained in violation of the free and voluntary rule, the confession may not be used either for the case in chief or for impeachment purposes.

While an extrajudicial confession obtained without administering the *Miranda* warnings may be used for impeachment purposes, the defendant's failure to tell the police an exculpatory story after being arrested may not be used to impeach him.103 In *Doyle v. Ohio,* the United States Supreme Court held that the use, for impeachment purposes, of the defendant's silence, after arrest and after receiving the *Miranda* warnings, violates the due process clause of the Fourteenth Amendment. The reasoning of the Court was that the accused has the right to remain silent, and that making reference to this fact violates his constitutional rights.

---

100 Miranda v. Arizona, 384 U.S. 436, 86 S. Ct. 1602, 16 L. Ed. 2d 694 (1966).
   See case in Part II, *infra,* and other cases relating to *Miranda* in Chapter 16.
101 Harris v. New York, 401 U.S. 222, 91 S. Ct. 643, 28 L. Ed. 2d 1 (1971);
   see also Oregon v. Hass, 420 U.S. 714, 915 S. Ct. 1215, 43 L. Ed. 2d 570 (1975).
102 Mincey v. Arizona, 437 U.S. 385, 98 S. Ct. 2408, 57 L. Ed. 2d 290 (1978).
103 Doyle v. Ohio, 426 U.S. 610, 96 S. Ct. 2240, 49 L. Ed. 2d 91 (1976).

However, in the case of *Greer v. Miller* in 1987, the Supreme Court decision, according to one of the dissenters, "saps *Doyle* of much of its vitality" and "eliminates much of the protection afforded by *Doyle.*"104 In the *Greer* case the prosecutor improperly asked the question, "Why didn't you tell this story to anybody when you got arrested?" The defense counsel immediately objected and, out of the jury's hearing, requested a mistrial on the ground that the prosecutor's question violated the respondent's right to remain silent after arrest. The judge denied the motion but instructed the jury to "ignore the question, for the time being."

The Court acknowledged the prosecutor's misconduct in trying to draw the jury's attention to the defendant's silence, but it held that improper conduct did not make the trial so unfair as to deny due process. The Court put quite a bit of weight on the fact that the defendant's post-arrest silence was not submitted to the jury as evidence from which it would have been allowed to draw any permissible inference, and the Court indicated that the trial court's prompt curative instructions made reference to the defendant's silence less damaging. However, the three dissenting justices noted that "a single comment is all the prosecutor needs to notify the jury that the defendant did not tell his story promptly after his arrest."

Notwithstanding the Court's decision in *Greer v. Miller,* the rule still remains that in most cases a defendant's failure to tell the police an exculpatory story after being arrested may not be used to impeach his testimony when the defendant takes the stand at trial.

§ 9.20   Rehabilitation of witness

When evidence has been offered to impeach a witness, other evidence may be offered to counteract the impeaching evidence. For example, a witness who has been impeached on the basis of prior inconsistency may endeavor to explain away the effect of supposed inconsistency by relating circumstances which would remove the inconsistency.105 In one case, a witness who had been impeached on the basis of prior inconsistent statements given to the FBI and a grand jury was allowed to explain that his earlier failure to mention the defendant's involvement was due to fear for his own and his family's safety.106

In a murder trial in which the defendant's credibility was critical, the defendant had a right to give a full explanation of his prior inconsistent

---

104 Greer v. Miller, 483 U.S. 756, 107 S. Ct. 3102, 97 L. Ed. 2d 618 (1987).
105 Schoppel v. United States, 270 F.2d 413 (4th Cir. 1959); Beghtol v. Michael, 80 Md. App. 387, 564 A.2d 82 (1989).
106 United States v. Franzese, 392 F.2d 954 (2d Cir. 1968).

statements, and failure to admit such testimony was reversible error.[107] In this case the defendant had been prohibited from testifying that he altered his prior statements at the conclusion of the polygraph examination because he had been assured by police authorities that they believed that he was truthful when he stated that he did not shoot his wife. Failure to allow the defendant to explain the inconsistencies called into question the defendant's credibility and was reversible error.

The same reasoning applies when the impeachment is sought by demonstrating bias or prejudice. If evidence is introduced to impeach the credibility of a witness by showing that the witness is prejudiced, other evidence may be introduced to contradict this. For example, when the defendant's counsel, during cross-examination of a police officer, used part of the police report to impeach the credibility of the police officer, it was proper to admit relevant portions of the remainder of police reports for the limited purpose of re-establishing the credibility of the police officer.[108]

If a declarant's credibility is attacked by pointing out that the declarant is lying to avoid conviction in a criminal case, then evidence that the declarant has a reputation for telling the truth is admissible to support his credibility.[109]

In some instances the court may admit evidence of the defendant's reputation for truthfulness as part of the rehabilitation process. For example, in one case a witness, whose testimony had been impeached because of prior inconsistent statements, attempted to introduce evidence of his reputation for truth and veracity. The Kentucky Court of Appeals refused to approve the introduction of this evidence, as it had nothing to do with the prior inconsistent statements.[110] In another case the defendant's counsel exposed several inconsistencies between a state trooper's testimony at the trial and statements that he made following the shooting. In rebuttal, the state, over the defendant's objection, called two highway patrol officers to testify to the trooper's reputation for honesty. The reviewing court found that the trial court erred in admitting evidence of the trooper's reputation for truthfulness because his character for truthfulness was never attacked.[111] However, in a Nebraska case, the reviewing court indicated that the admission of evidence of a witness' reputation for truthfulness after impeachment because of prior inconsistent statements made by the witness is within the discretion of the trial court.[112]

---

[107] Crumpton v. Commonwealth, 384 S.E.2d 339 (Va. App. 1989). *See* case in Part II, *infra.*

[108] Short v. United States, 271 F.2d 73 (9th Cir. 1959).

[109] United States v. Lechoco, 542 F.2d 84 (D.C. Cir. 1976).

[110] Ellis v. Ellis, 612 S.W.2d 747 (Ky. Ct. App. 1980), *cert. denied,* 452 U.S. 940, 101 S. Ct. 3085, 69 L. Ed. 2d 955 (1981).

[111] State v. Johnson, 784 P.2d 1135 (Utah 1989).

[112] State v. King, 197 Neb. 729, 250 N.W.2d 655 (1977).

In discussing the rule relating to the rehabilitation of a witness, one court explained the rule by stating that "it is well recognized that once a witness' credibility has been attacked, whether it be by the introduction of evidence of bad reputation, conviction of crime, inconsistent statements, evidence of misconduct, or by incisive cross-examination, the party calling the witness has a right to present evidence designed to rehabilitate the witness' credibility."[113]

§ 9.21 Summary

Although the testimony of witnesses is essential in a criminal case, not all witnesses who have information concerning the facts of the case are permitted to testify. Moreover, the witnesses who are authorized to testify are limited as to the manner and extent of the testimony given. The trial judge has a responsibility to apply the rules of evidence in determining whether a witness may testify at all, and as to the extent of his testimony. Usually the trial judge has wide discretion in making this determination.

Generally, to be eligible to testify, a witness must have a personal connection with the relevant occurrence, coupled with mental and physical faculties sufficient to observe the events at the time of their occurrence, and a witness must be able to recollect and relate the events to the jury or court in a manner which renders the testimony relevant. Before the witness gives substantive information, he is required to state under oath or affirmation that he will testify truthfully.

To prevent witnesses from being influenced by testimony of other witnesses, the judge has the discretion of separating the witnesses during the trial so that they are in the courtroom only when called upon to testify. As a general rule, police officers and other agents are considered officers of the court and are allowed to remain in the courtroom despite the fact that they will be called as witnesses.

After the witness is sworn, he is questioned by the attorney representing the party calling the witness. This is described as direct examination of the witness. As a rule, leading questions are not permitted on direct examination. However, there are certain exceptions to this rule. For example, introductory questions, such as the address of the witness, are allowed to be asked, and hostile witnesses may be asked leading questions. Also, leading questions may be permitted upon direct examination in order to correct an obviously erroneous statement, and children and others who have difficulty expressing themselves may, when necessary, be asked leading questions on direct examination.

---

113 State v. Bowden, 439 A.2d 263 (R.I. 1982).

Although it would be preferable for witnesses to testify from memory in all situations, it is clear that witnesses do not always remember the facts after a substantial period of time has passed. Recognizing this human weakness, witnesses are allowed in some instances and under very controlled conditions to refresh their memories by referring to written statements. This is known as refreshing memory or, in some courts, "present memory revived."

When the witness has no present recollection of the events which took place at the time of writing a report, but he remembers that he did record the facts concerning the action, this writing or memorandum of past recollection is admitted when a proper foundation is laid.

The right of cross-examination has for years been considered a constitutional right coexistent with the right of confrontation. The purpose of cross-examination is to give the opposing party an opportunity to challenge the credibility of the statements given by the witness on direct. With some exceptions, the cross-examination of the witness is limited to the scope of matters brought out on direct examination.

After a witness has been cross-examined, the party calling him may ask questions on redirect to explain matters brought out on cross-examination. Following this, the opposing party may then ask questions on recross-examination, but such questions are limited to new matters brought out on redirect examination.

Impeachment is a process of attempting to diminish the credibility of a witness by convincing the jury or court that the testimony may not be truthful or is unreliable. Common practices in the impeachment process are to show bias or prejudice on the part of the witness, to introduce evidence of conviction of certain crimes, and to introduce into court evidence of prior inconsistent statements. In some instances, a confession may be used for impeachment purposes even though the *Miranda* warnings were not administered. However, if a confession is not free and voluntary, it will not be admitted even for impeachment purposes.

An impeached witness may be rehabilitated, and evidence may be admitted to contradict the impeaching testimony.

Those involved in the criminal justice process are often confused and disappointed when they are not allowed to testify about what they think is pertinent. If the rules of evidence are fully understood and if justice personnel are familiar with the reasons for limiting the use of evidence, they will be more confident and better prepared for the contingencies.

CHAPTER 10
PRIVILEGES

Since it results in the exclusion of evidence, the doctrine of privileged communications between attorney and client runs counter to the fundamental theory of our judicial system that the fullest disclosure of facts will best lead to the truth and ultimately to the triumph of justice. In adjusting this conflict in policy our courts have uniformly recognized that the privilege is not absolute, but rather an exception to a more fundamental policy. It is therefore to be strictly limited to the purposes for which it exists.
In re Seiser, 15 N.J. 393, 105 A.2d 395 (1954)

§ 10.1 Introduction

> **Rule 501**
>
> **GENERAL RULE**
>
> Except as otherwise required by the Constitution of the United States or provided by Act of Congress or in rules prescribed by the Supreme Court pursuant to statutory authority, the privilege of a witness, person, government, State, or political subdivision thereof shall be governed by the principles of the common law as they may be interpreted by the courts of the United States in the light of reason and experience. However, in civil actions and proceedings, with respect to an element of a claim or defense as to which State law supplies the rule of decision, the privilege of a witness, person, government, State, or political subdivision thereof shall be determined in accordance with State law.[1]

Some otherwise admissible evidence is kept from the trier of fact because the courts, and, more recently, legislative bodies have determined that the protection of particular relationships, interests and rights is more important than making all relevant evidence admissible. The rule that protects the right of certain defined persons to refuse to give information acquired as the result of relationships with others and to refuse to disclose an informant in some instances is known in law as the "testimonial privilege rule," or the "privileged communications rule," or just "privilege."

Identifying the rule as the "privileged communications" rule is not completely accurate. In some instances, it is not the information that was derived from the communication but the disclosure of the person who gave the information that is privileged. Therefore, there are really two privilege rules: (1) the rule regarding privileged communications resulting from relationships such as husband-wife and attorney-client; and (2) the rule relating to disclosure of persons who made the communications. The second category is the privilege of the peace officer not to disclose an informant and the privilege of newspapermen in some jurisdictions not to disclose the source of their information.

These rules regarding privileges have developed over a long period of time and certainly are not without critics. Some authorities argue that the reasons for exclusion of valuable testimony because of these privilege rules are no longer valid and should be abandoned, or at least modified. As Chief Justice Burger observed, "Whatever their origin these exceptions to the

---

1 Fed. R. Evid. 501.

demand for everyman's evidence are not lightly created nor expansively construed, for they are in derogation of the search for truth."2 Those who oppose the use of the privilege argue that prohibiting the use of some evidence because of certain relationships alters the normal mode of proof in a trial by denying the trier of fact information that he would otherwise have before him. These arguments have had some effect, as there is an apparent tendency on the part of the courts to construe the rules narrowly, and certainly, there is a reluctance to expand the privilege to relationships other than those already covered by common law or existing statutes.

For example, a North Dakota court held that a conversation between a juvenile defendant and the executive director of a juvenile home where the defendant was an inmate, does not fall within any use of the recognized privileges and was therefore not privileged.3 In a Pennsylvania case, the court refused to recognize the privilege for statements were made by a rape victim to a counseling agency.4

The United States Supreme Court held that a United States Bankruptcy Court, sitting in the state of Georgia, did not err in refusing to recognize an accountant-client privilege as a matter of law.5 The judge in a North Carolina case indicated that North Carolina does not recognize accountant-client privilege either.6

The United States Supreme Court, in drafting the Rules of Evidence for Federal Courts and Magistrates in 1972, included comprehensive rules relating to privileges. The draft by the Supreme Court included guidelines relating to the traditional privileges, such as the lawyer-client privilege, husband-wife privilege and communications to clergymen. In addition, these guidelines set limits on the use of evidence concerning the political vote, trade secrets, identity of informers and state secrets.7 When the draft of the Federal Rules of Evidence reached Congress, it ran into legislative opposition, especially regarding the privilege section, because the Rules on privileges touched upon sensitive areas. As a result, the comprehensive codifications were deleted and only a general provision regarding privileges remained in the version that was finally adopted by both houses of Congress.

In discussing Rule 501 of the Federal Rules of Evidence, members of

---

2   United States v. Nixon, 418 U.S. 683, 94 S. Ct. 3090, 41 L. Ed. 2d 1039 (1974).

3   State v. Red Paint, 311 N.W.2d 182 (N.D. 1981).

4   In re Pittsburgh Action Against Rape, 494 Pa. 15, 428 A.2d 126 (1981).

5   United States v. Arthur Young & Co., 465 U.S. 805, 104 S. Ct. 1495, 80 L. Ed. 2d 456 (1984).

6   State v. Agnew, 294 N.C. 382, 241 S.E.2d 684 (1978).

7   MOORE'S RULES PAMPHLET, Federal Rules of Evidence, as effective July 1, 1975.

the Supreme Court explained that, by rejecting the proposed rules as submitted by the drafters and the Supreme Court and by enacting Federal Rule 501, Congress manifested an affirmative intention not to freeze the law of the privilege, and that the purpose of the rule was to provide courts with the flexibility to develop privilege rules on a case-by-case basis.[8]

Notwithstanding the fact that Congress rejected the draft prepared by the Supreme Court and deleted the articles relating to privileges, the definitions and requirements set forth are well worth studying. Some of these definitions are used in this chapter.

In the sections that follow, the relationships recognized by law in which the exchange of confidential information is encouraged are first discussed. Included in these relationships are: (1) attorney-client, (2) physician-patient, (3) husband-wife and (4) communications to clergymen. In addition, the law relating to privileges which protect the identity of informers and relate to the newsman-informant privilege are examined.

§ 10.2 Reasons for privileged communications

The rules of privilege have been designed to protect personal relationships or other rights and interests when the protection of the relationship is considered more important than the need for the evidence. Few privileges were recognized at common law, but a number of privileges have been created by statutory enactment. Generally, a statute conferring a privilege should be strictly construed.

The rationale for the privileged communication rules is that when persons occupy toward each other certain confidential relations, the law, on the ground of public policy, will not compel, or in some instances even allow, one of the persons to violate the confidence reposed in him by the other. This rule of privileged communications is not a rule of substantive law but a rule of evidence which does not affect the general competency of a witness but merely renders him incompetent to testify about certain particular matters.

Traditionally the relationships of (1) husband-wife, (2) attorney-client, (3) physician-patient and (4) clergyman-penitent are protected. In each instance, there are specific rules as to the scope of the privilege, who may claim the privilege, and and when the privilege may be claimed. There are also some general requirements that apply in all instances. First, the exchange must be between two persons whose relationship is recognized by law; second, the communication must have been exchanged because of the relationship; and third, the communication must be such that the interests of society will be benefited to a greater degree by keeping information secret than by revealing it.

---

8   Trammel v. United States, 445 U.S. 40, 100 S. Ct. 906, 63 L. Ed. 2d 186 (1980).

A communication is not privileged merely because a party, or both parties, or *all* parties regard it as confidential. There must be a relationship recognized by the courts or by statute.

One other general principle is that when a privileged communication is overheard, whether by accident or design, by some person not a member of the privileged relationship, such person may testify as to the communication.

In the sections that follow, the specific rules that apply to the respective privileged communications relationships are explored.

§ 10.3   Communications between husband and wife

In the case of *Funk v. United States*,9 the United States Supreme Court philosophized that a rule of evidence thought necessary at one time should yield to the experience of a succeeding generation whenever experience has clearly demonstrated the fallacy or unwisdom of the old rule. At no place is this more evident than in the law relating to the husband-wife privilege. In a 1980 case,10 *Trammel v. United States,* the Supreme Court set aside rules that had been established in the 1958 case of *Hawkins v. United States.*11 As a result of *Trammel* and other cases, it is necessary to approach the husband-wife privilege issue from two angles.

a.   Statement of the rules

(Rule 1) Information privately disclosed between husband and wife in the confidence of the marital relationship is privileged.12 This rule is followed in both the federal and state courts and is not changed by the decision in the *Trammel* case.

(Rule 2) One spouse is not permitted to testify regarding any acts observed before or during the marriage unless both spouses agree. This rule was established for federal courts in 1958 in the case of *Hawkins v. United States,*13 but it was set aside in the *Trammel* case. The rule is still followed in some states and, until it is changed by state statutes or decisions, it will remain in effect in those states.14

---

9   290 U.S. 371, 54 S. Ct. 212, 78 L. Ed. 369 (1933). *See* case in Part II, *infra.*
10   Trammel v. United States, 445 U.S. 40, 100 S. Ct. 906, 63 L. Ed. 2d 145 (1980). *See* case in Part II, *infra.*
11   Hawkins v. United States, 358 U.S. 74, 79 S. Ct. 141, 3 L. Ed. 2d (1958).
12   Blau v. United States, 340 U.S. 332, 71 S. Ct. 301, 95 L. Ed. 306 (1950).
13   Hawkins v. United States, *supra* n. 11.
14   See the footnotes by the Court in the *Trammel* case cited *supra* n. 10. *See also* Gallego v. State, 101 Nev. 782, 711 P.2d 856 (1985), in which the Nevada statute which precludes a wife from testifying for or against her husband without his consent is cited.

**b.	Scope of the privilege**

At common law, neither spouse was a competent witness for or against the other. This rule was based on the premise that man and wife were one, and at common law, if one was a party to a suit, whether civil or criminal, the other was not permitted to be a witness. This restrictive rule was abolished by court decisions and statutes, and it was replaced by the rule that a spouse may testify *for* the other in a criminal proceeding, but in some instances, a spouse may not testify *against* the other if either spouse objects.

The Court in *Trammel* referred to studies which revealed that in 1958, when *Hawkins* was decided, 31 states allowed a defendant the privilege to prevent adverse spousal testimony, but the Court indicated that the number had declined to 24 in 1980. The Court then said, "Here we must decide whether the privilege against adverse spousal testimony promotes sufficiently important interests to outweigh the need for probative evidence in the administration of criminal justice."15

In the case of *Blau v. United States,*16 the Supreme Court reaffirmed the rule that confidential communications between husband and wife are privileged. This means that neither spouse may be *required* to testify concerning these communications, nor is one *permitted* to testify if the other objects. This case did not decide, however, the issue of whether the spouse may be permitted to testify to an act observed before or during the marriage, nor did it settle the issue of communications made in the presence of a third party. The lower court in *Trammel* agreed that confidential communications between husband and wife were privileged and therefore inadmissible, but that they permitted the wife to testify about any acts that she observed before and during the marriage, and about any communications made in the presence of a third person.

After discussing the arguments for and against permitting a spouse to testify about criminal acts observed during their marriage, the Court concluded:

> Accordingly, we conclude that the existing rule should be modified so that the witness spouse alone has the privilege to refuse to testify adversely: the witness may be neither compelled to testify nor foreclosed from testifying. This modification—vesting the privilege in the witness spouse—furthers the important public interest in marital harmony without unduly burdening legitimate law enforcement needs.17

---

15 Trammel v. United States, *supra* n. 10.
16 Blau v. United States, *supra* n. 12.
17 Trammel v. United States, *supra* n. 10.

To summarize, the general rule in both state and federal courts is that information privately disclosed between husband and wife in the confidence of the marital relationship is protected in both federal and state courts. In federal courts, and in some states, the witness spouse alone has the privilege to testify or refuse to testify adversely regarding criminal acts observed during the marriage. In other states, where the rule has not been changed by statutes or court decisions, an accused may object not only to a spouse testifying about confidential communications, but also to that spouse's testimony about any act observed before or during the marriage.

The part of the marital privilege which concerns confidential communications during the marriage has come under scrutiny. The argument has been that if the marriage is in "utter shambles," the force behind the rule no longer exists, and the spouse should be required to testify.

Applying what the court termed reason and experience, a United States Court of Appeals commented that the federal courts should construe evidentiary privileges narrowly.18 In *United States v. Roberson,* Thomas and Rosie Roberson had been separated two months when he told her that he had raped and choked another woman. Two months earlier the defendant had instituted an action for dissolution of the marriage and had moved out of the home that he shared with his wife. In agreeing that the marital privilege no longer applied, the reviewing court approved the lower court's decision that the marital privilege was not applicable to prevent the defendant's wife from testifying in this rape trial as to statements made by the husband—even though the marriage was still valid under state law.

The court noted that, in making a determination regarding the irreconcilability of a marriage and the applicability of the marital privilege, the district court should consider whether, at the time of the communication, a divorce action had been filed, the relationship of the parties prior to the communication, and the parties' own statements about whether the marriage was reconcilable. In making this decision, the Ninth Circuit Court of Appeals referred to other federal cases and acknowledged the principle that the marital communication privilege is "an obstacle to the investigation of the truth that ought to be strictly confined within the narrowest possible limits consistent with the logic of its principle."

However, a Colorado court declared that the spousal testimonial privilege continues until such time as the bonds of marriage have been broken by death or dissolution, and that the privilege is not terminated by mere separation which has not yet resulted in a dissolution decree.19 While the principle that the marital communication privilege should not be applicable if a marriage is in utter shambles is probably still a minority view, the trend appears to be in that direction, especially in the federal courts.

---

18 United States v. Roberson, 859 F.2d 1376 (9th Cir. 1988).
19 In re Marriage of Bozarth, 779 P.2d 1346 (Colo. 1989).

c. Exceptions

(1) *The privilege generally is limited to confidential communications.* The privilege protects information privately disclosed between husband and wife. Therefore, the presence of third parties during the conversation between the defendant and his wife negates the confidentiality otherwise underlying the marital privilege.20 This is true even if the persons present are members of the family, including children, if the children are old enough to understand the communication.

(2) *Communications overheard by third parties.* Another exception, which is related to the first one mentioned, concerns the testimony of a third party who overheard the confidential communications. When a third party has overheard the conversation between the husband and wife, that person may testify about the communications.21 The reasoning for this is that the justification for the privilege rule does not exist, at least in whole, under the circumstances. Another rationale for this exception is that by failing to take precautions to prevent others from hearing, the spouses are deemed to have waived the right to secrecy.22

(3) *Prosecution against one spouse for acts against the other.* It would be a miscarriage of justice and not within the scope of the reasons for the rule to prohibit one spouse from testifying against the other when that spouse has been injured by the other.23 This exception applies in prosecutions for violation of the Mann Act, and in child abuse, bigamy and adultery cases.

In reaffirming this rule, a Michigan court said that, although the exception permitting testimony of a spouse in a case involving an assault by one spouse on the other is not provided for in the statute, the exception should apply since "any other result would, in principle, indeed be difficult to justify."24 As indicated, the privilege does not apply when the victim is the child of a spouse requested to testify. For example, in a Kentucky case, the court held that the husband-wife privilege is not applicable in the prosecution of a man for sexual abuse of his three-year-old adopted daughter.25

---

20 United States *ex rel.* Tores v. Brierton, 460 F. Supp. 704 (N.D. Ill. 1978).

21 Arnold v. State, 353 So. 2d 524 (Ala. 1977).

22 People v. Melski, 10 N.Y.2d 78, 176 N.E.2d 81 (1961); *See* People v. Gomez, 134 Cal. App. 3d 874, 185 Cal. Rptr. 155 (1982), which held that if the facts show that the communication was not intended to be kept confidential, the communication is not privileged.

23 United States v. Allery, 526 F. 2d 1362 (8th Cir. 1975). This same reasoning applies in a prosecution where a crime is committed by one spouse against the child of the other. *See* Wyatt v. United States, 362 U.S. 525, 80 S. Ct. 901, 4 L. Ed. 2d 931 (1960).

24 People v. Thompson, 111 Mich. App. 324, 314 N.W.2d 606 (1981).

25 Commonwealth v. Boarman, 619 S.W.2d 922 (Ky. Ct. App. 1980); *see also* Raborn v. State, 192 Ga. App. 99, 383 S.E. 2d 650 (1989).

Although a spouse may not be prohibited from testifying against the other spouse when the crime involves an act against the first spouse, one court has held that a wife of the defendant charged with assaulting her had the right to invoke the privilege not to testify against him.26 In this case the wife of the defendant did not voluntarily waive her privilege not to testify against him, as the record indicated that the wife had objected to testifying and that no one had informed her of her privilege to refuse to testify.

(4) *Conspiracy.* There is some evidence that if the husband and wife jointly participate in a criminal conspiracy, the person who is tried cannot claim the marital privilege. This was the decision of the Tenth Circuit in the case of *United States v. Trammel.*27 There the court upheld the testimony of the wife even though the husband objected, as the evidence was "the voluntary testimony of a spouse who appears as an unindicted co-conspirator under the grant of immunity from the government in return for her testimony."28

In one tax evasion case, the First Circuit decided that the statements made by a wife are not protected by the marital communication privilege when they are made in furtherance of a conspiracy to evade income taxes.29 In this case it was alleged that the wife was a co-conspirator and that the wife participated in discussions regarding laundering of cash proceeds of a drug smuggling operation and evading tax liability. The evidence also indicated that the wife delivered cash to an individual alleged to have helped launder the proceeds. The court concluded that communications concerning a crime in which the wife jointly participated do not fall within the protection of the marital communications privilege.

When one spouse described the possessions of the other spouse and their location, this was admissible, as the first spouse's knowledge of the possessions of the other spouse was not a spousal communication as to come within the privilege.30 But when a man revealed stolen objects to his wife, he was communicating to the same extent as if he had clearly told his wife, "I have a stolen gun and a camera."31

Several courts have considered the application of the privilege rule when a conversation between a husband and wife was intercepted by an authorized wiretap. In *United States v. Mendoza,* the Fifth Circuit held that the conversations between husband and wife about crimes in which they are jointly participating when the conversations occur are not marital commu-

---

26 Fuentes v. State, 775 S.W.2d 64 (Tex. App. 1989).
27 United States v. Trammel, 583 F.2d 1166 (10th Cir. 1978).
28 *Ibid.*
29 United States v. Picciandra, 788 F.2d 39 (1st Cir. 1986).
30 State v. Fowler, 101 Idaho 546, 617 P.2d 850 (1980), *cert. denied,* 450 U.S. 916, 67 L. Ed. 341 (1981).
31 State v. Smith, 384 A.2d 687 (Me. 1978).

nications for the purpose of the marital privilege, and thus, the conversations do not fall within the privilege.32

d. Duration of the privilege

The Supreme Court opinion in the *Trammel* case,33 allowing the witness spouse to make the decision whether to testify adversely, makes the question of the duration of the privilege less important. However, in some instances, it still must be determined whether the privilege continues after the marriage is dissolved.

Although in some states the rule still exists that the privilege continues after divorce regarding statements made in confidence during the marriage, a more logical approach is that the purpose of the rule is no longer applicable when the spouses are divorced at the time of the trial. In a New Jersey case, the state's witness was married to the defendant at the time that she overheard him making incriminating statements, but the couple was divorced at the time of the trial. The court accepted the arguments of the prosecutor that the ex-wife's testimony implicating the defendant as a receiver of stolen goods was admissible because the rationale behind the interspousal privilege was inapplicable.34

But the courts are not uniform in deciding whether the marital privilege should remain in effect when the parties are separated and not divorced. In a federal case the Ninth Circuit Court of Appeals declined to adopt a categorical test that the privilege would or would not be applied in the case of a failing marriage; instead, the court required trial judges to consider whether a separation exists based on all other circumstances bearing on the irreconcilability.35 In this case the reviewing court found that the trial judge's finding that the marriage was defunct was not clearly erroneous and, accordingly, the wife was permitted to testify to the statements made by the husband in which he admitted a charged rape.

In any event, the protection does not extend after a divorce to acts or utterances made prior to or subsequent to the marriage.36

The general rule is that the privilege exists when the parties are separated and there is no legal divorce. However, this rule appears to be eroding. Also, the privilege does not apply when the defendant is merely living with the person who is called as a witness,37 unless there is a recognized common law marriage.38

---

32 United States v. Mendoza, 574 F.2d 1373 (5th Cir.), *cert. denied*, 439 U.S. 988, 99 S. Ct. 584, 68 L. Ed. 2d 661 (1978).

33 Trammel v. United States, *supra* n. 10.

34 State v. Brown, 273 A.2d 783 (N.J. 1971); *see also* State v. Euell, 583 S.W.2d 173, 211 (Mo. 1979).

35 United States v. Robertson, 859 F.2d 1376 (9th Cir. 1988).

36 Pereira v. United States, 347 U.S. 1, 74 S. Ct. 358, 98 L. Ed. 435 (1954).

37 Mckee v. State, 452 P.2d 169 (Okla. 1969).

38 Lashley v. State, 132 Ga. App. 427, 208 S.E.2d 200 (1974).

§ 10.4   Communications between attorney and client

a.   Statement of the rule

The rule relating to the use of communications between attorney and client is that confidential communications made in the course of professional employment between an attorney and his client may not be divulged by the attorney without the consent of the client, nor may the client be compelled to testify regarding such communications.

This rule regarding confidential communications between client and attorney, as in the case of the husband-wife communications privilege, was recognized at common law. The rule is based on public policy, the reasoning being that the attorney's assistance can be made safely and readily available only when the client is free from the consequences of apprehension of discovery by reason of the subsequent statements of the lawyer. Thus the public policy factor outweighs the desirability of placing all facts before the jury.

A Pennsylvania court, however, cautioned that the privilege exists only to aid in the administration of justice, and when it is shown that the interests of justice would be frustrated by the exercise of the privilege, the trial judge may require that the communication be disclosed.[39]

In a 1981 case, the United States Supreme Court proclaimed the reason for the privilege and the extent of the privilege.[40] First explaining that the attorney-client privilege exists to protect not only the giving of professional advice to those who can act upon it, but also the giving of information to a lawyer to enable him to give sound and informed advice, the Court then indicated that the privilege is not without limits. The Court said that the attorney-client privilege only protects disclosures of communications, and that it does not protect disclosure of underlying facts by those who communicate with the attorney.

A party cannot conceal a fact merely by revealing it to his lawyer; a party who is testifying cannot refuse to answer questions concerning facts related to the case merely because he has at one time or another disclosed such facts to his lawyer. The witness may refuse to testify on other grounds, but not merely because he has communicated the facts to his attorney.

b.   Scope of the privilege

The doctrine is subject to statutory regulations and limitations. While it is desirable to protect communications between an attorney and his client, unless the facts are such that this relationship is in jeopardy, the rule should not apply.

---

39   Kohen v. Jenkintown Cab Co., 238 Pa. Super 456, 357 A.2d 689 (1976).
40   Upjohn Co. v. United States, 449 U.S. 383, 101 S. Ct. 677, 66 L. Ed. 2d 584 (1981).

A frequently quoted comment relating to the privilege is found in *United States v. United Shoe Machinery Corp.*41 In that case, the Court commented:

The privilege applies only if (1) the asserted holder of the privilege is or sought to become a client; (2) the person to whom the communication was made (a) is a member of the bar of a court, or his subordinate and (b) in connection with this communication is acting as a lawyer; (3) the communication relates to a fact of which the attorney was informed (a) by his client (b) without the presence of strangers (c) for the purpose of securing primarily either (i) an opinion on law or (ii) legal services or (iii) assistance in some legal proceeding, and not (d) for the purpose of committing a crime or tort; and (4) the privilege has been (a) claimed and (b) not waived by the client.

After making reference to previous cases, a federal court reiterated that the attorney-client privilege is intended to be strictly confined within the narrowest possible limits consistent with the logic of its principle. The court went on to explain that the privilege is designed to protect only such information as a client communicates to an attorney so that the attorney may properly and ethically carry out his responsibilities in representing his client.42

As indicated in the above requirement, the privilege only applies when the person to whom the communication was made is a member of the bar or his subordinate. It is clear that a statement made to one who is not an attorney, such as a prison inmate, is not privileged.43 Even when the prison inmate has knowledge of the law and is assigned to the law library to help prisoners with their legal problems by writing letters, preparing pleadings and giving them other advice, he is not a lawyer for the purposes of the privilege. Statements made to him are not privileged statements. However, statements made to an attorney's employee by a person seeking legal services from the attorney are covered by the privilege.44

Although the attorney-client privilege is recognized in all courts, not all of the relationships are protected. Some of the situations in which the protection is not applicable are discussed in the following sections.

---

41 89 F. Supp. 357 (D. Mass. 1950); *see also* United States v. Schmidt, 360 F. Supp. 339 (M.D. Pa. 1973) for a discussion of the scope of the privilege.

42 In re Witness before the Grand Jury, 631 F. Supp. 32 (E.D. Wis. 1985). *See* case in Part II, *infra.*

43 State v. Spell, 399 So. 2d 551 (La. 1981).

44 American National Water Mattress Corp. v. Manville, 642 P.2d 1330 (Alaska 1982).

c. Exceptions

(1) *Identity of client.* Generally, the identity of the attorney's client is not considered a privileged matter. The existence of the relation of attorney and client is not a privileged communication. The privilege pertains to the subject matter, and not to the fact of the employment as attorney, and as it presupposes the relationship of attorney and client, it does not attach to the creation of that relationship. The client or the attorney may be permitted or compelled to testify regarding the fact of his employment as attorney, or regarding the fact that the attorney advised his client about a certain matter, or performed certain services for the client.45

Neither the fact of employment nor the amount of fee paid is a confidential communication within the basic philosophy of the privilege. Thus, in a proceeding to require two attorneys to respond to an administrative summons in connection with the investigation of tax returns of the attorneys' clients, information as to the amount of fees paid, dates of payment, and by or through whom payments were made was not privileged.46

Although the authorities are substantially uniform against any privilege as applied to the fact of retainer or identity of the client, there is an exception to the general rule that is as firmly grounded as the rule itself. That exception is that the privilege may be recognized when so much of the actual communication has already been disclosed that identification of the client amounts to disclosure of a confidential communication.47

(2) *Advice in furtherance of crime.* The attorney-client relationship offers no shield to either client or attorney if either has been engaged in a plan to commit a crime or fraud in the future.48 The interests of public justice require that no shield such as the protection afforded to communications between attorney and client shall be interposed to protect a person who takes counsel on how he can safely commit a crime. This rule extends to one who, having committed a crime, seeks advice on how he can escape arrest and punishment. As an example, communications relating to advice regarding the destruction or disposition of the murder weapon or of the body following a murder are not within the privilege.49 Further, a client's plan to commit perjury is not protected, and a lawyer

---

45 Morris v. State, 242 A.2d 559 (Md. 1968). *See* case in Part II, *infra.*
46 In re Wasserman, 198 F. Supp. 564 (D.D.C. 1961).
47 In re Kaplan, 8 N.Y.2d 214, 168 N.E.2d 660 (1960); NLRB v. Harvey, 349 F.2d 900 (4th Cir. 1965); State v. Mullins, 26 Ohio App. 2d 13, 268 N.E.2d 603 (1971).
48 Clark v. United States, 289 U.S. 1, 53 S. Ct. 465, 77 L. Ed. 993 (1933); United States v. Weinberg, 226 F.2d 161 (3d Cir. 1955), *cited in* United States v. Hoffa, 349 F.2d 20 (6th Cir. 1965).
49 Clark v. State, 159 Tex. Crim. 187, 261 S.W.2d 339 (1953).

may testify concerning comments made to him by the defendant regarding such a plan.50

The announced intention of a client to commit a crime is not included within the confidences which the attorney is bound to respect. The attorney may properly make such disclosures as may be necessary to prevent the act or protect those against whom it is threatened.51

This exception to the attorney-client privilege was comprehensively explained by the United States Court of Appeals for the Fourth Circuit in the case of *In re Grand Jury Proceedings*, in which an attorney sought a writ requiring the reversal of an order directing him to testify concerning conversations between him and the three individuals.52 The attorney claimed that conversations between him and three others concerning a business relationship was confidential and that they should not be required to testify concerning such confidential communications. The reviewing court first explained that "the attorney-client privilege as traditionally recognized at common law and as now incorporated in the Federal Rules of Evidence controls in all federal judicial proceedings." The court continued, however, by stating that the privilege impedes the full and free discovery of the truth and is in derogation of the public's "right to have every man's evidence." Accordingly, the privilege's is to be construed within the narrowest possible limits consistent with the logic of its principle. In discussing the exception to the rule, the court noted that:

> Consonant with this policy, the privilege applies only when the person claiming the privilege has as a client consulted an attorney for the purpose of securing a legal opinion or services and not "for the purpose of committing a crime or tort," and in connection with that consultation has communicated information which was intended to be kept confidential.

In the case of *United States v. Zolin,* the United States Supreme Court considered the applicability of the "crime-fraud" exception to the attorney-client privilege.53 In this case the IRS, in investigating the tax returns of L. Ron Hubbard, founder of the Church of Scientology, sought documents, including two tapes, to assist the agents in the investigation. The founder of the church claimed, among other things, that the attorney-client privilege barred the tapes' disclosure. The IRS argued that the tapes fell within the exception of the attorney-client privilege for communications in furtherance of future illegal conduct—the so-called "crime-fraud" exception—and urged the district court to listen to the tapes in making this privilege determination.

---

50 State v. Phelps, 24 Or. App. 329, 545 P.2d 901 (1976).
51 Canons of Professional Ethics No. 37.
52 In re Grand Jury Proceedings, 727 F.2d 1352 (4th Cir. 1984).
53 United States v. Zolin, ___ U.S. ___, 109 S. Ct. 2619 (1989).

The Court acknowledged that the attorney-client privilege must necessarily protect the confidences of wrongdoers, but that the reason for the protection ceases to operate at a certain point, namely, when the desired advice refers not to a prior wrongdoing but to future wrongdoing. The Court advised that the purpose of the crime-fraud exception to the attorney-client privilege is to assure that the "seal of secrecy" between the lawyer and client does not extend to communications "made for the purpose of getting advice for the commission of fraud or crime."

As to the *in camera* review of the tapes to determine whether the exception applies, the court agreed that in appropriate circumstances an *in camera* review of allegedly privileged attorney-client communications may be used to determine whether the communications fall within the crime-fraud exception. However, before a district court may engage in an *in camera* review at the request of the party opposing the privilege, that party must present evidence sufficient to support a reasonable belief that such review may reveal evidence that establishes the exception's applicability.

(3) *Communications not intended to be confidential.*54 A communication is "confidential" if not intended to be disclosed to third parties other than those to whom its disclosure is in furtherance of the rendition of professional legal services to the client or those reasonably necessary for the transmission of the communication. If the communication is not intended to be confidential, then the reason for the rule is not present. The rule, within its limitations, is rigidly enforced as to attorneys in the interest of their clients. But as the rule tends to prevent a full disclosure of the truth, it should be strictly construed and limited to cases falling within the principle on which it is based.55

If a third party is present at the time the communication was made, the privilege does not generally apply. For example, in one case, the court reminded that communications between the defendant and his lawyer "were not privileged since third persons were present at the time the communications were made."56 However, in *United States v. Landof,* the Ninth Circuit determined that the presence of the client's father at the conference with the attorney does not necessarily vitiate the privilege and that the trial court did not abuse its discretion in permitting the attorney to invoke the privilege.57

In explaining that communications which are not intended to be confidential are not protected by the attorney-client privilege, a reviewing court indicated that an important requirement for invoking of the attorney-client

---

54 *See* FED. R. EVID. (as submitted to Congress in 1972).
55 Prichard v. United States, 181 F.2d 326 (6th Cir.), *aff'd,* 339 U.S. 974, 70 S. Ct. 1029, 94 L. Ed. 1380 (1950).
56 State v. Bigos, 459 F.2d 639 (1st Cir. 1972).
57 United States v. Landof, 591 F.2d 36 (9th Cir. 1978).

privilege is that the communication between the attorney and the client was made in confidence and under circumstances from which it could be reasonably assumed that the communication would remain in confidence.58

In justifying this exception to the privilege, a federal court in New York noted that a client's disclosure to a third party of a communication made during a confidential consultation with his attorney eliminates whatever privilege the communication may have already possessed.59 That court explained that the exception applies whether the disclosure is viewed as an indication that confidentiality is no longer intended, or as a waiver of the privilege.

(4) *Statements of the attorney relating to the client's mental or physical condition.* The privilege does not extend to information received by the attorney which does not relate to communications even though it was obtained while he was acting as an attorney. For example, testimony at the trial by the defendant's counsel concerning the defendant's mental competency does not violate the attorney-client privilege.60 The court in *Clanton v. United States* stated:

> Here the attorney's testimony did not relate to private, confidential communications with his client during the time of communications prior to and at the entry of the pleas of guilty. He was qualified as a layman to express a view as to his client's mental competency.

The same reasoning applies if the attorney acquired information from other sources, as the information was not communicated or confided to him by the client or by an agent of the client.61

d. Assertion and waiver

The privilege against disclosure of information confidentially revealed to an attorney is personal to the client and may be asserted only by him. The privilege belongs to the client, not to the attorney,62 but if the client is not present during the proceeding in which the attorney is called upon to testify, the attorney then may assert the privilege on behalf of his client, but not on his own behalf.63

---

58 United States v. Lopez, 777 F.2d 543 (10th Cir. 1985).

59 Bower v. Weisman, 669 F. Supp. 602 (S.D.N.Y. 1987).

60 Clanton v. United States, 488 F.2d 1069 (5th Cir. 1974).

61 United States v. Devasto, 52 F.2d 26 (2d Cir.), *cert. denied*, 284 U.S. 678, 52 S. Ct. 138, 76 L. Ed. 573 (1931).

62 Chadbourne, Inc. v. Superior Court, 36 Cal. Rptr. 60 Cal. 2d 733, 388 P.2d 700 (1964).

63 State v. Bean, 239 N.W.2d 556 (Iowa 1976).

Recent decisions have reaffirmed the rule that the waiver of the attorney-client privilege rests solely with the client, not the counsel. The attorney or agent may exercise that power only when acting with the client's authority.64 Therefore, to allow the district attorney to invoke the attorney-client privilege that existed between a murder victim and his attorney is error.65 But while the attorney-client privilege belongs to the client and not the attorney, an attorney may, and should, assert it, if he does so for the benefit of his client.66

Once a client has effectively waived the attorney-client privilege, the attorney is competent as a witness regarding matters otherwise within the scope of the privilege; he has no standing to invoke the privilege if the client does not wish to do so.67

This privilege is not a right effective without claim or assertion. It is a mere privilege that has no practical existence or effect unless personally and promptly claimed by its possessor. A claim of privilege must be promptly raised or it will be deemed to have been waived.

Testimony by the client or, at his request, by the attorney, revealing a portion of the communication, is a waiver as to the remainder of the communication. The client waives the privilege when he discloses what he claims were communications between himself and his attorney, especially when his version reflects on the attorney and calls for an explanation.68 If an attorney is accused of wrongdoing by his client, the attorney is not precluded from disclosing his explanation in respect to the accusation.69

§ 10.5　Communications between physician and patient

a.　Statement of the rule

At common law, there was no privilege protecting the confidences reposed by sick or injured persons in their physicians. Today, about two-thirds of the states have enacted statutes creating a testimonial privilege which prohibits a disclosure by the physician, when called to testify, of confidential communications made to him or information acquired by him in the course of his professional attendance upon the patient. A majority of the courts declare that the primary purpose of such a statute is to

---

64　State v. Davis, 116 N.J. 341, 561 A.2d 1082 (1989).

65　Smith v. State, 770 S.W.2d 70 (Tex. App. 1989).

66　United States v. Loften, 518 F. Supp. 839 (S.D.N.Y. 1981).

67　Barnes v. State, 460 So. 2d 126 (Miss. 1983).

68　Cooper v. United States, 5 F.2d 824 (6th Cir. 1925).

69　State v. Simmons, 57 Wis. 2d 285, 203 N.W.2d 887 (1973); Tasby v. United States, 504 F.2d 332 (8th Cir. 1975).

encourage the utmost confidence between the patient and his physician, and to preserve it inviolate.

In the Federal Rules of Evidence, as approved by the United States Supreme Court, the following definitions were included:[70]

(1) A "patient" is a person who consults or is examined or interviewed by a psychotherapist.

(2) A "psychotherapist" is (A) a person authorized to practice medicine in any state or nation, or reasonably believed by the patient so to be, while engaged in the diagnosis or treatment of a mental or emotional condition, including drug addiction, or (B) a person licensed or certified as a psychologist under the laws of any state or nation, while similarly engaged.

(3) A communication is "confidential" if not intended to be disclosed to third persons other than those present to further the interest of the patient in the consultation, examination, or interview, or persons reasonably necessary for the transmission of the communication, or persons who are participating in the diagnosis and treatment under the direction of the psychotherapist, including members of the patient's family.

Although this rule was omitted from the version of the Federal Rules that was passed on to the Senate by the House of Representatives, the definitions should be considered. It should be noted that the definition of "psychotherapist" has a broad coverage and includes not only physicians but psychologists and those "reasonably believed" by the patient so to be.

After quoting the guidelines prescribed in Rule 501 of the Federal Rules of Evidence, the Sixth Circuit reasoned that a psychotherapist-patient privilege may be recognized, but that the authority must be exercised with caution.[71] Making reference to the fact that at common law no physician-patient privilege existed and that no such privilege was recognized in federal courts in some prior federal cases, the court concluded that there is a compelling necessity for the privilege. However, the court cautioned, "Just as the recognition of privileges must be undertaken on a case-by-case basis, so too must the scope of the privilege be considered."

Two important prerequisites must be met before a communication can become privileged under the physician-patient doctrine. First, the communication must come in the course of lawful medical treatment of a patient. Second, the subject information that is sought to be privileged must be gained in the course of direct observation of the patient or in direct communication with him as to treatment.

---

70 Draft of Rule 504 of Federal Rules of Evidence.
71 In re Zuniga, 714 F.2d 632 (6th Cir. 1983).

b. Scope of the privilege

The privilege is for the protection of the patient and not the physician. The reason for the rule is not to protect third persons, and although others may incidentally benefit, such benefit is not intentional. For the privilege to apply, the relationship of physician-patient must have existed at the time when the physician acquired the information he is called upon to disclose. But a physician may testify about what he observed or learned about a person's condition before the relationship of physician and patient was established between himself and such person.72

c. Exceptions

While many states have by statute created the privilege, the exceptions which have been found necessary in order to obtain information required by the public interest or to avoid fraud are so numerous as to leave little basis for the privilege. Among the exclusions from the statutory privilege, the following may be enumerated: communications not made for purposes of diagnosis and treatment; commitment and restoration proceedings; issues as to wills or otherwise between parties claiming by succession from the patient; actions on insurance policies; required reports (venereal diseases, gunshot wounds, child abuse); communications in furtherance of crime or fraud; mental or physical condition put in issue by patient (personal injury cases); malpractice actions; and some or all criminal prosecutions. California, for example, excepts cases in which the patient puts his condition in issue, all criminal proceedings, will and similar contests, malpractice cases, and disciplinary proceedings, as well as certain other situations; thus the exceptions leave virtually nothing covered by the privilege.

Where a physician is required by state law to report to a law enforcement officer a gunshot wound or wound inflicted by a deadly weapon, the physician may testify, without violating the physician-patient privilege, concerning the description of the wounded person, his name and address if known, and the description of the nature and location of such wound. Knowledge in these areas may be obtained by examination, observation and treatment of the victim.73

In explaining that the privilege is not absolute, a federal appeals court admonished that while patients have a privacy interest under the Constitution of the United States in their medical records in the possession of their physicians, the protection afforded by the right to privacy is not absolute. The individual privacy interest in the patient's medical records must be balanced against the legitimate interest of the state in securing information contained therein.74 In this insurance fraud case a physician

---

72 Keeton v. State, 175 Miss. 631, 167 So. 68 (1936).
73 State v. Antill, 176 Ohio St. 61, 197 N.E.2d 548 (1964); Marcus v. Superior Court of Los Angeles, 18 Cal. App. 3d 22, 95 Cal. Rptr. 545 (1971).
74 In re Search/w warrant (sealed), 810 F.2d 67 (3d Cir. 1987).

being investigated made a motion to suppress certain of his medical records that were seized pursuant to a search warrant. While acknowledging that the physician had standing, as he was the only person in a position to protect the patient's privacy rights, the court refused to suppress the evidence because it recognized that "significant government interests in investigation clearly outweigh any individual privacy interests."

The privilege is justified only when disclosures are made in confidence. Therefore, when the communication is made in the presence of unnecessary third persons, the privilege is waived. For example, when the emergency medical technician was in the emergency room, but was not working under the supervision of the attending physician, he may testify about what he overheard the defendant say to the physician.[75]

If a psychiatrist gives information to police regarding the identity of a suspect, the privilege does not apply. In an Arkansas case, the defendant's psychiatrist gave police officers sufficient information about the defendant to enable the officer to identify the defendant and to obtain a warrant to search the defendant's home. Here the court agreed that evidence developed as a result of the search was not excluded by the privilege.[76]

d. Assertion and waiver

The physician-patient privilege definitely belongs to the patient, and the physician may be compelled to testify if the patient has waived the privilege.

State statutes creating a physician-patient privilege usually provide that if the patient voluntarily testifies about privileged matters, the physician may be compelled to testify on the same subject. The physician also may testify by express consent of his patient or, if the patient is deceased, by the express consent of the surviving spouse or the executor or administrator of the estate of the deceased patient. However, the physician may claim the privilege to records of his patients in the absence of evidence that the patient for whom he may serve as witness has waived his privilege.[77]

In making certain that the patient-physician privilege belongs to the patient, the Supreme Court of Vermont set forth:

> While the defendant has the power to invoke the privilege, it is based on the presumption that he speaks for the patient. Once it is clear that he does not speak for the patient, his power to invoke the privilege ceases.[78]

---

75 State v. LaRoche, 122 N.H. 231, 442 A.2d 602 (1982).
76 Gruzen v. State, 267 Ark. 380, 591 S.W.2d 342 (1979), *cert. denied,* 449 U.S. 852, 101 S. Ct. 144, 66 L. Ed. 2d 64 (1980).
77 People v. Bickham, 89 Ill. 2d 1, 431 N.E.2d 365 (1982).
78 State v. Chenette, 560 A.2d 365 (Vt. 1989).

In this case the defendant was found guilty of knowingly filing false Medicaid claims. His ground for challenging the conviction was that the court erred in allowing evidence of the medical records of the patients. However, as the patients participated fully in the investigation and did not object to discussing the records, the physician was not permitted to invoke the privilege.

Although a defendant does not waive the psychiatrist-patient privilege by pleading not guilty by reason of insanity, he does waive the privilege when he presents some evidence of insanity.[79] In the case of *State v. Soney,* the court explained that "when a patient testifies to a course of conduct directly opposed to that which he told a physician he followed, we see no reason why he should be entitled to rely on the physician's silence to hide the truth."[80]

§ 10.6 Communications to clergymen

a. Statement of the rule

A person has a privilege to refuse to disclose, and to prevent another from disclosing, a confidential communication by that person to a clergyman in his professional character as a spiritual adviser.[81]

In some statutes, the wording of the privilege is different. For example, in some states a clergyman or priest may not testify "concerning a confession made to him in his professional character in the course of discipline enjoined by the church to which he belongs."[82]

At common law, there was no privilege to communications or confessions to a spiritual adviser, and in the absence of statute, no privilege exists today.[83] But where there is an appropriate statute, the clergyman or priest may not disclose, over objection of the party so confiding, confessions or admissions made as a part of the practice of the church.[84]

---

[79] Ex parte Day, 378 So. 2d 1159 (Ala. 1979).

[80] State v. Soney, 177 N.J. Super 47, 424 A.2d 1182 (1980).

[81] Draft of Rule 506 of Federal Rules of Evidence.

[82] Mullen v. United States, 263 F.2d 275 (D.C. Cir. 1958); *see also* ARIZ. REV. STAT. ANN. § 12-2233 (1956); OHIO REV. CODE § 2317.02.

[83] State v. Morehous, 97 N.J. 285, 117 A. 296 (1922).

[84] Johnson v. Commonwealth, 310 Ky. 557, 221 S.W.2d 87 (1949). For a list of the jurisdictions recognizing the privilege, see WIGMORE ON EVIDENCE § 2395, Vol. 8, (1961 & Supp. 1990).

b.   Scope of the privilege

Generally, for the communication to be privileged, it must have been made in the understood pursuance of church discipline which gives rise to the confessional relation and not to communications of other tenor.[85] The privilege generally applies to a voluntary confession, as well as to one made under a mandate of the church, and to observations as well as to communications. A statute granting the privilege to "clergyman or other minister of any religion" does not limit the privilege to priests or clergymen of any one denomination.[86] The term "clergyman" as used in the the draft of Federal Rule of Evidence 506 and in other statutes includes a minister, priest, rabbi or other similar functionary of a religious organization.

Although the courts have been liberal in interpreting the definition of "clergyman" and other terms as used in the various statutes, a Louisiana court refused to include within the definition of "clergyman" a "born-again Christian" police officer.[87] In this case the defendant argued that statements made by him to a police officer who was a "born-again Christian" were inadmissible under the "priest-penitent privilege." The court refused to recognize this as privileged communication, even though the officer was a former deacon and conducted a prayer session with the defendant, as the officer never was ordained as a minister.

c.   Exceptions

In order for a communication to be privileged under the statute, it must be made to a clergyman in his professional capacity or character. A statement to a clergyman that does not meet this qualification may be repeated by the clergyman. Therefore, when the defendant speaks to the clergyman as a "friend" rather than as a "minister," there is no privilege.[88]

In 1979, the New York Court of Appeals again spelled out the limits on the priest-penitent privilege. In this case, the grand jury was investigating allegations that organized crime figures incarcerated in New York prisons received preferential treatment from corrections officials. The questions directed to a priest concerned his attempts to persuade a number of officials to grant work release to an inmate named Napoli. The priest made an effort to avoid answering the questions by cloaking himself with both the priest-penitent and First Amendment protections. Upon his failure to answer the questions, he was held in contempt and committed to prison for ten days, and he appealed. The Appellate Division affirmed, and the case was then appealed to the New York Court of Appeals. That court con-

---

85   In re Soeder, 7 Ohio App. 2d 271, 220 N.E.2d 547 (1966).
86   In re Swenson, 183 Minn. 602, 237 N.W. 589 (1931).
87   State v. Welch, 448 So. 2d 705 (La. App. 1984).
88   Wainscott v. Commonwealth, 562 S.W.2d 628 (Ky. 1978).

cluded that: "Neither asserted justification can serve to shield appellant from his obligation to respond to the Grand Jury's inquiries." Part of the statement of the court is as follows:

> It has been recognized, without serious disagreement, that there existed no common law priest-penitent privilege. . . . By statute, however, "a confession or confidence made to [a clergyman] in his professional character as spiritual advisor" shall not be disclosed "[u]nless the person confessing or confiding waives the privilege". . . . It is clear that the Legislature by enacting CPLR 4505 and its predecessors responded to the urgent need of people to confide in, without fear of reprisal, those entrusted with the pressing task of offering spiritual guidance so that harmony with one's self and others can be realized.[89]

The court explained that the law is designed to protect only confidential communications made to a clergyman in his spiritual capacity. In this case, the court found that the inquiries did not come within the wording or spirit of the law; therefore the grand jury was within its right to request testimony.[90]

When the communication is not made within the requisite nature of the confidential disclosure of a penitent seeking religious consolation from a clergyman, the privilege does not apply.[91] If the statements are not intended to be of a confidential nature, they are not privileged even though they are made to a person who comes within the definition of a minister as defined in the statute.[92]

Also, a minister's opinion regarding a person's soundness of mind does not come within the privilege. In such instance, there is not a confession or any communication covered by the privilege.[93]

d. Waiver

The majority of the jurisdictions consider the clergyman-penitent privileged communication relationship to be for the benefit of the penitent. Therefore, the penitent may claim the privilege or waive the privilege as he sees fit. The general rule is that if the penitent waives the privilege, the clergyman must testify about the communication.[94] On the other hand, in

---

89 Keenan v. Gigante, 47 N.Y.2d 160, 390 N.E.2d 1151 (1979), *affirming* 65 AD.2d. 585, 407 N.Y.S.2d 163 (1978).

90 *Ibid.*

91 State v. Berry, 324 So. 2d 822 (La. 1975), *cert. denied*, 425 U.S. 954, 96 S. Ct. 1731, 48 L. Ed. 2d (1976).

92 Bottoson v. State, 443 So. 2d 962 (Fla.), *cert. denied*, 469 U.S. 873, 105 S. Ct. 223, 83 L. Ed. 2d 153 (1983).

93 Buuck v. Kruckeberg, 121 Ind. App. 362, 95 N.E.2d 304 (1950).

94 WIGMORE ON EVIDENCE, § 2395 (Supp. 1979).

some jurisdictions the clergyman may also claim the privilege because the religious denomination holds that it is a violation of the church principles for the clergyman to reveal penitential communications.[95]

While evidence of statements made in confidence to a clergyman is subject to exclusion under certain statutes, the privilege is waived if the holder of the privilege voluntarily discloses a significant part of the privilege matter. In an Arkansas case, the court held that any privilege that the defendant might have claimed with respect to inculpatory statements made by him to his minister, the minister's wife, and a church elder were waived by the defendant's act in disclosing those statements to several others, including his mother-in-law.[96]

§ 10.7 Confidential informant privilege

There has been some confusion concerning the confidential informant privilege. Some of this confusion can be avoided by approaching the topic from two angles. One approach is to consider the confidential informant who gives information from which the court can determine "probable cause" for securing an arrest or a search warrant. This is different from the informer who was an integral part of the illegal transaction and whose identity is essential to the defense.

United States Supreme Court decisions have made it clear that in most instances the state does not have to disclose the name of the informant who gave information upon which probable cause for the search warrant was based. In *United States v. Ventresca*,[97] the Court stated:

> And, in *Aguilar*, we recognized "that an affidavit may be based upon hearsay information and need not reflect the direct personal observations of the affiant," so long as the magistrate is "informed of some of the underlying circumstances" supporting the affiant's conclusions and his belief that any informant involved "whose identity need not be disclosed . . . was 'credible' or his information 'reliable.' "

In the case of *Illinois v. Gates* in 1983, the Supreme Court again stated that it is not necessary to disclose the identity of an informant who only

---

95 Security Life Ins. Co. v. Newsome, 122 Ga. 137, 176 S.E.2d 463 (1970) (dissenting opinion).

96 Perry v. State, 280 Ark. 36, 655 S.W.2d 380 (1983); *see also* Snyder v. Poplett, 98 Ill. App. 3d, 424 N.E.2d 396 (1981).

97 380 U.S. 102, 85 S. Ct. 741, 13 L. Ed. 2d (1965); *see also* United States v. Harris, 403 U.S. 573, 91 S. Ct. 2075, 29 L. Ed. 2d 723 (1971), in which an informer refused to appear because he feared for his life and safety.

gives information concerning probable cause.98 Here, a search warrant for a residence and an automobile was obtained based on an affidavit setting forth facts made available by an undisclosed informant. The Supreme Court went even further than in previous cases and advised that neither is it necessary for the officer to disclose the informant, nor is it necessary to follow the two-pronged test stated in *Aguilar.* The test, according to the *Gates* case, in determining whether an informant's tip plus information is sufficient to justify the issuance of a search warrant, is the "totality of circumstances" test.

As a rule, therefore, the informant who only gives an officer information for a search warrant does not have to be identified if the officer can give information to the issuing official to insure that the magistrate has a substantial basis for concluding that probable cause exists.

Generally, communications made by informants to public officers engaged in the discovery of crime are privileged. This privilege exists in order to conceal the identity of the informant, thereby allowing him to continue as a source of future information as well as protecting him from reprisals for his actions in giving the information. The public policy encouraging others to assist in the prevention and detection of crime is deemed to outweigh the harm which is done to the defense by denying it the knowledge of the informant's identity.

This rule, however, has exceptions. This was clearly stated in one case, in which the court held:

> The State has the privilege to withhold from disclosure the identity of persons who furnish information to police officers concerning the commission of crimes. However, the privilege is not absolute. On the issue of guilt or innocence (not on Fourth Amendment issues) and only upon demand by the defendant, the trial court may, in the exercise of its judicial discretion compel such disclosure upon determination that it is necessary and relevant to a fair defense. Factors to be considered in ascertaining whether such disclosure is necessary and relevant to a fair defense include the nature of the crime charged; the importance of the informer's identity to determination of innocence, as for example, whether the informer was an integral part of the illegal transaction and the possible significance of his testimony; and the possible defenses. Whether the privilege must yield depends upon the facts and circumstances of the particular case. But if the informer testifies for the State the privilege may not be invoked by it.99

---

98 Illinois v. Gates, 462 U.S. 213, 103 S. Ct. 2317, 76 L. Ed. 2d 527 (1983).
99 Nutter v. State, 8 Md. App. 635, 262 A.2d 80 (1970).

Several examples may help to clarify this exception. In one case, the prosecutor was not privileged to withhold the name of the informant when the informant played a direct and prominent part as the sole participant with the accused in the very offense for which the latter was being tried.100 However, in another case, the accused was not entitled to know the identity of the informant when the record revealed only that the informant contacted the police and informed them that a pickup of narcotics was to take place, but the record was otherwise silent about the informant's participation in the transaction itself.101

Relying upon the *Roviaro v. United States* decision, a defendant who was convicted for the crime of unlawful distribution of a controlled dangerous substance appealed, claiming that failure to disclose the name of the informant violated his due process right to a fair trial.102 In this case, an undercover police officer testified that he received a phone call from his informant, during which the informant told him that he knew someone from whom the officer could purchase drugs. The officer picked up the informant, and they drove to a parking lot where the defendant approached to two of them, offering to sell the undercover agent a mixture of THC and cocaine. The Tenth Circuit in a *habeas corpus* action reversed the conviction, stating that:

> The court in *Roviaro* declared that fundamental requirements of fairness require restrictions on the government's privilege to refuse disclosure of an informant's identity.

The court explained that the public's interest in effective law enforcement is an important one. But at some point, withholding the identity of an informant who may be critical to the conduct of the defense infringes on the defendant's constitutional right to a fair trial, which obviously includes the right to prepare and present a defense. Here the informant set up the transaction and was the only witness to the sale other than the undercover officer and the seller. Thus, the informant could testify directly to the critical issue in the case—whether or not the defendant Gaines was the seller. The court concluded with this explanation:

> On these facts, it would violate Gaines' due process rights to deny disclosure if, in fact, the informant could provide potentially significant exculpatory testimony.

---

100 Roviaro v. United States, 353 U.S. 53, 77 S. Ct. 623, 1 L. Ed. 2d 639 (1957).
101 Jimenez v. United States, 397 F.2d 271 (5th Cir. 1968).
102 Gaines v. Hess, 662 F.2d 1364 (10th Cir. 1981).

The court did not say that the informant would have to be disclosed at a new trial, but stated that the trial judge in an *in camera* hearing should determine whether the informant's testimony would lend significant evidence to Gaines' defense. The justification was that such a procedure would limit the extent of the disclosure of the informant's identity and information, thereby protecting the state's interest in avoiding unnecessary disclosure, while at the same time the procedure would safeguard the defendant's right to the testimony of any accessible witness who may be significantly helpful to the defense.

If an informant only provides law enforcement officials with the location of the defendants, the trial court need not disclose the identity of the confidential reliable informant.103 If an informant does not disclose information regarding the substantive offense and was not present during the criminal act at issue, it is not error for a trial court to refuse to disclose the identity of the confidential informant. Even when an informant was present during the criminal transaction at issue, the fact that he did not actively participate in the crime favors nondisclosure of the identity of the informant.104

If the court decides that the informant can supply testimony necessary to a fair determination of the facts, the arguments for protecting the informant's identity must yield to the defendant's need for the evidence. At this point, the government must choose between revealing the informant's name—thereby risking his safety and its own investigative efficacy—and forfeiting the informant's testimony. As the issue of the disclosure of the informant is often critical, the defendant is required to explain to the court as precisely as possible what testimony he thinks the informant would give and how this testimony would be relevant to a material issue of guilt or innocence.105

The privilege belongs to the governmental authority, not to the informant, and thus it may be waived by the government.

§ 10.8   Secrets of state and other official information

The draft of Rule 509(b) of the Federal Rules of Evidence, which was prepared by the United States Supreme Court but not adopted by Congress provides that:

---

103 United States v. Given, 712 F.2d 1298 (8th Cir. 1983).

104 United States v. Torbide, 558 F.2d 1053 (2d Cir. 1979); *see also* United States v. Gonzales, 606 F.2d 70 (5th Cir. 1979).

105 Rugendorf v. United States, 376 U.S. 528, 84 S. Ct. 825, 11 L. Ed. 2d 887 (1964).

The government has a privilege to refuse to give evidence and to prevent any person from giving evidence upon a showing of reasonable likelihood of danger that the evidence will disclose a secret of state or official information, as defined in this rule.

The rule defines a secret of state as "a governmental secret relating to the national defense or the international relations of the United States." It defines official information as "information within the custody or control of a department or agency of the government, the disclosure of which is shown to be contrary to the public interest."

This principle, which protects military and state secrets, was described as "well-established in the law of evidence" in *United States v. Reynolds.*106 The policy basis of the rule is the desirability of encouraging candor in exchange of views within the government. Moreover, the privilege is consistent with the Freedom of Information Act.107

In order for the privilege to be allowed under the rule stated and under the general laws of evidence, the government must show a need for protecting the secret or other official information. The judge, in an *in camera* session, may require a showing of the entire text of the government's statements before granting the privilege. Then, if the privilege is successfully claimed by the government, the effect of such claim makes evidence unavailable as though the witness had died or claimed the privilege against self-incrimination.108

In pointing out the importance of the privilege, the United States Court of Appeals for the District of Columbia Circuit indicated that a ranking of the various privileges recognized in our courts would be a delicate undertaking at best, but that it is quite clear that the privilege to protect state secrets must head that list.109 In another case, a Fifth Circuit decision stated: that "to the extent that the documents withheld are internal working papers in which opinions are expressed, policies are formulated, and actions are recommended, they are privileged."110 However, the court went on to say that to the extent that the documents contain purely factual material in a form that can be separated without compromising the privileged portions of the document, the material is not privileged and is subject to discovery.

The "state secrets" privilege was comprehensively analyzed by the District of Columbia Circuit in the case of *Ellsberg v. Mitchell.*111 The plain-

---

106 345 U.S. 1, 73 S. Ct. 528, 97 L. Ed. 727 (1953).

107 5 U.S.C. § 552.

108 For a further discussion of the self-incrimination protection, *see* Chapter 16, *infra.*

109 Halkin v. Helms, 598 F.2d 1 (D.C. Cir. 1978).

110 Branch v. Phillips Petroleum Co., 638 F.2d 873 (5th Cir. 1981).

111 709 F.2d 51 (D.C. Cir. 1983), *cert. denied,* 462 U.S. 1038, 104 S. Ct. 1316, 79 L. Ed. 2d 712 (1984).

tiffs in this case were the defendants and their attorneys and advisers in the "Pentagon Papers" criminal prosecution. In the course of that proceeding, the plaintiffs here had learned that one or more of them had been the subject of a warrantless electronic surveillance by the federal government. They subsequently brought this damage action against all persons and agencies that they thought might be responsible. The defendants refused to respond to any of the plaintiff's remaining allegations or questions on the grounds that the information was privileged.

On appeal to the Court of Appeals, that court, after stating that it is now well established that the United States, by invoking its state secret privilege, may block discovery in a lawsuit of any information that, if disclosed, would adversely affect national security, laid down some principles distilled from the case law:

(1) The privilege may be asserted only by the government itself; neither a private party nor an individual official may seek its aid. Furthermore, in order to invoke it, "[t]here must be a formal claim of the privilege, lodged by the head of the department which has control over the matter, after actual personal consideration by that officer."

(2) When properly invoked, the state secrets privilege is absolute. No competing public or private interest can be advanced to compel disclosure of information found to be protected by a claim of privilege. However, because of the broad sweep of the privilege, the Supreme Court has made clear that "[i]t is not to be lightly invoked."

(3) [T]o insure that the state secrets privilege is asserted no more frequently and sweepingly than necessary, it is essential that the court continue critically to examine instances of its invocation. . . . [T]he trial judge should accord considerable deference to recommendations from the executive department.

In applying these principles in the case, the court concluded that there was a "reasonable danger" that revelation of the information in question would either enable a sophisticated analyst to gain insights into the nation's intelligence-gathering methods and capabilities, or it would disrupt diplomatic relations with foreign governments. Therefore, the trial court was correct in concluding that invocation of the state secrets privilege was proper.

If the granting of the privilege excludes evidence which may bear directly upon a substantive element of a criminal case, it may be necessary to require dismissal.112

---

112 United States v. Andolschek, 142 F.2d 503 (2d Cir. 1944).

§ 10.9 Newsman-informant privilege

In recent years, hundreds of federal and state courts have confronted the issue of whether a reporter has the privilege to refuse to testify concerning information procured in connection with that person's employment. Unlike communications between husband and wife and between attorney and client, there is no common law dealing with the newsman-informant privilege. The earlier cases made it clear that unless there is a statute, members of the journalistic profession are under the same duty as every other person to testify when properly called upon.113 In developing the law relating to the newsman-informant privilege, members of the journalistic profession have refused to testify on the grounds that the First Amendment protects such communications and that statutes enacted by the various states add to this First Amendment protection.

The United States Supreme Court first confronted the constitutional issue of whether a reporter has a privilege for confidential sources in *Branzburg v Hayes.*114 In that case, for which Justice White authored a plurality opinion,115 the Court acknowledged that news gathering qualified for some First Amendment protection, but found that the First Amendment does not guarantee the press a constitutional right of special access to information not generally available to the public.

Justice Douglas in the *Branzburg* case would have found an absolute immunity absent the reporter's personal involvement in the crime. Justice Stewart, writing for himself and two other justices, would have found a qualified privilege. Thus, four justices believed that there was no reporter's privilege, three believed in a qualified privilege, and one believed in an absolute privilege. Justice Powell authored the pivotal opinion, agreeing with the four justices, thereby making a majority, but he implied that there may be a form of privilege that should be considered on a case-by-case basis.

The justices of the Supreme Court disagreed at the time this case was decided, and the judges and justices of the federal courts and of the state courts continue to disagree on the issue. However, Justice White in the *Branzburg* decision invited Congress and the state legislatures to create statutory reporter's privileges.

Taking Justice White's invitation seriously, 26 states have enacted laws providing reporters with either an absolute or qualified privilege from divulging information received in confidence. These statutes have been labeled "shield laws." Congress has not enacted a federal shield law. The

---

113 Clein v. State, 52 So. 2d 117 (Fla. 1951).
114 408 U.S. 665, 92 S. Ct. 2646, 33 L. Ed. 2d 625 (1972).
115 For a discussion of the opinions of the various judges in the case of *Branzburg v. Hayes,* see the case of *Liggett v. Superior Court,* 260 Cal. Rptr. 161 (1989).

state laws differ in wording and have been interpreted differently by the respective state courts.

California's shield law was first enacted in 1935. This statute has undergone many amendments, and in 1980 the evidence code section relating to the News Gatherers Shield Law was incorporated into the California Constitution.116 The constitutional provision provides in pertinent part:

A publisher, editor, reporter or other person connected with or employed under a newspaper . . . shall not be adjudged in contempt by a judicial, legislative, administrative body or any other body . . . for refusing to disclose the source of any information procured while so connected or employed . . . or refusing to disclose any unpublished information obtained or prepared in gathering, receiving, or processing information for communication to the public.

As used in this subsection, "unpublished information" includes information not disseminated to the public by the person from whom disclosure is sought, whether or not related information has been disseminated and includes, but is not limited to all notes, out takes, photographs, tapes, or other data of whatever sort not itself disseminated to the public through a medium of communication, whether or not published information based or related to such material has been disseminated.

In the case of *Friedman v. Superior Court*, a reporter had written a news article about the Los Angeles Police Department. The plaintiff brought a defamation action and subpoenaed a non-party newspaper reporter to testify as to whether the plaintiff was his source of the information for a news article. The reporter made a motion to quash the subpoena, which was denied. On appeal, the court held that the shield law protected the reporter from being compelled to testify as to his source. The court noted that the shield law's protection of the reporter under these circumstances is absolute, not qualified. The court continued by asserting that the interest in nondisclosure need not be balanced against the policy of full disclosure of relevant evidence when petitioner is not a party to the underlying action.117

Even in those states which have shield laws, there are limitations on the application of the laws. To successfully raise a claim to the privilege, information must have been imparted to the reporter under a "cloak of confidentiality," and there must have been an understanding, express or implied, that the information would not be disclosed.118 If a reporter or a newspaper fails to assert that the interview in question was conducted under a cloak of

---

116 CAL. CONST. art. I, § 2, cl. (b).
117 Friedman v. Superior Court, 261 Cal. Rptr. 87 (Cal. App. 1989).
118 People v. Bova, 460 N.Y.S.2d 230 (1983).

confidentiality, a motion to reveal the reporter's notes, transcriptions, memoranda or tape recordings will not be denied.

While the legislative intent behind the shield laws is to protect the relationship between an informant who desires to give information to a news reporter and a radio, television or newspaper reporter, the trial court must take into consideration the Sixth Amendment rights of a criminal defendant before ruling that certain evidence is protected by the statute. In determining whether the statute protects the evidence, the court must consider the particular circumstances of the case, the crime charged, the possible defenses, the significance of the informant's testimony and other factors.[119]

In a New York case the court held that, in judging a claimed privilege against compelled disclosure by news media, there must be proper balance between the freedom of the press and the obligation of all citizens to give relevant testimony with respect to criminal conduct.[120]

In a Florida case that received national attention, a CBS reporter interviewed a defendant in a murder case while the defendant was on "Death Row" as part of a future story on serial killers. When the defendant became aware that the state planned to use part of the footage, he served subpoenas, upon CBS directing them to produce the videotape of the entire interview.[121] The lower court denied the CBS motion to quash the subpoenas, and CBS took the case to the Florida Court of Appeals. That court first recognized that the CBS petition was grounded in the First Amendment privilege that exists to protect journalists against unwarranted disclosure of their sources of information. The court explained that this privilege may be described as "limited" or "qualified" because it is not absolute and may be overcome under circumstances in which the fair administration of justice establishes a compelling need for disclosure.

The Florida Court of Appeals recognized that in judging a claimed privilege against compelled disclosure by the news media, there must be a striking of a proper balance between the freedom of the press and the rights of persons accused of crime. The court noted the difference between a criminal and civil case with these words:

> Certainly, the acquisition of helpful evidence in such a situation is more compelling than in the civil context, where the potential loss to a litigant is purely economic. The Sixth Amendment to the United States Constitution . . . provides that the accused in a criminal proceeding shall have the right of compulsory process for obtaining witnesses in his favor. When these constitutional provi-

---

119 State v. Geis, 441 N.E.2d 803 (Ohio App. 1981).
120 People v. Korkala, 467 N.Y.S.2d 517 (1983).
121 CBS, Inc. v. Cobb, 536 So. 2d 1067 (Fla. App. 1988). *See* case in Part II, *infra.*

sions conflict with the "shield laws" designed to protect the integrity of the print or broadcast media, some deference must be afforded to the rights of the accused.

In support of the finding that CBS had no constitutional right to withhold its work product, the court referred to a New Jersey Supreme Court case, in which that court stated: "[T]hat the rights of the accused must be protected is rather elementary and unassailable."122

As the discussion of the cases reveals, the law pertaining to the newsman-informant privilege remains unsettled. As the law now stands, a claim of the privilege may rest on constitutional grounds, on a state statute, or both. According to the California Court of Appeals, "the existence of a newsperson's privilege under the First Amendment is, at best, problematic." When the privilege is predicated on First Amendment grounds, it must give way to the rights of the accused if the accused's rights are in jeopardy.

Although at least 26 states have enacted shield laws, these laws differ from state to state. Some provide an absolute privilege from disclosing information received in confidence, some provide only a qualified privilege, and some provide that the newsperson shall not be held in contempt for refusing to disclose information. Even in those states that have shield laws, some deference must be afforded the accused if the accused's constitutional right to defend himself outweighs the right to withhold journalistic work products. However, before disclosure is ordered, there must be a showing that the information is highly material and relevant, and not obtainable from other available sources.123

§ 10.10 Summary

It is desirable that all relevant evidence be made available to the trier of fact in a criminal case. However, it is also desirable that certain rights, interests and relationships be protected. In balancing these two considerations, the courts and legislatures have developed rules whereby some testimony is not admitted. In these situations, the protection of the relationship or right is considered more important than the need for the evidence.

One privilege that has been developed over a period of many years is the husband-wife privilege. The general rule relating to communications between husband and wife is that testimony pertaining to communications arising out of the marital relationship is privileged and will not be required to be revealed unless both parties agree to do so.

---

122 In re Farber, 78 N.J. 259, 394 A.2d 330 (1978).
123 United States v. Burke, 700 F.2d 70 (2d Cir. 1983), cert. denied, 464 U.S. 816, 104 S. Ct. 72, 78 L. Ed. 2d 85 (1983).

However, there are several exceptions to this rule, and there is evidence that the trend is to abandon the privilege rule if the relationship between the two spouses is such that there is no longer any community interest in preserving the marriage.

A second common law privilege protects communications between the attorney and his client. Confidential communications made in the course of professional employment may not be divulged by the attorney. The privilege may not be claimed when the communication concerns the commission of a crime some time in the future. The privilege must be claimed by the client, and it may be waived by the client even if the attorney does not agree.

Although at common law there was no physician-patient privilege, most states have enacted statutes creating this testimonial privilege. Where statutes have been enacted, the privilege prohibits a disclosure by the physician, when called to testify, of confidential communications made to him or information acquired by him in the course of his professional attendance upon the patient. The privilege does not apply when a statute requires reports of gunshot wounds or wounds inflicted by deadly weapons. The privilege applies only when the disclosures are made in confidence. The privilege must be claimed by the patient, and only the patient may waive it.

At common law there was no privilege as to communications or confessions to a spiritual adviser, but when a statute exists, the clergyman or priest may not disclose, over objection of the party so confiding, confessions or admissions made as a part of the practice of the church. In order for the communication to be privileged under the statutes, it must be made to the clergyman in his professional capacity. The privilege may be claimed only by the communicator.

One privilege that is of greater concern to criminal justice personnel is that relating to the confidential informant. It can be said that, as a general rule, the name of the informant does not have to be disclosed, especially if his information relates only to facts from which probable cause can be based. However, if the informant played an integral part in the illegal transaction and his disclosure is necessary and relevant to a fair defense, his identity may be required to be disclosed. Much discretion in this regard is in the hands of the judge.

Testimony relating to secrets of state and other official information is sometimes privileged upon a showing of a reasonable likelihood of danger that the evidence will disclose a secret of state or official information.

The United States Supreme Court has determined that in the absence of statutes, communications to a newspaper editor or reporter are not privileged. However, some courts apply a balancing test that focuses on the need for the information and availability from other sources. If the information is available from other sources, the newsman privilege will prevail. Also, some states by statute have enacted newsman privilege laws.

Because of the common law privileges, as well as the statutory privileges, it is possible that much relevant evidence may be excluded at the trial. However, there are so many exclusions to the rules that much valuable evidence can be obtained if criminal justice personnel are familiar with the rules and the exceptions.

There is some indication that the courts and legislatures are modifying some of the privilege rules in order to prevent abuse. These changes should be watched carefully.

CHAPTER 11
OPINIONS AND EXPERT TESTIMONY

Opinion evidence, to be of any value, should be based either upon admitted facts or upon facts, within the knowledge of the witness, disclosed in the record. Opinion evidence that does not appear to be based upon disclosed facts is of little or no value.
Balaban & Katz Corp. v. Commissioner of Internal Revenue, 30 F.2d 807 (7th Cir. 1929)

§ 11.1 Introduction

When a witness takes the stand and testifies, the testimony is normally restricted to the facts within the personal knowledge, observation or recollection of the witness, as distinguished from opinions, inferences, impressions and conclusions. It is within the province of the jury to reach conclusions regarding matters in issue; therefore, an inference, opinion or conclusion of the witness, under this general rule, is incompetent and inadmissible evidence.

However, the rule that opinion evidence is not admissible is not absolute. Frequently, the only possible or practical method of getting proof of the fact in issue is by means of opinion evidence. If, from the nature of the subject matter, no better evidence can be obtained and opinion evidence will aid the triers of fact in their search for the truth, the judge in his discretion may admit the evidence even though it consists of an opinion. The law does

245

not look with favor on opinion evidence, and such evidence is not admitted unless it is required to prevent a failure of justice.

Over the years, the courts and legislatures have approved dozens of exceptions to the opinion evidence rule to the extent that some opinion evidence is admissible in almost every case. These rules of exception have developed in two areas: (1) opinions of non-experts and (2) opinions of expert witnesses. Admissibility rules that apply to non-expert witnesses do not necessarily apply to expert witnesses. Therefore, these rules are discussed separately.

Sometimes criminal justice personnel testify as expert witnesses when they have so qualified, as will be explained in future sections. However, in most instances, criminal justice personnel testify as non-expert witnesses; i.e., they testify as to facts within their personal knowledge, observation or recollection. Often it is unnecessary to determine whether a witness is an expert witness or a non-expert witness— even when opinion testimony is given—because some exceptions to the opinion rule are common to both expert and non-expert witnesses.

In the sections that follow, not only are the general rules relating to opinion evidence of non-expert and expert witnesses considered, but some of the specific instances, especially those instances that are common in criminal justice situations, are discussed in more detail.

§ 11.2 Definitions and distinctions

Before discussing the general rules and the exceptions relating to opinion testimony of expert and non-expert witnesses, some definitions are necessary to assist in understanding these rules.

a. Opinion evidence

Opinion evidence is defined in *Black's Law Dictionary*[1] as "evidence of what the witness thinks, believes, or infers in regard to facts in dispute, as distinguished from his personal knowledge of the facts themselves." The term refers to opinions declared from the witness stand, as distinguished from extrajudicial opinions.

b. Expert witness

An expert witness is a person who is particularly skilled, learned or experienced in a particular art, science, trade, business, profession or vocation, and is a person who has gained a thorough knowledge of a subject which is not possessed by the average layperson in regard to matters con-

---

1 BLACK'S LAW DICTIONARY (5th ed. 1979).

nected therewith. In *Black's Law Dictionary*2 an expert witness is defined as "one who by reason of education or specialized experience possesses superior knowledge respecting a subject about which persons having no particular training are incapable of forming an accurate opinion or deducing correct conclusions." In one case, an expert witness was defined as one who has acquired the ability to deduce correct inferences from hypothetically stated facts or from facts involving scientific or technical knowledge.3

c. Non-expert witness

A non-expert witness, or lay witness, is one who is not particularly skilled, learned or experienced in the particular area that is at issue in the court. One who is an expert in one field is deemed a lay witness when he is on the stand to testify in another area. The lay witness bases his conclusions on facts personally observed, while the expert witness, who must qualify as such by establishing that he has some special skill, knowledge or experience, may base his opinions on facts of his own observation or on evidence presented by other witnesses.

§ 11.3 Admissibility of non-expert opinions

Rule 701

Opinion Testimony by Lay Witnesses

If the witness is not testifying as an expert, the witness' testimony in the form of opinions or inferences is limited to those opinions or inferences which are (a) rationally based on the perception of the witness and (b) helpful to a clear understanding of the witness' testimony or the determination of a fact in issue.4

The general rule is that lay or "non-expert" witnesses must state facts or give evidence based upon their own knowledge and observations. They cannot give conclusions or opinions. Before looking at the exceptions, it should be noted that some observations, although appearing to be opinions, are not considered such at law. For example, when a person testifies as to what he observes, hears or smells, the testimony is considered a statement

---

2 BLACK'S LAW DICTIONARY (5th ed. 1979).

3 City of Chicago v. Lehmann, 262 Ill. 468, 104 N.E. 829 (1914). "Expert witness" will be further defined in later sections of this chapter.

4 FED. R. EVID. 701.

of fact and not a conclusion or opinion—even though in most instances what one states as what he saw is actually an opinion of what he saw.5 Much effort has been expended to confine the testimony of witnesses to statements of what they saw, heard or otherwise observed, as distinguished from inferences or opinions formed as a result of such observations. The distinction between opinion and fact is very difficult to draw.

The modern tendency is to regard it as more important to get to the truth of the matter than to quibble over distinctions which are in many cases imperceptible.6 When, however, the opinions of witnesses are clearly opinions or inferences based upon facts rather than opinions as to what the facts are, the opinion evidence rule comes into play.

The lay witness may state a relevant opinion if: (1) it is based on facts that he has observed; (2) the opinion is of a kind that normal persons form constantly and correctly; and (3) the witness cannot adequately or accurately describe the facts upon which his opinion is based.7 The general rule is that as a condition of stating his opinion, the witness must state the facts on which such opinion is based. The enumeration of facts not only goes to show the competency of the witness but also affords an opportunity for testing the reasonableness of the inference, as a witness will not be permitted to state an opinion inconsistent with, or finding no support in, the facts stated by him.

The purpose of authorizing a non-expert witness to testify as to his opinion is to help the jury or fact finder obtain a clear understanding of the testimony or the determination of a fact in issue. However, opinion testimony is admissible only after a showing that the witness' perceptions cannot adequately be conveyed except through opinions.8 To allow opinion testimony *absent* a showing of the inadequacy of other means of expression is to invade the province of the jury.

Apparently extending the use of opinion evidence by non-expert witnesses, Federal Rule of Evidence 701(b) allows opinions or inferences if they are merely "helpful" to clarify the witness' testimony or to aid in the determination of a factual issue. It would seem that the rule broadens the circumstances under which a lay witness may give an opinion or inference based upon his own personal observations. This rule also apparently eliminates the requirement that the witness state the facts that led to such an opinion. This is left for cross-examination.

---

5   State v. Riggs, 32 Wash. 2d 281, 201 P.2d 219 (1949).
6   Koslowski v. State, 248 Ala. 304, 27 So. 2d 818 (1946).
7   State v. Garver, 190 Or. 291, 225 P.2d 771 (1950); *see also* State v. Collins, 294 P. 957 (Mont. 1930); *see also* Hurst v. United States, 882 F.2d 306 (8th Cir. 1989).
8   Kight v. State, 512 So. 2d 922 (Fla. 1987).

Making reference to the guidelines provided in the Federal Rules of Evidence, a state court commented that, under the Federal Rules of Evidence, governing opinion testimony by lay witnesses, opinion testimony is admissible as long as the witness is competent to testify, that is, as long as the witness has perceived the events upon which his opinion is based.[9] After explaining that Pennsylvania had adopted Federal Rules 701 and 704, the Superior Court of Pennsylvania made this interpretation:

> Under these rules, opinion testimony is admissible as long as the witness is competent to testify—that is, as long as the witness has perceived the events upon which his opinion is based.

Rule 701, however, does not justify introduction of opinion evidence when the facts are clear and the jury can draw its own conclusion from the facts.[10]

Rule 701, although limiting the admissibility of opinion testimony, by lay witnesses, did not prohibit the defendant's cousin and parole officer from testifying that the person depicted in bank surveillance photographs taken during the robbery was the defendant.[11]

In interpreting Rule 701, a federal court determined that it was not an abuse of discretion, nor violative of the confrontation clause of the Constitution, to permit a parole officer to identify the defendant as the robber depicted in a bank surveillance photograph, in which the robber was wearing a scarf over his face, and when the defendant had grown a full beard prior to trial.[12]

It is obvious that some evidence would be unavailable to the fact finders if opinion evidence were not authorized. Examples of opinion testimony are discussed in the following section.

§ 11.4 Subjects of non-expert opinions

a. Age

A competent observer may be permitted to state his estimate or opinion as to the age of a person, whether the person is an adult, a minor or a young child.[13] Necessity often requires that the opinion of the witness as to the age of a person be used because it is often impossible to testify to the exact age of another person. For example, a North Carolina court commented:

---

9   Commonwealth v. Neiswonger, 338 Pa. Super. 625, 488 A.2d 68 (1985).
10 United States v. Carlock, 806 F.2d 535 (5th Cir. 1986), *cert. denied,* 480 U.S. 950, 107 S. Ct. 1611, 94 L.Ed. 2d 798 (1987).
11 United States v. Langford, 802 F.2d 1176 (9th Cir. 1986). *See* case in Part II, *infra.*
12 United States v. Farnsworth, 729 F.2d 1158 (8th Cir. 1984).
13 Watson v. State, 236 Ind. 239, 140 N.E.2d 109 (1957).

The opinion of a lay witness concerning the age of an accused is admissible into evidence when the witness has had adequate opportunity to observe the accused.14

To state the rule succinctly, if the witness has had adequate opportunity to observe the accused and if it is impossible to determine the exact age of the person, then opinion evidence of the lay witness concerning age is admissible. If, however, the exact age of an individual is available from documents or other sources, and all of the facts can be placed before the triers of fact, then an estimate of age is unnecessary and should be refused admission.15

b. Appearances

If the conditions mentioned in earlier sections are met, testimony concerning the appearance of another is admissible. For example, in a bank robbery case, testimony that the teller who handed over the money was "distraught and upset" was admissible.16 In a case involving the question of competency of an elderly person, a witness testified to circumstances of the person's irrational behavior, such as disgusting eating habits, irritability and wild expressions. When asked: "What was the appearance of this man at that time with reference to his being rational or irrational?", the witness' answer "irrational," was competent evidence. The court explained that to say that a man acts rationally or irrationally is merely to describe an outward manifestation drawn from observed facts. It is the ultimate fact, deduced from evidentiary facts coming under observation, but it is so transitory and evanescent as to be like drunkenness in that it is easy of detection and difficult of explanation.17

c. Conduct

A non-expert witness may describe the acts, conduct and demeanor of a person under investigation if necessary to enable the jury to draw a correct inference. In such instance, the witness should be required—as far as is possible—to state the facts on which he based his opinions. As stated in one case, the rule that witnesses in describing conduct should tell what they saw and heard does not preclude the use of words of summary description, and trials should not be delayed and witnesses made inarticulate by too many objections or rulings as to the use of such descriptive words.18

---

14 State v. Cobb, 295 N.C. 1, 243 S.E. 759 (1978).
15 State v. Robinson, 32 Or. 43, 48 P. 357 (1897).
16 Cole v. United States, 327 F.2d 360 (9th Cir. 1964); see also United States v. Brown, 490 F.2d 748 (D.C. Cir. 1973).
17 Holland v. Zollner, 102 Cal. 633, 36 P. 930 (1894).
18 Kane v. Fields Corner Grille, 341 Mass. 640, 171 N.E.2d 287 (1961).

In accordance with this rule of necessity, witnesses have been permitted to testify that a person acted "kind of sneaky,"[19] or "in an arrogant manner,"[20] and that a person was "trying to get away."[21]

In approving testimony concerning the appearance and conduct of a witness, a California court decided that the trial court erred in allowing a police officer to testify that when they interviewed the child they believed that she was truthful in her accusations against the defendant, which were repeated in her trial testimony. These opinions, as to the state of mind of the child, were conclusions of a lay witness without adequate facts to support the conclusions.[22]

However, testimony of customs investigators who observed legs and feet through the underside of a trailer and then concluded that the defendant and his companion had entered the trailer, was admissible under the Federal Rules of Evidence governing the admission of opinion testimony by lay witnesses.[23] Also, testimony by narcotic agents that a narcotic transaction was taking place was properly admitted as opinion testimony when the agents had offered opinions as to the nature of the events that they had personally viewed.[24]

d. Distance and space

In criminal cases it is often necessary to testify concerning distances and space between objects. While it is obviously preferable to introduce evidence to show exact distances, in some instances this is not practical and opinion evidence becomes necessary. As a result, an ordinary witness may give his estimate of distances, provided that he is cognizant of the facts on which the estimate is based. The courts have held that a witness may state the limitations in point of distance of human hearing or of human vision of objects under given conditions. For example, in one case the court admitted a sheriff's testimony that the plaintiff's taillights would not have been visible at 500 feet, as required by statute. The court allowed this, explaining that the sheriff was testifying from what he had learned from experience.[25] On the other hand, a witness will not be permitted to give an estimate of a distance when facts can be stated from which the jury could form a judgment as to the distance.[26]

19　Commonwealth v. Borasky, 214 Mass. 313, 101 N.E. 377 (1913).
20　*Ibid.*
21　Lewis v. State, 49 Ala. 1 (1871).
22　People v. Sergill, 138 Cal. App. 3d 34, 187 Cal. Rptr. 497 (1982).
23　United States v. Valdez, 880 F.2d 1230 (11th Cir. 1989).
24　United States v. Young, 745 F.2d 733 (2d Cir. 1984).
25　Mundy v. Olds, 120 N.W.2d 469 (Iowa 1963).
26　Alabama Power Co. v. Brown, 250 Ala. 167, 87 So. 608 (1921).

e. Time and duration

Relying on the same rationale as in the previous instances, the courts have authorized witnesses to make estimates of elapsed time.[27] However, if the witness can give specifics from which the jury can make its own estimate of time, then the opinion evidence regarding the passage of time is inadmissible.

f. Intoxication and drug use

When it is proper to permit non-expert opinion evidence, the witness may state his opinion without first detailing the facts on which he bases such opinion, if the matter testified about is not of a complex nature. Intoxication is such a matter.[28] Therefore, a police officer, who testified that during his years as an officer he had observed many persons under the influence of intoxicating liquor, was permitted to testify that he had observed the defendant on the day in question and had formed an opinion that the defendant "was drunk." A Rhode Island court noted that the better and more progressive rule is to allow the shorthand rendition of such external appearances as intoxication by lay witnesses as long as the witness has had an opportunity to observe the person and to give concrete details on which the inference or description is founded.[29] Opinion evidence of intoxication is not restricted to expert testimony.[30] However, the lay witness must show that he had ample opportunity to observe the defendant.

As more and more drug cases have reached the reviewing courts, a body of law has developed concerning the opinion testimony of agents relating to the identity and the use of drugs. As an example, in a federal case the court held that, although the government witness was not an expert on drugs and had used cocaine only once before, his testimony was admissible when he stated that the substance given to him by the accused—and used by the witness—was cocaine.[31] Also, lay witnesses were permitted to testify that the substance they obtained from the defendant in exchange for a car was cocaine; both men testified to sampling the alleged cocaine by injecting it into their veins, and both testified that they had previously used cocaine extensively.[32]

---

27 Allison v. Wall, 121 Ga. 822, 49 S.E. 831 (1905).
28 Gladden v. State, 36 Ala. App. 197, 54 So. 2d 607 (1951). *But see* State v. Steale, 211 N.W.2d 855 (N.D. 1973).
29 State v. Fogarty, 433 A.2d 972 (R.I. 1981).
30 People v. Ravey, 122 Cal. App. 2d 699, 265 P.2d 154 (1954); State v. Huff, 202 S.E.2d 342 (N.C. 1974).
31 United States v. Tyler, CMA, 17 M.J. 381 (1984).
32 State v. Haller, 363 S.E.2d 719 (W. Va. 1987).

It is error, however, for an arresting officer to give an opinion concerning the legal definition of driving "while impaired." The officer may give facts which would lead to this conclusion, but the trial court, not the witness, must explain and define the law to the jury.33

As indicated in a prior section, the Pennsylvania Superior Court held that, under the Federal Rules of Evidence governing opinion testimony by lay witnesses, opinion testimony is admissible as long as the witness is competent to testify, that is, as long as the witness perceived events upon which his opinion is based.34 In applying this rule, the court noted that, under Pennsylvania law, opinion testimony is admissible to prove a state of intoxication. The court explained that intoxication is not a condition outside the realm of understanding or powers of observation of ordinary persons. While expert opinions may be used to establish intoxication, this does not prohibit non-expert testimony. Therefore, a police officer, if he has perceived a defendant's appearance and acts, is competent to testify regarding his opinion as to the defendant's state of intoxication and ability to drive a vehicle safely.

After restating Rule 701, the Supreme Court of Rhode Island agreed that the rule permits a non-expert witness to testify to opinions that are (a) rationally based on the witness' perceptions and (b) helpful to determine a factual issue in the case.35 In this case the defendant was convicted of reckless driving and operating a motor vehicle under the influence of intoxicants, resulting in death. On appeal the defendant argued that the trial court erred in allowing a passenger of the other vehicle to give his opinion as to the speed of the defendant's oncoming car, as the defendant and the operator of the other vehicle were not allowed to give their opinion as to the speed of the two vehicles. The court held that, although the judge may have erred in the ruling concerning the defendant and the other vehicle's operator, this was no reason to allow the error to continue with respect to the passenger's testimony. As the witness perceived the events and that witness' perception was helpful to determine the issue in the case, the witness properly was allowed to testify even though she was a non-expert witness.

g. Sanity or mental condition

A non-expert witness, in response to purely hypothetical questions stating the facts, may not give an opinion on the question of sanity. But by the great weight of authority, one who, in the opinion of the trial judge, shows adequate means of becoming acquainted with the person whose mental condition is in issue, and who can detail the facts and circum-

---

33 State v. Harrell, 386 S.E.2d 103 (N.C. App. 1989).
34 Commonwealth v. Neiswonger, 338 Pa. Super. 626, 488 A.2d 68 (1985).
35 State v. St. Jean, 554 A.2d 206 (R.I. 1989).

stances concerning his acquaintance and the acts, conduct and conversation upon which his conclusion is based, may give his opinion on the question of sanity.36 Before a non-expert witness is competent to testify as to the sanity or insanity of another person, he must show an acquaintance of such intimacy and duration as to indicate clearly that his testimony would be of value in determining the issue. In some states the conclusion must be based upon the witness' testimony as to specific instances of behavior or conduct.37 This rule was applied in a Pennsylvania case, in which the court held that a layperson may express a general opinion as to mental capacity of the defendant if he states facts and observations upon which his opinion is based, and if the facts and observations are reasonably related in time and circumstance to the period during which sanity is at issue.38

There is no requirement as to the length of acquaintance. For example, the testimony of two police officers who were with the defendant for approximately ten and four hours respectively was not disqualified on the ground that the witnesses had insufficient opportunity of observing the defendant. The fact that the officers had not known the defendant for a longer period went to the weight of the testimony on the sanity question and not to its admissibility.39

h. Identification

Often the only adequate way that a person can be identified is by opinion. Therefore, the identification of a person need not be made in positive terms. A witness may testify that an accused "resembles" or "looks like" the person who committed the crime. He may testify that in his opinion the accused is the person who perpetrated the crime. The sound of a voice also may be the basis of an opinion as to the identity of a person.

This rule also applies to the identity of things. A person who has tasted alcoholic beverages before may testify as to the nature of a drink. In a prosecution for destroying property by means of dynamite, witnesses familiar with the odor were held properly permitted to testify to having smelled dynamite after the explosion.40 The court, in permitting the testimony, explained, "Most persons would probably find it difficult to describe the odor of a rose, whiskey, beer or Limburger cheese, but this difficulty could

---

36 Rupert v. People, 429 P.2d 276 (Colo. 1967); McCall v. State, 408 N.E.2d 1218 (Ind. 1980).
37 McKenzie v. United States, 266 F.2d 524 (10th Cir. 1959); United States v. Milne, 487 F.2d 1232 (5th Cir. 1973).
38 Commonwealth v. Young, 276 Pa. Super. 409, 419 A.2d 523 (1980); see also State v. Crenshaw, 27 Wash. App. 326, 617 P.2d 1041 (1980).
39 Kaufman v. United States, 350 F.2d 408 (8th Cir. 1965).
40 People v. Reed, 333 Ill. 397, 164 N.E. 847 (1929).

scarcely be regarded as affecting the value of their testimony that they were familiar with and recognized the particular odor."

Identification by law enforcement officials often becomes a critical issue at trial. If such identification is a crucial issue and if the officer had reasonable grounds for making the identification, the evidence will generally be admitted. For example, in the case of *People v. Mixon,* the testimony of a police officer identifying the defendant as the person shown in the surveillance photograph was proper, as adequate testimony was not available from other sources. The court held that, if the witness is testifying from personal knowledge of the defendant's appearance at or before the time when the photograph was taken, and if the testimony will aid the trier of fact in determining "the crucial identity issue," the evidence will be admitted.[41] In a federal case, the reviewing court explained that the trial court did not err in permitting a witness to testify that the man in the photograph taken by the bank's surveillance camera at the time of the bank robbery was the defendant, even though the witness had seen the defendant only once before at a party about four months prior to the robbery. The court held that the amount of time that the witness had to observe the defendant goes to the weight to be accorded to the testimony by the jury rather than to the admissibility of the testimony.[42]

When lay witnesses are able to make identifications based on their familiarity with the characteristics of the defendant that are not immediately observable by the jury at the trial, the lay-witness testimony is admissible. Following this reasoning, the Ninth Circuit affirmed the trial court's ruling that permitted the defendant's cousin, who had known the defendant all his life, and the defendant's parole officer, who had seen the defendant approximately 50 times, to testify that the person depicted in the bank surveillance photographs taken during the robbery was the defendant.[43]

i. Handwriting

The opinion of a lay witness as to a person's handwriting, of which he has knowledge, is admissible. As handwriting testimony involves a process of comparison, the lay witness is not permitted to fortify his opinion by making a physical comparison, in court, of the contested writing with genuine standards, for the reason that he has no more skill for making the comparison than do the jurors.[44] The lay witness must show that he had an

---

41 People v. Mixon, 129 Cal. App. 3d 118, 180 Cal. Rptr. 772 (1982).
42 United States v. Jackson, 688 F.2d 1121 (7th Cir. 1982), *cert. denied,* 460 U.S. 1043 (1983).
43 United States v. Langford, 802 F.2d 1176 (9th Cir. 1986). *See* case in Part II, *infra. See also* United States v. Farnsworth, 729 F.2d 1158 (8th Cir. 1984).
44 Bowles v. Kennemore, 139 F.2d 541 (4th Cir. 1944).

opportunity to become familiar with the handwriting at issue. This can be accomplished by showing that the witnesses corresponded with the writer, handled documents written by him, or by other means.45

In an action for misapplying and converting travelers checks, the Eleventh Circuit reasoned that the trial court did not err in admitting evidence of two co-workers' identification of the defendant's handwriting on the converted checks.46 In this case both lay witnesses testified that they were familiar with the defendant's handwriting and that, in their opinion, it matched or was similar to the handwriting on the checks. The court explained that this testimony was valid under Federal Rules 701 and 901B, which allow for the admission of non-expert opinion as to the genuineness of handwriting, based upon familiarity not acquired for the purpose of the litigation.

j. Speed

Most courts admit the testimony of a non-expert witness relating to the speed of a motor vehicle, provided that he had sufficient opportunity to observe the vehicle in motion. In automobile negligence suits, testimony of witnesses as to speed is admissible when the witnesses are experienced drivers and were in a position to observe under such circumstances and for a sufficient time to remove their conclusions from the realm of speculation.47 If a witness is shown to have been in a position to observe the speed of a train, and from such observation, he formed an opinion as to such speed, he should be permitted to give his opinion, whether he is shown to be experienced or inexperienced in estimating the speed of trains.48 While lay witnesses generally are permitted to express opinion estimates of vehicle speed in terms such as "fast," "slow," "excessive" and the like, some opinions have been found to be conclusory in nature as well as lacking in evidentiary value.49 The court in its discretion may disallow such opinion evidence.

---

45 State v. Fortier, 427 A.2d 1317 (R.I. 1981).

46 United States v. Barker, 735 F.2d 1280 (11th Cir. 1984).

47 Ohio Casualty Co. v. Landon, 1 Ohio App. 2d 317, 30 Ohio Op. 2d 313, 204 N.E.2d 566 (1961); Womack v. Pierson, 299 So. 2d 279 (La. 1974).

48 Central of Georgia R.R. v. Luther, 129 Ga. App. 178, 196 S.E.2d 149 (1973).

49 Catina v. Maree, 498 Pa. 433, 447 A.2d 228 (1982).

§ 11.5   Opinions of experts

> **Rule 702**
>
> **TESTIMONY BY EXPERTS**
>
> If scientific, technical, or other specialized knowledge will assist the trier of fact to understand the evidence or to determine a fact in issue, a witness qualified as an expert by knowledge, skill, experience, training, or education, may testify thereto in the form of an opinion or otherwise.50

Of particular importance in criminal cases is the opinion of expert witnesses. Without the testimony of experts, it would be very difficult for the jury to arrive at a conclusion concerning what took place. Over the years, laws relating to the use of expert opinion evidence have developed differently than those relating to the use of non-expert opinion evidence. While the non-expert, with some exceptions, may testify only if he has firsthand knowledge of the incident, the expert is generally permitted to give an opinion, even if he does not have firsthand knowledge, when he *establishes* himself as an expert and when the subject matter is such that the jury cannot necessarily be expected to draw correct information from the facts only.

To warrant the use of expert testimony, two elements are required: (1) the subject of the inference must be so distinctly related to some science, profession, business or occupation as to be beyond the knowledge of the average layperson; and (2) the witness must have such skill, knowledge or experience in the field or calling as to make it appear that his opinion or inference would probably aid the jury in its search for the truth.51 The trial court has broad discretion in determining whether to admit expert testimony.52 The judge decides initially whether the opinion evidence of the expert witness would aid the court or jury in reaching a conclusion and whether the witnesses offered as experts have the peculiar knowledge or experience that would make their opinions helpful to the court or jury in determining the question at issue.

Other rules for the use of expert testimony have been handed down in various cases. In one case an Indiana court agreed that an expert may base his opinion in part "on a report that is either not in evidence or

---

50 Fed. R. Evid. 702.

51 Jenkins v. United States, 307 F.2d 637 (D.C. Cir. 1962); *see also* Higgs v. Hodges, 697 S.W.2d 943 (Ark. App. 1985).

52 United States v. Watson, 587 F.2d 365 (7th Cir. 1978).

inadmissible as substantive evidence because of the hearsay rule." The court continued: "In order for the opinion to be admissible, (1) the expert must have sufficient expertise to evaluate the reliability and accuracy of the report, (2) the report must be of a type normally found reliable, and (3) the report must be of a type customarily relied upon by the expert in the practice of his profession or expertise."53

Even though a witness qualifies as an expert, his testimony may not be permitted if there is an indication that his opinion was based on information that did not go beyond the experience and understanding of the average juror. For example, in *United States v. Hudson,* the Seventh Circuit held that the trial court did not err in excluding the testimony of an expert because it would not assist the trier of fact.54 In this case, in which the defendants were charged with entering a credit union with intent to commit larceny, the defendants offered the testimony of a psychologist concerning: (1) the effect of stress upon identification; (2) the difficulty of cross-racial identification; (3) an overview of the memory process; and (4) the impact of a short viewing period on the accuracy of an identification. In rejecting this expert testimony, the court concluded that:

> Such expert testimony will not aid the jury because it addresses an issue of which the jury generally is aware, and it will not contribute to their understanding of the particular dispute.

An expert need not be a formally educated professional, such as a physician or scientist. He may just as easily be a plumber, a carpenter or a police officer, if his technical expertise in his occupation would help the jury to understand a particular point in evidence.

Rule 702 of the Federal Rules of Evidence defines the conditions which must be present before an expert may testify. The rule states that if the testimony would "assist the trier of fact to understand the evidence or to determine a fact in issue," then an expert witness may testify. As the expert may testify as to matters that are specialized as well as scientific or technical, the rule makes plain its intention to allow expert testimony on matters that are not necessarily beyond the understanding of laymen. However, in interpreting this section, one court indicated that in a criminal prosecution, a district court was well within its discretion when it found that proffered expert-witness testimony of a criminologist about the inherent inaccuracies of eyewitness identification did not concern matters sufficiently beyond the understanding of lay jurors to be admissible.55

---

53 Duncan v. George Moser Leather Co., 408 N.E.2d 1332 (Ind. App. 1980).
54 United States v. Hudson, 884 F.2d 1016 (7th Cir. 1989). *See* United States v. de Soto, 88 F.2d 354 (7th Cir. 1989), in Part II, *infra.*
55 United States v. Purham, 725 F.2d 450 (8th Cir. 1984).

In another case, the Ninth Circuit approved the use of evidence regarding the post-traumatic stress disorder following forced prostitution.56 In a prosecution for kidnapping and transporting women in interstate commerce for immoral purposes, the trial court properly determined that the subject matter of expert testimony regarding post-traumatic stress disorder following forced prostitution was beyond the common knowledge of the average layperson. Therefore, testimony that would assist the jury to understand the evidence was properly admitted.

§ 11.6 Qualifications of an expert

An expert has been defined as one who has acquired special knowledge of the subject matter about which he is to testify—either by study of the recognized authorities or by practical experience—and who can assist and guide the jury in solving a problem which the jury is not able to solve because its knowledge is inadequate. A witness who by education and experience has become an expert in any art, science, profession or calling may be permitted to state his opinion as to a matter in which he is versed and which is material to the case, and he may also state the reasons for such opinion.

One who has the necessary training, experience and skill, and who has familiarized himself retrospectively with the necessary data, can form an expert opinion which is substantially superior to that of the average person and that is therefore useful to the jury. Any difference between the reliability of information currently received and that which is retrospectively obtained is a difference which goes merely to the weight of the evidence.57 Absence of certificates, memberships and the like does not in and of itself detract from the competency of an expert witness.58

When a witness is offered as an expert upon a matter in issue, his competency with respect to special skill or experience is determined by the court as a question preliminary to the admission of the testimony. There must be a finding by the court, in the absence of an admission or a waiver by the adverse party, that the witness is qualified. As there is no presumption that a witness is competent to give an opinion, it is incumbent upon the party offering the witness to show that the witness possesses the necessary learning, knowledge, skill or practical experience to enable him to give opinion testimony.

---

56 United States v. Winters, 729 F.2d 602 (9th Cir. 1984).
57 United States v. 60.14 Acres of Land, 362 F.2d 660 (3d Cir. 1966); Ziegler v. Crorfont, 516 P.2d 954 (Kan. 1973); Kline v. Lorillard, 878 F.2d 791 (4th Cir. 1989).
58 Tank v. Comm'r of Internal Revenue. 270 F.2d 477 (6th Cir. 1959); see also Moran v. Ford Motor Co., 476 F.2d 289 (8th Cir. 1973).

The weight and value of the testimony of an expert witness depends largely upon his qualifications as an expert, and these qualifications may be the subject of intensive inquiry by the opposing counsel.

§ 11.7 Selection of expert witness

Rule 706

Court Appointed Experts

(a) **Appointment.** The court may on its own motion or on the motion of any party enter an order to show cause why expert witnesses should not be appointed, and may request the parties to submit nominations. The court may appoint any expert witnesses agreed upon by the parties, and may appoint expert witnesses of its own selection. An expert witness shall not be appointed by the court unless the witness consents to act. A witness so appointed shall be informed of the witness' duties by the court in writing, a copy of which shall be filed with the clerk, or at a conference in which the parties shall have opportunity to participate. A witness so appointed shall advise the parties of the witness' findings, if any; the witness' deposition may be taken by any party; and the witness may be called to testify by the court or any party. The witness shall be subject to cross-examination by each party, including a party calling the witness.

(b) **Compensation.** Expert witnesses so appointed are entitled to reasonable compensation in whatever sum the court may allow. The compensation thus fixed is payable from funds which may be provided by law in criminal cases and civil actions and proceedings involving just compensation under the fifth amendment. In other civil actions and proceedings the compensation shall be paid by the parties in such proportion and at such time as the court directs, and thereafter charged in like manner as other costs.

(c) **Disclosure of appointment.** In the exercise of its discretion, the court may authorize disclosure to the jury of the fact that the court appointed the expert witness.

(d) **Parties' experts of own selection.** Nothing in this rule limits the parties in calling expert witnesses of their own selection.[59]

Generally the prosecutor, the defense attorney, or both, may request that experts be called to testify in a case. Obviously, each party will attempt to

---

[59] Fed. R. Evid. 706.

find an expert who would testify most favorably for his side. In some jurisdictions, and under Federal Rule 706, the judge may, on his own motion, appoint expert witnesses agreed upon by the parties, and he may appoint witnesses of his own selection. A witness so appointed shall be informed of his duties by the judge in writing, a copy of which will be filed with the clerk, or at a conference in which the parties will have the opportunity to participate. When an expert is appointed by the court, that expert must advise the parties of his findings, if any; his deposition may be taken by any party; and he may be called upon to testify by the judge or any party. Also, the expert is subject to cross-examination by each party, and the judge in the exercise of his discretion may also authorize disclosure to the jury of the fact that the expert was appointed by the judge.[60]

Rule 706 of the Federal Rules of Evidence reaffirms the long-established rule that the court has the power to appoint expert witnesses. Section (c) of the rule authorizes the court to disclose to the jury the fact that the court appointed the expert witness. It is anticipated that it will be the practice, in most situations, to disclose that the expert witness was appointed by the court, and it appears that this disclosure would give the expert witness more credibility—everything else being equal.

Noting the provisions of Rule 706, one federal court commented that:

> District courts enjoy broad discretion in deciding whether to appoint independent experts under Rule 706. As the Court of Appeals for the Ninth Circuit has stated, "under Rule 706, the court is free to appoint an expert of its own choosing without the consent of either party. . . . Appointments made under Rule 706 are reviewable only for abuse of discretion."[61]

§ 11.8   Examination of expert witness

Rule 703

Bases of Opinion Testimony by Experts

The facts or data in the particular case upon which an expert bases an opinion or inference may be those perceived by or made known to the expert at or before the hearing. If of a type reasonably relied upon by experts in the particular field in forming opinions or inferences upon the subject, the facts or data need not be admissible in evidence.[62]

---

60   *Ibid.*
61   United States v. Michigan, 680 F. Supp. 928 (1987).
62   FED. R. EVID. 703.

Rule 704

Opinion on Ultimate Issue

(a) Except as provided in subdivision (b), testimony in the form of an opinion or inference otherwise admissible is not objectionable because it embraces an ultimate issue to be decided by the trier of fact.

(b) No expert witness testifying with respect to the mental state or condition of a defendant in a criminal case may state an opinion or inference as to whether the defendant did or did not have the mental state or condition constituting an element of the crime charged or of a defense thereto. Such ultimate issues are matters for the trier of fact alone.[63]

After the witness has qualified as an expert, he is first examined by the party calling him as a witness. There are two avenues through which expert evidence may be presented to the jury: (1) through testimony of the witness based on his personal knowledge or observation, and (2) through testimony of the witness based upon a hypothetical question addressed to him. In the hypothetical-question situation, the pertinent facts are assumed to be true, or rather, they are assumed to be found true by the jury. An expert witness may base his opinion partly on facts of his own observation and partly on factual evidence of other witnesses, that is, hypothetically presented.[64] A hypothetical question need not include all of the facts in evidence, nor facts or theories advanced by opposing counsel. A trial judge may properly accept expert testimony predicated on facts which have been previously admitted in evidence as testimony by witnesses who themselves made relevant observations of primary facts. For example, a doctor called to testify may give his expert opinion as to whether facts already in evidence support an inference or causation or support a particular diagnosis or prognosis. Also, the expert witness may base his testimony on information from his knowledge of textbooks, treatises, articles and other publications in his field.

As a rule, expert testimony must be based on facts and evidence presented in the record. The Federal Rules of Evidence provide, however, that if the facts or data are of a type reasonably relied upon by experts in the particular field in forming opinions or inferences on the subject, the facts or data need not be admissible in evidence.[65] As will be discussed in a following section, the credibility of both the witness and the evidence may be challenged on cross-examination.

---

[63] FED. R. EVID. 704, as amended (1984).

[64] State v. David, 222 N.C. 242, 22 S.E.2d 633 (1942).

[65] FED. R. EVID. 703.

The testimony of the expert witness must meet the other rules of evidence. For example, the evidence must be relevant.66 In accordance with the general rules concerning use of opinion testimony, the majority rule is that expert opinion testimony will not be admitted if such testimony would invade the province of the jury.67 The rationale is that experts may give opinions, but not as to the "ultimate issue"; according to this reasoning, only the jury has that responsibility.68 However, according to the comments made by those who drafted it, Rule 704 of the Federal Rules of Evidence is intended to abolish the "ultimate issue" rule. Although there are many arguments favoring that position, in some instances opinion testimony will be held objectionable if it embraces the "ultimate issue," and the jury is competent to draw its own conclusions on an issue.69 This rule was applied by the District of Columbia Court of Appeals in holding that reversible error occurred when an expert witness was allowed to testify that the defendant's activities were part of a "classic team effort" at picking pockets. The court indicated that this was a conclusion for the jury to draw.70 But despite the fact that some rules provide that an expert witness may give his opinion even if it embraces an ultimate issue to be decided by the trier of fact, the witness' opinion may not be given as to the legal implications of the conduct.71

---

66 United States v. Green, 548 F.2d 1261 (6th Cir. 1977); *see also* United States v. Greybear, 883 F.2d 1382 (8th Cir. 1989) which held that Rule 703 does not permit an expert witness to circumvent the rules of hearsay by testifying that other experts, not present in the courtroom, corroborate his views.

67 United States v. Brown, 540 F.2d 1048 (10th Cir. 1976).

68 People v. Wilson, 25 Cal. 2d 341, 153 P.2d 720 (1944).

69 32 C.J.S. *Evidence,* §§ 446, 447.

70 Lampkins v. United States, 401 A.2d 966 (D.C. Ct. App. 1979). *But see* United States v. Espinosa, 827 F.2d 604 (9th Cir. 1987), in which the court held that in a prosecution for possession of cocaine with intent to distribute, the trial court properly admitted expert testimony by a police detective that the defendant used the apartment as a "stash pad" for money and narcotics, that ledgers found in the apartment contained the names of defendant's cocaine buyers, and that an exchange of packages was an exchange of narcotics for money. The court agreed that under Rule 704 a law enforcement officer may testify as an expert that the defendant's activities indicated that he acted in accordance with the usual *modus operandi,* even if the officer's opinion encompassed an ultimate issue to be resolved by the trier of fact.

71 United States v. Baskes, 649 F.2d 471 (7th Cir.), *cert. denied,* 450 U.S. 1000 (1981).

§ 11.9 Cross-examination of expert witness

Rule 705

Disclosure of Facts or Data Underlying Expert Opinion

The expert may testify in terms of opinion or inference and give reasons therefor without prior disclosure of the underlying facts or data, unless the court requires otherwise. The expert may in any event be required to disclose the underlying facts or data on cross-examination.72

An expert witness is ordinarily exposed to a probing inquiry on cross-examination in an attempt to challenge the opinion, as well as the facts and data on which the opinion is based. The rules governing the cross-examination of witnesses generally apply, and the trial court has broad discretion in allowing cross-examination of expert witnesses both as to manner and scope of cross-examination.73 The failure to allow cross-examination is grounds for reversal.74

On cross-examination, a witness may be interrogated concerning his knowledge of textbooks, treatises, articles and other publications in the field; he may be confronted with extracts from them and may be asked whether he is familiar with them and whether he agrees with them. Rule 705 of the Federal Rules of Evidence indicates that the expert witness is not required to disclose facts on direct examination unless the court requires them, but he may be required to disclose underlying facts on cross-examination.

In applying Rule 705 of the North Carolina General Statutes, a court of that state held that prior disclosure of facts and data underlying the opinion of an expert witness may be requested by the adverse party. However, the appeals court found that the trial court did not err in not requiring a pathologist who testified as to the victim's injury to disclose facts underlying his opinion as the defendant made no specific request pursuant to this rule.75 In another North Carolina case, the reviewing court affirmed the use of the underlying data used by a doctor in reaching an opinion about the defendant's mental condition to impeach the credibility

---

72 FED. R. EVID. 705.
73 Dean v. State, 211 Iowa 143, 233 N.W. 36 (1930).
74 Delta Engineering Corp. v. Scott, 322 F.2d 11 (5th Cir. 1963), *cert. denied,* 377 U.S. 905, 84 S. Ct. 1164, 12 L. Ed. 2d 176 (1964).
75 State v. Fullwood, 373 S.E.2d 518 (N.C. 1988).

of the expert when the underlying data was directly contrary to the expert opinion expressed during direct examination.[76]

An expert witness who bases an opinion to a significant degree on his readings may be cross-examined as to that opinion by reference to other reputable works in the field. The rationale for this rule is that such cross-examination tests the expert witness' credibility and reliability by inquiring into the extent of his familiarity with the authorities in his specialty and by asking him whether he agrees with them. The extracts with which the witness is confronted on cross-examination do not, however, become affirmative evidence in the case.[77]

Although the confrontation clause of the United States Constitution guarantees an opportunity for effective cross-examination of expert witnesses, it does not guarantee that the cross-examination be effective in whatever way and to whatever extent the defense may wish.[78] This point was explored in a Delaware case in which the defendant was convicted of murdering his fiancée. The state's case was based on circumstantial evidence which proceeded on the theory that the defendant had strangled his fiancée with a cat leash. To establish that the cat leash was the murder weapon, the state sought to prove that two hairs found on the leash were similar to the victim's hair and that one of these hairs had been forcibly removed. To prove these theories, the state relied upon the testimony of a special agent of the FBI.

The FBI expert witness testified that he was unable to recall the basis for his opinion that one of the hairs had been forcibly removed. On appeal, the Delaware Supreme Court reversed the conviction, proclaiming that the agent's inability to recall the method whereby he arrived at his opinion rendered the admission of that opinion violative of the respondent's rights under the confrontation clause of the Constitution.

The United States Supreme Court disagreed and held that the expert witness' inability to recall the basis of his opinion may be considered by the jury and given weight, but that his inability alone does not render the opinion inadmissible. As to the confrontation clause, the Court made this comment:

> [T]he Confrontation Clause is generally satisfied when the defense is given a full and fair opportunity to probe and expose those infirmities through cross-examination, thereby calling to the attention of the factfinder the reasons for giving scant weight to the witness' testimony. Accordingly, we hold that the admission into evidence of Agent Robillard's opinion did not offend the Confrontation Clause despite his inability to recall the basis for that opinion.

---

76 State v. Allen, 367 S.E.2d 626 (N.C. 1988).
77 Stottlemire v. Cawood, 215 F. Supp. 266 (D.D.C. 1963).
78 Delaware v. Fensterer, 474 U.S. 15, 106 S. Ct. 292 (1985).

§ 11.10   Subjects of expert testimony

In previous sections of this chapter, some of the general rules relating to the testimony of expert witnesses were discussed. It is apparent that there are numerous areas in which the expert can meet the qualifications and in fact assist the trier of fact in reaching a logical conclusion. Although it would be impossible to discuss here all of the areas in which expert testimony would be valuable, especially in criminal cases, some of the most common areas or subjects of expert testimony are discussed.

a.   Automobile accidents

Expert testimony of a police officer who arrived at the scene of the accident within one-half hour after its occurrence and who made close observations and measurements as to the point of collision of approaching vehicles is properly admitted.[79] Under Oklahoma law, a police officer who has had proper training and experience in the investigation of traffic accidents and has made studies of reports on the facts and causes of accidents may give expert testimony as to the point of impact when his opinion is based upon physical evidence observed at the scene of the collision.[80]

A patrolman who had 15 years' experience as a highway patrolman, who had investigated a considerable number of automobile accidents during that time, and who had kept abreast of the field of automobile investigations by attending various refresher courses at institutions was qualified as an expert to testify as to the speed of automobiles involved in an accident.[81] When, however, the police officer was not a witness to a nighttime collision, did not arrive at the scene until sometime thereafter, and observed no skid marks, he was not sufficiently qualified as an expert to give an opinion as to the speed of the automobile.[82]

In a 1981 case, the opinion testimony of a police officer regarding the speed of a vehicle just before collision was not admissible. The court explained that "the officer did not observe the collision and his basis for testifying as to unsafe speed cannot be said to be based upon any rational perception of the facts."[83] However, expert testimony was proper when the expert estimated the speed of the vehicle by interpreting the remains of a collision.[84]

It is proper for an expert witness to reconstruct an accident by basing

---

79   Rhynard v. Filori, 315 F.2d 176 (8th Cir. 1963).
80   Parris v. Harris, 351 F.2d 52 (10th Cir. 1965); *see also* Tipsword v. Melrose, 301 N.E.2d 614 (Ill. 1973), in which the court took the same position.
81   Bonner v. Polacari, 350 F.2d 493 (10th Cir. 1965).
82   Chesapeake & Ohio R. Co. v. Schlink, 276 F.2d 114 (6th Cir. 1960).
83   Belitz v. Suhr, 208 Neb. 280, 303 N.W.2d 284 (1981).
84   Bernier v. Boston Edison Co., 380 Mass. 372, 403 N.E.2d 391 (1980).

his opinion upon exhibits showing the physical facts as well as upon numerous photographs.[85] In an action arising out of the death of an automobile driver in a head-on collision to which there were no eyewitnesses, testimony of a safety engineer, who saw one of the automobiles only after it had been brought into a salvage yard and altered, was admissible when, in his personal examination of the automobile in the salvage yard, he had considered pertinent to the subject of his investigation only those parts of the automobile that were photographed immediately after the collision.[86]

b. Airplane crashes

Witnesses may qualify as experts in airplane accident cases. For example, one witness, who had been an assistant chief flight engineer for an airline for 11 years, who had investigated about 30 cases of airplane engine overspeed, who was familiar with hundreds of other cases through air force reports and similar sources, whose work was to initiate corrective action and procedures necessary to cope with overspeeds, who had participated in the investigation of between 30 and 40 airplane crashes, and who was the inventor of devices having to do with propeller vibration and featherability, was qualified to testify as an expert witness in an action arising out of the crash of an airplane which had an overspeeding propeller which could not be feathered.[87]

c. Physical and mental condition

A general practitioner may testify concerning matters within a medical specialty if his education or experiences, or both, involve demonstrable knowledge of the subject. A skilled witness on a medical subject need not be duly licensed to practice medicine. The general rule is that anyone who is shown to have special knowledge and skill in diagnosing and treating human ailments is qualified to testify as an expert, if his learning and training show that he is qualified to give an opinion on the particular issue in question.

It is not essential that the witness be a medical practitioner. Thus, nonmedical witnesses who have had experience in electrical work may testify to the effects of electrical shock upon the human body. Optometrists, whose training includes instruction in the symptoms of certain eye diseases, may testify to the presence of a cataract discovered in the course of fitting glasses. A toxicologist has been permitted to testify to the effect of oxalic acid, a poison, upon the human eye.[88] In view of the long and extensive training and experience of a medical technician, his lack of certification or

---

85   Frank's Plastering Co. v. Koenig, 341 F.2d 257 (8th Cir. 1965); Edwards v. Rudowicz, 368 S.W.2d 503 (Mo. 1963).

86   Leeper v. Thornton, 344 P.2d 1101 (Okla. 1959).

87   Noel v. United Aircraft Corp., 342 F.2d 232 (3d Cir. 1964).

88   Jenkins v. United States, 307 F.2d 637 (D.C. Cir. 1962).

license is without significance and does not affect his competency to perform blood grouping tests.[89]

The trial court is given great discretion in deciding whether testimony of the defendant's mental condition should be admitted. Some cases exemplify the rules relating to the admissibility of such evidence. In a New York case, the trial court permitted a psychiatrist for the defense to testify generally on the subject of the defendant's condition after considering the defendant's alcohol and drug consumption. The court, however, felt constrained to draw the line at the expression of an opinion regarding the defendant's ability to form intent because such an opinion went to the ultimate question and would usurp the jury's function.[90]

The reviewing court reasoned, however, that the failure to allow the expert to testify concerning the defendant's ability to form intent was error, and that the trial court should have exercised its discretion to decide whether the testimony of the defendant's intent would have been helpful to the jury.

In a murder case, another court held that expert testimony tending to prove or disprove the defendant's capacity to form the requisite criminal intent was properly not admitted.[91] Finally, in a third case, the court declared that the trial court erred in excluding an "expert opinion that the defendant was severely impaired in his ability to form an intent to kill and an intent to injure."[92]

Attempting to clarify the issue, a Virginia court, in discussing a psychiatrist's testimony about the defendant's mental condition, stated that "in order for such testimony to become relevant, it must be brought out of the realm of speculation and into the realm of reasonable probability; the law in this area deals with probabilities and not possibilities."

d. Summaries

Summaries of various complex transactions prepared by an accountant are admissible in evidence. An accountant who is qualified as an expert may testify that the summaries are based on matters in evidence.[93] The originals of the records thus summarized must be made available to the opposing party for examination in advance of trial.

e. Handwriting comparisons

Of special importance in the investigation of crime is evidence relating to handwriting. Testimony that an individual piece of writing was written

---

89 Lew Moon Cheung v. Rogers, 272 F.2d 354 (9th Cir. 1959).

90 People v. Cronin, 60 N.Y.2d 430, 458 N.E.2d 351 (1983).

91 Steele v. State, 97 Wis. 2d 72, 294 N.W.2d 2 (1980).

92 State v. Edmon, 28 Wash. App. 98, 621 P.2d 1310 (1981).

93 United States v. Pollack, 417 F.2d 240 (5th Cir. 1969). *See also* § 13.8, *infra*.

by a certain person, in the absence of actual observation of the event is, in reality, an opinion to which a witness may testify only if he has special qualifications to do so. To be qualified he must have expert training and experience in handwriting analysis in general, or he must be familiar with the handwriting of the individual in question. A witness who is not qualified can merely express an untrained comparison of two writings which are in evidence; his testimony would supply nothing to aid the jury.[94] An expert handwriting witness is allowed, in the course of his testimony as well as before he takes the stand, to fortify his views by comparing the disputed document with genuine standards.

The opinion of an expert regarding handwriting need not be based upon absolute certainty in order to be admissible.[95] In a prosecution for conspiracy to import marijuana, the trial court was within its discretion in allowing a handwriting expert to testify that he had a "high degree of belief" that the handwriting on a motel bill was that of the codefendant. Even though the expert's opinion was "somewhat equivocal," the testimony of the expert was admissible and the jury was permitted to give whatever weight to the testimony that it felt was justified.

Especially as the United States Supreme Court has made it clear that submitting handwriting specimens for comparison purposes does not violate the Constitution, the use of this type of evidence is important. In *Gilbert v. California,*[96] the Court held that compelling the suspect to give handwriting specimens did not violate the Fifth Amendment protection against self-incrimination.

f.   Typewriter comparisons

In earlier years, the experts who could qualify to identify handwriting comparisons were more in demand than those who could give testimony regarding typewritten documents; however, as the typewriter has become more popular, expert testimony as to typewritten documents has become of considerable importance. In many criminal cases it becomes necessary to show that a certain typewritten document was written on a specific machine that can be identified as belonging to or that was available to the accused. Not only can the expert testify as to the identity of the machine that was used when the document was written, but in some instances evidence has also been admitted as to the identity of the person who used a particular machine.

Expert evidence is generally admissible to prove that a document was typed on a particular type of machine, such as an Underwood typewriter, even though the typewriter itself is not located. Expert evidence is generally

---

94 Ryan v. United States, 384 F.2d 379 (1st Cir. 1967).
95 United States v. Herrera, 832 F.2d 833 (4th Cir. 1987).
96 388 U.S. 263, 87 S. Ct. 1951, 18 L. Ed. 2d 1178 (1967).

admissible to prove that a document was typed on a particular machine that was located by the police officer during an investigation.97 In making comparisons, the expert usually points out the particular mechanical characteristics and peculiarities of the machine which produced the written instrument. As in other instances, in order to give opinion testimony, the expert witness must show that he is qualified by training and experience to be an expert in his field. Experts are available from the FBI laboratory in Washington who can testify not only that a certain document was typed on a specific machine, but who also can often testify as to the make of the machine even if no particular machine has been located by the investigator.

In some instances, the court has allowed the opinion of an expert as to the identification of the operator of the typewriter. In doing so, the expert points out the individuality of the person typing the instrument. This identification is primarily predicated upon the manner of punctuation, the length of the lines, the depth of the indentation, and other indications that each person has a different touch.98

g. Polygraph examination results

As was explained in Chapter 6, courts have not generally admitted the results of lie detector, or polygraph, tests because such tests are not yet sufficiently reliable. However, such tests will be admitted if all parties consent.99 Even if the defense consents to the admissibility of the polygraph results, he may cross-examine the expert who testifies concerning the results. In such instance, the person who administered the examination may be questioned concerning his training at a recognized school, his experience, and his general education which would enable him to interpret the results of the test.

Even if the witness qualifies as an expert polygraph examiner, his testimony may be disallowed if it relates to matters outside his area of expertise.100 In a case in which an FBI agent was prosecuted for bribery and conspiracy to commit espionage, the defendant sought to introduce an expert, a professor of psychology, who would have testified that the psychological impact of failing the polygraph test included making damaging admissions. The court disallowed this testimony, as the expert was not qualified as an expert on false confessions and the jury was adequately equipped to comprehend and evaluate the defendant's claim that the experience of being told that he had failed a polygraph was a psychologically devastating experience.

---

97 People v. Storrs, 207 N.Y. 147, 100 N.E. 730 (1912).
98 Thomas v. State, 197 Okla. 450, 172 P.2d 973 (1946).
99 *See* § 6.19, *supra. See also* § 15.5, *infra,* for a general description of polygraph tests.
100 United States v. Miller, 874 F.2d 1255 (9th Cir. 1989).

h.　Voice print identification

Although voice print identification has not yet gained the degree of general acceptance necessary to make spectrogram results admissible generally, some states do authorize the use of voice print evidence with proper instructions.101 In *United States v. Williams,* the United States Court of Appeals for the Second Circuit approved the admission of spectrographic voice print evidence, stating that "spectrographic voice analysis evidence is not so inherently unreliable or misleading as to require its exclusion from the jury's consideration in every case."102

The testimony of a spectrographic voice identification expert was approved in the case of *United States v. Smith* in 1989.103 In this case identical twins were prosecuted for bank fraud, credit card fraud and conspiracy, in which they posed as bank employees and telephoned banks authorizing them to make fictitious wire transfers of nonexistent funds. The reviewing court determined that the lower court did not err in allowing a spectrographic voice identification expert to testify on the issue of identity when sufficient evidence of the reliability of the spectrographic voice identification was introduced at trial, including the expert's testimony about a number of studies performed in the field, as well as his own spectrographic analysis. The court also determined that the testimony was not likely to mislead the jury, as the jury had an opportunity to hear both the voice exemplars and the recorded conversations and to see the spectrograms.

There is evidence that the admission of spectrographic voice print evidence is becoming more acceptable, despite the fear expressed in one case that there is a minimal reserve of experts.104 At the present time, one would not be justified in assuming that expert opinions regarding the voice print are acceptable in all jurisdictions, but should look to each jurisdiction for a decision which would apply in that jurisdiction.

i.　Neutron activation analysis

Although some courts have authorized expert witnesses to testify concerning the results of neutron activation analysis, some of these courts have expressed doubts concerning expert opinions. For example, in a Minnesota Supreme Court case, the neutron activation technique was used to show that the defendant, who was accused of shooting a policeman, had fired a pistol shortly before his arrest. After the suspect was taken into custody, but prior to the time he was booked in the county jail, his hands were swabbed with a nitric acid solution. These swabs were sent to the Treasury Department

---

101　*See* § 15.10, *infra,* for a thorough discussion of the use of voice print.
102　United States v. Williams, 583 F.2d 1194 (2d Cir. 1978).
103　United States v. Smith, 869 F.2d 348 (7th Cir. 1989).
104　United States v. Addison, 498 F.2d 741 (D.C. Cir. 1974).

laboratory in Washington for neutron activation analysis, a testing procedure which can determine the presence and amount of certain chemical elements. Although admitting the testimony of a representative of the Treasury Department, the court expressed concern about the sweeping and unqualified manner in which expert testimony was offered. The court said:

> An expert witness can be permitted to testify that in his opinion the chemicals present on the defendant's hand may have resulted from the firing of a gun. He should not have been permitted to state, as he did, that this defendant had definitely fired a gun. To allow this testimony to stand without a cautionary instruction to the jury was technical error.

Notwithstanding this caution, the evidence was admissible, and the court concluded by stating:

> We believe that neutron activation analysis is a useful law enforcement technique and that the increasing use of technology in criminal investigations should not be inhibited but encouraged where consistent with the rights of the accused.[105]

The Supreme Court of Louisiana upheld the use of the neutron activation analysis in a prosecution for second degree murder.[106] In this case the expert witness testified regarding a neutron activation test made on samples taken from the defendant's hands to determine whether the defendant had fired a weapon. The expert witness testified that amounts of antimony and barium found on the defendant's hands were of the typical amounts found on the hands of a person who had recently discharged a firearm.

j.   Fingerprint identification

The average officer may testify that he obtained latent prints at the scene of the crime, but to show that these fingerprints are the prints of a known suspect usually requires an expert. As in other situations, the expert must show that by study, training and experience he is qualified as such. Such experts are available in the FBI laboratory as well as in many of the large law enforcement agencies.

For example, in a prosecution for burglary, the court properly found that a police officer, who was a seven year veteran of the county sheriff's department and who had had special training in footprints and latent prints, was qualified to testify as an expert.[107]

---

[105] State v. Spencer, 216 N.W.2d 131 (Minn. 1974).
[106] State v. Boyer, 406 So. 2d 143 (La. 1981).
[107] State v. Oliver, 742 P.2d 999 (Mont. 1987); see also United States v. Dozier, 28 M.J. 550 (A.C.M.R. 1989).

To give more weight to his testimony, the fingerprint expert will in almost all cases use blown-up photographs or other means to show the points of similarity upon which he based his conclusion.

k. Testimony relating to drug operations

Expert witnesses may be authorized to testify regarding the identification, use and value of narcotics as well as the language used by narcotics dealers. To qualify as an expert, the witness must show that his training and experience made him more knowledgeable on this subject than the fact finders in the case.[108] Qualified witnesses may be permitted to express their opinions as to the meaning of "drug lingo" included in a tape-recorded conversation to the extent that those opinions otherwise comport with the Federal Rules of Evidence.[109] In one case the court found that there was no abuse of discretion in allowing a paid informant to testify as an expert witness about drug transactions when the evidence indicated that the informant had participated in over 50 similar drug sales.[110]

A police officer may testify as an expert regarding drug-related practices if the evidence introduced indicates that the officer is qualified by experience, training and education. For example, a reviewing court held that the trial court did not abuse its discretion in a drug-trafficking prosecution by admitting a police officer's expert testimony regarding countersurveillance techniques employed by a drug dealers to avoid detection.[111]

§ 11.11   Experts from crime laboratories

Because of the limitations placed on the use of confessions, more reliance is being placed upon the use of real evidence and other evidence obtained by laboratory technicians. With the addition of crime laboratories in all parts of the country, experts from these laboratories will become more readily available. These experts must qualify as any other experts, through experience, training or knowledge before they can give opinions concerning the significance of laboratory tests and other scientific evidence. Expert testimony of this type is especially important in the field of ballistics, that is, comparing bullets found at the scene with those fired from a known weapon. No attempt will be made here to list all of the other areas in which a crime laboratory expert can testify, but these include tool mark

---

108 United States v. Agyen, 842 F.2d 203 (8th Cir.), *cert. denied*, 486 U.S. 1035, 108 S. Ct. 2012, 100 L. Ed. 2d 608 (1988).
109 United States v. Nunez, 658 F. Supp. 828 (D. Colo. 1987).
110 United States v. Anderson, 813 F. 2d 1450 (9th Cir. 1987).
111 United States v. deSoto, 885 F.2d 354 (7th Cir. 1989). *See* case in Part II, *infra*.

comparisons and testimony concerning glass and glass fractures, clothing, hairs and fibers.

§ 11.12 Summary

The general rule is that witnesses may not testify as to their opinions but must confine their testimony to facts perceived. This rule is based on the principle that the witnesses are to furnish the facts and the jury has the responsibility of reaching conclusions based on these facts.

There are, however, necessary exceptions to the general rule. These common sense exceptions have been developed so that the jury will have better information and because the courts have recognized that it is often impossible to give facts to describe all situations. For example, it is difficult to give facts to explain that a person was "nervous" or "irrational."

The rules relating to the exceptions to the "opinion" rule are discussed in two categories: those relating to non-expert opinions and those relating to expert opinions. If the ordinary lay witness cannot adequately or accurately describe the facts so as to enable the jurors to draw an intelligent conclusion, the witness is allowed to give his opinion. For example, a lay witness, in the usual case and with certain limitations, may give opinion testimony as to age, appearance, conduct, distance, mental condition, handwriting, identifications and speed of a vehicle.

The expert witness, when properly qualified, may also give his opinion. However, this exception is based on different reasoning, and therefore the rules are different. This opinion testimony is allowed because the expert, due to training, experience or knowledge, can give information on a specific subject substantially superior to that of the average person. The opinion of the expert witness does not have to be, and usually is not, based on direct observations of incidents which brought about the trial. His opinions may be based on hypothetical questions and on facts already presented by other witnesses.

Examples of subjects of expert testimony are: (1) speed of automobile from tire marks, (2) cause of death, (3) handwriting comparisons, (4) typewriter comparisons and (5) fingerprint comparisons.

Although justice personnel will not present the case in court, it is important that they understand the "opinion" rule and the exceptions to it. Justice personnel will be called upon to testify, and they should be aware in advance that some opinion testimony will be challenged. Knowledge of this rule as well as other rules of evidence will give them more confidence and should result in more credible testimony.

CHAPTER 12
HEARSAY RULE AND EXCEPTIONS

The determination that a statement is hearsay does not end the inquiry into admissibility; there must still be a further examination of the need for the statement at trial and the circumstantial guaranty of trustworthiness surrounding the making of the statement.
Zippo Mfg. Co. v. Rogers Imports, Inc., 216 F. Supp. 670 (S.D.N.Y. 1963)

§ 12.1 Introduction

One of the most commonly known rules of evidence is the hearsay rule. Many of those who have heard about the rule itself, however, are not familiar with the fact that the rule has many exceptions. In fact, one can argue that the rule has so many exceptions that more hearsay evidence is admitted than excluded. If the hearsay rule were applied without exceptions, it would be very difficult in many criminal cases to present sufficient facts to prove guilt, and certainly much valuable evidence would be excluded from consideration.

The general rule excluding hearsay statements is justified on several grounds. It is important to understand the historical reasons for the rule in order to understand the exceptions. If the reasons for the rule do not exist in a particular situation, then the evidence should be admitted to assist in determining the facts of the case. Some of the reasons for the hearsay rule are discussed in the following paragraphs.[1]

(1) The declarant was not under oath to speak the truth. Although the person who has repeated what someone else has said is under oath, the person who actually made the statement is not under oath as are witnesses who testify in court. Therefore, it is reasoned that the statement lacks trustworthinesss.

(2) The demeanor or conduct of the person who actually makes the statement cannot be observed by the judge and jury. Because the declarant is not present, the trier of fact cannot observe the demeanor of the declarant, which may shed some light on his credibility.

(3) There is a danger that the in-court witness who is reporting what was said by an out-of-court person may repeat the statement inaccurately.

(4) The declarant cannot be cross-examined. As pointed out earlier, one of the purposes of cross-examination is to elicit the truth. In a hearsay situation the person who actually made the statement cannot be cross-examined; hence, the adverse party is deprived of the opportunity to challenge his memory or sincerity.

Obviously, some hearsay is more reliable than others. The courts, in seeking to allow as much evidence into court as possible while sifting out unreliable evidence, have developed many exceptions to the hearsay rule. For each exception, however, there exists some justification to assure trustworthiness of the hearsay evidence.

Some types of evidence which may be challenged as hearsay have been discussed in other chapters of the book. For example, an out-of-court confession when repeated by another in court is, technically, hearsay. However, this evidence is admissible under one of the exceptions as discussed in Chapter 16. In Chapter 9 "past recollections recorded" is discussed. "Official records," "ancient documents" and "learned treatises" are considered in Chapter 13.

In this chapter, the hearsay rule is stated and defined, and some of the other exceptions to the hearsay rule are discussed. These include declarations against interest, dying declarations, spontaneous and excited utterances and family history.

---

1   Gaines v. Thomas, 241 S.C. 412, 128 S.E.2d 692 (1962); Donnelly v. United States, 228 U.S. 243, 33 S. Ct. 449, 57 L. Ed. 820 (1913).

§ 12.2　Definitions and statement of the hearsay rule

Rule 801

Definitions

The following definitions apply under this article:

(a) Statement. A "statement" is (1) an oral or written assertion or (2) nonverbal conduct of a person, if it is intended by the person as an assertion.

(b) Declarant. A "declarant" is a person who makes a statement.

(c) Hearsay. "Hearsay" is a statement, other than one made by the declarant while testifying at the trial or hearing, offered in evidence to prove the truth of the matter asserted.

(d) Statements which are not hearsay. A statement is not hearsay if—

(1) Prior statement by witness.—The declarant testifies at the trial or hearing and is subject to cross-examination concerning the statement, and the statement is (A) inconsistent with the declarant's testimony, and was given under oath subject to the penalty of perjury at a trial, hearing, or other proceeding, or in a deposition, or (B) consistent with the declarant's testimony and is offered to rebut an express or implied charge against the declarant of recent fabrication or improper influence or motive, or (C) one of identification of a person made after perceiving the person; or

(2) Admission by party-opponent.—The statement is offered against a party and is (A) the party's own statement in either an individual or a representative capacity or (B) a statement of which the party has manifested an adoption or belief in its truth, or (C) a statement made by a person authorized by the party to make a statement concerning the subject, or (D) a statement by the party's agent or servant concerning a matter within the scope of the agency or employment, made during the existence of the relationship, or (E) a statement made by a coconspirator of a party during the course and in furtherance of the conspiracy.[2]

The federal courts have been called upon to interpret the provisions of the Federal Rules. For example, one court decided that evidence was "not hearsay" as defined in Rule 801(d)(1)(A) when a witness, although present and testifying at the trial, claimed no recollection of either the underlying events described in his prior grand jury testimony or of the giving of the

---

2　FED. R. EVID. 801.

testimony itself.3 The trial court did not abuse its discretion in admitting the witness' grand jury testimony, under Rule 801(d)(1)(A), pertaining to prior inconsistent statements. When prior inconsistent statements come within the rule, they are defined as not being hearsay and may be admitted as substantive evidence.

Under Rule 801(d)(1)(A) if an out-of-court statement is inconsistent with the declarant's trial testimony and was given under the penalty of perjury at a deposition, trial, hearing, or like proceeding, the prior statement may be received as evidence and is not considered hearsay. For purposes of this rule the word "inconsistent" does not include only statements diametrically opposed or logically incompatible, but inconsistency may be found in evasive answers, silence or changes in position and, in addition, in reported change in memory.4

The purpose of Rule 801(d)(1)(C) is to permit introduction of identifications made by a witness when memory was fresh and there had been less opportunity for influence to be exerted upon him.5

The United States Supreme Court has determined that an out-of-court identification by the victim naming the defendant as the assailant was admissible as nonhearsay although the victim could not remember seeing the assailant.6

Several courts have made an effort to determine the meaning of section 801(d)(2)(E) of the rule. In one case the court commented that statements are in furtherance of the conspiracy as mentioned in the rule if they are intended to further its objectives; however, mere conversations between conspirators, merely narrative declarations, and causal admissions of culpability are not statements in furtherance of the conspiracy.7

In another case the Third Circuit determined that to apply the co-conspirator exception to the hearsay rule, there must be independent evidence of the conspiracy, i.e., evidence independent of proffered hearsay itself; such evidence must establish by a "clear preponderance" that the conspiracy existed and that both the defendants and the declarant were members of the conspiracy.8

---

3   United States v. DiCaro, 772 F.2d 1314 (7th Cir. 1985).
4   United States v. Williams, 737 F.2d 594 (7th Cir. 1984).
5   United States v. Marchand, 564 F.2d 983 (2d Cir. 1977).
6   United States v. Owens, 484 U.S. 554, 108 S. Ct. 838, 98 L. Ed. 2d 951 (1988).
7   United States v. Tille, 729 F.2d 615 (9th Cir. 1984); *see also Bootstrapping of Hearsay under Federal Rule of Evidence* 801(d)(2)(E). 70 Iowa L. Rev. 467 (1989).
8   United States v. Jannotti, 729 F.2d 213 (3d Cir. 1984) (citing Fed. R. Evid. 801 (d)(2)(E)); *see also* United States v. Disbrow, 768 F.2d 976 (8th Cir. 1985).

> ## Rule 802
>
> ## HEARSAY RULE
>
> Hearsay is not admissible except as provided by these rules or by other rules prescribed by the Supreme Court pursuant to statutory authority or by Act of Congress.[9]

As defined in Rule 801 of the Federal Rules of Evidence, hearsay is "a statement other than one made by the declarant while testifying at the trial or hearing offered in evidence to prove the truth of the matter asserted."[10] Another definition is that hearsay evidence is evidence which derives its value, not from the credit to be given to the witness upon the stand, but at least in part from the veracity and competency of some other person who is not testifying.

A "statement" as used in the hearsay definition is: (1) an oral or written assertion or (2) nonverbal conduct of a person, if it is intended by him as an assertion. Therefore, a statement as defined may include an actual verbal statement, a written statement or nonverbal conduct such as pointing to identify a suspect in a lineup. In the latter instance, the burden is placed upon the party claiming that the intention existed to show such intention.

A "declarant" as used in the definition of hearsay is a person who makes a statement.

Rule 801 also adds subsection (d), which specifically provides that certain statements are not to be considered hearsay under the definition as stated in that section.

In the simplest of terms, the "hearsay rule" is merely that hearsay evidence is not admissible. To state this differently, the rule is that courts will not receive testimony of the witness if that witness is repeating what he heard another person state outside of court when such statement is offered as an assertion to show the truth of matters asserted therein.

A flat statement that hearsay evidence is not admissible is not factual. The hearsay rule has so many exceptions that much hearsay is necessarily admissible in evidence. In later sections of this chapter, some of those exceptions and the reasons that the courts have given for making them are discussed.

One other point before leaving definitions: testimony is not "hearsay" when it is introduced to prove only that a statement was made and not to prove the truth of the statement.

9　FED. R. EVID. 802.
10　For another definition, see State v. Gibson, 502 S.W.2d 310 (Mo. 1973).

§ 12.3 History and development of the hearsay rule

In 1813, Chief Justice Marshall, in explaining the justification for the hearsay rule, stated, "Our lives, our liberty, and our property, are all concerned in the support of these rules, which have been matured by the wisdom of ages, and are now revered from their antiquity and the good sense in which they are founded. One of these rules is that hearsay evidence is by its own nature inadmissible." Justice Marshall went on to say that "[i]ts intrinsic weakness, its incompetency to satisfy the mind of the existence of the fact, and the frauds which might be practiced under its cover, combine to support the rule that hearsay evidence is totally inadmissible."11

The hearsay rule as we know it had its origin in England in the sixteenth century. Prior to the 1500s, juries were permitted to obtain evidence by consulting persons who were not called as witnesses. During this period, the jurors were not bound to decide the case on the basis of testimony given in open court, but were in fact chosen because they had some knowledge of the case.

As the pendulum began to swing to the other side, that is, as jurors began to be chosen only if they had no knowledge of the case that would influence their decision, the hearsay rule began its development. By 1700, the rule prohibiting the admission of hearsay statements was formulated in criminal cases. Over the centuries, exceptions to the hearsay rule have developed because of the strict exclusionary nature of the rule.

§ 12.4 Exceptions to the hearsay rule—general

Despite the fact that Justice Marshall argued that hearsay evidence should not be admitted because of its intrinsic weakness and incompetency, and despite the fact that he concluded that "[t]his court is not inclined to extend the exceptions further than they have already been carried,"12 exceptions have been made and exceptions have been extended.

In Rules 803 and 804 of the Federal Rules of Evidence, at least 27 specific exceptions are listed. The rules also provide for recognition of other exceptions "not specifically covered by any of the foregoing exceptions, but having comparable circumstantial guarantees of trustworthiness."13

The reasons for the hearsay rule in the first instance are: (1) the declarant is not under oath to speak the truth; (2) the demeanor of the person

---

11 Mima Queen and Child v. Heburn, 7 U.S. (3 Cranch) 290 (1813). *See* Donnelly v. United States, 288 U.S. 243, 33 S. Ct. 449, 57 L. Ed. 820 (1913) for a discussion of the history of the rules.

12 Mima Queen and Child v. Hepburn, *supra* note 11.

13 FED. R. EVID. 803. The exceptions noted in Rules 803 and 804 are not

who actually makes the statement cannot be observed by the judge and jury; (3) there is danger that the statement may be repeated inaccurately; and (4) the declarant cannot be cross-examined. The argument for exceptions is that if the purpose of the hearsay rule is not present in a specific case and if the interests of justice will be best served by admission of the statement into evidence, then the evidence should be admitted despite the hearsay rule. The rationale for allowing evidence into court even though it is hearsay is that if the reasons for the hearsay rule or most of the reasons do not exist in a specific situation, then the evidence should be admitted as an exception to the hearsay rule.

In the following sections, some of the exceptions that are most frequently encountered by criminal justice personnel are discussed along with the reasons for the exceptions.

§ 12.5 —Spontaneous and excited utterances

Rule 803

HEARSAY EXCEPTIONS; AVAILABILITY OF DECLARANT IMMATERIAL

* * *

(2) Excited utterance. A statement relating to a startling event or condition made while the declarant was under the stress of excitement caused by the event or condition.14

* * *

Hearsay testimony as to a statement or declaration may be admissible under an exception to the hearsay rule for a spontaneous exclamation if the legal requirements are met. The theory of this exception is that circumstances produce a condition of excitement which temporarily stills the capacity for reflection and produces utterances free of conscious fabrication. Spontaneity is the key factor. In order for such statements to be admissible, the judge must find that: (a) there was some occurrence startling enough to produce a nervous excitement in the declarant, which was sufficient to still his reflective faculties and thereby make his statements and declarations the unreflective and sincere expression of his actual impressions and beliefs; (b) the statement or declaration, even if not strictly contemporaneous with

included in this section. These rules are included in the Appendix, *infra,* and they should be examined before continuing.

14 FED. R. EVID. 803.

its exciting cause, was made before there had been time for such nervous excitement to lose dominion over the declarant's reflective faculties; (c) the statement or declaration related to such startling occurrence or the circumstances of such startling occurrence; and (d) the declarant had an opportunity to observe personally the matters asserted in his statement or declaration.[15] To illustrate, it was proper to admit a statement by the victim to onlookers at the scene of the robbery and stabbing that two men had taken her purse. As the declaration from one who had recently suffered an overpowering experience, it was clearly within the exception.[16] In a murder case the defendant appealed on the grounds that the lower court admitted testimony by a police officer that the victim said to the officer, "Cheese shot me. He lives in the area of 92nd and Ada."[17] After noting the requirements for a statement to be admitted as a spontaneous declaration, the reviewing court agreed with the lower court that the testimony by the officer of the victim's statement was proper as the victim was observed to be hysterical, in great pain, frightened and bleeding profusely.

However, testimony of police officers as to statements made by a nontestifying woman and a crowd of people, identifying the defendant as the perpetrator in a tavern shooting, constituted inadmissible hearsay, not qualifying as a spontaneous declaration.[18] In this case the court first stated that for testimony to qualify as a spontaneous declaration, three factors must be present: (1) an occurrence sufficiently startling to produce a spontaneous and unreflecting statement; (2) absence of time to fabricate; and (3) the statement must relate to the circumstances of the occurrence. After noting these requirements, the reviewing court held that the first two factors had not been met. The unnamed women's or the crowd's identification of the defendant in the squadrol could not be characterized as spontaneous and unreflecting statements made in the absence of time to fabricate.

In a prosecution for interstate transportation of a stolen vehicle, the reviewing court determined that the trial court committed reversible error in permitting a state trooper to testify concerning a C.B. radio transmission he received "indicating that two white, shirtless males were seen leaving an abandoned truck," as such statement constituted hearsay.[19] In order for hearsay evidence to be admitted under the excited utterances exception,

---

15 Potter v. Baker, 162 Ohio St. 488, 55 Ohio Op. 389, 124 N.E.2d 140 (1955); People v. Washington, 81 Cal. Rptr. 5, 459 P.2d 259 (1969); Forssen v. Rieke, 295 N.E.2d 84 (Ill. 1973).

16 Anderson v. State, 471 N.E.2d 291 (Ind. 1984).

17 People v. Wofford, 509 N.E.2d 1026 (Ill. 1987). *See* case in Part II, *infra.*

18 People v. Lopez, 504 N.E.2d 862 (Ill. 1987).

19 United States v. Cain, 587 F.2d 678 (5th Cir. 1979) Since the defendants were not seen at the time the transmission was made and the declarant had no reason to be in a state of excitement when he observed the two men or when he spoke.

there must be evidence to show that the declarant was in fact under stress or excitement.

To be admissible, the repeated statement must have been spontaneous and not made as a result of a series of questions to which answers were given, and most courts admit into evidence only the fact of the complaint, not the details thereof.[20] The fact that the statement goes beyond a mere description of the event may be considered in deciding whether the statement was sufficiently related to the event to be spontaneous as required by the excited utterance exception to the hearsay rule or whether the statement was a product of conscious reflection.[21]

The fact that the excited witness was a law enforcement agent does not exclude the admissibility of statements under the excited utterance exception to the hearsay rule.[22]

There is no definite time interval following an exciting event which will make the utterance fall under the exception to the hearsay rule. The general rule is that an utterance following an exciting event must be made soon enough thereafter that it can reasonably be considered a product of the stress of the excitement, rather than of reflection or deliberation. In one case, the court affirmed a conviction of first degree sexual assault after approving the admission of testimony from two witnesses as to what the 18-year-old victim told them approximately three hours after the alleged assault. Here, under the circumstances, the court properly held that the statements were unpremeditated and so connected with the event as to preclude the idea that they were products of a calculated story.

In determining if the time interval between the event and the declaration is such that the statement is not an excited utterance, the trial court will focus on the declarant's state of mind at the time that the statement was made. The shock of the event must be present at the time that the statement was made in order for the exception to apply. For example, in one case the court held that a statement made 15 minutes after a startling event—a high speed flight—was admissible as a spontaneous or excited utterance.[23] The court indicated that what must be taken into account is not only the length of the intervening time period, but also an assessment of the declarant's activities and attitudes in the meantime. In any case, another court made it quite clear that the defendant's statements made over two years after an alleged theft took place were inadmissible hearsay when there was every indication that the declarant was not under stress when the statement was uttered.[24]

---

20 People v. Damen, 28 Ill. 2d 464, 193 N.E.2d 25 (1963).

21 United States v. More, 791 F.2d 566 (7th Cir. 1986).

22 United States v. Obayhebona, 467 F. Supp. 329 (E.D.N.Y. 1985).

23 States v. Golden, 671 F.2d 367 (10th Cir. 1982), *cert. denied,* 456 U.S. 919, 102 S. Ct. 1777, 72 L. Ed. 2d 179 (1982).

24 United States v. Jackson, 789 F.2d 1305 (7th Cir. 1986).

§ 12.6 —Business and public records

Rule 803
HEARSAY EXCEPTIONS; AVAILABILITY OF DECLARANT IMMATERIAL

* * *

(6) Records of regularly conducted activity. A memorandum, report, record, or data compilation, in any form, of acts, events, conditions, opinions, or diagnoses, made at or near the time by, or from information transmitted by, a person with knowledge, if kept in the course of a regularly conducted business activity, and if it was the regular practice of that business activity to make the memorandum, report, record, or data compilation, all as shown by the testimony of the custodian or other qualified witness, unless the source of information or the method or circumstances of preparation indicate lack of trustworthiness. The term "business" as used in this paragraph includes business, institution, association, profession, occupation, and calling of every kind, whether or not conducted for profit.

(7) Absence of entry in records kept in accordance with the provisions of paragraph (6). Evidence that a matter is not included in the memoranda reports, records, or data compilations, in any form, kept in accordance with the provisions of paragraph (6), to prove the nonoccurrence or nonexistence of the matter, if the matter was of a kind of which a memorandum, report, record, or data compilation was regularly made and preserved, unless the sources of information or other circumstances indicate lack of trusthworthiness.

(8) Public records and reports. Records, reports, statements, or data compilations, in any form, of public offices or agencies, setting forth (A) the activities of the office or agency, or (B) matters observed pursuant to duty imposed by law as to which matters there was a duty to report, excluding, however, in criminal cases matters observed by police officers and other law enforcement personnel, or (C) in civil actions and proceedings and against the Government in criminal cases, factual findings resulting from an investigation made pursuant to authority granted by law, unless the sources of information or other circumstances indicate lack of trustworthiness.[25]

* * *

---

25 Fed. R. Evid. 803. *See also* Fed. R. Evid. 803(9) & (10) in Appendix, *infra.*

Many states have adopted the uniform business records act. This law provides that the record of an act, condition or event, insofar as it is relevant, shall be competent evidence if the custodian or other qualified witness testifies to its identity and the modes of its preparation, and if it was made in the regular course of business, at or near the time of the act, condition, or event, and if, in the opinion of the court, the sources of information, method and time of preparation were such as to justify its admission.

The purpose of such statute is to provide, as an exception to the hearsay rule, an acceptable substitute for the specific authentification of records kept in the ordinary course of business. The underlying rationale permitting this exception is that business records have the "earmark of reliability" or "probability of trustworthiness," as they reflect the day-to-day operations of the enterprise and are relied upon in the conduct of business.

Under the Federal Rules of Evidence, the uniform law concerning records has been greatly expanded. According to these rules, various business and public records may be the source of evidence as exceptions to the hearsay rule. Some of these are records of regularly conducted activity, public records and reports, records of vital statistics, etc. Not only is information from the records admissible, but evidence also may be introduced to prove the absence of public records or entries or the absence of an entry in records of regularly conducted activities.26 All such records are admissible under this rule, but they are subject to exclusion if the sources of the information or other circumstances indicate lack of trustworthiness. In interpreting the Federal Rules of Evidence, one court approved the admission of a ledger book in which illegal drug transactions were recorded. Although the business activity was an unlawful business, the ledger book was kept as a record in the course of a regularly conducted business activity and is encompassed by the exception to the hearsay rule.27

The United States Court of Appeals for the District of Columbia Circuit determined that a telex communication sent from a Korean bank, and alleged to constitute or summarize certain financial records, was not admissible as a business record and did not come within the provisions of Federal Rule of Evidence 803(6). The court interpreted the exception strictly and found three reasons for disqualifying the telex of a business record. In explaining the reasons for disqualification, the court first indicated that the record was made over two years after the making of the first deposit that it was alleged to reflect. Secondly, the telex was created specifically in response to a government subpoena for the defendant's records, not for regular business purposes. Finally, the circumstances of trustworthiness surrounding the making of the telex justified the trial court in refusing to admit the message. The court went on to say that summaries of business

---

26 FED. R. EVID. 803.
27 United States v. Foster, 711 F.2d 871 (9th Cir. 1983).

records are sometimes admissible, but a proper foundation must be laid and that includes making the underlying data available for inspection by the opposing party.28

As there was some question concerning the exception of foreign records of regularly conducted business activity, Congress in 1984 included a provision relating to foreign evidence in the Crime Control Act of 1984.29 Section 3505 of the Act provided that in a criminal proceeding in a court of the United States, a foreign record of regularly conducted activity, or a copy of such records, will not be excluded as evidence by the hearsay rule if a foreign certification attests that:

(A) Such record was made, at or near the time of the occurrence of the matter set forth, by (or from information transmitted by) a person with knowledge of these matters;

(B) Such record was kept in the course of a regularly conducted business activity;

(C) The business activity made such a record as a regular practice; and

(D) If such record is not the original, such record is a duplicate of the original, unless the source of information or the method or circumstances of preparation indicate lack of trustworthiness.

As part of this provision by Congress to allow foreign evidence in courts of the United States under an exception to the hearsay rule, a section includes a definition of the terms used and provides that a "business," as used in the act, includes businesses, institutions, associations, professions, occupations and callings of every kind, whether or not conducted for profit.

Although police reports containing statements concerning the cause or responsibility for an accident are in a sense business or public records, they are often excluded for the reason that the person making the report is relying on what someone else told him, not affirming what he observed with his own senses. For example, investigative notes taken by the first law enforcement officer to arrive at the scene of the accident were not admissible under the "public records exception" to the hearsay rule in an action brought against a highway department for failure to correct an allegedly dangerous condition on the highway.30 The court noted that the portion of the records sought to be admitted was not a declaration of the officer's firsthand knowledge and did not contain factual findings of his investigation, but, at most, that portion contained certain factual assertions by the witness upon which the officer's finding may, or may not, have been based.

---

28 United States v. Kim, 595 F.2d 755 (D.C. Cir. 1979).

29 18 U.S.C. § 223 (1984).

30 Seaton v. State of Wyoming Highway District Number 1, 784 P.2d 197 (Wyo. 1989).

However, if the information in a police report of an accident is within the personal knowledge of the investigator (*e.g.,* the skid marks at the scene of the accident were more than 100 feet in length), such an item is admissible in evidence under the rule that written records of a public nature which public officers are required to keep are admissible as proof of the facts recorded therein.31 Although a police report stating that a car was reported stolen may not be admitted to establish that the car was in fact stolen, it would be admissible as proof that the car to which it referred had been *reported* stolen.32

A hospital record, so far as it pertains to the cause of an accident resulting in injuries to a person, causing his visit to a hospital and not to the medical or surgical treatment of the patient in the hospital, is inadmissible in evidence as a business record. The admissibility of hospital records in accident cases depends upon whether they relate to acts, transactions, occurrences or events incident to the hospital treatment.33

A time card and time sheet of the defendant's place of employment, although they are hearsay, were admissible in evidence as a record made in the regular course of business.34 Evidence as to long-distance telephone tickets, railway ticket records or hospital records is not the same as evidence concerning a book account. The elements necessary for admission of a telephone ticket are identification by one or more telephone employees who either make or have supervision and charge of the records, who know the ticket to be a genuine part of the records of the company, and who can testify that it was made at or about the time shown thereon. 35 Likewise, in a prosecution for transporting a minor in interstate commerce for purposes of prostitution, wherein the evidence showed that the defendant had induced the minor to accompany him from Montana to Florida by commercial airlines, the airline tickets used by the defendant and the minor were admissible under the business records law.36

---

31 Carswell v. State, 171 Ga. App. 455, 320 S.E.2d 249 (1984).
32 United States v. Graham, 391 F.2d 439 (6th Cir. 1968).
33 Melton v. St. Louis Public Service Co., 363 Mo. 474, 251 S.W.2d 663 (1952); *see also* State v. Griffin, 497 S.W.2d 133 (Mo. 1973), indicating a trend to admit certain hospital records.
34 United States v. Kennedy, 291 F.2d 457 (2d Cir. 1961); *see also* United States v. Ramsey, 785 F.2d 184 (7th Cir. 1986), which held that a victim's desk calendar, showing his calls to the defendant's fraudulent loan brokering enterprise, should not have been admitted in a mail and wire fraud prosecution under the business records exception to the hearsay rule, as the desk calendar was not maintained regularly in the course of business.
35 Oleson v. Henningsen, 247 Iowa 883, 77 N.W.2d 40 (1956).
36 Rotolo v. United States, 404 F.2d 316 (5th Cir. 1968).

Records stored on magnetic tape by data processing machines are unavailable and useless except by means of the print-out sheets. In admitting the print-out sheets, which reflect the record stored on the tape, the court is actually following the best evidence rule. This is not departing from the business records rule, but only extending its application to electronic record keeping.

Print-out sheets of business records stored on electronic computing equipment are admissible in evidence if they are relevant and material, without the necessity of identifying, locating and producing as witnesses the individuals who made the entries in the regular course of business. Before such sheets are admitted, it must be shown that the electronic computing equipment is recognized as standard equipment, that the entries are made in the regular course of business at or reasonably near the time of the happening of the event recorded, and that the foundation testimony satisfies the court that the source of information, method and time of preparation were such as to indicate its trustworthiness and justify its admission.[37]

§ 12.7 —Family history and records (pedigree)

> **Rule 803**
>
> **HEARSAY EXCEPTIONS; AVAILABILITY OF DECLARANT IMMATERIAL**
>
> * * *
>
> **(11) Records of religious organizations.** Statements of births, marriages, divorces, deaths, legitimacy, ancestry, relationship by blood or marriage, or other similar facts of personal or family history, contained in a regularly kept record of a religious organization.
>
> **(12) Marriage, baptismal, and similar certificates.** Statements of fact contained in a certificate that the maker performed a marriage or other ceremony or administered a sacrament, made by a clergyman, public official, or other person authorized by the rules or practices of a religious organization or by law to perform the act certified, and purporting to have been issued at the time of the act or within a reasonable time thereafter.
>
> **(13) Family records.** Statements of fact concerning personal or family history contained in family Bibles, genealogies, charts, engravings on rings, inscriptions on family portraits, engravings on urns, crypts, or tombstones, or the like.[38]
>
> * * *

---

37 King v. State ex rel. Murdock Acceptance Corp., 222 So. 2d 393 (Miss. 1969).
38 FED. R. EVID. 803.

Evidence relating to pedigree, genealogy and family history usually consists of hearsay and presents an exception to the general rule on that subject. The family history exception to the hearsay rule is based in part on the inherent trustworthiness of a declaration by a family member regarding matters of family history and on the usual unavailability of other evidence on these matters. As an example, testimony of a son that his mother told him that he was born in a certain place in the United States is admissible under the pedigree exception to the hearsay rule.[39] Such evidence is admissible if the declarant is related by blood or marriage to the other person, or has been so intimately associated with the other person's family as to be likely to have accurate information concerning the birth, marriage, divorce, death, ancestry or relationship.[40]

Generally, the courts have interpreted "member of the family" broadly. For example, the court in a Virginia case held that for purposes of the pedigree exception to the hearsay rule, the decedent in a wrongful death action is a "member of the family or [a person] related to the family" whose history the decedent's declaration of paternity concerns and, thus, hearsay evidence of the decedent's declaration is admissible provided no better evidence can be obtained.[41]

Not only are declarations by a family member regarding matters of family history admissible as an exception to the hearsay rule, such records as the family Bible are admissible where a proper showing is made as to the authority or authenticity of entries of the family record and where better evidence is not available. Such matters as births, deaths and marriages are competent in evidence.

In some states, entries in the family Bible or statements concerning the family history are not admitted where the person making them is alive or capable of being examined as a witness.[42] In some instances, however, the absence from the jurisdiction of the person who made the statements or made the entries, or insanity or illness hindering his presence at the trial is enough to make the evidence admissible. In some jurisdictions, entries in family Bibles are declared admissible by statute.[43]

Federal Rule of Evidence 803(11) provides that regularly kept records of a religious organization may be referred to to find information and that this information is admissible as an exception to the hearsay rule. Although such records are not as important today as they were at one time, this exception makes it clear that such evidence may now be admitted. In inter-

---

[39] Liacakos v. Kennedy, 195 F. Supp. 630 (D.D.C. Cir. 1961).

[40] FED. R. EVID. 804(b)(4).

[41] Smith v. Givens, 223 Va. 455, 290 S.E.2d 844 (1982).

[42] State v. Adkins, 146 S.E. 732 (Ga. 1929).

[43] FED. R. EVID. 803.

preting the rule, one federal court explained that the exception is limited to personal information and does not authorize evidence of statements of contributions to a church, as these do not fall within the religious records exception to the hearsay rule.44

§ 12.8 —Former testimony

Rule 804

HEARSAY EXCEPTIONS; DECLARANT UNAVAILABLE

* * *

(b) (1) **Former testimony.** Testimony given as a witness at another hearing of the same or a different proceeding, or in a deposition taken in compliance with law in the course of the same or another proceeding, if the party against whom the testimony is now offered, or, in a civil action or proceeding, a predecessor in interest, had an opportunity and similar motive to develop the testimony by direct, cross, or redirect examination.45

* * *

Some authorities assert that former testimony is actually not hearsay, as it was under oath and subject to cross-examination. Others, however, recognize former testimony as hearsay but recognize that it is admissible under an exception to the hearsay rule. Under either approach, when a witness for the prosecution or defendant is unavailable and cannot be produced at the present trial, the testimony of such witness at a formal criminal proceeding relating substantially to the same subject matter and between the same parties will usually be admitted.

Under various state statutes, the term "unavailable as a witness" means that the witness is unable to be present or to testify at the hearing because of death or then-existing physical or mental illness, or is beyond the jurisdiction of the court to compel his appearance by its process, or he is absent and his whereabouts cannot be ascertained through due diligence.

In criminal prosecutions, the mere temporary illness or disability of a witness is not sufficient to justify the reception of his former testimony; it must appear that the witness is in such a state, either mentally or physically, that in reasonable probability he will never be able to attend the trial.

---

44 Hall v. C.I.R., 729 F.2d 632 (9th Cir. 1984).
45 Fed. R. Evid. 804.

Therefore, testimony given at the former trial by a witness unable to attend the subsequent trial because of pregnancy was inadmissible on any issue at the subsequent trial, when she was neither dead, beyond the reach of process nor permanently incapacitated, and a continuance might have been requested to the time when the witness could probably be present.[46] Following like reasoning, the Eleventh Circuit agreed that the statement of defense counsel that the defendant's wife was unavailable to testify as a witness due to her child's illness, in and of itself, was insufficient to demonstrate the unavailability of the witness for purpose of securing the admission of the witness' testimony (given at a pre-trial suppression hearing) as an exception to the rule against hearsay.[47]

If the prosecution in a criminal case seeks to offer testimony taken at a previous trial, the burden is on the prosecution to establish that efforts have been made to locate the witness and that the witness is unavailable despite reasonable efforts made in good faith to secure his presence at the trial.[48] If, however, the prosecution can show that the witness cannot be procured to testify in a federal court proceeding and that reasonable means were used to obtain the presence of the witness, the witness' testimony in a prior state court hearing may be considered by a federal court in disposing of the defendant's motion to dismiss the indictment.[49]

In applying the rule, another federal court determined that an accomplice's refusal to testify concerning a confession rendered him unavailable for purposes of the hearsay rule, and therefore, the court permitted a law enforcement agent to recapitulate the confession at the defendant's trial.[50]

---

[46] Peterson v. United States, 344 F.2d 419 (5th Cir. 1965). *But compare* State v. Julian, 509 P.2d 1123 (Kan. 1973), which applies less strict requirements.

[47] United States v. Acosta, 769 F.2d 721 (11th Cir. 1985).

[48] State v. Keairns, 9 Ohio St. 3d 228, 460 N.E.2d 245 (1984); *see also* United States v. Winn, 767 F.2d 527 (9th Cir. 1985), which held that a witness is not "unavailable" within the meaning of the rule governing admittance of hearsay when the declarant is unavailable unless the prosecution makes a good faith effort to obtain the witness' presence.

[49] United States v. Smith, 577 F. Supp. 1232 (S.D. Ohio 1983).

[50] United States v. Coachman, 727 F.2d 1293 (D.C. Cir. 1984).

§ 12.9 —Dying declarations

Rule 804

HEARSAY EXCEPTIONS; DECLARANT UNAVAILABLE

(b) (2) **Statement under belief of impending death.** In a prosecution for homicide or in a civil action or proceeding, a statement made by a declarant while believing that the declarant's death was imminent, concerning the cause or circumstances of what the declarant believed to be impending death.[51]

A dying declaration is a statement by the victim concerning the cause and circumstances of a homicide, made under a fixed belief that death is impending. Dying declarations in homicide cases have from ancient times been admitted in evidence either: (1) because of solemnity—the solemnity of the occasion and the fear of punishment in the hereafter if one tells a lie just before death, or (2) because of necessity—as the victim of the homicide cannot testify, it is necessary to protect the public against homicidal criminals and to prevent a miscarriage of justice.

Generally, the dying declaration has the same effect as if it were made under oath. However, a number of authorities point out that, while it is a substitute for an oath and its credibility and weight is for the jury, the dying declaration is merely hearsay and is not the equivalent of nor does it have the same value or weight as testimony that is given under oath in open court and that is subject to cross-examination.[52]

The dying declaration is admissible only insofar as it relates to the circumstances immediately surrounding or leading up to the conduct which caused death. A dying declaration may be made in answer to a leading question or urgent solicitation. It is not necessary to prove expressions indicating apprehension of death if it is clear that the victim does not expect to survive the injury. This expectation may be shown by the circumstances of his condition or by his acts, such as sending for a minister of his church before making the declaration.

This exception to the hearsay rule is restricted in criminal cases to statements made by the victim of a homicide. In one case the court admitted evidence of the dying declaration of a woman who died as a result of an

---

51 Fed. R. Evid. 804.
52 Commonwealth v. Brown, 388 Pa. 613, 131 A.2d 367 (1957); *see also* Rodriguez v. State, 697 S.W.2d 463 (Tex. App. 1985) in Part II, *infra.*

abortion. The court in that case regarded death as an element of the offense.[53]

In the case of *Mattox v. United States*, the Supreme Court of the United States succinctly stated conditions under which the dying declaration exception to the hearsay rule is applicable, and it set forth the justification for the rule:[54]

> Dying declarations are admissible on a trial for murder, as to the fact of the homicide and the person by whom it was committed, in favor of the defendant as well as against him. . . . But it must be shown by the party offering them in evidence that they were made under a sense of impending death. This may be made to appear from what the injured person said; or from the nature and extent of the wounds inflicted, being obviously such that he must have felt or known that he could not survive; as well as from his conduct at the time and the communications, if any, made to him by medical advisors, if assented to or understandingly acquiesced in by him. The length of the time elapsing between the making of the declaration and the death is one of the elements to be considered. . . .

Approving the admission of the dying declarations in the case, the Court commented further:

> The admission of the testimony is justified on the ground of necessity, and in view of the consideration that certain expectation of almost immediate death will remove all temptation to falsehood and enforce as strict adherence to the truth as the obligation of an oath could impose. But the evidence must be received with the utmost caution, and, if the circumstances do not satisfactorily disclose that the awful and solemn situation in which he is placed is realized by the dying man because of the hope of recovery, it ought to be rejected.

In further explaining the rule relating to the knowledge of imminent death, the courts have determined that it is sufficient if the declarant believes his death is imminent even if he continues to fight for survival—so long as he believes that the odds are against him. In one case, a North Carolina court made this comment:

> The party seeking admission of the out-of-court statement need not show that the declarant stated he had given up all hope of living or considered himself to be in the throes of death. All that must be shown is that the declarant believes he is going to die.[55]

---

53   People v. Murawski, 2 Ill. 2d 143, 117 N.E.2d 88 (1954).
54   Mattox v. United States, 146 U.S. 140, 13 S. Ct. 50, 36 L. Ed. 917 (1892).
55   State v. Hamlett, 302 N.C. 490, 276 S.E.2d 338 (1981).

Even with these guidelines it is difficult to determine whether the statement is admissible under the dying declaration exception. For example, in a prosecution for murder, one court properly admitted into evidence statements that were made by the deceased. At trial, the police officer who interviewed the victim at the hospital testified that throughout the interview, in which the victim had recounted the attack that eventually led to his death, the victim repeatedly stated "Oh God, I'm dying; somebody please help me."[56] The court held there that it was not necessary that the declarant personally express his belief that he had no chance of recovery. On the other hand, a Texas court reasoned that the statements made by a shooting victim in an ambulance on the way to the hospital and to a relative in the hospital three days before the victim's death that "I don't believe I'm going to make it," "I'm trying to hang on," and "she came to kill me and it looks like she did" were insufficient to satisfy the consciousness of approaching death requirement of the dying declaration exception to the hearsay rule. Here, the victim never stated that he knew he was going to die.[57]

The length of time elapsing between the making of the declaration and the death is only one of the elements to be considered. Generally, the rule is that a dying declaration must be made at any time between the infliction of the fatal injury and the death of the declarant.[58] Nevertheless, if the prosecution seeks to introduce the dying declaration, the prosecutor must demonstrate that at the time the victim made the declaration, he believed that death was impending.

A dying declaration may be either written or oral and must relate to the killing of the declarant and not to the killing of a third party. Because in many instances the dying statements are made to officers, the officer should be aware that he will be cross-examined concerning what he heard. He should, therefore, make notes so that he can testify as to the exact words that he heard the declarant say.

---

[56] State v. Richardson, 308 N.C. 470, 302 S.E.2d 799 (1983).
[57] Rodriguez v. State, 697 S.W.2d 463 (Tex. App. 1985).
[58] Early v. State, 179 Ga. App. 158, 316 S.E.2d 527 (1984). The declarant in this case lived 54 days.

§ 12.10 —Declarations against interest

Rule 804

HEARSAY EXCEPTIONS; DECLARANT UNAVAILABLE

(b) (3) Statement against interest. A statement which was at the time of its making so far contrary to the declarant's pecuniary or proprietary interest, or so far tended to subject the declarant to civil or criminal liability, or to render invalid a claim by the declarant against another, that a reasonable person in the declarant's position would not have made the statement unless believing it to be true. A statement tending to expose the declarant to criminal liability and offered to exculpate the accused is not admissible unless corroborating circumstances clearly indicate the trustworthiness of the statement.[59]

a. Declarations against pecuniary interests

One of the exceptions to the hearsay rule, which has been found to be based on trustworthiness or a probability of truthfulness and veracity, and which has arisen due to necessity, is the exception admitting a declaration when it is against the interest of the declarant. The courts have reasoned that a person does not make statements against his own pecuniary interest unless they are true and have thus considered such statements trustworthy, even though there is no opportunity to confront or to cross-examine the witness.

A declaration against interest by one not a party or in privity with a party to an action is admissible in evidence where: (1) the person making such declaration is either dead or unavailable as a witness due to sickness, insanity or absence from the jurisdiction; (2) the declarant had peculiar means of knowing the facts which he stated; (3) the declaration was against his pecuniary or proprietary interest; and (4) he had no probable motive to falsify the facts stated.[60] Thus, in a civil action by an insured against his fidelity insurer to recover for defalcation by employees of the former, when such employees were unavailable as witnesses, (as they had been summoned and were not found in the jurisdiction by the sheriff) written and signed confessions of such employees were admissible in evidence as declarations against interest as to both the fact and the amount of the loss.[61]

---

59 FED. R. EVID. 804.
60 Gichner v. Antonio Troiano Tile Co., 410 F.2d 238 (D.C. Cir. 1969).
61 G.M. McKelvey Co. v. General Casualty Co., 166 Ohio St. 401, 2 Ohio Op. 2d 345, 142 N.E.2d 854 (1957).

A hearsay statement is against a declarant's pecuniary and proprietary interest, and therefore, it is susceptible to being admitted as a declaration against interest when it threatens loss of employment, reduces chances for future employment, or entails possible civil liability. Thus, a hearsay statement made by the lessee's employee to a fire investigator that he and others were smoking on the leased premises a few hours before the fire started was against the employee's pecuniary and proprietary interests, and since the statement also concerned a subject of which the employee was personally cognizant and there was no conceivable motive to falsify, the statement was admitted as a declaration against interest. The court in that case agreed, however, that the statement would not be admitted unless the employee was unavailable to testify at the trial.[62]

b.   Statements against penal interests—confessions and admissions

Closely related to the exception discussed in the preceding paragraphs is the exception concerning admissions and confessions. A confession as it is used in criminal law is an admission, declaration or acknowledgment made by one who has committed a crime stating that he committed the act or participated in its commission. The confession is the admission of the criminal act itself, not an admission of a fact or circumstances from which guilt may be inferred. An admission, as distinguished from a confession, is not an admission of the criminal act itself but an admission of incriminating acts or conduct which may tend to establish guilt.

When a police officer or corrections officer takes the stand and states what has been told to him by the accused, such testimony is hearsay, and as one court said, "since confessions are hearsay testimony, they are to be received with great caution."[63]

When confessions are brought to the attention of the court by other than those on trial, the evidence is hearsay. Such evidence is nevertheless admissible as an exception to the hearsay rule when certain conditions are met.[64] The reason for admitting the confession as an exception to the hearsay rule is that such statements are against the interest of the person making them and that a rational being does not make admissions prejudicial to his interest and safety unless urged by the promptings of conscience to tell the truth.

In the Federal Rules of Evidence, the statement against interest exception includes statements which are against penal interest as well as those against

---

62 Gichner v. Antonio Troiano Tile Co., *supra* n. 60.

63 Damas v. People, 62 Cal. 418, 163 P. 289 (1917).

64 *See* Chapter 16, *infra,* for a discussion of the constitutional issues concerning confessions and admissions; United States v. Coachman, 727 F.2d 1293 (D.C. Cir. 1984).

pecuniary and proprietary interests.65 Under this definition, a statement by a witness who repeated the statement of a third party which would tend to subject the witness to criminal liability would be admissible. This rule, however, provides: "A statement tending to expose the declarant to criminal liability and offered to exculpate the accused is not admissible unless corroborating circumstances clearly indicate the trustworthiness of the statement."

The Fifth Circuit reiterated that admitting out-of-court declarations against penal interest is an exception to the hearsay rule in accordance with Rule 804 of the Federal Rules of Evidence. There the court held that statements made by an alleged heroin trafficking conspirator asserting that heroin came from the defendant and that the conspirator was calling the defendant to set up heroin transactions were admissible declarations against the conspirator's penal interests.66 However, an out-of-court inculpatory assertion is not admitted as an exception to the hearsay rule if it was made to avoid the threat of physical harm.67

In a case that received national attention, the declaration against interest exception to the hearsay rule played a part in a trial which arose out of the murder of Congressman Leo Ryan in November 1978.68 Ryan was shot and killed at an airstrip in the Republic of Guyana after visiting Jonestown, a settlement of approximately 1200 members of the People's Temple, a religious cult headed by Jim Jones, who later led his followers in a mass suicide. At Laurence Layton's trial for the murder of Congressman Ryan, the government sought to introduce evidence of testimony by Jones's lawyer that shortly before the Ryan party left for the airstrip, Jones told him that Layton and another had taken all the weapons from Jonestown and were proceeding to the airstrip to carry out a mission of violence. The court agreed that this testimony was admissible as an exception to the hearsay rule as it was an assertion against Jones' penal interests and was admissible upon offer by the government.

In explaining that the remarks made by Jones were clearly against his penal interests and therefore admissible, the court pointed out that as Jones had already indicated a desire to kill Ryan and his remarks would tend to subject him to criminal responsibility for both the murder and participation in a conspiracy to murder Congressman Ryan, the evidence was admissible. The court made this comment in approving the admissibility of the evidence:

---

65 FED. R. EVID. 804(b)(3).
66 United States v. Alvarez, 584 F.2d 694 (5th Cir. 1978), interpreting FED. R. EVID. 804 (b). *See* case in Part II, *infra*.
67 United States v. Manshaw, 714 F.2d 785 (8th Cir. 1983).
68 United States v. Layton, 720 F.2d 548 (9th Cir. 1983).

We have held that remarks that tend to implicate the declarant in a conspiracy are statements against his penal interests. . . . It is inconceivable that, had Jones lived and been charged with conspiracy to murder, these statements would not have been admissible against him. It should not make any difference in the "against interest" finding that the statements are offered against Layton rather than Jones. We conclude that these statements clearly are against Jones' penal interest.

In interpreting Federal Rule 804(b) the Eighth Circuit set forth the factors to be considered when determining the trustworthiness of hearsay statements sought to be admitted as against the declarant's penal interest.[69] The court advised that admissibility is determined by an analysis of two elements: probable veracity of the in-court witness and the reliability of the out-of-court declarant. The court continued by stating that the factors to be considered in such an analysis include: whether there is any apparent motive for the out-of-court declarant to misrepresent the matter, the general character of the speaker, whether other people heard the out-of-court statement, whether the statement was made spontaneously, the timing of the declaration, and the relationship between the speaker and the witness.

§ 12.11 —Other exceptions

Rule 803

HEARSAY EXCEPTIONS; AVAILABILITY OF DECLARANT IMMATERIAL

(24) Other exceptions. A statement not specifically covered by any of the foregoing exceptions but having equivalent circumstantial guarantees of trustworthiness, if the court determines that (A) the statement is offered as evidence of a material fact; (B) the statement is more probative on the point for which it is offered than any other evidence which the proponent can procure through reasonable efforts; and (C) the general purposes of these rules and the interests of justice will best be served by admission of the statement into evidence. However, a statement may not be admitted under this exception unless the proponent of it makes known to the adverse party sufficiently in advance of the trial or hearing to provide the adverse party with a fair opportunity to prepare to meet it, the proponent's intention to offer the statement and the particulars of it, including the name and address of the declarant.[70]

---

69 United States v. Rasmussen, 790 F.2d 55 (8th Cir. 1986).
70 Fed. R. Evid. 803.

There are other specific exceptions, including those listed in Rules 803 and 804 of the Federal Rules of Evidence. The rules have made it clear that merely because some of the exceptions are listed, such listing does not close the door to the use of other hearsay evidence as exceptions to the hearsay rule. It would be presumptuous to assume that all possible desirable exceptions to the hearsay rule have been cataloged. Therefore, Rules 803(24) and 804(b)(5) specifically provide for other exceptions when certain conditions are met.

If the reasons for excluding hearsay evidence are not apparent and the interests of justice would best be served by admission of the statement into evidence, the court may find additional exceptions to the hearsay rule and allow hearsay evidence in certain cases. If such hearsay evidence is admitted, the court must find comparable circumstantial guarantees of trustworthiness.71

§ 12.12　Non-testimonial utterances

In the previous sections, the hearsay rule was defined and some of the exceptions to the hearsay rule were discussed. There is a category of evidence which is similar to hearsay but is not described as hearsay evidence. In some instances, a witness on the stand can repeat what was said by another person outside of court if the evidence is introduced not for the facts asserted but only to indicate that a statement was made. In some courts, this is distinguished as original evidence rather than pure hearsay. This evidence is not admitted as an exception to the hearsay rule but rather on the reasoning that it does not amount to testimonial hearsay as defined in the hearsay rule. This category of evidence consists of that evidence relating to the state of mind of a person.

When the sanity of a person accused of crime is at issue, the statements made at the time of the offense or immediately preceding or following the offense are admissible to prove his mental condition. Here the evidence is admitted not for its assertive or testimonial use but to show the state of mind of the person making the statements.72

On like reasoning it has been held that the hearsay rule does not exclude a statement if the utterance of the statement tends to prove an operative fact. For example, in *Braswell v. United States,* the police officers were permitted to testify that they heard words which were commonly used by narcotics addicts coming from a motel room that the officers were about to enter.73 The evidence was admitted not for the message that the words con-

---

71 United States v. Welsh, 774 F.2d 670 (4th Cir. 1985).
72 Bridges v. State, 247 Wis. 350, 19 N.W.2d 529 (1945).
73 Braswell v. United States, 200 F.2d 597 (5th Cir. 1952).

tained but as circumstantial evidence that narcotics were in the room.

To illustrate this concept further, another court found that there was no error in introducing evidence of an FBI agents' conversation with a client of the defendant, a defense attorney, because this was not offered to prove the truth of the content thereof, only that the conversation took place.[74] Also evidence was admissible in a prosecution of an attorney accused of conspiring to obstruct justice by convincing the client not to testify before the grand jury in a prosecution for arranging the murder of a government informant. The taped conversation between a second informant and the defendant was admissible as it was not admitted for the truth but only to show that the conversation took place.[75]

Under what is sometimes referred to as the verbal act doctrine, a statement which accompanies conduct is admissible to give legal significance to the act. Here the evidence is offered only to show that words were spoken, not as proof of the truth of what was said. As an example, in a prosecution for intimidating a witness, the witness' testimony as to the substance of what his wife had reported to him as having been said to her by the defendant was admissible but only as evidence of a "verbal act." The evidence was introduced for the purpose of proving the fact that statements which the wife testified she made to her husband were in fact made.[76]

§ 12.13 Summary

The general rule is that "hearsay evidence" is not admissible in court. Hearsay evidence is defined as testimony or written evidence presented in court from a statement made out of court, when such statement is offered to prove the truth of matters asserted therein. Thus, the evidence relies for its value on the credibility of the out-of-court declarant. Although this general rule is universally applied and is based on sound reasoning, there are many exceptions to the rule. If testimony comes within an exception, it is admissible even though it is hearsay.

Examples of exceptions to the hearsay rule are spontaneous and excited utterances, some business and public records, family history and records, former testimony, dying declarations and declarations against interest. Before evidence may be admitted as an exception to the hearsay rule, however, it must comply with specific qualifications that have been established for the particular exception.

---

74 United States v. Cintolo, 818 F.2d 980 (1st Cir.), *cert. denied,* 484 U.S. 913, 108 S. Ct. 259, 98 L. Ed. 2d 216 (1987).
75 United States v. Witman, 771 F.2d 1348 (9th Cir. 1985).
76 Overton v. United States, 403 F.2d 444 (5th Cir. 1968).

The hearsay rule is not applicable when the out-of-court statements are offered solely as evidence that a statement was made, and not for the content of that statement. Also, out-of-court statements may be repeated by another in court, not for the content of the statement but to indicate the person's physical or mental condition.

From the foregoing discussion, it is clear that some hearsay evidence is not admissible in court but that there are also many exceptions to the hearsay rule. One can argue that more evidence is admitted under the exceptions than is excluded under the general rule. It is therefore essential that criminal justice personnel be familiar not only with the rule that excludes hearsay evidence but also with the exceptions and the requirements for each exception.

E. EVIDENCE VIA DOCUMENTS AND REAL EVIDENCE

CHAPTER 13
DOCUMENTARY EVIDENCE

Before any writing will be admitted in evidence, it must be authenticated in some manner, i.e., its genuineness or execution must be proved. Even a competent public record or document must be properly identified, verified or authenticated by some recognized method before it may be introduced in evidence.

City of Randleman v. Hinshaw, 2 N.C. App. 381, 163 S.E.2d 95 (1968)

§ 13.1 Introduction

Evidence is divided into three categories: (1) oral testimony, (2) documentary evidence and (3) real evidence. The discussion in previous chapters related primarily to oral evidence. However, the general rules of admissibility are applicable to all types of evidence. In addition, there are certain rules that apply exclusively to documentary evidence. These rules are discussed in this chapter. In Chapter 14, the rules relating to the introduction of real evidence are discussed and explained.

Documentary evidence is that evidence furnished by written instruments, inscriptions and documents of all kinds. The term is broad enough to include every form of writing and applies to both public and private documents.

A document may be defined as any matter expressed or described upon any substance by means of letters, figures or marks, and intended to be used for the purpose of recording that matter. Examples of *private* documents are deeds, wills and agreements. Birth records, marriage records, registrations of various kinds, police records and licensing records are examples of public documents.

Documentary evidence is subject to the same rules of evidence as is

303

oral testimony with respect to relevancy, competency and materiality. In addition, the party that introduces a document must lay a foundation for the introduction of the documentary evidence with respect to the sufficiency of the proof to authenticate, verify or identify the document offered. There are two tests that are primarily peculiar to documentary evidence: the authentication test and the best evidence test. The general rules relating to these tests are discussed in this chapter with some specific examples.

§ 13.2 Authentication

Rule 901

REQUIREMENT OF AUTHENTICATION OR IDENTIFICATION

(a) **General provision.** The requirement of authentication or identification as a condition precedent to admissibility is satisfied by evidence sufficient to support a finding that the matter in question is what its proponent claims.[1]

* * *

A fundamental rule of evidence is that no document may be admitted into evidence without some proof of authentication. As one early writer stated, "A writing, of itself, is evidence of nothing, and therefore is not, unless accompanied by proof of some sort, admissible in evidence."[2] The required proof may be in the document itself, in that the document may become, by authority of statute or otherwise, "self-authenticating." Otherwise, outside proof is required in laying a foundation for admission of the evidence. Authentication merely means that there must be preliminary proof of genuineness, authenticity or identity of the document.

To authenticate a document, a proponent need only prove a rational basis for the claim that the document is what the proponent asserts it to be.[3] It is not necessary that the evidence introduced to authenticate a document be direct evidence, as the use of circumstantial evidence alone is sufficient to authenticate a document.[4]

Requirements as to authentication vary with the character of the document sought to be introduced into evidence. Authentication is usually

---

1   FED. R. EVID. 901. *See also* Rule 901(b) in Appendix, *infra,* for examples of evidence conforming with the requirements of Rule 901(a).
2   Stamper v. Griffin, 20 Ga. 312 (1856) (Vennine, J.).
3   United States v. Long, 857 F.2d 436 (8th Cir. 1988).
4   United States v. Elkins, 885 F.2d 775 (11th Cir. 1989).

accomplished by sworn testimony of a witness as to the source and genuineness of the writing. However, in some instances, such specific testimony is not required. For example, official records may be authenticated by an attesting certificate, which is a signed statement of the custodian of the records that the paper in question is the original or true copy thereof. In such cases, the attesting certificate must itself be authenticated by competent evidence. Also, in some cases the formal authenticity requirement may be dispensed with if the parties agree to the genuineness of the writing.

In an effort to save the time of the court, statutes have been designed to do away with the formal authentication requirements when such requirements obviously serve little purpose. But even when such statutes are in effect, the opposing party is not foreclosed from disputing authenticity by introducing evidence that the documents are not authentic.

Rule 901(b) of the Federal Rules of Evidence lists ten examples of authentication or identification as conforming with the requirement of the rule. Some of these deal with real evidence, which is discussed in the next chapter, while some refer to documentary evidence.

In interpreting Rule 901(b)(2), courts have agreed that a witness who is not an expert may identify a signature or handwriting if he is sufficiently familiar with the calligraphy so that his testimony will aid the jury. Knowledge of a person's writing may be acquired by any means as long as it is not obtained especially for the trial. The witness may become familiar with a person's handwriting by observing him write on previous occasions. No minimum number of occasions is required. However, evidence must be introduced to show that the witness was familiar with the handwriting. In a federal case the Fifth Circuit agreed that a prison official be permitted to testify that documents in the prison file were written by the defendant, when the official had seen the defendant write on approximately six occasions.[5]

A non-expert witness may be cross-examined in order to aid the jury in deciding how much weight to give his testimony, and his ability to identify the questioned handwriting or signature may be tested by asking him to identify a genuine specimen among false copies.

Rule 901(b)(7) provides that the requirement of authentication as a condition precedent to admissibility is satisfied if evidence is introduced to show that a writing was authorized by law to be recorded or filed in a public office. Under this section the proponent of the evidence need only show that the office from which the records were taken is the legal custodian of the records. The public records need not be in any particular form to be deemed authentic, and minor irregularities in appearance should not preclude admittance if the record is authentic.

Evidence may also be introduced to show that public records do not contain a specific entry. For example, when the government produced evi-

---

5   United States v. Mauchlin, 670 F.2d 746 (7th Cir. 1982).

dence that a record search had been made and no weapon registration in the defendant's name had been found, the evidence was admissible.6 While the record system may be challenged if there is evidence to impeach the quality of the system, the trial court's refusal, in a prosecution for possession of a registered semi-automatic weapon, to grant the defendant's motion to visit the National Firearms Registration and Transfer Record room in Washington, D.C. was not an abuse of discretion.7

Due to necessity, the rules have been relaxed concerning the authentication of ancient documents. Rule 901(b)(8) of the Federal Rules of Evidence liberalizes the common law "ancient document" rule. Rule 901(b)(8) provides that a document may be admitted when requirements pertaining to age, nonsuspicious condition and appropriate custody are satisfied. Under this rule a document must exist 20 years before it may be admitted as an "ancient document."

In interpreting the "ancient document" authentication rule, an Alabama court held that a coal company's cash books and its time and payroll book, which contained entries for the early 1940s, were established as authentic under the authenticity rule for ancient documents.8

Rule 901(b)(9) provides that evidence describing a process or system used to produce a result and showing that the process or system produced an accurate result satisfies the authentication requirements. Examples of evidence which have been held admissible under this subsection are X-rays, computer output, electrocardiograms, surveys and polls, and statistical examples. Typically such evidence produced by a process or system is presented to the jury or the judge by means of expert testimony, and usually the witness who conveys the substance of the evidence also lays the necessary foundation.

While this provision is used very sparingly in criminal cases, one court authorized the use of computer printouts prepared by a life insurance company that proposed to show commissions which the taxpayer had received but had not reported as income.9

Recognizing that evidence generated or gathered by means of a process or system is often highly technical and complex in nature, several courts have made it clear that the proponent who intends to introduce such evidence as a computer calculation will be required to make available the underlying data and material well before the trial. For example, in a federal case the Eighth Circuit warned that opposing counsel should be advised before the trial of the nature of the computer evidence and the likelihood that it will be offered in evidence so that the counsel can prepare for cross-examination or rebuttal.10

---

6   United States v. Rose, 695 F.2d 1356 (10th Cir. 1982).
7   *Ibid.*
8   Fulmer v. Connors, 665 F. Supp. 1472 (N.D. Ala. 1987).
9   United States v. Fendley, 522 F.2d 181 (5th Cir. 1975).
10 United States v. Scholle, 553 F.2d 1109 (8th Cir. 1977).

§ 13.3 Self-authentication

Rule 902
SELF AUTHENTICATION

Extrinsic evidence of authenticity as a condition precedent to admissibility is not required with respect to the following:

(1) **Domestic public documents under seal.** A document bearing a seal purporting to be that of the United States, or of any State, district, Commonwealth, territory, or insular possession thereof, or the Panama Canal Zone, or the Trust Territory of the Pacific Islands, or of a political subdivision, department, officer, or agency thereof, and a signature purporting to be an attestation or execution.

(2) **Domestic public documents not under seal.** A document purporting to bear the signature in the official capacity of an officer or employee of any entity included in paragraph (1) hereof, having no seal, if a public officer having a seal and having official duties in the district or political subdivision of the officer or employee certifies under seal that the signer has the official capacity and that the signature is genuine.

(3) **Foreign public documents.** A document purporting to be executed or attested in an official capacity by a person authorized by the laws of a foreign country to make the execution or attestation, and accompanied by a final certification as to the genuineness of the signature and official position (A) of the executing or attesting person, or (B) of any foreign official whose certificate of genuineness of signature and official position relates to the execution or attestation or is in a chain of certificates of genuineness of signature and official position relating to the execution or attestation.

(4) **Certified copies of public records.** A copy of an official record or report or entry therein, or of a document authorized by law to be recorded or filed and actually recorded or filed in a public office, including data compilations in any form, certified as correct by the custodian or other person authorized to make the certification, by certificate complying with paragraph (1), (2), or (3) of this rule, or complying with any Act of Congress or rule prescribed by the Supreme Court pursuant to statutory authority.

(5) **Official publications.** Books, pamphlets, or other publications purporting to be issued by public authority.

(6) **Newspapers and periodicals.** Printed materials purported to be newspapers or periodicals.

(7) **Trade inscriptions and the like.** Inscriptions, signs, tags, or labels purporting to have been affixed in the course of business and indicating ownership, control, or origin.

(8) **Acknowledged documents.** Documents accompanied by a certificate of acknowledgment executed in the manner provided by law by a notary public or other officer authorized by law to take acknowledgments.

(9) **Commercial paper and related documents.** Commercial paper, signatures thereon, and documents relating thereto to the extent provided by general commercial law.

(10) **Presumptions under Acts of Congress.** Any signature, document, or other matter declared by Act of Congress to be presumptively or prima facie genuine or authentic.[11]

Over the years, a substantial body of law has developed regarding instances in which authenticity is taken as sufficiently established for purposes of admissibility without extrinsic evidence to that effect. Under the early cases, there were only a few self-authenticating documents, such as ancient documents, documents bearing a certificate of acknowledgment and replies to letters.[12] However, to save the time of the court, the number of types of documents that are self-authenticating have grown. For example, the United States Supreme Court, in drafting the Federal Rules of Evidence, listed ten types of writings that are now to be considered self-authenticating. Rule 902 of the Federal Rules of Evidence, provides that extrinsic evidence of authenticity as a condition precedent to admissibility is not required with respect to the following: (1) domestic public documents under seal; (2) domestic public documents not under seal but certified by the appropriate public officer in charge of them; (3) foreign public documents accompanied by certification as to genuineness of signature and official position of executing or attesting person; (4) copies of public or official records certified by the custodian of the original record; (5) official publications issued by public authority; (6) newspapers and periodicals; (7) trade inscriptions and labels; (8) documents acknowledged by a notary public or other officer authorized by law to take acknowledgments; (9) commercial paper and related documents; and (10) documents declared by Congress to be presumptively authentic.

Extrinsic evidence is not required for documents coming within the self-authenticating group, and such documents are admissible without further authentication. However, it must be re-emphasized that the opposing party is not foreclosed from disputing authenticity by introducing evidence indicating that the documents are not what they purport to be.

---

11 FED. R. EVID. 902.
12 Tracy, HANDBOOK OF THE LAW OF EVIDENCE (1952).

§ 13.4   Methods of authentication

Unless the documents offered into evidence are in one of those categories that have been declared by statute or the court to be self-authenticating, it is necessary to lay the foundation of their admissibility. There are generally four methods of proof: (1) proof of signing, (2) proof of signature, (3) comparison of signatures, and (4) circumstantial evidence.13 All that is necessary is that there be some proof of the genuineness of the document, that the document was properly executed, and that the document correctly states what the party claims that it contains.

Probably the most common method of authentication is offering proof of signing. It is common for the witness to testify that he saw the person sign the document in question. The next most common method of authentication is proof of the signature. If the witness did not see the party sign but is familiar with and can identify the signature, this is sufficient authentication. Such evidence is as competent and valid as the testimony of the writers themselves and is in no sense secondary evidence.14

If a witness is not available who can either state that he witnessed the signing of the document or that he recognizes the signature, a document may be authenticated by comparison of signatures. In such instances, a handwriting expert may testify after comparing the signature on the document with the signature on another document signed by the party and recognized as the party's true signature.

If no witnesses are available to identify the signature or to compare signatures, then circumstantial evidence may be admitted to prove the genuineness of the document. This may include evidence that the purported writer of the document had indicated that he intended to write such a document, evidence that reference was made by the writer to the document, or other evidence that would lead one to believe that the document was authentic. The judge has much discretion in determining what evidence is admissible for proving the document to be authentic.

The procedure generally followed in qualifying a witness to identify a writing or a signature is to place the witness on the stand and ask the witness questions which will assure the jury and the judge that the witness is familiar with the writing. The witness may be asked, "Will you state whether you are acquainted with the handwriting of the writer?" If the witness answers in the affirmative, the witness will then be asked to look at the letter or signature and tell whether it is the handwriting of the writer. In addition, the witness may be asked questions which could confirm whether

---

13 Tracy, HANDBOOK OF THE LAW OF EVIDENCE (1952); selected writings, EVIDENCE AND TRIAL (1957).

14 United States v. Moreno, 68 U.S. 400 (1863).

he is or is not qualified. For example, he may be asked whether he has had an exchange of correspondence with the person, whether he has seen writing that the person has admitted to be his own, or whether the witness has become familiar with the person's writing by doing business with him on a day-to-day basis.15

§ 13.5 Specific examples of documentary evidence

Although most evidence introduced into court is oral evidence, documentary evidence plays an important part. Documentary evidence includes laws; judicial records and proceedings; public records; private documents such as business records, account books, corporate records, letters, telegrams, and other correspondence; books; church records; hospital records; hotel registers; and many others. In each instance, the general rules of evidence as well as the authentication requirements discussed in this chapter must be considered. Court decisions and statutes in various states must be consulted for more precise rules concerning the introduction of documentary evidence.

In order to develop a better understanding of some of the rules relating to documentary evidence, examples of specific types of such evidence are included here. These examples are selected as those most likely to be encountered by criminal justice personnel.

a.   Public records and documents

Public officers are under a duty to keep a record of transactions which occur in the course of their public service. The official records and writings made by such officers, or under their supervision, are of a public nature and are ordinarily admissible in evidence as proof of their contents, even though not proved by the person who actually made the entries. The extraordinary degree of confidence reposed in such documents is founded principally upon the fact that they have been made by authorized, accredited officers and deputies appointed for that purpose. However, a police report to the effect that a policeman was injured while in the performance of his duty without fault on his part was held inadmissible as a conclusion and as hearsay.16

While death certificates and autopsy reports are generally considered to be public records and documents and are therefore admissible, a statement in such a record that amounts to a mere opinion is not admissible because it violates other rules of evidence.17 However, a transcript of a trial was held to be

---

15 W.T. Rawleigh Co. v. Overstreet, 71 Ga. App. 873, 32 S.E.2d 574 (1944).

16 Bothner v. Keegan, 89 N.Y.S. 288, 275 A.D. 470 (1949).

17 Carson v. Metropolitan Life Ins. Co., 156 Ohio St. 104, 45 Ohio Op. 103, 100 N.E.2d 197 (1951).

a certified copy of a public record and was thus a prima facie correct statement of testimony; thus, it was properly admitted to evidence in a contempt hearing.[18]

In some states, the state statute, as interpreted by the courts, expressly provides for the use of certified copies. The Texas Court of Appeals, in interpreting a recently enacted statute pertaining to the authentication of public records, pointed out that the statute provides that "extrinsic evidence of authenticity is not required as a condition precedent to admissibility under Tex. R. Evid. 902(1) when the document bears the seal of the United States, or of any State, district, Commonwealth . . . or of a political subdivision, department, officer or agency thereof, and the signature, purporting to be an attestation of execution."[19]

The defendant in the case being reviewed had been convicted of aggravated assault and had appealed on the grounds that the documentary evidence of the defendant's prior federal conviction for escape should not have been admitted. He argued that documents introduced at the trial should have been evidenced by an official publication attested to by the custodian of the records. The reviewing court upheld the conviction, affirming that the seal of the Federal District Court's office and the attestation that the document was a certified copy of the original was sufficient authentication under the statute.

In other cases federal courts have held that the stamped signature and verifying initials on a domestic public document satisfied the requirement for self-authentication of public documents under seal as provided in Federal Rules of Evidence 902(1).[20] in a prosecution for possession of marijuana for purposes of importation, the reviewing judges in one case agreed that a diplomatic note demonstrating Panama's grant of permission to United States' officials to board Panamanian-registered vessels was properly admitted under Federal Evidence Rule 902(3), governing self-authentication of foreign public documents.[21]

While most public records and documents are generally admissible without extrinsic evidence of authenticity, the requirements as set out in the rules of evidence of state and federal statutes must be complied with. Therefore, the statutes for the respective states must be examined to determine whether there are any additional conditions, such as delivering a copy to the adverse party in a reasonable time before the trial.

b. Private writings

All private writings must be proved to be genuine before they are admissible in evidence. The genuineness may be proved by the testimony of

18 United States v. Lumumba, 794 F.2d 806 (2d Cir. 1986).
19 Mullins v. State, 699 S.W.2d 346 (Tex. App. 1985).
20 United States v. Wexler, 657 F. Supp. 966 (E.D. Pa. 1987).
21 United States v. Pena-Jessie, 763 F.2d 618 (4th Cir. 1985).

anyone who saw the writing executed or by indirect or circumstantial evidence, but the circumstantial evidence must be of such force and character that the person's authorship of the writing can be legitimately deduced from it.

Both expert and lay witnesses may testify to their opinions respecting authorship or genuineness of writings, provided that they are properly qualified to do so. A lay witness must be reasonably familiar with the handwriting of the person whose authorship of the contested document is at issue.[22] The necessary familiarity ordinarily is obtained by observing the person write or by receiving from him letters or other written material. For example, a bank teller frequently has the requisite familiarity with the signature of a depositor.

§ 13.6 Best evidence rule

Rule 1002

REQUIREMENT OF ORIGINAL

To prove the content of a writing, recording, or photograph, the original writing, recording, or photograph is required, except as otherwise provided in these rules or by Act of Congress.[23]

As indicated in the preceding sections, documentary evidence must be authenticated before it is admissible. Another rule peculiar to documentary evidence is the best evidence rule. In a broad sense, this elementary principle of the law of evidence embraces within its application every issue which may be in controversy. Briefly stated, the rule is that the best evidence that is obtainable in the circumstance of the case must be addressed to prove any disputed fact. However, the rule as now developed applies exclusively to documentary evidence.[24] Where proof is to be made of some fact which is recorded in a writing, the best evidence of the contents of the writing consists in the actual production of the document itself. Any proof of a lower degree is secondary evidence which will only be received as proof when nonproduction of the writing is properly demonstrated.

The real purpose of, and reasons for, the best evidence rule were well stated by Dean Wigmore:[25]

---

22 FED. R. EVID. 901(b)(2) specifies that the familiarity not be acquired for purposes of the litigation.

23 FED R. EVID. 1002.

24 Woods v. State, 14 Md. App. 267, 288 A.2d 215 (1972).

25 IV Wigmore, EVIDENCE, § 1179 (3d ed. 1940).

(1) As between a supposed literal copy and the original, the copy is always liable to errors on the part of the copyist, whether by wilfulness or by inadvertence; this contingency wholly disappears when the original is produced. Moreover, the original may contain, and the copy will lack, such features of handwriting, paper, and the like, as may afford the opponent valuable means of learning legitimate objections to the significance of the document. (2) As between oral testimony, based on recollection, and the original, the added risk, almost the certainty, exists, of errors of recollection due to the difficulty of carrying in the memory literally the tenor of the document.

The best evidence rule is aimed only at excluding evidence which concerns the contents of a writing; testimony as to other facts about a writing, such as its existence or identity, may be admissible. Thus, in a case in which the defendant was convicted of the unlawful possession of intoxicating liquor, police officers testified that they had seen a federal liquor license bearing the name of the defendant on the wall of a filling station where the intoxicants were found. Subsequently, a certified copy of the license was admitted in evidence. The court, after pointing out that the officers were allowed to testify to the fact that they had seen a liquor license, stated "but we have not permitted them to testify concerning the contents of the license as the license itself would be the evidence of what it contained."26

A federal court, in interpreting Rule 1002 of the Federal Rules of Evidence, reiterated that the best evidence rule comes into play only when terms of a writing are being established and an attempt is made to offer secondary evidence; the rule is not applicable when a witness testifies from personal knowledge of the matter even though the same information is contained in a writing.27 The best evidence rule does not require production of documents simply because the documents contain facts that were also testified to by the witness.28 In making reference to Federal Rule 1002, the court noted that:

---

26 Chambless v. State, 94 Okla. Cr. 140, 231 P.2d 711 (1951); see also United States v. Oiamin, 868 F.2d 130 (5th Cir. 1989) which held that the purpose of the best evidence rule is to prevent inaccuracy and fraud when attempting to prove the contents of a writing.

27 D'Angelo v. United States, 456 F. Supp. 127 (D. Del. 1978); see also R & R Associates, Inc. v. Visual Scene, Inc., 726 F.2d 36 (1st Cir. 1984), which held that the rule did not prohibit testimony when the witness was in no way attempting to prove the contents of the writing, but rather was attempting by his own direct testimony to prove a particular fact.

28 United States v. Finkielsteain, 718 F. Supp. 1187 (S.D.N.Y. 1989).

As to the best evidence rule, that canon requires the production of a document to prove its content when a witness testifies on the issue of what the document contains. It does not require production of a document simply because the document contains facts that are also testified to by a witness.

Some additional examples of decisions relating to the rule will clarify its application. In a prosecution for possession of a particular treasury check that had allegedly been stolen from an authorized mail depository, the receipt into evidence of a copy of the check rather than the check itself constituted a violation of the best evidence rule when the terms of the check were vitally material to the government's case and no reason was advanced why the check itself could not have been produced.29

With reference to letters written in duplicate or greater number by the use of carbon paper, all are made by the same mechanical act and are sometimes not excluded under the best evidence rule. For example, if the carbon copy is mailed and the original typed letter retained, the one mailed would certainly be a letter, as much so as the other, if sent, would be. Usually, then, carbon impressions are not considered copies but duplicate originals.30

A retained carbon copy of a letter was not subject to exclusion under the best evidence rule, when the carbon copy was signed, as was the other copy of it, by the person who prepared it, and this retained copy, as well as the copy sent, was a counterpart or duplicate.31

§ 13.7 Secondary evidence

Rule 1003

ADMISSIBILITY OF DUPLICATES

A duplicate is admissible to the same extent as an original unless (1) a genuine question is raised as to the authenticity of the original or (2) in the circumstances it would be unfair to admit the duplicate in lieu of the original.32

---

29 United States v. Alexander, 326 F.2d 736 (4th Cir. 1964).
30 Davis v. Williams Bros. Constr. Co., 207 Ky. 404, 269 S.W. 289 (1925); Hartstock v. Strong, 21 Md. App. 110, 318 A.2d 237 (1974).
31 Bruce v. United States, 361 F.2d 318 (5th Cir. 1965).
32 Fed. R. Evid. 1003.

Rule 1004

ADMISSIBILITY OF OTHER EVIDENCE OF CONTENTS

The original is not required, and other evidence of the contents of a writing, recording, or photograph is admissible if—

(1) Originals lost or destroyed. All originals are lost or have been destroyed, unless the proponent lost or destroyed them in bad faith; or

(2) Original not obtainable. No original can be obtained by any available judicial process or procedure; or

(3) Original in possession of opponent. At a time when an original was under the control of the party against whom offered, that party was put on notice, by the pleadings or otherwise, that the contents would be a subject of proof at the hearing, and that party does not produce the original at the hearing; or

(4) Collateral matters. The writing, recording, or photograph is not closely related to a controlling issue.[33]

When the original writing has been lost or destroyed, secondary evidence of its contents is admissible. A reasonable search should be made for the lost writing in the place where it was last known to have been, and inquiry should be made of persons most likely to have custody or who may have some knowledge of its whereabouts. Before secondary evidence may be offered, there must be proof that the writing was destroyed without fraudulent intent on the part of the proponent and that it was not intentionally destroyed for wholly innocent reasons.[34]

While there must be clear and convincing evidence that the document was lost or destroyed, sufficiency of the proof as to the loss of the document permitting the relaxation of the best evidence rule is largely a matter of judicial discretion.[35] The sufficiency of the evidence to show that it is not within the offering party's power to produce the original depends upon the circumstances of each case and is to a large degree within the discretion of the trial judge.[36]

Federal Rule of Evidence 1003, which has been adopted by many states, relaxes the rule concerning the admissibility of duplicates. Under this rule a duplicate is admissible to the same extent as is the original

---

33 FED. R. EVID. 1004.
34 United States v. England, 480 F.2d 1266 (5th Cir. 1973).
35 People v. Heckers, 37 Colo. App. 166, 543 P.2d 1311 (1975); Powell v. Hopkins, 288 Ala. 466, 262 So. 2d 289 (1971).
36 76 Ill. 2d 19, 389 N.E.2d 1200 (1979).

unless there is a question concerning authenticity of the original or it would be unfair to admit the duplicate in lieu of the original. In interpreting the rule, a state court noted that cases in that state have held that photocopies and copies produced by other similar processes are considered to be duplicate originals; as such, they may be admitted into evidence without explaining the reason for failure to produce the originals. When there is no suggestion of fraud or deception in the copying process, the photocopies are properly introduced.37

As indicated, if the original document or the primary evidence is not available, secondary evidence may be admitted. Rule 1004 of the Federal Rules of Evidence provides that the original is not required and secondary evidence of the contents of a writing (or recording or photograph) is admissible if: (1) originals are lost or destroyed (not in bad faith); (2) the original is not obtainable; (3) the original is in the possession of an opponent; or (4) the writing, recording or photograph is not related to the controlling issue.

The rule in most states is that before secondary evidence may be admitted the party requesting that it be admitted must lay a foundation. The party must show to the satisfaction of the court that the primary evidence or the original is unavailable through no fault of his own or because of one of the reasons indicated in Rule 1004.

As noted in the preceding section, carbon copies of documents made on the same typewriter are generally considered to be duplicate originals and may be introduced in evidence without accounting for the nonproduction of the original.38 Some cases hold to the contrary on the reasoning that the parties did not intend that the carbon be considered an original.39 Even if the carbon is not considered as the best evidence, it is certainly considered one of the best types of secondary evidence and may be introduced as such if the proper foundation has been laid.

In an action against the defendant for failing to return a rental car, the Missouri Court of Appeals found that no miscarriage of justice resulted from the trial court's admission of carbon copies of the automobile rental agreement.40 There the court reaffirmed that "carbon copies are admissible in lieu of the original when the unavailability of the original is established."

---

37 State v. Chance, 778 S.W.2d 457 (Tenn. 1989). *See* case in Part II, *infra.*
38 29 AM. JUR. 2D *Evidence* § 488; *see* Roberts v. State, 164 Ind. App. 354, 328 N.E.2d 429 (1975), which held that there is a well-established principle that signed carbon copies of documents are to be recorded as duplicates of originals, and any of these copies may be received in evidence without accounting for the original.
39 Mitchell v. United States, 214 Ga. 473, 105 S.E.2d 337 (1958).
40 State v. Harris, 636 S.W.2d 403 (Mo. App. 1982).

Unlike carbon copies, copies of documents made by a photographic or photostatic process or other similar processes are not considered to be the same as the original. This type of copy is inadmissible if the original can be produced in court and is admissible only as secondary evidence after the proper foundation has been laid.[41] Notwithstanding this general rule making photographic copies inadmissible except as secondary evidence, some states have adopted legislation making admissible photostatic copies that are regularly kept—without accounting for the original document.[42]

The Ninth Circuit held that under Rule 1003 a photostatic copy of a co-conspirator's drug ledger was admissible to the same extent as the original when there was no genuine issue as to authenticity of the original.[43] In this case the court, after stating that "first, pursuant to Federal Rule of Evidence 1003, a duplicate is admissible to the same extent as the original in many cases," agreed that the xerox copy of the original calendar/ledger was properly admitted after witnesses identified the calendar and testified that they did not alter any of the entries.

Often a question arises as to what type of secondary evidence is preferable. There is a category of evidence that may be considered as secondary to secondary evidence: a copy of a copy. Under the majority rule, if a copy of the original is available, the copy of the copy would not be admissible under the best evidence rule. However, when both the original and the copy have been destroyed or are not available, a copy of a copy is admissible.

The extensive use of the computer and the printout has introduced another question into the law of evidence. In at least one case, data and records stored on computer cards and magnetic tape have been held to fall within the bounds of "best evidence." Printouts are the best evidence because of the impossibility in practice of reading the original, which is a piece of tape or punch card.[44]

The rules relating to best and secondary evidence generally apply to recordings and photographs as well as documents. For example, when an original tape recording was available and would normally be the best evidence, one trial court nevertheless permitted introduction of a copy, which was conceded to be accurate. The court reasoned there that when a copy is proven accurate and serves to prove the substance of the original in a more easily understood form, the spirit of the rule permits the admission of the copy.[45]

---

41 Wath v. State, 143 Tex. Crim. 303, 158 S.W.2d 516 (1942).
42 State v. Walker, 230 Md. 133, 186 A.2d 472 (1962).
43 United States v. Smith, 893 F.2d 1573 (9th Cir. 1990).
44 FED. R. EVID. 1004.
45 Johns v. United States, 323 F.2d 421 (5th Cir. 1963); see also People v. Marcus, 107 Cal. Rptr. 264, 31 Cal. App. 3d 208 (1973).

The mere fact that a conversation was recorded does not exclude oral testimony concerning the issue. The best evidence rule does not require that a party prove the loss of a recording before offering testimony about the conversation.[46] In the case cited, the government sought to prove the contents of a conversation, the court explained, not the contents of the tape recording.

The best evidence rule does not require production of a police officer's written commission document in which the officer testifies that he was appointed to the police force.[47] In a prosecution for striking a police officer while the officer was engaged in the performance of his duty, the policeman was permitted to certify that he was appointed without the necessity of producing a written document stating that he was a police officer.

§ 13.8 Summaries

> ### Rule 1006
>
> ### SUMMARIES
>
> The contents of voluminous writings, recordings, or photographs which cannot conveniently be examined in court may be presented in the form of a chart, summary, or calculation. The originals, or duplicates, shall be made available for examination or copying, or both, by other parties at a reasonable time and place. The court may order that they be produced in court.[48]

The general rule is that the use of summary is a matter that rests within the sound discretion of the trial court. Certain criteria have evolved to guide the court in exercising its discretion. A proper foundation must be laid with reference to the admissibility of the originals. More importantly, it must be shown that the summation accurately summarizes the materials involved by only referring to information contained in the original. Usually the records or materials summarized must first be made accessible to the opposing party for inspections and for use in cross-examination.[49] A summary of the recon-

---

46 United States v. Rose, 590 F.2d 232 (7th Cir. 1978), *cert. denied,* 442 U.S. 929 (1979).

47 State v. Ramsdell, 285 A.2d 389 (R.I. 1971).

48 Fed. R. Evid. 1006.

49 Fed. R. Evid. 1006 requires that summaries or charts be made available to other parties at a reasonable time and place.

structed inventory was properly admitted in a mail fraud case, when the records which were the basis of the summary were available and the prosecution offered to produce the records in court.[50]

The preparation and submission to the jury of summaries prepared by an expert is almost indispensable to the understanding of a long and complicated set of facts. But when summaries are used and given to the jury, the court must ascertain with certainty that they are based upon, and fairly represent, competent evidence already before the jury. Such summaries, if given to the jury, must be accompanied by appropriate instructions concerning their nature and use. The jury should be advised that the summaries do not, in and of themselves, constitute evidence in the case but only purport to summarize the documentary and detailed evidence already admitted; that the jury should examine the basis upon which the summaries rest and be satisfied that they accurately reflect other evidence in the case; and that, if the jury is not so satisfied, the summaries should be disregarded. In addition, broad cross-examination should be permitted upon the summaries to afford a thorough test of their accuracy.

It was not error in a prosecution for wilfully subscribing to and filing of a false income tax return to permit the use of summaries of the evidence prepared by the revenue agent and given to the jury under proper instructions pertaining to summaries.[51]

In interpreting Rule 1006, the Fifth Circuit approved the use of summary charts when they were supported by sufficient evidence.[52] In this prosecution for making, presenting—and causing to be made and presented—false documents to an agency of the United States government, charts summarizing government documents which included almost 200 pages of material and substantial amounts of calculations were held admissible. The court explained that, although certain conclusions in the summary charge were the product of assumptions made by the government, the charts were supported by sufficient evidence offered by the government and their use was permitted under the Federal Rules of Evidence.

Interpreting a state rule of evidence similar to Federal Rule 1006, a Utah court approved the use of summaries. Here the court decided that when the original consists of numerous accounts or other documents which cannot be examined in court without great loss of time, and the evidence sought from the accounts, is only the general result of the whole, the evidence may be admitted.[53] The court reasoned that summaries are admissi-

---

50   Bruce v. United States, 361 F.2d 218 (5th Cir. 1965).

51   Conford v. United States, 336 F.2d 285 (10th Cir. 1964); *see also* United States v. Normile, 587 F.2d 784 (5th Cir. 1979).

52   United States v. Jennings, 724 F.2d 436 (5th Cir. 1984).

53   Harvester Co. v. Pioneer Tractor & Implement, Inc., 626 P.2d 418 (Utah 1981).

ble if they are submitted in writing and if the proponent has laid the foundation for admissibility of the underlying documents.

Obviously, if the underlying documents are not admissible for some reason, then the summary will also not be admissible. For example, in a case in Iowa, the court noted that a summary of voluminous records is admissible, but only when the underlying records are made available for examination by the opposing party and a foundation has been laid which would render the underlying records admissible.[54]

When a trial court authorizes the use of summary charts as a teaching device rather than as substantive evidence under Rule 1006, allowing admissions of such charts to summarize the contents of voluminous readings, recordings or photographs that cannot conveniently be examined in court, the preferred practice is for the court to give limiting instructions regarding the purpose of the use of the summaries.[55]

§ 13.9 Learned treatises

Medical books or treatises, even though properly identified and authenticated and shown to be recognized as standard authorities on the subjects to which they relate, are not admissible in evidence to prove the truth of the statements therein contained.

The decided weight of authority states that medical and other scientific treatises representing inductive reasoning are inadmissible as independent evidence of the theories and opinions therein expressed. The bases for exclusion are lack of certainty as to the validity of the opinions and conclusions set forth, the technical character of the language employed which is not understandable to the average person, the absence of an oath to substantiate the assertions made, the lack of opportunity to cross-examine the author, and the hearsay aspect of such matter.

A few states have adopted the rule that a published treatise, periodical or pamphlet on a subject of history, science or art may be admitted in evidence to prove the truth of a matter stated therein if the judge takes judicial notice or a expert witness in the subject area testifies, that the treatise, periodical or pamphlet is a reliable authority on the subject. Under a Massachusetts statute,[56] as a prerequisite to the admission of a medical treatise in evidence in a malpractice action, the party offering such evidence must satisfy the trial judge that the author was recognized in his profession or calling as an expert on the subject.[57]

---

54 State v. Fingert, 298 S.W.2d 249 (Iowa 1980).
55 United States v. Howard, 774 F.2d 838 (7th Cir. 1985).
56 MASS. GEN. LAWS ANN. ch. 233, § 79C.
57 Ramsland v. Shaw, 341 Mass. 56, 166 N.E.2d 894 (1960).

§ 13.10 Summary

In addition to oral testimony, documentary evidence may be used in court to assist the jury and judge in determining the ultimate facts. Documentary evidence includes all kinds of documents, records and writings. To be admissible, documentary evidence must meet the same requirements of relevancy, competency and materiality as does oral evidence, and must, in addition, meet other requirements. Documentary evidence must also be authenticated; i.e., competent evidence must as a rule be introduced to show that the writing is what it purports to be.

To save the time of the court, practical and simplified methods of authentication have been recognized in specific instances. By statute and court decisions, some documentary evidence such as domestic public documents under seal, certified copies of public records, and official publications are taken as sufficient to establish authenticity for purposes of admissibility without extrinsic evidence to that effect. Even in these situations, however, the opposing party is not foreclosed from disputing authenticity.

Although these are not necessarily exclusive, there are four general methods of authenticating a document: (1) by proof of signing; (2) by proof of signature; (3) by comparison of signatures, usually by an expert; and (4) by circumstantial evidence. The degree of proof varies with the type of document. As a general rule, public records and documents are admissible into evidence as an exception to the hearsay rule without the same degree of authenticity as is required for private writings. This is allowed because of the extraordinary degree of confidence reposed in documents drafted by authorized and credited officers. This same degree of competence is not placed in private writings, and such writings must be proved to be genuine before they are admissible in evidence.

The generally accepted principle of law is that the best evidence that can be obtained in the circumstances of the case must be introduced to prove a disputed fact. It follows that secondary evidence is admissible only if the primary evidence is unavailable. The historical basis for this rule is that a copy is more likely to have errors and that the copy will lack such features as handwriting and paper, which provide the opponent a means of finding legitimate objections to the admissibility.

Because of modern means of reproducing documents, some of the reasons for requiring the original are no longer valid and exceptions have been included in statutes and codes.

CHAPTER 14
REAL EVIDENCE

Stains of blood, found upon the person or clothing of the party accused, have always been recognized among the ordinary indicia of homicide. The practice of identifying them by circumstantial evidence and by the inspection of witnesses and jurors has the sanction of immemorial usage in all criminal tribunals. . . . the degree of force to which it is entitled may depend upon a variety of circumstances to be considered and weighed by the jury in each particular case; but its competency is too well settled to be questioned in a court of law.
People v. Gonzalez, 35 N.Y. 49 (1866)

§ 14.1 Introduction

In the previous chapter mention was made of the fact that evidence is categorized as oral testimony, documentary evidence and real evidence. Real evidence is evidence that is addressed directly to the senses without the intervention of witnesses, as by actual sight, hearing or taste. Real evidence has often been referred to by the terms "demonstrative" or "physical" evidence. Some authorities distinguish between demonstrative and real evidence by defining real evidence as that which involves the introduction of some object that had a direct part in the incident, such as the exhibition of injured parts of the body, while defining demonstrative evidence as that which involves the production in court of such things as models, maps, pho-

323

tographs or x-rays that have no probative value themselves but serve merely as visual aids to the triers of fact in comprehending the verbal testimony of a witness.[1] In this and the following chapter, real evidence includes both types.

Real evidence is generally considered to be a very persuasive class of evidence and, at least in some instances, to be more satisfactory than verbal descriptions of objects by those who have inspected the evidence outside of court.[2] Recent court decisions have emphasized the necessity of developing more sophisticated methods of obtaining and utilizing real evidence in criminal cases. Because of the limitations placed upon the use of confessions, more reliance is placed upon the use of real evidence. For example, in the case of *Schmerber v. California,*[3] the United States Supreme Court held that the Fifth Amendment self-incrimination protection applied to evidence of a testimonial or communicative nature, but that it did not apply to real evidence. There the Court stated:

> On the other hand, both federal and state courts have usually held that it [the Fifth Amendment] offers no protection against compulsion to submit to fingerprinting, photographing, or measurements, to write or speak for identification, to appear in court, to stand, to assume a stance, to walk, or to make a particular gesture.

The Court went on to say that:

> Compulsion which makes a suspect or accused the source of real or physical evidence does not violate it [the Fifth Amendment].

In the sections that follow, the general admissibility tests relating to real evidence are discussed, as well as some of the types of real evidence of particular concern to criminal justice personnel. In the next chapter, emphasis is placed upon the use of results of experiments and tests conducted in or out of court.

§ 14.2 Admissibility requirements

To be admissible, real evidence must generally meet the same requirements as to relevancy, competency and materiality as are required of documentary evidence and oral testimony. In addition, a foundation must be laid before real evidence is admissible. Generally, the foundation is laid by the attorney calling a witness and asking questions relating to the real evidence

---

1   32 C.J.S. *Evidence* § 602.
2   People v. Kinney, 124 Mich. 486, 83 N.W. 147 (1900).
3   384 U.S. 757, 86 S. Ct. 1826, 16 L. Ed. 2d 908 (1966). *See* case in Part II, *infra.* See Chapter 16 for discussion of constitutional safeguards.

to be introduced. In many instances, criminal justice personnel are most familiar with the evidence and can most correctly connect the evidence with the crime and the accused. Also, the attorney may call upon the victim to take the stand to establish the identity and relevancy of the real evidence.

Four general rules regarding the admissibility of real evidence are often applied. These are:

a. Establishment of a chain or continuity of custody

In order for real evidence to be admitted, the party introducing the evidence, for example, the prosecutor in a criminal case, must show that the evidence was not tampered with from the time it was first obtained until it is produced in court.[4] The trial court need only be satisfied that in reasonable probability the article has not been changed in important respects. In *West v. United States*,[5] the Eighth Circuit held that the trial court did not abuse its discretion in admitting in evidence packets containing marijuana on the ground that there was sufficient foundation to establish the chain of custody from the accused to the time of the analysis. In that case the testimony of an undercover officer was that he had purchased the packets and the packets had been kept by him and forwarded in sealed and initialed envelopes.

While it is preferable to introduce evidence to show that the chain of custody was not broken at any time, the fact that there was not a detailed chain of custody does not necessarily make the evidence inadmissible. In a well-considered case in 1984, the Supreme Court of North Carolina spelled out the rule relating to the standard of certainty in determining whether an object offered in evidence is the same as the object involved in the incident and is in an unchanged condition.[6]

In this first degree rape case, hair and blood samples from the victim, and vaginal and rectal smears and swabs were placed in a cylindrical container called a "rape kit," which was marked and sealed in the presence of the doctor taking the evidence and then placed in a refrigerator nearby. At the trial, a forensic serologist testified that blood stains found on the bedspread upon which the rape allegedly occurred were consistent with blood taken from the victim and that traces of semen found on the bedspread were consistent with that of a male with the defendant's blood groupings. The

---

4   Brewer v. United States, 353 F.2d 260 (8th Cir. 1965); *see also* United States v. Burris, 393 F.2d 81 (7th Cir. 1968) (held that prosecution established the chain of custody so that narcotics received from defendant and placed in a sealed envelope and later tested by a government chemist were admissible in evidence).

5   359 F.2d 50 (8th Cir. 1966); *see also* State v. Frotes, 160 Mont. 431, 503 P.2d 47 (1972).

6   Campbell v. State, 317 S.E.2d 391 (N.C. 1984).

defendant was convicted and sentenced to life imprisonment. He appealed directly to the Supreme Court of North Carolina as a matter of right.

On appeal, the defendant argued that the state failed to establish a chain of custody sufficient to allow the admission into evidence of either the rape kit or results obtained by analysis of its contents. The gist of the defendant's argument was that there was no evidence introduced about the location of the refrigerator in which the rape kit was placed and no indication that the refrigerator was locked. The defendant also claimed that the hospital's chief security officer in charge of the evidence was on vacation when the kit was prepared and that he had no knowledge of the kit until his return from vacation eight days after the preparation.

On behalf of the state, evidence was introduced to show that the samples were taken in the physician's presence, that he signed various forms for inclusion in the rape kit, that the rape kit identified by the physician on the witness stand was, without question, the same kit that he had completed as he examined the victim, that he recognized his handwriting on the kit, and that he recognized the victim's panties that he had included in the kit. He further testified that the kit was new when he prepared it, that it was sealed in his presence by the attending nurse, and that the nurse then placed the kit in the refrigerator at his request and reported that she had placed it there.

In approving the use of this evidence, the reviewing court explained that a detailed chain of custody need be established only when the evidence offered is not readily identifiable or is susceptible to alteration and there is reason to believe that it may have been altered. The court further noted that any weak links in a chain of custody under these situations relate only to the weight to be given to the evidence and not to its admissibility. Applying these rules to the case, the court determined that an adequate chain of custody had been established in this case to prove that the samples in the rape kit examined by the serologist were those placed in the kit by the physician.[7]

Agreeing with more recent decisions that an object should be admitted into evidence if it is sufficiently identified as being the same object involved in the incident giving rise to the trial and if the object is shown to have been unchanged in any material respect, the Supreme Court of North Carolina in 1984 upheld the admission into evidence of a hawkbill knife found in the glove compartment of the defendant's brother's car during an inventory search. The fact that the car had remained in a garage overnight did not contaminate the evidence as testimony disclosed that the car was locked before it was towed to the privately owned garage whose agents were experienced in handling vehicles involved in crime. Also, an officer

---

7   *See* Mosqueda v. State, 168 Ind. App. 181, 342 N.E.2d 679 (1976) which held that the chain of possession is proven if it is demonstrated that there is no reasonable doubt as to the continuous whereabouts of the property.

testified that when he arrived at the garage the vehicle was secured in a locked area, and the officer who processed the crime saw no change in the condition of the vehicle.

Quoting from other cases, the court held that "the trial judge possesses and must exercise a sound discretion in determining the standard of certainty required to show that the object offered is the same as the object involved in the incident giving rise to the trial, and that the object is in an unchanged condition." After examining the facts, the court concluded, "We believe that under the present facts the trial judge properly admitted the hawkbill knife into evidence."8

The federal courts, in interpreting Rules 901 and 101 of the Federal Rules of Evidence, have been fairly consistent in allowing real evidence to be admitted, even if the chain of evidence is not clear, when the items have been in official custody and there is no affirmative evidence of tampering.9 There is a "presumption of regularity which attends the official acts of public officers, and the courts presume that their official duties have been discharged properly."10

For example, in an armed robbery prosecution, the Seventh Circuit held that the trial court did not abuse its discretion in admitting several sweatshirts that allegedly belonged to the defendant, even though there had been a break in the chain of custody. In this case the sweatshirts, two of which fit the description of sweatshirts worn by the robber during two bank robberies, had originally been found by police during an investigatory search of the defendant's car. The police subsequently released the sweatshirts and the car to the defendant's brother. Six days after they were released, the FBI retrieved the sweatshirts from the brother's home, although not from the brother personally. As the government could not conclusively demonstrate that the sweatshirts that were recovered were the same ones thet were released to the brother, there was a break in the chain of custody. However, any discrepancies in the chain of custody went to the weight of the evidence, not to its admissibility.11

In a cocaine possession case, the Tenth Circuit held that the trial court did not abuse its discretion in admitting a plastic sack of cocaine that had been seized from the defendant's car, even though the police officer who had sealed and labeled the evidence and carried it to the evidence storage room was deceased and unable to testify as to the chain of custody.12 The court noted that for evidence (like cocaine) that is not readily identifiable and sus-

---

8   State v. Bell, 316 S.E.2d 611 (N.C. 1984).
9   United States v. Olson, 846 F.2d 1103 (11th Cir. 1988). *See* case in Part II, *infra.*
10 United States v. Olson, 846 F.2d 1103 (11th Cir. 1988). *See* case in Part II, *infra.*
11 United States v. L'Allier, 838 F.2d 234 (7th Cir. 1988).
12 United States v. Cardenas, 864 F.2d 1528 (10th Cir. 1989).

ceptible to alteration to be admissible under Rule 901(a), a chain of custody must be shown with sufficient completeness to render it improbable that the item has been exchanged with another or has been contaminated or altered. The court explained, however, that the trial court need not rule out every possibility that the evidence underwent alteration. The well-established rule is that deficiencies in the chain of custody go to the weight of the evidence.

Notwithstanding the fact that the courts have been reluctant to prohibit the use of evidence even if there has been a gap in the chain of custody, it is quite clear that if the prosecution cannot introduce evidence to show that it is improbable that the item has been contaminated or tampered with, it will not be admitted. Also, if there is some doubt created concerning the chain of custody of admitted evidence, a court or jury will give less weight to the evidence.

b.   Necessity

Because of the potential weight that may be placed upon the use of real evidence, the courts have reasoned that it should not be admitted unless good reason for its admission is offered. The admission or exclusion of real evidence rests largely within the discretion of the trial judge. In some instances, the party offering a demonstration of the real evidence is required to give good reason for its acceptance into evidence. As one court stated, the evidence should be admitted where it is both relevant and highly probative, better evidence cannot reasonably be anticipated, and the dangers are small in comparison to the advantages.[13] While the admission of real evidence is not improper merely because it is gruesome or because it may tend to influence the emotions, it should not be admitted merely for a dramatic effect or to arouse feelings.

c.   Relationship to crime

Evidence may be excluded at the discretion of the judge when the facts sought to be proved are only remotely connected with the issues. In other words, the evidence must be material. If the evidence would be likely to mislead or confuse the jury with a number of preliminary or collateral issues, the court in balancing the value of the evidence in relation to the confusion it might cause may exclude it.[14]

Before a physical object connected with the commission of a crime may properly be admitted into evidence, it must be satisfactorily identified and shown to have a direct relationship to the crime charged.[15] If there is insuffi-

---

13 Commonwealth v. Inhabitants of Holliston, 107 Mass. 232 (1871).
14 32 C.J.S. *Evidence* § 602.
15 State v. Campbell, 103 Wash. 2d 1, 691 P. 2d 929 (1984), *cert. denied,* 471 U.S. 1094, 105 S. Ct. 2169, 85 L. Ed. 2d 526 (1984).

cient evidence to show that the article is connected with the crime, it may not be admitted. For example, hairs found in the victim's apartment were not admissible in a murder and rape trial in which there was no evidence linking the hairs with another person who could have committed the crime.16

Although the burden is on the party introducing the evidence to show that it complies with the requirements, in most instances the court will admit real evidence if it has any logical bearing upon the case. The judge has the discretion as to whether the evidence is related to the crime, and his decision is not subject to review unless there has been a clear abuse of this discretion.

d. Proper identification

When an object, article, tool, weapon or similar tangible thing is to be used in evidence to prove a fact to which it is related, as of a previous time or event, the item is not competent evidence unless it is first identified as the same object and shown to be in substantially the same condition as of the time or event to which it is claimed to be related.17 The requirement of identification is designed not only to prevent the introduction of an object other than the one about which there has been testimony, but to insure that significant changes in the condition of the object have not occurred.18

Articles are sometimes admitted into evidence even though a slight alteration or change has occurred, e.g., a knife blade that was scraped for the purpose of obtaining a chemical analysis of the substance by which the blade was discolored;19 clothing worn by the deceased that was washed by his widow after having been returned by the police;20 a murder weapon dusted by the police for fingerprints and then wiped clean;21 a shell that was marked for identification by the sheriff, who scratched his initials into it;22 and counterfeit plates from which lacquer had been removed.23

---

16 State v. Bradfield, 29 Wash. App. 679, 630 P.2d 494 (1981).

17 Gutman v. Industrial Comm., 71 Ohio App. 383, 50 N.E.2d 187 (1942); *see also* State v. Campbell, 103 Wash. 2d 1, 691 P. 2d 929 (1984), which held that before a physical object connected with the commission of a crime may properly be admitted into evidence, it must be satisfactorily identified and shown to be in substantially the same condition as when the crime was committed. The factors to be considered include the nature of the article, circumstances surrounding its preservation and custody and the likelihood of intermeddlers tampering with it.

18 McElfresh v. Commonwealth, 243 S.W.2d 497 (Ky. 1951).

19 Fabian v. State, 97 Ohio St. 184, 119 N.E. 410 (1918).

20 Davidson v. State, 208 Ga. 834, 69 S.E.2d 757 (1952).

21 State v. Cooper, 10 N.J. 532, 91 A.2d 786 (1952).

22 Duke v. State, 257 Ala. 339, 58 So. 2d 764 (1952).

23 State v. Stewart, 1 Ohio App. 2d 260, 204 N.E.2d 397 (1963).

In the case of *Washington v. Commonwealth* the court held that the trial court did not err in admitting a shirt into evidence in a prosecution for capital murder, even though there were changes, including facts that the shirt had been worn, washed, ironed and folded after the crime had been committed where the changes were explained. The fact that bloodstains found on the shirt had been cut out for laboratory analysis, leaving small holes, did nothing to impair the admissibility or probative value of the exhibit where the changes were sufficiently explained to avoid any confusion of the jury.[24]

§ 14.3 Exhibition of person

Where in a criminal case the prosecution of the defendant is based on physical harm to the victim, it would seem that the best evidence of such harm would be the exhibition of the person of the victim to the jury. Such witness would be more valuable in determining what happened than would oral testimony, photographs or even x-rays, in some instances. Courts as a rule will allow the display of injuries to the jury—often in spite of the fact that the injury is gruesome.

The trial judge has much discretion in determining whether the physical display of the injury is so inflammatory as to unduly influence the jury in the decision. His discretionary decision is seldom overruled unless there is a clear abuse of discretion. However, if in the opinion of the judge the display of the person and the injury is determined to be so inflammatory as to prejudice the jury, the judge may require that the injury be described, rather than allowing the exhibition of the person and the display of the injury.

The person of the witness may be exhibited at the trial in a criminal case to assist the jury or judge in determining the nature and extent of the injury. For example, it is permissible for the prosecution to exhibit a child to the jury to prove the commission of the crime of statutory rape.[25] In a paternity proceeding, the court may generally require the alleged father to stand close to the illegitimate child to enable the jury to compare their physical features.[26]

Although the judge in his discretion may permit the witness to be exhibited at the trial in a criminal case in order to determine the extent of injury, the judge should not allow a defendant in a criminal case to appear

---

24 Washington v. Commonwealth, 228 Va. 535, 323 S.E.2d 577 (1984), *cert. denied,* 471 U.S. 1111, 105 S. Ct. 2347, 85 L. Ed. 863 (1984).
25 65 AM. JUR. 2D *Rape* § 60; State v. Danforth, 73 N.H. 215, 60 A. 839 (1905).
26 29 AM. JUR. 2D *Evidence* § 780; Kelly v. State, 133 Ala. 195, 32 So. 56 (1902).

before the jury in leg irons or handcuffs unless the prosecution can present to the court some clear justification for bringing a bound prisoner to court. In one case, the court stated that a defendant may not be subjected to physical restraints of any kind in the courtroom while in the jury's presence unless there is a showing of manifest need for such restraints.[27]

§ 14.4   Articles connected with the crime

Generally, devices and instruments used in the commission of a crime, as well as articles connected therewith, are admitted into evidence. To be admissible, the prosecution must show that there was or is a connection between the article and the accused.

Some examples of types of articles which have been acquired by investigators and submitted for consideration are discussed in the paragraphs that follow.

a.   Weapons

In a bank robbery prosecution in which the defendant was charged with the violation of a federal statute making it a crime to take money from a bank by intimidation, the trial court admitted into evidence the component parts of a non-explosive simulated bomb consisting of a brown paper bag, a small box, a short length of wire and an ordinary alarm clock. Although counsel for the defendant argued that these items were irrelevant to the proof of any element of the crime, the Eighth Circuit upheld the use of the real evidence on the theory that the introduction of such evidence helps to demonstrate the method by which the crime was committed.[28]

In the case of *People v. Riser,*[29] the court stated that if the specific type of weapon used to commit a homicide is not known, any weapons that are found in the defendant's possession after the crime and that might have been used in committing a homicide are admissible; however, if the prosecution relies on the specific weapon or type, it is error to admit evidence that other weapons were found in the defendant's possession. It was explained that to allow the introduction of other types of weapons would

---

27 People v. Duran, 16 Cal. 3d 282, 545 P.2d 1322 (1976).
28 Caldwell v. United States, 338 F.2d 385 (8th Cir. 1964). In Evans v. United States, 122 F.2d 461 (10th Cir. 1941), the court admitted a string and broom used in the commission of a homicide. In State v. Fulcher, 20 N.C. App. 259, a hammer found at the scene of a murder was admitted into evidence in view of bruise marks on the victim's body, even though there was no evidence particularly identifying the hammer as the murder weapon.
29 47 Cal. 2d 566, 305 P.2d 1 (1956).

not tend to show not that the defendant had committed the particular crime, but only that he was the sort of person who would carry deadly weapons.

Notwithstanding the general rule that other weapons found are inadmissible when the state's evidence indicates that the victim was shot by a specific caliber weapon, there are some exceptions. For example, in the case of *State v. Coury*, the Court of Criminal Appeals of Tennessee approved the introduction of evidence which showed that a .38 caliber pistol was found in the garage where the suspect was arrested even though the victim was shot by a .45 caliber pistol. At the time the defendant was arrested in the garage, some eleven hours after the shooting, the officers found a loaded .38 caliber pistol in a plastic bag. The bag was inside an "ammo case," and prior to the discovery of the pistol, the defendant was seen in the back of the garage and was seen placing a hat over the ammo case, obviously attempting to conceal it and the gun.

The defendant on appeal argued that as the state's evidence indicated that the victim was shot with a .45 caliber pistol, the .38 caliber pistol found in the garage was not relevant. The trial court and the reviewing court disagreed, reasoning that the jury was entitled to consider whether an additional weapon had been used or had been available for use in the shooting. Here the jury, according to this court, is entitled to consider the pistol and the defendant's action with reference thereto as this evidence would relate to the defendant's flight and attempt to avoid arrest.30

In a murder prosecution, the Eleventh Circuit Court found that the trial court did not abuse its discretion in admitting bullets and other physical evidence, even though the government failed to establish a continuous chain of custody, as it was shown that the evidence was connected with the crime.31 In another case, a murder weapon was admissible in evidence even though the detective who had seized the weapon was dead, as the detective had immediately delivered the weapon to another detective, who then delivered it to the forensic laboratory for examination. At the trial the weapon was identified by its serial number by a detective who indicated that the weapon possessed characteristics that are fairly unique, readily identifiable and relatively impervious to change.32

b. Instruments used in the crime

In a prosecution for the burglary of a tavern in which there was evidence that the front door had been forced open and the tavern proprietor testified that one of the burglars was trying to pry open the side door with a screwdriver and that one of the burglars wore gloves, the court autho-

---

30 State v. Coury, 697 S.W.2d 373 (Tenn. Crim. App. 1985).
31 United States v. Olson, 846 F.2d 1103 (11th Cir. 1988). *See* case in Part II.
32 Bassett v. Commonwealth, 222 Va. 844, 284 S.E.2d 844 (1981), *cert. denied,* 456 U.S. 938, 102 S. Ct. 1996, 72 L. Ed. 2d 458 (1981).

rized the introduction into evidence of a screwdriver and gloves found in a field where the defendant had admitted running. The court held that the items were sufficiently connected with the crime and the defendant to render them admissible.33 In another case, where there was direct positive evidence that tools found on the street had been used in a burglary, evidence tending to show that these tools had been in the possession of the defendants and thrown from their fleeing car was properly admitted.34

On the other hand, in the case of *People v. McCall*,35 in which the defendant testified that he struck the deceased in the deceased's car in self-defense and that the deceased fractured his skull when he fell to the pavement, the reviewing court held that the introduction into evidence of an auto crank, wrench, hammer handle and tire iron, all found in the car, was reversible error as there were no fingerprints or bloodstains on the implements to connect them with the defendant.

c. Clothing

Clothing that is identified by a witness as that worn by the accused at the time of the crime may be submitted to the jury for inspection. For example, in one case a coat and hat which were admittedly owned by the defendant and found in an abandoned automobile used by a bank robber, and which were identified as similar to those worn by the robber, were admissible as connecting the defendant with the bank robbery.36 In another case, a cap, jacket and trousers found in a washing machine a few minutes after a robber had allegedly entered the house wearing similar clothing were properly admitted. The court held that such evidence was relevant and that the obtaining of the evidence did not violate the Fifth Amendment.37

In order to be admissible, clothing and other articles must meet relevancy and materiality tests. In the case of *State v. Atkins*, a Missouri court of appeals agreed with the trial court that the victim's robe, nightgown and the sheets from her bed were relevant in a rape case.38 Here the defendant was convicted of first degree burglary, forcible rape and armed criminal action. The evidence indicated that the defendant forcibly entered the apartment of the victim by gaining entry through a window. It was alleged that after a struggle with the victim, the defendant overcame her will to resist by threatening to stab her with a knife which he displayed, and that he then forcibly raped her.

---

33 People v. Allen, 17 Ill. 2d 55, 160 N.E.2d 818 (1959).

34 McNeely v. United States, 353 F.2d 913 (8th Cir. 1965); *see also* Buck v. State, 503 S.W.2d 558 (Tex. 1974).

35 10 Cal. App. 2d 503, 52 P.2d 500 (1935).

36 Caldwell v. United States, 338 F.2d 385 (8th Cir. 1964); *see also* State v. Brierly, 509 P.2d 203 (Ariz. 1973).

37 Warden, Maryland Penitentiary v. Hayden, 387 U.S. 294, 18 L. Ed. 2d 782, 87 S. Ct. 1642 (1967).

38 State v. Atkins, 697 S.W.2d 226 (Mo. App. 1985).

The defendant argued on appeal that the trial court erred by admitting into evidence the victim's robe, nightgown and the sheets from her bed, claiming that the items failed to support any material fact. Disagreeing with the defendant's contention, the reviewing court decided:

> Evidence is relevant and admissible if it tends to logically prove or disprove facts in issue, or if it corroborates other material evidence. . . . The articles were found by the police at the crime scene. The robe and sheets contained seminal stains while the nightgown was torn and bloody. This evidence corroborated the victim's story that she had been raped and that her lip had been cut during the struggle with Atkins.

The court concluded by indicating that the evidence was relevant and material and that affirmed the sentence of the trial court.

In some instances an article of clothing may be introduced if it is properly authenticated in accordance with Rule 901 of the Federal Rules of Evidence, even though the description of the article of clothing does not exactly fit the seized article. For example, in a bank robbery case a witness testified that the robber wore a baseball cap that was navy blue without any white markings. In a search of the suspect's home, officers found a baseball cap which was light blue and had large white markings in the front. The trial court ruled that the cap found at the residence was sufficiently similar to the one identified and allowed its admission. The reviewing court concluded that the trial court was correct in finding that the cap taken from the residence was relevant and that the jury should be permitted to decide what, if any, weight that the cap should be given.[39]

d. Bloodstains

Stains of blood found upon the person or clothing of the party accused have been recognized as being among the ordinary indicia of homicide. The practice of identifying them by circumstantial evidence and by the inspection of witnesses and jurors has had the sanction of immemorial usage in criminal tribunals.[40]

Bloodstain evidence may be the subject of expert evaluation.[41] However, the state is required to show that evidence concerning the impact of bloodstain evidence is based upon a well-recognized scientific principle or tech-

---

39 United States v. Tyler, 878 F.2d 753 (3d Cir. 1989); *see also* State v. Simone 428 So. 2d 1226 (La. 1983), which held that it is constitutionally permissible for the police to clothe a suspect in attire similar to that worn by the perpetrator for purposes of identification.

40 People v. Gonzales, 35 N.Y. 49 (1866).

41 People v. Driver, 62 Ill. App. 3d 847, 379 N.E.2d 840 (1978).

nique which has gained general acceptance in the particular field to which it belongs.[42] If a police officer qualifies as an expert, he will generally be authorized to testify concerning blood patterns found at the scene of a crime.[43]

In a Tennessee case the supreme court of that state accepted the principles on which bloodstain pattern interpretation has been based and that expert testimony is recognized to explain the pattern of bloodstains.[44] In this case the trial court had permitted a witness to explain a pattern of bloodstains which were spread over the defendant's shirt, pants, cap and boots. In qualifying as an expert, the witness testified that he had trained over 300 people to testify regarding bloodstain patterns, and that he had "published many writings, conducted numerous seminars and done research over a long period of years in . . . the principles of physics as applied to blood patterns."

e. Other types of evidence

Other articles connected with the crime are also admissible if they meet the general tests. For example, in an Eighth Circuit case, paint chips and dust found on the clothing of the defendant which matched samples gathered from the scene of burglary—as well as debris found on some of the burglary tools—were found to have been properly admitted into evidence.[45]

Also, hair samples taken from an automobile 14 months after a collision were admissible in a wrongful death action.[46] In a prosecution for third degree burglary of a money depository, a wire hanger that the defendant may have used in removing money from a parking lot money collection box was properly admitted after a foundation was laid.[47]

In an arson case the reviewing court agreed that it was proper to admit a propane burner found lying on a bedspring in a burned trailer home when a fireman testified that the burner had remained there until the county fire marshal investigated the fire and picked up the burner and that there was no significant change in the burner after the state acquired it.[48]

§ 14.5 View of the scene

In almost all jurisdictions the trial judge has power in both civil and criminal cases to order the jurors to be conducted to a place where a material fact occurred or an offense was committed. The judge has considerable

---

42 People v. Milone, 43 Ill. App. 3d 385, 356 N.E.2d 1350 (1976).
43 People v. Knox, 121 Ill. App. 3d 579, 459 N.E.2d 1077 (1984).
44 State v. Melson, 638 S.W.2d 342 (Tenn. 1982).
45 McNeely v. United States, 353 F.2d 913 (8th Cir. 1965).
46 Wood v. Jones, 334 S.E.2d 9 (Ga. 1985).
47 People v. Garcia, 784 P.2d 823 (Colo. 1989).
48 State v. Conrad, 785 P.2d 185 (Mont. 1990).

discretion to grant or refuse a request for a view by the jury. Under a statute providing that "when it is proper for the jurors to have a view of the place at which a material fact occurred, the trial court may order them to be conducted in a body to such place," the word "may" implies discretion.[49] Over objection by the defendant and in the exercise of sound discretion, the trial court may, after it has been fully informed of the nature of the evidence to be offered and after proper safeguards are taken to protect the rights of the defendant, permit the jurors to view premises where the acts at issue are alleged to have been committed by the defendant.[50] Among the factors which the judge will consider are the degree of importance to the issue of the information to be gained by a view, the extent to which this information could be adequately secured from photographs, maps or diagrams, and the extent to which the premises or object have changed in appearance or condition since the occurrence.[51]

The decision as to whether the jury should be allowed to view the scene will not be reversed absent an abuse of discretion.[52] One court noted that in making this decision whether to grant or refuse a motion to view the scene, a court considers such factors as issues involved, status of the evidence and its inferences, and whether the view would aid the jury in understanding issues and appraising the evidence.[53] Even when a statute permits the court to have the jurors visit the scene, it does not mandate that visits be made even if requested.[54]

The procedure for viewing premises varies from state to state, and the manner of viewing the scene is often regulated by either statute or rule of court. Usually the jury is conducted to the place by an officer of the court, who directs the jurors' attention to features of the scene which will be or have been referred to in the testimony given in court. Ordinarily the parties and their counsel are allowed to be present; however, they are not permitted to discuss the case with members of the jury. In criminal cases some states permit the accused to be present; others hold that allowing the accused to be present is within the discretion of the judge. In one case, refusal to grant the defendant's request to be present, when his counsel was present and there was no showing of resulting injustice was not a denial of due process

---

49 Commonwealth v. Chance, 174 Mass. 245, 54 N.E. 551 (1899).
50 Commonwealth v. Gedzium, 259 Mass. 453, 156 N.E. 890 (1927); State v. Pigott, 1 Ohio App. 2d 22, 30 Ohio Op. 2d 56, 197 N.E.2d 911 (1964); People v. Crossan, 87 Cal. App. 5, 261 P. 531 (1927). *But see* Peyton v. Strickland, 203 S.E.2d 388 (S.C. 1974).
51 McCormick, Evidence § 183.
52 Kincaid v. Landing Development Corp., 344 S.E.2d 869 (S.C. 1986).
53 Parker v. Randolph County, 475 S.E.2d 1193 (Ala. 1985).
54 Swartz v. Wells, 449 N.E.2d 9 (Ohio 1982).

under the Fourteenth Amendment.55 However, in California, the trial judge must accompany the jury when it is taken to view the scene.56

The purpose of the view is to enable the jurors to observe places or objects which are pointed out to them, and thus, to provide them with a mental picture of the locality. There is a conflict in the law as to whether a view constitutes independent evidence. Some courts take a position that it does, while other courts hold that a view does not supply evidence but merely enables the jury to understand and apply the evidence offered at trial.57 Inevitably, what the jurors see on a view will be utilized in reaching a verdict, and in that sense, that which is disclosed on a view is evidence.

§ 14.6 Photographs

As was pointed out in previous sections, it is often possible to exhibit the person to the jury or judge, to introduce articles connected with the crime, or to have the jury view the scene of the crime. In other instances, it is impracticable to bring all of the tangible evidence before the court. On the other hand, it is often impossible to define tangible evidence by words alone, and photographs, if properly taken and explained, bring this type of evidence into court in a more convenient fashion. Photographs frequently convey information to the court and jury more accurately than words. Although photos are merely graphic representations of the oral testimony of witnesses, they often have far greater value than words.

Photographs are generally inadmissible as original or substantive evidence. They must be sponsored by a witness whose testimony they serve to explain or illustrate. To be admissible, a photograph must first be made a part of some qualified person's testimony. Someone, often a law enforcement officer, must stand forth as its testimonial sponsor; in other words, it must be verified. A photograph may not be received by itself; it must be verified by a witness.58

---

55 Snyder v. Massachusetts, 291 U.S. 97, 54 S. Ct. 330, 78 L. Ed. 674 (1934).

56 Rau v. Redwood City W. Club, 111 Cal. App. 2d 546, 245 P.2d 12 (1952).

57 In the case of City of Columbia v. Jennings, 339 S.E.2d 534 (S.C. 1986) the court noted that the purpose of the jury view is to enable the jury better to understand the evidence presented in the court room, and viewing the premises is not regarded as the taking of evidence.

58 3 Wigmore, EVIDENCE § 794 (3d ed.); see also Phillips v. State, 550 N.E.2d 1290 (Ind. 1990), which held that photographs are generally admissible if they depict an object or scene which a witness would be permitted to describe in his testimony.

Before a trial court will admit a photograph in evidence, a foundation must be laid. A competent witness who has personal knowledge must testify that the picture is an accurate representation of the objects or persons depicted. For example, in a case in which a bank teller examined photographs taken by an automatic camera and testified that they were fair and accurate representations of a bank robbery, the photographs were properly admitted into evidence.59

The correctness of such a representation may be established by any witness who is familiar with the scene, object or person portrayed, or who is competent to speak from personal observation. A witness qualifying a photograph does not have to be the photographer or see the picture taken; it is only necessary that the witness recognize and identify the object depicted and testify that the photograph fairly and correctly represents that object.60 Whether there is sufficient evidence of the correctness of a photograph to render it competent to be used by a witness for the purpose of illustrating or explaining his testimony is a preliminary question of fact for the trial judge.61

In addition to being properly identified or verified, photographic evidence will not be admitted unless it is relevant. Before a photograph may be introduced at trial, there must be a determination by the court of its relevancy and proof must be offered that it is a fair presentation of its subject.62 If a photograph is not relevant or material as discussed in previous chapters, it generally will not be admitted. However, a photograph which is relevant as to one issue should not be excluded merely because it is inadmissible on some other issue.63 If a photograph is challenged as being irrelevant on one issue but is admitted for another issue, the jury should be given a cautionary instruction directing it to consider the photograph for the limited purpose only.

---

59 United States v. Hobbs, 403 F.2d 977 (6th Cir. 1968); *see also* United States v. Rembert, 863 F.2d 1023 (D.C. Cir. 1988), which approved the admission of photographs taken by an automatic teller machine when the photographs were authenticated by the robbery victims, and the testimony of a bank official indicated that the cameras were properly loaded and secured.

60 Kleveland v. United States, 345 F.2d 134 (2d Cir. 1965).

61 State v. Gardner, 228 N.C. 567, 46 S.E.2d 824 (1948). In this case the trial judge, in admitting a photograph, instructed the jury: "You will not consider this photograph as substantive evidence—it is not competent for that purpose. It is only competent, and the court limits the evidence in the way of a photograph, to illustrating the testimony of the witness, and it is a question for you as to whether or not it does illustrate his testimony, and you will receive it and consider the photograph in no other way than as tending to illustrate the testimony of the witness, and not as substantive evidence."

62 *See* Fed. R. Evid. 401, discussed in § 7.2 of this book.

63 Williams v. State, 441 S.W.2d 853 (Tex. Crim. App. 1969).

In interpreting Rule 901 of the Federal Rules of Evidence, the Fifth Circuit agreed that the district court did not err in admitting photographs to show the juxtaposition of the defendant's van and rig, which contained marijuana, thereby tending to refute the defendant's claim that he knew nothing of the marijuana and thus did not join the conspiracy at issue. In authenticating the photograph, the prosecution established to a reasonable degree the time and place of the photographs by testimony that they depicted the scene of the arrest, thereby satisfying the prosecution's burden of authentication.[64]

In several cases, the question has arisen as to whether it is necessary to follow the rules relating to the chain of custody as discussed in Section 14.2. As photographs are not in the same category as such evidence as instruments used to commit the crime, the same rules do not apply. It generally is not necessary to show that the photographs have been in the possession of any one person until they were offered in evidence.[65] The fact that it is not necessary to establish the chain of custody of a photograph, however, does not mean that it may be used without verification. Evidence must be introduced (as indicated in the preceding paragraphs) to show that the photograph is a correct representation of the object portrayed.[66]

Not all photographs are admissible, even when a proper foundation is laid. If, in obtaining a photograph, the state violates a constitutional provision, the defendant has constitutional grounds to object to the admissibility. In the case of *California v. Ciraolo,* officers, after receiving a tip that the defendant was growing marijuana in his fenced backyard, took an airplane flight over the yard and observed and photographed what appeared to be marijuana under cultivation.[67] Although the California Court of Appeals reversed the conviction, the United States Supreme Court disagreed, holding that the photographs were taken from a public vantage where the officers had a right to be and that this action therefore did not violate the Fourth Amendment. However, if photographs are taken by an officer while violating the constitutional rights of the defendant, the evidence acquired will be inadmissible.

a. Posed photographs

There is a decided conflict of authority as to whether photographs of an attempted reproduction of the scene of a crime showing posed persons, dummies or other objects are admissible to illustrate the contention of the party offering them that they represent the relative positions of the movable objects so represented at the time and place of the crime involved in the prosecution

---

64 United States v. Mojica, 746 F.2d 242 (5th Cir. 1984).
65 United States v. Neal, 527 F.2d 63 (8th Cir. 1975), *cert. denied,* 429 U.S. 845, 97 S. Ct. 125, 50 L. Ed. 2d 134 (1976).
66 State v. Fournier, 2 Conn. Cir. Ct. 588, 203 A.2d 245 (1963).
67 California v. Ciraolo, 476 U.S. 267, 106 S. Ct. 1809, 90 L. Ed. 2d 210 (1986).

under consideration. In most jurisdictions where this question of admissibility has arisen, the courts have held such photographs admissible when a proper foundation has been laid by preliminary testimony showing that the objects and situations portrayed are faithfully represented as to position. An Oklahoma court held that posed photographs are admissible if they are properly identified and if they purport to represent conditions as they actually existed at some crucial time and place, but not if they are intended only to illustrate hypothetical situations and to explain certain theories of the parties.[68]

b. Gruesome photographs

Although a photograph may be rendered inadmissible by its inflammatory nature, the mere fact that it is gruesome or horrendous is not sufficient to render it inadmissible if the trial court, in the exercise of its discretion, feels that the photograph would prove useful to the jury. The critical question is whether the probative value of the photograph is outweighed by the danger of prejudice to the defendant.[69] For example, in the trial of a defendant charged with murder in the first degree, the admission or exclusion of photographs of the murder victim taken at the scene of the murder was properly within the sound discretion of the court.[70] In another case, a police photographer's gruesome pictures of a burned woman in her hospital bed on the day after the defendant allegedly set her afire were properly admitted in evidence.[71] Also, the admission of a photograph showing the decedent lying in a pool of blood was not an abuse of discretion, where it tended to assist the jury in understanding testimony of an autopsy surgeon concerning the injuries that the decedent suffered and the testimony of a criminologist regarding articles found in the vicinity of the body.[72] In another state case, the court found that the trial judge did not abuse his discretion in admitting photographs of the decedent's body, taken in a tavern where the shooting occurred, to corroborate testimony about the absence of powder burns on the flesh and on the deceased's shirt and undershirt.[73]

---

68 Roberts v. State, 166 P.2d 111 (Okla. 1946).

69 State v. Woodards, 6 Ohio St. 2d 14, 215 N.E.2d 568 (1966); Maxwell v. United States, 368 F.2d 735 (9th Cir. 1966); State v. Curry, 292 So. 2d 212 (La. 1974).

70 State v. Hill, 12 Ohio St. 88, 232 N.E.2d 394 (1967), in which the reviewing court found no abuse of discretion and held that "inspection of the photographs taken of decedent soon after his murder shows that they are not so gory or gruesome as to produce an inflammatory reaction by the jury against the defendant, and they were introduced in connection with the testimony of the state's witnesses to explain and clarify certain aspects of that testimony."

71 State v. McClain, 256 Iowa 175, 125 N.W.2d 764 (1964).

72 People v. Arguello, 37 Cal. Rptr. 601, 390 P.2d 377 (1964).

73 State v. O'Conner, 42 N.J. 502, 201 A.2d 705 (1964).

However, the Pennsylvania Supreme Court found that it was harmful error to admit at a murder trial a photograph showing in close and graphic detail the victim's distorted face, head wound, blood, flesh and brains scattered in the snow alongside the head. The court indicated that the gruesomeness and inflammatory nature of the photograph was patently obvious.[74] In this case, the court made reference to the balancing test when it stated that the important question is: "Is the photograph of such essential evidentiary value that its need clearly outweighs the likelihood of inflaming the minds and passions of jurors?" As other evidence had been introduced in this case to indicate that the victim was shot while lying on the ground and that the shooting took place after a robbery had occurred, the photograph was not of essential evidentiary value and should not have been admitted.

The line between photographs which are inadmissible because they unduly arouse passion or prejudice and those that are admissible is often a fine one. For example, the probative value of "hideous" color photographs in a prosecution for murder outweighed any allegedly prejudicial impact when the focus of the testimony involved two gunshot wounds were sustained by the victim, which paths these bullets took through the body, and which wounds were fatal.[75] However, the photographs of a murder victim's nude and partially decomposed body were inadmissible when the photographs were gruesome and lacked any evidentiary purpose and when their probative value was outweighed by their tendency to inflame and prejudice the jury.[76] In disallowing the photographs of the partially decomposed body, the court commented that when presented with gruesome photographs, the trial judge should carefully consider all facts and circumstances surrounding the admission of the photographs, including whether proof is absolute or in doubt as to the identity of the guilty party, as well as whether the photographs are necessary evidence or simply a ploy on the part of the prosecutor to arouse the passion and prejudice of the jury.

The rule is that if photographs are relevant, the mere fact that they are unpleasant or gruesome does not bar their admission.[77] If, however, the photographs have potential to distort the deliberative process and skew the trial's outcome, the potential for unfair prejudice is presumed to outweigh its probativeness, and the burden is on the prosecution to show otherwise.[78]

---

74 Commonwealth v. Rogers, 401 A.2d 329 (Pa. 1979). *See* case in Part II, *infra.*
75 People v. Lambkin, 193 Ill. App. 3d 570, 550 N.E.2d 278 (1990).
76 McNeal v. State, 551 So. 2d 151 (Miss. 1989).
77 Davis v. State, 551 So. 2d 165 (Miss. 1989).
78 State v. Dibello, 780 P.2d 1221 (Utah 1989).

c. Time of taking

In some instances, the correctness of the photograph depends upon the time it was taken. If the time between the incident and the taking of the photograph is so great as to make it unlikely that the photograph actually portrays the situation as it existed at the time of the incident, such a photograph will not be admissible. It is obvious that the nature of the thing photographed has great weight in determining the importance of the time element. Some examples will emphasize this point.

As a rule, photographs taken by an officer at the time of an accident will be admitted in evidence. However, in the case of *Hopper v. Reed,*[79] the court excluded photographs taken 14 months after a traffic accident (in which a boy was struck while crossing a highway) because the photographs did not show the traffic as it existed at the time of the accident. But a photograph of a section of a highway where a head-on collision between two trucks occurred was admitted in evidence even though they were taken some days after the accident, as the state trooper testified that the photograph correctly portrayed the same conditions as existed at the scene immediately after the collision.[80] In a prosecution for the illegal possession and sale of narcotics, it was not error to admit in evidence photographs that showed police surveillance of the defendant dealing with an informer, when the photographs were taken between the dates of the several indictments.[81]

Changes in conditions portrayed between the time of the event under investigation and the taking of a photograph do not render the photograph inadmissible where the changes can be explained by a witness and the changes are not of such a character as to render the photograph deceptive.[82] In an action for injuries sustained in an automobile accident, the court found admissible a photograph taken six years previously that showed the plaintiff in military uniform and that was accompanied by evidence to prove that the photograph accurately depicted the plaintiff's appearance two months before the accident.[83]

---

[79] 320 F.2d 433 (6th Cir. 1963).
[80] Jenkins v. Associated Transport, Inc., 330 F.2d 706 (6th Cir. 1964). In a prosecution for burglary of a tavern when the tavern door was open at the time of the burglary, it was proper to introduce in evidence the photograph of the open door. People v. Allen, 17 Ill. 2d 55, 160 N.E.2d 818 (1959).
[81] State v. Good, 110 Ohio App. 415, 165 N.E. 2d 28 (1960).
[82] McKee v. Chase, 73 Idaho 491, 253 P.2d 787 (1953).
[83] Highshew v. Kushto, 126 Ind. App. 584, 131 N.E.2d 652 (1956); *see also* Burnett v. Cabo, 7 Ill. App. 2d 266, 285 N.E.2d 619 (1972).

d. Color photographs

Color photographs and color slides are admissible in evidence subject to the same limitations and restrictions placed on black-and-white photographs. Even though color photographs are often more lifelike and consequently more gruesome and revolting, this in itself does not constitute grounds for exclusion of color photographs.[84] Because color photographs are subject to color distortion, however, it is more difficult to take photographs that show the actual colors as they existed at the scene, and the proponent is often subject to a strong cross-examination on the subject of distortion.

Some examples of cases in which color slides were admissible follow. In a murder trial, color slides of the nude body of the deceased showing the location of his wounds were admissible.[85] The admission of color slides taken during the course of an autopsy performed on a murder victim was not an abuse of discretion.[86] Color photographs of the deceased's body taken during an autopsy were admitted to give the jury a clear understanding of the cause of death,[87] and color photographs of injuries were admitted in a case in which the attending doctors identified the photographs as a fair representation of the plaintiff's condition as of the time they were taken.[88]

Apparently, color photography is used more in criminal cases than in civil cases, and the courts have recognized that the probative value of color photographs sometimes outweighs their probable adverse effect.[89] On the other hand, justice personnel must be cautioned that color photographs are sometimes overused. In a Pennsylvania case, the record showed that the trial lasted 4 1/2 days during which gruesome color slides were used during a third of that time. Although the conviction was not overturned on this ground, the court stated:

> Since the case will be remanded, we are constrained to suggest that the pictures should not if used be put before the jury for so long a time and although they were subjected to medical explanation we regard the duration of their view as excessive. Such pictures may be used as a fine point of demonstration but not as a bludgeon for winning the case.[90]

---

84 State v. Fulcher, 20 N.C. App. 259.
85 State v. Farley, 112 Ohio App. 448, 196 N.E.2d 232 (1960).
86 State v. Swafford, 520 P.2d 1151 (Ariz. 1942); State v. Woodards, 6 Ohio St. 2d 14, 215 N.E.2d 568 (1966).
87 State v. McClellan, 6 Ohio App. 2d 155, 217 N.E.2d 230 (1966).
88 Jenkins v. Associated Transport, Inc., 330 F.2d 706 (6th Cir. 1964).
89 People v. Love, 53 Cal. 2d 843, 350 P.2d 705 (1960).
90 Commonwealth v. Johnson, 402 Pa. 479, 167 A.2d 511 (1961). For an interesting discussion of the use of color photography, see the article by Edward C. Conrad which appears in *Fingerprint and Identification Magazine,* April 1961 issue.

e. Enlargements and aerial photographs

The mere fact that a photograph sought to be introduced in evidence is an enlarged one—while it is often made a ground of objection thereto—has not been considered a bar to its admission in either civil or criminal cases when the enlargement has been properly authenticated and is material to an issue in the case.91 Enlarged photographs are frequently used in cases involving the comparison of handwritings, or to show the place of an accident or the scene of a crime.

There seems to be no distinction between aerial and other types of photographs insofar as their admissibility is concerned. Aerial photographs have been admitted into evidence for the purpose of giving the jury an accurate picture of some relevant fact in issue; however, they may be excluded from evidence, at the discretion of the court, when other evidence gives the jury a sufficiently accurate picture of the subject matter involved.92

§ 14.7 Motion pictures and video tapes

Motion pictures are admissible in evidence, at the discretion of the court, when such pictures are relevant to the issue, when they are accurate reproductions of persons and objects introduced in oral examination before the jury, and the conditions under which such pictures were taken conform substantially to the facts related in open court.93 However, a California court has warned that:

> Motion pictures should be received as evidence with caution, because the modern art of photography and the devices of an ingenious director frequently produce results which may be quite deceiving. Telescopic lenses, ingenious settings of the stage, the elimination of unfavorable portions of a film, and angle from which a picture is taken, the ability to speed up the reproduction of the picture and the genius of a director may tend to create misleading impressions.94

Before motion pictures are admissible in evidence, their relevancy, authenticity and accuracy of portrayal must be established by the laying of

---

91 Annotation, *Admissibility in evidence of enlarged photographs or photostatic copies,* 72 A.L.R.2d 308 (1960).

92 Annotation, *Admissibility in evidence of aerial photographs,* 57 A.L.R.2d 1351 (1958).

93 Streit v. Kestel, 108 Ohio App. 241, 161 N.E.2d 409 (1959). In this case, the photographed experiment was one showing pictures of an automobile making turns at an intersection where the collision occurred. State v. Johnson, 18 N.C. App. 606, 197 S.E.2d 592 (1973).

94 Harmon v. San Joaquin L. & P. Corp., 37 Cal. App. 2d 169, 98 P.2d 1064 (1940).

an adequate foundation. Basically, the admissibility of motion pictures depends upon testimony by the operator of the camera that the film accurately portrays what he observed at the time and place of the action in question. Complete and formal laying of the foundation for admissibility would require:

1. Evidence as to the circumstances surrounding the taking of the pictures, which should include evidence as to the competency of the operator of the camera, the type of camera and operational methods used, the type of lens and lens adjustment, the sensitivity of the film, the lighting, visibility and the speed of the camera;
2. The manner and circumstances in regard to the development of the film;
3. Evidence in regard to the projection of the film, including the speed at which the projector was run and its distance from the screen; and
4. Testimony of one present when the pictures were taken that they accurately portray the subject matter filmed.[95]

In a Mississippi case,[96] the court held that a proper foundation had been laid for the introduction of films showing the injured party walking and running when the testimony established the identity and relevancy of the subject matter, the prevailing weather conditions, how the films would be projected, that the photographer was trained in the proper use of the camera and the making of films, that the camera was a standard make and in good working condition; that the camera was set and the pictures taken at a particular speed, and that the films accurately reproduced the scenes portrayed.

In a Texas case the court reasoned that motion pictures, like still photographs, may be admitted into evidence when they are properly authenticated, relevant to the issue and not violative of rules established for the admissibility of photographs.[97] The court noted that a new rule should not be adopted to govern admissibility of photographs merely because they were recorded as motion pictures instead of still photographs.

So long as sound motion pictures and video tapes are properly authenticated and portray the situations as they actually occurred, there is no serious question as to their admissibility—both as to the visual evidence and the audio evidence provided.[98] A sound motion picture of a defendant mak-

---

95 Richardson, MODERN SCIENTIFIC EVIDENCE § 16.22.
96 Barham v. Nowell, 243 Miss. 441, 138 So. 2d 493 (1962).
97 Gordon v. State, 784 S.W.2d 410 (Tex. 1990).
98 Miles Laboratories, Inc. v. Frolich, 195 F. Supp. 256 (S.D. Cal. 1961) (properly authenticated sound motion pictures of reaction test interviews of consumers to determine whether they would confuse an allegedly infringing brand name with a registered trademark were admissible); State v. Johnson, *supra* note 69.

ing a confession to police officers will be admitted in evidence provided a double foundation is laid, showing that the picture is an accurate reproduction and that the confession was voluntary.[99] Likewise, the court will admit into evidence a sound motion picture showing the defendants re-enacting the crime and admitting that they committed the crime in the manner depicted.[100]

Generally, the same rules that apply in the use of motion picture film apply when videotapes are sought to be introduced as evidence. Using videotapes has some advantages over using motion pictures, and videotapes are being used more in courts due to these advantages. The advantages of the use of videotape include the ability to use and edit videotape without cutting and splicing, the ability to freeze frames as needed, and the fact that videotape may be used in lighted rooms while motion picture films lose contrast when used in a lighted room. Perhaps the most valid arguments for using videotapes are that tapes are less expensive than film and that the equipment to tape the event and play it back is less cumbersome and more easily moved from place to place.

The admission of videotapes into evidence is largely within the discretion of the trial court. Several courts have equated videotape to motion picture film and have indicated that the two are subject to the same admissibility requirements.[101]

In deciding that videotapes are judged by the same general standards as motion pictures, the Eighth Circuit noted that a videotape is similar to a mug shot taken of an arrested person and may be used in a similar manner as is a mug shot.[102]

In a capital murder prosecution, a state court properly allowed into evidence a videotape of the crime scene, despite the defendant's contention that the tape was highly prejudicial in that it contained certain closeups of the victim's face showing decomposition.[103] To lay the foundation for admissibility of the videotape, a police officer testified that the videotape accurately portrayed and fairly depicted the interior of the victim's apartment.

---

[99] People v. Hayes, 21 Cal. App. 2d 320, 71 P.2d 321 (1937).

[100] People v. Dabb, 32 Cal. 2d 491, 197 P.2d 1 (1948). A rehearsal was first held, then the scene was shot, and the resulting film with sound was exhibited to the jury after a foundation was laid by testimony of the defendants' consent and of the authenticity of the film.

[101] International Union v. Russell, 264 Ala. 456, 88 So. 2d 175 (1956), aff'd, 356 U.S. 634, 78 S. Ct. 932, 2 L. Ed. 2d 1050 (1957).

[102] United States v. Houston, 892 F.2d 696 (8th Cir. 1989).

[103] Seibert v. State, 555 So. 2d 772 (Ala. 1989).

§ 14.8 X-rays

As an x-ray picture portrays only shadows of an internal part of the body that cannot be seen by the naked eye, it cannot be verified in the same manner as an ordinary photograph, that is, by testimony that it is a correct representation of the object that it purports to depict. The earlier decisions required that correctness be shown by comparison with what the witness saw through a fluoroscope or by proving skill in x-ray techniques, proper working conditions and accuracy of equipment, proper manner of taking the picture, and correctness of result based on experience.[104]

In more recent decisions, the courts have held that an x-ray is sufficiently authenticated if the evidence shows that the x-ray was taken by a qualified expert who is familiar with x-ray techniques and procedures, and that the x-ray is a true representation of what it purports to represent. There is no problem as to laying the foundation for an x-ray picture when the physician or roentgenologist under whose supervision and control the picture was taken interprets it in court for the jury.

Professional medical witnesses may illustrate x-rays through a view screen or illuminator in the courtroom.[105] In one state case, colored drawings prepared by a medical artist from x-rays were admitted in evidence when a doctor testified that the drawings were accurate reproductions of the x-rays, which were also admitted in evidence.[106]

§ 14.9 Sound recordings

Although the fantastic advances in the field of electronic communications constitute a great danger to the privacy of the individual, and the indiscriminate use of recording devices in law enforcement raises grave constitutional questions, sound recordings are frequently admitted into evidence. Before a sound recording is admitted into evidence, a foundation must be established by showing that: (1) the recording device was capable of taking the testimony or conversation offered in evidence; (2) the operator of the device was competent to operate it; (3) the recording is authentic and correct; (4) changes, additions or deletions have not been made in the recording; (5) the recording has been preserved in a manner that is shown to the court; (6) the speakers are identified; and (7) the conversation elicited was made voluntarily and in good faith, without any kind of duress.[107]

---

104 Stevens v. Illinois Cent. R. Co., 306 Ill. 370, 137 N.E. 859 (1923); Sim v. Weeks, 7 Cal. App. 2d 28, 45 P.2d 350 (1935).
105 Crocker v. Lee, 261 Ala. 439, 74 So. 2d 429 (1954).
106 Slow Development Co. v. Coulter, 88 Ariz. 122, 353 P.2d 890 (1960).
107 United States v. McKeever, 169 F. Supp. 426 (S.D.N.Y. 1958).

The North Carolina Supreme Court in 1984 reaffirmed the rule that a proper foundation must be laid before either a tape or a transcript of a tape will be admitted.[108] Quoting from a previous case, the court laid down seven requirements, which are worded a little differently than those mentioned in the previous paragraph. Here the court indicated that the following requirements must be met before a tape recorded statement may be admitted into evidence: (1) the recorded testimony was legally obtained and is otherwise competent; (2) the mechanical device was capable of recording the testimony, and it was operating properly at the time that the statement was recorded; (3) the operator was competent and operated the machine properly; (4) the recorded voices were identified; (5) the accuracy and authenticity of the recording was verified; (6) the defendant's entire statement was recorded and no changes, additions or deletions have since been made; and (7) evidence was introduced regarding the custody and manner in which the recording has been preserved since it was made.

The court further cautioned that when a transcript of a tape-recorded interview or conversation is sought to be admitted into evidence, additional foundational proof is required. A witness who was present when the interview was conducted must testify that it was recorded and later reduced to a transcript. It must also be shown that the transcript was compared with the tape recording and that the transcript is an accurate representation of the conversation. In absence of such a foundation, the recording will be inadmissible.

When a portable transmitting and receiving set or other device is used to overhear conversations, the initial qualification for admission of evidence so obtained involves two sets of interrelated problems: first, whether the device used is an effective means of communicating sound, and second, the identification of the alleged speaker.[109] Electronic recordings of conversations with one who is equipped with a wire recording device and also with a portable transmitting device are not secured in violation of the Fourth Amendment and are admissible in evidence.[110]

Before the jury is permitted to hear any part of a recording, there must be a preliminary hearing outside the jury's presence in order to determine the admissibility of the recording. The trial judge should first have the recording played before him, and he should afford counsel an opportunity to raise objections. If the recording includes incompetent, irrelevant or immaterial matter, or is inaudible, its admissibility will be questioned. When the recording contains incompetent matter, it will be rejected unless such mat-

---

108 State v. Toomer, 311 N.C. 183, 316 S.E.2d 66 (1984).
109 United States v. Sansone, 231 F.2d 887 (2d Cir. 1956).
110 Carbo v. United States, 314 F.2d 718 (9th Cir. 1963); United States v. White, 401 U.S. 745 (1971).

ter can be erased from the tape or the jury can be prevented from hearing the incompetent portion by stopping and starting the recording instrument. The deletion of inaudible, irrelevant or repetitive portions of a tape recording does not necessarily render the tape inadmissible at trial.[111]

In determining whether a tape recording is admissible, the judge must consider whether the probative value of the audiotape outweighs the danger of unfair prejudice to the accused. For example, in a narcotics case the court decided that the probative value of an audiotape of the defendant's sale of cocaine outweighed the danger of unfair prejudice that would allegedly result from the jury taking the recorded words out of context.[112] However, a reviewing court indicated that the trial court abused its discretion in admitting an unintelligible tape recording of a statement made by the defendant to a police officer, as the jury may have believed that the tape contained incriminating statements made by the defendants solely because the tape was introduced by the prosecution, thereby prejudicing the defendant.[113]

Even if the tape includes inaudible portions, it may be used as evidence if the inaudible portions of the recording are not substantial and do not render the audible parts unintelligible.[114] In interpreting Rule 901(a) of the Federal Rules of Evidence, a federal court held that the mere fact that portions of the tape recording are inaudible does not render the recording inadmissible per se.[115] In that case the court reasoned that the probative value of the tape recording of an alleged marijuana sale to establish the corpus delicti outweighed the prejudice that would result from inaudibility, even though the probative value was marginal.

The use of devices whereby one may overhear conversations beyond the area in which they might normally be heard does not in itself render the evidence thus obtained inadmissible.[116] Section 2511 of the United States Code states in detail the procedures which must be followed in the use of electronic surveillance devices to overhear and record conversations. Under

---

[111] United States v. Maxwell, 383 F.2d 437 (2d Cir. 1967), which held that although a taped conversation between the defendant and another was erased by the government, admitting into evidence a typewritten transcript previously made from the tape was not improper, as the tapes were not erased to prevent their production for trial. See also United States v. Young, 488 F.2d 1211 (8th Cir. 1973).

[112] State v. Foley, 234 Neb. 304, 450 N.W.2d 694 (1990).

[113] State v. Lane, 480 Ohio App. 3d 172, 549 N.E.2d 193 (1988).

[114] Hamm v. State, 301 Ark. 154, 782 S.W.2d 577 (1990); Middlebrook v. State, 550 So. 2d 1009 (Miss. 1990).

[115] Cape v. United States, 283 F.2d 439 (9th Cir. 1960).

[116] On Lee v. United States, 343 U.S. 747, 72 S. Ct. 967, 96 L. Ed. 1270 (1952); United States v. Vittoria, 284 F.2d 451 (7th Cir. 1960).

this provision, the admission of the recording of a telephone conversation or other conversation between two persons, including the defendant, is not unconstitutional if the recording is made with the consent of one party to the conversation.117

If one party does not agree to the recording of a conversation, the procedures specified in the statute must be followed to the letter if the recording is to be free from challenge on constitutional grounds.118 Even if the recordings meet constitutional standards, the evidence standards must also be met. Therefore, a taped confession was not admissible when a police captain admitted that the recorder on which the defendant's confession was originally recorded was not under his exclusive control and that some of the defendant's statements had not been recorded.119

The fact that the prosecution allowed a witness to retain custody of the original tape recording of a conversation between the witness, her attorney and the defendant, who was charged with endeavoring to influence the witness when she was under subpoena to appear before the grand jury, did not prevent the admission of a re-recording of the conversation on the ground that the prosecution should be held responsible for the loss of the original recording, as the original tape belonged to the witness and she insisted on keeping it.120

§ 14.10 Diagrams, maps, and models

The propriety of permitting a witness to explain his testimony by visual illustration is now firmly established; however, unless the illustration is essential to an understanding of the testimony, it is largely cumulative in effect, and the admission or exclusion rests within the discretion of the trial judge. The use of a map, drawing or plat for purposes of illustration must be distinguished from its admission in evidence. In the latter case, the map or plat possesses within itself evidentiary characteristics tending to establish a particular fact, while in the former case the testimony of the witness is the evidence and the map or diagram is merely an aid to its understanding.121

There is also a distinction between a diagram or chart which is in evidence or used for evidentiary purposes and one used only in counsel's argument; that is, the former may be exhibited throughout the trial or a portion

---

117 Harris v. United States, 400 F.2d 264 (5th Cir. 1968); United States v. White, 401 U.S. 745 (1971).
118 18 U.S.C. 2511 and cases.
119 Monts v. State, 214 Tenn. 171, 379 S.W.2d 34 (1964).
120 United States v. Knohl, 379 F.2d 427 (2d Cir. 1967).
121 Crocker v. Lee, 261 Ala. 439, 74 So. 2d 429 (1954).

thereof to which it is relevant, while the latter should be withdrawn from the jury's observation at the conclusion of the argument in which it is employed. The chart used by counsel in his argument should refer only to matters which are in evidence or to inferences which properly may be drawn from the evidence.[122]

The use of a blackboard for the purpose of illustrating testimony or in aid of counsel's argument has been held to be within the sound discretion of the trial judge. Although it is proper to use a blackboard, it is improper—according to one decision—to photograph it in the presence of the jury for purposes of the record on appeal, as this would unduly impress the jury with the importance of the material on the blackboard.[123] A witness should not be asked to indicate the place of impact or the location of skid marks by pointing to a place on the blackboard or map and saying merely "here" and "there"; instead he should indicate the particular point by means of a distinctive mark which is either numbered or identified by colored chalk or pencil. An advantage of a drawing on paper is that it can be identified and introduced in evidence when the testimony has been completed, and in jurisdictions where jurors are permitted to take exhibits with them, a drawing may be carried to the jury room during deliberations.

A map, diagram or drawing is admissible in evidence when a witness testifies that it is a correct portrayal of the existing facts; moreover, it is not essential that such witness be the one who made the map or diagram. When a map is used by a witness to illustrate the scene of an accident, it must be representative of the area at the time of the accident. When the map has been prepared long after the accident, it must be shown that the condition of the area has not changed materially from the date of the accident to the date when the map was prepared.

Models, when properly identified and authenticated, may be used for, illustration purposes if the evidence offered as a result of the use of a model is relevant and material to the ultimate fact to be demonstrated.[124] An exact model is not required if the original is substantially represented and there are no distortions which will mislead the jury. If a replica of the original is used, the jury should be instructed that the object is not the one used in the crime and that it is to be considered as evidence which demonstrates or illustrates what the object used in the crime looks like.[125] When the proper foundation is laid, models and replicas are valid means of making the evidence clear to the jury. For example, the state was

---

122 Ratner v. Arrington, 111 So. 2d 82 (Fla. 1959).
123 Affett v. Milwaukee & Sub. Transport Corp., 11 Wis. 2d 604, 106 N.W.2d 274 (1960).
124 State v. Mitchel, 56 Wash. App. 610, 784 P.2d 568 (1990).
125 Miskis v. State, 756 S.W.2d 350 (Tex. 1988).

properly allowed to use a knife and a styrofoam head as demonstrative exhibits in the prosecution of a defendant charged with stabbing the victim in the head.[126] The court noted that the knife and styrofoam were sufficiently accurate replicas of the objects involved in the crime.

Plastic models of the human skeleton and of the heart, brain, kidney or other organs—when injury to one of them is involved—are frequently used to illustrate the testimony of a medical expert.

§ 14.11 Courtroom demonstrations and experiments

While it is usually more convenient to videotape or photograph demonstrations or experiments that are done outside of court, in some instances, courtroom demonstrations are logically permitted because they more convincingly depict the situation to the jury. The standard for admission of experiments or demonstrations in the courtroom is that the experiment or demonstration must be substantially similar to the actual event.[127] As a general rule, virtually all of the same foundation and legal requirements and elements affecting the admissibility and use of demonstrative evidence are applicable to courtroom experiments and demonstrations.

To be admissible, the demonstration or experiment must be one that is designed to aid the jury in understanding or clarifying evidence or issues, and it must be relevant to the issues involved in the case. Also, the persons conducting the experiment must be qualified to do so, and the conditions under which the experiment or demonstration is to be performed must be substantially similar to those involved in the case.

In regard to the last of these requirements, i.e., that the experiment, to be legally relevant, must meet the test of "similarity of conditions," it is not necessary that the conditions be exactly the same, as this would be impossible. Also, it should be noted that even if the conditions are similar and the relevancy test has been met, the evidence may be rejected if its probative value is substantially outweighed by the danger of unfair prejudice or confusion of the issues, or if it would be misleading to the jury.[128]

In a case decided in 1981, a court of appeals in Maine reversed a conviction in the lower court on the grounds that an in-court demonstration re-enacting the crime in question should not have been admitted, as there were significant differences between the demonstration and the actual crime as shown by the evidence.[129]

---

126 Brown v. State, 550 So. 2d 527 (Fla. 1989). *See* case in Part II, *infra.*
127 Saldania v. Atchison, Topeka & Santa Fe Railway, 241 F.2d 321 (7th Cir. 1957).
128 *See* Kehm v. Procter & Gamble Co., 580 F. Supp. 890 (N.D. Iowa 1982).
129 State v. Philbrick, 436 A.2d 844 (Me. 1981).

§ 14.12   Preservation and disclosure of evidence favorable to the defense

Since 1963 various courts, including the United States Supreme Court, have pondered the extent to which due process requires law enforcement officers to preserve materials of unknown evidentiary value—that is, materials "of which no more can be said than it could have been subjected to test, the results of which might have exonerated the defendant." In the case of *Brady v. Maryland,* the United States Supreme Court decided that a defendant has a constitutionally protected privilege to request and obtain from the prosecution evidence that is either material to the guilt of the defendant or relevant to punishment to be imposed.[130] The Court in that case cautioned that failure to make disclosure of such evidence denies due process— irrespective of the good or bad faith of the prosecutor.

In *United States v. Agurs,* the Supreme Court again noted that even in the absence of a specific request, the prosecution has a constitutional duty to turn over exculpatory evidence that would raise a reasonable doubt about the defendant's guilt.[131] However, the Court at the same time rejected the argument that a "prosecutor has a constitutional duty routinely to deliver his entire file to the defense counsel."

In *Moore v. Illinois,* the Court observed that:

We know of no constitutional requirement that the prosecution make a complete and detailed accounting to the defense of all police investigatory work on a case.[132]

In 1984 the Supreme Court again considered the responsibility of the prosecution to make evidence available to the defense. In the case of *California v. Trombetta,* which involved the failure to preserve breath samples obtained by a breath test machine in a drunk driving prosecution, there was no constitutional violation when the breath samples were destroyed.[133] The Court explained that the police officers in that acting were acting "in good faith and in accord with their normal practice" and did not destroy the breath samples in a calculated effort to circumvent the due process requirement. Therefore, the conviction was affirmed.

When the United States Supreme Court decided the case of *Arizona v. Youngblood* in 1988, it reviewed the previous cases and held that the due process clause demands only that such evidence not be lost through bad

---

130 Brady v. Maryland, 373 U.S. 83, 83 S. Ct. 1194, 10 L. Ed. 2d 215 (1963).
131 United State v. Agurs, 427 U.S. 97, 96 S. Ct. 239, 49 L. Ed. 2d 342 (1976).
132 Moore v. Illinois, 408 U.S. 786, 92 S. Ct. 2562, 33 L. Ed. 2d 706 (1972).
133 California v. Trombetta, 467 U.S. 479, 104 S. Ct. 2528, 81 L. Ed. 2d 413
     (1984).

faith; otherwise, there is no due process requirement that police preserve for the defendant's possible use evidence of questionable exculpatory value.[134] In the Youngblood case the state court had thrown out all of the charges against the defendant on the ground that the police failed to preserve semen samples and test them in a timely fashion, thus depriving the defendant of evidence that might have exonerated him. The United States Supreme Court reversed the state court decision but noted that had the police acted in bad faith or had the state made use of any of the material in its case-in-chief, the decision would have been different. Three of the dissenting judges argued that the police should be required to preserve evidence if it might exonerate the defendant and if no comparable evidence is available.

From these cases emerges the rule that due process requires disclosure, upon the defendant's request, of evidence favorable to the defendant, but unless a criminal defendant can show bad faith on the part of the police, failure to preserve potentially useful evidence does not constitute a denial of due process of law. When the interests of justice clearly require it, the police and prosecutor have an obligation to preserve the evidence. If the evidence is destroyed through bad faith, the due process protection is violated.

§ 14.13 Summary

In addition to the use of oral testimony and documentary evidence, real evidence may be introduced to help the jury or other fact finders in determining what happened in a particular case. The use of real evidence to assist the court and jury in determining the guilt or innocence of the accused in criminal cases has had the sanction of immemorial usage. In many instances, real evidence is more persuasive and aids the jury more in reaching a decision than the testimony of the witness. The courts, in recognizing the desirability of obtaining all the facts, have actually encouraged the use of real evidence.

Notwithstanding this fact, certain rules have been established and must be followed if such evidence is to be admitted. For example, the prosecution must show that there is a connection between the instrument or article introduced and the accused; that the article is relevant to the particular case; and that the object is substantially in the same condition as when used in connection with the crime—or the change in condition, if any, is explained. Also, the prosecution must show a chain or continuity of custody concerning the article to be introduced.

---

134 Arizona v. Youngblood, 408 U.S. 51, 109 S. Ct. 333, 102 L. Ed. 2d 281 (1988).

There are various types of real evidence which have been held admissible, and for each type, certain conditions must be met. In some instances the exhibition of the person of the witness may be the best way to explain an injury. In this event, the judge in his discretion may allow such exhibition even though it may be somewhat gruesome.

Articles connected with the crime, such as weapons or clothing, may be introduced as real evidence if the prosecution can show that there was or is a connection between the article and the accused. Also, the judge may allow the jury to visit and view the scene of the incident, if in his discretion, this will help the jury in determining the facts of the case.

If it is not practicable to let the witness view the scene or to bring all of the evidence into court, photographs are admissible as a form of real evidence. Before a photograph may be introduced, a foundation must be laid, i.e., a competent witness who has personal knowledge of the area or thing photographed must testify that the picture is an accurate representation of the objects or persons depicted. In addition to photographs, motion pictures, x-rays and sound recordings may be introduced. As in the case of photographs, a foundation must be laid before such evidence is admitted into court.

Often it is possible for the witness to more effectively explain what took place by using diagrams, maps, charts and models. When reference is to be made to such a diagram, map or model, a witness must testify that it is a correct portrayal of the situation or thing represented.

Due process requires disclosure, upon the defendant's request, of evidence favorable to the defense, but unless the defendant can show bad faith on the part of the police or prosecutor, failure to preserve evidence does not ordinarily constitute a denial of due process.

CHAPTER 15
RESULTS OF EXAMINATIONS
AND TESTS

It is now well established that a witness who qualifies as an expert in the science of ballistics, may identify a gun from which a particular bullet was fired by comparing the markings on that bullet with those on a test bullet fired by the witness through the suspect gun.
Roberts. v. Florida, 164 So. 2d 817 (Fla. 1964)

§ 15.1 Introduction

In the previous chapter, some of the general rules concerning the collection, protection and introduction of real evidence were considered. Evidence is characterized as real evidence if it is the result of experiments and tests either in or out of court, even though in many cases the evidence is of little value unless it is accompanied by oral testimony.

Although a comparatively small part of the evidence produced at trial in the usual criminal case results from out-of-court tests and examinations, such evidence is often very convincing and is certainly important in helping the fact finders in determining what actually occurred.

According to the National Institute of Justice newsletter entitled "Research in Brief," dated October 1987, an analysis of prosecutor files for the years 1975, 1978 and 1981 revealed that laboratory reports were used in about one quarter to one third of felony cases that had survived initial screening. That report also indicated that police are about three times more likely to clear cases when scientific evidence is gathered and analyzed, and that prosecutors are less likely to agree to enter into plea negotiations if forensic evidence strongly associates the defendant with the crime. Equally important, such evidence can be unequivocal and can eliminate suspects who might otherwise be the focus of continuing investigative efforts.

While evidence concerning the results of examinations and tests has a great impact in criminal cases, such evidence is admissible only when it clears several evidence hurdles. First, forensic evidence must meet the same tests as must other evidence, such as the tests of relevancy, materiality and competency. Before such evidence is admitted, a foundation must be laid. For example, in one case the court held that the party seeking to introduce results must lay a proper foundation by connecting the specimen with its source, showing that it was properly labeled and preserved, properly transported for analysis, properly taken by authorized persons and properly tested.[1]

In interpreting rules 403 and 702 of the Federal Rules of Evidence, which have been adopted by many states, one court decided that under these rules of evidence, with regard to scientific tests, the burden of proof that the tests are reliable is on the proponent.[2] Another court determined that for scientific evidence to be admissible, there must be proof that the scientific tests used to gather such evidence are reliable and have been accepted and recognized by the scientific community.[3]

Because this book is prepared primarily for those involved in the criminal justice process and because in most instances the tests or examinations are conducted not by the prosecutor but by enforcement personnel, emphasis in this chapter is placed upon the most common tests and examinations.

§ 15.2 Examination of the person

Examination of the body of the defendant in a criminal case in a reasonable manner is not considered violative of his constitutional right of privacy or his privilege against self-incrimination. Both federal and state courts have usually held that the privilege against self-incrimination as protected by the Fifth Amendment to the United States Constitution offers no protection against compulsion to submit to fingerprinting, photographing or measurements, to write or speak for identification, to appear in court, to

---

1   Lawless v. New Orleans Police Department, 550 So. 2d 252 (La. App. 1989).
2   State v. Woodall, 385 S.E. 253 (W. Va. 1989). *See* case in Part II, *infra.*
3   Cavazos v. State, 779 P.2d 987 (Okla. 1989).

stand, to assume a stance, to walk, or to make a particular gesture.4 The courts have allowed procedures which involve minor interferences—for purposes of identification—with the person of individuals charged with crimes. Numerous cases uphold reasonable out-of-court identification procedures against claims of violation of the Fifth Amendment: for example, requiring the prisoner to try on a blouse that fitted him;5 requiring the accused to submit to a lineup;6 requiring the accused to speak for voice identification;7 examination of a defendant's body for traces of blood;8 examination of a defendant's body for marks and bruises;9 requiring defendant to remove items of clothing or to assume poses;10 and taking penis scrapings and saliva samples from defendant.11

In a case involving murder, a court of appeals in Alabama found that there was no error in taking fingernail scrapings, hair samples, and tennis shoes from a suspect who was being interviewed in a murder case.12 As the record did not indicate that the samples were taken against the suspect's will, his rights were not violated.

In both homicide and wrongful death cases, an examination of the body of the deceased by a trained pathologist is sometimes made, and the pathologist's testimony may be given on issues relating to the cause of death. The medical examiner's report is admissible as to his anatomical findings, anatomical diagnosis and cause of death.

§ 15.3   Intoxication tests

Intoxication may be scientifically determined by testing the subject's blood, breath, urine or saliva. Evidence resulting from such out-of-court

---

4   Schmerber v. California, 384 U.S. 757, 86 S. Ct. 1826, 16 L. Ed. 2d 908 (1966). *See* case in Part II, *infra,* at cases relating to Chapter 14. *See also* Chapter 16, *infra,* for additional discussion of the privilege against self-incrimination.

5   Holt v. United States, 218 U.S. 245, 31 S. Ct. 2, 54 L. Ed. 1021 (1910); State v. Lerner, 308 A.2d 324 (R.I. 1973).

6   Rigney v. Hendrick, 355 F.2d 710 (3d Cir. 1965); Bonaparte v. Smith, 362 F. Supp. 1315 (S.D. Ga. 1973).

7   Kennedy v. United States, 353 F.2d 462 (D.C. Cir. 1965).

8   McFarland v. United States, 150 F.2d 593 (D.C. Cir. 1945); Brattain v. Herron, 309 N.E.2d 150 (Ind. 1974).

9   Leeper v. Texas, 139 U.S. 462 (1891).

10   Gilbert v. United States, 366 F.2d 923 (9th Cir. 1966).

11   Brent v. White, 276 F. Supp. 386 (E.D. La. 1967).

12   Taylor v. State, 548 So. 2d 521 (Ala. Crim. App. 1988).

tests is usually admissible. Types of tests and limitations on the use of such evidence are discussed in the following paragraphs.

a. Blood tests

Statutes in numerous states have adopted the Uniform Vehicle Code, which incorporates recommendations of the National Safety Council and the American Medical Association with respect to chemical tests for alcohol. These statutes usually provide that:

1. Where there is less than 0.05 percent alcohol in the blood, or equivalent amounts in other body fluids or breath, the subject shall be presumed to be not under the influence of alcohol so far as the operation of a motor vehicle is concerned.
2. Where there is 0.15 (some say 0.10) percent of more alcohol in the blood, or equivalent amounts of other body fluids or breath, the subject is presumed to be under the influence of alcohol, as far as the operation of a motor vehicle is concerned.
3. Where there is between 0.05 percent and 0.15 (some say 0.10) percent alcohol in the blood, or equivalent amounts in other body fluids or breath, the results of such tests may be received along with other tests or observations for consideration by the court or jury as bearing upon the question of alcohol influence.[13]

Neither the National Safety Council nor the American Medical Association ever suggested that a strict line of demarcation could be drawn at which blood alcohol concentration could be used as a sole criterion by which to judge whether an individual was intoxicated or unfit to drive an automobile. On the contrary, all of the recommendations of these committees emphasized the desirability of introducing all available evidence of abnormal reactions or conditions. There was never any intimation that the results of chemical tests should be the only evidence or that the report of chemical tests should dominate other evidence in importance.[14]

In 1960 a joint National Safety Council and American Medical Associate Committee recommended that the percentage in the third category be lowered to 0.10 percent. In 1962 the Uniform Vehicle Code was amended to implement this recommendation, and most states have adopted the Uniform Vehicle Code's presumptions.[15] In 40 states the legislatures have adopted statutes making it a *per se* offense to drive with a certain

---

13 These percentage figures refer to alcohol in the blood. When breath or urine tests are used, the readings are converted into equivalant blood concentrations.

14 Gerber, S. R., *Practical Use of Results of Biochemical Tests for Alcohol*, 47 A.B.A.J. 477 (May 1961).

15 Drunk Driving in America, *"The Atlantic Monthly"* (October 1983).

blood- or breath-alcohol concentration—usually 0.10 percent.[16]

A number of cases involving blood tests to determine intoxication have reached the Supreme Court of the United States. In *Breithaupt v. Abram,*[17] police officers caused blood to be withdrawn from the driver of an automobile involved in an accident, and a blood-alcohol test was conducted. The Court found that there was ample justification for the conclusion that the driver was under the influence of alcohol. Because the extraction was made by a physician in a medically acceptable manner in a hospital environment, there was no violation of the driver's rights even though the driver was unconscious at the time the blood was withdrawn and had no opportunity to object to the procedure. The Court affirmed the conviction resulting from the use of the test, holding that under the circumstances the withdrawal did not offend a sense of justice.

In *Schmerber v. California,*[18] the Supreme Court held that the extraction of blood samples from the accused while he was in the hospital after being arrested for driving while under the influence of intoxicating liquor was a reasonable test to measure the accused's blood-alcohol level and did not violate his rights under the Fourth Amendment. The Court also decided that the physician's withdrawal, at the direction of a police officer, of a blood sample and the admission of the blood analysis in evidence did not deny the accused due process of law. Neither was the evidence inadmissible on the theory that it violated the Fifth Amendment privilege of any person not to be compelled in a criminal case to be a witness against himself.

In 1989 the Illinois Supreme Court considered the constitutionality of instructions to the jury that it "may presume" that the defendant was under the influence of intoxicating liquors if defendant's blood-alcohol level was 0.10% or more but that the presumption was "not binding." The court agreed that the instruction created a permissive presumption and that this did not violate the defendant's due process rights.[19]

b. Breath tests

A doctor, chemist or medical technician with the proper equipment can determine the percent of alcohol in the blood from a sample of blood from the body of the person. Because of the inconvenience of obtaining and ana-

---

16 The percentage in the other 10 states under the Uniform Code has been lowered to 0.08%.

17 352 U.S. 432, 77 S. Ct. 408, 1 L. Ed. 2d 448 (1957).

18 384 U.S. 757, 86 S. Ct. 1826, 16 L. Ed. 2d 908 (1966). *See* case in Part II, *infra,* at cases relating to Chapter 14. *See* the case of Winston v. Lee, 470 U.S. 753, 105 S. Ct. 1611, 84 L. Ed. 2d 662 (1985), in which reference was made to the balancing test approved in the *Schmerber* case.

19 People v. Hester, 131 Ill. 2d 91, 544 N.E.2d 797 (1989).

lyzing the blood sample, other means have been invented to determine blood-alcohol content without actually taking the blood. For example, the use of breath samples to determine blood-alcohol content is quite common and certainly has the advantage of being more convenient and less painful.[20] The breath test is also preferable because a trained officer may usually administer it, while generally a physician or nurse is needed when actual blood is to be withdrawn.

In the use of devices such as "Breathalyzers," "drunkometers" and "alcometers," the blood-alcohol content is determined by a formula applied to a test of the breath of the subject, who is required to blow into a balloon. The breath thus captured is allowed to expel itself through a tube containing a mixture of potassium permanganate and sulphuric acid until a certain shade or color is attained. By a measure of the water displaced by the breath that passed through this tube, it is determined how much air was required to create the color above described. This amount is determined from a reading of a calibrated scale. The number read from the calibrated scale must then be calculated and translated into a percentage of alcohol in the blood.[21]

Before evidence as to the results of breath tests is admissible, there must be proof (1) that the chemicals were compounded to the proper percentage for use in the machine; (2) that the operator and the machine were under periodic supervision of one who has an understanding of the scientific theory of the machine; and (3) that the witness is qualified to calculate and translate the reading of the machine into the percentage of alcohol in the blood.[22] An expert testifying as to the results of a test may testify that the result indicates intoxication, but not that the subject was in fact intoxicated.[23]

One question that has recently arisen is whether the state has a duty to preserve the Breathalyzer ampoules it uses to test for intoxication so that a drunk-driving defendant may later check the results by retesting. Although

---

20 Klebs v. State, 305 N.E.2d 781 (Ind. 1974).

21 Richardson, MODERN SCIENTIFIC EVIDENCE § 13.5. *See* Frankvoort, Mulder, and Neuteboom, "The Laboratory Testing of Evidential Breath Testing Machines," 35 FORENSIC SCIENCE INT'L 27 (1987), in which researchers found that although the results of breath testing machines in general were good, the machines tended to underestimate actual concentration. *See also* "Breathalyzer Accuracy in Actual Enforcement Practice," 32 J. FORENSIC SCI. 1235 (1987), in which it was found that the blood-alcohol concentration tended to be underestimated by the Breathalyzer.

22 Hill v. State, 158 Tex. Crim. 313, 256 S.W.2d 93 (1953); State v. Baker, 56 Wash. 2d 846, 355 P.2d 806 (1960); Klebs v. State, 305 N.E.2d 781 (Ind. 1974); Owens v. Commonwealth, 487 S.W.2d 877 (Ky. 1972).

23 Toms v. State, 95 Okla. Crim. 60, 239 P.2d 812 (1952).

three states have held that due process requires retention of ampoules for this purpose,24 a majority of the courts do not require that the Breathalyzer ampoules be reserved. In *State v. Canady,*25 the Washington Supreme Court concluded that it is not necessary to preserve the ampoules and that the defendants do not have a constitutional right to determine whether the testing officer properly conducted the Breathalyzer procedure. The court held that a defendant has an adequate opportunity to impeach the testing credibility through cross-examination. In this case, the court reasoned that other courts have found that the ampoule retesting procedures are not generally accepted as reliable evidence anyhow; therefore, the destruction and disposal of such ampoules does not violate any due process right of the defendant.

There is no deprivation of constitutional rights when a person charged with the offense of operating a motor vehicle while under the influence of intoxicating liquor voluntarily submits to a drunkometer test during a brief interrogation at police headquarters, in the absence of any coercion and after being informed that the test is voluntary and that he is not required to answer any questions.26 However, a complaint alleging that the arresting police officers beat the plaintiff with the intent of punishing him for his refusal to incriminate himself by taking a drunkometer test states a cause of action against the officers under the Civil Rights Act.27

The Supreme Court of Arkansas in 1985 considered the use of a device known as the Intoxilyzer. This device passes an infrared light beam through a sample of the accused's breath that he has blown into the device. The Intoxilyzer measures the amount of infrared energy that is absorbed by the alcohol vapor and converts that figure into a blood-alcohol reading.28

The defendant was convicted when the Intoxilyzer showed that his blood-alcohol level was 0.17 percent. He argued on appeal that the process was not a chemical analysis, as the Intoxilyzer does not satisfy the statutory requirement of being "a chemical analysis." The Supreme Court of Arkansas indicated that the question had only come up in three other cases and in all of these cases the test was approved as being a chemical analysis. The court observed that the process is not a "wet chemistry" process, but that it is nevertheless chemistry. The court also made the observation that even though the

---

24 Lauderdale v. State, 548 P.2d 376 (Ala. 1976); People v. Hitch, 117 Cal. Rptr. 9, 527 P.2d 361 (1974); State v. Michener, 25 Or. App. 523, 550 P.2d 449 (1976).

25 585 P.2d 1185 (Wash. 1978).

26 Toledo v. Dietz, 3 Ohio St. 2d 30, 209 N.E.2d 127 (1965).

27 Hardwick v. Hurley, 289 F.2d 529 (7th Cir. 1961).

28 Dollar v. State, 697 S.W.2d 93 (Ark. 1985); *see also* Smith, "Science, The Intoxilyzer and Breath Alcohol Testing." 11 THE CHAMPION 8 (May and June, 1987).

statute could have been more clear, the drafters of the statutory language exercised good judgment in leaving the exact details to the discretion of the board of health. Concluding that the test was a chemical analysis as used in the statute, the court upheld the conviction.

c. Urine tests

Although the use of urine to determine blood-alcohol content has some advantages, it also has disadvantages. One is that concentration of alcohol in the urine lags behind blood-alcohol concentration. Further, the test results are rendered unreliable by the fact that dilution is greater or lesser according to the amount of urine in the bladder, and this information is not known to the person making the test. In a case in which a sample of a suspect's urine was shown to have been taken at a time reasonably soon after the incident occurred, and to have been subjected to a test having general scientific recognition, with the results correlated to the probable blood concentration at the time of the violation charged, the court held that the results are properly admissible as evidence in a prosecution for drunkenness.[29]

Because of the doubts about blood-alcohol content estimated from urine, the National Highway Traffic Safety Administration has discouraged the use of such tests.[30] Some experts recommend that urinalysis be used only when a blood sample is unavailable or contaminated.[31]

d. Horizontal gaze nystagmus tests

Several states have approved the use of the Horizontal Gaze Nystagmus Test (HGN). Horizontal gaze nystagmus is the inability of the eyes to maintain visual fixation as they are turned to the side. This test was described in an Arizona case in 1986 in these terms:

> In the HGN test the driver is asked to cover one eye and focus the other on an object held by the officer at the driver's eye level. As the officer moves the object gradually out of the driver's field of vision toward his ear, he watches the driver's eyeball to detect involuntary jerking. The test is repeated with the other eye. By observing (1) the inability of each eye to track movement smoothly; (2) pronounced nystagmus at maximum deviation; and (3) onset of the nystagmus at an angle less than 45 degrees in relation to the center part, the officer can estimate whether the driver's blood-alcohol content (BAC) exceeds the legal limit of 0.10%.[32]

---

29 People v. Miller, 357 Mich. 400, 98 N.W.2d 524 (1960).

30 National Highway Traffic and Safety Administration Highway Safety Program Manual #8.

31 Winek and Esposito, "Comparative Study of Ethanol Levels in Blood v. Bone Marrow," 17 FORENSIC SCI. INTL. 27 (1981).

32 State v. Superior Court, 149 Ariz. 269, 718 P.2d 171 (1986).

According to that court, nystagmus is a well-known physiological phenomenon caused by, among other things, ingestion of alcohol. According to the study, which is cited in the case, the accuracy rate of the HGN test in estimating whether the level of BAC exceeds 0.10 percent is between 80 and 90 percent. The study found that the margin of inaccuracy is caused by the fact that certain drugs, such as barbituates, cause the same effects as alcohol.

In its conclusion the court summarized its findings:

> We find that the horizontal gaze nystagmus test properly administered by a trained police officer is sufficiently reliable to be a factor in establishing probable cause to arrest a driver for violating A.R.S. section 28-692 (B). [driving while intoxicated statute] We further find that the horizontal gaze nystagmus test satisfies the *Frye* test for reliability and may be admitted in evidence to corroborate or attack, but not to quantify, the chemical analysis of the accused's blood-alcohol content. It may not be used to establish the accused's level of blood alcohol in the absence of a chemical analysis showing the proscribed level in the accused's blood, breath or urine.

The Iowa Supreme Court, after making reference to cases from other states, determined that a police officer, who testified in a case in which the defendant was convicted of operating a vehicle while intoxicated, was fully qualified to testify to his specialized knowledge regarding the horizontal gaze nystagmus test.[33]

In the case of *State v. Murphy* the court noted that some courts have held that a police officer is not qualified to testify to the HGN test's scientific reliability[34] Other courts hold that HGN evidence, although it is of a scientific nature, is reliable and admissible if preceded by a proper foundation as to the techniques used and the officer's ability to conduct the test.[35]

Still other courts regard the HGN test as no more scientific than other field sobriety tests that require no expert interpretation.[36]

33　State v. Murphy, 451 N.W.2d 154 (Iowa 1990); *see also* State v. Nagel, 30 Ohio App. 3d 80, 506 N.E.2d 285 (1986), which includes a description of the HGN test.

34　State v. Borchardt, 224 Neb. 47, 395 N.W.2d 551 (1986); Commonwealth v. Miller, 367 Pa. Super. 359, 532 A.2d 1186 (1987); State v. Barker, 366 S.E.2d 642 (W .Va. 1988).

35　State v. Superior Court, 149 Ariz. 269, 718 P.2d 171 (1986); State v. Clark, 762 P 2d. 853 (Mont. 1988).

36　State v. Nagel, 30 Ohio App. 3d 80, 506 N.E.2d 285 (1986).

e. Implied consent statutes

Many states have enacted statutes providing that a driver, whether licensed locally, unlicensed or licensed in another state, is deemed to have given his consent, in return for the privilege of driving, to submit to an alcohol test if there are reasonable grounds to believe that he is driving while intoxicated; if he refuses to take the test, his license may be suspended. In upholding the constitutionality of such law, the Supreme Court of Nebraska agreed that:

> The validity of a sample of blood or urine under the implied consent law is not impaired by a request for legal counsel, or the failure of defendant's counsel to appear before the sample is taken. . . .
> A defendant loses no rights subject to protection by legal counsel when he is requested and furnishes a sample of blood or urine for chemical analysis to be used as evidence against him under the implied consent law.37

A Michigan court, reaffirming the constitutionality of an implied consent statute and explaining the reason for the provisions of the statute, held that a person who operates a motor vehicle on a public highway and who is arrested for operating the vehicle while under the influence of intoxicating liquor is considered to have consented to the chemical test for determining the amount of alcohol in his blood.38 Under the statute, the secretary of state may suspend or revoke, or deny issuance of an operator's license of a driver who refuses to take a chemical test.

A driver who is advised of his rights under the implied consent law but declines to submit to a chemical test to determine his blood-alcohol content is deemed to have refused the test so as to require revocation of his driver's license unless he objectively and unequivocally manifests, at the time that he is so advised, that he does not understand the rights and warning concerning the consequences of refusal, and is denied clarification.39 According to a Pennsylvania case, however, before the defendant's driver's license is revoked or suspended for refusal to submit to a Breathalyzer test, the Commonwealth is required to prove that the defendant was placed under arrest for driving under the influence; that the defendant was requested to submit to a chemical test; that the defendant was informed that his refusal to submit to such a test would result in suspension of his operating privilege; and the defendant refused to take the test.40

---

37 State v. Oleson, 180 Neb. 546, 143 N.W.2d 917 (1966).
38 Underwood v. Secretary of State, 181 Mich. App. 168, 448 N.W.2d 779 (1989).
39 Dudenhoeffer v. Director of Revenue, State of Missouri, 780 S.W.2d 701 (Mo. 1989).
40 Luckey v. Commonwealth, 569 A.2d 1008 (Pa. 1990).

In the case of *South Dakota v. Neville* in 1983, the United States Supreme Court examined not only the implied consent statutes but the constitutionality of prosecutors commenting on the failure of defendants to take a blood-alcohol test.[41] In this case, the defendant was arrested for driving while intoxicated. The arresting officer asked him to submit to a blood-alcohol test and warned him that he would lose his license if he refused. The South Dakota trial court granted a motion to suppress all evidence, and the South Dakota Supreme Court affirmed on the ground that the statute allowing the introduction of evidence of refusal violated the privilege against self-incrimination. The prosecution asked for a review by the United States Supreme Court.

First, the United States Supreme Court pointed out the reason for the implied consent law: that, as part of the program to deter drinkers from driving, South Dakota has enacted an "implied consent" law. This statute, the Court explained, declares that any person operating a vehicle is deemed to have consented to a chemical test of the alcohol content of his blood if arrested for driving intoxicated. In disagreeing with the South Dakota Supreme Court, the United States Supreme Court indicated that, as a blood test is "physical" or "real" evidence rather than testimonial evidence, such evidence is unprotected by the Fifth Amendment privilege.

As to the constitutionality of commenting on the failure to take the test, the Court stated that it is not fundamentally unfair, or in violation of due process, to use a defendant's refusal to take a blood-alcohol test as evidence of guilt, even though the police failed to warn him that the refusal could be used against him at trial. In making this decision, the Court explained that "the offer of taking the blood-alcohol test is clearly legitimate, and the action becomes no less legitimate when the state offers a second option of refusing the test, with the attendant penalties for making that choice." Summarizing the opinion, the Court concluded:

> We hold, therefore, that a refusal to take a blood-alcohol test, after a police officer has lawfully requested it, is not an act coerced by the officer, and thus is not protected by the privilege against self-incrimination.

§ 15.4 Blood grouping tests

Blood grouping tests often serve a useful purpose of identification in criminal prosecutions for rape,[42] assault and battery,[43] or non-support. In a

---

41 South Dakota v. Neville, 103 S. Ct. 916 (1983).
42 Shanks v. State, 185 Md. 437, 45 A.2d 85 (1945).
43 Commonwealth v. Statti, 16 Pa. Super. 577, 73 A.2d 688 (1950).

rape and murder case, the defendant argued on appeal that the trial court erred in admitting evidence of a serologist that the defendant was one of 35 percent of the male population who are "type O" secretors.[44] The evidence was offered to show that the defendant could have had intercourse with the victim. The reviewing court agreed that this was not improper evidence as it only indicated that the defendant fell into the suspect percentage.

Some other examples of the use of blood comparisons in criminal cases indicate the importance of this type of test. In a sexual assault prosecution, blood comparison evidence was properly admitted to show that the blood types of the defendant and the victim were different and that blood of the victim's blood type was found on the defendant's clothing.[45] In another case, the results from electrophoretic typing of aged, dried blood stains were admissible in a murder prosecution in which evidence indicated that the testing was performed by competent analysts using sufficient controls.[46] In approving the use of the blood test, this court noted that a trained technician who had been working with serological electrophoresis for five years examined the samples in question, and his readings were controlled by second readings as required by protocol.

The trial court has wide latitude in ruling on the admissibility of the results of blood grouping tests. The fact that the probative value is weak in its tendency to demonstrate a material fact goes to the weight of the evidence, not to its admissibility.[47] For example, in the *Jenkins* case cited, the lower court permitted a forensic serologist to testify concerning the results of blood grouping tests performed on samples obtained from the defendant and the vagina of the victim in a rape and burglary case. These results indicated that the defendant was a member of the class—consisting of 30 percent of the male population—which could have committed the rape. The reviewing court found no abuse of discretion on the part of the trial court and that the evidence was properly admitted—even though the group was a large one.

§ 15.5 Polygraph examinations[48]

The polygraph, also known as the lie detector, is an electronic device that, on being applied to the human body, graphically records changes in

---

44 State v. Duncan, 698 S.W.2d 63 (Tenn. 1985).
45 People v. Jiminez, 191 Ill. App. 3d 13, 547 N.E.2d 616 (1989).
46 State v. Fenney, 448 N.W.2d 54 (Minn. 1989).
47 Jenkins v. State, 485 N.E.2d 625 (Ind. 1985); *see also* State v. Woodall, 385 S.E.2d 253 (W. Va. 1989). *See* case in Part II, *infra.*
48 See Chapter 6, *supra,* for discussion of admissibility of polygraph results on stipulation.

blood pressure, heart rate and respiratory rate. These basic features may be supplemented with a unit for recording what is known as the galvanic skin reflex, based on changes in the activity of the sweat pores in a subject's hands, and another unit for recording muscular movements and pressures. A galvanometer, used alone, is totally inadequate for lie detector testing.

As an investigative technique, the use of the lie detector is based on the assumption that lying leads to conflict; that conflict causes fear and anxiety; that this mental state is the direct cause of measurable physical changes that can be accurately recorded; and that the polygraph operator, by a study of these reactions, can tell whether the subject is being deceptive or truthful. None of these assumptions is wholly true.[49]

In the case of *United States v. Piccinonna* in 1989, the United States Court of Appeals for the Eleventh Circuit revisited the issue of the admissibility at trial of polygraph expert testimony and examination evidence.[50] Three of the judges, who concurred in part and dissented in part in that case, described the polygraphy theory in these terms:

> The polygraph device records the subject's physiological activities (e.g., heart rate, blood pressure, respiration and perspiration) as he is questioned by a polygraph examiner. There are two major types of polygraph examinations: the "control question test" and the "concealed information test." The control question test is used most frequently in investigating specific incidents. The examiner compares the data corresponding to (a) questions relevant to the crime (b) "control" question designed to upset the subject but not directly relevant to the crime, and (c) neutral questions. If the subject reacts more strongly to the relevant questions than to the control and neutral questions, then the examiner infers that the subject is lying. . . .

> The concealed information test focuses on the fact that only the person involved in the crime could know the answers to certain questions. The examiner presents a series of multiple choice questions concerning the crime while the polygraph machine records the subject's physiological activities. If the subject has relatively strong physiological reactions to the correct alternatives, then the examiner infers that the subject is attempting to conceal information about the crime . . . The concealed information test assumes that information about the crime is protected, but in fact police often inform all suspects and even the media about the crime. . . .

---

49 Burkey, L. M., *The Case Against the Polygraph,* 51 A.B.A.J. 855 (Sept. 1965).
50 United States v. Piccinonna, 885 F.2d 1529 (11th Cir. 1989). *See* case in Part II, *infra.*

Lie detection is based on four assumptions: (1) that individuals cannot control their physiologies and behavior, (2) that specific emotions can be triggered by specific stimuli, (3) that there are specific relationships between the different aspects of behavior (such as what people say, how they behave, and how they respond physiologically), and (4) that there are no differences among people, so that most people will respond similarly.

The judges were of the opinion that testimony concerning the results of the polygraph examination should not be admitted into evidence. Their reasoning was that because the polygraph can predict whether a person is lying with accuracy that is only slightly greater than chance, it will be of little help to the trier of fact. These members of the court also noted that "the Ninth Circuit has found that polygraph evidence has an overwhelming potential for prejudicing the jury," and they cautioned that such evidence has the potential of confusing the issues and wasting time.

The majority of the court, after recognizing that significant progress had been made in the field of polygraph testing over the past 40 years and that it had gained increasingly widespread use, were of the opinion that the per se rule of exclusion should be reexamined and that new principles should be fashioned to govern the admissibility of polygraph evidence.

The court enumerated the three roughly identifiable approaches to the problem that have emerged. First, the traditional approach holds polygraph evidence inadmissible when offered by either party, either as substantive evidence or as relating to the credibility of a witness. Second, a significant number of jurisdictions permit the trial court, in its discretion, to receive polygraph evidence if the parties stipulate to the evidence's admissibility before the administration of the test and if certain other conditions are met. Third, some courts permit the trial judge to admit polygraph evidence even in the absence of a stipulation, but only when special circumstances exist. In these jurisdictions the issue is within the sound discretion of the trial judge.

Recognizing the fact that the federal courts are not in agreement, the Court indicated that the Fourth, Fifth and District of Columbia Circuits have historically adhered to the traditional approach of per se inadmissibility and that the Eighth Circuit has developed a more liberal approach which allows admission of polygraph evidence when the parties stipulate. Finally, the Third, Sixth, Seventh, Ninth and Tenth Circuits, and the Court of Military Appeals permit admission of polygraph evidence even in the absence of a stipulation—when special circumstances exist.

In the *Piccinonna* case the Eleventh Circuit concluded:

Because of the advances that have been achieved in the field which have led to the greater use of polygraph examinations, coupled with a lack of evidence that juries are unduly swayed by polygraph evidence, we agree with those courts which have found that a *per se* rule disallowing polygraph evidence is no longer warranted.

The court then established some rules to be applied:

A. Stipulation

The first rule governing admissibility of polygraph evidence is one easily applied. Polygraph expert testimony will be admissible in this circuit when both parties stipulate in advance as to the circumstances of the test and as to the scope of its admissibility. The stipulation as to circumstances must indicate that the parties agree on material matters such as the manner in which the test is conducted, the nature of the questions asked, and the identity of the examiner administering the test. The stipulation as to scope of admissibility must indicate the purpose or purposes for which the evidence will be introduced. Where the parties agree to both of these conditions in advance of the polygraph test, evidence of the test results is admissible.

B. Impeachment or Corroboration

The second situation in which polygraph evidence may be admitted is when used to impeach or corroborate the testimony of a witness at trial. Admission of polygraph evidence for these purposes is subject to three preliminary conditions. First, the party planning to use the evidence at trial must provide adequate notice to the opposing party that the expert testimony will be offered. Second, polygraph expert testimony by a party will be admissible only if the opposing party was given reasonable opportunity to have its own polygraph expert administer a test covering substantially the same questions. Failure to provide adequate notice or reasonable opportunity for the opposing side to administer its own test is proper grounds for exclusion of the evidence.

Finally, whether used to corroborate or impeach, the admissibility of the polygraph administrator's testimony will be governed by the Federal Rules of Evidence for the admissibility of corroboration or impeachment testimony. For example, Rule 608 limits the use of opinion or reputation evidence to establish the credibility of a witness in the following way: "[E]vidence of truthful character is admissible only after the character of the witness for truthfulness has been attacked by opinion or reputation evidence or otherwise." Thus, evidence that a witness passed a polygraph examination, used to corroborate that witness's in-court testimony, would not be admissible under Rule 608 unless or until the credibility of that witness were first attacked. Even where the above conditions are met, admission of polygraph evidence for impeachment or corroboration purposes is left entirely to the discretion of the trial judge.

Neither of these two modifications to the *per se* exclusionary rule should be construed to preempt or limit in any way the trial court's discretion to exclude polygraph expert testimony on other grounds under the Federal Rules of Evidence. Our holding states merely that in the limited circumstances delineated above, the *Frye* general acceptance test does not act as a bar to admission of polygraph evidence as a matter of law. As we have stated, the chief criterion in determining whether expert testimony is appropriate is whether it will help the trier of fact to resolve the issues. The expert testimony must also, of course, be relevant. Rule 401 defines relevant evidence as evidence "having any tendency to make the existence of any fact that is of consequence to the determination of the action more probable or less probable than it would be without the evidence." Further, Rule 403 states that even though relevant, evidence may be excluded by the trial court "if its probative value is substantially outweighed by the danger of unfair prejudice, confusion of the issues, or misleading the jury, or by consideration of undue delay, waste of time, or needless presentation of cumulative evidence." Thus, we agree with the Ninth Circuit "that polygraph evidence should not be admitted, even for limited purposes, unless the trial court has determined that 'the probative value of the polygraph evidence outweighs the potential prejudice and time consumption involved in presenting such evidence.'"

Thus under the Federal Rules of Evidence governing the admissibility of expert testimony, the trial court may exclude polygraph expert testimony because (1) the polygraph examiner's qualifications are unacceptable; (2) the test procedure was unfairly prejudicial or the test was poorly administered; or (3) the questions were irrelevant or improper. The trial judge has wide discretion in this area, and rulings on admissibility will not be reversed unless a clear abuse of discretion is shown.

In the concluding paragraph, the court explained again the status of the law concerning the use of polygraph evidence and the uncertainty of future decisions with this comment:

> We neither expect nor hope that today's holding will be the final word within our circuit on this increasingly important issue. The advent of new and developing technologies calls for flexibility within the legal system so that the ultimate ends of justice may be served. It is unwise to hold fast to a familiar rule when the basis for that rule ceases to be persuasive. We believe that the science of

polygraphy has progressed to a level of acceptance sufficient to allow the use of polygraph evidence in limited circumstances where the danger of unfair prejudice is minimized. We proceed with caution in this area because the reliability of polygraph testing remains a subject of intense scholarly debate. As the field of polygraph testing continues to progress, it may become necessary to reexamine the rules regarding the admissibility of polygraph evidence.

The law relating to the admissibility of testimony concerning the results of polygraph examinations in state courts is also unclear. Examples of recent cases indicate the diversity of decisions. Some state courts hold that questions asked by polygraph examiners and results of the examinations are not admissible evidence in any criminal prosecution.[51] Some courts refuse to allow the admissibility of such evidence when proffered by the defendant during the guilt phase of the trial because the reliability of the polygraph examination has not been sufficiently established.[52]

Another group of states have decided that polygraph tests are admissible in evidence when both parties stipulate their admission.[53] Other states have established criteria which must be met before evidence is admitted even though both parties stipulate the admissibility. For example, in one case the court noted that polygraph evidence may be admissible on stipulation, provided that: (1) the district attorney, defendant and defense counsel all sign a stipulation providing for admission; (2) the trial court, exercising its discretion, approves the admission; (3) the polygraph operator is available for cross-examination; and (4) the jury is instructed concerning the limited use of the evidence.[54]

In order for stipulated polygraph results to be admitted, the defendant's participation in the examination must be free and voluntary.[55] However, when an agreement was made with the prosecution that the results of the defendant's polygraph examination would be admissible at the trial, this agreement was binding between the state and the defendant, even though the district attorney did not sign the stipulation.[56]

Evidence of the refusal or willingness of a defendant to take a lie detector test is not admissible.[57] In a murder case, it was held to be reversible

---

51 State v. Juarez, 570 A.2d 118 (R.I. 1990).
52 Ex parte Hinton, 548 So. 2d 562 (Ala. 1989); State v. Hinton, 383 S.E.2d 704 (N.C. App. 1989).
53 Carr v. State, 380 S.E.2d 700 (Ga. 1989); State v. Fain, 774 P.2d 252 (Idaho 1989).
54 State v. Valdez, 371 P.2d 894 (Ariz. 1962).
55 State v. Fain, 774 P.2d 252 (Idaho 1989).
56 Miller v. State, 380 S.E.2d 690 (Ga. 1989).
57 Garmon v. Lumpkin County, Georgia, 878 F.2d 1406 (11th Cir. 1989); State v. McDavitt, 62 N.J. 36, 297 A.2d 849 (1972).

error to admit evidence that the defendant refused to submit to a polygraph examination in response to questions by a private detective.[58]

The examiner should receive his training in the lie detector technique under the guidance of an experienced examiner with a sufficient volume of actual cases to permit the trainee to make frequent observations of lie detector tests and to conduct tests himself under the instructor's personal supervision. In addition, the trainee should read and take courses in the pertinent phases of psychology and physiology, and should examine and interpret a considerable number of lie detector test records in verified cases.[59] Some states now require licensing of polygraph operators. Under the Illinois statute, an operator must have earned an academic degree at least at the baccalaureate level and have completed satisfactorily not less than six months of internship.

From the foregoing it is apparent that the laws relating to the use of polygraph evidence in court are still in the process of change. The majority view, however, is that the polygraph has attained a degree of validity and reliability, and that such evidence may be admitted if both parties stipulate as to its use and if the other requirements are met. Moreover, there are recent cases which support the admissibility of polygraph findings even without prior stipulation.[60]

§ 15.6 "Truth serum" results

The term "truth serum" has no precise medical or scientific meaning.[61] To refer to sodium amytal and sodium pentothal as "truth serum" is a misnomer, as they have no propensity or chemical effect to cause a person "to speak the truth." These drugs do not induce a state of mind in which a person tells the truth, but instead cause him to speak more freely than he otherwise might. The use of sodium amytal can produce any one of four results: truth, falsehood, fantasy or response to suggestion.[62]

---

58 Kosmas v. State, 316 Md. 587, 560 A.2d 1137 (1989).

59 Inbau, F.E. and J.E. Reid, *The Lie-Detector Technique: A Reliable and Valuable Investigative Aid,* 50 A.B.A.J. 470 (May, 1964).

60 Kadish, M. J. et al., The Polygraph . . . Admissibility in a Criminal Trial, 4 AM. J. TRIAL ADVOC. 593 (1981); *see also* L. Taylor, SCIENTIFIC INTERROGATION, Chapter 8 (1984).

61 *See* Townsend v. Sain, 372 U.S. 293, 83 S. Ct. 745, 768, 9 L. Ed. 2d 770 (1963) (Stewart, J., dissenting).

62 Freeman v. New York Central R. Co., 174 N.E.2d 550 (Ohio App. 1960), a civil action in which plaintiff told his psychiatrist that he was unable to recall the events leading up to his accident, and requested the doctor to try to restore his memory. The doctor administered a treatment of sodium amy-

It is generally recognized that the administration of sufficient doses of scopolamine will break down the will. The early literature on the subject designated scopolamine as a "truth serum," and it was thought to produce true confessions by criminal suspects.63 More recent commentators, however, state that scopolamine's use is not likely to produce true confessions, and that persons under the influence of drugs are very suggestible and may confess to crimes which they have not committed. False or misleading answers may be given, especially when questions are improperly phrased. For example, if the police officer asserts in a confident tone, "You did steal the money, didn't you?" a suggestible suspect might easily give a false affirmative answer.64

A confession induced by the administration of drugs is constitutionally inadmissible.65 In a prosecution for murder, the trial court properly refused to admit testimony of a psychiatrist that the defendant had been given a narcoanalysis test and that the test revealed that the defendant was telling the truth when he said that the shooting was an accident.66 Courts generally agree that the results of a sodium amytal test, sodium pentothal test or a brevital sodium test are not admissible for or against the defendant in a criminal case because of the lack of scientific certainty about the results.67

A judge in his discretion may exclude expert testimony by a psychiatrist explaining the effects of sodium amytal, especially when the psychiatrist admits that narcoanalysis does not reliably induce truthful statements.68 However, the fact that the witness underwent a sodium amytal interview does not preclude testimony of that witness concerning his current recollection of events. The court in *United States v. Solomon* determined that the admission of the testimony of a witness concerning his current recollection of events was not an abuse of discretion despite the claim that the witness' testimony could not be reliable after he underwent a sodium amytal interview. The court recognized that the defendant was not precluded from presenting evidence that the witness' testimony was enhanced by use of sodium amytal during narcoanalysis.

---

tal, which placed plaintiff in a hypnotic or semiconscious state—during which the doctor conversed with plaintiff and made a record of the questions and answers. At the trial, plaintiff's testimony was based upon his medically refreshed memory. The court did not expressly decide on the propriety of this method of refreshing one's memory.

63 *Why Truth Serum Should Be Made Legal,* 42 MEDICO-LEGAL J. 138 (1952).

64 MacDonald, *Truth Serum,* 46 J. CRIM. L. 259 (1955).

65 Townsend v. Sain, *supra,* note 61.

66 Dugan v. Commonwealth, 333 S.W.2d 755 (Ky. 1960).

67 State v. Heminger, 210 Kan. 587, 502 P.2d 791 (1972); People v. Cox, 85 Mich. App. 314, 271 N.W.2d 216 (1978).

68 United States v. Solomon, 753 F.2d 1522 (9th Cir. 1985).

After discussing the use of scientific evidence generally, the majority of the Supreme Court of Georgia indicated that neither the results of a truth serum test nor an opinion of an expert based on those results are admissible in evidence.[69] In this case the defendant was charged with murder but denied that he murdered the victim. The trial court excluded the opinion of a psychiatrist, based on his interview with the defendant while under the influence of sodium amytal that: (a) the defendant suffered from loss of memory, and (b) the defendant told the truth when he denied murdering the victim. Out of the presence of the jury the psychiatrist had told the judge that he had given a small dosage of sodium amytal, a so-called truth serum, in order to bring back the defendant's memory and to "find the truth." The trial court excluded this testimony on the ground that the reliability of the truth serum test had not been established with enough certainty to authorize it to be admitted into evidence. The trial judge in the case stated that, in reaching this conclusion, he had examined the authority of other states, the majority of which excluded evidence based on "truth serum tests."

On appeal, the Georgia Supreme Court considered the use of scientific principles and techniques in general. The court explained that an evaluation of whether a principle has gained acceptance will often be transmitted to the trial court by members of the appropriate scientific community testifying as an expert witness at a trial. The court pointed out, however, that it has been acknowledged that certain problems inhere in determining admissibility on the basis of this process:

> First, the expert is selected and compensated by a party seeking to demonstrate a specific premise; that the scientific process sought to be proved either is or is not accepted in the scientific community. Such a process may result in a battle between each party's experts at the trial. Also, there are limits on what any one "expert" may understand about a particular discipline. And, last, we acknowledged that wide variations in interdisciplinary opinions frequently exist. After much consideration, we conclude that the *Frye* rule of "counting heads" in the scientific community is not an appropriate way to determine the admissibility of a scientific procedure in evidence. Instead, we approve of the approach taken by the trial court in this case. We hold that it is proper for the trial judge to decide whether the procedure or technique in question has reached a scientific stage of verifiable certainty, or in the words of Professor Irving Younger, whether the procedure "rests upon the laws of nature."

---

[69] Harper v. State, 292 S.E.2d 389 (Ga. 1982).

Applying this reasoning, the court approved the denial of the admissibility of the evidence, explaining that the defendant did not undertake to establish the verifiable certainty that a person will tell the truth while under the influence of sodium amytal. Quoting from a number of other cases, the court here agreed that it had not yet been demonstrated with verifiable certainty that these tests were an accurate and reliable means of ascertaining whether a person is telling the truth. Concluding this part of the decision, the court made this comment:

> Furthermore, we agree with the trial court that, until it is proven with verifiable certainty that truth serum compels a person to tell the truth, neither the results of the truth-serum test nor the opinions of experts based on the results of these tests shall be admissible in evidence.

In an Idaho case, the defendant, in his motion to introduce statements made under the influence of sodium amytal, argued that such refreshed testimony should be admitted to the same extent that hypnotically refreshed testimony would be allowed.[70] The reviewing court agreed that the motion was properly denied, as there was no scientific basis to conclude that hypnosis and the use of sodium amytal produced comparable results. The court concluded that until the so-called "truth serum" test gains scientific acceptability, the results of such tests are inadmissible.

§ 15.7 Fingerprint comparisons

The science of fingerprint comparison for identification purposes is as old as civilization itself. The courts take judicial notice of the well-recognized fact that fingerprint identification is one of the surest methods of identification known. The primary purpose of fingerprinting is the positive identification of an accused. Another purpose of fingerprinting is an evidentiary purpose, e.g., to compare the fingerprints of the defendant with the fingerprints left at the scene of the crime. The evidentiary purpose may or may not be present in a given case.

The Fifth Amendment offers no protection against compulsion to submit to fingerprinting. Furthermore, fingerprinting of persons validly arrested or formally charged with a crime does not constitute a search and seizure within the meaning of the Fourth Amendment.[71]

---

70 State v. Rosencrantz, 110 Idaho 124, 714 P.2d 93 (1986).

71 United States v. Laub Baking Co., 283 F. Supp. 217 (N.D. Ohio 1968); Schmerber v. California, 384 U.S. 757, 86 S. Ct. 1826, 16 L. Ed. 2d 908 (1967); *see* Klotter & Kanovitz, CONSTITUTIONAL LAW, 6th Ed. (1991).

In a criminal case, an official police department fingerprint record may be authenticated for admission in evidence by the person who, having the duty to compile and file such records, is the lawful custodian thereof.[72] A fingerprint expert, to qualify as such, should have formal training in the science of fingerprinting and should be skilled in the photographic procedure of enlarging and developing photographs of fingerprints.[73] Thus, an officer who has been in the identification section of the county sheriff's office for two years, has received direct training in fingerprint work and has received instructions in fingerprinting under an expert in the department is qualified to testify as an expert on fingerprints.[74] Whether a witness possesses the requisite qualifications of a fingerprint expert is a question within the discretion of the trial court.

In a bank robbery case, five police fingerprint cards containing the defendant's genuine signature were offered in evidence for the limited purpose of establishing the fact that the defendant had bought travelers checks at the bank in question four days prior to the crime, and to prove the authenticity of his signature at the time of purchase. Nowhere on the cards was it expressly revealed that the defendant had been arrested, or that he had been charged with or convicted of a crime. The court carefully instructed the jury to disregard the cards except for the limited purpose for which they were offered.[75]

Palmprints left at the scene of a crime have been held to be just as reliable and accurate as fingerprints.[76] Likewise, a bare footprint may be photographed and compared with that of the defendant.[77]

Also, the admissibility of evidence concerning footprint comparisons has been approved—with one court finding that this new scientific technique has been shown to be reliable.[78] Indicating that this scientific technique has gained general acceptance in the particular field in which it belongs, this court explained that the process of making the footprint comparisons relied on scientifically established methods and that the measurements upon which the expert witness based her opinion could be verified by the jury.

The court may order the defendant to submit to palmprints for identification. In a North Carolina case, the prosecution moved that the defendant be ordered to submit to a second palmprint for identification purposes with the latent palmprint found on a bloody dollar bill which was found at the

---

72 State v. Shank, 115 Ohio App. 291, 185 N.E.2d 63 (1962).
73 McGarry v. State, 82 Tex. Crim. 597, 200 S.W. 527 (1918).
74 Todd v. State, 170 Tex. Crim. 552, 342 S.W.2d 575 (1961).
75 Duncan v. United States, 357 F.2d 195 (5th Cir. 1966).
76 People v. Les, 267 Mich. 648, 255 N.W. 407 (1934).
77 State v. Rogers, 233 N.C. 360, 64 S.W.2d 572 (1951).
78 People v. Knights, 212 Cal. Rptr. 307 (Cal. App. 1985).

crime scene. The trial court ordered the requested palmprint and granted a continuance for the defendant to consider the significance of the newly obtained palmprint. After examining the prints so acquired by a fingerprint expert, the witness testified that the defendant's palmprint matched the print found on the dollar bill.

On appeal, the defendant argued that the trial court's order requiring him to submit to a palmprinting during the trial was the equivalent of a non-testimonial identification order and therefore, that the palmprint obtained was inadmissible. The Supreme Court of North Carolina rejected the claim and upheld the validity of the trial court's order requiring the defendant to submit to taking a palmprint during trial.[79]

A court order is not necessary to take the fingerprints or palmprint of a person lawfully in custody. However, it is preferable to have a court order issued by the judge.

Although the police may take fingerprints at the scene of the crime and an expert may make comparisons, the state is not required to gather fingerprint evidence.[80] Even if the defendant argues that the police were attempting to frame him, the state is not required to gather evidence from articles allegedly touched by the defendant, and it is not incumbent on the state to account for the absence of such fingerprint evidence.[81]

§ 15.8 Ballistic experiments

The science of forensic ballistics is a well-recognized subject of expert testimony. Courts will allow such expert testimony to show that the bullet which killed a person was fired from a weapon belonging to the defendant in the case. Before a witness may testify in regard to the identification of firearms and bullets, his qualifications to give such testimony must be clearly shown. If he testifies as to his specialized training and his experience as a member of the criminal laboratory of a police department, the court will permit him to testify as an expert. On the subject of a witness' qualifications, it has been held proper to ask the witness if he has studied the techniques and methods of the Federal Bureau of Investigation at Washington, D.C., and of the crime laboratory at Northwestern University and compared them with the methods applied by him.[82]

A ballistics expert may testify that the firing-pin marking on cartridge shells found at the scene of a homicide corresponds to the marking on a

---

79 State v. Vereen, 312 N.C. 499, 324 S.E.2d 250 (1985).
80 State v. Beck, 785 S.W.2d 714 (Mo. 1990).
81 State v. Schneider, 736 S.W.2d 392 (Mo. 1987).
82 State v. Dallao, 187 La. 392, 175 So. 4 (1937).

test shell fired from the defendant's revolver.83 Likewise, a witness may testify that an empty shotgun shell found at the scene of a homicide had been fired from the defendant's shotgun, and he may base that opinion on breech-face markings revealed by a comparison microscope and photographs.84

Gunpowder-pattern test sheets of blotting paper which were identified, explained and testified to by a qualified ballistic expert who had made the tests were held to have been adequately authenticated and were properly admitted to illustrate his testimony.85 In a prosecution for murder, the trial court will exclude the testimony of an officer in regard to experiments as to distances at which powder burns might appear, when the experimental conditions are not shown to be similar to the actual event.86 When, however, a sheriff conducted experiments with respect to the distance at which a gun would powder-burn cloth, and used a piece of cloth similar to that worn by the deceased, the court admitted his testimony as to powder burns.87

In order for an expert to give opinion testimony concerning ballistics test results, the opinion must be based upon facts within the knowledge of the expert, or the expert may give an opinion based upon a hypothetical question which is itself based on facts already in evidence. This does not necessarily mean that real evidence itself must be admitted. For example, in the case of *Ex parte Hinton,* test bullets fired by the state's ballistics expert were compared with the bullets fired at the scene. Even though the bullets were not admitted into evidence, the reviewing court found that the decision of the lower court was not error, as the experts used the bullets only in analyzing the pieces of evidence that they were asked to examine. It was not required that those bullets be introduced, although they might have been relevant.88

The court reasoned that even if the bullets should have been introduced in evidence, they would have made no difference because the defendant's own expert used the test bullets and based his testimony on them. Also, as the markings of the bullets were microscopic and all the jury would have been able to examine would have been a couple of bullets, failure to introduce these bullets was not error.

---

83 Roberts v. State, 164 So. 2d 817 (Fla. 1964).

84 Ferrell v. Commonwealth, 177 Va. 861, 14 S.E.2d 293 (1941); *see also* Holland v. State, 268 So. 2d 883 (Ala. App. 1972).

85 Opie v. State, 389 P.2d 684 (Wyo. 1964).

86 Johnson v. State, 506 P.2d 963 (Okla. 1973); *see also* Wrenn v. State, 506 P.2d 418 (Nev. 1973).

87 State v. Truster, 334 S.W.2d 104 (Mo. 1961).

88 Ex parte Hinton, 548 So. 2d 562 (Ala. 1989).

§ 15.9   Speed detection readings

The principle of Radio Detection and Ranging (RADAR) is the use of exact laws of science and nature in the measurement of distance and speed. The radar speed-detecting devices commonly used in traffic control operate on what is known as the Doppler effect and utilize a continuous beam of microwaves sent out at a fixed frequency. The operation depends upon the physical law that when such waves are intercepted by a moving object, the frequency changes in such a ratio to the speed of the intercepted object that, by measuring the change of the frequency, the speed may be determined.[89]

In operation, the radar device is set up along the side of a road or street, usually in or upon a parked police car, with the beam being played along the highway. When a moving vehicle crosses that beam, the speed of the vehicle is registered on a graph or calibrated dial on the meter device. The speed, if it is excessive, is then transmitted by radio by the officer reading the graph or dial, along with a description of the vehicle, to another officer stationed some distance farther on, and the vehicle is intercepted by this officer.

For many years, the public has been aware of the widespread use of radio, microwaves and other electronic devices in detecting the speed of motor vehicles and other moving objects. While the intricacies of such devices were not fully understood, their general accuracy and effectiveness had few challenges.[90] The reasoning was that the radar speed meter was accepted in evidence just as courts have accepted photographs, x-rays, speedometer readings and the like without requiring expert testimony as to the scientific principles underlying them. In some cases, the courts had recognized by judicial knowledge—and those learned in electronics had confirmed—that a radar speed meter is a device which, within a reasonable engineering tolerance, and when properly functioning and properly operated, accurately measures speed in terms of miles per hour.[91]

However, in a Florida case in 1979, the accuracy of the devices used was seriously challenged. As the court stated, this was the first time that any court had been presented with so much testimony, so many exhibits, and so many highly qualified experts summoned from all parts of the country to determine the reliability of radar.[92] In this case, the court heard over 2,000 pages of testimony and arguments, and examined 33 exhibits pre-

---

89 Kopper, *The Scientific Reliability Of Radar Speedmeters,* 33 N.C.L. REV. 343 (1955).

90 Dooley v. Commonwealth, 198 Va. 32, 92 S.E.2d 348 (1956).

91 State v. Graham, 322 S.W.2d 188 (Mo. 1959).

92 State v. Aquilera, County Court for Dade County, Florida, decided May 7, 1979 (25 Cr. L. 2189).

sented by highly trained and experienced specialists in the fields of mathematics, electrical engineering, and the design, construction and testing of radar devices. The court made it clear that the hearing dealt only with radar used by police as a speed-measuring device in its present mode. The court asserted that there has been no argument with the Doppler system itself, but only as to its use by current units.

In finding that radar measuring devices as used in their present mode were not sufficiently reliable for courtroom use, the court pointed to possible errors inherent in varying degrees in the vast majority of radar units in present use. Among other things, the court referred to the cosine error, the batching error, panning and scanning errors, shadowing error and errors due to outside interference from billboards, overpasses, or passing CB radios, and many other similar errors. The court made it clear that this did not rule out the use of radar or other speed detection devices *per se,* stating that devices could and should be improved to the extent that they are accurate, and that the scientific and financial resources of manufacturers could be used to accomplish this in the very near future. In this particular case, the court stated:

> I find that the reliability of radar speed measuring devices as used
> in their present modes and particularly in these cases, has not been
> established beyond and to the exclusion of every reasonable doubt
> and it is, therefore, ordered and adjudged that the Motions to
> Suppress and/or Exclude herein be and they are hereby granted.

This is only one county court case and does not establish rules of evidence for the whole United States. Some courts seem to be relying on the reasoning of this case, but the majority still approve the use of radar evidence. Two things will probably result from this case: (1) manufacturers will improve upon the devices so as to make them more reliable; and (2) the use of speed detection devices will be challenged more frequently.

In a Nebraska case the officer was conducting stationary radar checks from his unmarked police cruiser when his radar sounded. He then observed a red Mercedes-Benz traveling at a high rate of speed in the center lane and the officer then pursued and finally stopped the vehicle. The defendant was convicted for traveling 75 miles per hour in a 45-mile-per-hour zone and appealed, arguing that there was inadequate evidence to establish that the radar unit was functioning properly and adequately.[93] This court upheld the conviction, explaining that the officer had testified that prior to using his radar unit he had performed an LED light segment test, an internal circuitry test, and a tuning fork test and had concluded that the radar was operating properly. The officer further testified that after issuing the cita-

---

93 State v. Kincaid, 235 Neb. 89, 453 N.W.2d 738 (1990).

tion, but prior to leaving the location, he performed the same tests and again concluded that the radar unit was functioning properly.

With regard to the tuning fork test, the officer testified that there were two forks, one stamped with a 35 m.p.h. marking and the other an 80 m.p.h. marking. The tuning forks were supplied by the manufacturer and were tested at the factory. He testified that he struck each tuning fork, held it approximately one inch in front of the radar antenna, and received a digital readout which correlated to the marking stamped on the fork. The court concluded that this was sufficient foundation to establish that the radar unit was operating properly.

In a decision decided by the Supreme Court of Hawaii, the scientific principles upon which the radar gun is based also were considered.[94] That court pointed out that every recent court which has dealt with the question has taken judicial notice of the scientific reliability of radar speedmeters as recorders of speed. The court referred to studies which indicate that the accuracy of a particular radar unit can be established by showing that the operator tested the device in accordance with accepted procedures to determine that the unit was functioning properly and that the operator was qualified by training and experience to operate the unit. The court concluded that the state's evidence, which consisted of the testimony of a single officer who relied upon a reading from a K-15 radar speed detection device, was sufficient to justify a judgment of conviction.

While the courts have generally taken judicial notice of the scientific reliability of radar speed detection devices, an Ohio reviewing court warned that judicial notice of the accuracy of a specific model of a radar device cannot automatically be extended to warrant judicial notice of the accuracy of another model of a radar device.[95] That reviewing court found that the trial court erred in taking judicial notice of the construction, operation and accuracy of the S-80 moving radar unit without the benefit of expert testimony before the trial court as to that specific model of moving radar.

Visual Average Speed Computer and Recorder (VASCAR) has been accepted in more than half of the states. The first VASCAR arrest was made in Indiana, in July 1966. Approximately the size of a cigar box, VASCAR can be fitted into a police car and is limited in portability only to the extent of the patrol cruiser in which it is used. Only one officer is needed to operate it, as opposed to the two required for radar.

The operation of VASCAR is very simple. A police officer feeds the distance covered and the time it takes to cover that distance into the unit. The speed of the vehicle being observed is then automatically computed by

---

94   State v. Tailo, 779 P.2d 11 (Haw. 1989). *See* case in Part II, *infra*.

95   Village of Moreland Hills v. Gazdak, 49 Ohio App. 3d 22, 550 N.E.2d 203 (1988).

the unit in miles per hour. The unit is then equipped with two toggle switches, one that controls the time-measuring mechanism and one that controls the distance-measuring mechanism. These switches are manually turned on and off by the operator of the machine to measure the distance between two fixed markers on the highway and the time taken by a vehicle to travel that same distance. The time may be placed into the unit before, during or after the distance measurement is made.

VASCAR computes the average speed for the amount of distance involved between the two location points used. The units are checked daily for accuracy. As slight variations are caused by the difference in wear of tires on each police car, the individual unit is checked with the patrol car in which it is to be used.

§ 15.10 Voice identification

A scientific technique designed to identify persons by means of a voiceprint, has presented evidentiary problems. Voiceprints, also known as speech spectrograms, were first developed in the United States in the 1930s at the Bell Telephone laboratories. The speech spectrogram, broadly speaking, is a picture showing the distribution of speech energy over the audio frequency spectrum, plotted against time. According to those who favor the use of this technique, every person's voice is unique and identifiable with the same accuracy as a fingerprint identification.

In the Michigan State University Department Information Service publication dated August 9, 1973, a Michigan State University audiology and speech scientist, Dr. Oscar Tosi, declared that in 39 cases, experts were authorized to testify in court for purposes of voice identification. In the paper Dr. Tosi explained that of 3,000 voice examinations made in cooperation with the Michigan State Police, 500 were positive identifications, 1600 were probable identifications and positive eliminations, and 850 were no-decisions. In criticizing a California judge's ruling which rejected the voiceprint, Dr. Tosi pointed out that voice identification is effective, but only if strict guidelines are observed, including:

1. The examination must include both aural and visual comparisons of the known voice with the unknown voice.
2. The examiner must be qualified, with at least two years of practical experience in an apprenticeship program.
3. In positively identifying the voice, the examiner cannot have the slightest hint of a doubt.

Although there are still arguments pro and con concerning the reliability and admissibility of the spectrogram to identify persons by showing similarities in spectrogram readings, more federal and state courts are authorizing the use of such evidence when all of the conditions are met. In the case of *United States v. Maivia*, the United States District Court for the District of Hawaii reviewed the decisions of federal courts and concluded that the use of spectrographic evidence to identify voices is no longer considered unreliable and that expert testimony is admissible for voice comparison purposes. The court first explained the principle and process in voice identification:

> The method of voice identification by spectrographic analysis is based upon the principle that a person's voice can be effectively identified and distinguished when its characteristics are registered by an instrument known as a "spectrograph." A spectrograph produces a readout or a linear representation of the voice on a "spectrogram." A spectrogram is . . . a graphic display of sound in three dimensions: frequency in hertz, time in seconds, and different levels of energy. Spectrograms display the fundamental frequencies (pitch) of a voice and its resonating characteristics, as well as rate of speech. Different formations of words result in different patterns on the spectrogram. Spectrograms are made by transferring a recorded voice to a machine, called a sound spectrograph, that transforms the sound on tape into electrical coordinates. These coordinates manifest themselves as different shadings on paper.[96]

In the *Maivia* case the defendant was prosecuted for conspiracy and extortion under the Hobbs Act. An important piece of evidence for the government was a threatening tape-recorded message of some 65 words, left on the alleged victim's telephone answering machine. One expert witness, if permitted to testify, would have stated that, in his opinion, based on his use of spectrographic voice analyses, the unknown caller was not the defendant. After discussing studies made by various experts in the area of spectrographic identification, the court concluded that in this case, the defendant met the burden of establishing the scientific basis and reliability of the proposed expert testimony. In the discussion of the case, the court explained that two experts agreed that aural spectrographic analysis is accurate if there are safeguards. These safeguards were proposed: (1) a minimum of two minutes of each speech sample; (2) a signal-to-noise ratio in which the signal is higher by 20 decibels; (3) a frequency of 3,000 hertz or better; (4) an example in the same words, the same rate, and the same way, spoken naturally and fluently; and (5) a responsible examiner.

---

96 United States v. Maivia, 728 F. Supp. 1471 (D. Haw. 1990). For a more detailed explanation of the scientific principles of speech mechanics, the spectrograph and the spectrogram, see United States v. Williams, 583 F.2d 1194 (2d Cir. 1978).

In 1989 the United States Court of Appeals for the Seventh Circuit approved the use of expert testimony concerning spectrographic voice analysis in cases in which the proponent of the testimony has established a proper foundation.97 In this case the defendant was convicted of conspiracy and fraud after an expert witness testified that the recorded voice of the person who called a bank and falsely identified herself as a bank employee was the defendant. The defendant challenged the admissibility of evidence, protesting that the use of the spectrographic voice identification testimony was not accepted by the scientific community.

In upholding the use of this evidence, the Seventh Circuit noted that expert testimony concerning spectrographic voice analysis is admissible in cases in which a proponent of the testimony has established a proper foundation. In this case, the government presented ample evidence of the reliability of spectrographic voice identification at trial.

In reviewing the admissibility of expert testimony concerning spectrographic voice analysis, the Seventh Circuit made reference to other circuits that have admitted such testimony. According to the court, the Second, Fourth and Sixth Circuits have held expert testimony concerning spectrographic voice identification admissible.98

The Seventh Circuit concluded that:

> We join these circuits today, and hold that expert testimony concerning spectrographic voice analysis is admissible in cases where the proponent of this testimony has established a proper foundation.

While some states have joined these circuits in finding that expert testimony concerning spectrographic analysis is admissible, other states have refused to join.99

From a review of the cases, there is an indication that even though the test has not been universally recognized, the tendency is to make use of the voiceprint as a means of identification when a proper foundation has been established and when evidence is introduced to show that the expert who performed the examination is qualified.

In 1989, an International Association of Chiefs of Police publication contained an article concerning research and development of the Computer

---

97 United States v. Smith, 869 F.2d 348 (7th Cir. 1989).
98 United States v. Williams, 583 F.2d 1194 (2d Cir. 1978); United States v. Baller, 519 F.2d 463 (4th Cir. 1975); United States v. Franks, 511 F.2d 25 (6th Cir. 1975). The Ninth Circuit has not directly addressed the issue; however, according to the case of *United States v. Maivia,* there were three opinions in which the court discussed the voice spectrogram evidence, and in none of them has the court held that such evidence was inadmissible.
99 Reed v. State, 283 Md. 374, 391 A.2d 364 (1978).

Assisted Voice Identification System (CAVIS). In the article entitled "A Breakthrough in Voice Identification," the spectrograph technique was compared with the CAVIS procedure. According to the article, the conventional method of comparing voices in criminal cases can take several hours, days, or even weeks, depending upon the nature of the recording. With the spectrograph, examiners need at least 20 words or approximately 30 seconds of speech to make an accurate comparison. But with the use of the computer, a voice examiner can compare the tone of the voice and the way that the energy vibrates from the vocal cords and make the identification in a shorter period of time. The article concluded that "although CAVIS is still in the testing stages, it is well on the way to having a tremendous impact on future criminal cases where audio identification is vital to solving the crime."100

§ 15.11 Neutron activation analysis

Neutron activation analysis is a relatively new process by which the chemical composition of materials can be determined.

This process was approved in a federal case involving the sending of a package bomb through the mail.101 In this case the court approved the explanation of the process which appeared in *American Jurisprudence's* "Proof of Facts," stating:

But we feel that the following description is the most understandable and succinct explanation which we have found available. *American Jurisprudence's* "Proof of Facts" describes the process thus:

One of the newest and most promising techniques of forensic science is neutron activation analysis. The ability of this nuclear method to detect traces of elements in minute samples enables it to solve many problems of identification that have heretofore been considered hopeless. . . . The process is essentially one whereby the material to be analyzed is first made radioactive—i.e., it is "charged" so that it will give off or emit radiation in the form of gamma rays. This radioactive sample is then exposed to a scintillation crystal; and every time a gamma ray from the radioactive material interacts with the crystal, it emits a flash of light, which is converted into an electrical pulse whose voltage is proportional to the energy of the gamma rays. An electronic device called a

---

100 International Association of Chiefs of Police News, Vol. 3, No. 10 (Oct. 1989).
101 United States v. Stifel, 433 F.2d 431 (6th Cir. 1970).

multi-channel differential analyzer then sorts the electrical impulses into different energy groups and adds up the pulses in each group. The result is a graph shown on an oscilloscope screen. The graph contains information related to the kind and amount of elements in the radioactive sample and can be transcribed immediately or stored on magnetic tape or punched paper tapes for future reference.

Virtually no sample of material is too small to be analyzed by activation analysis. A single hair, a shred of marijuana, or a fleck of automobile paint no longer than the period at the end of this sentence can be analyzed and correctly identified. Furthermore, activation analysis' high sensitivity allows quantitative measurement of elements in the parts per million and parts per billion range. For instance, if one thimbleful of arsenic poison were diluted in ten tankcars of water, the exact amount of arsenic present could be determined by activation analysis. In most cases the analysis is also nondestructive, so that material evidence may be preserved for presentation in court or saved for analysis by another method.

In a Minnesota case, the results of a neutron activation analysis were admitted to show that the suspect had fired a gun on the night of the shooting.[102] Here the neutron activation technique was used to determine if barium and antimony were on the hands of the accused. The court agreed that the neutron activation analysis can accurately detect the presence and amount of certain chemical elements and that the lower court did not err in admitting the test results. The Supreme Court of Minnesota, however, was concerned that the evidence may have been given more weight than warranted and that the testimony of the expert witness was too conclusive. In approving the use of the neutron activation analysis, the court stated:

> We believe that neutron activation analysis is a useful law enforcement technique and that the increasing use of technology in criminal investigations should not be inhibited but encouraged where consistent with rights of the accused.

In a case in which the defendant was convicted of murder and conspiracy to commit murder, the defendant on appeal objected to the admission of test results of atomic absorption—the tests having been made for the purpose of determining the presence of the elements barium and antimony, ingredients present in modern ammunition primer formulations.[103]

---

102 State v. Spencer, 216 N.W.2d 131 (Minn. 1974).
103 State v. Smith, 465 N.E.2d 1105 (Ind. 1984).

The expert had testified at the trial that the test can show that an individual from whom the tests were taken had significantly higher than normal amounts of these elements, which should be consistent with handling or firing a firearm. In this case the testimony indicated that the defendant's right hand had 27 times more barium and almost 50 times more antimony than would be normal. The reviewing court agreed that the evidence was properly admitted.

In a Florida case, the defendant was convicted of first degree murder, burglary and aggravated battery. He appealed, contending that the gunshot residue test results should not have been admitted into evidence because such tests are not scientifically accepted in general and because the tests used in this case were inconclusive and unreliable.104 The test in question was a neutron activation analysis which, according to the court, is designed to detect and measure the presence of barium and antimony on the suspect's hands. The court found that the test had attained sufficient standing among scientists to be accepted as reliable evidence in the courts. In citing other cases, the court observed that a majority of American jurisdictions have held the results of such tests to be admissible evidence in criminal proceedings.

While the neutron activation analysis does not conclusively establish whether the subject has recently fired a gun, the test results are generally admissible in evidence despite this inherent inconclusiveness. The evidence is admissible as relevant because it shows a probability that the suspect did or did not fire a gun; its probative value is for the jury to determine.

§ 15.12 Deoxyribonucleic acid (DNA) tests

Researchers have made a significant breakthrough in using the deoxyribonucleic acid (DNA) code present in blood and other body fluids to link evidence such as bloodstains or semen specimens to a specific individual, excluding all others. According to an article that appeared in a National Institute of Justice publication dated October 1987, DNA patterns are so distinguishably different between people who are not identical twins so as to provide virtually definite identification.

In the case of *State v. Schwartz,* the Supreme Court of Minnesota, in referring to DNA testing, included this statement:

Forensic DNA typing is heralded as a significant breakthrough because it promises greater specificity of results and may permit analysis of samples too small to be identified by traditional means, such as A.B.O. blood typing.105

---

104 Mills v. State, 476 So. 2d 172 (Fla. 1985).
105 State v. Schwartz, 447 N.W.2d 422 (Minn. 1989).

The court observed that DNA typing is an emerging scientific technique that reveals distinctive patterns in human genetic material of blood and other body fluids, hair and tissue. Citing a *Virginia Law Review* article, the court included this explanation of the basic scientific principles:

> DNA (deoxyribonucleic acid) is an extremely long, thread-like chain of molecules found in the nucleus of every cell of the body . . . . The DNA chains are tightly coiled into bodies called "chromosomes" of which humans have twenty-three . . . . No two individuals, except for identical twins, have identical DNA. Within a given person, however, DNA does not vary from cell to cell.

In the *Schwartz* case the defendant was indicted for murder in the first degree. The police, acting pursuant to a search warrant, had obtained a pair of bloodstained blue jeans from his residence and a shirt from the vicinity of the murder. The Minnesota Bureau of Criminal Apprehension performed blood group testing, which confirmed that the blood stains on the blue jeans and shirt were consistent with the blood of the victim.

The court of appeals, after noting that three commercial laboratories in the United States currently perform DNA analysis, held that DNA test results are admissible if performed in accordance with appropriate laboratory standards and controls to ensure reliability. However, the court cautioned that the test data and methodology must be available for independent review by the opposing party. The court warned that "as a direct corrollary, specific DNA test results are only as reliable and accurate as the testing procedures used by the particular laboratory." In this case, because the laboratory test did not comport with specific guidelines, the test results lacked fundamental adequacy and, without more, were inadmissible.

The Texas Court of Appeals first considered the reliability of DNA fingerprinting in the case of *Glover v. State* in 1990. Although noting that this was a case of first impression in Texas, the court, citing other state decisions, resolved that DNA fingerprint testing has been found to hold and enjoy a general acceptance in the scientific community.[106] The court concluded:

> DNA fingerprinting—its underlining principles, procedures and technology—is a scientific test that is reliable and has gained general acceptance in the scientific community in the particular field in which it belongs.

---

106 Glover v. State, 787 S.W.2d 544 (Tex. 1990) (citing Andrews v. State, 533 So. 2d 841 (Fla. Dist. Ct. App. 1988); Cobey v. State, 80 Md. App. 31, 559 A.2d 391 (1989); State v. Schwartz, 447 N.W.2d 422 (Minn. 1989); People v. Shi Fu Huang, 546 N.Y.S.2d 920 (1989); People v. Wesley, 533 N.Y.S.2d 643 (1988); People v. Castro, 545 N.Y.S.2d 985 (1989); Spencer v. Commonwealth, 238 Va. 275, 384 S.E.2d 775 (1989)).

The court made reference to the standard established in *Frye v. United States* for determining the admissibility of emerging scientific techniques.[107]

According to the New York Times News Service, a federal court in 1990 for the first time allowed the results of a "genetic fingerprinting" test to be admitted as evidence of a New York man accused of kidnapping a Vermont woman.[108] According to the New York Times information, DNA testing was first introduced in a criminal case in 1986 and has been used in at least 200 cases in some 30 states and in the military, but up to this time had not been used in a federal court. In this case, tried in federal court, the defendant was charged with rape.[109] The defendant's attorneys had argued that the technique used in DNA testing is unreliable and was an invasion of the defendant's right to privacy.

While DNA "fingerprinting" tests results are not universally accepted, in most cases, when the issue has been brought before the court, the results have been admissible if performed in accordance with appropriate laboratory standards and controls to ensure reliability.[110]

§ 15.13 Summary

Often real evidence is not admitted directly into court but is used for experiments and tests conducted out of court. General rules have been established concerning the admissibility of testimony concerning experiments and tests and the use of evidence such as charts and graphs resulting from experiments and tests. In recent years, the trend has been for the courts to allow and encourage the use of such evidence, and this has been held to be consistent with the rights of the accused.

As a general rule, examination of the body for evidence such as marks and bruises and the taking of samples such as saliva from the body do not violate the privilege against self-incrimination. Such evidence is admissible if proper safeguards are met. Also, the common practice of determining blood-alcohol content by testing the suspect's blood, breath or urine has

---

107 Frye v. United States, 293 F. 1013 (D.C. Cir. 1923).

108 *The Courier Journal,* Sept. 23, 1990.

109 In United States v. Jakobetz, 747 F. Supp. 250 (D. Vt. 1990), in which the federal court concluded that "DNA profiling was sufficiently reliable to support its admission in a criminal case to prove identity of a rapist; although there was no doubt that the evidence would have a substantial impact on the jury's verdict, the government established that DNA profiling was highly reliable and such reliability outweighed the increased potential for DNA profiling to unfairly prejudice the defendant or mislead or confuse the jury."

110 State v. Woodall, 358 S.E.2d 253 (W. Va. 1989). *See* case in Part II, *infra.*

been approved if the many conditions provided by the courts and legislative bodies are met.

Blood grouping test results are generally admissible in evidence for purposes of identification in criminal prosecutions for rape, assault and battery, and more often in determining nonpaternity when it is shown that the person who made the test is qualified, that proper safeguards were drawn around the testing procedure, and that no discrepancies were found in the testing methods.

Courts are divided concerning the admissibility of polygraph evidence. Three approaches have been taken by various federal and state courts: (1) the traditional approach of *per se* inadmissibility; (2) polygraph evidence is admissible only when both parties so stipulate; (3) polygraph evidence is admissible even in the absence of stipulation where special circumstances exist.

The reasoning that has been applied in the use of the polygraph is similar to that of most courts in finding that so-called "truth-serum" tests are not admissible for or against the defendant in a criminal case because of the lack of scientific certainty about the results. However, the courts take an entirely different view as to fingerprint comparisons. The results of fingerprint comparisons made out of court may be introduced to compare the fingerprints of the defendant with fingerprints left at the scene of the crime. This procedure has become so well recognized that the courts will take judicial notice of the fact that fingerprint identification is one of the surest methods of identification.

The science of forensic ballistics is also a well-recognized subject of expert testimony. The courts will generally allow such expert testimony to show, for example, that the bullet which entered the body was fired from a weapon belonging to the defendant in the case. Before such evidence is admissible, the introducing party must show that approved procedures were followed and that the person testifying is qualified as an expert in the field.

The use of speed detection devices such as radar has been generally approved, and testimony concerning the readings on such devices is generally accepted in evidence. However, test results are not admissible in court unless there is proof that the equipment was properly calibrated and the witness is qualified to testify concerning the meaning of such tests.

One of the more recent techniques is voice identification through the use of the spectrogram. Although the majority rule is that such evidence is probably admissible with very strict safeguards, there is still a strong minority that holds that such evidence is not reliable and not admissible. Another recently developed process is neutron activation analysis. Evidence concerning the results of such analysis is generally admissible, but here too the use of the equipment and the qualifications of the user must comply with strict standards.

Recent research has resulted in the development of forensic DNA analysis as a scientific technique that reveals distinctive patterns in human genetic material in blood and other body fluids, hair and tissue. The results of this "DNA fingerprint" test have been found in many courts to hold and enjoy a general acceptance in the scientific community. While not all courts have recognized this process, the trend is in that direction.

As many out-of-court examinations and tests are conducted by criminal justice personnel, it is essential that such criminal justice personnel be aware of the value of such evidence and be familiar with the requirements designed to protect the rights of those who are accused of crime.

F. EXCLUSION OF EVIDENCE ON CONSTITUTIONAL GROUNDS

CHAPTER 16
EVIDENCE
UNCONSTITUTIONALLY
OBTAINED

Today we once again examine Wolf's constitutional documentation of the right of privacy free from unreasonable state intrusions, and, after its dozen years on our books, are led by it to close the only courtroom door remaining open to evidence secured by official lawlessness in flagrant abuse of that basic right, reserved to all persons as a specific guarantee against that very same unlawful conduct. We hold that all evidence obtained by searches and seizures in violation of the Constitution is, by that same authority, inadmissible in a state court.
Mapp v. Ohio, 367 U.S. 643, 81 S. Ct. 1684, 6 L. Ed. 2d 1081 (1961)

Section

§ 16.1 Introduction

In the discussion of the reasons for the rules of evidence in Chapter 2, it was pointed out that recently developed rules exclude evidence obtained in violation of many of the rights protected by the Constitution. This is not because the evidence is not relevant or material. In fact, in many instances the evidence obtained in violation of the constitutional provisions as interpreted by the courts is highly relevant and material. The courts have reasoned that even though the evidence is relevant and material and would shed some light as to the actual happenings, such evidence should not be admitted because authorizing use of illegally obtained evidence would encourage violation of the individual rights as enumerated in the Constitution.

Although the exclusionary rules relating to the various types of evidence have been extended greatly in recent years, much doubt remains as to what evidence will be excluded and what will be admissible. Under the recent United States Supreme Court decisions, evidence is primarily excluded when the seizure of evidence violates the rights protected by the Fourth, Fifth or Sixth Amendments to the Constitution. The general rules concerning search and seizure, self-incrimination, right to counsel and other constitutional provisions cannot be discussed comprehensively due to space limitations. However, rules relating to the exclusion of the evidence so obtained are discussed briefly.[1]

§ 16.2 Development of the exclusionary rules

Comparatively speaking, the search and seizure exclusionary rule is of recent origin. This rule provides very succinctly that evidence which has been illegally obtained, or obtained in violation of the Constitution, will be excluded from use in court.

First, it should be pointed out that this exclusionary rule is certainly not universally applied. Today in England and in most of the other Anglo-Saxon countries, evidence is admitted even if obtained illegally. The principle that evidence should not be excluded merely because the constable blundered in obtaining evidence was followed in about half of the states as late as 1961. This rule, commonly called the common law of English Rule, was justified by an English judge, who explained:[2]

> I think it would be a dangerous obstacle to the administration of justice if we were to hold that because evidence was obtained by illegal means, it could not be used against the party charged with an offense. It therefore seems to me that the interests of the state must excuse the seizure of documents, which seizure would otherwise be unlawful, if it appears in fact that such documents were evidence of a crime committed by anyone.

Although the exclusionary rule as it relates to searches in violation of the Constitution was mentioned as far back as 1886 by the United States Supreme Court, it was not until 1914 that the Supreme Court, in the case

---

1 For a more comprehensive discussion of the constitutional limitations, see Klotter and Kanovitz, CONSTITUTIONAL LAW, Anderson Publishing Co. (6th ed. 1991).

2 Elias v. Pasmore, 2 K.B. 65 (1934).

of *Weeks v. United States,*[3] made the exclusionary rule applicable in federal courts in this country. The Supreme Court held that in a federal prosecution, the Fourth Amendment barred the use of evidence secured through an illegal search and seizure.

The reason for adopting the exclusionary rule is that the rule (according to the court) is the only way to insure that police and prosecutors will not violate or encourage violation of the rights protected by the Constitution and its amendments. While the English courts argue that the remedy is action against the officer who violates these provisions, the courts in this country emphasize that only by excluding the evidence can these privileges be sufficiently protected.

Although the exclusionary rule as it relates to search and seizure has been applied in federal courts since 1914, it was not until 1961 that the Supreme Court made the exclusionary rule applicable in search and seizure cases in state courts.[4]

Partially on the basis of the Fourth Amendment, but probably more as a result of legislation, wiretapping and eavesdropping evidence is often excluded if all statutory requirements are not met. However, if the state and federal laws are complied with some evidence obtained by wiretapping and eavesdropping is admissible.

The United States Supreme Court and other courts have established rules relating to the admissibility of confessions and other statements made by the accused. Such extrajudicial confessions are inadmissible if obtained contrary to the rules established by the courts. Some evidence is also excluded if obtained in violation of the self-incrimination provisions of the Fifth Amendment or the due process clause of the Fifth and Fourteenth Amendments. More recently, the courts have applied exclusionary reasoning to exclude evidence obtained in violation of the right to counsel provisions of the Constitution.

The degree of application of these rules of exclusion is discussed in the following sections.

§ 16.3 Search and seizure exclusions

The Fourth Amendment to the Constitution provides:

The right of the people to be secure in their persons, houses, papers and effects against unreasonable searches and seizures, shall not be violated, and no Warrants shall issue but upon probable cause supported by oath or affirmation, and particularly describing the place to be searched, and the persons or things to be seized.[5]

---

3   232 U.S. 383, 34 S. Ct. 341, 58 L. Ed. 652 (1914).
4   Mapp v. Ohio, 367 U.S. 643, 81 S. Ct. 1684, 6 L. Ed. 2d 1081 (1961).
5   U.S. CONST. amend IV.

This amendment was added to the Constitution in 1791 at the insistence of some of the leaders of the day, who complained that the Constitution itself, which was ratified in 1789, did not include some of the protections which should have been guaranteed to the people. At this point in history, the Fourth Amendment did not apply to state officials, but was added to prohibit the officials of a strong central government from abridging the rights of the citizens of the various states.

While it is true that initially the United States Supreme Court interpreted the Fourth Amendment to exclude evidence obtained by illegal search and seizure only in federal courts, the Court in 1961 extended the rule to all state as well as federal courts.[6] By making the exclusionary rule applicable to the states, the Court made it necessary for state prosecutors and judges to look to the decisions of the federal courts for minimum standards which must be met by state officials.

In the *Mapp* decision, the Supreme Court indicated that the decision closed the last courtroom door to the use of illegally seized evidence. However, in 1984, the Supreme Court modified the exclusionary rule. In the case of *United States v. Leon,* police officers acting in good faith executed a search warrant instructing them to search residences for controlled substances.[7] Although it was later determined that the search warrant was invalid because the affidavit was insufficient to establish probable cause, the Court made this comment:

> We conclude that the marginal or nonexistent benefits produced by suppressing evidence obtained in objectively reasonable reliance on a subsequently invalidated search warrant cannot justify the substantial costs of exclusion.

The Supreme Court acknowledged that the exclusionary rule had been modified, but included this warning:

> We do not suggest, however, that exclusion is always inappropriate in cases where an officer has obtained a warrant and abided by its terms. . . . Nevertheless, the officer's reliance on the magistrate's probable cause of determination and on the technical sufficiency of the warrant he issues must be objectively reasonable . . . and it is clear that in some circumstances the officer will have no reasonable grounds for believing that the warrant was properly issued.

In a second case decided on the same day as *Leon,* the Supreme Court upheld a search for real evidence when the search was executed in good faith by the officers.[8] Here the Court determined that the evidence should

---

6   Mapp v. Ohio, *infra.* note 4.
7   104 S. Ct. 3405, 82 L. Ed. 2d 677 (1984).
8   Massachusetts v. Shepherd, 468 U.S. 897, 104 S. Ct. 3424, 82 L. Ed. 2d 677 (1984).

be admitted even though it was later found by a reviewing court that the description in the search warrant did not meet constitutional standards.

In both the *Leon* and the *Shephard* cases, police officers executed what they believed to be valid warrants. Soon after these cases were decided, the question arose as to whether the "good faith" rationale would be applied in situations in which officers acted without a warrant. In the case of *Illinois v. Krull,* officers, acting pursuant to a statute, made an inspection of an automobile wrecking yard and discovered several stolen cars.9 The state statute, similar to those in many other states, regulated the business of buying and selling motor vehicles, parts and scrap metal. The day after the warrantless search, a federal court ruled that such a statute was unconstitutional, and at the trial a motion was made to exclude the evidence obtained by the officers even though the officers acted in good faith under the statute. On review, the United States Supreme Court reversed the lower court decision and decided that the evidence should have been admitted, as the application of the exclusionary rule in these circumstances would have little deterrent effect on police conduct, and that effect is the basic purpose of the exclusionary rule.

Although the court in the *Krull* case did not extend the "good faith" exception to a considerable extent, it did clarify the reasoning concerning the exclusionary rule with these comments:

> Application of the Exclusionary Rule "is neither intended nor able to cure the invasion of the defendant's rights which he has already suffered". . . . Rather, the rule "operates as a judicially created remedy designed to safeguard Fourth Amendment rights generally through its deterrent affect, rather than as a personal constitutional right of the party aggrieved". . . . As with any remedial device, application of the exclusionary rule properly has been restricted to those situations in which its remedial purpose is effectively advanced.

These cases indicate a trend by the Supreme Court to apply less technical rules in search and seizure cases. However, the exclusionary rule is still applicable in the majority of the cases when evidence has been obtained illegally. Therefore, it is essential that the rules concerning the constitutionality of searches be followed.

One type of search which is universally recognized as legal is a search with a warrant. Both the United States Constitution and the constitutions of the various states describe the circumstances upon which search warrants may be issued.

---

9 Illinois v. Krull, 475 U.S. 868, 107 S. Ct. 1160, 94 L. Ed. 2d 364 (1987). *See* Klotter and Kanovitz, Constitutional Law, Anderson Publishing Co. (6th ed. 1991) for a more thorough discussion of the search and seizure requirements

The United States Supreme Court, as well as other courts, has encouraged the use of a search warrant in making a search. In 1983, the Court, in reinforcing this preference and in indicating a trend to approve less technical procedures, modified the probable cause requirements for a search warrant. In previous cases, the Court had approved the use of undisclosed informants in determining probable cause and had established what was known as the "two-pronged" test.[10] This standard for testing the credibility of an informant's tip upon which a magistrate is asked to rely was: (1) that the magistrate must be given some of the underlying circumstances from which the affiant concluded that the informant was credible or that his information was reliable; and (2) that the magistrate must be given some of the underlying circumstances from which the informant reached the conclusion conveyed in the tip.

In the case of *Illinois v. Gates,* the Court abandoned the two-pronged requirement and established the "totality of circumstances" test.[11] While agreeing with the Illinois Supreme Court that an informant's veracity, reliability and basis of knowledge are all highly relevant in determining the value of an informant's report, the Court indicated that the totality of circumstances approach is far more consistent with the Court's prior treatment of probable cause, and that this would now be the test applied by reviewing courts. Under this test, the issuing magistrate is simply required to make a practical, common-sense decision, given all the circumstances set forth in the affidavit before him, that there is a fair probability that contraband or evidence of a crime will be found in a particular place.

Although preference is given to the search warrant as a means of making a search, and the search warrant is the only such means mentioned in the Constitution as proper, the courts have recognized over the years the necessity to make searches without warrants. These exceptions to the warrant rule have been clearly stated by the courts. In each instance an exception applies only when certain requirements are met. The most important examples of these exceptions are discussed in the paragraphs that follow.

a.   Search incident to a lawful arrest

The right to make a search incident to a lawful arrest has been repeatedly recognized by all the courts, including the United States Supreme Court.[12] In order for a search incident to a lawful arrest to be valid, the arrest must be lawful, the search must be made contemporaneously with the arrest, and the arrest upon which the search is based must have been made in good faith.

---

10 Aguilar v. Texas, 378 U.S. 108, 84 S. Ct. 1509, 12 L. Ed. 2d 723 (1964).
11 462 U.S. 213, 103 S. Ct. 2317, 76 L. Ed. 2d 527 (1983).
12 Chimel v. California, 395 U.S. 752, 89 S. Ct. 2034, 23 L. Ed. 2d 685 (1969).

While the United States Supreme Court has left no doubt that a search of the person incident to a lawful arrest may occur before the actual arrest if the arrest occurs contemporaneously with the search, it is preferable to advise the person apprehended that he is being arrested.13 In the case of *Smith v. Ohio*, the United States Supreme Court was asked to answer the single question of "whether a warrantless search that provides probable cause for an arrest can nonetheless be justified as an incident of that arrest."14 Here, the defendant, when asked by an officer to "come here a minute" threw onto the hood of his car a paper grocery sack that he was carrying. The officer, *before* making an arrest, pushed the defendant's hand away and opened the bag, which contained drug paraphernalia.

As the defendant was not arrested until *after* the contraband was discovered, the contraband could not serve as a part of the justification for a lawful search. The Court concluded that:

> The exception for searches incident to arrest permits the police to search a lawfully arrested person and areas within his immediate control . . . it does not permit police to search any citizen without a warrant or probable cause so long as an arrest immediately follows.

As a search incident to a lawful arrest is intended to protect the searching officer and to prevent the destruction of evidence, the scope of the area of search is limited. In the case of *Chimel v. California,* the area of search was defined as "the area within his immediate control—construing that phrase to mean the area from which he might gain possession of a weapon or destructible evidence."15 In 1981, the Supreme Court extended the area of search when the search is made of an automobile incident to a lawful arrest.16 In explaining the area of search, the Court indicated that:

> Accordingly we hold that when a policeman has made a lawful custodial arrest of the occupant of an automobile, he may, as a contemporaneous incident of that arrest, search the passenger compartment of the automobile.

---

13 Rawlings v. Kentucky 448 U.S. 98, 100 S. Ct. 2556, 65 L. Ed. 2d 633 (1980).

14 Smith v. Ohio, ___ U.S. ___, 110 S. Ct. 1288 (1990).

15 Chimel v. California, 395 U.S. 762, 89 S. Ct. 2034, 23 L. Ed. 2d 685 (1969); *see also* United States v. Robinson, 414 U.S. 218 (1973), which held that the authority to search incident to a lawful arrest includes the right to search the person arrested for evidence not related to the crime.

16 New York v. Belton, 453 U.S. 454, 101 S. Ct. 2960, 69 L. Ed. 2d 768 (1981).

However, in applying the *Chimel* rule when the search is made of a residence incident to a lawful arrest, the Court refused to justify a full search of an apartment when the arrest was made in one room of that apartment.[17] If an arrest is made in one part of the house, the Fourth Amendment permits a properly limited protective sweep in conjunction with the in-home arrest when the searching officers possess a reasonable belief, based on specific and articulable facts, that the area to be swept harbors an individual posing a danger to those on the arrest scene. However, the fact that an arrest is made in the living room does not justify a full search of the whole house without a warrant unless there is consent by one who has authority to consent.[18]

b.   Search after a waiver of constitutional rights
In accordance with the general principles which allow a person to waive his constitutional rights, the rights protected by the Fourth Amendment to the Constitution and the state provisions concerning search and seizure may be waived. In order for this exception to the warrant rule to apply, the prosecution must show that the consent was voluntary and that the person who gave the consent had the capacity to consent. The general rule is that the consent of one who possesses common authority over the premises or effects is valid against the absent non-consenting person with whom the authority is shared.[19]

In considering the waiver of constitutional rights, the court must carefully observe any limitations placed upon the consent—either directly or by inference. The consent to search a portion of one's premises is not a consent to search other portions. Also, even if the person consents to a search, that person may revoke the consent during the process of the search.[20] If the consent is revoked, evidence obtained from a continuing search is not admissible unless justified on other grounds.

c.   Search of a vehicle which is moving or about to be moved
Recognizing a necessary difference between the search of a dwelling house, for which a warrant can be readily obtained, and the search of an automobile, ship, wagon, airplane or other moveable object, for which it is

---

17 Harris v. United States, 395 U.S. 752, 89 S. Ct. 2034, 23 L. Ed. 2d 685 (1969).

18 Maryland v. Buie, ___ U.S. ___, 110 S. Ct. 1093, (1990).

19 United States v. Matlock, 415 U.S. 164, 94 S. Ct. 988, 39 L. Ed. 2d 242 (1974). See Klotter and Kanovitz, Constitutional Law, Anderson Publishing Co. (6th ed. 1991), for a discussion of the authority of a spouse, a minor child and a parent to consent to a search.

20 Strong v. United States, 46 F.2d 257 (1st Cir. 1931).

not practical to secure a warrant, the courts have approved some searches of vehicles that are about to be moved out of the jurisdiction in which the warrant must be sought.[21] Three requirements which must be met in order for a search of this type to be valid are: (1) that the officer must have probable cause which would justify a search warrant if one could be obtained; (2) that the vehicle must be moving or is about to be moved; and (3) that the facts must indicate that the warrant cannot be readily obtained.

In 1982, the United States Supreme Court reexamined the scope of the search under the moving vehicle doctrine and held that police acting under the automobile exception to the Fourth Amendment warrant requirements may search every part of the vehicle, including closed containers in the trunk, that might conceal the contraband for which the police are looking.[22]

As a general rule the moving vehicle/probable cause doctrine, which authorizes the search of a vehicle that is moving or about to be moved, applies to automobiles, boats and airplanes if the criteria are met. The Supreme Court has indicated that the doctrine also applies when the search is of a motor home temporarily parked in a downtown parking lot.[23] The Court, in applying this reasoning, stated:

> When a vehicle is being used on a highway, or if it is readily capable of such use and is found stationary in a place not regularly used for residential purposes . . . the two justifications for the vehicle exception come into play. First, the vehicle is obviously readily mobile . . . . Second, there is a reduced expectation of privacy stemming from its use as a licensed motor vehicle subject to a range of police regulations inapplicable to a fixed dwelling."

d.   The seizure of evidence when no search is required (plain view)

Because the Fourth Amendment prohibits searches and seizures, the seizure of evidence when there is no search does not violate the Constitution. Under the "plain view" doctrine, evidence may be seized if the officer is in a position where he can legally observe the evidence.[24] In the *Brown* case, the United States Supreme Court reaffirmed that "absolute certainty" that the evidence seized is contraband or illegally possessed is not a requirement. All that is necessary is for the officer to have probable cause to believe that the evidence is subject to seizure. The Court also made it clear that an officer may use a flashlight to enhance his view without violating the Constitution.

---

21 Chambers v. Maroney, 339 U.S. 42, 90 S. Ct. 1975, 26 L. Ed. 2d 419 (1970).
22 United States v. Ross, 456 U.S. 798, 102 S. Ct. 2157, 72 L. Ed. 2d 572 (1982).
23 California v. Carney, 471 U.S. 386, 195 S. Ct. 2066, 85 L. Ed. 2d 406 (1985).
24 Texas v. Brown, 460 U.S. 730, 103 S. Ct. 1535, 75 L. Ed. 2d 502 (1983).

Does the plain view exception justify the seizing of a gun observed by police under the seat of a car while attempting to get the vehicle identification number? The Supreme Court held such evidence admissible when the officer had to remove some papers which obscured the area on the dashboard where the VIN was located.25 The Court noted that the officer met the requirement of being legitimately in a position to view the article that was seized. The Court cautioned, however, that "our holding today does not authorize police officers to enter a vehicle to obtain a dashboard-mounted VIN when the VIN is visible from outside the automobile."

As indicated, for the plain view exception to apply, there must be a seizure *without* a search. If a search is required in order to determine whether an item is stolen, the "seizure without a warrant" exception will not apply and evidence seized will not be admissible.26 In *Arizona v. Hicks,* the officers were legally in the apartment of a suspect, as they were investigating a report that a bullet was fired through the floor of the respondent's apartment, injuring a man on the floor below. While in the suspect's apartment, one of the officers noticed two sets of expensive stereo components and, suspecting that they were stolen, the officer read and recorded their serial numbers, and he moved some of the equipment, including a turntable, to do so. Even though further investigation revealed that the equipment had been stolen, the evidence was not admissible because the moving of the components amounted to a "search" in violation of the Constitution.

To summarize, the requirements for applying the "plain view" exception are: (1) that the officer must legitimately be in a position to view the object; and (2) that the officer must have probable cause to associate the property with criminal activity.

e. Seizure of evidence from premises not protected by the Fourth Amendment (open fields)

In 1984, the United States Supreme Court confirmed the rule that only "houses, papers, and effects" are protected by the Constitution and that a search of open fields does not violate the Fourth Amendment.27 The closing paragraph of the Supreme Court opinion in this case summarizes the decision with these words:

> We conclude that the open fields doctrine, as enunciated in *Hester,* is consistent with the plain language of the Fourth Amendment and its historical purposes.

---

25 New York v. Class, 475 U.S. 106, 106 S. Ct. 960, 89 L. Ed. 2d 81 (1986).
26 Arizona v. Hicks, 489 U.S. 321, 107 S. Ct. 1149, 94 L. Ed. 2d 347 (1987).
27 Oliver v. United States, 466 U.S. 170, 104 S. Ct. 1735, 80 L. Ed. 2d 214 (1984).

While the Constitution protects houses, including the curtilage, evidence obtained from outside the curtilage is admissible even if entry amounts to a trespass. In the case of *United States v. Dunn*, the United States Supreme Court set out some guidelines to be applied in determining whether an area is within the curtilage for Fourth Amendment purposes.28 The Court enumerated four factors to be considered in determining the extent-of-curtilage questions:

1. The proximity of area to the home;
2. Whether the area is within an enclosure surrounding the home;
3. The nature and uses to which the area is put; and
4. The steps taken by the resident to protect the area from observation by passers-by.

Applying these criteria, the Court ruled that a barn which was located 60 yards from the house and which was not within the area enclosed by a fence surrounding the house was not within the curtilage of the home.

After a long debate in the lower courts, the United States Supreme Court in 1988 concluded that the Fourth Amendment does not prohibit the warrantless seizure of garbage left for collection outside of the curtilage of the home.29 As the evidence was seized from garbage bags left on the curb in front of the defendant's house, it was admissible.

f. Search by a private individual

The Fourth Amendment provisions apply to governmental officials, not to private individuals who are not acting as agents of the government or with participation or knowledge of any government official. In the case of *United States v. Jacobsen* in 1984, the Supreme Court determined that employees of a private carrier who made an examination of a package did not violate the Fourth Amendment; therefore, the evidence obtained in the examination was admissible.30

This exception to the warrant requirement is applicable only if the private individual makes, without the knowledge or participation of a government agent, what would be an illegal search if it were made by government personnel. If the individual works in conjunction with an agent, the activity is official and the Fourth Amendment applies.

In 1985, the United States Supreme Court held that school officials are government officials for Fourth Amendment purposes, but the Court

---

28 United States v. Dunn, 480 U.S. 294, 107 S. Ct. 1134, 94 L. Ed. 2d 326 (1987).
29 California v. Greenwood, 486 U.S. 35, 108 S. Ct. 1625, 100 L. Ed. 2d 30 (1988). See the case for a review of lower court decisions.
30 466 U.S. 109, 104 S. Ct. 1652, 80 L. Ed. 2d 85 (1984).

justified the search of students when there are reasonable grounds for suspecting that the search would turn up evidence that either the law or the rules of the school have been violated.31

Probation officers, too, are government officials for Fourth Amendment purposes. However, a probation officer may search a probationer's home without a warrant if there are "reasonable grounds" to believe that contraband is present there and if the officer acts under a state statute which authorizes such a search.32 The United States Supreme Court held that, although probation officers are government officials for Fourth Amendment purposes, the standard for justifying the search is less than probable cause, which is normally required for a search warrant.

g. Search after lawful impoundment

Often the police have the duty and responsibility to impound a car that has been abandoned, is blocking traffic, is illegally parked, or has been left without a driver after the driver has been arrested. In such instances the officer is usually required, either by law or regulations, to search the vehicle and make a list of its contents before impounding it. If, during this routine inventory, illegally seized evidence or contraband is in plain view, it may be admitted into evidence.33 The issues of the reasonableness of inventory seizures reached the United States Supreme Court in the case of *Colorado v. Burtine* in 1987.34 In approving the opening of closed containers found in a van which was lawfully impounded, the Court held that important government interests were served by inventory searches.

Two caveats apply here:

1. The decisions do not give officers *carte blanche* authority to search all stopped or impounded vehicles; only when an inventory is justified and contraband is observed is the evidence legally admissible.
2. The respective states, under their own constitutional authority, may prescribe additional limitations.

h. Stop and frisk search

To complete the discussion concerning the admissibility of search and seizure evidence, mention must be made of the stop and frisk search. In 1968, the United States Supreme Court authorized the admission of evidence obtained by a police officer who articulated his reasons for "frisking"

---

31 New Jersey v. T.L.O., 469 U.S. 325, 105 S. Ct. 733, 83 L. Ed. 2d 720 (1985).
32 Griffin v. Wisconsin, 483 U.S. 868, 107 S. Ct. 3164, 97 L. Ed. 2d 709 (1987).
33 South Dakota v. Opperman, 328 U.S. 364, 96 S. Ct. 3092, 49 L. Ed. 2d 1000 (1976).
34 Colorado v. Burtine, 479 U.S. 367, 107 S. Ct. 738, 93 L. Ed. 2d 739 (1987).

a person that the officer suspected was "casing a job."[35] The Court explained the limitation of such seizure in this language:

> The sole justification of the search in the present situation is the protection of the police officer and others nearby, and it must, therefore, be confined in scope to an intrusion reasonably designed to discover guns, knives, clubs, or other hidden instruments for the assault of the police officer.

The frisk which is authorized by the *Terry v. Ohio* case is limited to a frisk for weapons; that is, a frisk may not be made for evidence that may otherwise be gathered when the search is made incident to a lawful arrest.

Applying the *Terry* reasoning, the Supreme Court upheld the investigatory stop of a motorist and the search of a paper bag located in his car.[36] The Court reasoned that the protective search of the passenger compartment of an automobile was reasonable under the principles articulated in *Terry*. According to the *Michigan v. Long* decision, when an officer stops a car to issue a traffic citation, he may, for his protection, order the driver to step out of the car and, if the facts available warrant a man of reasonable caution to conclude that the person is armed and poses a serious and present danger to the safety of the officer, the officer may pat down the person stopped and frisk for weapons. If weapons are found under these circumstances, they may be introduced into evidence.

The *Terry* rule was also applied in holding that law enforcement agents may temporarily detain luggage on suspicion amounting to less than probable cause that the luggage contains narcotics.[37] The Supreme Court noted that if an officer's observation leads him reasonably to believe that a traveler is carrying luggage that contains narcotics, the officer may detain the luggage briefly to investigate the circumstances that aroused his suspicion, *provided* that the investigative detention is properly limited in scope. In this case the 90 minute time span between the luggage seizure and its exposure to a search by a trained narcotic-detection dog was too long; therefore, the evidence was not admitted.

From the foregoing, it is obvious that some evidence obtained in a search is inadmissible under the rules of evidence, even though the evidence seized may meet the requirements of relevancy and materiality. Evidence will be excluded if the search is illegal or if the search does not come within one of the recognized exceptions.

---

35 Terry v. Ohio, 392 U.S. 1, 88 S. Ct. 1868, 20 L. Ed. 2d 720 (1968).
36 Michigan v. Long, 463 U.S. 1032, 103 S. Ct. 3469, 77 L. Ed. 2d 1201 (1983).
37 United States v. Place, 462 U.S. 696, 103 S. Ct. 2637, 77 L. Ed. 2d 110 (1983).

§ 16.4 Exclusion of evidence obtained by illegal wiretapping or eavesdropping

The United States Supreme Court at one time refused to include wiretapping within the scope of the Fourth Amendment. In the case of *Olmstead v. United States,*38 after reviewing the historical context in which the Fourth Amendment was adopted, the Court concluded that the proscription was limited to search and seizure of material things and did not apply to evidence procured by the sense of hearing. However, in a later decision, *Nardone v. United States,*39 the Supreme Court held that, although wiretapping did not violate the Constitution, it did violate the Federal Communications Act of 1934, and the Court ruled that evidence obtained by officers who violated the provisions of this Act was inadmissible in federal court. This rule was not originally applied to the state courts, but many of the states adopted the rule, either by legislation or by court interpretation. In a landmark decision in 1967, *Katz v. United States,*40 the Supreme Court rejected the contention that surveillance without trespass and without the seizure of material fell outside the purview of the Constitution. This and other decisions make it clear that wiretapping and eavesdropping are within the protection of the Fourth Amendment.

After several efforts, Congress in 1968 finally enacted a comprehensive scheme designed to regulate eavesdropping and wiretapping on a uniform nationwide basis.41 This law as amended must be studied thoroughly in order to understand the requirements for wiretapping or eavesdropping. Broadly speaking, the interception of wire or oral communications is illegal unless conducted in conformity with statutory procedures. To be admissible, evidence obtained by wiretapping or eavesdropping must comply with the standards established by federal law as interpreted by the courts.

Title 18 U.S.C. §§ 3121-3126 sets forth the procedures for wiretapping and eavesdropping. Section 2511 prohibits the interception and disclosure of wire, oral or electronic communications except when in compliance with a detailed statutory procedure. Section 2516 states the procedures by which an investigative agency may apply for an order authorizing the interception of a wire or oral communication. In effect, this portion of the statute authorizes designated federal and state officers to apply for a court order, similar

---

38 277 U.S. 438, 48 S. Ct. 564, 72 L. Ed. 944 (1928).

39 302 U.S. 379, 58 S. Ct. 275, 82 L. Ed. 314 (1937).

40 389 U.S. 347, 88 S. Ct. 507, 19 L. Ed. 2d 576 (1967).

41 *See* Chapter 119 of the Omnibus Crime Control Act of 1968, 18 U.S.C. § 2510. (amended in 1986 by Pub. L. No. 99-508, and codified at 18 U.S.C. 2510 *et. seq.*)

to a search warrant, to intercept wire or oral communication when the crimes charged are specifically enumerated.

In addition, some evidence obtained by means of wiretapping and eavesdropping is admissible if one party to the conversation consents. Section 2511(2)(c) authorizes law enforcement officers to intercept wire, oral or electronic communications with the consent of one party without a court order unless a state statute prohibits such interception.

In a 1983 case, the United States Supreme Court upheld the use of the "bumper beeper," a small radio transmitter which is used to keep track of moving vehicles or other moving subjects. However, the Electronic Communication Privacy Act of 1986 now prohibits the use of evidence obtained in this manner unless a court order is obtained.

One federal court also approved the use of the "pen register," a device attached to a telephone line which records numbers dialed from a particular phone.42 Both federal and state courts had held that, as this device does not record any conversation but merely ascertains the number dialed from a particular phone, no court order was required. However, the 1986 act prohibits the use of the "pen register" without a court order and establishes procedures for obtaining such an order. Unless these procedures are followed, the evidence seized will not be admissible.

As the state laws are still inconsistent, one must look to the statutes and decisions of the various states as well as the federal statutes to determine whether wiretapping and eavesdropping is permissible in the particular state. If the evidence is obtained in violation of federal or state laws or decisions, it usually may not be admitted into court.43

§ 16.5 Exclusion of confessions obtained in violation of constitutional provisions

Although a confession or an admission of guilt would seem to be the best kind of relevant evidence, in many instances evidence of a confession is not admissible because the officer obtaining the confession violated certain constitutional provisions. Over the years the courts (especially the United States Supreme Court) have developed rules concerning the admissibility of confessions and other statements. Not only have the rules changed over a period of time, but the rationale justifying the rules has changed.

At early common law, an admission or confession was admissible as evidence of guilt despite the fact that it was a product of force or duress. The

---

42 United States v. John, 508 F.2d 1134 (8th Cir. 1984).

43 For further discussions of the use of wiretap and eavesdrop evidence *see* Klotter and Kanovitz, Constitutional Law, Anderson Publishing Co. (6th ed. 1991).

rule allowing the admissibility of such evidence was abandoned because it was found by experience that persons accused of a crime would admit to committing the crime in order to avoid torture. As a result, the courts developed what came to be known as the "free and voluntary" rule.

The free and voluntary rule states that a confession of a person accused of crime is admissible against the accused only if freely and voluntarily made, without fear, duress or compulsion in its inducement and with full knowledge of the nature and consequences of the confession. This was first justified on the theory that only free and voluntary confessions are reliable. Later cases, however, stated that the free and voluntary rule was predicated on the Fifth Amendment requirement that no person shall be compelled in a criminal case to be a witness against himself.44

The United States Supreme Court in 1985 reaffirmed its authority to review state cases in which the confession was admitted as part of the evidence. The Court noted that the voluntariness of a confession is a matter that is subject to review by federal courts.45 Although in this case the New Jersey Supreme Court had determined that the petitioner's confession was voluntary, the United States Supreme Court announced that it was not bound by a state court finding as to voluntariness.

Regardless of which historical approach is most persuasive, at the present time, a confession obtained by force or duress, or by promises of reward, whether the confession is a judicial confession or an extrajudicial confession, is not admissible.46

Judges in various courts have often disagreed as to the amount of evidence required to determine whether a confession is voluntary. This was partially reconciled in the 1972 case of *Lego v. Twomey*,47 in which the judge in the lower court had not found the confession voluntary "beyond a reasonable doubt" and the defendant argued that this made the admission of the confession erroneous. The Supreme Court, however, disagreed. The Court explained that the defendant is presumed innocent, and that the burden falls on the prosecution to prove guilt beyond a reasonable doubt; how-

---

44 Bram v. United States, 168 U.S. 532, 18 S. Ct. 187, 42 L. Ed. 568 (1897).
45 Miller v. Fenton, 474 U.S. 104, 106 S. Ct. 445, 88 L. Ed. 2d 405 (1985).
46 The United States Supreme Court in the case of Arizona v. Fulminante, 499 U.S. ___, 113 L. Ed. 2d 302, 111 S. Ct. ___ (1991), ruled that defendants whose coerced confessions were improperly used as evidence are not always entitled to a new trial. The use of such confessions may be considered "harmless error" if other trial evidence was sufficent to convict the defendant. In this case, the U.S. Supreme Court affirmed the decision of the Arizona Supreme Court that the harmless error analysis could not be used to save the conviction, and remanded the case for a new trial without the use of the confession.
47 Lego v. Twomey, 404 U.S. 477, 92 S. Ct. 619, 30 L. Ed. 2d 618 (1972).

ever, the Court continued, "This is not the same burden that applies in determining the admissibility of a confession." The Court agreed that the prosecution must prove the confession to be "free and voluntary" by a "preponderance" of the evidence, but that it was not required to prove the confession to be free and voluntary "beyond a reasonable doubt."

In addition to the free and voluntary rule, the United States Supreme Court has more recently applied what has become known as the "delay in arraignment" rule. This rule provides that if there has been a delay in bringing the accused person before a magistrate and that if a confession has been obtained during this unnecessary delay, the confession may not be admitted even though it was voluntarily made.[48] In the *Mallory v. United States* case, the defendant was convicted of rape in a District of Columbia court, and the jury returned a sentence of death. The defendant appealed on the ground that the confession obtained was improperly admitted into evidence. The facts indicate that the defendant was apprehended between 2:00 and 2:30 on the afternoon following the rape, along with his older nephews who were also suspects. After being questioned by police, the three suspects were asked to submit to polygraph tests at about 4:00 p.m. It took about two hours to locate the operator of the polygraph, during which time the suspects received food and drink. The questioning started at about 8:00 p.m., and one and one-half hours later, the defendant stated that he might have done the crime. It was not until after 10:00 p.m. that an effort was made to locate the United States Commissioner, and in fact, the defendant was not taken before the Commissioner until the following morning. The Court, in reversing the conviction, stated:

> We cannot sanction this extended delay resulting in a confession, without subordinating the general rule of prompt arraignment to the discretion of the arresting officers in finding exceptional circumstances for its disregard.

Here the Court did not rely on the free and voluntary rule, but reversed the decision because there had been a delay in bringing the accused before the United States Commissioner, in violation of the United States Code.

Both the free and voluntary rule and the delay in arraignment rule are now applicable to the states. The free and voluntary rule was made applicable to the states at an early date, when the Supreme Court using the Fourteenth Amendment due process clause again as the vehicle for applying the Fifth Amendment to the states. It was not, however, until the *Miranda* decision in 1966 that the delay in arraignment rule was applied to the states.[49]

---

48 Mallory v. United States, 354 U.S. 449, 77 S. Ct. 1356, 1 L. Ed. 2d 1479 (1957).

49 Miranda v. Arizona, 384 U.S. 436, 86 S. Ct. 1602, 16 L. Ed. 2d 694 (1966). *See* case in Part II, *infra*.

The restrictions concerning the use of the confession as evidence were broadened in 1966. The confessions in the case of *Miranda v. Arizona* and its three companion cases were declared inadmissible by the Supreme Court because the suspects were not given the required warnings. The Supreme Court held that for a confession to be deemed admissible, the person who has been taken into custody or otherwise deprived of his freedom of action in any significant way must be warned before questioning that: (1) he has a right to remain silent; (2) if he does make a statement, anything he says can and will be used against him in court; (3) he has a right to have an attorney present or to consult with an attorney; and (4) if he cannot afford an attorney, one will be appointed prior to any questioning if he so desires.

Although the earlier cases interpreting the requirements of *Miranda* held that the warning must be given in the exact terms as stated in the case, more recent cases have modified those requirements. In the case of *Duckworth v. Eagan,* the United States Supreme Court found that the warning need not be given in the exact terms as stated in *Miranda,* but that the warning must reasonably convey to a suspect his rights as required by *Miranda.*50

Not only must the warnings be given initially, but the opportunity to exercise the rights must be afforded throughout the questioning. If the accused indicates at any stage of the questioning that he does not wish to be interrogated, or that he wishes to consult an attorney, the questioning must stop.

Also, at any stage of the questioning the person in custody may waive his rights and make a statement. There has been some question as what amounts to a waiver; i.e., is an express waiver an essential requirement or may the facts taken as a whole indicate that the waiver has been made? In *North Carolina v. Butler,*51 the United States Supreme Court held that the *Miranda* rule does not require the prosecution to show that an in-custody suspect make a specific written or oral waiver of his right to counsel. The burden is on the prosecution to show that the defendant has waived his rights. However, in making this determination, the court must consider the particular facts and circumstances surrounding each case, including the background, experience and conduct of the accused. If, after considering all the facts, the court determines that the accused understood and implicitly waived his rights, an explicit statement of waiver is not required. The Constitution does not require suppression of incriminating oral statements if the proper *Miranda* warnings were administered.52 Even if the suspect has indicated that he will not make a written statement, the oral statements are still admissible.

Due to these restrictions on the use of confessions, there are many who claim that the confession can no longer be used as an investigative tool.

---

50 ___ U.S. ___, 109 S. Ct. 2875 (1989).
51 441 U.S. 369, 99 S. Ct. 1755, 60 L. Ed. 2d 286 (1979).
52 Connecticut v. Barrett, 479 U.S. 523, 107 S. Ct. 828, 93 L. Ed. 2d 920 (1987).

However, experience has indicated that this is not true. In fact, the Supreme Court in the *Miranda* case stated that confessions remain a proper element in law enforcement and that any statement given freely and voluntarily without any compelling influence is admissible in evidence. The Court went on to say that there is no requirement for the police to stop a person who enters a police station and states that he wishes to confess to a crime or a person who calls the police to offer a confession or some other statement. The Court further asserted that voluntary statements of any kind are not barred by the Fifth Amendment and that their admissibility is not affected by the holding.[53]

Confessions continue to be admitted into evidence, and the skilled and informed investigator can obtain confessions or statements and comply with the requirements established by the courts. Even if the strict requirements of *Miranda* are not complied with fully, as long as the confession is voluntarily given, the evidence may be admitted for impeachment purposes.[54]

In the case of *Harris v. New York*, the defendant was charged with selling heroin, and at the trial, he took the stand in his own defense. The prosecution did not offer a confession made by the defendant during its case in chief because there was some question as to whether *Miranda* warnings had been given. The prosecution did, however, offer a confession to impeach the testimony of the defendant after he took the stand. The United States Supreme Court allowed the admission of the confession even though *Miranda* warnings had not been given, explaining that a confession may be used for impeachment purposes if it is freely and voluntarily made. In so doing, the Court reasoned that:

> Having voluntarily taken the stand, petitioner was under an obligation to speak truthfully and accurately, and the prosecution did no more than utilize the traditional truth-testing devices of the adversary process.

However, if a confession is not voluntary even though *Miranda* warnings are given, the confession is not admissible in evidence even for impeachment purposes.[55]

In a 1984 case, the Supreme Court added another rule under which a confession may be admitted even though the *Miranda* warnings have not been administered. Here the Supreme Court recognized a "narrow exception" to the *Miranda* rule. Briefly stated, the exception is that statements elicited from the defendant, as well as real evidence resulting from such

---

53 Miranda v. Arizona, *supra* note 49.
54 Harris v. New York, 401 U.S. 222, 91 S. Ct. 643, 28 L. Ed. 2d 1 (1971).
   Oregon v. Hass, 420 U.S. 714, 91 S. Ct. 1215, 43 L. Ed. 2d 570 (1975).
55 Mincey v. Arizona, 437 U.S. 385, 98 S. Ct. 2408, 57 L. Ed. 2d 290 (1978).

statements, may be used in evidence even if the officers do not recite the *Miranda* warnings before asking the questions, as long as the officer's safety or the safety of others is in jeopardy.[56]

Recognizing a "public safety" exception to the *Miranda* rule, the Court concluded that if the officer is in danger or others nearby are in danger, as in this case, the threat to the public safety outweighs the need for the rule protecting the Fifth Amendment privilege against self-incrimination, and evidence resulting from questions not preceded by *Miranda* warnings is admissible under these limited circumstances.

The discussion concerning the admissibility of confessions would not be complete without mention of the Omnibus Crime Control and Safe Streets Act of 1968. The applicable part of this Act is section 3501(c), which reads as follows:

> In any criminal prosecution by the United States or by the District of Columbia, a confession made or given by a person who is a defendant therein, while such person was under arrest or other detention in the custody of any law enforcement officer or law enforcement agency, shall not be inadmissible solely because of delay in bringing such person before a commissioner or other officer empowered to commit persons charged with offenses against the laws of the United States or of the District of Columbia if such confession is found by the trial judge to have been made voluntarily and if the weight to be given the confession is left the jury and if such confession was made or given by such person within six hours immediately following his arrest or other detention: Provided, That the time limitation contained in this sub-section shall not apply in any case in which the delay in bringing such person before such commissioner or other officer beyond such six-hour period is found by the trial judge to be reasonable considering the means of transportation and the distance to be traveled to the nearest available commissioner or other such officer.[57]

This section states in effect that a confession will not be deemed inadmissible in evidence in a federal court solely because the confession was obtained during a delay in arraignment. It also establishes a maximum allowable time of six hours between the arrest and the making of the con-

---

56 New York v. Quarles, 467 U.S. 649, 104 S. Ct. 2626, 81 L. Ed. 2d 550 (1984).

57 Two United States Courts of Appeals have considered the application of this Act. Both courts held that more than a six-hour delay does not necessarily make the confession inadmissible. U.S. v. Hathorn, 451 F.2d 1337 (5th Cir. 1971) and U.S. v. Halbert, 436 F.2d 1226 (9th Cir. 1970).

fession, but gives the judge discretion to admit the confession when more than six hours have elapsed if the judge finds the delay reasonable. In effect, Congress has attempted by legislation to nullify the delay in arraignment rule as established by the *McNabb* and *Mallory* cases.58

Another section of the Omnibus Crime Control and Safety Streets Act of 1968 attempts to modify some of the legal requirements as interpreted by the United States Supreme Court in the *Miranda v. Arizona* case. Section 3501 of the Act, which would change the requirements for warning prior to custodial interrogations, reads as follows:

> (a) In any criminal prosecution brought by the United States or by the District of Columbia, a confession, as defined in subsection (e) hereof, shall be admissible in evidence if it is voluntarily given. Before such confession is received in evidence, the trial judge shall, out of the presence of the jury, determine any issue as to voluntariness. If the trial judge determines that the confession was voluntarily made, it shall be admitted in evidence and the trial judge shall permit the jury to hear relevant evidence on the issue of voluntariness and shall instruct the jury to give such weight to the confession as the jury feels it deserves under all the circumstances.

> (b) The trial judge in determining the issue of voluntariness shall take into consideration all the circumstances surrounding the giving of the confession, including (1) the time elapsing between arrest and arraignment of the defendant making the confession, if it was made after arrest and before arraignment, (2) whether such defendant knew the nature of the offense with which he was charged or of which he was suspected at the time of making the confession, (3) whether or not such defendant was advised or knew that he was not required to make any statement and that any such statement could be used against him, (4) whether or not such defendant had been advised prior to questioning of his right to the assistance of counsel, and (5) whether or not such defendant was without the assistance of counsel when questioned and when giving such confession. The presence or absence of any of the above-mentioned factors to be taken into consideration by the judge need not be conclusive on the issue of voluntariness of the confession.

Two questions arise concerning these congressional enactments. One of these is: will the provisions be declared unconstitutional when considered by the United States Supreme Court, which would make the confessions inadmissible even though declared to be admissible by the Congress? The second question is: how do these congressional acts affect the admissibility of confessions in state courts?

---

58 McNabb v. United States, 318 U.S. 332, 63 S. Ct. 608, 87 L. Ed. 2d 816 (1943); Mallory v. United States, *supra* note 48.

There is a good possibility that at least part of this Act will be upheld as constitutional, but there is no certainty until a case is appealed to the Supreme Court.

As to the second question, there is every reason to believe that if a state court authorizes the use of confessions obtained in accordance with the congressional enactment, the Supreme Court would have difficulty applying higher standards to state proceedings than those required in federal criminal prosecutions.

It is apparent from this discussion concerning confessions and other statements that, although the courts have established strict rules concerning their admissibility, confessions and admissions are still admissible and continue to be valuable tools in the investigative process. Generally, statements obtained in accordance with the requirements established by the Supreme Court will be admissible evidence.

§ 16.6 Self-incrimination and related protections

Often evidence is challenged because the officer, in obtaining the evidence, violated the Fifth Amendment privilege against self-incrimination. The pertinent section concerning self-incrimination provides that: "No person . . . shall be compelled in any criminal case to be a witness against himself." This provision, like the Fourth Amendment search and seizure provision, was included as a part of the Bill of Rights and was ratified so as to become a part of the Constitution in 1791. The Fifth Amendment restrictions were not made applicable to the states until 1964.[59] The United States Supreme Court in the case of *Malloy v. Hogan* stated in its holding:

> We hold today that the Fifth Amendment's exception from compulsory self-incrimination is also protected by the Fourteenth Amendment against abridgement by the states.

This means, in effect that the standards to be applied are the standards as determined by the Supreme Court and not the standards that were developed by the state courts. After many conflicting decisions, the Supreme Court in the case of *Schmerber v. California*[60] clearly limited the application of the self-incrimination provisions, stating:

> We hold that the privilege protects the accused only from being compelled to testify against himself, or otherwise provide the state with evidence of a testimonial or communicative nature, and that the withdrawal of blood and use of the analysis in question in this case did not involve compulsion to these ends.

59 Malloy v. Hogan, 378 U.S. 1, 84 S. Ct. 1489, 12 L. Ed. 2d 653 (1964).
60 384 U.S. 757, 86 S. Ct. 1826, 16 L. Ed. 2d 908 (1966). *See* case in Part II, *infra,* and cases relating to Chapter 14.

Following this interpretation, obtaining fingerprints and photographs, requiring appearance in a lineup, taking blood samples and taking handwriting specimens do not violate the self-incrimination protection. On the other hand, if an accused is forced to take a lie detector test or to give other evidence of a testimonial or a communicative nature, the self-incrimination provisions are violated, and evidence so obtained will be inadmissible.

In the case of *South Dakota v. Neville,* the United States Supreme Court approved the admission of evidence of the defendant's refusal to submit to a blood-alcohol test.61 Not only did the Court uphold the use of the test itself, but it indicated that evidence relating to the defendant's refusal to take a blood-alcohol test may be introduced. Summarizing its opinion, the Court stated:

> We hold, therefore, that a refusal to take a blood-alcohol test, after a police officer has lawfully requested it, is not an act coerced by the officer, and thus is not protected by the privilege against self-incrimination.

The procedures followed in introducing evidence have also been challenged as violating the Fifth Amendment. The procedure in most courts had been for the defendant to take the stand in his own defense before other defense witnesses if he was to take the stand at all. As a matter of fact, most states had either rules or laws which required the defendant to take the stand before any other witnesses for the defense. This requirement was challenged in the case of *Brooks v. Tennessee.*62 The Supreme Court there held that the requirement that the defendant take the stand before other defense witnesses violates the self-incrimination protection of the Fifth Amendment and the due process protection of the Fourteenth Amendment. The Court stated: "This rule requiring the defendant to take the stand first cuts down on the privilege to remain silent by making its assertion costly." Now the rule of law is that the defense attorney is authorized to put the defendant on the stand at any time during the defendant's case in chief.

§ 16.7 Due process exclusions

Closely related to the self-incrimination protections are the limitations which the due process clause of the Fourteenth Amendment imposes on the conduct of criminal proceedings of the states. If investigators, in

---

61 South Dakota v. Neville, 459 U.S. 553, 103 S. Ct. 916, 75 L. Ed. 2d 748 (1983).

62 406 U.S. 605, 92 S. Ct. 1891, 32 L. Ed. 2d 358 (1972).

obtaining evidence, violate the due process clause, evidence obtained thereby will not be admissible. The reasoning here, as in other instances, is that to allow the admission of such evidence would encourage conduct which is prohibited by the Constitution.

Although the courts have refused to define specifically what is included in the due process protection, some examples help to clarify what evidence will be excluded on these grounds. One example is the case of *Rochin v. California*.[63] In this case, deputy sheriffs in Los Angeles, after forcing their way into the defendant's room, attempted to extract capsules from his mouth. Failing in this attempt, the defendant was taken to a hospital and at the officers' insistence his stomach was pumped and two capsules containing morphine were obtained. These were used in evidence against the defendant. The United States Supreme Court reversed the conviction and directed that this evidence not be used against the defendant, not on the grounds that this violated the self-incrimination protection, but that such conduct violated the due process clause of the Fourteenth Amendment. The Court said, "To sanction the brutal conduct would be to afford brutality the cloak of law."

Also, evidence obtained as a result of an improper lineup is not admissible. If a lineup or other confrontation for identification is held in such a way as to be suggestive, i.e., to suggest to the witnesses who make the identification which person in the lineup is the suspect, then the in-court identification would be contaminated.[64] The same reasoning applies when photographs are used for identification purposes in such a way as to be suggestive and to deny due process. Therefore, evidence so acquired and used in this way is admissible.[65] But the taking of blood, breath or urine samples—if done properly—does not violate the due process clause, and such evidence is admissible if other conditions are met.[66]

To summarize, if evidence is obtained by federal agents in violation of the due process clause of the Fifth Amendment, or by state agents in violation of the due process clause of the Fourteenth Amendment, such evidence is inadmissible.

§ 16.8   Right to counsel as it relates to the exclusion of evidence

One of the protections of the Bill of Rights which has been very broadly interpreted in recent years is the section of the Sixth Amendment providing that: "In all criminal prosecutions, the accused shall enjoy the

---

63 342 U.S. 165, 72 S. Ct. 205, 96 L. Ed. 183 (1952).
64 Foster v. California, 394 U.S. 440, 89 S. Ct. 1127, 22 L. Ed. 2d 402 (1969).
65 Workman v. Cardwell, 471 F.2d 909 (6th Cir. 1972).
66 Davis v. District of Columbia, 247 A.2d 417 (D.C. App. 1968).

right . . . to have the assistance of counsel for his defense." In early decisions, this right was made available to the accused only at the trial, but later it was made applicable during the investigation.[67]

As a means of enforcing the right to counsel provisions, a confession or statement obtained when the right to counsel is not protected will be excluded from evidence. For example, in *Escobedo v. Illinois*, the defendant moved to suppress the use of incriminating statements taken after he had requested counsel and had been refused. In reversing the state court decision, the United States Supreme Court stated:

> [W]here, as here, the investigation is no longer a general inquiry into an unsolved crime but has begun to focus on a particular suspect, the suspect has been taken into police custody, the police carry out a process of interrogation that lends itself to eliciting incriminating statements, the suspect has requested and has been denied an opportunity to consult with his lawyer and the police have not effectively warned him of his absolute constitutional rights to remain silent, the accused has been denied the "assistance of counsel" in violation of the Sixth Amendment to the Constitution as "made obligatory upon the States by the Fourteenth Amendment. . ." and no statement elicited by the police during interrogation may be used against him at a criminal trial.

Although in the *Escobedo* case the accused requested counsel, the Supreme Court in *Miranda*[68] stated that such a request was not necessary. Under the *Miranda* ruling, if the suspect is in custody, the burden is placed upon the police to inform the suspect of his constitutional right and to refrain from asking any questions unless the accused knowingly waives his right to counsel.

From these and other cases it is obvious that if the accused requests counsel during the interrogation and counsel is not allowed, statements obtained will not be admissible. Under the *Miranda* reasoning, if a person is taken into custody or questioned with the view to obtaining incriminating statements, the police must advise him of his right to counsel—either retained or appointed.

The suspect may waive the right to counsel provided the waiver is made voluntarily, knowingly and intelligently. However, the Supreme Court in *Edwards v. Arizona* determined that if the accused has expressed his desire to deal with police only through counsel, interrogation must cease until counsel has been made available to the accused or until the accused himself initiates further communications.[69] Although the Court there did not define

---

67 Escobedo v. Illinois, 378 U.S. 478, 84 S. Ct. 1758, 12 L. Ed. 2d 977 (1964).
68 Miranda v. Arizona, *supra* note 49.
69 Edwards v. Arizona, 451 U.S. 477, 101 S. Ct. 1880, 68 L. Ed. 2d 378 (1981).

"initiation of further communications," the Court in a later case determined that the question from the suspect, "Well, what is going to happen to me now?" really amounted to an attempt by the defendant to initiate further questioning, and that ensuing statements given by the defendant, even after he was warned further of his rights, were admissible.70

The rationale that was framed in *Edwards v. Arizona* was applied when the Supreme Court decided that if police initiate an interrogation after a defendant's assertion of his right to counsel at the arraignment or similar proceedings, a waiver of that right, after police-initiated interrogation, is invalid unless counsel is present. Once a suspect has been arraigned and has requested counsel at the arraignment or preliminary hearing, a police officer may not initiate questioning. Questioning may be initiated by the suspect, but the burden is on the prosecution to show that the suspect did, in fact, initiate further questioning.71

In *Edwards* and in *Michigan v. Jackson*, the rule was established that once a suspect invokes his Sixth Amendment right to counsel, a subsequent waiver of that right is presumed invalid if it is secured pursuant to a police-initiated conversation. In these circumstances the evidence obtained may not be admitted for the prosecution's case in chief. However, according to the ruling set forth in *Michigan v. Harvey*, statements elicited without a valid waiver may be used to impeach the defendant's false or inconsistent testimony if he elects to take the stand, even though the same statement may not be used as substantive evidence.72 The court explained that while the Sixth Amendment prohibits the use of evidence obtained after the defendant has invoked his Sixth Amendment right to counsel for his case in chief, this shield should not be perverted into a license to use perjury by way of a defense, free from the risk of confrontation with prior inconsistent utterances.

Another case which has had quite a bit of influence on the admissibility of evidence when the right to counsel is in issue is *United States v. Wade*.73 The case concerned the right to counsel during a police lineup. In *Wade*, the Supreme Court stated that both the defendant Wade and his counsel should have been notified of the impending post-indictment lineup and that counsel's presence should have been a requisite to conduct of the lineup, absent an intelligent waiver. The Court asserted that the best method of enforcing this right to counsel at the lineup is to prohibit in-court identification by witnesses if the court finds that the pretrial confrontation or lineup tainted

---

70 Oregon v Bradshaw, 463 U.S. 1039, 103 S. Ct. 2830, 77 L. Ed. 2d 405 (1983).
71 Michigan v. Jackson, 475 U.S. 625, 106 S. Ct. 1404, 89 L. Ed. 2d 631 (1986).
72 Michigan v. Harvey, ___ U.S. ___, 110 S. Ct. 1176 (1990). *See* case in Part II, *infra.*
73 388 U.S. 218, 87 S. Ct. 1926, 18 L. Ed. 2d 1149 (1967).

the in-court identification. In other words, the Court reasoned that the post-indictment lineup was a critical stage of the proceedings and that counsel should be present—unless the right is waived—if the identifying witness is to testify in court. In justifying this stand, the Court stated:

> Since it appears that there is a grave potential for prejudice, intentional or not, in the pretrial lineup, which may not be capable of reconstruction at trial, and since presence of counsel itself can often avert prejudice and assure a meaningful confrontation at trial, there can be little doubt that for Wade the post-indictment lineup was a critical stage of the prosecution.

If the accused's attorney is present or if the accused intelligently waives the right to an attorney, then a witness may be called upon in court to identify the accused. It is not the lineup itself that is prohibited without counsel, and a lineup is appropriate when the witness making the identification will not be called upon to identify the accused at trial. Also, there is some indication that the prosecutor may be authorized to show that the pretrial confrontation for identification did not taint the in-court identification. In such circumstances the in-court identification may be admissible even though counsel was not present at the pretrial confrontation.

In 1972, the United States Supreme Court placed limitations on the right to counsel at a lineup.[74] After reiterating the opinion that the lineup does not deprive the accused of the right to protection from self-incrimination, the Court further explained that counsel is not required at a pre-arrest, pre-indictment identification confrontation. The Court distinguished this situation from the *Wade* post-indictment confrontation for identification, explaining:

> The initiation of judicial criminal proceedings is far from a mere formalism. It is the starting point of our whole system of adversary criminal justice. For it is only then that the government has committed itself to prosecute, and only then that the adverse positions of government and defendant have solidified. . . . It is this point, therefore, that marks the commencement of the "criminal prosecution" to which alone the explicit guarantees of the Sixth Amendment are applicable.

The modified rule, therefore, is that the post-indictment lineup or confrontation for identification is a critical stage, and the right to counsel attaches if the witness is to identify the accused at trial. However, the pre-arrest, pre-indictment confrontation is not a critical stage, and identifying evidence may be offered at trial even if counsel was not present at the lineup or showup.

---

74 Kirby v. Illinois, 406 U.S. 682, 92 S. Ct. 1877, 32 L. Ed. 2d 411 (1972).

§ 16.9 Summary

Although the traditional common law doctrine was that evidence would be admissible if relevant even though obtained illegally, much evidence is not admissible if a constitutional provision is violated. Exclusionary rules were developed over a period of years and made applicable both to federal and state courts on a piecemeal basis.

Under the present rules as established by the United States Supreme Court and lower courts, most evidence obtained by search and seizure in violation of the Constitution is inadmissible in both federal and state courts. The cases must be examined thoroughly to determine what is considered an illegal search and under what circumstances the exclusionary rules apply.

Although wiretap evidence at first was not considered to be within the constitutional provisions, recent cases have held that wiretapping and eavesdropping fall within the protection of the Fourth Amendment. Under the Omnibus Crime Control Act of 1968, certain wiretap and eavesdrop evidence is admissible if the statutory requirements are met and if one party to the conversation consents. Evidence obtained in violation of the statute will not be admitted into court.

As a means of insuring that confessions will be obtained freely and voluntarily, courts have established rules which prohibit the admissibility of confessions obtained in violation of established standards. Although evidence has been challenged because it was obtained in violation of the self-incrimination protection, this protection is generally limited to evidence of a testimonial or a communicative nature. Evidence which is interpreted to be of a testimonial or communicative nature is inadmissible unless this protection is waived.

Evidence acquired in violation of the due process clauses of the Fifth and Fourteenth Amendments is inadmissible. Court opinions must be studied to determine what constitutes such a violation.

Evidence is also excluded if the right to counsel provisions of the Sixth Amendment are violated. Again, it is essential that cases be studied carefully to determine the various courts' interpretations as to what is considered a violation of the Sixth Amendment.

Although certain evidence is excluded because constitutional provisions have been violated, criminal justice personnel should not take a negative attitude. The investigator who understands that the limitations, protect the rights of the individual can generally obtain evidence which will be admitted into court.

PART II
JUDICIAL DECISIONS

TABLE OF CASES IN PART II

Case relating to Chapter 1
HISTORY AND DEVELOPMENT OF RULES OF EVIDENCE

FUNK v. UNITED STATES

290 U.S. 371, 54 S. Ct. 212, 78 L. Ed. 369 (1933)

Mr. Justice SUTHERLAND delivered the opinion of the Court.

The sole inquiry to be made in this case is whether in a federal court the wife of the defendant on trial for a criminal offense is a competent witness in his behalf. Her competency to testify against him is not involved.

The petitioner was twice tried and convicted in a federal District Court upon an indictment for conspiracy to violate the prohibition law. His conviction on the first trial was reversed by the Circuit Court of Appeals upon a ground not material here. 46 F.(2d) 417. Upon the second trial, as upon the first, defendant called his wife to testify in his behalf. At both trials she was excluded upon the ground of incompetency. The Circuit Court of Appeals sustained this ruling upon the first appeal, and also upon the appeal which followed the second trial. 66 F.(2d) 70. We granted certiorari, limited to the question as to what law is applicable to the determination of the competency of the wife of the petitioner as a witness.

Both the petitioner and the government, in presenting the case here, put their chief reliance on prior decisions of this court. The government relies on *United States v. Reid*, 12 How. 361, 13 L.Ed. 1023; *Logan v. United States*, 144 U.S. 263, 12 S.Ct. 617, 36 L.Ed. 429; *Hendrix v. United States*, 219 U.S. 79, 31 S.Ct. 193, 196, 55 L.Ed. 102; and *Jin Fuey Moy v. United States*, 254 U.S. 189, 41 S.Ct. 98, 65 L.Ed. 214. Petitioner contends that these cases, if not directly contrary to the decisions in *Benson v. United States*, 146 U.S. 325, 13 S.Ct. 60, 36 L.Ed. 991, and *Rosen v. United States*, 245 U.S. 467, 38 S.Ct. 148, 150, 62 L.Ed. 406, are so in principle. We shall first briefly review these cases, with the exceptions of the Hendrix Case and the Jin Fuey Moy Case, which we leave for consideration until a later point in this opinion.

In the Reid Case, two persons had been jointly indicted for a murder committed upon the high seas. They were tried separately, and it was held that one of them was not a competent witness in behalf of the other who was first tried. The trial was held in Virginia; and by a statute of that state passed in 1849, if applicable in a federal court, the evidence would have been competent. Section 34 of the Judiciary Act of 1789 (28 USCA § 725) declares that the laws of the several states, except where the Constitution, treaties, or statutes of the United States otherwise provide, shall be regarded as rules of decision in trials at common law in the courts of the United States in cases where they apply; but the court said that this referred only to civil cases, and did not apply in the trial of criminal offenses against the United States. It was conceded that there was no act of Congress prescribing in express words the rule by which the federal courts would be governed in the admission of testimony in criminal cases. "But," the court said (page 363 of 12 How.), "we think it may be found with sufficient certainty, not indeed in direct terms, but by necessary implication, in the acts of 1789 and 1790, establishing the courts of the United States, and providing for the punishment of certain offences."

The court pointed out that the Judiciary Act regulated certain proceedings to be had prior to impaneling the jury, but contained no express provision concerning the mode of conducting the trial after the jury was sworn, and prescribed no rule in respect of the testimony to be taken. Obviously, however, it was said, some certain and established rule upon the subject was necessary to enable the courts to administer the criminal jurisprudence of the United States, and Congress must have intended to refer them to some known and established rule "which was supposed to be so familiar and well understood in the trial by jury that legislation upon the subject would be deemed superfluous. This is necessarily to be im-

plied from what these acts of Congress omit, as well as from what they contain." Page 365 of 12 How. The court concluded that this could not be the common law as it existed at the time of the emigration of the colonists or the rule which then prevailed in England, and [therefore] the only known rule which could be supposed to have been in the mind of Congress was that which was in force in the respective states when the federal courts were established by the Judiciary Act of 1789. Applying this rule, it was decided that the witness was incompetent.

In the Logan Case it was held that the competency of a witness to testify in a federal court sitting in one state was not affected by his conviction and sentence for felony in another state; and that the competency of another witness was not affected by his conviction of felony in a Texas state court, where the witness had since been pardoned. The indictment was for an offense committed in Texas and there tried. The decision was based, not upon any statute of the United States, but upon the ground that the subject "is governed by the common law, which, as has been seen, was the law of Texas * * * at the time of the admission of Texas into the Union as a state." Page 303 of 144 U.S., 12 S.Ct. 617, 630.

We next consider the two cases upon which petitioner relies. In the Benson Case two persons were jointly indicted for murder. On motion of the government there was a severance, and Benson was first tried. His codefendant was called as a witness on behalf of the government. The Reid Case had been cited as practically decisive of the question. But the court, after pointing out what it conceived to be distinguishing features in that case, said (page 335 of 146 U.S., 13 S.Ct. 60, 63): "We do not feel ourselves, therefore, precluded by that case from examining this question in the light of general authority and sound reason." The alleged incompetency of the codefendant was rested upon two reasons, first, that he was interested, and, second, that he was a party to the record, the basis for the exclusion at common law being fear of perjury. "Nor," the court said, "were those named the only grounds of exclusion from the witness stand. Conviction of crime, want of religious belief, and other matters were held sufficient. Indeed, the theory of the common law was to admit to the witness stand only those presumably honest, appreciating the sanctity of an oath, unaffected as a party by the result, and free from any of the temptations of interest. The courts were afraid to trust the intelligence of jurors. But the last 50 years have wrought a great change in these respects, and today the tendency is to enlarge the domain of competency, and to submit to the jury for their consideration as to the credibility of the witness those matters which heretofore were ruled sufficient to justify his exclusion. This change has been wrought partially by legislation and partially by judicial construction." Attention then is called to the fact that Congress in 1864 had enacted that no witness should be excluded from testifying in any civil action, with certain exceptions, because he was a party to or interested in the issue tried; and that in 1878 (c. 37, 20 Stat. 30 [28 USCA § 632]) Congress made

the defendant in any criminal case a competent witness at his own request. The opinion then continues (page 337 of 146 U.S., 13 S.Ct. 60, 64):

"Legislation of similar import prevails in most of the states. The spirit of this legislation has controlled the decisions of the courts, and steadily, one by one, the merely technical barriers which excluded witnesses from the stand have been removed, till now it is generally, though perhaps not universally, true that no one is excluded therefrom unless the lips of the originally adverse party are closed by death, or unless some one of those peculiarly confidential relations, like that of husband and wife, forbids the breaking of silence.

"* * * If interest and being party to the record do not exclude a defendant on trial from the witness stand, upon what reasoning can a codefendant, not on trial, be adjudged incompetent?"

That case was decided December 5, 1892. Twenty-five years later this court had before it for consideration the case of *Rosen v. United States,* supra. Rosen had been tried and convicted in a Federal District Court for conspiracy. A person jointly indicted with Rosen, who had been convicted upon his plea of guilty, was called as a witness by the government and allowed to testify over Rosen's objection. This court sustained the competency of the witness. After saying that, while the decision in the Reid Case had not been specifically overruled, its authority was seriously shaken by the decisions in both the Logan and Benson Cases, the court proceeded to dispose of the question, as it had been disposed of in the Benson Case, "in the light of general authority and of sound reason."

"In the almost twenty [twenty-five] years," the court said, "which have elapsed since the decision of the Benson Case, the disposition of courts and of legislative bodies to remove disabilities from witnesses has continued, as that decision shows it had been going forward before, under dominance of the conviction of our time that the truth is more likely to be arrived at by hearing the testimony of all persons of competent understanding who may seem to have knowledge of the facts involved in a case, leaving the credit and weight of such testimony to be determined by the jury or by the court, rather than by rejecting witnesses as incompetent, with the result that this principle has come to be widely, almost universally, accepted in this country and in Great Britain.

"Since the decision in the Benson Case we have significant evidence of the trend of congressional opinion upon this subject in the removal of the disability of witnesses convicted of perjury, Rev. St. § 5392, by the enactment of the federal Criminal Code in 1909 with this provision omitted and section 5392 repealed. This is significant, because the disability to testify, of persons convicted of perjury, survived in some jurisdictions much longer than many of the other common-law disabilities, for the reason that the offense concerns directly the giving of testimony in a court of justice, and conviction of it was accepted

as showing a greater disregard for the truth than it was thought should be implied from a conviction of other crime.

"Satisfied as we are that the legislation and the very great weight of judicial authority which have developed in support of this modern rule, especially as applied to the competency of witnesses convicted of crime, proceed upon sound principle, we conclude that the dead hand of the common-law rule of 1789 should no longer be applied to such cases as we have here, and that the ruling of the lower courts on this first claim of error should be approved."

It is well to pause at this point to state a little more concisely what was held in these cases. It will be noted, in the first place, that the decision in the Reid Case was not based upon any express statutory provision. The court found from what the congressional legislation omitted to say, as well as from what it actually said, that in establishing the federal courts in 1789 some definite rule in respect of the testimony to be taken in criminal cases must have been in the mind of Congress; and the rule which the court thought was in the mind of that body was that of the common law as it existed in the thirteen original states in 1789. The Logan Case in part rejected that view, and held that the controlling rule was that of the common law in force at the time of the admission of the state in which the particular trial was held. Taking the two cases together, it is plain enough that the ultimate doctrine announced is that, in the taking of testimony in criminal cases, the federal courts are bound by the rules of the common law as they existed at a definitely specified time in the respective states, unless Congress has otherwise provided.

With the conclusion that the controlling rule is that of the common law, the Benson Case and the Rosen Case do not conflict; but both cases reject the notion, which the two earlier ones seem to accept, that the courts, in the face of greatly changed conditions, are still chained to the ancient formulae and are powerless to declare and enforce modifications deemed to have been wrought in the common law itself by force of these changed conditions. Thus, as we have seen, the court in the Benson Case pointed to the tendency during the preceding years to enlarge the domain of competency, significantly saying that the changes had been wrought not only by legislation but also "partially by judicial construction"; and that it was the *spirit* (not the *letter* be it observed) of this legislation which had controlled the decisions of the courts and steadily removed the merely technical barriers in respect of incompetency, until generally no one was excluded from giving testimony, except under certain peculiar conditions which are set forth. It seems difficult to escape the conclusion that the specific ground upon which the court there rested its determination as to the competency of a codefendant was that, since the defendant had been rendered competent, the competency of the codefendant followed as a natural consequence.

This view of the matter is made more positive by the decision in the Rosen Case. The question of the testimonial competency of a person jointly indicted with the defendant was disposed of, as the question had been in the Benson Case, "in the light of general authority and of sound reason." The conclusion which the court reached was based, not upon any definite act of legislation, but upon the trend of congressional opinion and of legislation (that is to say of legislation generally), and upon the great weight of judicial authority which, since the earlier decisions, had developed in support of a more modern rule. In both cases the court necessarily proceeded upon the theory that the resultant modification which these important considerations had wrought in the rules of the old common law was within the power of the courts to declare and make operative.

That the present case falls within the principles of the Benson and Rosen Cases, and especially of the latter, we think does not reasonably admit of doubt.

The rules of the common law which disqualified as witnesses persons having an interest long since in the main have been abolished both in England and in this country; and what was once regarded as a sufficient ground for excluding the testimony of such persons altogether has come to be uniformly and more sensibly regarded as affecting the credit of the witness only. Whatever was the danger that an interested witness would not speak the truth—and the danger never was as great as claimed—its effect has been minimized almost to the vanishing point by the test of cross-examination, the increased intelligence of jurors, and perhaps other circumstances. The modern rule which has removed the disqualification from persons accused of crime gradually came into force after the middle of the last century, and is today universally accepted. The exclusion of the husband or wife is said by this court to be based upon his or her interest in the event. *Jin Fuey Moy* v. *United States*, supra. And whether by this is meant a practical interest in the result of the prosecution or merely a sentimental interest because of the marital relationship makes little difference. In either case, a refusal to permit the wife upon the ground of interest to testify in behalf of her husband, while permitting him, who has the greater interest, to testify for himself, presents a manifest incongruity.

Nor can the exclusion of the wife's testimony, in the face of the broad and liberal extension of the rules in respect of the competency of witnesses generally, be any longer justified, if it ever was justified, on any ground of public policy. It has been said that to admit such testimony is against public policy because it would endanger the harmony and confidence of marital relations, and, moreover, would subject the witness to the temptation to commit perjury. Modern legislation, in making either spouse competent to testify in behalf of the other in criminal cases, has definitely rejected these notions, and in the light of such legislation and of modern thought they seem to be altogether fanciful. The public policy of one generation may not, under changed conditions, be the public policy of another. *Patton* v. *United States*, 281 U.S. 276, 306, 50 S.Ct. 253, 74 L.Ed. 854, 70 A.L.R. 263.

The fundamental basis upon which all rules of evidence must rest—if they are to rest upon reason —is their adaptation to the successful development of the truth. And, since experience is of all teachers the most dependable, and since experience also is a continuous process, it follows that a rule of evidence at one time thought necessary to the ascertainment of truth should yield to the experience of a succeeding generation whenever that experience has clearly demonstrated the fallacy or unwisdom of the old rule.

It may be said that the court should continue to enforce the old rule, however contrary to modern experience and thought, and however opposed, in principle, to the general current of legislation and of judicial opinion it may have become, leaving to Congress the responsibility of changing it. Of course, Congress has that power; but, if Congress fails to act, as it has failed in respect of the matter now under review, and the court be called upon to decide the question, is it not the duty of the court, if it possess the power, to decide it in accordance with present-day standards of wisdom and justice rather than in accordance with some outworn and antiquated rule of the past? That this court has the power to do so is necessarily implicit in the opinions delivered in deciding the Benson and Rosen Cases. And that implication, we think, rests upon substantial ground. The rule of the common law which denies the competency of one spouse to testify in behalf of the other in a criminal prosecution has not been modified by congressional legislation; nor has Congress directed the federal courts to follow state law upon that subject, as it has in respect of some other subjects. That this court and the other federal courts, in this situation and by right of their own powers, may decline to enforce the ancient rule of the common law under conditions as they now exist, we think is not fairly open to doubt. In *Hurtado* v. *California*, 110 U.S. 516, 530, 4 S.Ct. 111, 118, 28 L.Ed. 232, this court, after suggesting that it was better not to go too far back into antiquity for the best securities of our liberties, said:

"It is more consonant to the true philosophy of our historical legal institutions to say that the spirit of personal liberty and individual right, which they embodied, was preserved and developed by a progressive growth and wise adaptation to new circumstances and situations of the forms and processes found fit to give, from time to time, new expression and greater effect to modern ideas of self-government.

"This flexibility and capacity for growth and adaptation is the peculiar boast and excellence of the common law. * * * And as it was the characteristic principle of the common law to draw its inspiration from every fountain of justice, we are not to assume that the sources of its supply have been exhausted. On the contrary, we should expect that the new and various experiences of our own situation and system will mould and shape it into new and not less useful forms."

Compare *Holden* v. *Hardy*, 169 U.S. 366, 385-387, 18 S.Ct. 383, 42 L.Ed. 780.

To concede this capacity for growth and change in the common law by drawing "its inspiration from every fountain of justice," and at the same time to say that the courts of this country are forever bound to perpetuate such of its rules as, by every reasonable test, are found to be neither wise nor just, because we have once adopted them as suited to our situation and institutions at a particular time, is to deny to the common law in the place of its adoption a "flexibility and capacity for growth and adaptation" which was "the peculiar boast and excellence" of the system in the place of its origin.

The final question to which we are thus brought is not that of the power of the federal courts to amend or repeal any given rule or principle of the common law, for they neither have nor claim that power, but it is the question of the power of these courts, in the complete absence of congressional legislation on the subject, to declare and effectuate, upon common-law principles, what is the present rule upon a given subject in the light of fundamentally altered conditions, without regard to what has previously been declared and practiced. It has been said so often as to have become axiomatic that the common law is not immutable but flexible, and by its own principles adapts itself to varying conditions. In *Ketelsen* v. *Stilz*, 184 Ind. 702, 111 N.E. 423, L.R.A. 1918D, 303, Ann Cas. 1918A, 965, the Supreme Court of that state, after pointing out that the common law of England was based upon usages, customs, and institutions of the English people as declared from time to time by the courts, said (page 707, of 184 Ind.,

111 N.E. 423, 425):

"The rules so deduced from this system, however, were continually changing and expanding with the progress of society in the application of this system to more diversified circumstances and under more advanced periods. The common law by its own principles adapted itself to varying conditions and modified its own rules so as to serve the ends of justice as prompted by a course of reasoning which was guided by these generally accepted truths. One of its oldest maxims was that where the reason of a rule ceased the rule also ceased, and it logically followed that when it occurred to the courts that a particular rule had never been founded upon reason, and that no reason existed in support thereof, that rule likewise ceased, and perhaps another sprang up in its place which was based upon reason and justice as then conceived. No rule of the common law could survive the reason on which it was founded. It needed no statute to change it but abrogated itself."

That court then refers to the settled doctrine that an adoption of the common law in general terms does not require, without regard to local circumstances, an unqualified application of all its rules; that the rules, as declared by the English courts at one period or another, have been controlling in this country only so far as they were suited to and in harmony with the genius, spirit, and objects of American institutions; and that the rules of the. common law considered proper in the eighteenth century are not necessarily so considered in the twentieth. "Since courts have had an existence in America," that court said (page 708 of 184 Ind., 111 N.E. 423, 425), "they have never hesitated to take upon themselves the responsibility of saying what are the proper rules of the common law."

And the Virginia Supreme Court of Appeals, in *Hanriot* v. *Sherwood,* 82 Va. 1, 15, after pointing to the fact that the common law of England is the law of that commonwealth except so far as it has been altered by statute, or so far as its principles are inapplicable to the state of the country, and that the rules of the common law had undergone modification in the courts of England, notes with obvious approval that "the rules of evidence have been in the courts of this country undergoing such modification and changes, according to the circumstances of the country and the manner and genius of the people."

The Supreme Court of Connecticut, in *Beardsley* v. *City of Hartford,* 50 Conn. 529, 542, 47 Am. Rep. 677, after quoting the maxim of the common law, cessante ratione legis, cessat ipsa lex, said:

"This means that no law can survive the reasons on which it is founded. It needs no statute to change it; it abrogates itself. If the reasons on which a law rests are overborne by opposing reasons, which in the progress of society gain a controlling force, the old law, though still good as an abstract principle, and good in its application to some circumstances, must cease to apply as a controlling principle to the new circumstances."

The same thought is expressed in People v. Randolph, 2 Parker, Cr. R. (N.Y.) 174, 177:

"Its rules [the rules of the common law] are modified upon its own principles and not in violation of them. Those rules being founded in reason, one of its oldest maxims is, that where the reason of the rule ceases the rule also ceases."

Judgment reversed.

Mr. Justice CARDOZO concurs in the result.

Mr. Justice McREYNOLDS and Mr. Justice BUTLER are of opinion that the judgment of the court below is right and should be affirmed.

Case relating to Chapter 2
APPROACH TO THE STUDY
OF CRIMINAL EVIDENCE

STATE v. PERKINS

130 W.Va. 708,

45 S.E.2d 17 (1947)

KENNA, Judge.

Katherine Perkins was indicted by a grand jury of Wayne County for the murder of her husband, P. P. Perkins. She pleaded not guilty, was tried and convicted of murder of the second degree, and sentenced to imprisonment for a term of five to eighteen years. She brings the case here by writ of error.

On the evening of September 1, 1944, defendant, while riding in the automobile of a friend on Monroe Avenue in the City of Huntington, observed her husband in his automobile embracing a woman. At the request of defendant, the automobile was stopped, and defendant then went to the vehicle in which her husband and his companion were seated, and there engaged in a fight with the woman. The husband interfered in the struggle, enjoined defendant not to hurt his companion, and finally hit and kicked defendant several times. The defendant reentered her friend's automobile and returned to her home in the Town of Ceredo.

About ten o'clock p.m. of the same day, the husband returned to his home, and, according to defen-dant's testimony, he was angry and inclined to be violent. The quarrel between defendant and her husband was renewed and ended by the husband striking and kicking the defendant. After committing the second assault on defendant, the husband left his home and did not return until about midnight. Upon his return home he occupied a room on the second floor of his residence different from that which he and defendant had been wont to occupy. The defendant slept for the greater portion of the night in the room of her son and daughter-in-law.

On the morning of September 2, 1944, defendant prepared breakfast for a boarder, herself and her family. She and her daughter-in-law ate breakfast together, after which defendant went to the business section of the town for the purpose of paying a grocery bill. At some time during the morning defendant went to the home of a witness who testified for the State, where the witness said she saw a firearm in the possession of defendant, and that defendant indicated that trouble was about to occur.

Defendant returned to her home,

went to an upstairs bedroom, and began combing her hair. While doing so her husband came to the door; severely criticized defendant on her conduct in fighting the night before; said in substance that he was not further interested as he was leaving and started toward defendant, saying, "I will break your God damned neck."

The record is not clear as to what took place after the threat had been made by the husband. Defendant does not admit shooting her husband, but it is a reasonable inference, well supported by the facts, that she shot the deceased three times. One bullet entered his right shoulder, one about the middle of his right thigh, and another at the ninth dorsal vertebra. All bullets entered from the back. It is also a reasonable inference that defendant shot herself in the forehead, a pistol having been found near her body in the upstairs hall, and she was bleeding from a gunshot wound in her head.

The pistol found near defendant's body was offered as an exhibit, and was fairly well identified as belonging to a boarder and roomer, who stayed at the home of defendant and her husband, and whose room was on the first floor thereof. The neighbors of defendant were summoned and upon their arrival at the scene of the shooting, the husband, who had fallen down the stairway to first floor, requested them to go upstairs and see about "Kate", adding that he was to blame for the shooting. Another witness testified that on the way to the hospital in the ambulance defendant stated she was sorry she had not killed her husband and applied to him a vile epithet.

The husband was taken to a hospital, where he remained under treatment until the 8th day of April, 1945, when he left the hospital and returned to his home, where he died on April 16, 1945.

Defendant contends that the court committed the following errors: (1) In permitting an attending physician, prior to any proof of the cause of death, to give in evidence his opinion as to the cause of deceased's death; (2) in refusing to give defendant's instruction No. 3; and (3) by overruling defendant's objection to the cross-examination of defendant by the judge.

* * *

Instruction No. 3 embodied a statement of the law of self-defense. The instruction was refused on the ground that there was no evidence, either on the part of the State or defendant, supporting an instruction on self-defense. The record in this case has been carefully examined. The acts of violence perpetrated by the deceased on defendant on the night preceding the shooting, as well as the threat made by deceased just prior thereto, have been considered. Mere words, unaccompanied by an overt act, are not sufficient to justify an instruction to the jury on the theory of self-defense. *State* v. *Snider*, 81 W.Va. 522, 94 S.E. 981. Defendant was probably smarting from the indignities occasioned by the two assaults committed on her prior to the shooting, but when the deceased encountered defendant at the time of the shooting, there was no overt act committed by deceased. There is testimony that he started toward defendant at the time of the threat but that fact does not constitute an overt act. The record does not disclose what took place after the threat was made, as the defendant states that her mind is blank as to what was done by her or the deceased after the threat. Instruction No. 3 assumes that deceased made an attack on defendant. There is no showing of such fact in the record, nor is there sufficient evidence which tends to prove that such attack was made. The instruction comes within the rule laid down in the third point of the syllabus in *State* v. *Barker,* 92 W.Va. 583, 115 S.E. 421. See *State* v. *Weissengoff*, 89 W.Va. 279, 109 S.E. 707; *State* v. *Frank Zinn*, 95 W.Va. 148, 120 S.E. 387; *State* v. *Newman*, 101 W.Va. 356, 132 S.E. 728.

Facts necessary to support the theory of self-defense are not shown in this record. On the contrary, it is undisputed that all of the bullets inflicting wounds on deceased entered from the rear, which militates against the idea that deceased had assumed an aggressive attitude toward defendant at the time of the shooting. The refusal of the trial court to give defendant's instruction No. 3 is not error.

Defendant testified in her own behalf. At the commencement of her re-direct examination, her counsel asked one question, which she did not answer. At that time the judge of the trial court commenced to cross-examine defendant in the presence of the jury and asked, without intermission, forty-one questions. It would unduly prolong this opinion to quote all the questions asked by the judge and answered by defendant. Such questions related to the ownership of the revolver, and also how the revolver came to be on the

second floor when the room of the owner thereof was on the first floor. The cross-examination also elicited the fact that defendant had made the roomer's bed on the morning of the shooting; that deceased was shot three times in the back; and that defendant also suffered a gunshot wound.

After developing these two subjects, the judge of the trial court then asked defendant the following questions:

"Q. Mrs. Perkins, you have told the jury you had a blackout up there on the evening when you found your husband with this woman and you don't remember anything except what your husband did to you, is that right?

"A. That is right, exactly right.

"Q. You remember everything that happened from then on until this shooting?

"A. Yes, sir.

"Q. You remember your husband standing with a flashlight in his hand and his gun in his hand?

"A. Yes, sir.

"Q. You remember that?

"A. Yes, sir.

"Q. Then you testified to the jury that you had a blackout from that time on, is that right?

"A. Yes, sir.

"Q. You don't know what happened?

"A. I don't remember anything that happened until late that evening in the hospital.

"Q. When that blackout struck you where were you standing?

"A. In the doorway.

"Q. Room No. 2?

"A. Yes, sir.

"Q. Where was he?

"A. In the hall.

"Q. Facing each other?

"A. Yes.

"Q. And you don't know how that gun which has been exhibited in evidence got there in the hallway and found there after you were shot?

"A. I don't remember ever having that gun in my hands.

"Q. You didn't have a blackout except on those two occasions, is that right?

"A. I don't understand what you mean.

"Q. You told the jury your mind was a blank at the time of the trouble with this woman, now you tell the jury your mind was a blank from the time your husband was standing there in the hall and you were in the room facing him.

"A. I guess I was so mad, I don't know anything else."

Thereupon defendant objected to the questions asked by the trial judge and rested her case.

The question presented by the third assignment of error has been before this Court several times. In disposing of a similar question presented in the case of State v. Hurst, 11 W.Va. 54, this Court laid down the following rule: "It is error for a court in the trial of a criminal cause, to make a remark to, or in the presence of the jury, in reference to matters of fact, which might in any degree influence them in their verdict." In the case of State v. Thompson, 21 W.Va. 741, 756, this Court again adverted to the rule laid down in the Hurst case.

The rule is amplified and restated in the seventh point of the syllabus in the case of State v. Austin, 93 W.Va. 704, 117 S.E. 607, as follows: "In the trial of a criminal case, the jurors, not the court, are the triers of the facts, and the court should be extremely cautious not to intimate in any manner, by word, tone, or demeanor, his opinion upon any fact in issue." In the case of State v. Hively, 103 W.Va. 237, 136 S.E. 862, this Court held: "Under the practice in this State, the trial judge should express to the jury no opinion on the testimony, either directly or by innuendo."

The action of the trial judge in the case of State v. Songer, 117 W.Va. 529, 186 S.E. 118, was somewhat similar to that of the trial judge in the instant case. In the Songer case, this Court, citing with approval the case of State v. Austin, supra, reversed the trial court, using the following language: "Edgar Martin was a witness for the state though friendly to defendant. The court virtually conducted his examination in chief asking him in all, sixty questions. Reed Mullens was a witness for defendant. Reed testified (without objection) that he did not know they were stealing the car; that Martin told him Bias had the car borrowed. (Martin was not questioned on that point). While Reed's examination in chief was in progress, the court interposed and asked him thirty-three questions. Upon Reed's cross examination, the court again asked a number of questions. Some of the court's questions were brusque and his interrogations generally, both of Martin and Mullens, tended to indicate to the jury that he did not credit the innocence of defendant. This was prejudicial error."

*   *   *

In this case the demeanor of the trial judge is not portrayed by the record, nor is it shown whether the questions were brusque or otherwise. But it suffices to say that the trial judge in this case conducted a vigorous, searching and sustained cross-examination of the defendant. Upon consideration of any single question, we could not say that there was prejudice. But upon consideration of the forty-one questions asked defendant by the trial judge, the conclusion is inescapable that the trial judge by such cross-examination of defendant in the manner here shown intimated to the jury his opinion upon the facts in issue.

We cannot say to what extent the minds of the jurors who tried defendant were influenced by the cross-examination conducted by the trial judge, but we must assume that if the trial judge indicated to the jury his belief in her guilt, such belief influenced the jury in arriving at its verdict.

We do not intend to say that a trial judge should not ask questions during the progress of a criminal trial at proper times and in a proper manner. Clarifying questions are necessary, but we see no occasion for the trial judge to take over the duties of a prosecuting officer.

In accordance with the foregoing we reverse the judgment of the Circuit Court of Wayne County, set aside the verdict, and award the defendant a new trial.

Judgment reversed; verdict set aside; new trial awarded.

HAYMOND, Judge (dissenting). Though I fully agree with the principle stated in the syllabus, it does not apply to the situation which existed, as shown by the record, in the trial of this case. For that reason I dissent from the decision of the majority.

In my opinion the defendant had a fair trial which was free from prejudicial error and in which the evidence was ample to support the verdict of the jury finding her guilty of murder of the second degree. The sole ground upon which the majority sets aside that verdict and reverses the judgment is the action of the trial judge in propounding certain questions to the defendant while she was testifying in her own behalf after examination by her attorney and cross-examination by the prosecuting attorney had not succeeded in developing pertinent facts relative to her conduct shortly before or at the time she shot and killed her husband. I emphatically disapprove any act or conduct of a judge of any trial court which indicates the slightest bias or unfairness toward any party or any opinion entertained by him with respect to any factual question, and I would promptly act to reverse the judgment and award a new trial whenever behavior of that nature occurs. But I would not require a judge of a trial court to act the part of a mere umpire in charge of a game between contestants or deprive him of his unquestioned right and duty to exercise his judicial power to direct and conduct the trial of a case. A trial is not a game. It is a solemn judicial inquiry to determine the merits of the conflicting claims of the parties for the sole purpose of administering justice between them according to law and the right of the case.

The judge of a trial court should, at all times, carefully refrain from encroachment upon the function of the attorneys who represent the litigants. Rarely should he engage in the examination of witnesses. That is the work of counsel. When, however, a witness is unwilling to tell the facts within his knowledge, and counsel are not disposed, or are unable, to elicit the facts, it may be proper for the judge, within recognized limits, to interrogate a witness. In such instances his failure to do so would risk his proper control of the case or require him to submit to the whim of an unruly witness. He is not required to do either.

* * *

I am unable to find, in this record, any act of the circuit judge who conducted the trial of this case indicative of any partiality or lack of fairness upon his part toward either party, or any conduct by which any opinion entertained by him concerning the guilt or the innocence of the defendant, or as to any other fact, was or could have been communicated or disclosed to the jury. Nothing prejudicial to any right of the defendant appears to have resulted from the conduct of the trial judge.

The defendant was fairly tried. The verdict of guilty of murder of the second degree was fully warranted by the evidence. In fact, upon the evidence, a verdict for any offense less than murder, or of not guilty, would not have been justified. The verdict was approved by the court and a proper judgment was rendered upon it. Perceiving no prejudice or injustice to the defendant, I am unwilling to disturb that judgment.

I am authorized to say that Judge FOX concurs in the views expressed in this dissent.

Cases relating to Chapter 3
BURDEN OF PROOF

IN RE WINSHIP

397 U.S. 358, 51 Ohio Op.2d 323, 90 S. Ct. 1068, 25 L. Ed. 2d 368 (1970)

[Footnotes omitted]

Mr. Justice BRENNAN delivered the opinion of the Court.

Constitutional questions decided by this Court concerning the juvenile process have centered on the adjudicatory stage at "which a determination is made as to whether a juvenile is a 'delinquent' as a result of alleged misconduct on his part, with the consequence that he may be committed to a state institution." *In re Gault*, 387 U.S. 1, 13, 40 Ohio Op.(2d) 378, 383 (1967). *Gault* decided that, although the Fourteenth Amendment does not require that the hearing at this stage conform with all the requirements of a criminal trial or even of the usual administrative proceeding, the Due Process Clause does require application during the adjudicatory hearing of " 'the essentials of due process and fair treatment.' " *Id.*, at 30. This case presents the single, narrow question whether proof beyond a reasonable doubt is among the "essentials of due process and fair treatment" required during the adjudicatory stage when a juvenile is charged with an act which would constitute a crime if committed by an adult.

Section 712 of the New York Family Court Act defines a juvenile delinquent as "a person over seven and less than sixteen years of age who does any act which, if done by an adult, would constitute a crime." During a 1967 adjudicatory hearing, conducted pursuant to § 742 of the Act, a judge in New York Family Court found that appellant, then a 12-year-old boy, had entered a locker and stolen $112 from a woman's pocketbook. The petition which charged appellant with delinquency alleged that his act, "if done by an adult, would constitute the crime or crimes of Larceny." The judge acknowledged that the proof might not establish guilt beyond a reasonable doubt, but rejected appellant's contention that such proof was required by the Fourteenth Amendment. The judge relied instead on § 744(b) of the New York Family Court Act which provides that "[a]ny determination at the conclusion of [an adjudicatory] hearing that a [juvenile] did an act or acts must be based on a preponderance of the evidence." During a subsequent dispositional hearing, appellant was ordered placed in a train-

441

ing school for an initial period of 18 months, subject to annual extensions of his commitment until his 18th birthday—six years in appellant's case. The Appellate Division of the New York Supreme Court, First Judicial Department, affirmed without opinion, 30 App. Div. 2d 781, 291 N.Y.S. 2d 1005 (1968). The New York Court of Appeals then affirmed by a four-to-three vote, expressly sustaining the constitutionality of § 744(b), 24 N.Y.2d 196, 247 N.E.2d 253 (1969). We noted probable jurisdiction, 396 U.S. 885 (1969). We reverse.

The requirement that guilt of a criminal charge be established by proof beyond a reasonable doubt dates at least from our early years as a Nation. The "demand for a higher degree of persuasion in criminal cases was recurrently expressed from ancient times, [though] its crystallization into the formula 'beyond a reasonable doubt' seems to have occurred as late as 1798. It is now accepted in common law jurisdictions as the measure of persuasion by which the prosecution must convince the trier of all the essential elements of guilt." C. McCormick, Evidence § 321, pp. 681-682 (1954); see also 9 J. Wigmore, Evidence § 2497 (3d ed. 1940). Although virtually unanimous adherence to the reasonable-doubt standard in common-law jurisdictions may not conclusively establish it as a requirement of due process, such adherence does "reflect a profound judgment about the way in which law should be enforced and justice administered." Duncan v. Louisiana, 391 U.S. 145, 155, 45 OhioOp. (2d) 198, 203 (1968).

Expressions in many opinions of

this Court indicate that it has long been assumed that proof of a criminal charge beyond a reasonable doubt is constitutionally required. See, for example, Miles v. United States, 103 U.S. 304, 312 (1881); Davis v. United States, 160 U.S. 469, 488 (1895); Holt v. United States, 218 U.S. 245, 253 (1910); Wilson v. United States, 232 U.S. 563, 569-570 (1914); Brinegar v. United States, 338 U.S. 160, 174 (1949); Leland v. Oregon, 343 U.S. 790, 795 (1952); Holland v. United States, 348 U.S. 121, 138 (1954); Speiser v. Randall, 357 U.S. 513, 525-526 (1958). Cf. Coffin v. United States, 156 U.S. 432 (1895). Mr. Justice Frankfurter stated that "[i]t is the duty of the Government to establish . . . guilt beyond a reasonable doubt. This notion—basic in our law and rightly one of the boasts of a free society— is a requirement and a safeguard of due process of law in the historic, procedural content of 'due process.'" Leland v. Oregon, supra, at 802-803 (dissenting opinion). In a similar vein, the Court said in Brinegar v. United States, supra, at 174, that "[g]uilt in a criminal case must be proved beyond a reasonable doubt and by evidence confined to that which long experience in the common-law tradition, to some extent embodied in the Constitution, has crystallized into rules of evidence consistent with that standard. These rules are historically grounded rights of our system, developed to safeguard men from dubious and unjust convictions, with resulting forfeitures of life, liberty and property." Davis v. United States, supra, at 488, stated that the requirement is implicit in "constitutions . . . [which] recognize the fundamental principles that are deemed essential for the protection of life and liberty." In *Davis* a murder conviction was reversed because the trial judge instructed the jury that it was their duty to convict when the evidence was equally balanced regarding the sanity of the accused. This Court said: "On the contrary, he is entitled to an acquittal of the specific crime charged if upon all the evidence there is reasonable doubt whether he was capable in law of committing crime. . . . No man should be deprived of his life under the forms of law unless the jurors who try him are able, upon their consciences, to say that the evidence before them . . . is sufficient to show beyond a reasonable doubt the existence of every fact necessary to constitute the crime charged." *Id.*, at 484, 493.

The reasonable-doubt standard plays a vital role in the American scheme of criminal procedure. It is a prime instrument for reducing the risk of convictions resting on factual error. The standard provides concrete substance for the presumption of innocence—that bedrock "axiomatic and elementary" principle whose "enforcement lies at the foundation of the administration of our criminal law." *Coffin v. United States, supra,* at 453. As the dissenters in the New York Court of Appeals observed, and we agree, "a person accused of a crime . . . would be at a severe disadvantage, a disadvantage amounting to a lack of fundamental fairness, if he could be adjudged guilty and imprisoned for years on the strength of the same evidence as would suffice in a civil case." 24 N.Y.2d, at 205, 247 N.E.2d, at 259.

The requirement of proof be-yond a reasonable doubt has this vital role in our criminal procedure for cogent reasons. The accused during a criminal prosecution has at stake interests of immense importance, both because of the possibility that he may lose his liberty upon conviction and because of the certainty that he would be stigmatized by the conviction. Accordingly, a society that values the good name and freedom of every individual should not condemn a man for commission of a crime when there is reasonable doubt about his guilt. As we said in *Speiser v. Randall, supra,* at 525-526: "There is always in litigation a margin of error, representing error in factfinding, which both parties must take into account. Where one party has at stake an interest of transcending value—as a criminal defendant his liberty—this margin of error is reduced as to him by the process of placing on the other party the burden of . . . persuading the factfinder at the conclusion of the trial of his guilt beyond a reasonable doubt. Due process commands that no man shall lose his liberty unless the Government has borne the burden of . . . convincing the factfinder of his guilt." To this end, the reasonable-doubt standard is indispensable, for it "impresses on the trier of fact the necessity of reaching a subjective state of certitude of the facts in issue." Dorsen & Rezneck, In Re Gault and the Future of Juvenile Law, 1 Family Law Quarterly, No. 4, pp. 1, 26 (1967).

Moreover, use of the reasonable-doubt standard is indispensable to command the respect and confidence of the community in applications of the criminal law. It is critical that the moral force of the criminal law not be diluted by a standard of proof that leaves people in doubt whether innocent men are being condemned. It is also important in our free society that every individual going about his ordinary affairs have confidence that his government cannot adjudge him guilty of a criminal offense without convincing a proper factfinder of his guilt with utmost certainty.

Lest there remain any doubt about the constitutional stature of the reasonable-doubt standard, we explicitly hold that the Due Process Clause protects the accused against conviction except upon proof beyond a reasonable doubt of every fact necessary to constitute the crime with which he is charged.

We turn to the question whether juveniles, like adults, are constitutionally entitled to proof beyond a reasonable doubt when they are charged with violation of a criminal law. The same considerations that demand extreme caution in factfinding to protect the innocent adult apply as well to the innocent child. We do not find convincing the contrary arguments of the New York Court of Appeals. *Gault* rendered untenable much of the reasoning relied upon by that court to sustain the constitutionality of § 744 (b). The Court of Appeals indicated that a delinquency adjudication "is not a 'conviction' (§ 781); that it affects no right or privilege, including the right to hold public office or to obtain a licence (§ 782); and a cloak of protective confidentiality is thrown around all the proceedings (§§ 783-784)." 24 N.Y.2d, at 200, 247 N.E.2d, at 255-256. The court said further: "The delinquency status is not made a crime;

and the proceedings are not criminal. There is, hence, no deprivation of due process in the statutory provision [challenged by appellant]. . . ." 24 N.Y.2d, at 203, 247 N.E.2d, at 257. In effect the Court of Appeals distinguished the proceedings in question here from a criminal prosecution by use of what *Gault* called the "'civil' label-of-convenience which has been attached to juvenile proceedings." 387 U.S., at 50. But *Gault* expressly rejected that distinction as a reason for holding the Due Process Clause inapplicable to a juvenile proceeding. 387 U.S., at 50-51. The Court of Appeals also attempted to justify the preponderance standard on the related ground that juvenile proceedings are designed "not to punish, but to save the child." 24 N.Y. 2d, at 197, 247 N.E.2d, at 254. Again, however, *Gault* expressly rejected this justification. 387 U.S., at 27, 40 OhioOp.(2d), at 389. We made clear in that decision that civil labels and good intentions do not themselves obviate the need for criminal due process safeguards in juvenile courts, for "[a] proceeding where the issue is whether the child will be found to be 'delinquent' and subjected to the loss of his liberty for years is comparable in seriousness to a felony prosecution." *Id.*, at 36.

Nor do we perceive any merit in the argument that to afford juveniles the protection of proof beyond a reasonable doubt would risk destruction of beneficial aspects of the juvenile process. Use of the reasonable-doubt standard during the adjudicatory hearing will not disturb New York's policies that a finding that a child has violated a criminal law does not constitute a criminal conviction, that such a finding does not deprive the child of his civil rights, and that juvenile proceedings are confidential. Nor will there be any effect on the informality, flexibility, or speed of the hearing at which the factfinding takes place. And the opportunity during the post-adjudicatory or dispositional hearing for a wide-ranging review of the child's social history and for his individualized treatment will remain unimpaired. Similarly, there will be no effect on the procedures distinctive to juvenile proceedings that are employed prior to the adjudicatory hearing.

The Court of Appeals observed that "a child's best interest is not necessarily, or even probably, promoted if he wins in the particular inquiry which may bring him to the juvenile court." 24 N.Y.2d, at 199, 247 N.E.2d, at 255. It is true, of course, that the juvenile may be engaging in a general course of conduct inimical to his welfare that calls for judicial intervention. But that intervention cannot take the form of subjecting the child to the stigma of a finding that he violated a criminal law and to the possibility of institutional confinement on proof insufficient to convict him were he an adult.

We conclude, as we concluded regarding the essential due process safeguards applied in *Gault*, that the observance of the standard of proof beyond a reasonable doubt "will not compel the States to abandon or displace any of the substantive benefits of the juvenile process." *Gault, supra*, at 21.

Finally, we reject the Court of Appeals' suggestion that there is, in any event, only a "tenuous differ-ence" between the reasonable-doubt and preponderance standards. The suggestion is singularly unpersuasive. In this very case, the trial judge's ability to distinguish between the two standards enabled him to make a finding of guilt that he conceded he might not have made under the standard of proof beyond a reasonable doubt. Indeed, the trial judge's action evidences the accuracy of the observation of commentators that "the preponderance test is susceptible to the misinterpretation that it calls on the trier of fact merely to perform an abstract weighing of the evidence in order to determine which side has produced the greater quantum, without regard to its effect in convincing his mind of the truth of the proposition asserted." Dorsen & Rezneck, *supra*, at 26-27.

In sum, the constitutional safeguard of proof beyond a reasonable doubt is as much required during the adjudicatory stage of a delinquency proceeding as are those constitutional safeguards applied in *Gault*—notice of charges, right to counsel, the rights of confrontation and examination, and the privilege against self-incrimination. We therefore hold, in agreement with Chief Judge Fuld in dissent in the Court of Appeals, "that, where a 12-year-old child is charged with an act of stealing which renders him liable to confinement for as long as six years, then, as a matter of due process . . . the case against him must be proved beyond a reasonable doubt." 24 N.Y.2d, at 207, 247 N.E.2d, at 260.

Reversed.

Concurring and dissenting opinions not included.

COMMONWEALTH v. MUNOZ

426 N.E.2d 1161 (Mass. 1981)

NOLAN, Justice.

The defendant was convicted of unauthorized possession of a controlled substance, G.L. c. 94C, § 34, and of operating an uninsured motor vehicle, G.L. c. 90, § 34J, by a jury of six in a District Court. The Appeals Court affirmed both convictions. *Commonwealth v. Munoz*, Mass.App.Ct.Adv.Sh. (1980) 2175, 413 N.E.2d 773. The defendant sought further appellate review on the charge of operating an uninsured motor vehicle. We granted the defendant's application. The defendant asserts that the trial judge's instructions to the jury on the uninsured motor vehicle charge were improper because they shifted to the defendant the burden of proof on an essential element of the crime. We conclude that the "overall impact" of the instructions (*Commonwealth v. Sellon*, Mass.Adv.Sh. [1980] 789, 800, 402 N.E.2d 1329) was to place the burden of proof on the defendant as to the absence of insurance, an essential element of the crime. Therefore, we reverse the judgment of conviction of operating an uninsured vehicle.

We summarize only the facts relevant to the issue before us on appeal. The commonwealth introduced evidence that the defendant had been observed on July 12, 1979, operating a 1972 brown Pontiac automobile on a public way. When asked for his license and registration, the defendant produced a license, a registration certificate for a 1967 Mercury Cougar automobile, and a certificate of title for the Pontiac in the name of a third person. The title certificate for the Pontiac had not been completed to indicate a proper transfer of the vehicle, although the assignment of title on the back of the title certificate had been signed by the third person and the certificate contained a notation that a bank lien on the car had been released six days prior to the incident. Copies of the registration for the Mercury and the title certificate for the Pontiac were introduced as exhibits by the Commonwealth. Neither the Commonwealth nor the defendant introduced any evidence touching the question whether the Pontiac was properly insured.

In instructing the jury on the presumption of innocence and the burden of proof, the judge stated: "[The defendant] is presumed to be innocent when he first stands before you. It is the Commonwealth's burden then to show beyond a reasonable doubt that that presumption is not founded and that he is, in fact, guilty. Now, let us talk a little bit about the defendant's burden and he has none with a minor exception on which I will instruct you a little later in this case. The defendant has no burden. He does not have to take the stand. He does not have to prove anything to you. The whole of the proof is left to the Commonwealth as I said with an exception which I will explain to you in a little while."

The judge subsequently instructed the jury on the charge of operating an uninsured vehicle in the following language: "The second complaint that you have before you alleges that the defendant did operate a motor vehicle without having the motor vehicle insured as is required under our law. And here the Commonwealth is required to prove two things to you. First, that the defendant operated a motor vehicle. Secondly, that the motor vehicle was operated on a public way or on a way to which the public had a right of access or had access by way of being an invitee or a licensee. Then the Commonwealth also has to allege that the vehicle was uninsured. And here is where the presumption that I have indicated to you before stands in favor of the defendant. It changes a little bit.

"Once the Commonwealth has shown that there was operation of the motor vehicle and that the operation took place on a public way or a way to which the public had a right of access, then if they further allege that the motor vehicle was uninsured, the defendant has the responsibility and the obligation of showing that, as a matter of fact, it was insured. And that presumption that we talked about shifts a little bit. It shifts because it is very difficult if not impossible to prove a negative. It is very difficult to show that something does not exist.

"Under this special circumstance, our law requires, one, the Commonwealth has made out those two elements and alleges there was no insurance on the vehicle. It is up to the defendant to show there was insurance. The law in Massachusetts requires that there be at least a minimum amount of insurance on a motor vehicle for it to be operated on the highway. And that is called

compulsory motor vehicle insurance requirements."

The defendant made a timely objection to this portion of the charge and contends that the instructions inpermissibly shifted to him the burden of proof of an element of the crime and invaded the fact-finding function of the jury.

The Commonwealth contends that the judge's instructions represent a correct application of the law because G.L. c. 278, § 7, which places the burden on the defendant to produce evidence of license or authority, applies to a prosecution under G.L. c. 90, § 34J, for operating an uninsured motor vehicle. The Commonwealth argues that the instructions at issue comply with G.L. c. 278, § 7, since they did not shift the burden of proof to the defendant but merely placed on the defendant the burden of producing some evidence of automobile insurance.

General Laws c. 278, § 7, provides that "[a] defendant in a criminal prosecution, relying for his justification upon a license, appointment, admission to practice as an attorney at law, or authority, shall prove the same; and, until so proved, the presumption shall be that he is not so authorized." In *Commonwealth* v. *Jones*, 372 Mass. 403, 361 N.E.2d 1308 (1977), we discussed the history and interpretation of this statute and ruled that the statute applied to prosecutions under G.L. c. 269, § 10, which prohibits the carrying of a firearm. We indicated in *Jones* that, under G.L. c. 278, § 7, the burden is on a defendant to come forward with evidence of his license to carry a firearm; that, if he does, "the burden is on the prosecution to persuade the trier of the facts beyond a reasonable doubt that the defense does not exist"; and that, if the defendant does not, there is no jury issue as to licensing or authority. Id. at 406-407, 361 N.E.2d 1308. In *Commonwealth* v. *Jefferson*, 377 Mass. 716, 387 N.E.2d 579 (1979), we held that the same principles apply to a prosecution under G.L. c. 94C, § 27, which prohibits the unlawful possession of hypodermic needles and syringes, and ruled that where there was no evidence bearing on the defendant's justification for possession of the needles and syringes, the judge's charge properly removed justification from the jury's consideration. As we stated in *Jones*, G.L. c. 278, § 7, is applicable to situations where "[a]s [a] matter of statutory construction, the prohibition is general, the license is exceptional." *Commonwealth* v. *Jones, supra* 372 Mass. at 405, 361 N.E.2d 1308, quoting from *Commonwealth* v. *Nickerson*, 236 Mass. 281, 305, 128 N.E.273 (1920). In the absence of evidence with respect to licensing or authority, the issue of licensing or authority is removed from consideration and no jury issue is presented. Accordingly, if a defendant is relying on licensing or authority, he must come forward with evidence of license or authority. If he fails in this particular, the issue is not presented.

These considerations are inapplicable, however, in the case at bar because insurance is an element of the crime charged, not a mere license or authority. See J. R. Nolan, Criminal Law § 583 (1976). Therefore, the issue of insurance cannot be viewed as an affirmative defense

and, of course, it cannot be removed from jury consideration. In a prosecution under G.L. c. 90, § 34J, the Commonwealth must prove as an element of the crime charged that the motor vehicle was in fact uninsured. The defendant cannot be under any obligation to aid the Commonwealth in its proof of this central element of the case against him. If the Commonwealth fails to carry its burden of proof on this element, its entire case must fail.

The Commonwealth, in urging us to apply G.L. c. 278, § 7, to this case and to require the defendant to bear the burden of producing evidence showing insurance, points to the relative ease with which the defendant could produce a document proving insurance if the car were in fact insured as compared with the difficulty the Commonwealth has in proving noninsurance. The Commonwealth acknowledges, however, that under G.L. c. 90, § 34J, the Registrar of Motor Vehicles is obliged to maintain information as to insurance on every car registered in the Commonwealth and is required to make this information available to any person on request. Even assuming that it may be difficult for the Commonwealth to prove noninsurance, this obstacle does not warrant the application of c. 278, § 7, in view of the fact that noninsurance is an element, in fact, the central element of a prosecutions under G.L. c. 90, § 34J. Accordingly, we conclude that G.L. c. 278, § 7, is inapplicable to prosecution under G.L. c. 90, § 34J.

Because G.L. c. 278, § 7, does not apply to the issue of insurance under prosecutions for driving an uninsured motor vehicle, that statute cannot save the instructions given to the jury in this case. As we stated in *Jones* and *Jefferson*, G.L. c. 278, § 7, merely places on the defendant the burden of coming forward with evidence of his justification. General Laws c. 278, § 7, does not, and could not constitutionally, shift the burden of proof to the defendant as to an element of the crime charged. We believe that the judge's charge involved in this case had the effect of placing on the defendant the burden of proving insurance.

The judge, after instructing the jury that the defendant is presumed to be innocent and that the Commonwealth has the burden of proving guilt beyond a reasonable doubt, stated "let us talk a little bit about the defendant's burden and he has none *with a minor exception....* The whole of the proof is left to the Commonwealth as I said *with an exception*" (emphasis added). In instructing the jury on the charge of operating an uninsured motor vehicle the judge stated that the "Commonwealth is required to prove two things"—that the defendant operated a motor vehicle and that this occurred on a public way. He then stated that the Commonwealth "has to *allege* that the vehicle was uninsured...then...the defendant has the responsibility and the obligation of showing that, as a matter of fact, it was insured.... It is up to the defendant to show there was insurance." (Emphasis added.)

As we stated in *Commonwealth* v. *Medina*, Mass.Adv.Sh. (1980) 1143, 404 N.E.2d 1228, " 'whether a defendant has been accorded his constitutional rights depends upon the way in which a reasonable juror

could have interpreted the instruction...,' and...error is avoided if the charge, read as a whole, makes clear the Commonwealth's burden." *Id.* at 1155, 404 N.E.2d 1228, quoting from *Sandstrom* v. *Montana*, 442 U.S. 510, 514, 99 S.Ct. 2450, 2454, 61 L.Ed.2d 39(1979). Viewing these instructions as a whole, we think it clear that a reasonable juror could have interpreted them as placing a burden on the defendant to prove that the car was insured. A reasonable juror would have further concluded that, absent such proof, the jury were obliged to find that the defendant's car was in fact not insured, once the Commonwealth had alleged noninsurance, even if the Commonwealth has presented no evidence tending to show the absence of insurance. Since the defendant here did not present any evidence pertaining to insurance, the judge in his instructions, effectively (though not formally) directed a verdict against the defendant. As we stated in *Commonwealth* v. *Pauley*, 368 Mass. 286, 291, 331 N.E2d 901, appeal dismissed, 423 U.S. 887, 96 S.Ct. 181, 46 L.Ed.2d 119 (1975), it is an "established principle that a verdict may not be directed against a defendant in a criminal prosecution, see Wigmore, Evidence, § 7495, p. 312 (2d ed. 1940), with the corollary proposition that the trier of fact, judge or jury, cannot be compelled to find against the defendant as to any element of the crime."

Nor can the burden of persuasion be shifted to the defendant by means of a mandatory presumption. In *Commonwealth* v. *Callahan*, Mass.Adv.Sh. (1980) 1411, 406 N.E.2d 385, we struck down a jury instruction which had the effect of imposing a mandatory presumption of malice arising from the use of a deadly weapon. The judge's charge in *Callahan* "clearly stated that unless some evidence were introduced to the contrary, presumably by the defendant, the implication' of malice was required to be drawn from the intentional use of a deadly weapon. This language clearly reflects the shifting of some burden onto the defendant.... Such a shift of the burden of proof is clearly contrary to the constitutional requirement that the Commonwealth must prove every essential element of a crime beyond a reasonable doubt" (citations omitted). *Id.* at 1414-1415, 406 N.E.2d 385.

It has long been the rule that "the Due Process Clause protects the accused against conviction except upon proof beyond a reasonable doubt of every fact necessary to constitute the crime with which he is charged." *In re Winship*, 397 U.S. 358, 364, 90 S.Ct. 1068, 1072, 25 L.Ed.2d 368 (1970). This constitutional requirement cannot be altered because of any difficulty the Commonwealth may have in proving the absence of insurance as compared to the relative ease with which the defendant could prove that his car was insured. Justice Powell wrote in *Mullaney* v. *Wilbur*, 421 U.S. 684, 701, 95 S.Ct. 1881, 1890, 44 L.Ed.2d 508 (1975): "It has been suggested...that because of the difficulties in negating an argument that the homicide was committed in the heat of passion the burden of proving this fact should rest on the defendant. No doubt this is often a heavy burden for the prosecution to satisfy. The same may be said of the requirement of proof beyond a reasonable doubt of many controverted facts in a criminal trial. But this is the traditional burden which our system of criminal justice deems essential."

We also point out, so as to avoid future confusion in this area, that the recommended instruction for operating a motor vehicle without insurance (Instruction 5.11 of the Model Jury Instructions for Criminal Offenses Tried in the District Courts [1980]) is improper. The model instruction states that the Commonwealth must prove beyond a reasonable doubt that the defendant operated a motor vehicle upon a public way. It then reads: "Once the Commonwealth has proved these two things and has alleged that the defendant failed to produce proof of insurance, the burden is upon the defendant to prove that he does have the required insurance coverage." This instruction shifts the burden of proof to the defendant as to this element of the crime and is therefore improper.

For the foregoing reasons we reverse the defendant's conviction on the charge of operating an uninsured motor vehicle.

Judgment reversed.
Verdict set aside.
Judgment for the defendant.

MARTIN v. OHIO

480 U.S. 228, 107 S. Ct. 1098, 94 L. Ed. 2d 267 (1987)

Justice WHITE delivered the opinion of the Court.

The Ohio Code provides that "[e]very person accused of an offense is presumed innocent until proven guilty beyond a reasonable doubt, and the burden of proof for all elements of the offense is upon the prosecution. The burden of going forward with the evidence of an affirmative defense, and the burden of proof by a preponderance of the evidence, is upon the accused." Ohio Rev. Code Ann. §2901.05(A) (1982). An affirmative defense is one involving "an excuse or justification peculiarly with the knowledge of the accused, on which he can fairly be required to adduce supporting evidence." Ohio Rev. Code Ann. §2901.-05(C)(2) (1982). The Ohio courts have "long determined that self-defense is an affirmative defense," 21 Ohio St. 3d 91, 93, 488 N.E.2d 166, 168 (1986), and that the defendant has the burden of proving it as required by §2901.05(A).

As defined by the trial court in its instructions in this case, the elements of self-defense that the defendant must prove are (1) that the defendant was not at fault in creating the situation giving rise to the argument; (2) the defendant had an honest belief that she was in imminent danger of death or great bodily harm and that her only means of escape from such

danger was in the use of such force; and (3) the defendant must not have violated any duty to retreat or avoid danger. App. 19. The question before us is whether the Due Process Clause of the Fourteenth Amendment forbids placing the burden of proving self-defense on the defendant when she is charged by the State of Ohio with committing the crime of aggravated murder, which, as relevant to this case, is defined by the Revised Code of Ohio as "purposely, and with prior calculation and design, caus[ing] the death of another." Ohio Rev. Code Ann. §2903.01 (1982).

The facts of this case, taken from the opinions of the courts below, may be succinctly stated. On July 21, 1983, petitioner Earline Martin and her husband, Walter Martin, argued over grocery money. Petitioner claimed that her husband struck her in the head during the argument. Petitioner's version of what then transpired was that she went upstairs, put on a robe, and later came back down with her husband's gun which she intended to dispose of. Her husband saw something in her hand and questioned her about it. He came at her, she lost her head and fired the gun at him. Five or six shots were fired, three of them striking and killing Mr. Martin. She was charged with and tried for aggravated murder. She pleaded self-defense and testified in her own defense. The judge charged the jury with respect to the elements of the crime and of self-defense and rejected petitioner's Due Process Clause challenge to the charge placing on her the burden of proving self-defense. The jury found her guilty.

Both the Ohio Court of Appeals and the Supreme Court of Ohio affirmed the conviction. Both rejected constitutional challenge to the instruction requiring petitioner to prove self-defense. The latter court, relying upon our opinion in *Patterson v. New York*, 432 U.S. 197, 97 S. Ct. 2319, 53 L. Ed. 2d 281 (1977), concluded that, the State was required to prove the three elements of aggravated murder but that *Patterson* did not require it to disprove self-defense, which is a separate issue that did not require Mrs. Martin to disprove any element of the offense with which she was charged. The court said, "the state proved beyond a reasonable doubt that appellant purposely, and with prior calculation and design, caused the death of her husband. Appellant did not dispute the existence of these elements, but rather sought to justify her actions on grounds she acted in self-defense." 21 Ohio St. 3d, at 94, 488 N.E.2d, at 168. There was thus no infirmity in her conviction. We granted certiorari, 475 U.S. __, 106 S. Ct. 1634, 90 L. Ed. 2d 180 (1986), and affirm the decision of the Supreme Court of Ohio.

In re Winship, 397 U.S. 358, 364, 90 S. Ct. 1068, 25 1. Ed. 2d 368 (1970), declared that the Due Process Clause "protects the accused against conviction except upon proof beyond a reasonable doubt of every fact necessary to constitute the crime with which he is charged." A few years later, we held that *Winship*'s mandate was fully satisfied where the State of New York had proved beyond reasonable doubt, each of the elements of murder, but placed on the defendant the burden of proving the affirmative defense of extreme emotional disturbance, which, if proved, would have reduced the crime from murder to manslaughter. *Patterson v. New York, supra*. We there emphasized the preeminent role of the States in preventing and dealing with crime and the reluctance of the Court to disturb a State's decision with respect to the definition of criminal conduct and the procedures by which the criminal laws are to be enforced in the courts, including the burden of producing evidence and allocating the burden of persuasion. 432 U.S., at 201-202, 97 S. Ct. at 2322. New York had the authority to define murder as the intentional killing of another person. It had chosen, however, to reduce the crime to manslaughter if the defendant proved by a preponderance of the evidence that he had acted under the influence of extreme emotional distress. To convict of murder, the jury was required to find beyond a reasonable doubt, based on all the evidence, including that related to the defendant's mental state at the time of the crime, each of the elements of murder and also to conclude that the defendant had not proved his affirmative defense. The jury convicted Patterson, and we held that there was no violation of the Fourteenth Amendment as construed in *Winship*. Referring to *Leland v. Oregon*, 343 U.S. 790, 72 S. Ct. 1002, 96 L. Ed. 1302 (1952) and *Rivera v. Delaware*, 429 U.S. 877, 97 S. Ct. 226, 50 L. Ed. 2d (1976), we added that New York "did no more than *Leland* and *Rivera* permitted it to do without violating the Due Process Clause" and declined to reconsider those cases. 432 U.S., at 206, 207, 97 S. Ct., at 2324, 2325. It was also observed that "the fact that a majority of the States have now assumed the burden of disproving affirmative defenses—for whatever reasons—[does not] mean that those States that strike a different balance are in violation of the Constitution." Id., at 211, 97 S. Ct., at 2327.

As in *Patterson*, the jury was here instructed that to convict it must find, in light of all the evidence, that each of elements of the crime of aggravated murder must be proved by the State beyond reasonable doubt and that the burden of proof with respect to these elements did not shift. To find guilt, the jury had to be convinced that none of the evidence, whether offered by the State or by Martin in connection with her plea of self-defense, raised a reasonable doubt that Martin had killed her husband, that she had the specific purpose and intent to cause his death, or that she had done so with prior calculation and design. It was also told, however, that it could acquit if it found by a preponderance of the evidence that Martin had not precipitated the confrontation, that she had an

honest belief that she was in imminent danger of death or great bodily harm, and that she had satisfied any duty to retreat or avoid danger. The jury convicted Martin.

We agree with the State and its Supreme Court that this conviction did not violate the Due Process Clause. The State did not exceed its authority in defining the crime of murder as purposely causing the death of another with prior calculation or design. It did not seek to shift to Martin the burden of proving any of those elements, and the jury's verdict reflects that none of her self-defense evidence raised a reasonable doubt about the state's proof that she purposefully killed with prior calculation and design. She nevertheless had the opportunity under state law and the instructions given to justify the killing and show herself to be blameless by showing that she acted in self-defense. The jury thought she had failed to do so, and Ohio is as entitled to punish Martin as one guilty of murder as New York to punish Patterson.

It would be quite different if the jury had been instructed that the self-defense evidence could not be considered in determining whether there was reasonable doubt about the state's case, i.e., that self-defense evidence must be put aside for all purposes unless it satisfied the preponderance standard. Such instruction would relieve the state of its burden and plainly run afoul of *Winship*'s mandate. 397 U.S., at 364, 90 S. Ct., at 1072. The instructions in this case could be clearer in this respect, but when read as a whole, we think they are adequate to convey to the jury that all of the evidence, including the evidence going to self-defense, must be considered in deciding whether there was a reasonable doubt about the sufficiency of the state's proof of the elements of the crime.

We are thus not moved by assertions that the elements of aggravated murder and self-defense overlap in the sense that evidence to prove the latter will often tend to negate the former. It may be that most encounters in which self-defense is claimed arise suddenly and involve no prior plan or specific purpose to take life. In those cases, evidence offered to support the defense may negate a purposeful killing by prior calculation and design, but Ohio does not shift to the defendant the burden of disproving any element in the state's case. When the prosecution has made out a *prima facie* case and survives a motion to acquit, the jury may nevertheless not convict if the evidence offered by the defendant raises any reasonable doubt about the existence of any fact necessary for the finding of guilt. Evidence creating a reasonable doubt could easily fall short of proving self-defense by a preponderance of the evidence. Of course, if such doubt is not raised in the jury's mind and each juror is convinced that the defendant purposely and with prior calculation and design took life, the killing will still be excused if the elements for the defense are satisfactorily established. We note here, but need not rely on it, the observation of the Supreme Court of Ohio that "Appellant did not dispute the existence of [the elements of aggravated murder], but rather sought to justify her actions on grounds she acted in self-defense." 21 Ohio St. 3d, at 94, 488 N.E.2d, at 168.[**]

Petitioner submits that there can be no conviction under Ohio law unless the defendant's conduct is unlawful and that because self-defense renders lawful what would otherwise be a crime, unlawfulness is an element of the offense that the state must prove by disproving self-defense. This argument founders on state law, for it has been rejected by the Ohio Supreme Court and by the Court of Appeals for the Sixth Circuit. *White v. Arn*, 788 F.2d 338, 346-347 (CA6 1986); *State v. Morris*, 8 Ohio App. 3d 12, 18-19, 455 N.E.2d 1352, 1359-1360 (1982). It is true that unlawfulness is essential for conviction, but the Ohio courts hold that the unlawfulness in cases like this is the conduct satisfying the elements of aggravated murder—an interpretation of

---

[**]   The dissent believes that the self-defense instruction might have led the jury to believe that the defendant had the burden of proving prior calculation and design. Indeed, its position is that no instruction could be clear enough not to mislead the jury. As is evident from the test, we disagree. We do not harbor the dissent's mistrust of the jury; and the instructions were sufficiently clear to convey to the jury that the state's burden of proving prior calculation did not shift and that self-defense evidence had to be considered in determining whether the state's burden had been discharged. We do not depart from Patterson v. New York, 432 U.S. 197, 97 S. Ct. 2319, 53 L. Ed. 2d 281 (1977), in this respect, or in any other.

state law that we are not in a position to dispute. The same is true of the claim that it is necessary to prove a "criminal" intent to convict for serious crimes, which cannot occur if self-defense is shown: the necessary mental state for aggravated murder under Ohio law is the specific purpose to take life pursuant to prior calculation and design. See *White v. Arn, supra,* at 346.

As we noted in *Patterson,* the common law rule was that affirmative defenses, including self-defense, were matters for the defendant to prove. "This was the rule when the Fifth Amendment was adopted, and it was the American rule when the Fourteenth Amendment was ratified." 432 U.S., at 202 97 S. Ct., at 2322. Indeed, well into this century, a number of States followed the common law rule and required a defendant to shoulder the burden of proving that he acted in self-defense. Fletcher, Two Kinds of Legal Rules: A Comparative Study of Burden-of-Persuasion Practices in Criminal Cases, 77 Yale L.J. 880, 882, and n. 10 (1968). We are aware that all but two of the States, Ohio and South Carolina, have abandoned the common law rule and require the prosecution to prove the absence of self-defense when it is properly raised by the defendant. But the question remains whether those States are in violation of the Constitution; and, as we observed in *Patterson,* that question is not answered by cataloging the practices of other States. We are no more convinced that the Ohio practice of requiring self-defense to be proved

by the defendant is unconstitutional than we are that the Constitution requires the prosecution to prove the sanity of a defendant who pleads not guilty by reason of insanity. We have had the opportunity to depart from *Leland v. Oregon* but have refused to do so. *Rivera v. Delaware,* 429 U.S. 877, 97 S. Ct. 226, 50 L. Ed. 2d 160 (1976). These cases were important to the *Patterson* decision and they, along with *Patterson,* are authority for our decision today.

The judgment of the Ohio Supreme Court is accordingly

Affirmed.

Justice Powell, with whom Justice BRENNAN and Justice MARSHALL join, and with whom Justice BLACKMUN joins with respect to Parts I and III, dissenting.

Today the Court holds that a defendant can be convicted of aggravated murder even though the jury may have a reasonable doubt whether the accused acted in self-defense, and thus, whether he is guilty of a crime. Because I think this decision is inconsistent with both precedent and fundamental fairness, I dissent.

I

Petitioner Earline Martin was tried in state court for the aggravated murder of her husband. Under Ohio law, the elements of the crime are that the defendant have purposely killed another with "prior calculation and design." Ohio Rev. Code Ann.

§2903.01 (1982). Martin admitted that she shot her husband, but claimed that she acted in self-defense. Because self-defense is classified as an "affirmative" defense in Ohio, the jury was instructed that Martin had the burden of proving her claim by a preponderance of the evidence. Martin apparently failed to carry this burden, and the jury found her guilty.

The Ohio Supreme Court upheld the conviction, relying in part on this Court's opinion in *Patterson v. New York*, 432 U.S. 197, 53 L. Ed. 2d 281, 97 S. Ct. 2319 (1977). The Court today also relies on the *Patterson* reasoning in affirming the Ohio decision. If one accepts *Patterson* as the proper method of analysis for this case, I believe that the Court's opinion ignores its central meaning.

In *Patterson*, the Court upheld a state statute that shifted the burden of proof for an affirmative defense to the accused. New York law required the prosecutor to prove all of the statutorily defined elements of murder beyond a reasonable doubt, but permitted a defendant to reduce the charge to manslaughter by showing that he acted while suffering an "extreme emotional disturbance." See N.Y. Penal Law §§ 125.25, 125.20 (McKinney 1975 and Supp. 1987). The Court found that this burden-shifting did not violate due process, largely because the affirmative defense did "not serve to negative any facts of the crime which the State is to prove in order to convict of murder." 432 U.S., at 207, 97 S. Ct., at 2325. The clear implication of this ruling is

that when an affirmative defense does negate an element of the crime, the state may not shift the burden. See *White v. Arn*, 788 F.2d 338, 344-345 (CA6 1986). In such a case, *In re Winship*, 397 U.S. 358, 90 S. Ct. 1068, 25 L. Ed. 2d (1970), requires the state to prove the nonexistence of the defense beyond a reasonable doubt.

The reason for treating a defense that negates an element of the crime differently from other affirmative defenses is plain. If the jury is told that the prosecution has the burden of proving all the elements of a crime, but then also is instructed that the defendant has the same burden of disproving one of these elements, there is a danger that the jurors will resolve the inconsistency in a way that lessens the presumption of innocence. For example, the jury might reasonably believe that by raising the defense, the accused has assumed the ultimate burden of proving that particular element. Or, it might reconcile the instructions simply by balancing the evidence that supports the prosecutor's case against the evidence supporting the affirmative defense, and conclude that the state has satisfied its burden if the prosecution's version is more persuasive. In either case, the jury is given the unmistakable but erroneous impression that the defendant shares the risk of nonpersuasion as to a fact necessary for conviction.[1]

---

[1] Indeed, this type of instruction has an inherently illogical aspect. It makes no sense to say that the prosecution has the burden of proving an element beyond a reasonable doubt and that

Given these principles, the Court's reliance on *Patterson* is puzzling. Under Ohio law, the element of "prior calculation and design" is satisfied only when the accused has engaged in a "definite process of reasoning *in advance* of the killing," *i.e.*, when he has given the plan at least some "studied consideration." App. 14 (jury instructions, emphasis added). In contrast, when a defendant such as Martin raises a claim of self-defense, the jury also is instructed that the accused must prove that she "had an honest belief that she was in imminent danger of death or great bodily harm." Id., at 19 (emphasis added). In many cases, a defendant who finds himself in immediate danger and reacts with deadly force will not have formed a

_____

the defense has the burden of proving the contrary by a preponderance of the evidence. If the jury finds that the prosecutor has not met his burden, it of course will have no occasion to consider the affirmative defense. And if the jury finds that each element of the crime has been proved beyond a reasonable doubt, it necessarily has decided that the defendant has not disproved an element of the crime. In either situation the instructions on the affirmative defense are surplusage. Because a reasonable jury will attempt to ascribe some significance to the court's instructions, the likelihood that it will impermissibly shift the burden is increased.

Of course, whether the jury will in fact improperly shift the burden away from the state is uncertain. But it is "settled law . . . that when there exists a reasonable possibility that the jury relied on an unconstitutional understanding of the law in reaching a guilty verdict, that verdict must be must be set aside." Francis v. Franklin, 471 U.S. 307; 323 n. 8, 105 S. Ct. 1965, 1976 n. 8, 85 L. Ed. 2d 344 (1985).

prior intent to kill. The Court recognizes this when it states:

"It may be that most encounters in which self-defense is claimed arise suddenly and involve no prior plan or specific purpose to take life. In those cases, evidence offered to support the defense may negate a purposeful killing by prior calculation and design. . . ." *Ante*, at 1102.

Under *Patterson*, this conclusion should suggest that Ohio is precluded from shifting the burden as to self-defense. The Court nevertheless concludes that Martin was properly required to prove self-defense, simply because "Ohio does not shift to the defendant the burden of disproving any element of the state's case." *Ibid.*

The Court gives no explanation for this apparent rejection of *Patterson*. The only justification advanced for the Court's decision is that the jury could have used the evidence of self-defense to find that the state failed to carry its burden of proof. Because the jurors were free to consider both Martin's and the state's evidence, the argument goes, the verdict of guilt necessarily means that they were convinced that the defendant acted with prior calculation and design, and were unpersuaded that she acted in self-defense. *Ante*, at 1101. The Court thus seems to conclude that as long as the jury is told that the state has the burden of proving all elements of the crime, the overlap between the offense and defense is immaterial.

This reasoning is flawed in two respects. First, it simply ignores the problem that arises from inconsistent jury instructions in a criminal case. The Court's holding implicitly assumes that the jury in fact understands that the ultimate burden remains with the prosecutor at all times, despite a conflicting instruction that places the burden on the accused to disprove the same element. But as pointed out above, the *Patterson* distinction between defenses that negate an element of the crime and those that do not is based on the legitimate concern that the jury *will* mistakenly lower the state's burden. In short, the Court's rationale fails to explain why the overlap in this case does not create the risk that *Patterson* suggested was unacceptable.

Second, the Court significantly, and without explanation, extends the deference granted to state legislatures in this area. Today's decision could be read to say that virtually all state attempts to shift the burden of proof for affirmative defenses will be upheld, regardless of the relationship between the elements of the defense and the elements of the crime. As I understand it, *Patterson* allowed burden-shifting because evidence of an extreme emotional disturbance did not negate the *mens rea* of the underlying offense. After today's decision, however, even if proof of the defense does negate an element of the offense, burden-shifting still may be permitted because the jury can consider the defendant's evidence when reaching its verdict.

I agree, of course, that States must have substantial leeway in defining their criminal laws and administering their criminal justice systems. But none of our precedents suggests that courts must give complete deference to a State's judgment about whether a shift in the burden of proof is consistent with the presumption of innocence. In the past we have emphasized that in some circumstances it may be necessary to look beyond the text of the State's burden-shifting laws to satisfy ourselves that the requirements of *Winship* have been satisfied. In *Mullaney v. Wilbur*, 421 U.S. 684, 698-699, 95 S. Ct. 1881, 1889, 44 L. Ed. 2d 508 (1975) we explicitly noted the danger of granting the State unchecked discretion to shift the burden as to any element of proof in a criminal case. The Court today fails to discuss or even cite *Mullaney*, despite our unanimous agreement in that case that this danger would justify judicial intervention in some cases. Even *Patterson*, from which I dissented, recognized that "there are obviously constitutional limits beyond which the States may not go [in labeling elements of a crime as an affirmative defense]." Today, however, the Court simply asserts that Ohio law properly allocates the burdens, without giving any indication of where those limits lie.

Because our precedent establishes that the burden of proof may not be shifted when the elements of the defense and the elements of the offense conflict, and because it seems clear that they do so in this case, I would reverse the decision of the Ohio Supreme Court.

II

Although I believe that this case is wrongly decided even under the principles set forth in *Patterson*, my differences with the Court's approach are more fundamental. I continue to believe that the better method for deciding when a state may shift the burden of proof is outlined in the Court's opinion in *Mullaney* and in my dissenting opinion in *Patterson*. In *Mullaney*, we emphasized that the state's obligation to prove certain facts beyond a reasonable doubt was not necessarily restricted to legislative distinctions between offenses and affirmative defenses. The boundaries of the state's authority in this respect were elaborated in the *Patterson* dissent, where I proposed a two-part inquiry:

"The Due Process Clause requires that the prosecutor bear the burden of persuasion beyond a reasonable doubt only if the factor at issue makes a substantial difference in punishment and stigma. The requirement of course applies *a fortiori* if the factor makes the difference between guilt and innocence. . . . It also must be shown that in the Anglo-American legal tradition the factor in question historically has held that level of importance. If either branch of the test is not met, then the legislature retains its traditional authority over matters of proof." 432 U.S., at

226-227, 97 S. Ct., at 2335 (footnotes omitted).

Cf. *McMillan v. Pennsylvania*, 477 U.S. ___, ___, 106 S. Ct. 2411, 2421, 91 L. Ed. 2d 67 (1986) (STEVENS, J., dissenting) ("if a State provides that a specific component of a prohibited transaction shall give rise both to a special stigma and to a special punishment, that component must be treated as a 'fact necessary to constitute the crime' within the meaning of our holding in *In re Winship*").

There are at least two benefits to this approach. First, it ensures that the critical facts necessary to sustain a conviction will be proved by the state. Because the Court would be willing to look beyond the text of a state statute, legislatures would have no incentive to redefine essential elements of an offense to make them part of an affirmative defense, thereby shifting the burden of proof in a manner inconsistent with *Winship* and *Mullaney*. Second, it would leave the states free in all other respects to recognize new factors that may mitigate the degree of criminality or punishment, without requiring that they also bear the burden of disproving these defenses. See *Patterson v. New York*, 432 U.S., at 229-230, 97 S. Ct., at 2336-2337 (POWELL, J., dissenting) ("New ameliorative affirmative defenses . . . generally remain undisturbed by the holdings in *Winship* and *Mullaney*" (footnote omitted)).

Under this analysis, it plainly is impermissible to require the accused to prove self-defense. If petitioner could have carried her burden, the result would have been decisively different as to both guilt and punishment. There also is no dispute that self-defense historically is one of the primary justifications for otherwise unlawful conduct. See *e.g.*, *Beard v. United States*, 158 U.S. 550, 562, 15 S. Ct. 962, 39 L. Ed. 1086 (1895). Thus, while I acknowledge that the two-part test may be difficult to apply at times, it is hard to imagine a more clear-cut application than the one presented here.

III

In its willingness to defer to the State's legislative definitions of crimes and defenses, the Court apparently has failed to recognize the practical effect of its decision. Martin alleged that she was innocent because she acted in self-defense, a complete justification under Ohio law. See *State v. Nolton*, 19 Ohio St. 2d 133, 249 N.E.2d 797 (1969). Because she had the burden of proof on this issue, the jury could have believed that it was just as likely as not that Martin's conduct was justified, and yet still have voted to convict. In other words, even thought the jury may have had a substantial doubt whether Martin committed a crime, she was found guilty under Ohio law. I do not agree that the Court's authority to review state legislative choices is so limited that it justifies increasing the risk of convicting a person who may not be blameworthy. See *Patterson v. New York*, *supra*, 432 U.S., at 201-202, 97 S. Ct., at 2322 (state definition of criminal law must yield when it "'offends some principle of justice so rooted in the traditions and conscience of our people as to be ranked as fundamental'" (quoting *Speiser v. Randall*, 357 U.S. 513, 523, 78 S. Ct. 1332, 1340, 2 L. Ed. 2d 1460 (1958)). The complexity of the inquiry as to when a state may shift the burden of proof should not lead the Court to fashion simple rules of deference that could lead to such unjust results.

Cases relating to Chapter 4
PROOF VIA EVIDENCE

MADDOX v. MONTGOMERY

718 F.2d 1033 (11th Cir. 1983)

Before FAY, VANCE and KRA-VITCH, Circuit Judges.

PER CURIAM:

Appellant Jimmy Maddox was convicted of rape in a Georgia state court and sentenced to life imprisonment. At the trial, appellant and the alleged victim, Kathy Elder, gave radically different accounts of the events in question. Elder testified that on a number of occasions prior to the alleged rape, appellant had approached her purportedly seeking to sell her an insurance policy. On the morning in question, while Elder was dressing her two sons, appellant appeared at her apartment and again asked whether she wanted the insurance. After explaining that she had discovered that she could get insurance at work, Elder went into the bedroom to retrieve coats for the boys. Elder testified that appellant followed her into the room and forcibly raped her on the bed. Another witness for the prosecution, Debbie Phillips, testified that she had once taken out insurance with appellant, but had dropped it after he had come to her home on a Saturday night. Appellant testified that he and Elder had had voluntary sexual relations on several occasions prior to the alleged rape and that Elder

had consented to their sexual relations on the morning in question.

Having unsuccessfully pursued his direct appeal and the state post-conviction remedy, appellant filed a federal habeas corpus petition alleging prosecutorial suppression of exculpatory evidence in violation of the doctrine of *Brady v. Maryland,* 373 U.S. 83, 83 S.Ct. 1194, 10 L.Ed.2d 215 (1963). Specifically, appellant asserted that his right to due process was violated by the state's failure to disclose (1) a photograph taken by the police shortly after the alleged rape showing Elder's bed neatly made, (2) the results of a police examination of the bedspread which revealed no blood, semen or other fluid, and (3) a written statement by another witness, Brenda Phelps, that Debbie Phillips had stated that she dropped her insurance with appellant for financial reasons. Appellant appeals the denial of habeas relief. We affirm.

There are four types of situations in which the *Brady* doctrine applies:

(1) the prosecutor has not disclosed information despite a specific defense request; (2) the prosecutor has not disclosed information despite a general defense

461

request for all exculpatory information or without any defense request at all; (3) the prosecutor knows or should know that the conviction is based on false evidence[;(4)] the prosecutor fails to disclose purely impeaching evidence not concerning a substantive issue, in the absence of a specific defense request. *United States* v. *Anderson*, 574 F.2d 1347, 1353 (5th Cir. 1978). Inasmuch as appellant filed no pretrial request—specific or general—for exculpatory information, the present case falls within the second category with respect to the photograph of the bed and the results of the police examination of the bedspread and within the fourth category with respect to Phelps' statement.

In order to prevail on a *Brady* claim, one must establish the materiality of the exculpatory information suppressed by the prosecution. The applicable threshold of materiality, however, varies depending on the type of situation. Where, as here, the state failed to disclose substantive evidence favorable to the defendant for which there was no specific request, the standard set forth in *United States* v. *Agurs*, 427 U.S. 97, 96 S.Ct. 2392, 49 L.Ed.2d 342 (1976), governs. In *Agurs*, the Supreme Court stated that such a failure to disclose violates due process only "if the omitted evidence creates a reasonable doubt that did not otherwise exist." *Id.* at 112, 96 S.Ct. at 2401; *accord United States* v. *Kubiak*, 704 F.2d 1545, 1551 (11th Cir. 1983). In *Cannon* v. *Alabama*, 558 F.2d 1211 (5th Cir. 1977), cert. denied, 434 U.S. 1087, 98 S.Ct. 1281, 55 L.Ed.2d 792 (1978), the former Fifth Circuit explained:

Applying this standard requires an analysis of the evidence adduced at trial and of the probable impact of the undisclosed information. In this context, we cannot merely consider the evidence in the light most favorable to the government but must instead evaluate all the evidence as it would bear on the deliberations of a factfinder. *Id.* at 1213-14.

With regard to the photograph of the bed, we agree with the district court that "the undisclosed photograph does not create a reasonable doubt as to [appellant's] guilt that did not otherwise exist," Order, p. 8, and thus is not material under *Agurs*. Similarly, the results of the police examination of the bedspread do not give rise to a reasonable doubt and again are immaterial under *Agurs*. Although both pieces of evidence, if admitted at trial, might conceivably have affected the jury's verdict, the constitutional threshold of materiality is higher. See *Agurs*, 427 U.S. at 108-09, 96 S.Ct. at 2400. Insofar as this information is merely consistent with appellant's version of the incident and scarcely contradicts the alleged victim's testimony, and in view of the substantial inculpatory evidence in the record, the evidence at issue is not sufficiently material to render the state's failure to disclose unconstitutional.

The standard of materiality in a case, such as this one, involving the prosecution's suppression of impeaching evidence absent a specific request was recently discussed in *United States* v. *Blasco*, 702 F.2d 1315 (11th Cir.), cert. denied, _____ U.S. ____, ____, 104 S.Ct. 275, 276,

78 L.Ed.2d 256 (1983). There this Court noted, "[i]f the suppressed evidence is purely impeaching evidence and no defense request has been made, the suppressed evidence is material only if its introduction probably would have resulted in acquittal." *Id.* at 1328; *accord Anderson,* 574 F.2d at 1354. Given the relatively minor role of Phillips' testimony and the limited impact that Phelps' statement would likely have had on the jury's assessment of Phillips' credibility, appellant is unable to demonstrate that the undisclosed evidence probably would have resulted in an acquittal. Accordingly, the evidence is immaterial under *Blasco,* and its suppression did not violate appellant's due process right.

For the foregoing reasons, the district court's dismissal of appellant's habeas petition is AFFIRMED.

UNITED STATES v. NELSON

419 F.2d 1237 (9th Cir. 1969)

[Footnotes omitted]

BROWNING, Circuit Judge:

Roy Arthur Nelson and Frank Brewton were indicted for robbery of a federally-insured institution in violation of 18 U.S.C. § 2113(a) (1964). Brewton was found incompetent to stand trial. Nelson was tried separately and convicted. He has appealed on three grounds, all of which relate to the use of circumstantial evidence to secure his conviction.

The government offered direct evidence of the following facts. Brewton entered a bank and presented a teller with a written demand for money. The teller handed Brewton $627 in currency, including five marked $20 bills. Meanwhile, an unidentified person was observed sitting in a car in an adjacent parking lot, racing the engine. Brewton fled from the bank to the waiting car and entered on the passenger side. The car immediately sped away. Shortly thereafter, a police officer, alerted to these incidents, observed the car, with two male occupants, at an intersection some blocks away. The car fled. The officer pursued at high speed. After a chase the car slowed down, defendant alighted from the driver's side and ran, and was captured. Currency in the amount of $125 was taken from his person. The car, driverless, crashed into a tree. Brewton emerged from the wreck, and was arrested after attempting to conceal $502 in currency, including the marked bills taken from the bank, under an adjacent building. Ten to fifteen minutes elapsed between the robbery of the bank and defendant's flight from the car.

Defendant asserts that since he was charged as a principal in the bank robbery rather than as an accessory after the fact, the government was required to prove that he had actual knowledge that Brewton intended to rob the bank. We assume, arguendo, that proof of precisely that specific knowledge was required.

Defendant contended below, and

in this court, that such proof was lacking. He argued that if such knowledge could be inferred at all, the inference must be based upon the prior inference that he was the man waiting in the car while the robbery occurred—and such an "inference upon an inference" was precluded by law. Further, he argued that even if the jury were permitted to infer that he knowingly acted as the "get-away" driver, there was no evidence that he knew Brewton planned to commit a robbery, as distinguished from some other illegal act, or planned to rob the bank, and not one of the several stores and offices in the area, and that circumstantial evidence which does not "exclude every hypothesis but that of guilt" is insufficient as a matter of law.

The court denied a motion for acquittal based on these grounds, and rejected proposed instructions embodying the theories that a conviction could not be based upon inferences drawn from other inferences, or upon circumstances "which while consistent with guilt, are not inconsistent with innocence."

The legal theories upon which defendant relies, although clearly wrong, are repeatedly asserted in the trial courts of this circuit and in fruitless appeals to this court. It would be a boon to both the parties and the courts if they could be laid finally to rest.

For at least a third of a century this court has rejected the notion that it is improper to infer a fact at issue from other facts which have been established by circumstantial evidence. *E. K. Wood Lumber Co. v. Anderson*, 81 F.2d 161, 166 (9th Cir. 1936); *Ross v. United States*, 103 F.2d 600, 606 (9th Cir. 1939);

Fegles Construction Co. v. McLaughlin Construction Co., 205 F.2d 637, 639-640 (9th Cir. 1953); *Toliver v. United States*, 224 F.2d 742, 745 (9th Cir. 1955); *Medrano v. United States*, 315 F.2d 361, 362 (9th Cir. 1963); *Devore v. United States*, 368 F.2d 396, 399 (9th Cir. 1966). As Professor Wigmore has said, "[t]here is no such orthodox rule; nor can be. If there were, hardly a single trial could be adequately presented." 1 Wigmore, Evidence, § 41, at 435 (3rd ed. 1940).

The error in this discredited doctrine is clearly reflected in the defendant's formulation: it assumes that a fact established by circumstantial evidence is not a "proven fact." But as we have repeatedly said, circumstantial evidence is not inherently less probative than direct evidence. Under some conditions it may even be more reliable, as this case illustrates.

The intermediate fact at issue here was whether defendant was the driver of the car waiting in the parking lot. That fact was established to a moral certainty by circumstances proven by uncontradicted and unquestioned testimony. Unless defendant was Brewton's accomplice waiting in the get-away car, it is all but inconceivable that he would have been driving that car with Brewton as a passenger a few minutes after Brewton ran from the bank to the car and was driven from the scene; that he would have had part of the stolen currency in his possession, and Brewton the rest; and that upon seeing the police officer he would have driven away at high speed, and later fled from the officer on foot.

If none of this circumstantial evidence had been available and the only evidence offered had been a courtroom identification of the defendant by a witness who had a fleeting glimpse of the driver as the car stood in the parking lot, the truth of the fact that defendant was that man would not have been established with equal certainty.

Of course either direct or circumstantial evidence may fail to prove the fact in issue—direct evidence because the credibility of the witness is destroyed; circumstantial evidence for that reason, or because the inference from the proven circumstances to the fact in issue is too speculative, or remote. Whether such a failure has occurred is an appropriate inquiry in any case—be the evidence direct, circumstantial, or both. But since under some conditions circumstantial evidence may be equally or more reliable than direct evidence, it would be wholly irrational to impose an absolute bar upon the use of circumstantial evidence to prove any fact, including a fact from which another fact is to be inferred.

The trial court therefore properly refused to instruct the jury that "one inference may not be based upon another inference to support a conclusion of fact." It would be error for the jury, the trial court, or this court, to apply such an arbitrary formula in the performance of their respective roles in the fact-finding process.

It is also clear that the court properly rejected defendant's proposed instruction embodying a variation on the theme that circumstantial evidence must exclude every hypothesis but that of guilt. This much, at least, is settled by

Holland v. *United States,* 348 U.S. 121, 75 S.Ct. 127, 99 L.Ed. 150 (1955). What the *Holland* court said is brief, and well worth repeating in full:

"The petitioners assail the refusal of the trial judge to instruct that where the Government's evidence is circumstantial it must be such as to exclude every reasonable hypothesis other than that of guilt. There is some support for this type of instruction in the lower court decisions, *Garst* v. *United States,* 4 Cir., 180 F. 339, 343; *Anderson* v. *United States,* 5 Cir., 30 F.2d 485-487; *Stutz* v. *United States,* 5 Cir., 47 F.2d 1029, 1030; *Hanson* v. *United States,* 6 Cir., 208 F.2d 914, 916, but the better rule is that where the jury is properly instructed on the standards for reasonable doubt, such an additional instruction on circumstantial evidence is confusing and incorrect, *United States* v. *Austin-Bagley Corp.,* 2 Cir., 31 F.2d 229, 234, cert. denied, 279 U.S. 863, 49 S.Ct. 479, 73 L.Ed. 1002; *United States* v. *Becker,* 2 Cir., 62 F.2d 1007, 1010; 1 Wigmore, Evidence (3d ed.), § § 25-26.

Circumstantial evidence in this respect is intrinsically no different from testimonial evidence. Admittedly, circumstantial evidence may in some cases point to a wholly incorrect result. Yet this is equally true of testimonial evidence. In both instances, a jury is asked to weigh the chances that the evidence correctly points to guilt against the possibility of inaccuracy or ambiguous inference. In both, the jury must use its experience with people and events in weighing the probabilities. If the jury is convinced beyond a reasonable doubt, we can require no more." 348 U.S. at 139-140, 75 S.Ct. at 137 (emphasis added).

The Supreme Court did more than reject the particular instruction before it; it clearly stated that *no* instruction is to be given distinguishing the manner in which direct and circumstantial evidence are to be weighed. Since circumstantial and testimonial evidence are indistinguishable so far as the jury's fact-finding function is concerned, all that is to be required of the jury is that it weigh *all* of the evidence, direct or circumstantial, against the standard of reasonable doubt.

Our holdings are in accord with this interpretation of *Holland*. *Mull v. United States*, 402 F.2d 571, 575 (9th Cir. 1968); *Ramirez v. United States*, 350 F.2d 306, 307-308 (9th Cir. 1965); *Armstrong v. United States*, 327 F.2d 189, 194 (9th Cir. 1964); *Strangway v. United States*, 312 F.2d 283, 285 (9th Cir. 1963). Indeed, this was the rule in this circuit prior to *Holland*. *Samuel v. United States*, 169 F.2d 787, 791 (9th Cir. 1948); *McCoy v. United States*, 169 F.2d 776, 784 (9th Cir. 1948); *see also Penosi v. United States*, 206 F.2d 529, 530 (9th Cir. 1953).

Thus the trial court properly instructed the jury that "the law makes no distinction between direct and circumstantial evidence but simply requires that the jury be satisfied of the defendant's guilt beyond a reasonable doubt from all the evidence in the case," including "such reasonable inferences as seem justified, in the light of your own experience." Under *Holland* and the

uniform decisions of this court, no additional instruction was required, and none would have been proper. The contrary dictum in *Matthews v. United States*, 394 F.2d 104, 105 (9th Cir. 1968), must therefore be disregarded.

* * *

The second question is that specifically raised by the defendant, namely, whether the court is also to inquire whether the evidence "excludes every hypothesis but that of guilt."

Precisely as put, the test is unquestionably wrong. Although we have frequently stated the rule as defendant does, it has never been held that the evidence must exclude "*every* hypothesis," as distinguished from every reasonable hypothesis, of innocence. Furthermore, in applying the test, the question is not whether the court itself would find that every reasonable hypothesis of innocence had been excluded, but rather whether the jurors could reasonably arrive at that conclusion.

Thus, as first stated in this court in *Stoppelli v. United States*, 183 F.2d 391, 393 (9th Cir. 1950), the test was as follows:

"The testimony * * * was sufficient to go to the jury if its nature was such that reasonable minds could differ as to whether inferences other than guilt could be drawn from it. It is not for us to say that the evidence was insufficient because we, or any of us, believe that inferences inconsistent with guilt may be drawn from it. To say that would make us triers of the fact. We may say that the evidence is insufficient to sustain the verdict only if we can conclude *as a matter of law* that reasonable minds, as triers of the fact, must be in agreement that reasonable hypotheses other than guilt could be drawn from the evidence."

This formulation, commonly condensed to "whether 'reasonable minds could find the evidence excludes every hypothesis but that of guilt,'" appears frequently in our opinions.

Yet this is precisely the standard which was rejected by the Supreme Court in *Holland* v. *United States, supra,* 348 U.S. at 139, 75 S.Ct. 127, as a guide for the jury, on the ground that it was "confusing and incorrect." *Id.* at 140, 75 S.Ct. 127. Our opinions demonstrate that it is equally confusing as a guide for the reviewing court. Moreover, if it is "incorrect" as an instruction defining the jury's duty, it must be equally "incorrect" as a test for determining whether the jury has performed its duty within the limits fixed by the instructions. Accordingly, most courts have held that its use as a test of the sufficiency of the evidence on review is inconsistent with *Holland*.

The "reasonable hypothesis" test was formulated for the evaluation of circumstantial evidence; it is often referred to as the "circumstantial evidence test." *See, e.g.,* Comment, Sufficiency of Circumstantial Evidence in a Criminal Case, 55 Colum. L.Rev. 549 (1955). As we have noted, the Supreme Court rejected the test in *Holland* on the premise that there is no essential difference in the mental processes required of the jury in weighing direct and circumstantial evidence. As to both, "the jury must use its experience with people and events in weighing the probabilities. If the jury is convinced beyond a reasonable doubt, we can require no more." *Holland,* 348 U.S. at 140, 75 S.Ct. at 138.

The key word is "probabilities." The jury cannot determine that a proposition is true or false, but only that it is more or less probable. Guilt "is proved beyond a reasonable doubt if it is proved not only to be more probable than its contradictory but to be much more probable than its contradictory." Adler & Michael, The Trial of an Issue of Fact I, 34 Colum.L.Rev. 1224, 1256 (1934). The required degree of probability is reached if the jury is free of "the kind of doubt that would make a person hesitate to act" in the more serious and important affairs of his own life. *Holland* v. *United States, supra,* 348 U.S. at 140, 75 S.Ct. at 138.

It adds only an illusion of certainty, and is both misleading and wrong, to attempt to describe this broad exercise of practical judgment in abstract generalizations borrowed from the terminology of formal logic.

The "reasonable hypothesis" test does not reflect what juries and reviewing courts in reality do. Juries constantly convict, and the convictions are duly affirmed, on evidence upon which none would hesitate to act but which cannot be said to exclude as a matter of inexorable logic, every reasonable hypothetical consistent with innocence.

Moreover, the impression left by appellate court opinions is that the "reasonable hypothesis" standard may lead to serious departures from the proper appellate role in evaluating the sufficiency of evidence. Courts following the rule exhibit a noticeable tendency to divide the evidence into separate lines of proof, and analyze and test each line of proof independently of others rather than considering the evidence as an interrelated whole. The sufficiency of the evidence is often tested against theoretical and speculative possibilities not fairly raised by the record, and inferences are sometimes considered which, though entirely possible or even probable, are drawn from evidence which the jury may have disbelieved.

We affirm the denial of the motion for acquittal in this case because we are satisfied that the jurors reasonably could decide that they would not hesitate to act in their own serious affairs upon factual assumptions as probable as the conclusion that defendant planned and executed the robbery of the bank as a joint venture with Brewton in which each carried out a prearranged role.

Affirmed.

Cases relating to Chapter 5
JUDICIAL NOTICE

STATE v. VEJVODA

231 Neb. 668, 438 N.W.2d 461 (1989)

HASTINGS, C.J., and BOSLAUGH, WHITE, CAPORALE, SHANAHAN, and FAHRNBRUCH, JJ.

SHANAHAN, Justice.

In a bench trial in the county court for Hall County, Mark Vejvoda was convicted of drunk driving and received an enhanced sentence as the result of his second conviction for drunk driving. See Neb.Rev.Stat. §39-669.07 (Reissue 1988). On appeal, the district court affirmed Vejvoda's conviction and sentence. Vejvoda contends that the evidence is insufficient to sustain his conviction for drunk driving and that the State failed to prove that Hall County was the venue for his trial because the court improperly took judicial notice that locations mentioned in Vejvoda's trial were within Hall County.

VEJVODA'S TRIAL

Officer Elmer Edwards of the Grand Island Police Department was the sole witness at Vejvoda's trial. Edwards testified that on May 1, 1987, at 2:14 a.m., he was in the vicinity of 7th and Vine Streets and noticed a vehicle proceeding west on 7th Street, "weaving back and forth

across the entire width of the street." Edwards had observed the vehicle for 2 1/2 to 3 blocks," when the car commenced a wide right turn from 7th Street onto Oak Street and "ran over the curb section located at the . . . northeast corner of the intersection." In pursuit, Edwards followed the car northbound on Oak Street to 8th Street, where Edwards stopped the pursued vehicle.

On confronting the car's driver, whom Edwards eventually identified as Vejvoda, Edwards observed that Vejvoda's eyes were bloodshot and watery, and a strong odor of alcohol emanated from Vejvoda's car. According to Edwards, Vejvoda's reactions were "slow and sluggish" while he fumbled to produce a driver's license. Edwards then asked Vejvoda to step out of his car for field sobriety tests. Vejvoda was "swaying and wobbling" and had difficulty maintaining his balance during the field sobriety tests. In Edwards' opinion, Vejvoda was under the influence of alcohol when stopped by the officer, who later arrested Vejvoda for drunk driving. In all his testimony concerning his observations, pursuit, and stop of the vehicle, Edwards never mentioned the city or county where the events occurred. Defense counsel did not cross-examine Edwards, and the prosecution rested.

After Vejvoda offered no evidence, the prosecutor apparently realized that Edwards had not testified that the events involving Vejvoda occurred in Hall County. When the prosecutor asked leave to recall Edwards for testimony concerning the location of the events, the court responded, "The Court will take judicial notice of the fact that all of the addresses and areas described are those—are those within the city limits of the city of Grand Island which lies wholly within Hall County." Vejvoda objected to the court's "taking judicial notice after the . . . State has rested." In closing argument, Vejvoda argued, among other things, that the State had failed to prove proper venue. The court then found Vejvoda guilty of drunk driving.

Vejvoda contends, first, that there is insufficient evidence to sustain his conviction for drunk driving, and, second, the court improperly took judicial notice of facts establishing the site of the events on which his conviction is based. In essence, Vejvoda's venue claim is an assertion that the court improperly took judicial notice that Grand Island in Hall County was the site of the events in question and, as the result of the improper judicial notice, determined that venue was evidentially established as Hall County.

SUFFICIENCY OF EVIDENCE

In determining whether evidence is sufficient to sustain a conviction in a bench trial, the Supreme Court does not resolve conflicts of evidence, pass on credibility of witnesses, evaluate explanations, or reweigh evidence presented, which are within a fact finder's province for disposition. A conviction in a bench trial of a criminal case is sustained if the evidence, viewed and construed most favorably to the State, is sufficient to support that conviction. See *State v. Brown*, 225 Neb. 418, 405 N.W.2d 600 (1987).

With no explanation for the obvious or further comment necessary, we find that the evidence supports Vejvoda's conviction for drunk driving, the substantive offense charged against Vejvoda.

GUARANTEE OF VENUE

The venue problem in this appeal could have been easily avoided by the court's merely granting the State's motion to withdraw its rest and present evidence on venue. "Even in criminal prosecutions the withdrawal of a rest in a trial on the merits is within the discretion of the trial court." *State v. Putnam*, 178 Neb. 445, 448-449, 133 N.W.2d 605, 608 (1965). Unfortunately, however, instead of allowing the State to recall Edwards to answer a single, simple question identifying venue, the court chose to try to remedy the evidential situation and created the venue problem presented in Vejvoda's appeal.

Vejvoda claims that "an accused is guaranteed the right to be tried in the county where the offense is committed by Article 1, Section 11 of the Constitution of the State of Nebraska." Brief for appellant at 3. Vejvoda, however, incorrectly interprets the constitutional guarantee in article I, § 11, of the Nebraska Constitution, which grants to a criminal defendant the right to "a speedy public trial by an impartial jury of the county or district in which the offense is alleged to have been committed." We have characterized the preceding constitutional language as "too plain to require interpretation." *Marino v. State*, 111 Neb. 623, 625, 197 N.W. 396, 397 (1924). Article I, § 11, of the Nebraska Constitution relates to an impartial jury in a criminal case for which a jury trial is constitutionally guaranteed, but does not grant a defendant a constitutional right to be tried in a particular county. In the present case, Vejvoda was convicted in a bench trial. Therefore, article I, § 11, of the Nebraska Constitution concerning a jury trial is inapplicable to Vejvoda's case.

Vejvoda's right to be tried in the county in which the criminal offense is alleged to have been committed is secured by statute rather than by the Nebraska Constitution. Neb.Rev.Stat. §29-1301 (Reissue 1985) provides that "[a]ll criminal cases shall be tried in the county where the offense was committed . . . unless it shall appear to the court by affidavits that a fair and impartial trial cannot be had therein." While proper venue in a criminal case

may be established by circumstantial evidence, we have held that the State must prove proper venue beyond a reasonable doubt. *Union P.R. Co. v. State*, 88 Neb. 547, 130 N.W. 277 (1911); *Keeler v. State*, 73 Neb. 441, 103 N.W. 64 (1905). It is clear from Nebraska decisions that a defendant may waive the statutorily designated venue for the trial of a criminal case in accordance with § 29-1301 concerning a change of venue. See Kennison v. State, 83 Neb. 391, 119 N.W. 768 (1909). Whether venue is an element of the substantive offense charged against an accused is apparently an unresolved issue in Nebraska. See, however, *State v. Harris*, 48 Wash.App. 279, 281-82, 738 P.2d 1059, 1061 (1987): "As a general rule, proof of venue is necessary in a criminal prosecution. [Citations omitted.] However, venue is not an element of the crime [citations omitted], and it need not be proved beyond a reasonable doubt [citation omitted]." See, further, *State v. Grayceck*, 335 N.W.2d 572, 574 (S.D. 1983): "Venue, not being an integral part of a criminal offense, does not affect the question of guilt or innocence of the accused [and may be proved] by a preponderance of the evidence. . . ." Cf., *State v. Barnes*, 7 Ohio App.3d 83, 84, 454 N.E.2d 572, 574 (1982): "Venue with respect to the situs of a crime is ordinarily considered an element of the offense which must be proved along with the other elements"; *State v. Hester*, 145 Ariz. 574, 703 P.2d 518 (1985) (venue is an essential element).

WAIVER OF VENUE

If the rules regarding waiver of venue in a civil action were applicable in the present appeal, Vejvoda's appellate claim based on venue would undoubtedly fail. At the risk of waiver, to preserve a claim of improper venue in a civil case, a defendant must raise the venue issue before or in the defendant's answer. In a civil action, if a defendant fails to timely raise the issue of proper venue, the defendant waives any venue question. See, *In re Interest of Adams*, 230 Neb. 109, 430 N.W.2d 295 (1988) (venue under the Nebraska Mental Health Commitment Act waived by failure to request transfer at appropriate time); *Blitzkie v. State*, 228 Neb. 409, 422 N.W.2d 773 (1988) (venue in a transitory civil action under the State Tort Claims Act waived unless raised in the answer or earlier). Unlike venue in a civil case, however, a statutorily designated venue in a criminal case may not be waived by a defendant's failure to raise the venue issue before or at trial. *Union P.R. Co. v. State, supra; State v. Lindsey*, 193 Neb. 442, 227 N.W.2d 599 (1975). In *Union P.R. Co. v. State, supra*, involving a prosecution for violation of the state's "anti-pass law" regarding railroads, the court was faced with a situation in which "the matter of venue was entirely overlooked by both the prosecutor and the trial court. . . ." *Union P.R. Co., supra*, 88 Neb. at 550, 130 N.W. at 278. Despite the fact that the defendant apparently did not raise the venue issue at trial, the court held,

over dissent, that the defendant's conviction should be reversed "[f]or the sole reason that the state failed to prove the venue. . . ." *Union P.R. Co., supra* at 551, 130 N.W. at 279. (In *Union P.R. Co. v. State, supra*, the dissent argued that the "ancient rule" that venue must be proved beyond a reasonable doubt was not "based upon reason," and further noted that "the rule that a defendant may waive the right to insist upon a trial in any particular county, and that if he goes to trial without objection he does so, is in accord with reason and modern conditions. . . ." (Sedgwick, J., dissenting.) *Union P.R. Co., supra* at 552, 130 N.W. at 279.)

Thus, Nebraska cases indicate that a defendant in a criminal case may waive the issue of a statutorily designated venue by requesting a change of venue in accordance with §29-1301, but a defendant does not waive the venue issue by failure to raise the issue before or during trial. See *State v. Lindsey, supra*. In the absence of a defendant's waiver of venue, the State has the burden to prove proper venue beyond a reasonable doubt. *State v. Lindsey, supra; Union P.R. Co. v. State, supra; Keeler v. State, supra*. With this in mind, we turn to Vejvoda's claim that proper venue was not sufficiently proved in his case.

PROOF OF VENUE

The venue of an offense may be proven like any other fact in a criminal case. It need not be established by positive testimony, nor in the words of the information; but if from the facts appearing in evidence the only rational conclusion which can be drawn is that the offense was committed in the county alleged, it is sufficient.

Weinecke v. State, 34 Neb. 14, 24, 51 N.W. 307, 310 (1892). See, also, *Gates v. State*, 160 Neb. 722, 71 N.W.2d 460 (1955); *State v. Liberator*, 197 Neb. 857, 251 N.W.2d 709 (1977); *State v. Laflin*, 201 Neb. 824, 272 N.W.2d 376 (1978); *State v. Ellis*, 208 Neb. 379, 303 N.W.2d 741 (1981).

The only testimony regarding venue was that of Edwards', a Grand Island police officer, who observed Vejvoda's car at "7th and Vine Streets" and later apprehended Vejvoda on a street called "Oak." Edwards never identified the city or county where he observed and apprehended Vejvoda. As this court noted in *State v. Bouwens*, 167 Neb. 244, 247, 92 N.W.2d 564, 566 (1958), the fact that a defendant was arrested by policemen of a particular city "is not proof that the offense was committed within the jurisdiction... of the city...." When the judicial notice in question is disregarded, the evidence offered in Vejvoda's case fails to establish that either a Vine Street or an Oak Street exists in Grand Island or Hall County. A defendant's arrest by a law enforcement officer of a particular political subdivision does not identify or establish the political subdivision as the proper venue in a criminal case. *State v. Bouwens, supra*. Therefore,

without the court's judicial notice that events concerning Vejvoda occurred in Grand Island within Hall County, the evidence fails to establish venue.

In this appeal, the State does not challenge the current Nebraska rule that a waiver does not result from a defendant's inaction on a venue question in a criminal case, nor does the State take issue with the necessity of evidence beyond a reasonable doubt regarding proof of venue.

JUDICAL NOTICE

Neb.Evid.R. 201(2), Neb. Rev. Stat. §27-201(2) (Reissue 1985), pertains to judicial notice of adjudicative facts and states: "A judicially noticed fact must be one not subject to reasonable dispute in that it is either (a) generally known within the territorial jurisdiction of the trial court or (b) capable of accurate and ready determination by resort to sources whose accuracy cannot reasonably be questioned."

A fact is adjudicative if the fact affects the determination of a controverted issue in litigation, or, as one author has characterized adjudicative facts:

> When a court or an agency finds facts concerning the immediate parties—who did what, where, when, how, and what motive or intent—the court or agency is performing an adjudicative function, and the facts so determined are conveniently called adjudicative facts. . . .

Stated in other terms, the adjudicative facts are those to which the law is applied in the process of adjudication. They are the facts that normally go to the jury in a jury case. They relate to the parties, their activities, their properties, their businesses.

Davis, *Judicial Notice*, 55 Colum.L.Rev. 945, 952 (1955).

Concerning judicial notice of adjudicative facts, Weinstein observes:

The obvious cost of establishing adjudicative facts in an adversary proceeding—in terms of time, energy, and money—justifies dispensing with formal proof when a matter is not really disputable. . . . When facts do not possess this requisite degree of certainty, our traditional approach has been to require proof within the framework of the adversary system for reasons well-expressed by Professor Davis: "The reason we use trial-type procedure, I think, is that we make the practical judgment, on the basis of experience, that taking evidence subject to cross-examination and rebuttal, is the best way to resolve controversies involving disputes of adjudicative facts, that is, facts pertaining to the parties. The reason we require a determination on the record is that we think fair procedure in resolving disputes of adjudicative facts calls for giving each party a chance to meet in the appropriate fashion the facts that come to the tribunal's attention, and the appropriate fashion

for meeting disputed adjudicative facts includes rebuttal evidence, cross-examination, usually confrontation, and argument (either written or oral or both)." [Quoting from K. Davis, *A System of Judicial Notice Based on Fairness and Convenience*, in Perspectives of Law 69 (1964)]

1 J. Weinstein & M. Berger, Weinstein's Evidence §201[03] at 201-23 to 201-24 (1988).

When neither of the alternative tests prescribed in Neb.Evid.R. 201(2) is satisfied, judicial notice of an adjudicative fact is improper. See *Cardio-Medical Assoc. v. Crozer-Chester Med. Ctr.*, 721 F.2d 68 (3d Cir. 1983). See, also, 1 J. Weinstein & M. Berger, *supra*.

A judge or court may take judicial notice, whether requested or not. Neb.Evid.R. 201 (3). Judicial notice of an adjudicative fact may be taken at any stage of the proceedings. Neb.Evid.R. 201 (6).

JUDICIAL NOTICE;
A SPECIES OF EVIDENCE

Judicial notice of an adjudicative fact is a species of evidence which, if relevant as an ultimate fact or a fact from which an ultimate fact may be inferred, is received without adherence to the Nebraska Evidence Rules otherwise applicable to admissibility of evidence and establishes a fact without formal evidentiary proof. See, *In re Samaha*, 130 Cal.App. 116, 19 P.2d 839 (1933) (judicial notice is a form of evidence); *Moss v. Aetna Life Ins. Co.*, 267 S.C. 370, 377, 228

S.E.2d 108, 112 (1976): judicial notice "means that the court will admit into evidence and consider, without proof of the facts, matters of common and general knowledge"; *National Aircraft Leasing v. American Airlines*, 74 Ill.App. 3d 1014, 1017, 31 Ill.Dec. 268, 394 N.E.2d 470, 474 (1979): "Judicial notice is an evidentiary concept which operates to admit matters into evidence without formal proof...." Although Neb.Evid.R. 201 does not expressly require relevance for judicial notice, an irrelevant fact cannot be validly classified as an "adjudicative fact," the only type of fact noticeable under Neb.Evid.R. 201.

JUDICIAL NOTICE V.
A JUDGE'S
PERSONAL KNOWLEDGE

Judicial notice, however, is not the same as extrajudicial or personal knowledge of a judge. "What a judge knows and what facts a judge may judicially notice are not identical data banks. . . . [A]ctual private knowledge by the judge is no sufficient ground for taking judicial notice of a fact as a basis for a finding or a final judgment. . . ." McCormick on Evidence § 329 at 922-23 (E. Cleary 3d ed. 1984). As Wigmore observes:

There is a real but elusive line between the judge's *personal knowledge* as a private man and these matters of which he takes judicial notice as a judge. The latter does not necessarily include the former, as a judge, indeed, he may have to ignore what he knows as a man and contrariwise.

. . .

It is therefore plainly acceptable that the judge is not to use from the bench, under the guise of judicial knowledge, that which he knows *only as an individual* observer outside of court. The former is in truth "known" to him merely in the fictional sense that is known and notorious to all men, and the dilemma is only the result of using the term "knowledge" in two senses. Where to draw the line between the knowledge by personal observation may sometimes be difficult but the principle is plain.

(Emphasis in original). 9 J. Wigmore, Evidence in Trials at Common Law §2569(a) at 722-23 (J. Chadbourn rev. 1981).

JUDICIAL NOTICE
IN CRIMINAL CASES

In function and effect, judicial notice in a civil action is fundamentally different from judicial notice in a criminal case. "In a civil action or proceeding, the judge shall instruct the jury that it may, but is not required to, accept as conclusive any fact judicially noticed. Neb.Evid.R. 201(7). In a civil action, the adjudicative fact judicially noticed is conclusively established and binds the jury, whereas in a criminal case a jury ultimately has the freedom to find that an adjudicative fact has not been established notwithstanding judicial notice by the trial court. If the conclusive effect of judicial notice in a civil action were transposed to the trial of a criminal case, judicial notice might supply proof of an element in the charge against an accused and thereby have the practical effect of a directed verdict on the issue of the defendant's guilt. The actual danger of judicial notice as a directed verdict against an accused was carefully considered in *State v. Lawrence*, 120 Utah 323, 234 P.2d 600 (1951), which involved a conviction of grand larceny, that is, theft of property with value in excess of $50. As recounted by the court in *Lawrence*:

> At the conclusion of the evidence, the defendant's counsel moved the court for a directed verdict on the ground that there had been no evidence of value of the stolen car. The State's attorney might properly and with little difficulty have moved to reopen and supply the missing evidence. He did not do so but instead argued that judicial notice could be taken of the value of the car. The court denied defendant's motion and included in its instructions to the jury the following:
>
> . . .
>
> "In this case you will take the value of this property as being in excess of $50.00 and therefore the defendant, if he is guilty at all, is guilty of grand larceny."

In that setting, the *Lawrence* court directed its attention to the prosecution's argument that the court could take judicial notice of the automobile's value and instruct the jury accordingly. Rejecting the State's argument the court concluded:

> It is to be admitted that upon the surface there doesn't appear to be much logic to the thought that a jury would not be bound to find that the car involved here (1947 Ford 2-Door Sedan) is worth more than $50. However, under our jury system, it is traditional that in criminal cases juries can, and sometimes do, make findings which are not based on logic, nor even common sense. No matter how positive the evidence of a man's guilt may be, the jury may find him not guilty and no court has any power to do anything about it. Notwithstanding the occasional incongruous result, this system of submitting all of the facts in criminal cases to the jury and letting them be the exclusive judges thereof has lasted for some little time now and with a fair degree of success. If the result in individual cases at times seems illogical, we can be consoled by the words of Mr. Justice Holmes, that in some areas of the law, "a page of history is worth a volume of logic." We, who live with it, have a fervent devotion to the jury system, in spite of its faults. We would not like to see it destroyed nor whittled away. If a court can take one important element of an offense from the jury and determine the facts for them because such fact seems plain enough to him, then which element cannot be similarly taken away, and where would the process stop?

120 Utah at 330-31, 234 P.2d at 603. The court then reversed Lawrence's conviction and ordered a new trial.

In *U.S. Mentz*, 840 F.2d 315 (6th Cir. 1988), the government prosecuted Mentz in a jury trial on charges of bank robbery. To convict Mentz, the government had to prove that Mentz robbed a financial institution insured by the Federal Deposit Insurance Corporation. See 18 U.S.C. §2113(a) and (f) (1982). When Mentz moved for dismissal of the charges at the close of the government's case, claiming that evidence failed to establish that the banks were FDIC-insured at the time of the robberies, the court overruled Mentz' motion and, although there was no evidence of FDIC insurance, instructed the jury that each of the banks, which Mentz was accused of robbing, was "insured by the Federal Deposit Insurance Corporation at the time of the offense alleged in the indictment." (Emphasis omitted.) 840 F.2d at 318-319. In reversing Mentz' conviction, the court stated:

> Regardless of how overwhelming the evidence be, the Constitution delegates to the jury, not to the trial judge, the important task of deciding guilt or innocence. "[The jury's] overriding responsibility is to stand between the accused and a potentially arbitrary or abusive Government that is in command of the criminal sanction. For this reason, a trial judge is prohibited from entering a judgment of conviction or directing the jury to come

> forward with such a verdict, regardless of how overwhelming the evidence may point in that direction. The trial judge is thereby barred from attempting to override or interfere with the juror's independent judgment in a manner contrary to the interests of the accused." *United States v. Martin Linen Supply Co.* [430 U.S. 564, 97 S. Ct. 1349, 51 L. Ed. 2d 642 (1977)] [citation omitted].

840 F.2d at 319.

The *Mentz* court continued:

> We agree with Mentz that the trial judge invaded the jury's province by instructing that body, in clear and unequivocal language, that the banks were FDIC insured at the time the robberies occurred. His conclusive statement left no room for the jury to believe otherwise. The judge improperly cast himself in the role of trier of fact, and directed a verdict on an essential element of the bank robbery charge. His instructions had the effect of relieving the government of its burden of proving, beyond the *jury's* reasonable doubt that the accused committed the crimes charged. . . .

> It is not important that the jury might have reached a similar conclusion had it been given an opportunity to decide the issue under a correct instruction. A plea of not guilty places all issues in despite, "even the most patent truths." [Citations omitted.] The First Circuit has suc-

cinctly stated this point: "Whatever probative force the government's proof possessed, the jury had the power to accept or reject it-or to find it insufficiently persuasive. The defendant had a correlative right to free and unhampered exercise by the jury of all its powers." [Quoting from *U.S. v. Argentine*, 814 F.2d 783 (1st Cir. 1987).]

840 F.2d at 320.

The court in *Mentz* then noted: "Since the government's evidence on this issue consisted mainly of witness testimony, the trial judge replaced the jury by reaching a conclusion based on assessing the credibility of witnesses and weighing the probative value of the evidence." 840 F.2d at 320 n. 8.

Specifically referring to judicial notice under Fed.R.Evid. 201(g), the counterpart to Neb.Evid.R. 201(7), the court concluded in *Mentz*:

A court may take judicial notice of adjudicative facts in a criminal case, whether requested or not. Rule 201(c), (f), Fed.R.Evid. When the court does so, however, there will normally be a record of this. "Care should be taken by the court to identify the fact it is noticing, and its justification for doing so." *Colonial Leasing Company of New England v. Logistics Control Group International*, 762 F.2d 454, 459 (5th Cir. 1985). This facilitates intelligent appellate review, and is particularly necessary when the fact noticed is an essential element of the crime charged. . . .

. . . In a criminal case, a trial court that takes judicial notice of an adjudicative fact must "instruct the jury that it may, but is not required to, accept as conclusive any fact judicially noticed." Rule 201(g), Fed.R.Evid. This provision "contemplates that the jury in a criminal case [will] pass upon facts which are judicially noticed." *United States v. Jones*, 580 F.2d 219, 224 (6th Cir. 1978). As so construed, Rule 201(g) preserves the jury's "traditional prerogative to ignore even uncontroverted facts in reaching a verdict," and thereby prevents the trial court from transgressing the spirit, if not the letter, of the Sixth Amendment right to a jury trial by directing a partial verdict as to the facts. [Citations omitted.]

A trial court commits constitutional error when it takes judicial notice of facts constituting an essential element of the crime charged, but fails to instruct the jury according to Rule 201(g). The court's decision to accept the element as established conflicts with the bedrock principle that the government must prove, beyond the *jury's* reasonable doubt, every essential element of the crime. [Citation omitted.]

Even assuming the district court in this case judicially noticed the insurance coverage by the FDIC, it was obligated to inform the jury that it could disregard the facts noticed. The court's failure to make such a statement permitted the jury to convict Mentz without ever examining the evidence concerning an element of the crime charged, and thus violated his Sixth Amendment right to a jury trial.

840 F.2d at 322-23.

As one commentator has remarked concerning judicial notice and Fed.R.Evid. 201(g), which remark is equally applicable to Neb.Evid.R. 201(7).

> With respect to criminal cases, Rule 201(g) apparently contemplates that contrary evidence is admissible, which of course means that evidence, if any, in support of the fact judicially noticed may also be admitted. Problems arising with respect to the court considering inadmissible evidence in determining the proprietary of taking judicial notice coupled with the confusion that naturally would be expected to rise in the jury's mind when presented with judicial notice accompanied by conflicting evidence, makes resort to judicial notice in criminal cases where the opposing party is prepared to introduce contrary evidence highly undesirable.

M. Graham, Handbook of Federal Evidence § 201.7 at 83 (2d ed. 1986).

JUDICIAL NOTICE IN A BENCH TRIAL

Potential problems from judicial notice in a bench trial are discussed in 21 C. Wright & K. Graham, Federal Practice and Procedure § 5104 at 488 (1977):

> [T]he high degree of indisputability required before a fact can be judicially noticed applies to both forms of litigation [jury trials and court or bench trials]. However, the procedural context in which notice is taken makes the process quite different in court trials. Since the judge is not insulated, as the jury is, from the material consulted in deciding whether or not to take notice, it may make little difference whether he takes formal judicial notice based on the material or whether he is simply convinced of the fact as a result of having examined the sources. Technically, the source material is not in evidence, and thus a finding that was without other support in the record could not stand unless the matter was properly noticeable; but otherwise, the line between judicial notice and proof-taking is blurred in court trials.

From all the foregoing observations, we believe, and for that reason suggest, that judicial notice should be sparingly used in a criminal case lest prejudicial error result from denial of a defendant's constitutional or statutory rights in the trial of a criminal case.

JUDICIAL NOTICE IN VEJVODA'S CASE

Under the Nebraska Evidence Rules, the trial court's sua sponte judicial notice was permissible at the point in Vejvoda's trial where adduction of evidence had been concluded and the case was ready for submission to the factfinding process. See Neb.Evid.R. 201(4): "A judge or court shall take judicial notice if requested by a party and supplied with the necessary information." See, also, Neb.Evid.R. 201(6): "Judicial notice may be taken at any stage of the proceeding."

However, from the record in Vejvoda's case, one cannot conclude that the location of the municipal microcosm known as Vine Street or 8th and Oak Streets was known throughout the length and breadth of Hall County and, therefore, a fact "known within the territorial jurisdiction of the trial court." Neb.Evid.R. 201(2)(a). Consequently, we must focus on the alternative expressed in Neb.Evid.R. 201(2)(b), that is, whether the location of Vine and Oak streets in Grand Island are adjudicative facts "capable of accurate and ready determination by resort to sources whose accuracy cannot reasonably be questioned."

For resolution of Vejvoda's claim regarding the impropriety of the trial court's judicial notice, we must first identify and characterize the scope of the trial court's "judicial notice," which actually has two components: (1) Vine, Oak, 7th, and 8th Streets exist in Grand Island, which is located in Hall County, and (2) Vejvoda's drunk driving occurred at 8th and Oak in Grand Island. Thus, existence of Grand Island streets is inferentially correlated with Edwards' testimony, producing a conclusion judicially noticed by the trial court, namely, the judicially noticed streets are the same

streets mentioned in Edwards' testimony, and, therefore, Vejvoda was arrested in Grand Island.

An inference may be entirely reasonable, yet nevertheless an improper subject for judicial notice.

[Neb.Evid.R. 201] puts judges and attorneys on notice that underlying assumptions must be analyzed to ascertain whether their validity can be verified and placed beyond practical dispute. Attorneys must be alert to instances . . . where a court's statement, although plausible on the surface, may be based on unverified [and unverifiable] hypotheses.

1 J. Weinstein & M. Berger, Weinstein's Evidence § 201[03] at 201-34 (1988).

When a fact is not generally known within the territorial jurisdiction of the trial court, judicial notice may be taken only if an adjudicative fact can be verified by "sources whose accuracy cannot reasonably be questioned." Neb.Evid.R. 201(2)(b). The inference that Vejvoda was arrested in Grand Island is not "capable of accurate and ready determination by resort to sources whose accuracy cannot reasonably be questioned." Neb.Evid.R. 201(2)(b). We cannot imagine any unimpeachable source or sources which quickly and accurately verify the trial court's inferential determination that Vejvoda's drunk driving occurred in Grand Island. While a map of Grand Island would verify existence of Vine and Oak Streets within the city, a Grand Island map would not indisputably establish that Vejvoda was driving in that city.

As a matter of judicial notice, the trial court's conclusion that Vejvoda's drunk driving occurred in Grand Island is verifiable only by the cumbersome process of examining all locations outside Grand Island, which might match Edwards' description of a site with "Vine" and "Oak" streets, and then eliminating those locations which are inconsistent with Edwards' testimony about the direction traveled by Vejvoda's vehicle, for example, Vejvoda's car traveled west on 7th Street, turned right from 7th Street onto Oak Street, and stopped at 8th and Oak Streets. In the foregoing process of comparison and elimination, a court would have to consult not only a map of Grand Island, but also maps of cities and towns outside Grand Island and Hall County which have streets designated "Vine," "Oak," and "8th." Although a court might, after a laborious comparison of virtually innumerable city maps, confirm Edwards' identification of "Vine" and "Oak" as the streets traveled by Vejvoda within Grand Island, such an unavoidably burdensome procedure is not only impracticable but contrary to Neb.Evid.R. 201(2)(b), which specifies that a judicially noticed adjudicative fact must be "capable of . . . ready determination."

A court may take judicial notice concerning the location of streets in a particular subdivision within the court's jurisdiction. *State v. Scramuzza*, 408 So.2d 1316 (La. 1982);

Evans Associated Industries, Inc. v. Evans, 493 S.W.2d 547 (Tex.Civ.App. 1973); *State v. Martin*, 270 N.C. 286, 154 S.E.2d 96 (1967); *Cascio v. State*, 213 Ark. 418, 210 S.W.2d 897 (1948); *United States v. Hughes*, 542 F.2d 246 (5th Cir. 1976). See, also, Annot., Judicial Notice as to Location of Street Address Within Particular Political Subdivision, 86 A.L.R.3d 485 (1978). In the trial of a criminal case, whether a political subdivision has a street identified by a particular name used in evidence is an adjudicative fact for judicial notice, but whether the street location mentioned in testimony is actually within the political subdivision is a matter of reasonable inference by the factfinder. *United States v. Mendell*, 447 F.2d 639 (7th Cir. 1971).

In Vejvoda's case, the trial court could properly take notice that Grand Island, which is wholly within Hall County, has streets named "Vine" and "Oak." Furthermore, by simply referring to a map of Grand Island, the court could properly take judicial notice that the intersection of 7th and Vine Streets is within two blocks of the intersection of 8th and Oak Streets. At that point the site of the offense was an issue submissible to the trier of fact.

Although the location of streets within Grand Island is readily verifiable by reference to a city map, a source capable of ready verification and a cartographic source of information which cannot reasonably be questioned, the county court took another and impermissible step by judicially noticing the inference that Vejvoda was driving in Grand Island. The court's locational inference necessary for venue was not an adjudicative fact "capable of accurate and ready determination by resort to sources whose accuracy cannot reasonably be questioned." The county court erred in taking judicial notice of the inference that Vejvoda was driving in Grand Island and, therefore, that Vejvoda's drunk driving occurred in Grand Island.

If Vejvoda had been convicted in a jury trial, we would reverse Vejvoda's conviction on account of the trial court's invasion of the factfinding process within a jury's province in the trial of a criminal case. However, as mentioned, Vejvoda's case was tried to court. Although Vejvoda's arrest by Edwards, a Grand Island police officer, does not establish venue, Edwards' official affiliation as a Grand Island police officer was a circumstance bearing on the issue of venue. When combined with other evidence, namely, the trial court's judicial notice of "Vine" and "Oak" as streets in Grand Island, Edwards' testimony supplied a sufficient evidentiary basis for a fact finder's determination that Vejvoda's drunk driving occurred in Grand Island, Hall County, Nebraska. "Harmless error exists in a jury trial of a criminal case when there is some incorrect conduct by the trial court, which, on review of the entire record, did not materially influence the jury in a verdict adverse to a substantial right of the defendant." *State v. Watkins*, 227 Neb. 677, 686, 419

N.W.2d 660, 666 (1988). The preceding principle applicable in a jury trial of a criminal case is equally applicable to a judgment embodying a factfinding in the bench trial of a criminal case.

Therefore, the trial court's error in judicially noticing the inferential location of Vejvoda's conduct, namely, drunk driving, is harmless error beyond a reasonable doubt. Vejvoda's conviction is affirmed.

AFFIRMED.

WHITE, Justice, dissenting.

Today, the majority holds that harmless error occurred during a bench trial of a criminal case when the trial court took judicial notice of venue.

Today's holding conflicts with our holding in *State v. Bouwens*, 167 Neb. 244, 92 N.W.2d 564 (1958). In *Bouwens*, this court affirmed the decision of the district court which dismissed a complaint against the defendant for disturbing the peace. While noting that "[i]t is fundamental that venue must be proven as any other essential fact," id. at 246, 92 N.W.2d at 566, the court held that the mere reference to streets and addresses in an unnamed city, standing alone, will not be deemed sufficient evidence for the court to take judicial notice of venue.

Second, as I first noted in my dissent in *State v. Foster*, 230 Neb. 607, 433 N.W.2d 167 (1988), today's holding is another step in the continuing process of making the trial court an active participant in criminal proceedings. Again, I submit this active participation offends notions of fairness and due process.

STATE v. SCOTT

3 Ohio App.2d 239, 32 Ohio Op.2d 360, N.E.2d 289 (1965)

LYNCH, Judge.

This is an appeal on questions of law from a conviction of defendant-appellant in the Newton Falls Municipal Court for operation of a motor vehicle while under the influence of alcohol as the result of an arrest on the Ohio Turnpike by a State Highway Patrolman.

Defendant-appellant's first assignment of error is that the state has failed to prove that the offense was committed within the territorial jurisdiction of the trial court.

The Newton Falls Municipal Court was created by Section 1901.01, Revised Code, of the Uniform Municipal Court Act, and its territorial jurisdiction as provided by Section 1901.02, Revised Code, in addition to the corporate limits of Newton Falls, includes Bristol, Bloomfield, Lordstown, Newton, Braceville, Southington, Farmington and Mesoptamia [sic] Townships in Trumbull County.

Section 1901.20, Revised Code, provides, in part, as follows:

"The municipal court has jurisdiction of the violation of any ordinance of any municipal corporation within its territory and of any misdemeanor committed within the limits of its territory. * * *."

Section 2938.10, Revised Code, provides, in part, as follows:

"The state or municipality in all cases must prove the offense committed within the territorial jurisdiction of the court * * *."

The pertinent testimony as to the location of this traffic violation is as follows:

Mr. Lloyd Wiseman, a serviceman of Passarelli Brothers, who works on service breakdowns on the Ohio Turnpike, first saw defendant parked at the Niles-Youngstown interchange. Mr. Wiseman was going to Milepost 209, which he later indicated was the Warren interchange. Mr. Wiseman radioed the State Patrol from the Niles-Youngstown interchange as to defendant's condition. Mr. Wiseman followed defendant's car for about seven miles until about Milepost 212, when the State Patrolman passed him. The State Patrolman followed defendant's car for about three miles and ordered defendant's car to stop. Mr. Wiseman then passed them and went to the Warren interchange.

State Patrolman Thomas G. Summer testified that while on duty on the Ohio Turnpike he received a radio report on defendant, and he first observed defendant driving his car westbound on the Ohio Turnpike at approximately Milepost 212 on the Ohio Turnpike. He followed him approximately three miles and then ordered him to stop and arrested him. He then took defendant to the Newton Falls Police Department.

At the conclusion of the case, the attorney for defendant-appellant moved for a directed verdict and for dismissal of the case on the ground that the state failed to prove jurisdiction. The court overruled this motion "for the reason it is my recollection that the Patrol Officer and this last witness, Mr. Wiseman, both or either of them have testified as to the milepost and the area of where the occurrences have happened, and I take judicial notice that the area in which this alleged offense is said to have occurred is within the territorial limits of this court, and in the County of Trumbull and State of Ohio."

Defendant-appellant contends that the record of the trial does not disclose sufficient evidence to warrant the determination that the offense committed by the defendant was committed within the territorial jurisdiction of the trial court, and cited as authority for his position the unreported case of State v. Baker, Trumbull County Common Pleas Case No. 71889, which has been the subject of considerable interest in this area. The Baker case was not appealed, and this is the first time that this issue has been presented in this court.

In the Baker case the arrest for driving while intoxicated was made by a State Highway Patrolman on the Ohio Turnpike, and the defendant was convicted in the County Court of Newton Falls which pre-ceded the present Municipal Court of Newton Falls. The defendant appealed to the Common Pleas Court of Trumbull County, which reversed the judgment of the Newton Falls County Court and discharged the defendant for several reasons, among which was that the state failed to prove that the offenses were committed within the territorial jurisdiction of the trial court. The only evidence in the record was that Baker was observed in the area of Milepost 210, and the Trumbull County Common Pleas Court held that the Newton Falls County Court could not take judicial notice as to the location of Milepost 210 on the Ohio Turnpike.

The issue thus presents itself as follows: May a trial judge take judicial notice of the existence of the Ohio Turnpike and an interchange of such Turnpike within the territorial jurisdiction of his court? If the Ohio Turnpike does pass through the territorial jurisdiction of his court, may a trial judge take judicial notice of the location of specific mileposts of the Ohio Turnpike for the purpose of determining whether such mileposts are within the territorial jurisdiction of his court?

A research of the law applicable to this case was made but no reported Ohio case on the issue of judicial notice of the jurisdiction of a court as to an offense occurring on the Ohio Turnpike was found. None of the briefs of the respective parties contained any reported Ohio cases.

15 Ohio Jurisprudence 2d 474, Criminal Law, Section 299, states:

"The general rule may be stated broadly that courts will take judicial notice of whatever is generally known or ought to be generally known within the limits of their jurisdiction, for the court is presumed to know what is of common knowledge. * * *"

Courts may take judicial notice of geographical facts which are matters of common knowledge, particularly those existing within the jurisdiction of the court. 21 Ohio Jurisprudence 2d 58, Evidence, Section 43; 31 C.J.S. Evidence § 32, p. 935; 20 American Jurisprudence 74-75, Evidence, Section 50. 20 American Jurisprudence 76, Evidence, Section 50, states:

"The question whether a specific geographical fact is entitled to judicial notice is considerably simplified if such fact is the creature of statute; for in such case the court will take notice of the statute and incidentally the geographical fact, regardless of the notoriety of the latter."

It is generally held that a court will take judicial notice of the limits of its jurisdiction and the extent of the territory therein included. Zimmerman v. Rockford Stone Co., Ohio Com.Pl., 196 N.E.2d 474; 21 Ohio Jurisprudence 2d 70, Evidence, Section 57; 20 American Jurisprudence 103, Evidence, Section 85.

In State v. Neff, 104 Ohio App. 289, 148 N.E.2d 236, the court held that in a criminal case venue need not be proved in express terms but may be established by all the facts and circumstances in the case, and that the Findlay Municipal Court could take judicial notice that an intersection at a Main Street and a Front Street is located within the city of Findlay.

31 C.J.S. Evidence § 12, pp. 833-835, states:

"Since judicial cognizance may extend to matters beyond the actual knowledge of the judge, he may, in ascertaining facts to be judicially noticed, resort to, or obtain information from, any source of knowledge which he feels would be helpful to him, always seeking that which is most appropriate. * * *

"The judge may inform himself as to the facts of geography, such as the navigable character of a river, the distance between two points, or the location of a given place within the jurisdiction, by resort to * * * public documents, maps, etc."

See Zimmerman v. Rockford Stone Co., Ohio Com.Pl., 196 N.E.2d 474.

In Wainright, Admr. v. Lake Shore & Michigan Southern Ry. Co., 11 Ohio Cir. Dec. 530, the court took judicial notice of a map of a city in order to determine the distance between certain points on a railroad track within its limits.

The Ohio Turnpike was created under authority of Chapter 5537 of the Revised Code, and has been in existence for over ten years. It is a distinctive geographical feature, and it appears on all official highway maps, whether issued by the State of Ohio or County Engineers. It certainly has become a matter of common knowledge, and we hold that a court may take judicial notice whether the Ohio Turnpike passes through the territorial jurisdiction of the court.

One of the features of the Ohio Turnpike is interchanges. These are at fixed geographical locations, and their locations appear on all official maps. These interchanges are a matter of common knowledge, and we hold that a court may take judicial notice whether a specific interchange is located within the territorial jurisdiction of the court.

In this case, the evidence showed that the Warren interchange was Milepost 209, and that defendant was first observed at Milepost 212 driving west towards Milepost 209, and that the State Highway Patrolman followed defendant approximately three miles and then arrested him. By deduction, the arrest of defendant had to be in the vicinity of the Warren interchange. The trial judge may take judicial notice of whether the Warren interchange is within the territorial jurisdiction of the Newton Falls Municipal Court. Since the trial court took judicial notice that this offense occurred within the territorial jurisdiction of the Newton Falls Municipal Court, this court must presume that the vicinity of the Warren interchange is within the jurisdiction of his court. If this is not true, the defendant could produce evidence to dispute this fact.

For purposes of designating distances or locations, the Ohio Turnpike uses mileposts as reference points. For those who have use of the Ohio Turnpike, it is a practical and accurate system of identifying a specific location. General maps do not designate the mileposts, but the Ohio Turnpike Commission has a pamphlet for general distribution showing the milepost numbers of each interchange, and they also have a chart of the mileposts on the Ohio Turnpike showing, among other things, the location of the county lines, disabled vehicle service zones, ambulance service zones, fire department service zones,

etc. This chart is available to all who have need of such information.

Thus, a particular milepost designation on the Ohio Turnpike can be readily and accurately ascertained by checking this chart of the Ohio Turnpike Commission. For this reason we hold that a court may take judicial notice whether a particular milepost is within the territorial jurisdiction of its court.

We, therefore, hold that there was sufficient evidence in this case to warrant the trial court to determine that the offense committed by defendant was committed within the territorial jurisdiction of the Newton Falls Municipal Court.

Defendant-appellant's second assignment of error is that the state failed to identify the defendant. This contention is based on the fact that at no time during the trial was any of the witnesses for the state specifically asked if the person in the courtroom was the same William R. Scott who was charged by the State Highway Patrol for driving while intoxicated.

The general rule is that to warrant conviction the evidence must establish beyond a reasonable doubt the identity of the accused as the person who committed the crime. 23 C.J.S. Criminal Law § 920, p. 643; 1 Wharton's Criminal Evidence, Twelfth Edition, 46; 1 Underhill's Criminal Evidence, Fifth Edition, 243. 23 C.J.S. Criminal Law § 920, p. 645, states:

"The probative value of an identification depends on the circumstances under which it was made. * * *

" * * * It is not necessary that the identification be made positively by a witness, * * * . Lack of positiveness does not destroy the value of the identification, but goes to the weight of the testimony. * * *

  " * * *

"Identity may be established by direct evidence, but direct evidence of identification is not required; circumstantial evidence may be sufficient to establish the identity of accused as the person who committed the crime, * * * . The circumstances proved must, however, lead to but one fair and reasonable conclusion pointing to accused to the exclusion of all others as the guilty person and exclude every other reasonable hypothesis except that of accused's guilt. * * * ."

In this case, the State Highway Patrolman testified that he came in contact with defendant, William Scott, on September 1, 1964, and eventually arrested him. His testimony thereafter referred to the accused as "defendant." However, he testified that the person he arrested wore eyeglasses, and that he thought that the defendant in the courtroom was wearing the same glasses that he had on the night of the arrest.

When Mr. Wiseman testified, he was asked the following question:

"Q. On September 17, 1964, did you have occasion to come in contact with the defendant here, William Scott? * * * A. Yes, I did."

His testimony thereafter referred to the accused as "defendant."

We hold that there was sufficient evidence of probative value to identify the defendant as the same person who was arrested, beyond a reasonable doubt.

Defendant-appellant's third assignment of error is that the judgment is against the manifest weight of the evidence and is contrary to law. A review of the transcript and bill of exceptions reveals that there was ample evidence to sustain the conviction.

Judgment affirmed.

JOHNSON, P. J., and JONES, J., concur.

Cases relating to Chapter 6
PRESUMPTIONS, INFERENCES AND STIPULATIONS

STATE v. JACKSON

112 Wash. 2d 867, 774 P.2d 1211 (1989)

CALLOW, Chief Justice.

The defendant, Destin L. Jackson was convicted of attempted second degree burglary. He contends the trial court erred in giving an inference of intent instruction.

The issues presented are:

1. In an attempted burglary case, is it error to instruct the jury that it may infer the defendant acted with the intent to commit a crime within the building from the fact that the defendant may have attempted entrance into the building?

2. Is malicious mischief in the third degree a lesser included offense within attempted burglary in the second degree, where a substantial step taken in the furtherance of the burglary is the malicious destruction of property?

3. Does federal due process require the state to plead the nature of the crime a defendant intended to commit inside the building he tried to enter? See and compare State v. Bergeron, 105 Wash.2d 1, 711 P.2d 100 (1985), overruling, *State v. Johnson*,

100 Wash.2d 607, 674 P.2d 145 (1983).

We hold the trial court cannot instruct the jury where the charge is attempted burglary, that it may infer the defendant acted with intent to commit a crime within a building, where the evidence is that the defendant may have attempted entrance into a building, but there exist other equally reasonable conclusions which follow from the circumstances.

On the evening of February 2, 1986, a Seattle police officer received a dispatch call to proceed to Neal's Tailoring and Beverage Shop. As the officer was coming around a corner he saw the defendant kicking the front door of the shop. The defendant was taking short running kicks at the window area of the door. Once the defendant spotted the officer, he proceeded to briskly walk away. The officer placed the defendant under arrest. The officer testified that no one else was in the vicinity and that the defendant was constantly in his sight. When the door was examined it was found that about 10 inches of Plexiglas had been pushed inward and part of the wood stock around the Plexiglas and they appeared to match the shoes of the defendant. The Plexiglas was not taken into custody, even though the right edge had been pushed inward, as it still prevented entry into the business. The molding which holds the glass in the door was broken on the inside, and there was wood on the floor. The pressure from the outside tore the molding off on the inside.

The defendant was charged with attempted second degree burglary. At trial, the defendant denied kicking the door. He claimed he noticed the broken door as he was walking by the shop and was arrested as he continued on his way.

At the conclusion of the State's case, the defendant moved for a dismissal asserting:

This may get to attempting malicious mischief, but to stack inferences of intent as to what was intended in terms of kicking or knocking out the door, then another inference if he intended to break in, he intended to commit a crime is beyond the limits of reasonable inferences. One inference is not enough. There is evidence to support one inference that he intended to break in, but you are asking, or the State would be asking, your honor, for the jury to do is to stack inferences. First of all, you have to infer he intended to break in based on his conduct. If you believe that once—that he did it, then

that he intended to commit a crime. Stacking inferences is something that is beyond a prima facie case. Therefore, the case should proceed only on attempted criminal trespass or malicious mischief.

The trial court denied the motion. At the conclusion of the trial, the court heard exceptions to the proposed instructions to the jury.

[Defense Counsel] The defense would except to your Honor's failure to give the lesser included. The defense would suggest that the attempt statute is so broad. When you get down to what is alleged, namely, Destin Jackson broke the door in an attempt to get in that, indeed, legally and factually you would have to commit malicious mischief, or attempted burglary, which in a manner which has been charged in this case. For that reason, I would except to your Honor's failure to give that lesser included instruction.

. . . . .

[Defense Counsel] In addition, the defense would except to your Honor's giving the inference Instruction No. 10. Factually, the cases do not support that inference. The instruction reads, "A person who remains unlawfully in a building with intent to commit a crime." However, the record does not support the allegation Mr. Jackson—even if you assume it was Mr. Jackson who entered or remained unlawfully, he is charged with attempting to do so. Again, in the motion to dismiss at the end of the State's case, you are asking the jury first to infer what his intent is, then asking them to infer what his intent was assuming the inference, that is inappropriate. It is clear on the face of the instruction it doesn't apply here because no injury was—or entry was actually made. That is the reason this instruction is inappropriate and the defense would except to it being given.

[Defense Counsel] Your Honor, in terms of our record, then having changed that, the defense would still suggest it is inappropriate because it stacks inferences, then, based on that conclusion, suggests they make another inference. It is a permissive inference as obtained here, but it is a comment on the evidence, if you find this then you can find that, then move on from there. The defense believes it is stacking inferences and would rely on that as previously explained.

Over the defendant's objection the court gave the following jury instruction:

A person who *attempts* to enter or remain unlawfully in a building may be inferred to have acted with intent to commit a crime against a person or property therein unless such entering or remaining shall be explained by evidence satisfactory to the jury to have been made without such

criminal intent. This inference is not binding upon you and it is for you to determine what weight, if any, such inference is to be given.

(Italics ours.) WPIC 60.05 does not include the underlined words "attempts to". The defendant objected to the trial court's failure to give a lesser included instruction. (See WPIC 4.11) However, the defendant did not propose an instruction setting out the crime, nor did he except to the instruction which defined burglary. These issues were not raised in the petition for review; only the objection to the inference of intent instruction and whether there is evidence of an actual entry are raised before us. The jury found the defendant guilty as charged.

In ruling on the motion for new trial the trial court stated in part:

THE COURT: [C]ounsel reminded me that there was a motion for a new trial brought by the defense in regard to an instruction, . . . which I gave to the jury, in regard to the inference of intent to commit a crime therein, this being an attempted burglary in the second degree in which the jury found defendant was guilty of the crime of attempted burglary in the second degree.

The trial court denied the motion for new trial, the defendant appealed and we granted a petition for review after the Court of Appeals affirmed his decision.

I

QUAERE: What Is the Function of
An Inference and When Is an
Inference Permissible?

" ' "Presumptions" . . . "*may be
looked on as the bats of the law, flit-
ting in the twilight but disappearing
in the sunshine of actual facts.*" . . .' "
Bradley v. S.L. Savidge, Inc. 13
Wash.2d 28, 123 P.2d 780 (1942)
(citing *Beeman v. Puget Sound Trac-
tion Light & Power Co.*, 79 Wash.
137, 139, 139 P. 1087 (1914),
(quoting *Paul v. United Rys. Co.*, 152
Mo.App. 577, 134 S.W. 3 (1911))).

The basic notions upon which
presumptions are grounded are
simple. When fact A (the basic
fact) exists for certain purposes
and with certain limitations. This
specific assumption or inference
by application of a general rule is
a presumption.

K. Tegland, Wash. Prac., *Evidence*
§65, at 127 (2d ed. 1982).

Most presumptions have come
into existence primarily because
the judges have believed that
proof of fact B renders the inference of the existence of fact A so
probable that it is sensible and
timesaving to assume the truth of
fact A until the adversary dis-
proves it.

E. Cleary, *McCormick on Evidence*
§343, at 969 (3d ed. 1984).

We follow *Bradley v. S.L.
Savidge, Inc.*, *supra*, in quoting the
definition of a presumption as defined
in *Heidelbach v. Campbell*, 95 Wash.
661, 668, 164 P. 247 (1917):

A presumption is an inference,
affirmative or disaffirmative, of
the truth of a proposition of fact
which is drawn by a process of
reasoning from some one or
more matters of known fact. The
presumption arises from a want
of knowledge of the truth of the
proposition. It is in the nature of
evidence, and if it be known
whether the given proposition is
true or false, there can be no presumption because the fact is established which the presumption
tends to prove or disprove.

[2, 3] Presumptions are one
thing; inferences another. Presumptions are assumptions of fact which
the law requires to be made from another fact or group of facts; inferences
are logical deductions or conclusions
from an established fact. Presumptions deal with legal processes,
whereas inferences deal with mental
processes. *Lappin v. Lucurell*, 13
Wash.App. 277, 284, 534 P.2d 1038,
94 A.L.R.3d 594 (1975). "An inference is simply a logical deduction or
conclusion which the law allows, but
does not require, following the establishment of the basic facts." 5 K.
Tegland, at 127-28.

RCW 9A.52.040 creates an
"inference of intent" as applied to
burglary and trespass as follows:

In any prosecution for burglary, any person who enters or remains unlawfully in a building may be inferred to have acted with intent to commit a crime against a person or property therein, unless such entering or remaining shall be explained by evidence satisfactory to the trier of fact to have been made without such criminal intent.

RCW 9A.52.040 is reflected in WPIC 60.05 to read:

A person who enters or remains unlawfully in a building may be inferred to have acted with intent to commit a crime against a person or property therein [unless such entering or remaining shall be explained by evidence satisfactory to the jury to have been made without such criminal intent]. This inference is not binding upon you and it is for you to determine what weight, if any, such inference is to be given.

Both RCW 9A.52.040 and WPIC 60.05 permit the inference of one fact from another as a presumption. Burglary consists of two elements; entry or unlawfully remaining upon another's premises, and intent. RCW 9A.52.030. RCW 9A52.040 provides that a burglary may be inferred (intent exists) if one either unlawfully remains upon another's premises or an entry occurs. "Inferences and presumptions are a staple of our adversary system of factfinding. It is often necessary for the trier of fact to de-termine the existence of an element of the crime—that is, an 'ultimate' or 'basic' facts." County Court v. Allen, 442 U.S. 140, 156, 99 S. Ct. 2213, 60 L. Ed. 2d 777 (1979). "The most common evidentiary device is the en-tirely permissive inference or pre-sumption, which allows—but does not require—the trier of fact to infer the elemental fact from proof by the pros-ecutor of the basic one and which places no burden of any kind on the defendant." County Court, at 157, 99 S. Ct. at 2224.

WPIC 60.05 provides for a per-missive inference or presumption, which allows the trier of fact to either infer the elemental fact from proof by the prosecutor, or reject the inference. WPIC 60.05 does not apply to those attempting to enter or remain unlaw-fully "unless it can at least be said with substantial assurance that the presumed fact is more likely than not to flow from the proved fact on which it is made to depend." Leary v. United States, 395 U.S. 6, 36, 89 S. Ct. 1532, 1548, 23 L. Ed. 2d 57 (1969). See also Sandstrom v. Montana, 442 U.S. 510, 99 S. Ct. 2450, 61 L. Ed. 2d 39 (1979).

For a trier of fact to draw infer-ences from proven circumstances, the inferences must be "rationally related" to the proven facts. State v. Jeffries, 105 Wash.2d 398, 442, 717, P.2d, cert. denied 479 U.S. 922, 107 S. Ct. 328, 93 L. Ed. 2d 301 (1986). A ratio-nal connection must exist between the initial fact proven and the further fact presumed. "The jury is permitted to infer from one fact the existence of another essential to guilt, if reason and experience support the inference." *Tot v. United States*, 319 U.S. 463, 467, 63 S. Ct. 1241, 1244, 87 L. Ed. 1519 (1943).

For a criminal statutory presumption to meet the test of constitutionality the presumed fact must follow beyond a reasonable doubt from the proven fact. *State v. Blight*, 89 Wash. 2d 38, 569 P.2d 1129 (1977). See also *State v. Odom*, 83 Wash.2d 541, 520 P.2d 152, *cert. denied* 419 U.S. 1013, 95 S. Ct. 333, 42 L. Ed. 2d 287 (1974); *State v. Rogers*, 83 Wash. 2d 553, 520 P.2d 159, *cert. denied* 419 U.S. 1053, 95 S. Ct. 633, 42 L. Ed. 2d 650 (1974).

WPIC 60.05 may be given as a proper instruction in a burglary case. However, where the state pleads and proves only attempted burglary, as here, this instruction is improper. In *State v. Bergeron, supra,* the defendant signed a statement wherein he admitted that when he threw a rock through a window he intended to enter the premises. In *Bergeron* we reasoned that while intent may be inferred from all the facts and circumstances surrounding the commission of an act, intent may not be inferred "from conduct that is patently equivocal." In order to give an instruction that an inference of an intent to commit a crime existed in a burglary case, there must be evidence of entering or remaining unlawfully in a building. The instruction on intent cannot be given without evidence to support it and that must place the defendant within a building. *State v. Ogden*, 21 Wash.App. 44, 49, 584 P.2d 957 (1978).

A presumption is only permissible when no more than one conclusion can be drawn from any set of circumstances. An inference should not arise where there exist other reasonable conclusions that would follow from the circumstances. Here the inferences are twofold: (1) attempted burglary or (2) vandalism or malicious destruction. Therefore, an inference can not follow that there was intent to commit a crime within the building just by the defendants' shattering of the window in the door. This evidence is consistent with two different interpretations; one indicating attempted burglary, a felony; and the other malicious mischief, a misdemeanor.

II

QUAERE: Could the Giving of the Instruction Be Considered Harmless Error?

"A 'harmless error' is one which is ' "*trivial, or formal, or merely academic,* and was not prejudicial to the substantial rights of the party assigning it, and *in no way affected the final outcome of the case.*" ' " *State v. Pam*, 98 Wash.2d 748, 754, 659 P.2d 454 (1983) (quoting *State v. Wanrow*, 88 Wash.2d 221, 237, 559 P.2d 548 (1977)). Here, the giving of the instruction could not be harmless error since it tended to prove an element of the commission of a crime. The instruction coming from the trial judge indicated that the defendant had entered the building and did so with the intent to commit a crime against the property therein. We do not need to determine whether the "overwhelming evidence" test would be applicable since we are convinced the inference of intent of instruction was not harmless. See *State v. Guloy*, 104 Wash.2d 412, 426, 705 P.2d 1182 (1985).

III

QUAERE: Is Malicious Mischief a Lesser Included Offense of Attempted Burglary?

"Under the Washington rule, a defendant is entitled to an instruction on a lesser included offense if two conditions are met. First, each of the elements of the lesser offense must be a necessary element of the offense charged. Second, the evidence in the case must support an inference that the lesser crime was committed." (Citations omitted.) *State v. Workman*, 90 Wash.2d 443, 447-48, 584 P.2d 382 (1978). Here, the defendant contends that an instruction defining malicious mischief in the third degree should have been given to the jury. RCW 9A.48.090 defines malicious mischief in the third degree as:

(1) A person is guilty of malicious mischief in the third degree if he knowingly and maliciously causes physical damage to the property of another, . . .
(2) Malicious mischief in the third degree is a gross misdemeanor if the damage to the property is in an amount ex-

ceeding fifty dollars; otherwise, it is a misdemeanor.

The defendant is charged with attempted burglary. RCW 9A.52.030 defines burglary in the second degree as:

(1) A person is guilty of burglary in the second degree if, with intent to commit a crime against a person or property therein, he enters or remains unlawfully in a building other than a vehicle.

Criminal attempt is defined by RCW 9A.28.020 as:

(1) A person is guilty of an attempt to commit crime if, with intent to commit a specific crime, he does any act which is a substantial step toward the commission of that crime.
(2) If the conduct in which a person engages otherwise constitutes an attempt to commit a crime, it is no defense to a prosecution of such attempt that the crime charged to have been attempted was, under the attendant circumstances, factually or legally impossible of commission.

Since the first condition of the test has not been met, we need not go any further in determining whether the second condition applies. Malicious mischief is not a lesser offense of attempted burglary because one does not invariably cause physical damage while attempting a burglary. One who enters a premises through an unlocked door without permission may be committing burglary, but he has not physically damaged property. The prosecution should have charged the defendant in the alternative; by not doing so the prosecution's choice was to seek a conviction of attempted burglary or nothing.

IV

QUAERE: Must the State Specify the Crime a Defendant Intended To Commit Upon Entry into Property?

We have held that our burglary statutes simply require an intent to commit a crime against a person or property inside the burglarized premises. As stated in *State v. Bergeron*, 105 Wash.2d 1, 4, 711 P.2d 1000 (1985):

> The intent to commit a specific named crime inside the burglarized premises is not an "element" of the crime of burglary in the State of Washington. . . . The intent required by our burglary statutes is simply the intent to commit any crime against a person or property inside the burglarized premises.

We adhere to the decision in *Bergeron*. The conviction of attempted second degree burglary is reversed and the cause is remanded for a new trial.

DORE, C.J., and UTTER, DOLLIVER, PEARSON and ANDERSEN, JJ., concur.

SMITH, J., concurs in the result only.

DURHAM, Justice (dissenting).

The majority remands for a new trial after concluding that the trial court committed reversible error by giving the following instruction in a prosecution for attempted burglary:

> A person who attempts to enter or remain unlawfully in a building may be inferred to have acted with intent to commit a crime against a person or property therein unless such entering or remaining shall be explained by evidence satisfactory to the jury to have been made without such criminal intent. This inference is not binding upon you and it is for you to determine what weight, if any, such inference is to be given.

This instruction is derived from a Washington pattern jury instruction, WPIC 60.-05, which in turn is based on RCW 9A52.-040. Both WPIC 60.05 and RCW 9A.52.-040 allow juries in burglary prosecutions to infer that a defendant intended to commit a crime on the premises when he unlawfully entered or remained in a building. An instruction of this nature is appropriate not only in a burglary case, but also in a prosecution for attempted burglary where the evidence shows that the defendant illegally entered the building. *State v. Bassett*, 50 Wash.App. 23, 26, 746 P.2d 1240 (1987), *review denied*, 110 Wash.2d 1016 (1988). The Legislature has broadly defined an entry in this context to include the insertion of any part of [a person's] body" into a building. RCW 9A.52.010(2); *see also Bassett*, at 26, 746 P.2d 1240 (insertion of finger through window constitutes entry). *State v. Couch*, 44 Wash.App. 26, 31-32, 720 P.2d 1387 (1986) (pushing open a trap door constitutes entry). Because the jury reasonably could have found that an entry occurred in the present case—Jackson kicked the Plexiglas window some 10 inches back into the building—the instruction was proper. So reasoned the Court of Appeals in this case, and so should we. See *State v. Jackson*, 51 Wash.App. 100, 102-05, 751 P.2d 1248 (1988).

Instead, the majority engages in an abstract and protracted discussion of the nature of presumptions and inferences. Unfortunately, the court does not discuss the case that addresses presumptions and inferences in the very context at issue here, jury instructions based on RCW 9A.52.040. In *State v. Johnson*, 100 Wash.2d 607, 674 P.2d 145 (1983), overruled on other grounds in *State v. Bergeron*, 105 Wash.2d 1, 711 P.2d 1000 (1985), this court explained that there are four fundamental types of presumptions: conclusive presumptions, persuasion-shifting presumptions, production-shifting presumptions, and permissive inferences. Instructions based on RCW 9A.52.040 are analyzed as permissive inferences when the defendant presents evidence in his own case, as occurred here. *Johnson*, 100 Wash.2d at 616-20, 674

P.2d 145. Permissive inferences are "constitutionally impermissible only when 'under the facts of the case, there is no rational way the trier couÚd make the connection permitted by the inference.' " Johnson, at 616, 674 P.2d 145 (quoting *County Court of Ulster Cy. v. Allen*, 442 U.S. 140, 157, 99 S. Ct. 2213, 2225, 60 L. Ed. 2d 777 (1979)).

By contrast, the majority concludes that "[a]n inference should not arise where there exists other reasonable conclusions that would follow from the circumstances." Majority, at 1215. The majority's conclusion conflicts with the well-accepted notion that juries are not bound to find for the defendant merely because reasonable inferences can be drawn either in favor of guilt or innocence. See *State v. Gosby*, 85 Wash.2d 758, 764-68, 539 P.2d 680 (1975) (rejecting the requirement of a multiple-hypothesis instruction); *State v. Randecker*, 79 Wash.2d 512, 517, 487 P.2d 1295 (1971). The mere existence of contrary reasonable inferences does not necessarily preclude juries from finding guilt. *Randecker*, at 517, 487 P.2d 1295. The *Johnson* standard recognizes these principles, the majority does not.

Applying the *Johnson* standard to the present case is not difficult. There is, of course, a rational connection between Jackson's act of kicking in a window and an inference of an intent to commit a crime inside the building. Because the requisite rational connection exists in this case regardless of the existence of other rational inferences, the instruction was properly given to the jury.

The majority concludes not only that the trial court erred in using this instruction, but that the error was prejudicial, requiring a reversal of the conviction below. The majority presents the basis for its holding as follows:

> Here, the giving of the instruction could not be harmless error since it tended to prove an element of the commission of a crime. The instruction coming from the trial judge indicated that the defendant had entered the building and did so with the intent to commit a crime against the property therein. We do not need to determine whether the "overwhelming evidence" test would be applicable since we are convinced the inference of intent instruction was not harmless.

Majority, at 1216.

I disagree both with the majority's interpretation of the instruction and with its application of the law of harmless error. The instruction in no way "indicated" that Jackson intended to commit another crime, it merely informed the jurors that they were permitted to infer this intent from the evidence presented. As for the test of harmless error, the majority implies that an error relating to presumptions or inferences can never be harmless when it relates to an element of the crime. The case law holds directly to the contrary. See Rose v. Clark, 478 U.S. 570, 579-82, 106 S. Ct. 3101, 3106-09, 92 L. Ed. 2d 460 (1986); State v. Johnson, supra, 100 Wash.2d at 620-21, 674 P.2d 145.

If I were to reach the issue of harmless error, I would adopt the approach taken by the Court of Appeals in this case. The Court of Appeals reasoned that any error in instructing the jury based on RCW 9A.52.040 would be harmless because the jury would have been permitted to make the inference as to Jackson's intent even if the RCW 9A.52.040 instruction were not used. See Jackson, at 104 n. 3, 751 P.2d 1248 n. 3.

Accordingly, I dissent from the majority's holdings in sections I and II of its opinion. I would affirm the Court of Appeals in upholding the conviction below.

BRACHTENBACH, J., concurs.

COMMONWEALTH OF KENTUCKY v. WHORTON

441 U.S. 786, 99 S. Ct. 2088, 60 L. Ed. 2d 640 (1979)

[Footnotes omitted]

PER CURIAM.

In *Taylor* v. *Kentucky*, 436 U.S. 478, 98 S.Ct. 1930, 56 L.Ed.2d 468, this Court reversed a criminal conviction resulting from a trial in which the judge had refused to give a requested jury instruction on the presumption of innocence. Relying on its understanding of that decision, the Kentucky Supreme Court in the present case held that such an instruction is constitutionally required in all criminal trials, and that the failure of a trial judge to give it cannot be harmless error. Ky., 570 S.W.2d 627. We granted certiorari to consider whether the Kentucky Supreme Court correctly interpreted our holding in *Taylor*. 439 U.S. 1067, 99 S.Ct. 832, 59 L.Ed.2d 31.

I.

The respondent was charged in three separate indictments with the commission of several armed robberies. At trial, numerous eyewitnesses identified the respondent as the perpetrator. Weapons, stolen money, and other incriminating evidence found in the respondent's automobile were introduced in evidence. The respondent did not take the stand in his own defense. The only evidence on his behalf was given by his wife and sister who offered alibi testimony concerning his whereabouts during the time of the commission of one of the robberies. The respondent's counsel requested that the jury be instructed on the presumption of innocence. This instruction was refused by the trial judge. An instruction was given, however, to the effect that the jury could return a verdict of guilty only if they found beyond a reasonable doubt that the respondent had committed the acts charged in the indictment with the requisite criminal intent.

The jury found the respondent guilty of 10 counts of first-degree robbery, two counts of first-degree wanton endangerment, and two counts of first-degree attempted robbery. The respondent was sentenced to consecutive terms of imprisonment totalling 230 years.

On appeal, the respondent argued that he had been denied Due Process of Law in violation of the Fourteenth Amendment by reason of the trial judge's refusal to give an instruction on the presumption of innocence. A divided Kentucky Supreme Court agreed, interpreting this Court's decision in *Taylor* "to mean that when an instruction on the presumption of innocence is asked for and denied there is a reversible error." Ky., 570 S.W.2d 627.

Two Justices filed separate dissenting opinions. In their view, the *Taylor* case should be understood as dealing with the factual situation there presented, and not as establishing a constitutional rule that failure to instruct the jury on the presumption of innocence requires automatic reversal of a conviction.

Since these Justices concluded that the respondent received a fair trial, they would have affirmed the convictions.

II.

While this Court in *Taylor* reversed a conviction resulting from a trial in which the judge had refused to give a requested instruction on the presumption of innocence, the Court did not there fashion a new rule of constitutional law requiring that such an instruction be given in every criminal case. Rather, the Court's opinion focused on the failure to give the instruction as it related to the overall fairness of the trial considered in its entirety.

The Court observed, for example, that the trial judge's instructions were "Spartan," 436 U.S., at 486, 98 S.Ct., at 1935, that the prosecutor improperly referred to the indictment and otherwise made remarks of dubious propriety, *id.*, at 486-488, 98 S.Ct., at 1935-1936, and that the evidence against the defendant was weak. *Id.*, at 488, 98 S.Ct., at 1936. "[T]he combination of the skeletal instructions, the possible harmful inferences from the references to the indictment, and the repeated suggestions that petitioner's status as a defendant tended to establish his guilt created a genuine danger that the jury would convict petitioner on the basis of those extraneous considerations, rather than on the evidence introduced at trial." *Id.*, at 487-488, 98 S.Ct., at 1936.

It was under these circumstances that the Court held that the failure of the trial court to instruct the jury on the presumption of innocence denied the defendant due process of law. Indeed, the Court's holding was expressly limited to the facts: "We hold that *on the facts of this case* the trial court's refusal to give petitioner's requested instruction on the presumption of innocence resulted in a violation of his right to a fair trial as guaranteed by the Due Process Clause of the Fourteenth Amendment." *Id.*, at 490, 98 S.Ct., at 1937 (emphasis added). This explicitly limited holding, and the Court's detailed discussion of the circumstances of the defendant's trial, belie any intention to create a rule that an instruction on the presumption of innocence is constitutionally required in every case.

In short, the failure to give a requested instruction on the presumption of innocence does not in and of itself violate the Constitution. Under *Taylor*, such a failure must be evaluated in light of the totality of the circumstances—including all the instructions to the jury, the arguments of counsel, whether the weight of the evidence was overwhelming, and other relevant factors—to determine whether the defendant received a constitutionally fair trial.

The Kentucky Supreme Court thus erred in interpreting *Taylor* to hold that the Due Process Clause of the Fourteenth Amendment absolutely requires that an instruction on the presumption of innocence must be given in every criminal case. The court's inquiry should have been directed to a determination of whether the failure to give such an instruction in the present case deprived the respondent of Due Process of Law in light of the totality of the circumstances.

Accordingly, the judgment is reversed and the case is remanded to the Supreme Court of Kentucky for further proceedings not inconsistent with this opinion.

Mr. Justice STEWART, with whom Mr. Justice BRENNAN and Mr. Justice MARSHALL join, dissenting.

No principle is more firmly established in our system of criminal justice than the presumption of innocence that is accorded to the defendant in every criminal trial. In *In re Winship*, 397 U.S. 358, 90 S.Ct. 1068, 25 L.Ed.2d 368, the Court held that the Due Process Clause of the Fourteenth Amendment requires proof beyond a reasonable doubt of a defendant's guilt. I believe that the Due Process Clause of the Fourteenth Amendment equally requires the presumption that a defendant is innocent until he has been proven guilty.

Almost 85 years ago the Court said: "The principle that there is a presumption of innocence in favor of the accused is the undoubted law, axiomatic and elementary, and its enforcement lies at the foundation of the administration of our criminal law." *Coffin* v. *United States*, 156 U.S. 432, 453, 15 S.Ct. 394, 403, 39 L.Ed. 481. Only three years ago the Court reaffirmed that the presumption of innocence "is a basic component of a fair trial under our system of criminal justice." *Estelle* v. *Williams*, 425 U.S. 501, 503, 96 S.Ct. 1691, 1692, 48 L.Ed.2d 126. See also *Cool* v. *United States*, 409 U.S. 100, 104, 93 S.Ct. 354, 357, 34 L.Ed.2d 335. And a fair trial, after all, is what the Due Process Clause of the Fourteenth Amendment above all else guarantees.

While an instruction on the presumption of innocence in one sense only serves to remind the jury that the prosecutor has the burden of proof beyond a reasonable doubt, it also has a separate and distinct function. Quite apart from considerations of the burden of proof, the presumption of innocence "cautions the jury to put away from their minds all the suspicion that arises from the arrest, the indictment, and the arraignment, and to reach their conclusion solely from the evidence adduced." 9 Wigmore on Evidence § 2511, at 407 (3d ed. 1940). And because every defendant, regardless of the totality of the circumstances, is entitled to have his guilt determined only on the basis of the evidence properly introduced against him at trial, I would hold that an instruction on the presumption of innocence is constitutionally required in every case where a timely request has been made.

There may be cases where the failure to give such an instruction could not have affected the outcome of the trial. If that conclusion can be drawn beyond a reasonable doubt, failure to give the instruction would be harmless error. Cf. *Chapman* v. *California*, 386 U.S. 18, 87 S.Ct. 824, 17 L.Ed.2d 705; *Harrington* v. *California*, 395 U.S. 250, 89 S.Ct. 1726, 23 L.Ed.2d 284. Since the Kentucky Supreme Court did not consider this possibility, I would vacate its judgment and remand the case to that court, but only for consideration of whether the failure to give the instruction in the circumstances presented here was harmless error.

STATE v. FORD

725 S.W.2d 689 (Tenn. Crim. App. 1986)

OPINION

SCOTT, Judge

The appellant was convicted of driving under the influence of an intoxicant, third offense. He was sentenced to serve eleven months and twenty-nine days in the county jail and was fined $1,000.00. On appeal he has presented four issues. In the first he challenges the sufficiency of the convicting evidence. In the second he contends that his motion for judgment of acquittal should have been granted since he was not shown to be driving or in "physical control" of the automobile.

The state's proof consisted of the testimony of Randy Hartselle, a member of the Tennessee Highway Patrol. At approximately 2:45 A.M. on October 9, 1983, Mr. Hartselle received a call that there had been a wreck on Interstate 40 near the Cave Church Road overpass. Upon arriving at the scene, he found the appellant's car had struck a guardrail, damaging the front fender of the passenger side. The car was still in gear and the keys were in the ignition. The appellant was behind the steering wheel, either asleep or "passed out." Mr. Hartselle noted "the odor of alcohol beverage about this person." In addition, the appellant was "very unsteady on his feet" and had bloodshot eyes. Seven full cans of beer and two empty cans were in his car. The appellant agreed to take a breath test. Later, he changed his mind, and stated that he wanted a lawyer present at the time of the test. Mr. Hartselle let the appellant call two different attorneys. However, both refused to go to the police station.

The appellant's proof consisted of the testimony of one of the attorneys and a stipulation of the other attorney's expected testimony. Both stated that when they spoke with the appellant by telephone that he did not sound drunk to them.

Based upon this controverted proof, the jury found the appellant guilty of driving under the influence of an intoxicant. Proof was also introduced to show his prior convictions and the jury enhanced the verdict to DUI, third offense.

A jury verdict of guilty, approved by the trial judge, accredits the testimony of the state's witnesses and resolves all conflicts in favor of the theory of the state. *State v. Hatchett*, 560 S.W.2d 627, 630 (Tenn. 1978). On appeal the state is entitled to the strongest legitimate view of the evidence and all reasonable and legitimate inferences which may be drawn therefrom, *State v. Cabbage*, 571 S.W.2d 832, 835 (Tenn. 1978).

The crime of driving under the influence is a continuing offense.

State v. Adkins, 619 S.W.2d 147, 149 (Tenn. Cr. App. 1981). Our Supreme Court has sustained convictions for driving under the influence even though no one saw the car in motion or saw the accused driving the car. *E.g., Hopson v. State*, 201 Tenn. 337, 299 S.W.2d 11, 13 (1957), (defendant "alighted from the driver's seat"); *Farmer v. State*, 208 Tenn. 75, 343 S.W.2d 895, 897 (1961) (defendant, as in this case, found drunk and asleep at the wheel). Like any other crime, driving under the influence of an intoxicant can be established by circumstantial evidence. *State v. Harless*, 607 S.W.2d 492, 493 (Tenn. Cr. App. 1980).

There was ample, indeed overwhelming, evidence from which any rational trier of fact would conclude that the appellant was guilty of driving under the influence of an intoxicant, third offense, beyond a reasonable doubt. Rule 13(e), T.R.A.P., *Jackson v. Virginia*, 443 U.S. 307, 99 S. Ct. 2781, 2786-2792, 61 L. Ed. 2d 560 (1979).

In another issue it is asserted that the trial judge erred by stipulating the testimony of Mr. Leibrock without the appellant's consent. The appellant contends in his brief that a hearing was held the day before the trial and the trial judge then decided to allow Mr. Leibrock, a practicing attorney, to disobey the subpoena issued for him and to not appear at trial. At trial, the court stated in substance what Mr. Leibrock's testimony would have been had he appeared. The appellant contends that these statements were entered as evidence without his consent and over his objection.

The transcript of the hearing the day before the trial is not in the record. Whether a verbatim stenographic report of the proceedings was made or not, it is the appellant who has the responsibility to have prepared a transcript "of such part of the evidence of proceedings as is necessary to convey a fair, accurate and complete account of what transpired with respect to those issues that are the bases of appeal." Rule 24(b) and (c), T.R.A.P. Thus, were are unable to review what occurred at that hearing.

However, the record does reveal that the defense counsel objected to Mr. Leibrock being released from the subpoena prior to the beginning of the trial. Later, when the stipulation was stated to the jury by the judge, it appeared to be with the appellant's consent. Furthermore, after the stipulation was stated by the judge, the state objected to the way he worded the stipulation. The judge responded that he had stated it accurately, and defense counsel noted his concurrence with the way the stipulation was presented.

A stipulation is an *agreement between counsel* with respect to business before a court. 83 C.J.S. (Stipulations) § 1, p. 2. (emphasis added) Stipulations are favored and should be encouraged and enforced by the courts, since they expedite the business of the courts. *Brown v. McCulloch*, 24 Tenn. App. 324, 144 S.W.2d 1, 4 (1940). However, it is not the duty or function of a trial court to require one of the parties to the litigation to stipulate with his adversary. 83 C.J.S. (Stipulations) § 2, p. 3.

Certainly, it is not the business of the trial judge to decide what will be stipulated, or as in this case, to state to the jury the substance of the absent witness's testimony. The impropriety of this unusual procedure is illustrated by the fact that both the state and the appellant were dissatisfied with the stipulation. The appellant was dissatisfied that the stipulation replaced the witness and the state was dissatisfied that the judge couched the stipulation in terms too favorable to the appellant. The danger of courts getting involved in the stipulation process is evident. It was clearly error for the trial judge to have required the appellant to present the testimony of the witness by stipulation.

However, the error was harmless. Rule 52(a), T.P.Cr.P. Stated differently, it cannot be said that the stipulation was an error involving a substantial right which more probably than not affected the judgment or resulted in prejudice to the judicial process. Rule 36(b), T.R.A.P. The appellant presented the live testimony of Ben Hooper, a well known attorney in Cocke County, who testified in his behalf. Mr. Leibrock's testimony was merely cumulative to Mr. Hooper's and absolutely no prejudice resulted from this procedure. This issue has no merit.

Finally, the appellant contends that the trial judge erred by allowing a conviction for driving under the influence, third offense, to stand because he did not receive proper notice that he was being prosecuted for a third offense.

The indictment in this case charged the appellant with driving under the influence of an intoxicant in October 1983, having been previously convicted of the same offense on four occasions. The indictment sets forth the docket numbers of the cases in the Cocke County Circuit Court and the date on which each conviction occurred. That was, without any question, sufficient notice to apprise the appellant that he was charged with driving under the influence after having been previously convicted on the other occasions. This issue has no merit.

Finding no merit to any of the issues, the judgment is affirmed.

DUNCAN and DAUGHTREY, JJ., concur.

Cases relating to Chapter 7
RELEVANCY AND MATERIALITY

UNITED STATES v. SCHWARTZ

790 F.2d 1059 (3d. Cir. 1986)

Before GARTH and STAPLETON, Circuit Judges and FULLAM, District Judge.

PER CURIAM.

Convicted of distributing small quantities of cocaine (about one-half ounce) and sentenced to a 10-year prison term, appellant Jeffrey Schwartz seeks reversal of his conviction. He asserts that he was deprived of his right to a fundamentally fair trial in three ways: (1) by the erroneous admission of evidence of other crimes, in violation of Federal Rule of Evidence 404; (2) by the trial judge's hostility and bias; and (3) by the trial judge's receipt, from extra-judicial sources, of (false) information adverse to the defendant, the judge's reliance thereon, and the denial of a recusal motion filed when the alleged incident came to light shortly after the conclusion of the trial. We agree with the first of these three contentions, and remand for a new trial. In view of this disposition, it is unnecessary to dwell at length upon the other two assertions.

I. BACKGROUND

Appellant, in his mid-30s, has lived for several years in an intimate relationship with a young lady named Joyce Marker. She is the daughter of a government official in the Western Pennsylvania area. Her parents strongly disapprove of the relationship and of the appellant. However, her younger brother, Scott Marker— aged about 20 when the relevant events occurred— has maintained close ties with both the appellant and his sister over the years.

On the evening of November 23, 1983, Scott Marker and a friend of his were engaged in helping the appellant and Joyce Marker move their furniture to a new residence. Later the same night, at about 1:30 a.m. on November 24, 1983, local police officers spotted a suspicious van in the parking lot of a closed restaurant in a rural area. Upon investigation, they learned that the van was occupied by Scott Marker, in the driver's seat; a young man named Kevin Morelli, in the passenger seat; and a young lady named Diane Smidansky— Scott Marker's girlfriend— seated between the two. After ordering these persons to get out of the van, the police conducted a pat-down search. In Scott Marker's pocket was a small plastic bag containing about one-half ounce of cocaine and a razor blade; some envelopes which had apparently contained a white powder at some earlier time; and an empty "Bic" pen casing with evidence that it had earlier been used for sniffing cocaine. Searches of the van at the scene and later on disclosed a kitchen-type cutting board with a whitish powder residue thereon; vestiges of marijuana; and other miscellaneous drug paraphernalia.

The van was owned by Kevin Morrelli's brother. No drugs were found in the actual possession of either Diane Smidansky or Kevin Morrelli, and they were not charged.

Scott Marker was charged under state law with the criminal possession of cocaine, but in exchange for his agreement to cooperate with the authorities was granted use-immunity and was placed in an accelerated rehabilitation program (ARD). He told the police that he had obtained the cocaine from the appellant earlier in the evening. His testimony to that effect at appellant's trial provided the principal evidentiary support for the conviction appealed from.

The Indictment contains but a single count, charging appellant with having distributed cocaine on or about November 24, 1983. At the start of the trial, the prosecuting attorney in-

formed defense counsel that he intended to elicit from Scott Marker testimony not only about the November 24 incident, but also to the effect that appellant had furnished him with cocaine on innumerable occasions over a four-or-five-year period.

Before any evidence was presented, defendant's counsel made a formal motion to exclude proffered testimony about other crimes. After considering the arguments of counsel, and after a recess in which further research was apparently conducted, the trial judge overruled all objections to this evidence. Thereupon, as part of the government's case in chief, Scott Marker testified that the defendant supplied him with cocaine, not only on the occasion charged in the Indictment, but also on numerous other occasions, beginning when Scott Marker was a 16-year-old high school student. In addition, he provided the further information that he had shared with other high school students the cocaine obtained from the defendant.

The record makes clear that appellant, by repeated objections and motions throughout the trial, preserved his right to appellate review of the various rulings of the trial judge admitting this evidence.

II. DISCUSSION

Federal Rule of Evidence 404(b) provides:

"(b) Other crimes, wrongs, or acts. Evidence of other crimes, wrongs, or acts is not admissible to prove the character of a person in order to show that he acted in conformity therewith. It may, however, be admissible for other purposes, such as proof of motive, opportunity, intent, preparation, plan, knowledge, identity, or absence of mistake or accident."

As the notes of the Advisory Committee point out

"Subdivision (b) deals with a specialized but important application of the general rule excluding circumstantial use of character evidence. Consistently with that rule, evidence of other crimes, wrongs, or acts is not admissible to prove character as a basis for suggesting the inference that conduct on a particular occasion was in conformity with it. However, the evidence may be offered for another purpose, such as proof of motive, opportunity, and so on, which does not fall within the prohibition. In this situation, the rule does not require that the evidence be excluded. No mechanical solution is offered. The determination must be made whether the danger of undue prejudice outweighs the probative value of the evidence in view of the availability of other means of proof and other factors appropriate for making decisions of this kind under Rule 403."

And, of course, Federal Rule of Evidence 403 provides that

"Although relevant, evidence may be excluded if its probative value is substantially outweighed by the danger of unfair prejudice, confusion of the issues, or misleading the jury, or by considerations of undue delay, waste of time, or needless presentation of cumulative evidence."

There is a great deal of uncertainty in the record as to the purpose for which the evidence of other crimes was offered, and as to the basis on which it was admitted. At no point—during the lengthy arguments over the admissibility of the evidence in the course of trial, or in the court's rulings, or in the charge to the jury, or even in the government's briefs on appeal—can there be found anything more specific than a reference to the entire laundry-list of possible exceptions to the general rule excluding such evidence. Trial counsel for the defendant repeatedly stressed this ambiguity, and offered sweeping stipulations relieving the government of the need to prove anything other than that the substance possessed by Scott Marker when he was arrested had been obtained from the defendant. That is, the defendant offered to stipulate that if the jury concluded that Scott Marker had obtained the substance from the defendant, the defendant readily conceded that the substance was indeed cocaine, that the defendant knew it was cocaine, and that the defendant acted intentionally, and not by accident or mistake. Defendant's sole defense was limited to the issue of distribution: the defendant presented evidence, through cross-examination of Scott Marker and through the testimony of of defense witnesses, to the effect that Scott Marker had journeyed to the University of Pittsburgh to keep an appointment with a friend earlier in the evening, and thereafter had been seen in possession of a substantial quantity of cocaine both before and at the time of his arrival at the defendant's residence that evening.

The defendant's expressed willingness to stipulate to substantial portions of the government's case does not, of course, preclude the government from presenting relevant, admissible, evidence. See *United States v. Chaimson*, 760 F.2d 798, 805-06 (7th Cir. 1985). But see *United States v. Manafzadeh*, 592 F.2d 81, 87 (2d Cir. 1979). Generally speaking, it is for the prosecutor, not the defendant, to shape the government's trial strategy with a view toward sustaining its heavy burden of proof. On the other hand, the presence or absence of a genuine need for the questioned evidence is a legitimate part of the balancing analysis required by Federal Rules of Evidence 403. *See United States v. Herman*, 589 F.2d 1191, 1198 (3d Cir. 1978).

In the circumstances of this case, there is room for argument that the evidence about earlier alleged drug dealings between defendant and Scott Marker neither proved nor tended to prove anything more than the defendant's propensity for criminal activity of that kind. The government's repeated assertions that the evidence was admissible to prove all of the matters covered by the listed exceptions, and (unspecified) other legitimate purposes as well, seemingly strengthens that argument. For surely, if one or more of the exceptions is applicable, it should be possible to specify which, and to provide a reasoned explanation of the alleged relevance.

We deem it unnecessary to reach a firm conclusion on that score, however. Assuming that the "other crimes" evidence had some relevance to an issue other than character/propensity, in the circumstances of this case its relevance was marginal at best, and the prejudice to the defendant was very great. If the trial judge had undertaken the balancing analysis required by Federal Rule of Evidence 403, we are confident that he would have realized that, irrespective of its possible technical admissibility under Rule 404(b), the evidence should have been excluded.

It bears mention that the prejudice to the defendant arises not only from the implication that, since he had committed other crimes, he must be guilty of the crime on trial, but also from the fact that the generalized nature of the testimony precluded any meaningful refutation except a similarly generalized denial. It should be noted that the Indictment charged the defendant with having given away a small quantity of cocaine in a social setting; generalized testimony suggesting that the defendant was a large-scale and longstanding supplier of cocaine to high school students made a fair trial on this Indictment unlikely. We therefore conclude that the district court abused its discretion in admitting the disputed evidence. Since we cannot say that it is "highly probable that the evidence . . . did not contribute to the jury's judgment of conviction," *Government of the Virgin Islands v. Toto*, 529 F.2d 278, 284 (3d Cir. 1976), the error cannot be regarded as harmless, and we therefore remand for a new trial.

The appellant also contends that the trial judge exhibited bias against appellant and his counsel throughout the trial, and should have recused himself because of his (alleged) improper receipt of ex parte communications concerning the appellant. Since a new trial is required because of the erroneous evidentiary ruling discussed above, it is unnecessary to consider whether the trial was marred in other respects. With regard to the recusal motion—filed after the trial was concluded—it is apparent (1) that, rightly or wrongly, appellant and his counsel sincerely believe that appellant's sentence was improperly influenced by *ex parte* communications; (2) that the charges of bias and the filing and pursuit of the recusal motion, both in the district court and on appeal, might tend to generate or exacerbate adverse emotional reactions; and (3) that an evidentiary hearing would be required in order to lay to rest the recusal question. In these circumstances, the interests of efficient administration of justice would best be served by pretermitting the recusal matter, by the simple expedient of suggesting that the retrial be conducted before a judge who has had not involvement in the case to date.

We emphasize that this suggestion is grounded solely upon expediency, and is no way a reflection upon the fairness and impartiality of the highly respected jurist who presided at the first trial.

III. CONCLUSION

The judgment appealed from will be reversed, and the case remanded for a new trial.

STATE of Missouri v. HEMPHILL

699 S.W. 2283 (1985)

SMITH, Presiding Judge.

Defendant appeals from his conviction of capital murder and the sentence of life imprisonment without possibility of probation or parole for fifty years. We affirm.

The victim, Cornell Hamilton, was shot to death on July 12, 1983 in his front yard. A man armed with a rifle was seen in an alley next door to Hamilton's residence by two women residing in the house next door. One of these witnesses saw the man move to the front of her house raise the rifle, and fire a shot. She identified defendant as the armed man. The second witness could not identify the man she saw. The next day two police officers were questioning Hamilton's sister about the killing and about defendant who had at one time been her paramour. Because of the presence of a large group of relatives and friends gathered at the victim's home the interrogation took place in the detectives' unmarked car down the street. During the course of the interrogation several shots were heard causing the people at the Hamilton house to take cover. Defendant carrying a rifle then ran from a vacant building in close proximity to the detectives' vehicle, jumped into the passenger side of a waiting car and left the area. The detectives gave chase and stopped the fleeing vehicle within four blocks. A 30-30 Winchester Western rifle was found on the street a short distance from the end of the chase. A broken piece of the stock of the rifle and two parts of the gun's sights were also found in close proximity to the rifle. Defendant was apprehended in the vehicle. The driver was his cousin. Defendant had a live round of 30-30 rifle ammunition in his pocket. His fingerprints were on the rifle. An empty shell casing was found near the spot where the defendant was seen the night of the killing, and three empty shell casings were found in the house from which the defendant fled the next day. All four casings had been discharged by the rifle. The bullet found in Hamilton's body was fired from the rifle.

Defendant's first point is that the trial court committed error in admitting testimony and evidence concerning the occurrences on the day after the killing which we have outlined above. He invokes the oft-cited rule prohibiting evidence of uncharged crimes. *State* v. *Williams*, 652 S.W.2d 102 (Mo. banc 1983) [9]. The rule is inapplicable where as here the evidence has a legitimate tendency to establish the identity of the killer. *State* v. *Williams, supra.* Defendant was seen on the day after the murder in possession of a rifle after shots were fired. A rifle, containing his fingerprints, was found in a location and in a condition warranting an inference that it had been thrown from a vehicle in which defendant was a passenger during a brief instant while the pursuing police vehicle was negotiating a turn and its occupants were not in visual contact with the pursued vehicle. That rifle was utilized to fire the shots on the day after the killing and was the weapon which killed Hamilton. That evidence serves to identify defendant as the murderer.

Defendant next objects to testimony relating to an episode involving defendant and Hamilton occurring approximately a month prior to the killing. This evidence established that after defendant and Hamilton's sister discontinued their relationship, defendant physically prevented the sister's daughter from leaving a store where she had been sent by Hamilton and his brother. Hamilton and the brother went to the store and after some undefined unpleasantries left with the girl. Upon their return to their home, a jack was thrown through the window of the front door and defendant was seen in front of the house. Assuming that this evidence also implicates the rule against evidence of uncharged crimes, it also is admissible under the motive and intent exceptions to the general rule. *State* v. *Williams, supra.* This evidence combined with defendant's actions the day after the killing establish a continuing vendetta by defendant against the family of his former girl friend and thus establishes a hatred motive in the otherwise inexplicable shooting of Hamilton.

The crime charged here was capital murder which required at the time of trial that the state prove defendant unlawfully, willfully, knowingly, deliberately, and with premeditation killed Hamilton. Defendant's mental state, in this case deliberation and premeditation, was a necessary element of the state's case. Mental state is rarely capable of direct proof. *State* v. *Flynn*, 541 S.W.2d 344 (Mo.App 1976)[2, 3]. It is frequently established by inferences reasonably drawn from the evidence and the circumstances surrounding the act. *State* v. *Wood*, 596 S.W.2d 394 (Mo. banc 1980) [7-10]. Conduct before and after the commission of the charged crime is relevant where it relates to the elements of the crime charged. *State* v. *Williams, supra*, [10]. Defendant's virtual kidnapping of the victim's niece, his altercation with the victim and his brother, the throwing of the jack through a window, the shooting of Hamilton from ambush, and the subsequent shooting of multiple shots in the presence of the victims's grieving family, which included small children, is evidence that the killing of Hamilton was performed in a cool, albeit evil, state of mind as a free act of will not under the influence of violent passion suddenly aroused by some provocation. *State* v. *Zeitvogel*, 655 S.W.2d 678 (Mo.App. 1983) [20]. The evidence was relevant and its admission was not error.

Defendant next complains of the admission into evidence of a "mugshot" of defendant. Specifically he objects because the date upon which the pictures were taken was not blanked out, allowing the jury to surmise that defendant had been previously arrested. The date, however, was relevant. The witness who identified the defendant at the scene of the crime was unable to identify defendant from the picture. Not surprisingly the defense capitalized on this failure. The picture was taken a year prior to the killing and the defendant's appearance had arguably changed since the taking. The date of the picture was therefore relevant to explain the witness' inability to make an identification from the picture. Furthermore, the picture was shown to the witness prior to the arrest of the defendant for the murder. The jury was therefore aware that it was taken by the police department for some reason other than this crime. That that reason occurred at any particular time prior to the murder could not have prejudiced the defendant. Mugshots are themselves neutral and do not constitute evidence of prior crimes. *State v. Lorenze*, 592 S.W.2d 523

(Mo.App. 1979) [13, 14]; *State v. Hamell*, 561 S.W.2d 357 (Mo.App. 1977) [10]. We find no error in the admission of the photograph.

Defendant's final point concerns the closing argument of the state. We find no abuse of the trial court's broad discretion in allowing the argument. *State v. Newlon*, 627 S.W.2d 606 (Mo. banc 1982) [12-14].

Judgment affirmed.

SNYDER and SATZ, JJ., concur.

HUDDLESTON v. UNITED STATES

485 U.S. 681, 108 S. Ct. 1496, 96 L. Ed. 2d 771 (1988)

Chief Justice REHNQUIST delivered the opinion of the Court.

Federal Rule of Evidence 404(b) provides:

"Other crimes, wrongs, or acts.—Evidence of other crimes, wrongs, or acts is not admissible to prove the character of a person in order to show that he acted in conformity therewith. It may, however, be admissible for other purposes, such as proof of motive, opportunity, intent, preparation, plan, knowledge, identity, or absence of mistake or accident."

This case presents the question whether the district court must itself make a preliminary finding that the Government has proved the "other act" by a preponderance of the evidence before it submits the evidence to the jury. We hold that it need not do so.

Petitioner, Guy Rufus Huddleston, was charged with one count of selling stolen goods in interstate commerce, 18 U.S.C. § 2315, and one count of possessing stolen property in interstate commerce, 18 U.S.C. § 659. The two counts related to two portions of a shipment of stolen Memorex video cassette tapes that petitioner was alleged to have possessed and sold, knowing that they were stolen.

The evidence at trial showed that a trailer containing over 32,000 blank Memorex video cassette tapes with a manufacturing cost of $4.53 per tape was stolen from the Overnight Express yard in South Holland, Illinois, sometime between April 11 and 15, 1985. On April 17, 1985, petitioner contacted Karen Curry, the manager of the Magic Rent-to-Own in Ypsilanti, Michigan, seeking her assistance in selling a large number of blank Memorex video cassette tapes. After assuring Curry that the tapes were not stolen, he told her he wished to sell them in lots of at least 500 at $2.75 to $3.00 per tape. Curry subsequently arranged for the sale of a total of 5,000 tapes, which petitioner delivered to the various purchasers—who apparently believed the sales were legitimate.

There was no dispute that the tapes which petitioner sold were stolen; the only material issue at trial was whether petitioner knew that they were stolen. The District Court allowed the Government to introduce evidence of "similar acts" under Rule 404(b), concluding that such evidence had "clear relevance as to [petitioner's knowledge]." App. 11. The first piece of similar act evidence offered by the Government was the testimony of Paul Toney, a record store owner. He testified that in February, 1985, petitioner offered to sell new 12" black and white televisions for $28 a piece. According to Toney, petitioner indicated that he could obtain several thousand of these televisions. Petitioner and Toney eventually traveled to Magic Rent-to-Own, where Toney purchased 20 of the televisions. Several days later, Toney purchased 18 more televisions.

The second piece of similar act evidence was the testimony of Robert Nelson, an undercover FBI agent posing as a buyer for an appliance store. Nelson testified in May 1985,

petitioner offered to sell him a large quantity of Amana appliances—28 refrigerators, 2 ranges, and 40 icemakers. Nelson agreed to pay $8,000 for the appliances. Petitioner was arrested shortly after he arrived at the parking lot where he and Nelson had agreed to transfer the appliances. A truck containing the appliances was stopped a short distance from the parking lot, and Leroy Wesby, who was driving the truck, was also arrested. It was determined that the appliances had a value of approximately $20,000 and were part of a shipment that had been stolen.

Petitioner testified that the Memorex tapes, the televisions, and the appliances had all been provided by Leroy Wesby, who had represented that all of the merchandise was obtained   legitimately.   Petitioner stated that he had sold 6,500 Memorex tapes for Wesby on a commission basis. Petitioner maintained that all of the sales for Wesby had been on a commission basis and that he had no knowledge that any of the goods were stolen.

In closing, the prosecution explained that petitioner was not on trial for his dealings with the appliances or the televisions. The District Court instructed the jury that the similar acts evidence was to be used only to establish petitioner's knowledge, and not to prove his character. The jury convicted petitioner on the possession count only.

A divided panel of the United States Court of Appeals for the Sixth Circuit initially reversed the conviction, concluding that because the Government had failed to prove by clear and convincing evidence that the televisions were stolen, the District Court erred in admitting the testimony concerning the televisions. 802 F.2d 874 (1986).[1] The panel subsequently granted rehearing to address the decision in *United States v. Ebens*, 800 F.2d 1422 (CA6 1986), in which a different panel had held: "Courts may admit evidence of prior bad acts if the proof shows by a preponderance of the evidence that the defendant did in fact commit the act." *Id.* at 1432. On rehearing, the court affirmed the conviction. "Applying the preponderance of the evidence standard adopted in *Ebens*, we cannot say that the district court abused its discretion in admitting evidence of the similar acts in question here." 811 F.2d 974, 975 (1987) (*per curiam*). The court noted that the evidence concerning the televisions was admitted for a proper purpose and that the probative value of this evidence was not outweighed by its potential prejudicial effect.

We granted certiorari, 484 U.S. ____, 108 S. Ct. 226, 98 L. Ed. 2d 185 (1987), to resolve a conflict among the Courts of Appeals as to whether the trial court must make a preliminary finding before "similar act" and other Rule 404(b) evidence is

submitted to the jury.[2] We conclude that such evidence should be admitted if there is sufficient evidence to support a finding by the jury that the defendant committed the similar act.

Federal Rule of Evidence 404(b)—which applies in both civil and criminal cases—generally prohibits the introduction of evidence of extrinsic acts that might adversely reflect on the actor's character, unless that evidence bears upon a relevant is-

---

[1] "[T]he government's only support for the assertion that the televisions were stolen was [petitioner's] failure to produce a bill of sale at trial and the fact that the televisions were sold at a low price." 802 F.2d at 876, n. 5.

[2] The First, Fourth, Fifth and Eleventh Circuits allow the admission of similar act evidence if the evidence is sufficient to allow the jury to find that the defendant committed the act. *United States v. Ingraham*, 832 F.2d 229, 235 (CA1 1987); *United States v. Martin*, 773 F.2d 579, 582 (CA4 1985); *United States v. Beechum*, 582 F.2d 898, 914 (CA5 1978) (en banc), *cert. denied*, 440 U.S. 920, 99 S. Ct. 1244, 59, L. Ed. 2d 472 (1979); *United States v. Dothard*, 666 F.2d 498, 502 (CA11 1982). Consistent with the Sixth Circuit, the Second Circuit prohibits the introduction of similar act evidence unless the trial court finds by a preponderance of the evidence that the defendant committed the act. *United States v. Leonard*, 524 F.2d 1076, 1090-1091 (CA2 1975). The Seventh, Eighth, Ninth, and District of Columbia Circuits require the Government to prove to the court by clear and convincing evidence that the defendant committed the similar act. *United States v. Leight*, 818 F.2d 1297, 1302 (CA7), *cert. denied*, 484 U.S. ____, 108 S. Ct. 356, 98 L. Ed. 2d 381 (1987); *United States v. Weber*, 818 F.2d 14 (CA8 1987); *United States v. Vaccaro*, 816 F.2d 443, 452 (CA9), *cert. denied, sub. non. Alvis v. United States*, 484 U.S. ____, 108 S. Ct. 262, 98 L. Ed. 2d 220 (1987); *United States v. Lavelle*, 243 U.S. Ap. D.C. 46, 57, 751 F.2d 1266, 1276, *cert. denied*, 474 U.S. 817, 106 S. Ct. 62, 88 L. Ed. 2d 51 (1985).

sue in the case such as motive, opportunity, or knowledge. Extrinsic acts evidence may be critical to the establishment of the truth as to a disputed issue, especially when that issue involves the actor's state of mind and the only means of ascertaining that mental state is by drawing inferences from conduct. The actor in the instant case was a criminal defendant, and the act in question was "similar" to the one with which he was charged. Our use of these terms is not meant to suggest that our analysis is limited to such circumstances.

Before this Court, petitioner argues that the District Court erred in admitting Toney's testimony as to petitioner's sale of the televisions.[3] The threshold inquiry a court must make before admitting similar acts evidence under Rule 404(b) is whether that evidence is probative of a material issue other than character. The Government's theory of relevance was that the televisions were stolen, and proof that petitioner had engaged in a series of sales of stolen merchandise from the same suspicious source would be strong evidence that he was aware that each of these items, including the Memorex tapes, was stolen.[4]   As

such, the sale of the televisions was a "similar act" only if the televisions were stolen. Petitioner acknowledges that this evidence was admitted for the proper purpose of showing his knowledge that the Memorex tapes were stolen. He asserts, however, that the evidence should not have been admitted because the Government failed to prove to the District Court that the televisions were in fact stolen.

Petitioner argues from the premise that evidence of similar acts has a grave potential for causing improper prejudice. For instance, the jury may choose to punish the defendant for the similar rather than the charged act, or the jury may infer that the defendant is an evil person inclined to violate the law. Because of this danger, petitioner maintains, the jury ought not to be exposed to similar act evidence until the trial court has heard the evidence and made a determination under Federal Rules of Evidence 104(a) that the defendant committed the similar act. Rule 104(a) provides that "[p]reliminary questions concerning the qualification of a person to be a witness, the existence of a privilege, or the admissibility of evidence shall be determined by the court, subject to the provisions of subdivision (b)." According to petitioner, the trial court must make this preliminary finding by at least a preponderance of the evidence.[5]

---

[3] Petitioner does not dispute that Nelson's testimony concerning the Amana appliances was properly admitted under Rule 404(b).

[4] The Government also argues before this Court that the evidence concerning the televisions is relevant even if the jury could not conclude that the sets were stolen. We have found nothing in the record indicating that this theory was suggested to or relied upon by the courts

below, and in light of our ruling, we need not address this alternate theory.

[5] In his brief, petitioner argued that the Government was required to prove to the trial court

We reject petitioner's position, for it is inconsistent with the structure of the Rules of Evidence and with the plain language of Rule 404(b). Article IV of the Rules of Evidence deals with the relevancy of evidence. Rules 401 and 402 establish the broad principle that relevant evidence—evidence that makes the existence of any fact at issue more or less probable—is admissible unless the Rules provide otherwise. Rule 403 allows the trial judge to exclude relevant evidence if, among other things, "its probative value is substantially outweighed by the danger of unfair prejudice." Rules 404 through 412 address specific types of evidence that have generated problems. Generally, these latter Rules do not flatly prohibit the introduction of such evidence but instead limit the purpose for which it may be introduced. Rule 404(b), for example, protects against the introduction of extrinsic act evidence when that evidence is offered

---

the commission of the similar act by clear and convincing proof. At oral argument, his counsel conceded that such a position is untenable in light of our decision last term in *Bourjaily v. United States*, 483 U.S. ___, 107 S. Ct. 268, 93 L. Ed. 2d 246 (1987), in which we concluded that preliminary factual findings under Rule 104(a) are subject to the preponderance of the evidence standard. Tr. of Oral Arg. 12. Petitioner now asserts that although the Sixth Circuit correctly held that the Government must prove the similar act by preponderant evidence before it is admitted, the court erred in applying that test to these facts. We consider first what preliminary finding, if any, the trial court must make before letting similar acts evidence go to jury.

solely to prove character. The text contains no intimation, however, that any preliminary showing is necessary before such evidence may be introduced for a proper purpose. If offered for such a proper purpose, the evidence is subject only to general strictures limiting admissibility such as Rules 402 and 403.

Petitioner's reading of Rule 404(b) as mandating a preliminary finding by the trial court that the act in question occurred not only superimposes a level of judicial oversight that is nowhere apparent from the language of that provision, but it is simply inconsistent with the legislative history behind Rule 404(b). The Advisory Committee specifically declined to offer any "mechanical solution" to the admission of evidence under Rule 404(b). The Advisory Committee specifically declined to offer any "mechanical solution" to the admission of evidence under 404(b). Advisory Committee's Notes on Fed. Rule Evid. 404(b), 28 U.S.C. App., p. 691. Rather, the Committee indicated that the trial court should assess such evidence under the usual rules for admissibility: "The determination must be made whether the danger of undue prejudice outweighs the probative value of the evidence in view of the availability of other means of proof and other factors appropriate for making decisions of this kind under Rule 403." *Ibid*; see also S. Rep. No. 93-1277, p.25 (1974) ("[I]t is anticipated that with respect to permissible uses for such evidence, the trial judge may exclude it only on the basis of those considerations set forth in Rule 403, *i.e.* prejudice, confusion or waste of time").

Petitioner's suggestion that a preliminary finding is necessary to protect the defendant from the potential for unfair prejudice is also belied by the Reports of the House of Representatives and the Senate. The House made clear that the version of Rule 404(b) which became law was intended to "plac[e] greater emphasis on admissibility than did the final Court version." H.R. Rep. No. 93-650, p. 7 (1973). The Senate echoed this theme: "[T]he use of the discretionary word 'may' with respect to the admissibility of evidence of crimes, wrongs, or other acts is not intended to confer any arbitrary discretion on the trial judge." S. Rep. No. 93-1277, at 24. Thus, Congress was not nearly so concerned with the potential prejudicial effect of Rule 404(b) evidence as it was with ensuring that restrictions would not be placed on the admission of such evidence.

We conclude that a preliminary finding by the court that the Government has proved the act by a preponderance of the evidence is not called for under Rule 104(a).[6] This is not to

say, however, that the Government may parade past the jury a litany of potentially prejudicial similar acts that have been established or connected to the defendant only by unsubstantiated innuendo. Evidence is admissible under Rule 404(b) only if it is relevant. "Relevancy is not an inherent characteristic of any item of evidence but exists only as a relation between an item of evidence and a matter properly provable in the case." Advisory Committee's Notes on Fed. Rule Evid. 401, 28 U.S.C. App., p. 688. In the Rule 404(b) context, similar act evidence is relevant only if the jury can reasonably conclude that the act occurred and that the defendant was the actor. See *United States v. Beechum*, 582 F.2d 898, 912-913 (CA5 1978) (en banc). In the instant case, the evidence that petitioner was selling the televisions was relevant under the Government's theory only if the jury could reasonably find that the televisions were stolen.

Such questions of relevance conditioned on a fact are dealt with under Federal Rule of Evidence 104(b). *Beechum, supra,* at 912-913; see also E. Imwinkelried, Uncharged Misconduct Evidence § 2.06 (1984). Rule 104(b) provides:

"When the relevancy of evidence depends upon the fulfillment of a

---

[6] Petitioner also suggests that in performing the balancing prescribed by Federal Rule of Evidence 403, the trial court must find that the prejudicial potential of similar acts evidence substantially outweighs its probative value unless the court concludes by a preponderance of the evidence that the defendant committed the similar act. We reject this suggestion because such a holding would be erroneous for the same reasons that a preliminary finding under Rule

104(a) is inappropriate. We do, however, agree with the Government's concession at oral argument that the strength of the evidence establishing the similar act is one of the factors the court may consider when conducting the Rule 403 balancing. Tr. of Oral Arg. 26.

condition of fact, the court shall admit it upon, or subject to, the introduction of evidence sufficient to support a finding of the fulfillment of the condition."

In determining whether the Government has introduced sufficient evidence to meet Rule 104(b), the trial court neither weighs credibility nor makes a finding that the Government has proved the conditional fact by a preponderance of the evidence. The court simply examines all the evidence in the case and decides whether the jury could reasonably find the conditional fact—here, that the televisions were stolen—by a preponderance of the evidence. See 21 C. Wright & K. Graham, Federal Practice and Procedure § 5054, p. 269 (1977). The trial court has traditionally exercised the broadest sort of discretion in controlling the order of proof at trial, and we see nothing in the Rules of Evidence that would change this practice. Often the trial court may decide to allow the proponent to introduce evidence concerning a similar act, and at a later point in the trial assess whether sufficient evidence has been offered to permit the jury to make the requisite finding.[7] If

the proponent has failed to meet this minimal standard of proof, the trial court must instruct the jury to disregard the evidence.

We emphasize that in assessing the sufficiency of the evidence under Rule 104(b), the trial court must consider all evidence presented to the jury. "[I]ndividual pieces of evidence, insufficient in themselves to prove a point, may in cumulation prove it. The sum of an evidentiary presentation may well be greater than its constituent parts." *Bourjaily v. United States*, 483 U.S. ____, 107 S. Ct. 268, 93 L. Ed. 2d 246 (1987). In assessing whether the evidence was sufficient to support a finding that the televisions were stolen, the court here was required to consider not only the direct evidence at that point—the low price of the televisions, the large quantity offered for sale, and petitioner's inability to produce a bill of sale—but also the evidence concerning petitioner's involvement in the sales of other stolen merchandise obtained from Wesby, such as the Memorex tapes and the Amana appliances. Given this evidence, the jury reasonably could have concluded that the televisions were stolen, and the trial court therefore properly allowed the evidence to go to the jury.

---

[7] "When an item of evidence is conditionally relevant, it is often not possible for the offeror to prove the fact upon which relevance is conditioned at the time the evidence is offered. In such cases it is customary to permit him to introduce the evidence and 'connect it up' later. Rule 104(b) continues this practice, specifically authorizing the judge to admit the evidence 'subject to' proof of the preliminary fact. It is, of course, not the responsibility of the judge sua sponte to insure that the foundation evidence is offered; the objector must move to strike the evidence if at the close of the trial the offeror has failed to satisfy the condition." 21 C. Wright & Graham, Federal Practice and Procedure § 5054 pp. 269-270 (1977) (footnotes omitted).

We share petitioner's concern that unduly prejudicial evidence might be introduced under Rule 404(b). See *Michelson v. United States*, 335 U.S. 469, 475-476, 69 S. Ct. 213, 218-219, 93 L. Ed. 168 (1948). We think, however, that the protection against such unfair prejudice emanates not from a requirement of a preliminary finding by the trial court, but rather from four other sources: first, from the requirement of Rule 404(b) that the evidence be offered for a proper purpose; second, from the relevancy requirement of Rule 402—as enforced through Rule 104(b); third, from the assessment the trial court must make under Rule 403 to determine whether the probative value of the similar acts evidence is substantially outweighed by its potential for unfair prejudice, see Advisory Committee's Notes on Fed. Rule Evid. 404(b), 28 U.S.C. App., p. 691; S. Rep. No. 93-177, at 25; and fourth, from Federal Rule of Evidence 105, which provides that the similar acts evidence is to be considered only for the proper purpose for which it was admitted. See *United States v. Ingraham*, 832 F.2d 229, 235 (CA1 1987).

Affirmed.

Cases relating to Chapter 8
COMPETENCY OF EVIDENCE AND WITNESSES

UNITED STATES v. LIGHTLY

675 F.2d 825 (4th Cir. 1982)

ERVIN, Circuit Judge:

On December 19, 1979, Terrance McKinley, an inmate at Lorton Reformatory in northern Virginia, sustained serious stab wounds from an assault in his cell. Two of McKinley's fellow inmates, Randy Lightly and Clifton McDuffie, were investigated, but only Lightly was formally charged. McDuffie was not indicted by the grand jury because a court appointed psychiatrist found him incompetent to stand trial and criminally insane at the time of the offense. He is presently confined in a mental hospital.

On May 22, 1980, Lightly was convicted of assault with intent to commit murder, and sentenced to ten years imprisonment to run consecutively with the sentence he already was serving. Lightly had also been charged with conspiracy to commit murder, but this charge was dropped.

At trial two different accounts of the stabbing developed. The government's case included testimony from the victim, Terrance McKinley, inmates Harvey Boyd and Robert Thomas, and McKinley's treating physician, Dr. Lance Weaver, which indicated that McDuffie and Lightly cornered McKinley in his cell and repeatedly stabbed him with half pairs of scissors. Lightly received a severe cut on his hand in the assault. Lightly's account of the stabbing was that he was walking along cell block three when he saw McDuffie and McKinley fighting in McKinley's cell. Lightly said he went into the cell to stop the fight and while he was pulling McDuffie off of McKinley, McDuffie turned around and cut him. His testimony was corroborated by three other inmates.

The defense also attempted to have McDuffie testify. McDuffie would have testified that only he and not Lightly had assaulted McKinley. The court ruled McDuffie incompetent to testify because he had been found to be criminally insane and incompetent to stand trial, and was subject to hallucinations. We believe this was error and that Lightly is entitled to a new trial.

Every witness is presumed competent to testify, Fed.R.Evid. 601, unless it can be shown that the witness does not have personal knowledge of the matters about which he is to testify, that he does not have the capacity to recall, or that he does not understand the duty to testify truthfully. This rule applies to persons considered to be insane to the same extent that it applies to other persons. *United States* v. *Lopez*, 611 F.2d 44 (4th Cir. 1979); *Shuler* v. *Wainwright*, 491 F.2d 1213, 1223 (5th Cir. 1974). In this case, the testimony of McDuffie's treating physician indicated that McDuffie had a sufficient memory, that he understood the oath, and that he could communicate what he saw. The district judge chose not to conduct an *in camera* examination of McDuffie. On this record, it was clearly improper for the court to disqualify McDuffie from testifying.

The government argues in this appeal that it was not error to disqualify McDuffie because he did not understand the incriminating nature of his anticipated testimony. If McDuffie is incompetent to stand trial, the government asserts, he also lacks the requisite mental capacity to waive his right against self-incrimination and for that reason should be disqualified from testifying. The privilege against self-incrimination, however, is personal and generally cannot be raised by anyone other than the potential witness. See *United States* v. *Nobles*, 422 U.S. 225, 95 S.Ct. 2160, 45 L.Ed.2d 141 (1975). The government, therefore, does not have standing to raise this issue.

McDuffie's potential testimony would have substantially corroborated Lightly's testimony. His disqualification from testifying, therefore, cannot be considered harmless error. In finding Lightly entitled to a new trial on this ground, we decline to rule on the other issues he raised in this appeal.

REVERSED and REMANDED.

FUENTES v. STATE

775 S.W.2d 64 (Tex. Crim. App. 1989)

O'CONNOR, Justice

A jury convicted appellant, Emanuel Fuentes, Jr., of assault and assessed punishment at 120 days confinement and a fine of $125. In his sole point of error, appellant contends the trial court erred in compelling his wife to testify against him. Appellant's spouse, Ms. Fuentes, is the complainant in this case. The information alleged that appellant struck Ms. Fuentes with his fist.

I. THE PRE-TRIAL HEARING ON THE PRIVILEGE

Before the trial on the merits, the trial court held a hearing outside the presence of the jury on the issue of Ms. Fuentes' privilege not to testify against her husband. At the hearing, the State questioned Ms. Fuentes and insisted she admit she testified against her husband at an earlier hearing on July 20, 1988. Ms. Fuentes finally admitted it, but repeatedly stated that she did not want to testify against her husband.

As part of the hearing, defense counsel presented the trial court with a certified copy of the statement of facts of the July 20 hearing. The record indicated Ms. Fuentes had objected to testifying then, and that no one had informed her of her privilege to refuse to testify.

The trial court made two rulings. First, the court ruled Ms. Fuentes did not waive the privilege when she testified at the July 20 hearing. Second, the trial court ruled Ms. Fuentes was required to testify as to appellant's actions against her under Rule 504, sections 2(a) and (b), Texas Rules of Criminal Evidence.

II. THE TRIAL ON GUILT

The first witness to testify at trial was Officer McCord, who testified he went to the Fuenteses' apartment on March 24, 1988, in response to a disturbance call. He saw Ms. Fuentes sitting on stairs outside the apartment crying when he arrived. She told the officer that appellant hit her with his fist and that he was inside the apartment. The officer went inside with Ms. Fuentes and called for a back-up unit. The officer stated Ms. Fuentes had a bump on her head and a black eye.

Under protest, Ms. Fuentes testified that her husband came home, and she told him to go away and threw his clothes outside because he did not come home the night before. She said they got into a fight, and appellant hit her in the eye. She called the police. Ms. Fuentes stated she did not want to testify against her husband nor did she want the State to prosecute him.

III. THE PRIVILEGE NOT TO TESTIFY AND ITS EXCEPTIONS

The Texas Rules of Criminal Evidence grant a privilege to the spouse of the accused not to testify against the accused.

> The spouse of the accused has a privilege not to be called as a witness for the state. This rule does not prohibit the spouse from testifying voluntarily for the state, even over objection by the accused. . . .

Tex. R. Crim. Evid. 504(2)(a). There is an exception to the privilege not to testify: When the accused is charged with violence against any member of either spouse's household, the spouse may not assert the privilege not to testify. Tex. R. Crim. Evid. 504(2)(b). There is also an exception to the exception: When the accused is charged with a crime committed against the spouse during the marriage, the spouse may assert the privilege not to testify. *Id.* This last exception applies here: Ms. Fuentes had a right to assert the privilege not to testify against her husband. The trial court erred when it compelled her to testify against her husband at his trial.

The State argues Ms. Fuentes waived her privilege not to testify when she testified at the July 20 hearing. Rule 511, on which the State relies, says:

> A person upon whom these rules confer a privilege against disclosure waives the privilege if (1) he or his predecessor while holder of the privilege voluntarily discloses or consents to disclosure of any significant part of the privileged matter. . . .

The State's premise is that Ms. Fuentes waived her privilege because she voluntarily testified at the July 20 hearing. The trial court, however, found that she did not voluntarily waive her privilege. We agree with the trial court's ruling.

The State also contends it could have introduced her former testimony under the "unavailable witness" rule. See Tex. R. Crim. Evid. 804. Rule 804 permits a party to introduce the former testimony of a witness who is exempted from testifying because of a privilege. Rule 804 would only permit the State to introduce her earlier testimony if it were itself admissible. The trial court found that Ms. Fuentes did not waive her privilege at the July 20 hearing. That testimony, therefore, was not admissible under rule 804. See Tex. R. Crim. Evid. 512. Without a waiver, the testimony from the earlier hearing was not admissible.

We hold that the trial court compelled Ms. Fuentes to testify contrary to rule 504. On this record, we cannot say beyond a reasonable doubt that the error in forcing Ms. Fuentes to testify did not contribute to appellant's conviction. See Tex. R. App. P. 81(b)(2).

We reverse the judgment of the trial court and remand the case for a new trial.

GILLARS v. UNITED STATES

182 F.2d 962 (D.C. Cir. 1950)

FAHY, Circuit Judge.

Appellant was convicted of treason in a jury trial in the United States District Court for the District of Columbia. Treason alone of crimes is defined in the Constitution, as follows:

> "Treason against the United States, shall consist only in levying War against them, or in ad-

hering to their Enemies, giving them Aid and Comfort. * * *" U.S. Const. Art. III, § 3.

The First Congress, in 1790, provided by statute,

"* * * That if any person or persons, owing allegiance to the United States of America, shall levy war against them, or shall adhere to their enemies, giving them aid and comfort within the United States or elsewhere, and shall be thereof convicted, on confession in open court, or on the testimony of two witnesses to the same overt act of the treason whereof he or they shall stand indicted, such person or persons shall be adjudged guilty of treason against the United States, * * *." 1 Stat. 112 (1790).

The indictment alleges that appellant was born in Maine, was a citizen of and owed allegiance to the United States, that within the German Reich, after December 11, 1941, to and including May 8, 1945, in violation of her duty of allegiance she knowingly and intentionally adhered to the enemies of the United States, to wit, the Government of the German Reich, its agents, instrumentalities, representatives and subjects with which the United States was at war, and gave to said enemies aid and comfort within the United States and elsewhere, by participating in the psychological warfare of the German Government against the United States. This participation is alleged to have consisted of radio broadcasts and the making of phonographic recordings with the intent that they would be used in broadcasts to the United States and to American Expedition-

ary Forces in French North Africa, Italy, France and England. The indictment charges the commission of ten overt acts, each of which is described, and, finally, that following commission of the offense the District of Columbia was the first Federal Judicial District into which appellant was brought.

Eight of the ten alleged overt acts were submitted to the jury. A verdict of guilty was returned, based on the commission of overt act No. 10, which is set forth in the indictment as follows:

"10. That on a day between January 1, 1944 an June 6, 1944, the exact date being to the Grand Jurors unknown, said defendant, at Berlin, Germany, did speak into a microphone in a recording studio of the German Radio Broadcasting Company, and thereby did participate in a phonographic recording and cause to be phonographically recorded a radio drama entitled "Vision of Invasion," said defendant then and there well knowing that said recorded radio drama was to be subsequently broadcast by the German Radio Broadcasting Company to the United States and to its citizens and soldiers at home and abroad as an element of German propaganda and an instrument of psychological warfare."

We now discuss the several matters raised by appellant as grounds for reversal.

I
The Sufficiency and Weight of the Evidence

Appellant contends the verdict was contrary to the evidence and to the weight of the evidence. The argument runs as follows: The indictment charged that at various times appellant spoke into a microphone and her voice was later sent over the radio; that two of the ten overt acts of this character were withdrawn, leaving eight for jury consideration; that of these she was acquitted of seven; that she admitted speaking into the microphone and sending her views over the radio but denied any intention to betray; and that therefore the jury, having in mind this admission, concluded there was no intent to betray in the case of seven overt acts. From this it is argued that the finding of treasonable intention as to one overt act could not have been made consistently with acquittal of these other overt acts.

If, however, there is sufficient evidence to support the verdict of guilty based on the commission of the tenth overt act alone we may not reverse even were we of opinion that the evidence was equally strong to support a conviction based on other alleged overt acts as to which appellant was acquitted. A jury verdict need not be consistent.

"Consistency in the verdict is not necessary. Each count in an indictment is regarded as if it was a separate indictment. *Latham* v. *The Queen*, 5 Best & Smith 635, 642, 643; *Selvester* v. *United States*, 170 U.S. 262, 18 S.Ct. 580, 42 L.Ed. 1029. * * *." *Dunn* v. *United States*, 1931, 284 U.S. 390, 393, 52 S.Ct. 189, 190, 76 L.Ed. 356, 80 A.L.R. 161.

The evidence was sufficient to support the verdict on the tenth overt act. There was before the jury evidence from which they could find the following: Appellant was

a native born citizen of the United States and therefore owed allegiance to the United States; in 1940 she was thirty-nine years of age; she had studied dramatics and had been employed in the United States as an actress; she left the United States in 1933, and took up residence in Berlin in 1934; on May 6, 1940, she was employed there by the German Broadcasting Company as announcer on the European Services; within a few months after this employment she was made mistress of ceremonies of the European Services; in 1941 she took part also in an overseas service program broadcast to the United States; the United States declared war on Germany December 11, 1941; the German Radio Broadcasting Company was a tax-supported agency of the German Government; it consisted of two main branches, the Home Branch and the Foreign Branch; the Foreign Branch in turn consisted of the European Service and the Overseas Service; the purpose of the broadcasts by the Foreign Branch was to disseminate to the Armed Forces and civilians of the United States and her allies propaganda along lines laid down by the German Propaganda Ministry and the Foreign Office to aid Germany and to weaken the war effort of the nations at war with her; daily conferences were held among Goebbels, head of the Ministry of Public Enlightenment and Propaganda of the German Government, and representatives of the Foreign Office to formulate propaganda lines; these were followed by conferences of the Director of the Foreign Branch with the officials of the Overseas Service about the propaganda lines to be pursued; the employees of the Overseas Service followed the propaganda instructions then announced; the lines of propaganda for broadcast to the citizens and Armed Forces of the United States were that Germany was superior in various ways; she was fighting against Communistic domination of the world; the United States was improperly influenced to enter and remain in the war by Jewish interests; German fighting forces were superior; Germany had secret military weapons such as the V-1 and V-2 rockets; an attempted invasion of Germany would be disastrous; the United States should not oppose Germany in its fight to save Christianity and world salvation from the Communists; the President would sell his country to the Russians and was improperly influenced by Jewish advisers; the people of the United States should not follow the policy of the war effort of their Government; the war was a British war.

☆   ☆   ☆

In the light of the uncontradicted evidence of her participation in the recording of *Vision of Invasion*, testified to by more than two witnesses, as a part of her employment by an agency of the German Government, and the evidence as to the nature and purpose of this employment, of the intended use of the recordings and programs, the evidence of her citizenship, and the fact of war between the United States and Germany, we hold that the evidence furnished an adequate basis for the jury to find that appellant, while owing allegiance to the United States, adhered to the enemy, giving such enemy aid and comfort,

and that this was done knowingly and with the intention of aiding the enemy in the war in which it was then engaged with the United States. Furthermore, we find no necessary inconsistency between the jury's conviction on overt Act No. 10 and their acquittal on others. They might reasonably have distinguished between the nature of *Vision of Invasion* and other recordings.

II

The Question of the Competency and Credibility of Certain Witnesses

(A) As a subsidiary to her attack on the sufficiency of the evidence appellant contends that the witness Schnell, who was one of three who testified to her participation in the recording of *Vision of Invasion*, was an incompetent witness because he stated that he did not believe in the God of the Bible. He also testified that he did not believe in rewards or punishments after death. It appears from his full statement, set forth in the margin, that he recognized a right and duty of society to force members to speak the truth. He was permitted to testify on affirmation.

The D.C. Code, Title 14, Section 101, reads as follows:

"All evidence shall be given under oath according to the forms of the common law, except that where a witness has conscientious scruples against taking an oath, he may, in lieu thereof, solemnly, sincerely, and truly declare and affirm; ☆ ☆ ☆"

The Government contends that Schnell affirmed in accordance with this provision. We read the permission to affirm because of conscientious scruples against taking an oath to apply to one who believes in God but does not believe in oath-taking in court. The witness Schnell was not of that character. He did not believe in the God before whom an oath is taken "according to the forms of the common law," Who is indeed the God of the Bible. *United States v. Lee*, C.C.D.C. 1834, 26 Fed.Cas. page 908, No. 15,586; *United States v. Kennedy*, C.C.D.Ill. 1843, 26 Fed. Cas. page 761, No. 15,524; *Wakefield v. Ross*, C.C.D.R.I. 1827, 28 Fed.Cas. page 1346, No. 17,050; Anonymous, 1839, 1 Fed.Cas. page 999, No. 446. The early common law rule, and therefore the rule which at an earlier period would have prevailed under the Code might well have rendered Schnell incompetent. But the Code must now be read with Rule 26 of the Federal Rules of Criminal Procedure, 18 U.S.C.A., which provides, *inter alia:*

"* * * competency and privileges of witnesses shall be governed, except when an act of Congress or these rules otherwise provide, by the principles of the common law as they may be interpreted by the courts of the United States in the light of reason and experience."

A fair reading together of the Code and the Rule leads to the conclusion that the common law rule in the District of Columbia is to be interpreted now in the light of reason and experience. This brings into the area of competence witnesses who were under disability under the older criteria. For example, in *Rosen v. United States,* 1917, 245 U.S. 467, 38 S.Ct. 148, 62 L.Ed. 406,

the Supreme Court in substance held that the former common law rule disqualifying criminals from being witnesses could no longer be followed; conviction of crime will be considered in testing the credibility of a witness but will not exclude him from the stand. See, also, *United States v. Peterson,* D.C.E.D. Pa. 1938, 24 F.Supp. 470; *United States v. Segelman,* D.C.W.D.Pa. 1949, 83 F.Supp. 890. In *Gantz v. State,* 1916, 18 Ga.App. 154, 88 S.E. 993, 994, a similar rationale was applied where the witness disclaimed any belief in God. The court said:

"* * * The sufficiency of the test as to the competency of a witness is necessarily largely a matter of judicial discretion * * *

"* * * In our view it is not essential to the competency of a witness that he shall know where he will go after death. Although lack of faith on this subject might affect his credit with the jury, it would not disqualify him from being a witness. * * *"

The course of change is traced in Underhill, Criminal Evidence, 4th Ed. Ch. 28. See, also, Wigmore on Evidence, 3rd Ed. Vol. VI, § 1816 et seq. Even therefore if we assume that the Code provision is a test of competency and not merely a prescription of the sanction under which one shall testify, it does not, when read with Rule 26, exclude as incompetent the nonbeliever in the God of the Bible.

We note that the affirmation in this case was not in the words of the Code, "* * * he may, in lieu thereof, solemnly, sincerely, and truly declare and affirm"; but such an affirmation, as we have said, is for one who believes but does not wish to swear. No words are prescribed for the affirmation of such a witness as Schnell. It was for the court to adopt appropriate words. Those used were adequate for an affirmation under pain and penalty of perjury.

(B) Some argument seems to be made that the testimony of the witness von Richter, who like Schnell testified to the participation by appellant in the recording of *Vision of Invasion*, could not be relied upon in support of an overt act of treason because he was a member of the Nazi party and had been seen wearing a Nazi membership button during the war. This argument is without legal significance. Whether or not the witness should be believed was for the jury. It is not clear appellant contends von Richter could not qualify as a witness; we refer to the matter only because counsel has done so though we are not certain his reference was intended to evoke a ruling.

(C) Appellant urges that the witness Haupt should not have been heard in support of proof of an overt act because he testified that his own participation in *Vision of Invasion* was under compulsion and fear of death. The suggested conclusion that this rendered incredible his testimony regarding the participation of the accused does not follow. It is not claimed his testimony regarding her participation was elicited by fear or compulsion and no reason is advanced why it necessarily should have been disregarded by the jury.

We note at this point that no question was raised at the trial as to the competency of von Richter or Haupt. Furthermore, appellant admitted her participation in the recording of *Vision of Invasion*. Nevertheless our above rulings on competency and the admissibility of testimony are not based upon this admission. We do not discuss the question whether her admission dispensed with the need of other testimony as to the commission of overt act No. 10 (see *Cramer v. United States*, 325 U.S. 1, dissenting opinion at page 63, 65 S.Ct. 918, 89 L.Ed. 1441) because independently of her testimony the constitutional requirement of two witnesses to the same overt act was met.

*   *   *

Judgment affirmed.

Cases relating to Chapter 9
EXAMINATION OF WITNESSES

UNITED STATES v. GIBSON

675 F.2d 825 (6th Cir. 1982)

BOYCE F. MARTIN, Jr., Circuit Judge.

This is a direct criminal appeal from embezzlement and conspiracy convictions. John F. Gibson was found guilty by a jury of misappropriating union property in violation of 29 U.S.C. § 501(c). Gibson is the General Secretary-Treasurer of the Hotel and Restaurant Employees'and Bartenders' International Union ("The International"). In March, 1979, a Grand Jury sitting in the Southern District of Ohio returned an 18-count indictment against Gibson, alleging numerous acts of embezzlement from the Union. The counts that concern us charged that Gibson has misused the Union's jet airplane or personal travel. Gibson was also charged with conspiring with James Stamos and Herbert Schiffman to misuse the Union jet for a fishing trip.

After a jury trial on all but two of the original counts, Gibson was convicted of one count of overstating unreimbursed employee business expenses on his tax returns. The jury acquitted Gibson of another tax count; one unauthorized travel count; and all unauthorized salary counts. The jury was unable to reach verdicts on six other counts. Accordingly, the trial judge declared a partial mistrial.

Gibson was retried in May, 1980. He was convicted of misusing the Union jet for pleasure trips to Gaspe, Canada and Sacramento, California. He was also found guilty of conspiracy. The jury acquitted Gibson of the other charges. The District Court sentenced Gibson to serve three concurrent four-month terms.

Gibson now appeals, raising four contentions. First, he challenges the sufficiency of the evidence supporting the guilty verdicts. Second, he contends that he was prejudiced by an erroneous evidentiary ruling excluding certain testimony as hearsay. Third, Gibson argues that the District Court abused its discretion by prohibiting a defense witness from testifying as a sanction because the witness violated a sequestration order. Finally, Gibson complains of prosecutorial misconduct during closing argument. For the following reasons we affirm.

* * *

531

II. HEARSAY EXCLUSION

Gibson contends that he was prejudiced by an evidentiary ruling excluding as hearsay a defense witness' proffered testimony that he heard Hanley say to Gibson: "get her over here and let's find out what's going on." The defense called Anthony Smieca, Secretary-Treasurer of the Palm Springs Local, who travelled with Hanley and Gibson in 1975 when they toured Bay Area Locals. Defense counsel asked Smieca to recount any discussions he overheard between Gibson and Hanley about Local 28. The prosecution objected that any answer would be inadmissible hearsay. At side bar the defense counsel made an offer of proof that the woman Hanley's utterance referred to was Hallett. The District Court sustained the objection as inadmissible hearsay.

Gibson now argues that the exclusion of Smieca's statement was reversible error because: (1) the utterance was not hearsay because it was not offered for the truth of its contents; (2) the statement would have corroborated Hanley's earlier testimony to the same effect; and (3) the statement was relevant to Gibson's state of mind at the time he invited Hallett to journey to Sacramento. We agree with Gibson that Smieca's statement should not have been excluded as hearsay. However, we conclude that the improper exclusion was harmless error.

We have no doubt that the statement should have been received. First, the hearsay rule bans in-court repetition of extra-judicial utterances only when they are offered to prove the truth or falsity of their contents. The rule does not apply to statements offered merely to show that they were made. E.g. *United States* v. *Miriana*, 442 F.2d 150, 153 (6th Cir.), *cert. denied.*, 399 U.S. 910, 90 S.Ct. 2199, 26 L.Ed.2d 561 (1970); *United States* v. *Press*, 336 F.2d 1003 (2nd Cir. 1964), *cert. denied.*, 379 U.S. 965, 85 S.Ct. 658, 13 LEd2d 559 (1965). Smieca's proffered statement was not hearsay under Federal Rule of Evidence 801(c): it was not offered to show that the substance of Hanley's utterance was either true or false. Indeed, a suggestion or an order is not subject to verification at all because such utterances do not assert facts. Gibson offered the utterance solely for the fact that it was made by Hanley and heard by Gibson. Smieca's account of Hanley's suggestion was testimony about a circumstantial utterance; which could have been received properly on the issue of Gibson's belief or state of mind in consequence of the utterance. See *United States* v. *Herrera*, 600 F.2d 502 (5th Cir. 1979); *United States* v. *Rubin*, 591 F.2d 278 (5th Cir.), *cert. denied.*, 444 U.S. 864, 100 S.Ct. 133, 62 L.Ed.2d 87 (1979); *United States* v. *Wilson*, 532 F.2d 641 (8th Cir.), *cert. denied*, 429 U.S. 846, 97 S.Ct. 128, 50 L.Ed.2d 117 (1976); *United States* v. *Chason*, 451 F.2d 301 (2nd Cir. 1971), *cert. denied*, 405 U.S. 1016, 92 S.Ct. 1291, 31 L.Ed.2d 479 (1972). See also, VI Wigmore on Evidence § 1789 at 235 (3rd ed. 1940); McCormick on Evidence § 225 at 460-463 (1954 ed.).

We conclude that the District Court's error was harmless beyond a reasonable doubt and that it did not affect Gibson's substantial rights. First, Smieca's testimony would not have provided the jury with any new information about Gibson's purpose or belief in transporting Hallett to Sacramento. Hanley himself had already testified, without objection, that he suggested to Gibson that he bring Hallett to Sacramento. Evidence bearing on Gibson's good faith belief that Hallett's trip would serve a legitimate purpose was already before the jury in the form of the declarant's own testimony. Thus, the jury had ample opportunity to draw the inference that Hanley and Gibson discussed Hallett's potential as an informant. Therefore, the greatest evidentiary value Smieca's version could have secured for the defense was corroboration of Hanley's previous testimony that he had in fact made such a suggestion to Gibson. In short, Smieca's testimony had only minor "incremental probity." *United States* v. *Mock*, 640 F.2d 629 (5th Cir. 1981). Smieca's statement in itself would not have added new dimensions to the issue of Gibson's good faith. We conclude that had the jury heard Smieca's statement, its verdict would not have differed. See *United States* v. *Chason*, 451 F.2d 301 (2nd Cir. 1971), *cert. denied*, 405 U.S. 1016, 92 S.Ct. 1291, 31 L.Ed.2d 479 (1972).

Second, we reject Gibson's argument that he was prejudiced because he was denied the opportunity to bolster Hanley's credibility. It is always within the discretion of the trial judge to deny a party the opportunity to present cumulative evidence bearing solely on credibility. *United States* v. *Dennis*, 625 F.2d 782 (8th Cir. 1980); *United States* v. *Medical Therapy Sciences, Inc.*, 583 F.2d 36, 41 n.6 (2nd Cir. 1978), *cert. denied*, 439 U.S. 1130, 99 S.Ct. 1049, 59 L.Ed.2d 91 (1979). See also *United States* v. *Hoffa*, 349 F.2d 20 (6th Cir. 1965), *aff'd*, 385

U.S. 293, 87 S.Ct. 408, 17 L.Ed.2d 374 (1966); *Boeing Airplane Co.* v. *O'Malley*, 329 F.2d 585 (8th Cir. 1964); *Harvey* v. *United States*, 23 F.2d 561 (2nd Cir. 1928). Furthermore, Hanley was not impeached on cross-examination about whether he had in fact made such an utterance to Gibson, nor did the government directly or impliedly suggest that Hanley's testimony was a recent fabrication. Therefore Smieca's statement was not essential to rehabilitate Hanley. Hanley's credibility would not have been bolstered by mere repetition. Repetition simply does not ensure veracity:

> When the witness has merely testified on direct examination, without any impeachment, proof of consistent statements is unnecessary and valueless. The witness is not helped by it; for even if it is an improbable or untrustworthy story, it is not made more probable or more trustworthy by any number of repetitions of it. Such evidence would ordinarily be cumbersome to the trial and is ordinarily rejected.

Because Smieca's testimony was cumulative and repetitious, and would therefore not have influenced the jury's verdict, its exclusion was harmless error beyond a reasonable doubt.

III. SEQUESTRATION ORDER

We reject Gibson's third contention that the District Court erroneously denied his motion for a new trial based on the court's refusal to allow a witness to testify who had remained in court despite a sequestration order. The defense tried to establish through Hanley's testimony that Hallett's trip had been the catalyst for a special internal audit of Local 28. According to Hanley, the audit commenced after November 11, 1975. In earlier testimony, however, Hanley had stated that the post-Sacramento audit revealed various fiscal irregularities, including the unauthorized life insurance policy Ray Lane had bought for himself. To corroborate his testimony, Hanley produced a letter to Lane written in October, 1975, denying authorization for the policy and pointing out various irregularities. On cross-examination, the prosecution seized upon the apparent discrepancy in dates. Hanley failed to state that the audit mentioned in the October letter was a routine audit, but that another special audit was made after November.

The defense maintains that Hanley was merely confused about the number and dates of the audits because he was largely unfamiliar with audit procedures. To correct Hanley's testimony, defense counsel attempted to call Joseph Clair to the stand. Clair had been assigned to audit Local 28 to replace an auditor who had recently died. The District Court denied Gibson' request to call Clair because the latter had been present to assist defense counsel throughout the trial. Gibson was allowed to call Kenneally to the stand, however, to give the same information that Clair would have given about the dates and depth of the various audits.

Federal Rule of Evidence 615 provides that: "at the request of a party the court shall order witnesses excluded so that they cannot hear the testimony of other witnesses." The witness rule has been part of our law for centuries, and has its origins in the English common law. As Wigmore notes sequestration "already had in English practice an independent and continuous existence, even in the time of those earlier modes of trial which preceded the jury and were a part of our inheritance of the common Germanic law." VI Wigmore on Evidence § 1837 at 348 (3rd ed. 1940) *quoted in Geders* v. *United States*, 425 U.S. 80, 87, 96 S.Ct. 1330, 1334, 47 L.Ed.2d 592 (1976). The rule serves two salutary purposes: (1) it prevents witnesses from tailoring testimony to that of other witnesses; and (2) it aids in detecting false testimony. *United States* v. *Warren*, 578 F.2d 1058 (5th Cir. 1978) (en banc) on reh. 612 F.2d 887 (en banc), *cert. denied*, 446 U.S. 956, 100 S.Ct. 2928, 64 L.Ed.2d 815 (1980)

Our review of the District Court's action is limited to whether the court abused its discretion in denying Gibson's request to call Clair. The decision whether a witness who fails to obey a sequestration order may subsequently take the stand is undoubtedly one for the trial court. The controlling principle in this Circuit is that violation of an order directing that witnesses be separated does not automatically bar a witness' testimony. *United States* v. *Bostic*, 327 F.2d 983 (6th Cir. 1964). We have always heeded the following pronouncement of the Supreme Court:

If a witness disobeys the order of withdrawal, while he may be proceeded against for contempt and his testimony is open to comment to the jury by reason of his conduct, he is not thereby disqualified, and the weight of authority is that he cannot be excluded on that ground merely, although the right to exclude under particular circumstances may be supported as within the sound discretion of the trial court. Most authorities agree that "particular circumstances" sufficient to justify exclusion of a witness are indications that the witness has remained in court with the "consent, connivance, procurement or knowledge" of the party seeking his testimony. *United States* v. *Kiliyan*, 456 F.2d at 560; *Taylor* v. *United States*, 388 F.2d 786 (9th Cir. 1967).

Applying this test to the facts, it is clear that the court did not abuse its discretion in excluding Clair.

First, we note that the government requested a Rule 615 order in open court without objection. Second, Gibson concedes that Clair remained in court with his knowledge and consent. In this regard we are not persuaded by Gibson's claim that his need to call Clair was unexpected. Defense counsel should have anticipated that Clairs' testimony concerning the dates and scope of each audit might be necessary, if as defense counsel claimed, Clair was the only Union official suf-

ficiently competent to describe the nature of the audits. In fact, Clair would have been the logical choice to give this allegedly crucial testimony initially. Furthermore, Clair had testified at Gibson's first trial, although in a limited capacity.

We conclude that Gibson has failed to show any prejudice because Kenneally, defense counsel's substitute witness, gave substantially identical testimony to that Clair would have given, according to Gibson's offer of proof. Kenneally testified quite specifically that Gibson instructed Clair to "take a good look at Local 28's books" and "to do a good job on them and it's to be an in-depth audit." Gibson thus had an adequate opportunity to correct the mistakes Hanley had made in his testimony. In our view the District Court properly excluded Clair from the stand.

IV. CONCLUSION

We find no merit in Gibson's final contention that the prosecutor's closing arguments constituted misconduct. Accordingly, we affirm the judgment below in all respects.

ROCK v. ARKANSAS

483 U.S. 44, 107 S. Ct. 2704, 97 L. Ed. 2d 37 (1987)

(Syllabus only)

Syllabus

Petitioner was charged with manslaughter for shooting her husband. In order to refresh her memory as to the precise details of the shooting, she twice underwent hypnosis by a trained neuropsychologist. These sessions were tape-recorded. After the hypnosis, she remembered details indicating that her gun was defective and had misfired, which was corroborated by an expert witness' testimony. However, the trial court ruled that no hypnotically refreshed testimony would be admitted, and limited petitioner's testimony to a reiteration of her statements to the doctor prior to hypnosis, as reported in the doctor's notes. The Arkansas Supreme Court affirmed her conviction, ruling that the limitations on her testimony did not violate her constitutional right to testify, and that criminal defendants' hypnotically refreshed testimony is inadmissible per se because it is unreliable.

Held:

1. Criminal defendants have a right to testify in their own behalf under the Due Process Clause of the Fourteenth Amendment, the Compulsory Process Clause of the Sixth Amendment, and the Fifth Amendment's privilege against self-incrimination.

2. Although the right to present relevant testimony is not without limitation, restrictions placed on a defendant's constitutional right to testify by a State's evidentiary rules may not be arbitrary or disproportionate to the purposes they are designed to serve.

3. Arkansas' *per se* rule excluding all hypnotically refreshed testimony infringes impermissibly on a criminal defendant's right to testify on his or her own behalf. Despite any unreliability that hypnosis may introduce into testimony, the procedure has been credited as instrumental in obtaining particular types of information. Moreover, hypnotically refreshed testimony is subject to verification by corroborating evidence and other traditional means of assessing accuracy, and inaccuracies can be reduced by procedural safeguards such as the use of tape or video recording. The State's legitimate interest in barring unreliable evidence does not justify a per se exclusion because the evidence may be reliable in an individual case. Here, the expert's corroboration of petitioner's hypnotically enhanced memories and the trial judge's conclusion that the tape recordings indicated that the doctor did not suggest responses with leading questions are circumstances that the trial court should have considered in determining admissibility.

288 Ark. 566, 708 S.W.2d 78 (1986), vacated and remanded.

UNITED STATES v. SPIVEY

841 F.2d 799 (7th Cir. 1988)

BAUER, Chief Judge.

Anthony Spivey appeals from his conviction for conspiracy to possess and actual possession of goods stolen from an interstate shipment, knowing that the goods were stolen. 18 U.S.C.

§§ 371, 659. He contends on appeal that the district court violated his sixth amendment right to confront witnesses against him by limiting the cross-examination of his co-conspirator, and that the district court's treatment of his trial counsel deprived him of a fair trial. We reject both claims and affirm Spivey's conviction.

I.

A.

Spivey and Albert "Rick" Crumble were long-time friends. Both men frequented a tavern on Chicago's West Side called "The Karate Club," which was owned by the family of their mutual friends, David, Randy, and Tom Johnson. Spivey apparently worked sporadically as a volunteer bouncer at the club. In September, 1984, Crumble was a truck driver for Cargo, Incorporated, a Chicago trucking company.

On Friday, September 21, 1984, Crumble invited Spivey to join him in looking for a trailerload of goods to steal. Spivey accepted the invitation, so Crumble went to work that night, picked up his tractor, then picked up Spivey. After Crumble delivered one load of goods, the two men drove around the Santa Fe rail yard in Chicago looking for a trailer to steal. Finding nothing that suited their fancy, they drove to the Burlington rail yard. There they found an overseas trailer, which Crumble attached to his tractor.

Crumble and Spivey drove the trailer to Cargo's yard, parked in a se-cluded spot, and broke the trailer's seal. Inside was a thief's dream: Sharp Electronics calculators, turntables, speakers, receivers, and cassette decks. Spivey and Crumble agreed that it was a good load, then began contemplating what to do with it. Spivey contacted a fence of stolen goods, who met with Spivey and Crumble, then left with Spivey to look for another fence, to whom they would offer the load. After nothing came of that idea, Spivey and the fence drove to a warehouse to see if they could hide the stolen goods there. The warehouse door was too low for the trailer, however, and they went back to tell Crumble the bad news. Apparently, they left the trailer at Cargo's yard.

On Saturday, September 22, 1984, Crumble went back to work at Cargo, taking Spivey with him. After work, the two men went to the Karate Club Lounge, where they told David Johnson and another friend, Pierre Cameron, of their theft, and recruited Cameron and Johnson to help unload the trailer. The four men then returned to Cargo, got the trailer of stolen goods, stole another empty trailer marked "AVAZ" from the yard across the street from Cargo, and began transferring the goods from one trailer to the other. The four men unloaded all of the Sharp stereo equipment and calculators from the overseas trailer until they reached copying equipment. At that point, the men moved the AVAZ trailer, now loaded with the stolen stereo equipment and calcula-tors, to a secluded spot. Next, they loaded David Johnson's truck with some of the stolen goods, which each would try to sell individually.

Late Sunday or early Monday, during the night of September 23 and 24, 1984, Crumble moved the AVAZ trailer, first to a restaurant parking lot in Chicago and then back to the Cargo yard, while David Johnson and Spivey followed in Johnson's pickup. At the Cargo yard, the three men loaded more of the loot into Johnson's truck and departed. Unfortunately for them, another Cargo employee who was waiting for the return of his tractor saw Crumble, Spivey, and Johnson leave in Johnson's pickup.

B.

FBI Agent Thomas Dillon, brought into the investigation by the Chicago police, spoke to Crumble about the theft on September 28, 1984. Crumble denied everything in a lengthy, elaborate statement, all of it lies. On October 4, 1984, the Chicago police arrested Crumble. While in custody, he asked to speak to Agent Dillon. This time Crumble admitted his participation in the theft and gave Dillon the names of several others he said were involved in taking, unloading, and fencing the merchandise. He also agreed to cooperate with the government. In November, 1984, Crumble was indicted on federal charges of theft and conspiracy. On March 8, 1985, he pled guilty pursuant to a plea agreement and the court, aware that Crumble was cooperating with the government, gave him a suspended sentence of five years plus five years probation, the first six months to be spent in custody.

Spivey admitted his participation in the theft in a written statement taken by Agent Dillon on February 22, 1985. Spivey's statement was substantially similar to Crumble's confession, except that Spivey said he thought that the theft of the goods and the subsequent transfer into the empty AVAZ container all may have occurred on Saturday (and not Friday) night, September 22, 1984, although he was not sure. Spivey was indicted in September, 1985. At trial, he proffered an alibi defense. Randy Johnson, one of the Johnson brothers, testified that Spivey was working at the Karate Club Lounge on Saturday, September 22, 1984. Johnson said he remembered that night because there was a large birthday party held that evening for one of the club's regulars. Thomas Johnson, the club's manager, testified, however, that that birthday party had been cancelled. Other members of the Johnson family testified that Spivey was working at the club on the night of the theft. The key witness for the government was, of course, Crumble.

II.

A.

Spivey first argued that the district court violated his sixth amendment right to confront witnesses against him by terminating his cross-examination of Crumble before he was able to question Crumble about prior convictions and other bad acts. The government called Crumble to the stand on the afternoon of January 14, 1987. On direct examination, Crumble testified about the events of September 22 through 24, 1984. He also testified that he had pled guilty and served a jail term for his role in the theft, that he was testifying under a grant of immunity, and that he had lied to Agent Dillon on September 28, 1984 when he denied his involvement in the theft.

Defense counsel's cross-examination of Crumble lasted the remainder of the afternoon and early evening. During the cross-examination, defense counsel elicited the following information: that Crumble would not have testified unless granted immunity; that Crumble's September 28, 1984 statement to Agent Dillon was "all lies"; that Crumble admitted his participation in the crime to the FBI only after the Chicago police had arrested and jailed him; that the FBI never charged Crumble with the crime of giving a false statement; that after the government informed the court of his cooperation, Crumble was sentenced to only six months of incarceration; that the government had interviewed Crumble three or four times for up to seven hours before trial; and that during these interviews, Crumble overcame his confusion about when the theft actually occurred.

Late in the day, after defense counsel repeatedly asked Crumble whether he had ever attempted to sell any of the stolen merchandise at the Karate Club, to which Crumble repeatedly answered "no," counsel informed the court in a sidebar that he had an additional half-hour of cross-examination concerning prior bad acts. It was approximately 5:20 p.m. Although the government asked the court to limit defense counsel's questioning concerning Crumble's prior acts, the court refused to do so, stating that it was "going to allow a lot of latitude on the cross-examination of [Crumble] in light of the grant of immunity and other matters brought to the attention of the jury." The court then denied defense counsel's request to continue Crumble's cross-examination the next morning.

Defense counsel then questioned Crumble for twenty minutes concerning his second statement to Agent Dillon, after which counsel pointed out that it was 5:40 and that he was now going to delve into whether Crumble lied to the FBI in other earlier investigations. The court ruled that counsel could not inquire into these areas but that he could not prove any lies with extrinsic evidence. Defense counsel then twice more asked to continue the cross-examination until the following morning, but the court refused, stating that "you cannot move as slowly as you are and then say you're not getting enough time."

Defense counsel then questioned Crumble about statements made to the FBI in May, 1984 regarding a trailer Crumble owned in which some stolen Craig radios were found. Crumble admitted on the stand that he knew of the theft of the radios, but said he was not involved in the theft. He also admitted that he had lied to the FBI about his knowledge of the them. Defense counsel then started taking Crumble through the May, 1984 statement line by line, asking which statements were and were not lies. The court sustained a government objection, advising counsel that "the jury has heard enough about this conversation. . . . Move to another area of inquiry, if any." After informing the court that he had an additional half-hour to forty five minutes worth of cross-examination, defense counsel proceeded to ask more questions about the Craig merchandise theft. After a number of such questions, the court *sua sponte* terminated the cross-examination. The following morning, defense counsel arrived after the 10:00 a.m. starting time, and the court refused to hear his motion to reopen the cross-examination of Crumble. The jury subsequently convicted Spivey.

B.

The sixth amendment guarantees a defendant the right to cross-examine hostile witnesses. *Davis v. Alaska*, 415 U.S. 306, 315, 94 S. Ct. 1105, 1109, 39 L. Ed. 2d 347 (1973). Thus, a defendant must be granted the opportunity to expose facts from which a defendant could argue that the witness is incredible. *Delaware v. Van Arsdall*, 475 U.S. 673, 106 S. Ct. 1431, 1435, 89 L. Ed. 2d 674 (1986)

(citing *Davis v. Alaska*, 415 U.S. at 316-17), and we have stated that defense counsel should be afforded every opportunity to effectively cross-examine a government witness. *United States v. Castro*, 788 F.2d 1240, 1244 (7th Cir. 1986).

This does not mean, however, that the right to cross-examine is unlimited. "[T]he Confrontation Clause guarantees an *opportunity* for effective cross-examination, not cross-examination that is effective in whatever way, and to whatever extent the defense might wish." *Delaware v. Fensterer*, 474 U.S. 15, 106 S. Ct. 292, 296, 88 L. Ed. 2d 15 (1986) (emphasis in original). Hence, the trial court has discretion to impose reasonable limitations on cross-examination based upon concerns about, *inter alia*, harassment, confusion of issues, and repetitive or marginally relevant interrogation. *Delaware v. Van Arsdall*, 106 S. Ct. at 1435; see also *United States v. Silva*, 174 F.2d 106, 110 (7th Cir. 1986). The question in review is whether the jury had sufficient information to make a discriminating appraisal of the witness's motive or bias. *United States v. Rodgers*, 755 F. 2d 523, 548 (7th Cir.), *cert. denied*, 473 U.S. 127, 105 S. Ct. 3532, 87 L. Ed. 2d 656 (1985).

In this case, we believe the answer to that question is an obvious affirmative. Before the court terminated the Crumble cross-examination, defense counsel exposed facts showing virtually every possible motive or bias Crumble might have for testifying against Spivey. Defense counsel elicited that Crumble would not have testified but for his grant of immunity, that Crumble cooperated with the FBI only after he was arrested by Chicago police, that thereafter Crumble's state criminal case disappeared, that the government had interviewed Crumble extensively before trial, and that, during these interviews, Crumble crystallized in his mind the times and dates of the theft. Defense counsel also exposed that Crumble's first statement to the FBI was "all lies," and that Crumble had lied to the FBI during the 1984 investigation of the stolen Craig merchandise. Together, this was sufficient information for the jury to make a discriminating appraisal of Crumble's possible motives and biases. That Spivey was not able to pursue certain other avenues of impeachment does not change this conclusion.

Thus, the district court's termination of defense counsel's cross-examination of Crumble did not violate Spivey's sixth amendment rights. Defense counsel had cross-examined Crumble for most of the afternoon and evening. It was only after defense counsel backtracked, persistently asking improper questions, and repeatedly revised his estimates of how much cross-examination he had left that the court interceded. Even at the court's prodding, defense counsel refused to move on to new areas of inquiry. When it became clear that defense counsel was stalling, the court terminated the cross-examination. Cutting off the repetitive interrogation was within the court's discretion. In-

deed, our review of the record indicates that the district court allowed defense counsel a good deal of latitude in his questioning of Crumble, and carefully weighed the consequences of terminating the cross-examination before doing so. In short, there was no sixth amendment violation.

III.

Spivey next argues that, by terminating defense counsel's cross-examination of Crumble and another witness, Agent Dillon, and by making certain other statements to defense counsel during the trial, the court destroyed the credibility of Spivey's attorney in the eyes of the jury and deprived Spivey of a fair trial. A judge, of course, "should be and be seen to be even-handed." *United States v. Kwiat*, 817 F.2d 440, 470 (7th Cir. 1987). Because "the influence of the trial judge on the jury is necessarily and properly of great weight," *United States v. Dellinger*, 472 F.2d 340, 386 (7th Cir.), *cert. denied*, 410 U.S. 970, 93 S. Ct. 1443, 35 L. Ed. 2d 706 (1972), "the judge should reserve extensive and harsh criticism of counsel for times when the jury is absent," *Kwiat*, 817 F.2d at 447. Where the trial judge's remarks effectively destroy counsel's credibility in the eyes of the jury, we will reverse a criminal conviction. *United States v. Blakey*, 607 F.2d 779, 788 (7th Cir. 1979). Our review of the record, however, indicates that no such thing occurred in this case.

Spivey argues that the court's termination of defense counsel's cross-examinations of both Crumble and Dillon, coupled with other, for the most part unidentified, remarks addressed to defense counsel destroyed counsel's credibility. We disagree. We have already found no fault with the court's handling of the cross-examination of Crumble, and Spivey does not argue on appeal that the court's termination of defense counsel's cross-examination of Dillon was improper. As to the other remarks, Spivey points to none that fall outside the court's discretion to regulate the conduct of the trial, which, at certain points, requires the court to take positions and remind counsel, sometimes repeatedly, to ask proper questions. *Kwait*, 817 F.2d at 447; *see also Blakey*, 607 F.2d at 788. Obviously, some of defense counsel's tactics taxed the court's patience below, but the record does not reveal any overt display of contempt for the defense that occurred in the presence of the jury. What our review shows is a no-nonsense judge properly controlling the tempo of the trial before him. In short, the court was doing its job, not prejudicing the jury.

For the foregoing reasons, the defendant-appellant's conviction is AFFIRMED.

CRUMPTON v. COMMONWEALTH

384 S.E. 2d 339 (Va. App. 1989)

KOONTZ, Chief Judge

In a trial by jury in the Circuit Court of Pittsylvania County, Bobby Lee Crumpton was convicted of the first degree murder of his wife. Pursuant to the jury verdict he was sentenced to life imprisonment. On appeal Crumpton raises the following issues: (1) whether Crumpton was improperly prosecuted in violation of an agreement made with the Commonwealth; (2) whether Crumpton, under the particular facts of this case, has a right to explain the circumstances that prompted him to alter his prior inconsistent statements; (3) whether evidence of the deceased's character was admissible to disprove a defense of suicide; (4) whether the trial court improperly limited the testimony of Crumpton's expert witness; (5) whether improper evidence of Crumpton's bad character was admitted; (6) whether the Commonwealth Attorney's closing argument was improper; (7) whether the jury was properly instructed; (8) whether the evidence was sufficient to prove first degree murder; and (9) whether at the post-trial hearing Crumpton proved by clear and convincing evidence that the testimony of Elvis Redd was perjured. For the reasons that follow, we reverse Crumpton's conviction and remand for a new trial. In doing so, we address only those issues raised by Crumpton which are necessarily subject to repetition upon retrial.

I. Facts.

On the evening of April 6, 1986, Bobby Lee Crumpton's wife, Lynn Ward Crumpton, died of a shotgun wound to the chest. The death occurred in the couple's home. The shotgun belonged to Crumpton, and he was the only person present when the fatality occurred. For clarity, the details of the pertinent evidence will be related where appropriate to resolve the issues addressed in this appeal.

II. The Agreement with the Commonwealth.

Crumpton asserts that certain officers of the Pittsylvania County Sheriff's Department separately or in conjunction with the Pittsylvania County Commonwealth Attorney promised him that if he took and "passed" a polygraph examination no charges would be brought against him for the death of his wife. Crumpton further asserts that he took and "passed" a polygraph examination and therefore the Commonwealth should have been bound by this agreement.

Neither the trial court nor this Court need decide whether Crumpton "passed" the polygraph examination. Upon evidence presented at a pre-trial hearing on this issue the trial court found that while Crumpton took a polygraph examination the Common-

wealth had not agreed not to charge Crumpton with the murder of his wife if he "passed" the examination. We hold that the trial court's finding is supported by the evidence. Accordingly, Crumpton's assertion of an agreement not to prosecute him is without merit.

III. The Prior Inconsistent Statements and Polygraph Examination.

On April 6 and again on April 11, 1986, following the death of his wife, Crumpton gave the police authorities recorded statements in which he asserted that the death resulted from an accident while his wife was holding and cleaning his shotgun. While no charges were placed against Crumpton at that time, the authorities continued their investigation. On July 11, 1986, Crumpton willingly took a polygraph examination. Upon completion of the polygraph examination, Crumpton altered his prior statements, and, for the first time, asserted that his wife had committed suicide rather than having died by accident. Crumpton was indicted for the murder of his wife on October 26, 1986.

At trial, Crumpton's inconsistent statements and the polygraph examination became issues which arose repeatedly in different procedural contexts. As we have previously noted, in a pre-trial hearing Crumpton first asserted that he had an agreement with the Commonwealth that if he "passed" the polygraph examination no criminal charges would be placed against him. For the reasons previously stated, the trial court correctly determined that no such agreement existed. At that time the court did not rule on the admissibility of the polygraph evidence as it might relate to future incidents of the trial. During the trial, counsel for Crumpton, for reasons not apparent from the record, alternately referred to Crumpton's statements as "confessions" and "statements" and took several contradictory positions regarding the admissibility of these statements and the evidence relating to the polygraph examination. Counsel argued that Crumpton had no objection to the admission of his statements and that the polygraph evidence was admissible to show his "state of mind." Further, counsel argued that evidence of the "results" of the polygraph was admissible on the issue of voluntariness of the statements, although counsel also stated that he did not intend to offer evidence of the results of the polygraph. These contradictory and at best confusing positions taken by defense counsel provide the procedural background in which the issue we address here arose.

As the trial court noted, the "general issue" of the polygraph examination had been raised from the first day of the trial. Ultimately, during the Commonwealth's case-in-chief in a hearing out of the presence of the jury, the trial court was advised that Crumpton intended to testify concerning the circumstances surrounding his giving of the July 11 statement and specifically his reasons for altering his prior inconsistent statements. Crumpton asserted that he had a right to testify that he had been assured by

the police authorities that if he told them "exactly what happened" the public and especially his father-in-law, a prominent member of the local community, would not be told what happened. Crumpton maintained that he and his father-in-law were "the best of friends." Crumpton further asserted that upon completion of the polygraph examination George Watts, the polygraph examiner employed by the Virginia State Police, told him that the polygraph examination indicated that Crumpton was not lying when Crumpton said that he did not kill his wife. In the context that he had been assured that his father-in-law would not be told what happened and that the police authorities believed he did not kill his wife, Crumpton asserted that he altered his prior statements and gave that statement that his wife had committed suicide. The trial court ruled that the results of the polygraph examination were not admissible and that Crumpton could not "testify at any time that you testify about a polygraph or results of a polygraph test."

Subsequently, the Commonwealth introduced all three of Crumpton's statements. Following the conclusion of the Commonwealth's case, Crumpton testified that his wife's death resulted from suicide. Pertinent to his prior inconsistent statements, Crumpton was permitted to testify that the police had promised him if he told them exactly what happened "the case would be closed and the public and especially [his wife's father] would not be told what happened." He was also permitted to testify that George Watts "had information that said that I did not shoot my wife" and that for these reasons he had changed his account of the death. Crumpton was not permitted to testify that George Watts was a polygraph examiner or that the "information" allegedly possessed by Watts came from or concerned a polygraph examination. In short, consistent with the trial court's ruling, Crumpton was not permitted to testify "about a polygraph or results of a polygraph test."

To the extent that the trial court ruled that the *results* of the polygraph examination were not admissible, we agree. The law of this Commonwealth on that point is clear:

> [P]olygraph examinations are so thoroughly unreliable as to be of no proper evidentiary use whether they favor the accused, implicate the accused, or are agreed to by both parties. The point . . . is that the lie-detector or polygraph has an aura of authority while being wholly unreliable.

Robinson v. Commonwealth, 231 Va. 142, 156, 341 S.E.2d 159, 167 (1986) (citations omitted). The rule is so firmly embedded in our law that even "[e]vidence of a person's willingness or unwillingness to submit to a polygraph examination is inadmissible." *Gray v. Graham*, 231 Va. 1, 10, 341 S.E.2d 153, 158 (1986). See also *Taylor v. Commonwealth*, 3 Va. App. 59, 348 S.E.2d 36 (1986) (holding that to conclude an unreliable test can yield results which are definite and conclusive is a *non sequiter* and there-

fore polygraph results are inadmissible even under a stipulation by the parties that the results will be admissible if not shown to be indefinite or inconclusive). We do not retreat from or attempt to create exceptions to this clear precedent. An unreliable test cannot determine the truth; that determination is properly left to the judge or jury as the fact finder.

The application of the rule barring the polygraph examination *results*, however, does not resolve the issue presented by this appeal. Just as firmly embedded in our law as the rule against the admissibility of polygraph examination results is the rule that "[a] witness may be allowed to explain a prior inconsistent statement, and his explanation should be received and considered by the jury." *Brown v. Peters*, 202 Va. 382, 389, 117 S.E.2d 695, 699 (1961). A witness must be permitted to explain a prior inconsistent statement because his credibility as a witness at trial may be impeached by the fact that he made statements inconsistent with his trial testimony. The weight and credibility of a witness' testimony are for the jury to determine, and that determination, as we have previously held, may not be usurped by an unreliable polygraph examination. Nevertheless, in this case the polygraph examination and the alleged statements made by the polygraph examiner were a part of Crumpton's explanation for altering his prior inconsistent statements concerning his wife's death. In this context, we must reconcile these two rules as they apply to the specifics of this case.

Crumpton was the sole witness to the death of his wife. The Commonwealth's evidence tending to prove that she died as a result of a criminal act of Crumpton, with the exception of certain statements alleged to have been made to Crumpton by Elvis Redd, was wholly circumstantial. While admittedly inconsistent, Crumpton's statements to police authorities as well as his trial testimony were not per se admissions or confessions of criminal culpability; that is, the content of the statements if believed would not incriminate Crumpton. Similarly, the Commonwealth did not offer these statements for the truth of the content of the statements. Obviously, the Commonwealth did not intend to prove either accident or suicide as the cause of death. However, because these statements were offered into evidence by the Commonwealth when Crumpton subsequently testified his credibility as a witness was called into question by them. Crumpton's credibility was critical to the ultimate issue to be determined by the jury, which was whether Crumpton was telling the truth when he testified that his wife committed suicide. Moreover, once Crumpton's credibility was called into question by the admission of his prior inconsistent statements, Crumpton's reasons and the circumstances attendant to his giving those statements were just as critical to the jury's determination of his credibility as the fact that he had made them.

In reconciling Crumpton's right to explain his prior inconsistent statements with the rule prohibiting the admission of polygraph examination evidence, we begin with the premise that these rules are not inherently contradictory; that is, they may be reconciled so that the objectives of both rules are fulfilled. In our view, under the particular facts and procedural posture in which the application of these rules arose in this trial, Crumpton had a right to give a full explanation of his prior inconsistent statements so long as that explanation did not also necessarily invoke the polygraph examination results as proof that he had been truthful when he stated that his wife committed suicide.

It is clear from the record that Crumpton was not permitted to give a full explanation of his prior inconsistent statements. He was permitted to testify that the police authorities had promised him essentially that if he told the truth the case would be closed and the public and his father-in-law would not be told what happened. This, however, was only part of his explanation and perhaps the least significant part. A more significant part of his explanation was the fact that he altered his prior statements at the conclusion of a polygraph examination under circumstances in which he asserted that he had been assured by the police authorities that they believed he was truthful when he stated that he did not shoot his wife. Without explaining that George Watts was a polygraph examiner and that whatever "information" Watts had came from his interpretation of the polygraph examination, the jury could not have appreciated the significance of this evidence. Moreover, without any reference to "results" of the polygraph examination, coupled with appropriate cautionary instruction from the court that no inference favorable or unfavorable to Crumpton should be drawn from the reference to the polygraph examination, Crumpton could and should have been permitted to fully explain the surrounding circumstances and reasons for which he gave his July 11 statement which was introduced by the Commonwealth. Such a procedure would have preserved both the integrity of the rule prohibiting admissibility of polygraph results and the integrity of the rule permitting Crumpton to give a full explanation of his prior inconsistent statements. For these reasons we hold that the failure to permit Crumpton to give a full explanation of his prior inconsistent statements was error.

Finally, we disagree with the Commonwealth's assertion that Crumpton has shown no prejudice. Error will be presumed to be prejudicial unless it plainly appears that it could not have affected the result. *Sargent v. Commonwealth*, 5 Va. App. 143, 155, 360 S.E.2d 895, 902 (1987). The Commonwealth attacked Crumpton's credibility with his prior inconsistent statements. We cannot determine that a full explanation under the limitations set out above rather than Crumpton's restricted explanation would not have affected the jury's determination of Crumpton's credibility and ultimately his guilt or innocence of the charge against him.

For these reasons, we reverse Crumpton's conviction and remand for a new trial consistent with the holding of this opinion.

Reversed and remanded.

Cases relating to Chapter 10
TESTIMONIAL PRIVILEGES

TRAMMEL v. UNITED STATES

445 U.S. 40, 100 S. Ct. 906 (1980)

[Selected footnotes omitted]

Mr. Chief Justice BURGER delivered the opinion of the Court.

We granted certiorari to consider whether an accused may invoke the privilege against adverse spousal testimony so as to exclude the voluntary testimony of his wife. ___U.S.___ (1979). This calls for a re-examination of *Hawkins* v. *United States*, 358 U.S. 74 (1958).

I

On March 10, 1976, petitioner Otis Trammel was indicted with two others, Edwin Lee Roberts and Joseph Freeman, for importing heroin into the United States from Thailand and the Philippine Islands and for conspiracy to import heroin in violation of 21 U.S.C. § § 952(a), 962(a), and 963. The indictment also named six unindicted co-conspirators, including petitioner's wife Elizabeth Ann Trammel.

According to the indictment, petitioner and his wife flew from the Philippines to California in August 1975, carrying with them a quantity of heroin. Freeman and Roberts assisted them in its distribution. Elizabeth Trammel then travelled to Thailand where she purchased another supply of the drug. On November 3, 1975, with four ounces of heroin on her person, she boarded a plane for the United States. During a routine customs search in Hawaii, she was searched, the heroin was discovered, and she was arrested. After discussions with Drug Enforcement Administration agents, she agreed to cooperate with the Government.

Prior to trial on this indictment, petitioner moved to sever his case from that of Roberts and Freeman. He advised the court that the Government intended to call his wife as an adverse witness and asserted his claim to a privilege to prevent her from testifying against him. At a hearing on the motion, Mrs. Trammel was called as a Government witness under a grant of use immunity. She testified that she and petitioner were married in May 1975 and that they remained married. She explained that her cooperation with the Government was based on assurances that she would be given lenient treatment. She then described, in considerable detail, her role and that of her husband in the heroin distribution conspiracy.

After hearing this testimony, the District Court ruled that Mrs. Trammel could testify in support of the Government's case to any act she observed during the marriage and to any communication "made in the presence of a third person"; however, confidential communications between petitioner and his wife were held to be privileged and inadmissible. The motion to sever was denied.

At trial, Elizabeth Trammel testified within the limits of the court's pretrial ruling; her testimony, as the Government concedes, constituted virtually its entire case against petitioner. He was found guilty on both the substantive and conspiracy charges and sentenced to an indeterminate term of years pursuant to the Federal Youth Corrections Act, 18 U.S.C. § 5010(b).

In the Court of Appeals petitioner's only claim of error was that the admission of the adverse testimony of his wife, over his objection, contravened this Court's teaching in *Hawkins* v. *United States,* 358 U.S. 74 (1958), and therefore constituted reversible error. The Court of Appeals rejected this contention. It concluded that *Hawkins* did not prohibit "the voluntary testimony of a spouse who appears as an unindicted co-conspirator under grant of immunity from the Government in return for her testimony." 583 F.2d 1166, 1168 (CA10 1978).

II

The privilege claimed by petitioner has ancient roots. Writing in 1628, Lord Coke observed that "it hath been resolved by the Justices that a wife cannot be produced ei-

ther against or for her husband." 1 Coke, A Commentarie upon Littleton 6b (1628). See, generally, 8 J. Wigmore, Evidence § 2227, (McNaughton rev. 1961). This spousal disqualification sprang from two canons of medieval jurisprudence: first, the rule that an accused was not permitted to testify in his own behalf because of his interest in the proceeding; second, the concept that husband and wife were one, and that since the woman had no recognized separate legal existence, the husband was that one. From those two now long-abandoned doctrines, it followed that what was inadmissible from the lips of the defendant-husband was also inadmissible from his wife.

Despite its medieval origins, this rule of spousal disqualification remained intact in most common-law jurisdictions well into the 19th century. See 8 Wigmore, § 2333. It was applied by this Court in *Stein* v. *Bowman,* 13 Pet. 209, 220-223 (1839), in *Graves* v. *United States,* 150 U.S. 118 (1893), and again in *Jin Fuey Moy* v. *United States,* 254 U.S. 189, 195 (1920), where it was deemed so well established a proposition as to "hardly requir[e] mention." Indeed, it was not until 1933, in *Funk* v. *United States,* 290 U.S. 371, that this Court abolished the testimonial disqualification in the federal courts, so as to permit the spouse of a defendant to testify in the defendant's behalf. *Funk,* however, left undisturbed the rule that either spouse could prevent the other from giving adverse testimony. *Id.,* at 373. The rule thus evolved into one of privilege rather than one of absolute disqualification. See J. Maguire, Evidence, Common Sense and Common Law, at 78-92 (1947).

The modern justification for this privilege against adverse spousal testimony is its perceived role in fostering the harmony and sanctity of the marriage relationship. Notwithstanding this benign purpose, the rule was sharply criticized. Professor Wigmore termed it "the merest anachronism in legal theory and an indefensible obstruction to truth in practice." 8 Wigmore, § 2228, at 221. The Committee on the Improvement of the Law of Evidence of the American Bar Association called for its abolition. 63 American Bar Association Reports, at 594-595 (1938). In its place, Wigmore and others suggested a privilege protecting only private marital communications, modeled on the privilege between priest and penitent, attorney and client, and physician and patient. See 8 Wigmore, § 2332 *et seq.*

These criticisms influenced the American Law Institute, which, in its 1942 Model Code of Evidence, advocated a privilege for marital confidences, but expressly rejected a rule vesting in the defendant the right to exclude all adverse testimony of his spouse. See American Law Institute, Model Code of Evidence, Rule 215 (1942). In 1953 the Uniform Rules of Evidence, drafted by the National Conference of Commissioners on Uniform State Laws, followed a similar course; it limited the privilege to confidential communications and "abolishe[d] the rule, still existing in some states, and largely a sentimental relic, of not requiring one spouse to testify against the other in a criminal action." See Rule 23 (2) and comments. Several state legislatures enacted similarly patterned provisions into law.

In *Hawkins* v. *United States,* 358 U.S. 74 (1958), this Court considered the continued vitality of the privilege against adverse spousal testimony in the federal courts. There the District Court had permitted petitioner's wife, over his objection, to testify against him. With one questioning concurring opinion, the Court held the wife's testimony inadmissible; it took note of the critical comments that the common-law rule had engendered, *id.,* at 76, and n. 4, but chose not to abandon it. Also rejected was the Government's suggestion that the Court modify the privilege by vesting it in the witness spouse, with freedom to testify or not independent of the defendant's control. The Court viewed this proposed modification as antithetical to the widespread belief, evidenced in the rules then in effect in a majority of the States and in England, "that the law should not force or encourage testimony which might alienate husband and wife, or further inflame existing domestic differences." *Id.,* at 79.

Hawkins, then, left the federal privilege for adverse spousal testimony where it found it, continuing "a rule which bars the testimony of one spouse against the other unless both consent." *Id.,* at 78. Accord, *Wyatt* v. *United States,* 362 U.S. 525, 528 (1960). However, in so doing, the Court made clear that its decision was not meant to "foreclose whatever changes in the rule may eventually be dictated by 'reason and experience.'" 358 U.S., at 79.

III

A

The Federal Rules of Evidence acknowledge the authority of the federal courts to continue the evolutionary development of testimonial privileges in federal criminal trials "governed by the principles of the common law as they may be interpreted . . . in the light of reason and experience." Fed. Rule Evid. 501. Cf. *Wolfle* v. *United States, supra,* at 12 (1934). The general mandate of Rule 501 was substituted by the Congress for a set of privilege rules drafted by the Judicial Conference Advisory Committee on Rules of Evidence and approved by the Judicial Conference of the United States and by this Court. That proposal defined nine specific privileges, including a husband-wife privilege which would have codified the *Hawkins* rule and eliminated the privilege for confidential marital communications. See Fed. Rule of Evid., Proposed Rule 505. In rejecting the proposed rules and enacting Rule 501, Congress manifested an affirmative intention not to freeze the law of privilege. Its purpose rather was to "provide the courts with the flexibility to develop rules of privilege on a case-by-case basis," 120 Cong. Rec. 40891 (1974) (statement of Rep. Hungate), and to leave the door open to change. See also S. Rep. No. 93-1277, 93d Cong., 2d Sess., 11 (1974); H. R. Rep. No. 93-650, 93d Cong., 1st Sess., 8 (1973).

Although Rule 501 confirms the authority of the federal courts to reconsider the continued validity of the *Hawkins* rule, the long history of the privilege suggests that it ought not to be casually cast aside. That the privilege is one affecting marriage, home, and family relationships—already subject to much erosion in our day—also counsels caution. At the same time we cannot escape the reality that the law on occasion adheres to doctrinal concepts long after the reasons which gave them birth have disappeared and after experience suggests the need for change. This was recognized in *Funk* where the Court "decline[d] to enforce . . . ancient rule[s] of the common law under conditions as they now exist." 290 U.S., at 382. For, as Mr. Justice Black admonished in another setting, "[w]hen precedent and precedent alone is all the argument that can be made to support a court-fashioned rule, it is time for the rule's creator to destroy it." *Francis* v. *Southern Pacific Co.,* 333 U.S. 445, 471 (1948) (Black, J., dissenting).

B

Since 1958, when *Hawkins* was decided, support for the privilege against adverse spousal testimony has been eroded further. Thirty-one jurisdictions, including Alaska and Hawaii, then allowed an accused a privilege to prevent adverse spousal testimony. 358 U.S., at 81, n. 3 (STEWART, J., concurring). The number has now declined to 24.* In

---

*Eight states provide that one spouse is incompetent to testify against the other in a criminal proceeding: see Haw. Rev. Stat. § 621-18 (1968); Iowa Code § 622.7 (1979); Miss. Code Ann. § 13-1-5 (Cum. Supp. 1978); N. C. Gen. Stat § 8-57 (Cum. Supp. 1977); Ohio Rev. Code Ann. § 2945.42, Pa. Stat. Ann., Tit. 42, §§ 5913, 5915 (Purdon Supp. 1979); Tex. Crim. Pro. Code Ann. Art. 38.11 (Vernon 1979); Wyo. Stat. § 1-12-104 (1977).

Sixteen states provide a privilege against adverse spousal testimony and vest the privilege in both spouses or in the defendant-spouse alone: see Alaska Crim. Proc. Rules 26(b)(2) (Supp. Sept. 1968);

1974, the National Conference on Uniform States Laws revised its Uniform Rules of Evidence, but again rejected the *Hawkins* rule in favor of a limited privilege for confidential communications. See Uniform Rules of Evidence, Rule 504. That proposed rule has been enacted in Arkansas, North Dakota, and Oklahoma—each of which in 1958 permitted an accused to exclude adverse spousal testimony.** The trend in state law toward divesting the accused of the privilege to bar adverse spousal testimony has special relevance because the law of marriage and domestic relations are concerns traditionally reserved to the states. See *Sosna* v. *Iowa*, 419 U.S. 393, 404 (1975). Scholarly criticism of the *Hawkins* rule has also continued unabated.

Colo. Rev. Stat. § 13-90-107 (1974); Idaho Code § 9-203. (Cum. Supp. 1978); Mich. Comp. Laws § 600.2162 (Mich. Stat. Ann. § 27A.2162 (Callaghan 1976)); Minn. Stat. Ann. § 595.02 (West Cum. Supp. 1978); Mo. Ann. Stat. § 546.260 (Vernon 1953); Mont. Rev. Codes Ann. § 95-3011 (Cum. Supp. 1975); Neb. Rev. Stat. § 27-505 (1975); Nev. Rev. Stat. § 49.295 (1977); N. J. Stat. Ann. § 2A:84A-17 (West 1976); N. M. Stat. Ann. § 20-4-505 (Cum. Supp. 1975); Ore. Rev. Stat. § 44.040 (1977); Utah Code Ann. § 78-24-8 (1977); Va. Code § 19.2-271.2 (Cum. Supp. 1978); Wash. Rev. Code Ann. § 5.60.060 (Supp. 1979); W. Va. Code § 57-3-3 (1966).

Nine states entitle the witness-spouse alone to assert a privilege against adverse spousal testimony: see Ala. Code, Tit. 12, § 21-227 (1977); Cal. Evid. Code §§ 970-973 (West 1966); Conn. Gen. Stat. Ann. § 54-84 (West Cum. Supp. 1979); Ga. Code Ann. § 38-1604 (1974); Ky. Rev. Stat. § 421.210 (Cum. Supp. 1978); La. Rev. Stat. Ann. § 15:461 (West 1967); Md. Cts. and Jud. Proc. Code Ann. §§ 9-101, 9-106 (1974); Mass. Ann. Laws ch. 233, § 20 (Law, Co-op 1974); R. I. Gen. Laws § 12-17-10 (1970).

The remaining 17 states have abolished the privilege in criminal cases: see Ariz. Rev. Stat. Ann. § 12-2231 (Supp. 1978); Ark. Stat. Ann. § 28-1001, Rules 501 and 504 (Cum. Supp. 1977); Del. Code Ann., Tit. 11, § 3502 (1975); Fla. Stat. Ann. §§ 90.501, 90.504 (West Supp. 1979); Ill. Ann. Stat. ch 38, § 155-1 (Smith-Hurd Cum. Supp. 1979); Ind. Code Ann. §§ 34-1-14-4, 34-1-14-5 (Burns 1973); Kan. Stat. Ann. §§ 60-407, 60-428 (1976); Me. Rev. Stat. Ann., Maine Rules of Evidence,

Rules 501, 504 (West Supp. 1978); N. H. Rev. Stat. Ann. § 516.27 (1974); N. Y. Crim. Proc. Law § 60.10 (McKinney 1971); N. Y. Civ. Proc. Law §§ 4502, 4512 (McKinney 1963), N. D. Cent. Code, N. D. Rules of Evidence, Rules 501, 504 (Supp. 1977); Okla. Stat. Ann., Tit. 12, §§ 2103, 2501, 2504 (West Cum. Supp. 1978-1979); S. C. Code § 19-11-30 (1977); S. D. Compiled Laws Ann. §§ 19-13-1, 19-13-12 thru 19-13-15 (Supp. 1978); Tenn. Code Ann. § 40-2404 (1975); Vt. Stat. Ann., Tit. 12, § 1605 (1973); Wis. Stat. Ann. §§ 905.01, 905.05 (West 1975).

In 1901, Congress enacted a rule of evidence for the District of Columbia that made husband and wife "competent but not compellable to testify for or against each other," except as to confidential communications. This provision, which vests the privilege against adverse spousal testimony in the witness spouse, remains in effect. See 31 Stat. 1358 § § 1068, 1069, recodified as D. C. Code § 14-306 (1973).

** In 1965, California took the privilege from the defendant-spouse and vested it in the witness-spouse, accepting a study commission recommendation that the "latter [was] more likely than the former to determine whether or not to claim the privilege on the basis of the probable effect on the marital relationship." See Cal. Evi. Code §§ 970-973 and 1 California Law Revision Commission, Recommendation and Study relating to The Marital "For or Against" Testimonial Privilege at F-5 (1956). See also 6 California Law Revision Commission, Tentative Privileges Recommendations—Rule 27.5, at 243-244 (1964).

C

Testimonial exclusionary rules and privileges contravene the fundamental principle that "the public . . . has a right to every man's evidence." *United States* v. *Bryan,* 339 U.S. 323, 331 (1950). As such, they must be strictly construed and accepted "only to the very limited extent that permitting a refusal to testify or excluding relevant evidence has a public good transcending the normally predominant principle of utilizing all rational means for ascertaining truth." *Elkins* v. *United States,* 364 U.S. 206, 234 (1960) (Frankfurter, J., dissenting). Accord, *United States* v. *Nixon,* 418 U.S. 683, 709-710 (1974). Here we must decide whether the privilege against adverse spousal testimony promotes sufficiently important interests to outweigh the need for probative evidence in the administration of criminal justice.

It is essential to remember that the *Hawkins* privilege is not needed to protect information privately disclosed between husband and wife in the confidence of the marital relationship—once described by this Court as "the best solace of human existence." *Stein* v. *Bowman,* 13 Pet., at 223. Those confidences are privileged under the independent rule protecting confidential marital communications. *Blau* v. *United States,* 340 U.S. 332 (1951); see n. 5, *supra.* The *Hawkins* privilege is invoked, not to exclude private marital communications, but rather to exclude evidence of criminal acts and of communications made in the presence of third persons.

No other testimonial privilege sweeps so broadly. The privileges between priest and penitent, attor-

ney and client, and physician and patient limit protection to private communications. These privileges are rooted in the imperative need for confidence and trust. The priest-penitent privilege recognizes the human need to disclose to a spiritual counselor, in total and absolute confidence, what are believed to be flawed acts or thoughts and to receive priestly consolation and guidance in return. The lawyer-client privilege rests on the need for the advocate and counselor to know all that relates to the client's reasons for seeking representation if the professional mission is to be carried out. Similarly, the physician must know all that a patient can articulate in order to identify and to treat disease; barriers to full disclosure would impair diagnosis and treatment.

The *Hawkins* rule stands in marked contrast to these three privileges. Its protection is not limited to confidential communications; rather it permits an accused to exclude all adverse spousal testimony. As Jeremy Bentham observed more than a century and a half ago, such a privilege goes far beyond making "every man's house his castle," and permits a person to convert his house into "a den of thieves." 5 Rationale of Judicial Evidence 340 (1827). It "secures, to every man, one safe and unquestionable and ever ready accomplice for every imaginable crime." *Id.,* at 338.

The ancient foundations for so sweeping a privilege have long since disappeared. Nowhere in the common-law world—indeed in any modern society—is a woman regarded as chattel or demeaned by denial of a separate legal identity and the dignity associated with recognition as a whole human being. Chip by chip, over the years those archaic notions have been cast aside so that "[n]o longer is the female destined solely for the home and the rearing of the family, and only the male for the marketplace and the world of ideas." *Stanton* v. *Stanton*, 421 U.S. 7, 14, 15 (1975).

The contemporary justification for affording an accused such a privilege is also unpersuasive. When one spouse is willing to testify against the other in a criminal proceeding—whatever the motivation—their relationship is almost certainly in disrepair; there is probably little in the way of marital harmony for the privilege to preserve. In these circumstances, a rule of evidence that permits an accused to prevent adverse spousal testimony seems far more likely to frustrate justice than to foster family peace. Indeed, there is reason to believe that vesting the privilege in the accused could actually undermine the marital relationship. For example, in a case such as this, the Government is unlikely to offer a wife immunity and lenient treatment if it knows that her husband can prevent her from giving adverse testimony. If the Government is dissuaded from making such an offer, the privilege can have the untoward effect of permitting one spouse to escape justice at the expense of the other. It hardly seems conducive to the preservation of the marital relation to place a wife in jeopardy solely by virtue of her husband's control over her testimony.

IV

Our consideration of the foundations for the privilege and its history

satisfy us that "reason and experience" no longer justify so sweeping a rule as that found acceptable by the Court in *Hawkins*. Accordingly, we conclude that the existing rule should be modified so that the witness spouse alone has a privilege to refuse to testify adversely; the witness may be neither compelled to testify nor foreclosed from testifying. This modification—vesting the privilege in the witness spouse—furthers the important public interest in marital harmony without unduly burdening legitimate law enforcement needs.

Here, petitioner's spouse chose to testify against him. That she did so after a grant of immunity and assurances of lenient treatment does not render her testimony involuntary. Cf. *Bordenkircher* v. *Hayes*, 434 U.S. 357 (1978). Accordingly, the District Court and the Court of Appeals were correct in rejecting petitioner's claim of privilege, and the judgment of the Court of Appeals is affirmed.

Affirmed.

MR. JUSTICE STEWART, concurring in the judgment.

Although agreeing with much of what the Court has to say, I cannot join an opinion that implies that "reason and experience" have worked a vast change since the *Hawkins* case was decided in 1958. In that case the Court upheld the privilege of a defendant in a criminal case to prevent adverse spousal testimony, in an all-but-unanimous opinion by Mr. Justice Black. Today the Court, in another all-but-unanimous opinion, obliterates that privilege because of the purported change in perception that "reason and experience" have wrought.

The fact of the matter is that the Court in this case simply accepts the very same arguments that the Court rejected when the Government first made them in the *Hawkins* case in 1958. I thought those arguments were valid then, and I think so now.

The Court is correct when it says that "[t]he ancient foundations for so sweeping a privilege have long since disappeared." But those foundations had disappeared well before 1958; their disappearance certainly did not occur in the few years that have elapsed between the *Hawkins* decision and this one. To paraphrase what Mr. Justice Jackson once said in another context, there is reason to believe that today's opinion of the Court will be of greater interest to students of human psychology than to students of law.

In re WITNESS BEFORE THE GRAND JURY

631 F. Supp. 32 (E.D. Wis. 1985)

ORDER

CURRAN, District Judge

The government has filed a Motion to Compel Testimony of a witness who testified before the grand jury on March 5, 1985, and declined to answer two questions: (1) who brought up the idea of listing income as "fees and commissions" on his federal income tax return, and (2) whether he and his tax attorney had any conversation as to how much the witness earned and how much he spent. The witness refused to answer these questions on the ground of attorney-client privilege. He has submitted a brief in response to this motion which is now ready for decision.

The attorney-client privilege is an evidentiary privilege, not a constitutional right. See Federal Rule of Evidence 501. The privilege only prohibits the disclosure of the substance of communications made in confidence by a client to his attorney for the purpose of obtaining legal advice. The attorney-client privilege is intended to be strictly confined with the narrowest possible limits consistent with the logic of its principle, and the privilege is designed to protect only such information a client communicates to his attorney so that the attorney may properly, competently and ethically carry out his representation. *United States v. Weger*, 709 F.2d 1151, 1154 (7th Cir. 1983).

A party seeking to invoke the attorney-client privilege has the burden of establishing all of its essential elements. *United States v. First State Bank*, 691 F.2d 332, 335 (7th Cir. 1982). These elements were set forth in *Radiant Burners Inc. v. American Gas Association*, 320 F.2d 314, 319

(7th Cir.), *cert. denied*, 375 U.S. 929, 84 S. Ct. 330, 11 L. Ed. 2d 262 (1963):

(1) Where legal advice of any kind is sought (2) from a professional legal adviser in his capacity as such, (3) the communications relating to that purpose, (4) made in confidence (5) by the client, (6) are at his instance permanently protected (7) from disclosure by himself or by the legal adviser, (8) except the protection be waived.

The claim of privilege must be made and sustained on a question-by-question or document-by-document basis. *First State Bank*, 691 F.2d at 335.

The instant case is unusual in that the client who is asserting the privilege is not the target of the grand jury investigation. In this case the lawyer is the target. The witness has cited no authority for the proposition that the attorney-client privilege is meant to cover this type of situation.

The subject matter of the testimony the government seeks to elicit concerns the preparation of the witnesses' federal income taxes. Other courts in this circuit have held that "where the attorney acts as a business advisor or collection agent, gives investment advice, or handles financial transactions for his client, the communications between him and his client are not protected by the privilege." *In re Shapiro*, 381 F. Supp. 21, 22 (N.D. Ill. 1974) (footnotes omitted). See also *First Wisconsin Mortgage Trust v. First Wisconsin Corpo-*

ration, 86 F.R.D. 160, 174 (E.D. Wis. 1980). More specifically, the preparation of tax returns is generally not considered legal advice within the scope of the attorney-client privilege. The Seventh Circuit Court of Appeals has explicitly held that "information transmitted for the purpose of preparation of a tax return, though transmitted to an attorney, is not privileged information." *United States v. Lawless*, 709 F.2d 485, 488 (7th Cir. 1983). "[A]lthough preparation of tax returns by itself may require some knowledge of the law, it is primarily an accounting service. Communications relating to that service should therefore not be privileged, even though performed by a lawyer." *United States v. Davis*, 636 F.2d 1028, 1043 (5th Cir.), *cert. denied*, 454 U.S. 862, 102 S. Ct. 320, 70 L. Ed. 2d 162 (1981). *See also United States v. El Paso Company*, 682 F.2d 530 (10th Cir. 1982), *cert. denied*, 466 U.S. 944, 104 S. Ct. 1927, 80 L. Ed. 2d 473 (1984); *United States v. Willis*, 565 F. Supp. 1186 (S.D. Ia. 1983). The government has submitted a transcript of the March 5, 1985, grand jury proceedings in connection with its motion. During those proceedings the witness testified that he sought advice from his attorney regarding his gem business (Transcript at 9) and the preparation of his income tax return (Id. at 13). The two questions for which the privilege has been asserted clearly relate to the preparation of the tax returns. Thus, the information sought is not privileged.

A second basis for compelling this testimony from the witness is that it appears to fall within the continuing or contemplated crime or fraud exception to the attorney-client privilege. If the government makes a prima facie showing that the professional attorney-client relationship was intended to further a criminal enterprise, the privilege does not exist. *See In re Special September 1978 Grand Jury*, 640 F.2d 49, 59 (7th Cir. 1980). This is so even if the lawyer is an unwitting participant in the fraud or crime. *See In re Grand Jury Proceedings*, 680 F.2d 1026, 1029 (5th Cir. 1982). During the grand jury proceedings the witness testified that he had profited from the sale of cocaine (Transcript at 16) and that he did not report this profit on the income tax return prepared by his attorney. (Id. at 17). By his own admission the witness filed a false income tax return for the year 1980. It follows, therefore, that the preparation of the 1980 return was part of a fraudulent, if not criminal act. In 1984 a jury convicted the witness of dealing in narcotics and of engaging in a continuing criminal enterprise. The court finds that this conviction, plus the witnesses' subsequent grand jury testimony constitutes a prima facie showing that the preparation of the 1980 tax returns furthered his criminal conduct. Therefore, the crime-fraud exception to the attorney-client privilege applies in this situation. See *Ohio-Sealy Mattress Manufacturing Company v. Kaplan*, 90 F.R.D. 21, 29-30 (N.D. Ill. 1980).

Accordingly, the court ORDERS that the Government's Motion to Compel Testimony (filed May 14, 1984) IS GRANTED.

CBS, INC. v. COBB

536 So. 2d 1067 (Fla. Dist. Ct. App. 1988)

PER CURIAM

CBS, Inc. and reporter Victoria Corderi seek an emergency writ of certiorari to quash an order of the circuit court requiring them to relinquish unpublished film footage to the defendant in a pending criminal case. We deny the petition.

This controversy arose during the trial of Bobby Joe Long, charged with first degree murder. Long has been convicted of this same murder once before, but the supreme court reversed that conviction and ordered a new trial. *Long v. State*, 517 So.2d 664 (Fla. 1987), *cert. denied*, ____ U.S. ____, 108 S. Ct. 1754, 100 L. Ed. 2d 216 (1988). In the interim between Long's first conviction and the present trial, Corderi interviewed Long on Florida's "Death Row" as part of a feature story on serial killers. The broadcast included certain admissions by Long to the effect "I've probably destroyed about a hundred people." The state has obtained this broadcast footage and, over Long's objection, has been permitted to introduce it during its case-in-chief. When he became aware of the state's plan to use the footage, Long served subpoenas upon the petitioners, directing them to produce the videotape of the entire Long interview. The circuit court denied petitioner's motion to quash the subpoenas, resulting in the matter now before us.

The CBS petition is, of course, grounded in the First Amendment privilege that exists to protect journalists against unwarranted disclosure of their sources of information. *See, e.g., Branzburg v. Hayes,* 408 U.S. 665, 92 S. Ct. 2646, 33 L. Ed. 2d 626 (1972); *Tribune Co. v. Huffstetler,* 489 So.2d 722 (Fla. 1976). *Morgan v. State,* 337 S.2d 951 (Fla. 1976). This privilege may be described as "limited" or "qualified" because it is not absolute and may be overcome under circumstances where the fair administration of justice establishes a compelling need for disclosure. *Gadsden County Times v. Horne,* 426 So.2d 1234 (Fla. 1st DCA), *petition for review denied,* 441 So.2d 631 (Fla. 1983). On the other hand, where such a compelling need has not been established, this court has refused to distinguish between information received in confidence, such as through an "informer," and that which was not. *Tribune Co. v. Green,* 440 So.2d 484 (Fla. 2d DCA 1983), *petition for review denied,* 447 So.2d 886 (Fla.

1984). *Contra, Miami Herald Publishing Co. v. Morejon,* 529 So.2d 1204 (Fla. 3d DCA 1988).

Initially, there is some question whether the materials requested by Long are the sort to which a strong presumption of privilege should attach. At the hearing on the CBS motion to quash Long's counsel raised the interesting point, "[W]hat chilling effect is there if a person talks to a reporter and asks for a copy of what he told them?" Furthermore, we cannot help but note that CBS, by soliciting the damaging comments of a condemned killer (even one apparently willing to make such admissions to a nationwide audience), may have contributed to the controversy. *Cf. Waterman Broadcasting of Florida, Inc. v. Reese,* 523 So.2d 1161 (Fla. 2d DCA 1988) (murder suspect's admissions to television interviewer were "unique," thus their relevancy was "obvious," supporting requirement of disclosure). Yet this court has extended protection beyond the revelation of sources and reporter's notes to non-testimonial items, finding that "unpublished photographs taken by a newspaper photographer stand on the same footing as any other information acquired by a news-gatherer." *Johnson v. Bentley,* 457 So.2d 507, 509 (Fla. 2d DCA 1984). "The autonomy of the press would be jeopardized if resort to its resource materials, by litigants seeking to utilize the news-gathering effects of journalists for their private purposes, were routinely permitted." *O'Neill v. Oakgrove Construction, Inc.* 71 N.Y.2d 521, 526,

528 N.Y.S.2d 1, 2, 523 N.E.2d 277, 279 (1988). That is, the scope of the First Amendment's protection may be broader than is necessary to protect confidential informants, extending to the expense and harassment that might be foreseeable if litigants were allowed unlimited access to journalistic archives.

Assuming that some privilege attaches to the CBS outtakes, the question follows whether the trial court, in requiring their disclosure to Long, satisfied the three-pronged test adopted by *Gadsden County Times v. Horne* and *Tribune Co. v. Green*, *supra*. Briefly, the criteria for determining the necessity of disclosure are: (1) whether the information sought is relevant to issues in the case; (2) whether any alternative source exists for the information; (3) whether there is compelling interest in the information. Only if all three questions can be answered in the affirmative may a journalist be required to relinquish or disclose privileged matters.

In determining that CBS should furnish the tapes, the trial court expressed its opinion that the cases relied upon by CBS "all regard sources, not just a finished product." Therefore, the network reasons, the trial court totally failed to apply the so-called *Garland* test, let alone make the specific findings of fact that CBS believes are required. We disagree. Notwithstanding certain language in *Gadsden County Times v. Horne*, regarding an absence of facts "set out in the lower court's order," 426 So.2d at 1242, we do not accept the argument that the failure of the court to make detailed findings of fact, or to reduce such findings to writing, is necessarily fatal to the party seeking to compel disclosure. As stated by counsel for Long, it is clear from the record before us "regardless whether the lower court specifically articulated the findings [that] the three-part test has been met."

As to the first prong of the test, CBS argues that *none* of Long's statements, whether contained within the broadcast portion of the interview or not, should be admissible at trial, and therefore the outtakes sought by Long are not relevant. More specifically, they contend that Long's damaging admissions were not shown to relate to the murder for which he is now being tried, nor do they display sufficient similarity to the facts of that murder to justify their admission as "Williams Rule" evidence. *Williams v. State*, 110 So.2d 654 (Fla.), cert. denied, 361 U.S. 847, 80 S. Ct. 102, 4 L. Ed. 2d 86 (1959). Furthermore, the only conceivable use Long would have for the outtakes would be if they contained "self-serving exculpatory statements," inadmissible under the hearsay rule. *Moore v. State*, 530 So.2d 61 (Fla. 1st DCA 1988).

Be that as it may, the trial court has determined, since the time CBS filed its petition with this court, that the state will be allowed to introduce the interview excerpt in its possession. It is not within our present authority to rule upon the correctness of this decision, except to state that it strongly bolsters Long's claim of relevancy. Whenever part of a written or recorded statement is introduced by a party, an adverse party may require the introduction of any other part of the statement that in fairness ought to be considered contemporaneously. §90.108, Fla. Stat. (1987). Concededly, Long is at somewhat of a disadvantage in that he cannot determine whether such "fairness" arises in this case—or even whether there is anything on the tape he may want the jury to hear—without first viewing the entire statement. Yet we must take care not to confuse relevancy with the ultimate question of the admissibility of that evidence. The record in this case strongly suggests that if any segment of the interview is relevant, there is a good chance the rest of it is relevant also. Whether, beyond that, it is "pertinent and proper to be considered in reaching a decision" is for the trial court to decide.

We further find that Long has adequately demonstrated the lack of an alternative source for the same information. CBS considers this alternative source obvious—Long himself. At the hearing in circuit court Long's counsel countered that Long does not remember everything he said to reporter Corderi during the course of the interview. CBS considers this "naked assertion" insufficient. However, the trial court indicated that "I don't know how we can expect him to remember how the questions and his answers were organized," and we are not persuaded that this conclusion was unreasonable. In *Colonial Penn Insurance Co. v. Blair*, 380 So.2d 1305,

1306 (Fla. 5th DCA 1980), the court overruled an objection based on attorney work product and required production of the transcript of a civil defendant's traffic court testimony that had been prepared at the behest of the plaintiff, noting that "[t]he memories of the parties [are] a poor and possibly fallible substitute for statements close in time to the accident." That rationale has since been extended to "unique" pictures of allegedly hazardous road conditions, relevant to issues in a civil action, which were taken by a newspaper photographer. *Carroll Contracting, Inc. v. Edwards*, 528 So.2d 951 (Fla. 5th DCA 1988). The taped interview is the best evidence of what was said by Long, including the context of Long's remarks.

Finally, we hold that Long has demonstrated a compelling need for the information currently in the possession of CBS, notwithstanding his apparent inability to summarize the exact nature of that information without first being allowed to examine it. This is not merely a "fishing expedition" for evidence which theoretically could be useful to Long in the preparation of his defense. Rather, it is "a necessary step in [defendant's] due and proper preparation for trial." *Gulliver's Periodicals, Ltd. v. Chas. Levy Circulating Co.*, 455 F. Sup. 1197 (N.D. Ill. 1978). A small portion of the interview already has been utilized to Long's detriment, and he considers it imperative to determine whether this segment was edited, properly or otherwise, in a manner which rendered it unduly suggestive or distorted its content. We must not lose sight of the fact that Long is, literally, fighting for his life. Certainly, the acquisition of helpful evidence in such a situation is more compelling than in the civil context, where the potential loss to a litigant is purely economic. The Sixth Amendment to the United States Constitution, as well as Article 1, Section 16, of the Florida Constitution, provides that the accused in a criminal proceeding shall have the right of compulsory process for obtaining witnesses in his favor. When these constitutional provisions conflict with "shield laws" designed to protect the integrity of the print or broadcast media, some deference must be made afforded to the rights of the accused. So held the Supreme Court of New Jersey, describing this "rather elementary, but entirely sound proposition" as "unassailable." *In the Matter of Farber*, 78 N.J. 259, 394 A.2d 330, 336, *cert. denied sub. nom. New York Times Co. v. New Jersey*, 439 U.S. 997, 99 S. Ct. 598, 58 L. Ed. 2d 670 (1978). We are satisfied that, under the facts of this case as presented to us, the trial court's order constitutes a reasonable determination that Long's constitutional right to defend himself outweighs the constitutional right of CBS to withhold journalistic work product.

In closing, we would observe that, given the time constraints generated by the petition's emergency status, the excellent presentation of the issues by all the attorneys who have submitted pleadings in this proceeding is worthy of commendation.

Petition denied.

CAMPBELL, C.J., and HALL and THREADGILL, JJ., concur.

Cases relating to Chapter 11
OPINIONS AND EXPERT TESTIMONY

UNITED STATES v. LANGFORD

802 F.2d 1176 (9th Cir. 1986)

FARRIS, Circuit Judge:

Charles Langford appeals his conviction of unarmed bank robbery 18 U.S.C. § 2113(a)). We have jurisdiction under 28 U.S.C. §§ 1291 and 1294. We affirm.

By indictment handed down February 6, 1985, Langford was charged with armed bank robbery (18 U.S.C. § 2113(d)). He was tried before a jury and convicted of unarmed bank robbery (18 U.S.C. § 2113(a)). On April 19, 1985, the district court granted Langford's motion for a new trial and permitted his counsel to withdraw upon the latter's representation that he had "conflicts" with Langford. The matter was set to be retried on May 13, 1985. On May 8, 1985, substitute counsel for moved for a continuance to prepare for trial. The motion was heard and granted on May 13, 1985. The matter was reset for July 8, 1985. On June 7, 1985, Langford filed a discovery motion that was heard June 13, 1985. The time between the filing and disposition of these motions was excludable for Speedy Trial Act purposes. 18 U.S.C. § 3161(h)(1)(F). Thus, while the second trial commenced some 80 calendar days after the motion for a new trial was granted, the 70-day time limit for retrial established under the Act, 18 U.S.C. § 3161(e), was not violated. Accordingly, we do not decide whether the trial court improperly granted original trial counsel leave to withdraw, thereby prejudicing Langford's right to a speedy trial.

At trial Langford's cousin, Jerry Lankford, and his parole officer, Richard Wood, testified that the person depicted in bank surveillance photographs taken during the robbery was Langford. Such opinion testimony by lay witnesses is admissible under Fed. R. Evid. 701 if it is "limited to those opinions or inferences which are (a) rationally based on the perception of the witness and (b) helpful to a clear understanding of his testimony or the determination of a fact in issue." *United States v. Young Buffalo*, 591 F.2d 506, 513 (9th Cir.), *cert. denied*, 441 U.S. 950, 99 S. Ct. 2178, 60 L. Ed. 2d 1055 (1979);

United States v. Butcher, 557 F.2d 666, 669-70 (9th Cir. 1977). Such testimony is particularly valuable where, as in the present case, the lay witnesses are able to make the challenged identifications based on their familiarity with characteristics of the defendant not immediately observable by the jury at trial. *See, e.g., United States v. Barrett*, 703 F.2d 1076, 1086 (9th Cir. 1983); *United States v. Young Buffalo*, 591 F.2d at 513. We conclude that, because Wood had met with Langford approximately 50 times and Lankford had known Langford most of his life, the opinions testified to by Lankford and Wood were rationally based and helpful to the jury in determining a fact in issue. Fed. R. Evid. 701.

Langford suggests that opinion testimony on ultimate issues of fact is inadmissible. Opinion testimony on ultimate issues of fact is admissible unless the testimony concerns the mental state or condition of a defendant in a criminal case. Fed. R. Evid. 704. Because the testimony Langford objects to was neither given by an expert nor concerned with Langford's mental state or condition, Langford's objection is untenable.

Langford additionally maintains that the trial court abused its discretion in balancing the probative value of the lay opinion testimony against its potential for prejudice. Rule 403 of the Federal Rules of Evidence provides that "[a]lthough relevant, evidence may be excluded if its probative value is outweighed by the danger of unfair prejudice . . ." Fed. R. Evid. 403. We conclude that, given the familiarity both Lankford and Wood had with Langford, their testimony was sufficiently probative to outweigh the danger of unfair prejudice. The district court thus did not abuse its discretion in this respect.

Upon Langford's ex parte application, the trial court appointed an expert in the field of eyewitness identification to assist in preparation of Langford's defense. Such an appointment requires a finding that the services of the expert "are necessary for an adequate defense." 18 U.S.C. §3006A(e)(1). Nevertheless, at trial the court excluded the expert's testimony concerning the unreliability of eyewitness identification:

> I rather think in all of these situations it is a balancing question. The ruling of the court (excluding the proffered testimony) is in no way predicated upon the absence of qualifications of the witness who has been identified in his professional field of psychology. The ruling, including the use of his testimony as an expert, is that it goes beyond the field of expertise to which such testimony should be directed or can be directed, and is basically argumentative and intrusive upon the jury's responsibility as triers of the facts of the case.

Even if the admission of expert testimony concerning eyewitness identification is proper under certain circumstances, "there is no federal authority for the proposition that such testimony *must* be admitted." *United States v. Moore*, 786 F.2d 13008, 1312-13 (5th Cir. 1986). We have repeatedly upheld the exclusion of such testimony. See *United States v. Brewer*, 783 F.2d 841, 842 (9th Cir. 1986); *United States v. Amaral*, 488 F.2d 1148, 1153 (9th Cir. 1973). It was within the broad discretion of the trial court to conclude that, on balance, the jury would not benefit from admission of the proffered evidence. *See United States v. Solomon*, 753 F.2d 1522, 1525 (9th Cir. 1985) (quoting *United States v. Awkard*, 597 F.2d 667, 669 (9th Cir.), *cert. denied*, 444 U.S. 885, 100 S. Ct. 179, 62 L. Ed. 2d 116 and 444 U.S. 969, 100 S. Ct. 460, 62 L. Ed. 2d 383 (1979)("Expert testimony is admissible if the jury may receive 'appreciable help' from it.". See also *Brown v. Darcy*, 783 F.2d 1389, 1396 (9th Cir. 1986) (Expert testimony is properly excluded where it "infringes on the jury's role"; *United States v. Binder*, 769 F.2d 595, 602 (9th Cir. 1985) ("Expert testimony should not be permitted if it concerns a subject... that invades the province of the jury."); *Amaral*, 488 F.2d at 1153 ("It is the responsibility of counsel during cross-examination to inquire into the witness' opportunity for observation, his capacity for observation, his attention and interest and his distraction or division of attention." As exclusion was not "manifestly erroneous," the judgment will not be disturbed. *See Salem v. United States Lines Co.* 370 U.S. 31, 35, 82 S. Ct. 1119, 1122, 8 L. Ed. 2d 313 (1962).

At Langford's behest, the professional relationship between Langford and Parole Officer Richard Wood was not revealed to the jury when Wood identified Langford in the bank surveillance photographs. Sworn declarations submitted by Langford in connection with his post-trial motion for a new trial establish (1) that during a recess in trial proceedings Wood entered and exited the probation office in view of the jury, and (2) that post-trial interviews with an undisclosed number of jurors revealed that three had determined that Wood was Langford's probation or parole officer.

Langford contends that the affidavits establish that the jury was improperly exposed to "extraneous and prejudicial matter" and that the trial court erred in failing to grant his motion for a second new trial. His argument is that Wood's presence in the probation office gave rise to the inference that Langford had previously been convicted of a federal offense. That information, he continues, prejudiced Langford's defense, necessitating reversal and a third trial. In the alternative, Langford contends that the matter should be remanded for a hearing concerning the nature of any extraneous information that reached the jury. We disagree.

When information not admitted into evidence reaches the jury, "the defendant is entitled to a new trial if 'there existed a reasonable possibility that the extrinsic material could have affected the verdict.' " *United States v. Bagley*, 641 F.2d 1235, 1240 (9th Cir.) (citing *United States v. Vasquez,*

597 F.2d 192, 193 (9th Cir. 1979)), cert. denied, 454 U.S. 942, 102 S. Ct. 480, 70 L. Ed. 2d 251 (1981). While we independently review allegations of juror misconduct to determine whether a new trial is required, *United States v. Halbert*, 712 F.2d 388, 389 (9th Cir.), cert. denied, 465 U.S. 1005, 104 S. Ct. 997, 79 L. Ed. 2d 230 (1984), we give substantial weight to the district court's conclusion about the effect of the juror misconduct. *Id.* The tenuous connection between Wood's emergence from the probation office and knowledge of Langford's prior conviction is insufficient to support a finding of a reasonable possibility that the event complained of could have affected the verdict. While we recognize that where a trial court learns of a possible incident of jury misconduct, it is preferable to hold an evidentiary hearing "to determine the precise nature of the extraneous information," *United States v. Bagnariol*, 665 F.2d 877, 885 (9th Cir.) cert. denied, 456 U.S. 962, 102 S. Ct. 2040, 72 L. Ed. 2d 487 (1982), not every allegation that extraneous information has reached the jury requires a full-dress hearing. United States v. Halbert, 712 F.2d at 389 (hearing not required where the trial court knew the exact scope and nature of the extraneous information). The district court did not abuse its discretion by failing to conduct such a hearing. *Cf. Halbert*, 712 F.2d at 389.

We have reviewed the additional assignments of error urged by Langford in his pro se briefs and find them to be uniformly meritless.

AFFIRMED

FERGUSON, Circuit Judge, dissenting:

It is time for this circuit to reexamine the importance of expert testimony concerning the reliability of eyewitness identification and to provide guidance to the district courts for exercising discretion to exclude such testimony. I therefore dissent from the majority's unquestioning reliance on *United States v. Amaral*, 488 F.2d 1148 (9th Cir. 1973). We should instead adopt the guidelines emerging from cases that actually consider this issue. *See United States v. Downing*, 753 F.2d 1224 (3d Circ. 1985); *United States v. Smith*, 736 F.2d 1103 (6th Cir.), cert. denied, 469 U.S. 868, 105 S. Ct. 213, 83 L. Ed. 2d 143 (1984). I would vote to reverse Langford's conviction because the district court abused its discretion by refusing to admit expert testimony regarding eyewitness reliability.

....

Expert testimony that can explain to a jury the problems inherent in eyewitness identification is extremely relevant. Given the unreliability and pervasive influence of eyewitness testimony, expert testimony is not only more probative than prejudicial, it prevents the eyewitness testimony from having an overly prejudicial effect. Courts and scholars have long recognized the untrustworthiness of eyewitness testimony. *E.g. Watkins v. Sowders*, 449 U.S. 341, 350, 101 S. Ct. 654, 659-60, 66 L. Ed. 2d 549 (1981) (Brennan, J., dissenting) ("eyewitness identification evidence is notoriously unreliable"); *United States v. Wade*, 388 U.s. 218, 228, 87 S. Ct. 1926, 1933, 18 L. Ed. 2d 1149 (1967) ("The vagaries of eyewitness identification are well-known; the annals of criminal law are rife with instances of mistaken identification."); *Jackson v. Fogg*, 589 F.2d 108, 112 (2d Cir. 1978) ("Centuries of experience in the administration of criminal justice have shown that convictions based solely on testimony that identifies a defendant previously unknown to the witness [are] highly suspect."; E. Borchard, *Convicting the Innocent: Errors of Criminal Justice* (3d ed. 1970). The problem is compounded because juries almost unquestioningly accept eyewitness testimony. *See, e.g. Watkins*, 449 U.S. at 352, 101 S. Ct. at 660-61 (Brennan, J., dissenting) ("[D]espite its inherent unreliability, much eyewitness identification evidence has a powerful impact on juries."); E. Loftus, *Eyewitness Testimony* 9 (1979) (eyewitness identification is "overwhelmingly influential"); P. Wall, *Eye-Witness Identification in Criminal Cases* 19 (1965) ("[J]uries are unduly receptive to identification evidence and are not sufficiently aware of its dangers.").

Expert testimony on this issue is important because it reveals the reasons why a witness may truthfully, but mistakenly, believe that the defendant was the culprit. *See United States v. Moore*, 786 F.2d 1308, 1312

(5th Cir. 1986); I. Horowitz & T. Willging, *The Psychology of Law: Integrations and Applications* 238-41 (1984). We can no longer believe that the jurors come to the courtroom already equipped with such knowledge. *See United States v. Downing*, 753 F.2d 1224, 1230-31 (3d Cir. 1985) (factors regarding reliability are "beyond what an average juror might know as a matter of common knowledge and indeed some of them directly contradict 'common sense' "); *United States v. Smith*, 736 F.2d 1103, 1106 (6th Cir.), *cert. denied*, 469 U.S. 868, 105 S. Ct. 213, 83 L. Ed. 2d 143 (1984).

....

IV.

We should follow the guidelines for admitting expert testimony on eyewitness identification presented in the recent decisions favoring admissibility. Each provides extensive guidance to the trial courts in resolving this question. Each examined the expert's qualifications, the reliability of the evidence, the likelihood of misleading or confusing the jury, and the link between the proffered testimony and the particular facts of the case in deciding whether such testimony is admissible. *See Downing*, 753 F.2d at 1237-43; *Smith*, 736 F.2d at 1105-07.

Establishing such guidelines would prevent the continued application of a mechanical rule against admitting expert testimony on the reliability of eyewitness identification. Defendant contends that the district court used such a mechanical rule here. I agree. Under the circumstances of this case, the trial court abused its discretion by excluding the proffered testimony. The government relied almost entirely on eyewitness testimony to link the defendant to the crime. If expert testimony is ever appropriate, it is here. One of the eyewitnesses, Clemente, initially misidentified another person as the robber. The other, Bitanga, stated that she did not get a "good look" at the robber and could not identify the defendant in the police's first photo lineup. Both viewed the robber under similarly stressful conditions. *See Moore*, 786 F.2d at 1313 ("We emphasize that in a case in which the sole testimony is casual eyewitness identification, expert testimony regarding the accuracy of that identification is admissible and properly may be encouraged.").

In certain cases, there may be sufficient reason to exclude the evidence, but I cannot condone the practice of a blanket rule of exclusion in every case. More important, this court has never provided any guidance in exercising that discretion. Without such guidance, the review for "abuse of discretion" becomes a meaningful charade. If we are to abdicate our appellate responsibilities in this fashion, let us do so openly.

If these facts do not cry out for reversing for abuse of discretion, none will. I would reverse.

UNITED STATES v. DE SOTO

885 F.2d 354 (7th Cir. 1989)

Only the part of the case which relates to opinion and expert testimony is included here.

Before CUDAHY, POSNER and RIPPLE, Circuit Judges.

RIPPLE, Circuit Judge.

The defendants—Gustavo Chaverra Cardona, Ruth Urrego Chaverra, and Maria Urrego de Soto—appeal their convictions for various drug trafficking offenses; a jury found each defendant guilty of conspiring to distribute cocaine in violation of 21 U.S.C. §846 and of several counts of possession of cocaine with intent to distribute in violation of 21 U.S.C. §841(a)(1). The defendants appeal on a multitude of grounds. We affirm.

I

FACTS

A tangled web of actions, spun by the three defendants and a number of their associates in a north Chicago neighborhood over the course of 1986, forms the basis of the case now before us. The three defendants are all related to each other: Gustavo Chaverra Cardona and Ruth Urrego Chaverra are husband and wife, and

Maria Urrego de Soto is Ruth Urrego Chaverra's sister.[1] Other participants in the conspiracy were also closely tied to the defendants by bonds of family or friendship: Alvaro Chaverra (Alvaro) is Mr. Chaverra's brother and Ramon Sanchez (Sanchez) is a close associate of the family members. Also involved in the organization was Fanny Bertha Altamirano, who served in the Chaverra and de Soto homes as a housekeeper, and later became a principal government witness in the case against her former employers. The locations used by the conspiracy operated out of three primary households: (1) Alvaro's apartment at 5752 North Campbell Avenue, which served as a stash house; (2) Ms. de Soto's apartment at 5812 North Campbell Avenue, which served as a meeting place to carry out the transactions; and (3) Mr. and Mrs. Chaverra's former home at 5306 North California Avenue. (Just prior to Mr. Chaverra's arrest, the Chaverras moved to a new home at 5143 North Oakley Avenue.)

In August 1984, Mrs. Altamirano started working as a housekeeper for the Chaverras. Ms. de Soto often came home to visit her sister and brother-in-law's home, and thus Mrs. Altamirano came to know Ms. de Soto as well. After becoming acquainted, Ms. de Soto occasionally hired Mrs. Altamirano to do house-

hold chores at her home. In early 1986, Mrs. Altamirano testified, she came to notice large amounts of cash in the Chaverra home. This money was stacked in a closet to which Mr. Chaverra would go often, and alone, during each day; she also noticed a safe in a closet of another room. By the month of May 1986, Mrs. Altamirano began to see even larger amounts of cash in the Chaverra home. For example, she saw Mrs. Chaverra and Ms. de Soto counting stacks of money and separating them by denomination. At Ms. de Soto's apartment, Mrs. Altamirano witnessed similar activity—once, the money counting occurred immediately before the visit of a woman named Mona, who was a friend of Ms. de Soto's. Another time, while she was cleaning Ms. de Soto's dresser, Mrs. Altamirano found a box containing a white powdery substance. Mrs. Altamirano later observed Ms. de Soto sell the powder to an unidentified man for $900.

Mrs. Altamirano was not simply a detached observer of the goings-on in the Chaverra and de Soto homes. She herself sold cocaine, supplied by Mrs. Chaverra, to a confidential informer. Sometime in early May 1986, this confidential informer introduced undercover FBI Agent Gregorio Rodriguez—then known to her as Jorge Castro. On May 28, Agent Rodriguez met Mrs. Altamirano to purchase a sample of the cocaine that she said she could provide through her Colombian employers—the Chaverras. He paid her $150, and she entered the Chaverra home; a short time later,

---

[1] In this opinion, we shall refer to Gustavo Chaverra Cardona as Mr. Chaverra, Ruth Urrego Chaverra as Mrs. Chaverra, and Maria Urrego de Soto as Ms. de Soto.

Mrs. Altamirano returned with a small packet of cocaine. Mrs. Altamirano testified that Mrs. Chaverra provided her with the cocaine and instructed her to use the code word "movies" for any future cocaine purchases. On May 30, Agent Rodriguez arranged another purchase through Mrs. Altamirano. First, she called Mrs. Chaverra and told her she wanted a "movie"; then, Agent Rodriguez gave her $1,200 to buy an ounce of cocaine. At 3:00 p.m., Mrs. Altamirano went into the Chaverra house and soon returned to Agent Rodriguez' car with a plastic bag containing 28 grams of 93 percent pure cocaine. Mrs. Altamirano testified that Mrs. Chaverra provided her with the cocaine and that Mrs. Chaverra gave her $50 for arranging the deal.

On June 3, Agent Rodriguez again met with Mrs. Altamirano to buy another ounce of cocaine. They again drove to the same area, Agent Rodriguez paid $1,200, and Mrs. Altamirano went into the Chaverra home. On this occasion, however, the transaction did not proceed as smoothly as on May 30. Upon entering the Chaverra home, Mrs. Altamirano was told by Mrs. Chaverra that the cocaine was not ready. Mr. Chaverra then arrived; he and Mrs. Chaverra had a conversation. Mrs. Chaverra soon broke down in tears and explained that Alvaro had not yet delivered "it." Mr. Chaverra was not satisfied with his wife's response and called Alvaro on the phone, telling Mrs. Chaverra that Alvero "has to obey." Alvaro soon arrived, carrying a

paper bag containing one ounce of cocaine, which was given to Mrs. Altamirano. She then returned to Agent Rodriguez and delivered the drugs. Agent Rodriguez made a third one-ounce purchase on June 11. This time the transaction proceeded without incident. Mrs. Altamirano told her undercover customer that Mrs. Chaverra was her supplier and that the Chaverra house contained a stash of cocaine and large amounts of cash. With regard to this cocaine sale, Mrs. Altamirano testified that Alvaro delivered the cocaine, which Mrs. Chaverra then turned over to her housekeeper. Mr. Chaverra observed the transaction.

On June 21, 1986, Agent Rodriguez visited Mrs. Altamirano at her home. She indicated that she had just returned from Ecuador carrying one kilogram of cocaine. Agent Rodriguez testified that Mrs. Altamirano then explained how Maria de Soto's home at 5812 North California was used as a cocaine selling place, and that, at another apartment one-half block away, Ms. de Soto and some friends stored, packaged, and weighed cocaine. According to Agent Rodriguez, Mrs. Altamirano also told him that she would continue to deal with him directly because Ms. de Soto and Mrs. Chaverra did not want to deal with Agent Rodriguez.

The government offered as evidence numerous telephone pen register records from the telephone numbers of the Chaverras, Ms. de Soto, and Alvaro covering the period between April and October 1986. These records revealed numerous calls of short duration from the various residences to Florida and Colombia. For example, Ms. de Soto called numbers in Florida 300 times and numbers in Colombia 142 times during this period. One of her monthly phone bills totaled $1,596.

The investigation conducted by Agent Rodriguez did not bear immediate fruit because the investigation was not approved by his supervisors as a "Group 2 undercover operation" until January 1987. See Tr. IV at 68. Consequently, the relevant facts of this case next occur in mid-October 1986. On October 15, 1986, several officers from the Chicago Police Department-Drug Enforcement Administration Task Force (Task Force) were conducting a surveillance of Ms. de Soto's building at 5812 North Campbell because they had received an informer's tip that a cocaine delivery would soon be made to that address. That afternoon, they observed Mr. Chaverra drive up in front of the building in a gray Mercury Cougar, enter the building, and then exit ten minutes later. Agents attempted to follow him, but they eventually lost him in traffic.

At approximately 5:00 a.m. the following morning, the agents spotted a brown Mercury Marquis slowly circling the block. After three tours of the area, the car stopped in front of Ms. de Soto's building. Two persons got out of the car and went into the building; the agents could not tell which apartment they entered in the two-apartment building. Suspecting

that this was the delivery vehicle, Chicago Police Lt. Maurice Dailey radioed for a canine narcotics team to inspect the car. A narcotics dog named Rex was walked by the car; its handler reported that Rex reacted positively to the presence of drugs in the rear of the Marquis.

About an hour later, 5812 North Campbell started bustling with activity. First, Sanchez was dropped by a passing car and entered the building. Next, an Hispanic man arrived, walked up to the stoop, and entered. About fifteen minutes later, an empty-handed Sanchez walked out of 5812 North Campbell and stopped on the stoop. He looked up and down the street and then walked to Alvaro's building—5752 North Campbell. Five to ten minutes later, Sanchez returned to 5812 North Campbell carrying a small paper bag. However, moments after entering the building, Sanchez again left. This time, he was accompanied by Ms. de Soto. The two looked up and down the street, and then together walked to and entered 5852 North Campbell. Ten to fifteen minutes later, Sanchez and Ms. de Soto, now toting a gray flight bag, left 5752 North Campbell. The Hispanic man who had earlier entered Ms. de Soto's building then left, carrying a brown paper bag.

At around 12:15 p.m., Ms. de Soto left her building with two children and a man. They all entered the brown Marquis to which Rex had earlier reacted positively. Members of the surveillance team stopped the car and arrested Ms. de Soto and the man.

A later search of the car revealed a secret compartment hidden in the interior of the gas tank. Inside that compartment was discovered more than ten kilograms of 91 percent pure cocaine.

At around 12:30-12:45 p.m., Mr. Chaverra, accompanied by two other men, arrived at 5812 North Campbell. They were stopped by the police. Upon their indicating that they were entering Ms. de Soto's building, they were arrested.

Members of the Task Force secured Ms. de Soto's apartment at 5812 North Campbell and Alvaro's apartment at 5752 North Campbell. Subsequently, the officers executed searches of these premises pursuant to search warrants. These searches produced a variety of incriminating evidence, including, from Ms. de Soto's apartment, large amounts of cash and ledgers and journals listing the names and information later interpreted as being drug related. A triple-beam scale, a revolver, a safe, and four kilograms of cocaine were recovered from Alvaro's apartment.

In October 1986, just before the arrests at Ms. de Soto's apartment, Agent Rodriguez re-established contact with Mrs. Altamirano, who still did not know his undercover status. After the arrest of Mr. Chaverra and Ms. de Soto, a number of conversations between Agent Rodriguez and Mrs. Altamirano were recorded. In those conversations, she described the organization of the distribution operation and stated that Mrs. Chaverra was still willing and able to sell cocaine despite the arrest of her husband and her sister. No further undercover purchases ever occurred, however.

II

ANALYSIS

Each defendant raises a number of issues on appeal. We shall address each defendant's arguments separately.

A. Mr. Chaverra's Appeal

1. Admission of Testimony of Lt. Dailey

Mr. Chaverra submits that the district court abused its discretion in allowing Lt. Dailey to testify as an expert witness. Specifically, he contends that the district court erred in allowing Lt. Dailey to testify as to (1) his opinion on the manner in which drug dealers operate, including countersurveillance activities, (2) his opinion on the true nature of certain activities that he observed, and (3) his interpretation of certain documents seized at Ms. de Soto's apartment. See Mr. Chaverra's Br. with Counsel at 16-17.

We begin our evaluation of these contentions by stating the basic principles that must guide our inquiry:

1. Federal Rule of Evidence 702, governing the admission of testimony in federal courts states that:

> If scientific, technical, or other specialized knowledge will assist the trier of fact to understand the evidence or to determine a fact in

issue, a witness qualified as an expert by knowledge, skill, experience, training, or education, may testify thereto in the form of opinion or otherwise.

Fed. R. Evid. 702. Courts have recognized that "[t]he subject matter of the expert testimony here, i.e., the clandestine manner in which drugs are bought and sold, is unlikely to be within the knowledge of the average layman." *United States v. Carson*, 702 F.2d 351, 369 (2d Cir.), *cert. denied*, 462 U.S. 1108, 103 S. Ct. 2456, 2457, 77 L. Ed. 2d 1335 (1983); *see also United States v. Young*, 745 F.2d 733, 760 (2d Cir. 1984), *cert. denied*, 470 U.S. 1084, 105 S. Ct. 1842, 85 L. Ed. 2d 142 (1985); *United States v. Borrone-Iglar*, 468 F.2d 419, 421 (2d Cir. 1972), *cert. denied*, 410 U.S. 927, 93 S. Ct. 1360, 35 L. Ed. 2d 588 (1973). Therefore, law enforcement experts may testify in order to assist the jury in understanding particular transactions. However, like all expert testimony, this testimony must be evaluated under the qualification and helpfulness requirements of Rule 702. In short, each witness must be qualified as an expert and the district court must determine that testimony "will assist the trier of fact to understand the evidence or to determine a fact in issue." Fed. R. Evid. 702.

2. The admission of expert testimony, like all evidentiary determinations, constitutes a ground for reversal by a court of appeals "only where the district court commits a clear abuse of discretion." *United*

States v. Marshall, 856 F.2d 896, 901 (7th Cir. 1988); *see also United States v. Peco*, 784 F.2d 798, 800 (7th Cir.), *cert. denied*, 476 U.S. 1160, 106 S. Ct. 2281, 90 L. Ed. 2d 723 (1986). However, the abuse of discretion standard of review does not mean the absence of any review at all. *See In re Ronco, Inc.*, 838 F.2d 212, 217 (7th cir. 1988) ("Review under an abuse of discretion standard does not mean no appellate review.") An appellate court always must be mindful of the context in which an evidentiary decision is made. When the litigation context presents circumstances particularly susceptible to abuse, we must be especially alert to the possibility of prejudice. Such a situation exists here. Lieutenant Daily was called by the government to testify both as an eyewitness to the events of October 16 and as an expert on law enforcement and drug dealer methodology. Testifying as both eyewitness and expert is permissible. *See Young*, 745 F.2d at 760; *Carson*, 702 F.2d at 369. However, when these two roles are intertwined, the possibility of juror confusion is increased. Here, for instance, this intermingling of the two roles increased the possibility that the jurors would not distinguish between Lt. Dailey's role as eyewitness and his role as expert. This situation placed an especially heavy burden on the district court to ensure that the jury understood its function in evaluating the evidence. In reviewing the record, we must pay special attention to the manner in which the district court discharged this responsibility. We now turn to the precise situations presented for our review.

a. countersurveillance testimony

Lieutenant Dailey testified as an expert with respect to "counter-surveillance" techniques employed by drug dealers to avoid detection by competitors or the police. As an example of such a technique, the Lieutenant noted that when "on the street when they are on foot they constantly stop and look back and forth at the street traffic to see if anyone is watching them." Tr. II at 123. Later on in his testimony, while describing the events of October 16, Lt. Dailey recounted how he twice witnessed Sanchez emerge from Mrs. de Soto's building (once accompanied by the Ms. de Soto) and look up and down the street while standing on the stoop. When asked by the prosecutor to describe Sanchez' activity more precisely, Lt. Dailey stated that Sanchez "was looking for either us, the police, or any type agents or, again, competitors that may be concerned what his activities were." Sanchez' actions "definitely" constituted counter-surveillance, in Lt. Dailey's opinion. Mr. Chaverra now submits that Lt. Dailey's interpretation of these outwardly commonplace and innocuous actions—looking up and down a street—was based on mere speculation and improperly imposed the imprimatur of expert testimony on an otherwise straightforward narrative. Therefore, the defendant further argues, Lt. Dailey's testimony should

have been excluded as intruding on the exclusive province of the jury. Under the circumstances set forth in this record, we cannot agree.

As we have noted earlier, testimony by law enforcement officers regarding drug countersurveillance may be admitted as expert testimony. For example, in *United States v. Stewart*, 770 F.2d 825, 831 (9th Cir. 1985), *cert. denied*, 474 U.S. 1103, 106 S. Ct. 888, 88 L. Ed. 2d 922 (1986), the Ninth Circuit "upheld the admission of DEA agents' opinion testimony that the defendant's activities were similar to the *modus operandi* of persons conducting countersurveillance while transporting drugs." (testimony regarding modus operandi). The particular conduct as to which the agents testified in *Stewart* and *Maher* was the manner in which the defendants drove their cars—circuitously touring the drop-off point several times before stopping. Such activity, especially in city streets with congested parking spaces, may appear, to the outside observer to be perfectly normal and innocent—just like looking up and down a street. As the Ninth Circuit concluded, however, the everyday appearance of the activity is not an automatic bar to the admission of expert testimony which may attribute a more sinister motive to the actions.

However, because such activities are usually innocent, the district court must be especially vigilant in ensuring that a law enforcement expert's testimony does not unfairly prejudice the defendant or usurp the jury's function. Consequently, there are limits to admission of this type of testimony: the expert must not base his opinion on mere speculation; nor can he speak, as an expert, to matters that the jury can evaluate for itself. See *United States v. Arenal*, 768 F.2d 263, 269 (8th Cir. 1985) (law enforcement expert "testimony is still subject to exclusion if the subject matter is within the knowledge or experience of the jury, because the testimony does not meet the helpfulness requirement of Rule 702"); *Young*, 745 F.2d at 760 (court questioned need to have expert police testimony that "25 to 30 people milling around outside a building" indicated presence of heroin den).

Our review of the record convinces us that, in this case, the district court was well aware of its special responsibilities and proceeded with the utmost caution. Immediately before Lt. Dailey testified, the district court carefully considered the defendants' arguments to exclude this expert testimony. It stated that:

> What we're dealing with here, as I understand it, is the projected testimony of someone who has observed a lot of narcotics transactions, and has observed conduct that might, to someone who has not had that as part of his or her common experience, appear either perfectly innocuous or perhaps with argument might view that with some degree of suspicion.

After that characterization of Lt. Dailey's proposed testimony, the court allowed admission of the evidence.

However, later on, during the testimony of Lt. Dailey, the district court admonished the jury "that the fact that an expert has given an opinion does not meant that it[']s binding on you.... You should assess the weight that's to be accorded to this expert opinion in the light of all of the evidence in the case." This instruction was repeated to the jury at the conclusion of the trial. Finally, and most importantly, the jury had an opportunity to hear the defendants' arguments, which cast all these activities in an innocent light. *Id.* at 108-112; *see also id.* at 108 ("[A]n American jury needs something more than a policeman saying looking up and down a street is countersurveillance and he was engaged in countersurveillance and that's it"). On this record, we cannot say that the district court abused its discretion in admitting Lt. Dailey's testimony regarding countersurveillance.

b. "dope deals" testimony

The district court's concern that the jury appreciate its role in evaluating Lt. Dailey's testimony is further illustrated by its decision to strike his opinion that two of the defendants were conducting "dope deals" in Ms. de Soto's building. Tr. II at 150. In the course of his narrative, Lt. Dailey had testified that he saw Ms. de Soto and Sanchez enter Ms. de Soto's building carrying a gray flight bag, and shortly afterwards, an Hispanic man, who previously had entered the building empty-handed, emerged carrying a paper bag. Lieutenant Dailey did not see whether the Hispanic man had entered Ms. de Soto's apartment. When asked to describe the nature of the activities inside the building, Lt. Dailey testified that they were "dope deals or drug sales, purchases." *Id.* The district court struck the answer. Even though the answer was stricken and the jury was cautioned to disregard the statement, Mr. Chaverra now submits that the comment nevertheless constituted reversible error. The government responds that the district court erred in striking the statement. Relying on *Young*, 745 F.2d at 760 (court affirmed admission of eyewitness police officer's opinion that certain activities constituted drug sales), and *Carson*, 702 F.2d at 369-70 (court affirmed admission of eyewitness agent's opinion that street-corner deals "appeared to him to be drug transactions"), the government suggests that the district court was overly cautious and that Lt. Dailey should have been permitted to testify that he regarded the pattern of activity he witnessed to be a "dope deal." *See generally* Fed. R. Evid. 704 (opinion testimony on ultimate issue permitted).

There does appear to be authority for the government's position—at least in the abstract. However, a district court must be given great latitude in any evidentiary judgment call and, in a context as delicate as the one before us, we should certainly be most circumspect about second-guessing a district court's determination to proceed cautiously. Here, where Lt. Dailey was unable to see the activities within Ms. de Soto's apartment, the court's conservative approach is certainly understandable and we certainly shall not express disapproval of its judgment. Nor shall we presume that the jury ignored the court's explicit cautionary instruction. In making this determination, we note that, like the district court's decision regarding the proper scope of Lt. Dailey's countersurveillance testimony, this evidentiary decision was informed and careful. Prior to the government's embarking on this line of questioning, the court held a prolonged sidebar discussion, when the government persisted in pursuing this improper evidence, apparently through a misunderstanding, the court made its evidentiary ruling and then called another conference, outside the hearing of the jury, to explain its decision and stress that Lt. Dailey's testimony must be restricted to matters within his past experience. It is clear that no reversible error was committed.

c. testimony concerning documents retrieved from Ms. de Soto's apartment

As a final evidentiary challenge, Mr. Chaverra also submits that Lt. Dailey's testimony interpreting documents seized at Ms. de Soto's apartment constituted plain error. These documents appear to be informal business records: all but one contain numbers and most also contain names and comments cryptically entered, in Spanish, in the margins. Names including "Gustavo," "Ruth," and

"Mona" appear on some of the documents. For example, on the most formal ledger-type sheet, there is an entry for "Gustavo's rent" and a corresponding figure. Mr. Chaverra now challenges Lt. Dailey's tying the records to drug sales, despite no mention of the words drugs, cocaine, heroin, or similar terminology in the records, and his explanation of numbers listed on certain documents as representing records of drug sales in quantities of kilograms or ounces. When testifying, Lt. Dailey stated that drug dealers often drop the zeros in thousand-dollar calculations, and he referred to various numerals as representing kilograms or ounces of cocaine. He also stated that he did not know who authored these documents.

The admission of this testimony was not plain error. The seized records were quite obscure and Lt. Dailey's expert interpretation could be considered helpful to the jury. See Fed. R. Evid. 702. Additionally, we note that the witness himself never linked these documents to the defendants on trial; the government argued that connection during its closing statement. Furthermore, Lt. Dailey's interpretation received some corroboration: Government Exhibit 16T features a notation for a $345 expense for the repair of a brown car; also found in the search of Ms. de Soto's apartment was a $345 car repair receipt for repairs made on the Mercury Marquis-a brown car. Mr. Chaverra's Br. with Counsel at A-5. Accordingly, we refuse to hold that the admission of Lt. Dailey's testimony interpreting these seized documents constituted plain error.

CONCLUSION

For the preceding reasons, we affirm the convictions of Gustavo Cardona Chaverra, Ruth Urrego Chaverra, and Maria Urrego de Soto.

AFFIRMED.

Cases relating to Chapter 12
HEARSAY RULE AND EXCEPTIONS

PEOPLE v. WOFFORD

509 N.E.2d 1026 (Ill. App. 1987)

Justice FREEMAN delivered the opinion of the court:

Following a jury trial, defendant, David Wofford, was convicted on two counts of murder, (Ill. Rev. Stat. 1981, ch. 38, sec. 9-1(a)(1)(2)), and sentenced to 40 years in the Illinois Department of Corrections. Defendant appeals his conviction, contending: (1) he was denied a fair trial due to the cumulative effect of the trial court's conduct; (2) the trial court committed error in allowing certain testimony into evidence under the "spontaneous declaration" exception to the hearsay rule, and (3) the evidence presented was not sufficient to prove defendant guilty beyond a reasonable doubt.

The facts of the case relevant to this appeal are as follows. At approximately 7:45 p.m. on March 3, 1983, a caller informed the police that gunshots had been fired and a man injured at 1314 West 90th Street in Chicago. When police arrived at that address, several people confirmed that shots had been fired; however, they told the officers that those involved ran east on 90th Street. The police subsequently received a second call, informing them the possible victim was somewhere around 8937 South Elizabeth. There they found the victim, Harold Crawford, lying in the grass surrounded by a group of people.

Several minutes later, three Chicago police detectives arrived at the scene. Detective Joe Paladino approached the victim, determined his identity, and observe he was bleeding profusely from the abdominal area. Paladino testified that when he asked the victim who shot him, the victim responded "Cheese shot me. He lives in the area of 92nd and Ada." When the ambulance still did not arrive after several minutes, the victim was taken by squad car to the hospital. He later died of a gunshot wound to the abdomen.

At the scene, the police spoke with Vincent James and David Brown who where with the victim when he was shot. They explained that they went to the park to play basketball and, while there, James spent some time talking with his girl friend. They left for awhile to go to the grocery store and then headed back to the park. As they walked, a green Thunderbird approached, and the driver shouted some gang slogans at them. They responded they were not affiliated with the gang. The driver proceeded, then stopped the car and got out. He spoke with three girls whom James, Brown and Crawford saw and briefly spoke to earlier in the evening. As the three men passed the alleyway where the others were standing, a man identified as defendant came up to James and put a pistol to his face. James quickly walked away and, when he, Brown and Crawford were around the corner, a car came by and the driver fired two shots, one of which struck Crawford. They described his car as a green, 1977 Ford Thunderbird, license plate number AV5760. The car was registered to the Wofford family near 92nd and South Ada Streets. The detectives drove James and Brown west on 90th Street and, when they reached Ada, the men indicated they saw two of the girls with whom the assailant was talking when he pulled a gun on James prior to shooting the victim. The girls told the detectives they did not know anyone named "Cheese" and, further, knew nothing about the shooting. Detective Paladino drove to 92nd and Ada where James and Brown recognized a parked green Thunderbird. The detective testified that its hood and grill were still warm.

He went to the address to which the car was registered. The woman who answered the door identified herself as Evertedine Wofford. When asked if "Cheese" was there, she responded that he recently had parked the car and left with the keys.

Later that evening James and Brown went to police headquarters where they each viewed six photographs. Both identified defendant as the victim's assailant. After the police made several visits to defendant's home without locating him, defendant turned himself in and was arrested on June 2, 1983. The police conducted two lineups; both James and Brown identified defendant as the person who shot the victim. The trial commenced on February 6, 1984. The jury returned a finding of guilt, and defendant appeals.

Defendant next contends that the trial court erred when it permitted into evidence testimony regarding statements of the deceased as to who shot him. As mentioned earlier, Officer Paladino testified that he asked the victim who shot him and the victim responded, "Cheese shot me. He lives in the area of 92nd and Ada." Prior to the arrival of Paladino, another officer noticed the victim was frightened and hysterical. Defendant claims that the circumstances surrounding the statement removed it from the "spontaneous declaration" exception to the hearsay rule because, among other reasons, the victim made the statement at a location other than where the shooting took place, he made it in response to questioning, and he did not make it immediately after the occurrence.

In order for a statement to be admitted as a spontaneous declaration, the following factors must be present: (1) the occurrence of an event startling enough to produce a spontaneous unreflecting statement; (2) the absence of time to fabricate, and (3) the statement must relate to the startling event or condition. (*People v. Damen* (1963), 28 Ill.2d 464, 471, 193 N.E.2d 25 quoting *People v. Poland* (1961), 22 Ill.2d 175, 181, 174 N.E.2d 804.) Although the time elapsed between the occurrence and the utterance is material, the court must determine from the entirety of the circumstances whether time existed for reflection and invention. (*People v. Smith* (1984), 127 Ill. App. 3d 622, 627, 83 Ill. Dec. 27, 469 N.E.2d 634.) As to the distance the declarant traveled before making the statement, the court again will consider the surrounding events to determine whether the declarant deliberated in making a false statement. *People v. Cherry* (1980), 88 Ill. App. 3d 1048, 1053054, 44 Ill. Dec. 155, 411 N.E.2d 61.

Applying all the above factors to the instant case, the State proposes that the trial court was correct in ruling the statement was admissible as a spontaneous declaration. In support of its position, the State cites *People v. Sanchez* (1982), 105 Ill. App. 3d 488, 492, 61 Ill. Dec. 242, 434 N.E.2d 395, in which testimony that the victim was in great pain, shivering, and groaning was sufficient to establish he

did not engage in reflective thought. Further, the court determined that asking the victim who committed the offense did not destroy the spontaneity of the response. (195 Ill. App. 3d 488, 491, 61 Ill. Dec. 242, 434 N.E.2d 395.) Additionally, in *People v. Wilson* (1980), 87 Ill. App. 3d 693, 702, 42 Ill. Dec. 729, 409 N.E.2d 344, the court looked to the totality of the circumstances in a rape case to determine that the victim was in such a state of continuing emotional upset so as to negate the possibility of a reflective thought process.

We agree with the State's position. In *People v. Damen* (1963), 28 Ill.2d 464, 472, 193 N.E.2d 25, the supreme court specifically indicated that a response to questioning is sufficient to destroy spontaneity. In *People v. Poland* (1961), 22 Ill.2d 175, 174 N.E.2d 804, the court also found that statements made at locations other than where the occurrence took place were admissible. The primary question to be addressed in such a situation was whether there was time for reflection and invention. (22 Ill.2d 175, 181, 174 N.E.2d 804.) In the instant case, the testimony revealed that the victim was shot, ran down the street, and then collapsed. He was observed to be in great pain, frightened, and bleeding profusely. We believe that the circumstances did not provide time for fabrication or reflection and invention. The factors necessary for the admission of the statement were present. Therefore, the court did not err in admitting the statement under the spontaneous declaration exception to the hearsay rule.

Finally, defendant contends that the evidence was not sufficient to establish his guilt beyond a reasonable doubt. He maintains that the testimony of James and Brown was incredible, unbelievable, and conflicting. Defendant indicates that, as to the time of the incident, James and Brown differ by an hour. He alleges the two men could not have seen so well at approximately 7:30 p.m. on a March evening, that someone else could have been driving the car, and that the two merely wanted to revenge defendant because of jealousy over the girls to whom they had been talking. Further, he points out that two of the girls testified the trio was swearing at them and carrying clubs. Defendant additionally alleges that it is beyond comprehension that an hysterical, dying boy would respond to Officer Paladino's question as the officer indicated he did.

The State, in contrast, points out that both Brown and James gave a description of the assailant's car, which they found minutes later parked near the defendant's home with the hood and grill still warm. Also, the defendant appeared in two lineups, posed in two different positions and was positively identified on both occasions as the perpetrator of the crime. The State further notes that the witness, who testified she saw fifteen to twenty boys carrying bats and sticks while shouting gang slogans, testified at trial that the boys came from a direction different than the one she had

earlier indicated. Also, one of the girls stated the boys scattered in different directions while another testified the boys walked in front of her and defendant.

The sufficiency of eyewitness testimony, the witnesses' credibility, the weight to be given the testimony, and the inferences to be drawn are within the province of the jury to decide. (*People v. Pearson* (1978), 67 Ill. App. 3d 300, 310, 24 Ill. Dec. 173, 384 N.E.2d 1331, *cert. denied* (1980), 445 U.S. 960, 100 S. Ct. 1645, 64 L. Ed. 2d 235.) We will not disturb the jury's determination unless the evidence is so improbable as to raise a reasonable doubt of guilt. (*People v. Randall* (1980), 84 Ill. App. 3d 888, 893, 40 Ill. Dec. 177, 405 N.E.2d 1269.) Any discrepancies in the testimony of James and Brown could possibly be explained as differences in the knowledge of the two or the way they interpreted questions asked of them. What was important was that their statements regarding identification were positive and consistent. (*People v. Winfield* (1983), 113 Ill. App. 3d 818, 827, 69 Ill. Dec. 594, 447 N.E.2d 1029.) As to defendant's argument that James identified defendant as "Cee" and "T" before being told by the prosecutor the name was "Cheese," we note that he never waivered in his identification of defendant as the assailant even if there was confusion as to his name. (*People v. Miller* (1981), 98 Ill. App. 3d 453, 456, 53 Ill. Dec. 833, 424 N.E.2d 624). We have examined the record and believe that, viewed as a whole, the evidence was sufficient to prove the defendant guilty beyond a reasonable doubt.

For all the foregoing reasons, the judgment of the circuit court of Cook County is affirmed.

AFFIRMED.

McNAMARA, P.J., and WHITE, J., concur.

RODRIGUEZ v. STATE

697 S.W.2d 463 (Tex. App. 1985)

OPINION

ESQUIVEL, Justice.

Appellant was indicted for the murder of Jimmy Ellingwood. After a change of venue, appellant was convicted by a jury for the offense of murder and assessed punishment of twenty-two years' confinement in the Texas Department of Corrections. Appellant presents three grounds of error.

In the early morning of May 15, 1983, Jimmy Ellingwood was shot twice at his home in Menard, Texas. Although his condition improved for a time, he suffered a relapse and died on May 25, 1983. Appellant complains of the State's introduction of statements made by Ellingwood in which he named appellant, a girlfriend, as having shot him. Appellant put on several alibi witnesses whose testimony was that the appellant was elsewhere and could not have shot Ellingwood.

In ground of error number one, appellant alleges the trial court erred in admitting prejudicial opinion evidence, concerning facts in issue, as to the thoughts of Ellingwood.

In ground of error number two, appellant alleges the trial court erred in admitting, over her timely objection, dying declarations of Ellingwood without a proper predicate.

In ground of error number three, appellant alleges the trial court erred in holding the evidence sufficient to sustain the conviction because the evidence was insufficient to establish the appellant's identity as the actor perpetrating the alleged offense. Appellant alleges the trial court erred in holding the evidence sufficient to sustain the conviction because there was insufficient evidence to establish the identity of the appellant as the actor perpetrating the alleged offense. In support of her contention, appellant argues that the State only had two items of evidence which implicated appellant in Ellingwood's death—the statements submitted as dying declarations and the statement by Trina Ellingwood that she heard her father yelling "Lydia" and appellant saying "be quiet."

Appellant appears to argue that the trial court erred in admitting hearsay statements of Ellingwood as related to Terry Zimmerman, Steve Whitson and Bobby Danford in the ambulance on the way to the hospital and to James Lobstein, an uncle, at the hospital three days before his death, and that if such testimony is properly excluded, the remainder of the record does not sufficiently show her connection with the death of Ellingwood in order to sustain a conviction.

The significance of the contention is that if it is sustained a retrial would be barred. *Burks* v. *United States*, 437 U.S. 1, 98 S.Ct. 2141, 57 L.Ed.2d 1 (1978); *Greene* v. *Massey*, 437 U.S. 19, 98 S.Ct. 2151, 57 L.Ed.2d 15 (1978). Therefore we will first consider appellant's third ground of error even though reversal may be based on another ground. See *Hooker* v. *State*, 621 S.W.2d 597 (Tex.Crim.App. 1980). We will first eliminate from considération the hearsay statements of Ellingwood to Zimmerman, Whitson, Danford and to his uncle, James Lobstein and we will examine the evidence of the other witnesses to ascertain if there is any inculpatory evidence which tends to connect the accused with the commission of the offense and to sustain the conviction.

The evidence identifying appellant is circumstantial and thus is sufficient to support a conviction only if the facts proved support a reasonable inference that appellant committed the crime and exclude to a moral certainty any inference consistent with appellant's innocence. *Burns* v. *State*, 676 S.W.2d 118, 120 (Tex.Crim.App. 1984); *Galvan* v. *State*, 598 S.W.2d 624, 627 (Tex.Crim.App. 1979). The evidence in support of conviction must exclude every other reasonable hypothesis except that of appellant's guilt. *Burns*, 676 S.W.2d at 120. The standard of review for sufficiency of the evidence is whether "any rational trier of fact could have found the essential elements of the crime beyond a reasonable doubt." *Wilson* v. *State*, 654 S.W.2d 465, 471 (Tex.Crim.App. 1983). If the evidence supports an inference other than the guilt of appellant or an inference other than a finding of one of the essential elements of the crime, a trier of fact cannot rationally find an accused guilty beyond a reasonable doubt. *Id.* at 472. To answer this ground of error, we must review the evidence adduced in an attempt to prove that appellant was in fact the perpetrator of the offense.

* * *

We hold the circumstantial evidence presented by the State was sufficient to exclude every reasonable hypothesis except appellant's guilt. The trial court did not err in holding the evidence sufficient to sustain the conviction because the evidence was sufficient to establish the identity of appellant as the actor perpetrating the offense. Appellant's ground of error number three is overruled.

Certain witnesses were permitted to testify, over appellant's objection, about statements made by Ellingwood in two instances concerning the circumstances of his shooting and in particular, that appellant had shot him. These statements were allegedly made by Ellingwood while in the ambulance on the way to the San Angelo Hospital and in his hospital room three days before his death. In her grounds of error numbers one and two appellant complains that the court erred in permitting the witnesses Terry Zimmerman, Steve Whitson and Bobby Danford to testify as to Ellingwood's statements while in the ambulance, and permitting the witness James Lobstein, to testify as to Ellingwood's statements to him at the hospital. Appellant contends that these statements were not dying declarations and therefore were inadmissible. We agree with appellant.

The statements of the deceased are hearsay and inadmissible unless they fit into an exception to the hearsay rule. In Texas, the admission of a dying declaration is regulated by statute. See TEX.CODE CRIM. PROC.ANN. art. 38.20 (Vernon 1979). That article provides:

The dying declaration of a deceased person may be offered in evidence, either for or against a Defendant charged with the homicide of such person, under the restrictions hereafter provided. To render the declarations of the deceased competent evidence, it must be satisfactorily proved:

1. That at the time of the making such declaration he was conscious of approaching death, and believed there was no hope of recovery.

2. That such declaration was voluntarily made, and not through the persuasion of any person.

3. That such declaration was not made, in answer to interrogatories calculated to lead the deceased to make any particular statement.

4. That he was of sane mind at the time of making the declaration.

* * *

In support of her contention in ground of error number one, appellant states that the trial court wrongfully allowed the State to ask witnesses Terry Zimmerman, Steve Whitson and Bobby Danford whether or not, in their opinions, the deceased appreciated that he might die and had no hope of recovery.

Appellant argues, and we agree, that while the State is permitted to elicit testimony from the witnesses that would permit the jury to infer the fact that the deceased was conscious of approaching death and believed there was no hope of recovery at the time he made the declaration, the State is not permitted to ask and a witness is not allowed to give an opinion as to whether a deceased thought he was going to die and whether he had given up hope of recovery. A witness is not allowed to give an opinion on an ultimate fact as questions of fact are to be determined by the trier of fact from all of the circumstances and the evidence.... There are many cases in the jurisprudence of this State that have disallowed opinion testimony on an ultimate issue of fact that was to be determined by the jury. See, e.g., *Stein v. State*, 514 S.W.2d 927, 931 (Tex.Crim.App. 1974) (testimony that another was surprised prohibited as calling for speculation on part of witness); *Witty*

v. *State*, 203 S.W.2d 212, 220 (Tex.Crim.App. 1947) (State authorized to show declarant nervous but not have witness express opinion that declarant "expecting something to happen"); *Casey* v. *State*, 116 Tex.Cr.R. 111, 32 S.W.2d 461, 462 (1930) (game warden could testify appellant had jug of water and gun but error for warden to express opinion that appellant hunting out of season). Involving the issue of self-defense, Texas courts have long excluded opinion testimony by bystanders as to whether defendants perceived themselves to be in danger. If this were not done, the "rules requiring that witnesses state facts would be abrogated and cases be tried on a constantly broadening rule of conjecture and opinion." *Dunne* v. *State*, 98 Tex.Cr.R. 7, 263 S.W. 608, 612 (1923). If witnesses were allowed to so testify, trials would "soon resolve themselves unto a contest of conclusions and opinions of bystanders as to whether or not the appellant was apprehensive of an infliction of death or serious injury at the hands of his adversary." *Pounds* v. *State*, 150 S.W.2d 798, 801 (Tex.Crim.App. 1941). If witnesses cannot testify as to whether a defendant was apprehensive of an infliction of death, surely they should not be able to testify as to whether a deceased thought he was going to die and whether he had given up hope of recovery.

The questions of whether Ellingwood appreciated the fact that he might die and of whether he had any hope of recovery were clearly questions to be determined by the jury. Allowing the witnesses to express their opinion was prejudicial to appellant. When the jury is in possession of the same information as

the witness and can draw its own inferences and conclusions, a witness' opinion is unnecessary and inadmissible....

In ground of error number two, appellant alleges the trial court erred in admitting, over her timely objection, dying declarations of the deceased without a proper predicate. In support of this contention, the appellant argues the State failed to establish the first part of the predicate necessary for the admission of such dying declarations, to wit: that at the time of making such declaration he was conscious of approaching death, and believed there was no hope of recovery. The trial court limited the dying declarations to those made in the ambulance while transporting Ellingwood from the Menard Hospital Emergency Room to the San Angelo Hospital. Further, all statements made at the San Angelo Hospital were suppressed with the exception of the statement made to Ellingwood's uncle, James Lobstein, some three days before his death. The trial court determined the admissibility of the declarations in the absence of a jury during a pretrial hearing.

The opinion in the case of *Craven* v. *State*, 49 Tex.Cr.R. 78, 90 S.W. 311 (Tex.Crim.App. 1905), is particularly instructive on the degree of consciousness of approaching death necessary to be proved. In Craven, the deceased made the statement "I believe I am fatally shot." The court held:

This did not exclude the hope of recovery; nor does it show that he was conscious of approaching death, in the sense in which this statute means approaching death. Of course, every man knows, as a matter of fact, that ultimately he must die, and the fact that he may state a belief of the fact does not show, within the meaning of our statute with reference to dying declarations, a consciousness of approaching death. The predicate must exclude hopes of life. It must reach the point of a certainty in the mind of declarant that all hope of recovery is gone, and that he is conscious of then approaching death, and in his mind it must be the inevitable result.

* * *

If the deceased had the slightest hope of recovery when the declarations, they were inadmissible. The words of our statute 'lost all hope of recovery' means that it is a belief in death which does exclude any hope of recovery.

* * *

The declarant must be in extremis, and under the solemn conviction that he is bound to die and that all hope of recovery is eliminated from his mind.
Id. at 311.

The witness, Terry Zimmerman, testified that she sat next to Ellingwood's head on the trip to San Angelo, that he was stable, and that he expressed no concern about whether he would make the trip to San Angelo. So long as the declarant was unsure what would happen, he had hope of recovery. Unlike the declarant in *Whitson* v. *State*, 495 S.W.2d 944, 947 (Tex.Crim.App. 1973), Ellingwood never stated that he "knew" he was going to die. Neither did the circumstances demonstrate that all hope of recovery were eliminated from his mind The statements made by Ellingwood were in terms of "I don't believe I'm going to make it," and "I'm trying to hang

on." We hold that the evidence illustrating the circumstances of the deceased's ambulance trip from Menard to San Angelo, although showing Ellingwood in pain and worrying about his condition, did not rise to that level of certainty that death was imminent and that he had no hope of recovery.

We also find the evidence elicited through Ellingwood's uncle, James Lobstein, regarding what was said by Ellingwood to his uncle on May 22, 1983, in the hospital room some three days before Ellingwood's death, is insufficient to show that Ellingwood thought he was dying and had no hope of recovery. Aside from opinion testimony which was objected to on the same ground as the opinions elicited from other witnesses, the only evidence elicited by the State through Ellingwood's uncle, James Lobstein. was the following:

MR. SUTTON:

Q: What did he say when you were standing there by the bed?

THE WITNESS:

A: Said, 'She came to kill me and it looks like she did.'

We hold that evidence insufficient to satisfy the first part of the predicate for its admission.

Whether the improper admission of hearsay evidence requires the reversal of conviction is determined on a case by case basis. *Torres* v. *State*, 552 S.W.2d 821 (Tex.Crim.App. 1977). our duty is to determine from the record the probable impact of the erroneously admitted evidence upon "the minds of the average jury." *Schneble* v. *Flann*, 405 U.S. 427, 92 S.Ct. 1056, 31 L.Ed.2d 340 (1972). Unless there is a reasonable possibility that the improperly admitted evidence contributed to the defendant's conviction, reversal is not required. *Wilder, v. State*, 583 S.W.2d 349 (Tex.Crim.App. 1979).

We cannot conclude that the admission of hearsay testimony of Zimmerman, Whitson, Danford and Lobstein that Ellingwood said appellant shot him was reversible error where the evidence, absent such hearsay testimony, was sufficient to uphold the jury's finding of appellant's participation in the instant offense. There was no reasonable possibility that the improperly admitted evidence contributed to appellant's conviction.

We hold the evidence to be sufficient to sustain the conviction. The judgment of the trial court is affirmed.

BUTTS, Justice, concurring in result.

I agree that a rational trier of fact could have found the essential elements of the crime beyond a reasonable doubt in this case, thus, the evidence is sufficient to support the conviction.

But I differ with the majority ruling that the dying declaration should be excluded from evidence because of deficiency in the predicate laid for its introduction.

The State introduced two dying declarations, therefore, the predicate for each hearsay statement must be found inadequate to deny admissibility. The criminal law in Texas at this time retains the well known exception to the hearsay rule, the dying declaration. TEX.CODE CRIM.PROC.ANN. art. 38.20 (Vernon 1979).

It is the first prong of the fact predicate which appellant argues falls short of the requirement, that is, the showing that the decedent was conscious of approaching death and believed there was no hope of recovery. The three other facts (or prongs) which must be shown are not challenged.

It is argued that permitting the witnesses to state their "opinion" of an ultimate fact issue, whether or not the decedent "appreciated" the fact that he might die, does not satisfy the statute.

The trial court first conducted a pretrial hearing and eliminated the testimony of other witnesses, but left these four as competent to testify to the fact predicate. At trial the State then submitted to the jury the testimony of the four witnesses. The pretrial ruling of the trial court was that the predicate as shown by the four witnesses was properly laid.

Texas is different when it come to dying declarations. What was done in the present case is permissible under Texas law. The trial court in this case followed Texas law and submitted to the jury the four-prong predicate in the form of fact questions. Thus, the jury was required to make findings on the fact issues. See 1A R. RAY, EVIDENCE § 975 (3rd ed. 1980).

I would hold under these circumstances that the predicate had been established; proof of the first fact may be considered a "short hand rendition," similar to describing intoxication. It was properly shown. The dying declaration became admissible in the case. Only to the majority ruling on the dying declaration do I respectfully dissent.

UNITED STATES v. ALVAREZ

584 F.2d 694 (5th Cir. 1978)

[Footnotes omitted]

LEWIS R. MORGAN, Circuit Judge:

The appellant, Gilberto Alvarez, was convicted of heroin trafficking charges by the words of a dead man. The decedent's statements allegedly implicating Alvarez were heard only by Lopez, the prosecution's principal witness, who had earlier pled guilty to narcotics charges and received probation. In addition to other alleged trial errors, the appellant urges that Lopez' in-court testimony of the out-of-court statements by the decedent constituted inadmissible hearsay and violated his constitutional right of confrontation. We agree, and therefore reverse the judgment of the court below.

Alvarez' arrest and conviction followed a government investigation of heroin dealing in Rio Grande, Texas during the fall of 1975. An agent working undercover made contact with Jose "Chema" Lopez, the alleged "out front" man for the operation. The agent succeeded in purchasing almost 20 ounces of heroin from Lopez. Lopez would later testify that he in turn, had obtained the heroin from Lucio Mejorado, the middleman, who supposedly told Lopez that the heroin was supplied by the appellant Alvarez. At no time, however, did Lopez or any government agent communicate directly with Alvarez. Nor was Alvarez ever seen meeting with Mejorado or any other alleged members of the conspiracy. In January, 1976, indictments were issued charging Lopez, Mejorado, Alvarez, and several others with violating narcotics laws. Within a few days, Alvarez left for Mexico where he remained for most of a year until extradition was effected. Meanwhile, Lopez pled guilty, received probation, and became the government's most communicative witness. Mejorado was convicted but died in a car accident prior to Alvarez' return to this country. When Alvarez finally came to trial, the critical evidence connecting him to the conspiracy was Lopez' report that Mejorado had identified Alvarez as the supplier. Thus, the government's case depends mightily upon the admission of the decedent's out-of-court statements. Such evidence is rank hearsay which, prior to 1975, would have been patently inadmissible. E.g., *United States v. Oliva*, 497 F.2d 130, 134 (5th Cir. 1974). With the adoption of the new Federal Rules of Evidence, however, the realm of admissibility has been significantly expanded. These rules infuse the government's claim for admission with much more serious merit than would previously have existed. Applying these new rules of evidence, and recent decisions construing them, we turn to the government's arguments that the deceased witness' words were properly used to convict the appellant.

Rule 801(d)(2)(E): Statement By a Coconspirator

The first argument raised by the government is that Lopez' in-court testimony of Mejorado's out-of-court declaration was admissible as a statement by a co-conspirator under Federal Rule 801(d)(2)(E). This rule provides that a "statement by a coconspirator of a party during the course and in furtherance of the conspiracy" is admissible because it is not hearsay at all. Traditionally, the co-conspirator exception was predicated upon the fulfillment of several requirements, one of which poses an especially serious obstacle to the admission of Mejorado's incriminating words: "(S)uch declarations are admissible over the objection of an alleged co-conspirator, who was not present when they were made, only if there is proof *aliunde* that he is connected with the conspiracy." *Glasser* v. *United States*, 315 U.S. 60, 74, 62 S.Ct. 457, 467, 86 L.Ed. 680 (1942). The appellant contends that the district court incorrectly applied the *Glasser* rule by allowing the introduction of alleged hearsay to rest on insufficient independent evidence of the defendant's conspiratorial complicity. . . .*

Rule 804(b)(3): Declaration Against Penal Interest

Rejecting the government's contention that Lopez' testimony was admissible under the coconspirator's exception, we consider the claim that the hearsay fell within the exemption of Federal Rule 804 (b)(3). The revised rules permit the admission of an out-of-court declaration against the declarant's penal interest when three tests are

met: (1) the declarant must be unavailable, (2) the statement must so far tend to subject the declarant to criminal liability " 'that a reasonable man in his position would not have made the statement unless he believed it to be true'; and [(3)] if offered to exculpate the accused, [the statement] must be corroborated by circumstances clearly indicating its trustworthiness." *United States* v. *Thomas*, 571 F.2d 285, 288 (5th Cir. 1978). In the present case, the unavailability of the declarant, the deceased Lucio Mejorado, is manifest.

Turning to the second test, we conclude that Mejorado's statement was sufficiently contrary to his penal interest for Rule 804(b)(3) purposes. The incriminating declarations by Mejorado include his statement that "the heroin was Gilberto Alvarez'" and assertions that he was calling Alvarez to set up the transaction. The appellant urges that these declarations did not really contravene the interest of Mejorado, but instead served primarily to incriminate Alvarez. This court, however, has not limited the "against interest" exception to the declarant's direct confession of guilt. *United States* v. *Bagley*, 537 F.2d 162, 167 (5th Cir. 1976). "Rather, by referring to statements that 'tend' to subject the declarant to criminal liability, the Rule encompasses disserving statements by a declarant that would have probative value in a trial against the declarant." *United States* v. *Thomas, supra*, at 288. In the present case Mejorado's remarks

---

*NOTE—Parts of opinion are omitted. The court found that the exception stated in Federal Rule 801(d)(2)(E) did not apply as there was insufficient independent evidence that the alleged co-conspirator was connected with the conspiracy.

"strongly implied his personal participation in the . . . crimes and hence would tend to subject him to criminal liability." *Id.* at 289, *citing United States* v. *Barrett,* 539 F.2d 244, 251 (1st Cir. 1976). Examined in context, Mejorado's statements clearly indicated his participation "since (they) strengthened the impression that he had an insider's knowledge of the crimes." *United States* v. *Barrett,* 539 F.2d at 252. Accordingly, we hold that Mejorado's out-of-court statements readily meet the expansive test this circuit has adopted for determining whether remarks contravene the declarant's interest.

Rule 804(b)(3) explicitly adds a third requisite to admissibility for statements offered to exculpate the accused. In such cases, there must be corroborating circumstances that "clearly indicate the trustworthiness of the statement." Fed.R.Evid. 804 (b)(3). In this case, however, we consider a statement offered to *inculpate* the accused. No express provision safeguards declarations against a defendant; the reasoning behind this omission is reflected in legislative history:

> The House amended this exception to add a sentence making inadmissible a statement or confession offered against the accused in a criminal case, made by a codefendant or other person implicating both himself and the accused. The sentence was added to codify the constitutional principle announced in *Bruton* v. *United States,* 391 U.S. 123, 88 S.Ct. 1620, 20 L.Ed.2d 476 (1968). Bruton held that the admission of the extrajudicial hearsay statement of

one codefendant inculpating a second codefendant violated the confrontation clause of the sixth amendment.

> The committee decided to delete this provision because the basic approach of the rules is to avoid codifying, or attempting to codify, constitutional evidentiary principles, such as the fifth amendment's right against self-incrimination and, here, the sixth amendment's right of confrontation. Codification of a constitutional principle is unnecessary and, where the principle is under development, often unwise.

S.Rep.No. 93-1277, 93d Cong., 2d Sess., *reprinted in* 1974 U.S. Code Cong. and Admin. News pp. 7051, 7068.

Thus, while specifically addressing exculpatory statements, the draftsmen of the new rules left to the courts the task of delineating prerequisites to the admissibility of inculpatory against-interest hearsay. As Congress recognized, the central underpinning of such a safeguard must be the confrontation clause of the United States Constitution.

In the mid-1960's, a series of Supreme Court decisions mold the sixth amendment right of confrontation into a shield against condemnation spoken by declarants who could not be questioned. *Roberts* v. *Russell,* 392 U.S. 293, 88 S.Ct. 1921, 20 L.Ed.2d 1100 (1968); *Bruton* v. *United States,* 391 U.S. 123, 88 S.Ct. 1620, 20 L.Ed.2d 476 (1968); *Barber* v. *Page,* 390 U.S. 719, 88 S.Ct. 1318, 20 L.Ed.2d 255 (1968); *Brookhart* v. *Janis,* 384 U.S. 1, 86 S.Ct. 1245, 16 L.Ed.2d 314 (1966); *Douglas* v. *Alabama,* 380 U.S. 415,

85 S.Ct. 1074, 13 L.Ed.2d 934 (1965); *Pointer* v. *Texas*, 380 U.S. 400, 85 S.Ct. 1065, 13 L.Ed.2d 923 (1965). Initially, the Court appeared to generally proscribe the admission of incriminating hearsay unless a traditional exception applied. *Cf. Bruton* v. *United States*, 391 U.S. at 128 n.3, 88 S.Ct. 1620. With subsequent decisions, though, the contours of the right of confrontation shifted to permit the introduction of out-of-court statements so long as cross-examination of the declarant was permitted at some stage of the proceedings. *California* v. *Green*, 399 U.S. 149, 158, 90 S.Ct. 1930, 26 L.Ed.2d 489 (1970). The most recent in this line of decisions enunciated a new threshold for admissibility:

> The decisions of this Court make it clear that the mission of the Confrontation Clause is to advance a practical concern for the accuracy of the truth-determining process in criminal trials by assuring that "trier of fact (has) a satisfactory basis for evaluating the truth of the prior statement."

Dutton v. *Evans*, 400 U.S. 74, 89, 91 S.Ct. 210, 220, 27 L.Ed.2d 213 (1970) quoting, *California* v. *Green, supra.* Thus, the central feature of Confrontation Clause analysis became the "practical concern" for the reliability of inculpatory hearsay.

To bring Rule 804(b)(3) within this mandate for reliability, we hold that the admissibility of *inculpatory* declarations against interest requires corroborating circumstances that "clearly indicate the trustworthiness of the statement." We believe that this construction fully corre-

sponds to the Court's directive in *Dutton* v. *Evans, supra,* and will thus avoid the constitutional difficulties that Congress acknowledged but deferred to judicial resolution. Further, by transplanting the language governing exculpatory statements onto the analysis for admitting inculpatory hearsay, a unitary standard is derived which offers the most workable basis for applying Rule 804(b)(3).

Moreover, attaching a requirement of trustworthy circumstances to the declaration against interest exception is necessary to a logical interrelation between that rule and the earlier discussed exemption for a coconspirator's "hearsay" under Rule 801(d)(2)(E). The great majority of statements traditionally evaluated under the coconspirator's exception may now fall within the markedly reduced threshold for against-interest hearsay. Most of the things conspirator "A" might say that could incriminate conspirator "B" could also *tend* to incriminate "A" because such a remark could "strengthened the impression that he (A) had an insider's knowledge of the crimes." *United States* v. *Barrett, supra.* "A's" hearsay could not be admitted against "B" under the coconspirator's exception absent proof *aliunde* of "B's" complicity in the conspiracy. *United States* v. *Glasser, supra.* By its terms, however, the against-interest exception would generally authorize admission irrespective of *Glasser* so long as the declarant is unavailable. Thus, there is a serious danger that the declaration against interest exception will swallow the coconspirator's exception with its attendant *Glasser* safeguard. The danger of this incongruity fortifies our conviction that the availability of Rule 804(b)(3) is predicated upon establishing circumstances of trustworthiness.

Accordingly, we hold that Lopez' hearsay testimony is admissible under Rule 804(b)(3) only if "corroborating circumstances clearly indicate the trustworthiness of the statement." Cf. *United States* v. *Thomas, supra* at 290. While the against-interest component of this exception poses a legal issue, the consideration of the statement's trustworthiness raises a question of fact ordinarily to be reviewed according to a clearly erroneous standard. *United States* v. *Bagley, supra* at 166-167. However, "(b)ecause the trial judge never reached this final question under Rule 804(b)(3), we are not bound to the 'clearly erroneous' standard . . . (r)ather, we look to the record to adduce the corroboration" for Lopez' testimony. *United States* v. *Thomas, supra* at 290.

Examining the record, we conclude that the trustworthiness of Lopez' testimony has not been sufficiently established. Under Rule 804(b)(3), trustworthiness is determined primarily by analysis of two elements: the probable veracity of the in-court witness, and the reliability of the out-of-court declarant. *United States* v. *Bagley, supra* at 167. Applying the first standard, we note that Lopez presumably testified in the hope of receiving preferential treatment and thus could have been motivated by a desire to "curry favor with the authorities." Cf. *United States* v. *Gonzales*, 559 F.2d 1271, 1272 (5th Cir. 1977). Turning to the second facet of trustworthiness, we observe that the traditional surety of reliability for this hearsay exception, the statement's contravention of the declarant's interest, is extremely weak in this case. *United States* v. *Hoyos*, 573 F.2d 1111, 1115 (9th Cir. 1978).

Moreover, both aspects of trustworthiness are seriously undermined by the virtual dearth of circumstances corroborating the hearsay accusation against Alvarez. "This requirement goes beyond minimal corroboration." *United States* v. *Barrett*, 539 F.2d 244, 253 (1st Cir. 1976). Indeed, the standard mandates "clear" corroboration. *United States* v. *Hoyos, supra.* For largely the same reasons that we earlier found the independent evidence in this case insufficient to invoke the coconspirator's exemption, we also rule that the circumstances do not clearly corroborate and indicate the trustworthiness of the hearsay within the meaning of Rule 804(b)(3). Therefore, we hold that Lopez' hearsay testimony may not be admitted into evidence under the exemption for declarations against interest.

Our ruling that the hearsay testimony may not be used removes the government's principal evidence from the case against the appellant. The remaining ingredients, including Alvarez' apparent flight from prosecution, Mejorado's parking habits, and the fact of a phone call from Mejorado to Alvarez would not permit a verdict of guilty to stand. On substantially similar facts, this court reversed a judgment of conviction and directed the lower court to dismiss the indictment in *United States* v. *Oliva*, 497 F.2d 130, 134 (5th Cir. 1974). We believe that such a disposition is proper for the present case. "Since this hearsay formed a vital link in the appellee's case, we render rather than reverse for new trial." 497 F.2d at 131. Accordingly, judgment is

Reversed and rendered.

Cases relating to Chapter 13
DOCUMENTARY EVIDENCE

MULLINS v. STATE

699 S.W.2d 346 (Tex. App. 1985)

Before PAUL W. NYE, C.J., and BENAVIDES and DORSEY, J.J.

OPINION

NYE, Chief Justice.

Appellant pled guilty to aggravated sexual assault and was sentenced by a jury to eighty-five years in the Texas Department of Corrections. On appeal, he challenges the photographic lineup, the evidence of his prior convictions admitted at trial, the testimony of the victim's psychologist, and the refusal of the trial court to allow one of the victim's attorneys to testify. We find no reversible error and affirm.

On May 21, 1984, the complainant left her office in the First City Bank Tower at about 3:30 p.m. and elevator alone headed for the parking garage. The elevator stopped on the first floor, appellant entered, punched the "stop" switch, pointed a knife at her and forced her to have sexual intercourse with him. He then fled the scene.

At the punishment stage, the state called a psychologist who testified that the victim suffered from exaggerated fearfulness, withdrawal, hypervigilance, sleep disturbances,

nightmares and depression, which are symptoms of a post-traumatic stress disorder she was experiencing. She testified that the victim would probably suffer permanent damage to her sense of personal security.

* * *

In appellant's third ground of error he contends that the trial court erred in admitting a prior federal conviction into evidence. He claims that the proper predicate was not laid because it was not properly authenticated. The State offered a document entitled "Judgment and Probation/Commitment Order," which showed that appellant had been convicted for escape from federal custody. The certification of the Clerk of the district court in which appellant was convicted was attached to the judgment.

Appellant argues that the documents should have been evidenced by an official publication attested to by the custodian of the records. Authentication of documents, such as the one at bar, was formerly governed by TEX. REV. CIV. STAT. ANN. art. 3731a. See *Todd* v. *State*, 598 S.W.2d 286 (Tex. Crim. App.

595

1980). This statute, as it relates to civil cases, was repealed when the Texas Supreme Court adopted the new Texas Rules of Evidence. It is unclear whether these rules are applicable in criminal cases. TEX.CODE.CRIM.PROC.ANN. art. 38.02 provides:

The rules of evidence prescribed in the statute of law of this State in civil suits shall, so far as applicable, govern also in criminal actions when not in conflict with the provisions of this Code or of the Penal Code.

Neither the Code of Criminal Procedure nor the Penal Code provides guidance for the admission of documentary evidence. It is logical, therefore, that the "statute law of this State in civil suits," which is now the Texas Rules of Evidence, should apply here, and we so hold.

TEX.R.EVID. 901(b)(7), pertaining to authentication of public records or reports states:

Evidence that a writing authorized by law to be recorded or filed and in fact recorded or filed in a public office, or a purported public record, report, statement, or data compilation in any form, is from the public office where items of this nature are kept.

TEX.R.EVID. 902, dealing with self-authentication, provides that extrinsic evidence of authenticity is not required as a condition precedent to admissibility under TEX.R.EVID. 902(1) when the document bears the seal "of the United States, or of any State, district, Commonwealth, . . . or of a political subdivision, department, officer, or agency thereof, and a signature purporting to be an attestation or execu-

tion." TEX.R.EVID. 902(4) further provides that a "copy of an official record or report or entry therein, or of a document authorized by law to be recorded or filed and actually recorded or filed in a public office, including data compilations in any form, certified as correct by the custodian or other person authorized to make the certification, by certificate complying with paragraph (1), (2) or (3) of this rule or complying with any statute or other rule prescribed by the Supreme Court pursuant to statutory authority."

The State's exhibits bear the seal of the federal district clerk's office, her attestation that the document was a certified copy of the original and her signature. We hold that this is sufficient authentication under either TEX.R.EVID. 901 (b)(7) or 902 (1) or (4). Appellant's third ground of error is overruled.

Appellant argues in his fourth ground of error that the trial court erred in admitting evidence concerning his federal escape charge because the exhibit had no formal sentence attached to it. Exhibit 2(c)-1 entitled Judgment and Probation/Commitment Order contains a section entitled "Sentence or Probation Order" which reads:

The court asked whether defendant had anything to say why judgment should not be pronounced. Because no sufficient cause to the contrary was shown, or appeared to the court, the court adjudged the defendant guilty as charged and convicted and ordered that: The defendant is hereby committed to the custody of the Attorney General or his authorized representative for imprisonment for a period of THREE (3) YEARS.

The exhibit shows that appellant was sentenced to three years' imprisonment. The document shows on its face that there was a final conviction, and it was properly admissible.

Appellant's fourth ground of error is overruled.

Appellant, in his fifth ground of error argues that the identity proof inadequately links him to the federal escape conviction. In order to use a prior criminal offense at trial, the State must prove that the defendant is the person charged with the offense and found guilty. *Rios* v. *State*, 557 S.W.2d 87 (Tex.Crim. App. 1977). In this case, the State attempted to prove appellant's identity through the testimony of Dick Leonard, appellant's probation officer. Leonard testified that appellant reported to him from November 9, 1981 until March 7, 1982. He identified appellant as the individual who had reported to him as a parolee on the escape charge. Leonard also testified that he was not in the courtroom when appellant was sentenced.

In *Daniel* v. *State*, 585 S.W.2d 688 (Tex.Crim.App. 1979), the Court of Criminal Appeals specified means whereby the prosecution could prove convictions constituting a prior criminal record to include: (1) testimony of a witness who personally knows the defendant and the fact of his prior conviction and identified him; (2) a stipulation or judicial admission of the defendant that he has been convicted; (3) introduction of certified copies of the judgment and sentence, including fingerprints of the accused supported by expert testimony identifying them with fingerprints of the defendant or comparison of the record of conviction containing photographs and a detailed physical description of the person in those records, with the appearance of the person in count. *Daniel*, 585 S.W.2d at 690, 691. The testimony of Leonard satisfies the requirements in Daniel because Leonard personally knew the defendant, the facts of his conviction, and he identified him. Similar proof was held sufficient to show identity in *Bautista* v. *State*, 642 S.W.2d 233 (Tex.App.-Houston [14th Dist] 1982, pet. ref'd). Appellant's fifth ground of error is overruled.

In appellant's sixth ground of error he urges that the trial court erred by refusing his request to allow the testimony of an attorney whom the victim had hired to represent her in a related civil lawsuit. Appellant claims that his testimony would have established bias and motive on the part of the victim to embellish the injuries she received during the assault.

The right of the accused to confront witnesses against him and, through reasonable cross examination, place the witness in his proper setting and test the weight and credibility of his testimony has long been held essential to a fair trial. An accused should be allowed wide latitude in showing any fact which would tend to establish bias or interest on the part of any witness testifying against him. Harris v. State, 642 S.W.2d 471 (Tex.Crim.App. 1982); *Zuniga* v. *State*, 664 S.W.2d at 369.

Appellant argued that there was a discrepancy in the victim's written statement to police after the indictment and her testimony at trial. The victim said in her written statement that appellant had pointed a knife at her. At trial she testified that appellant had put a knife to her throat. Appellant apparently theorizes that this was a "change" in her testimony, and it was motivated by her civil lawsuit in order to make her damages appear worse than they actually were.

Appellant was allowed to cross-examine the complainant on this point. She testified that she had filed a lawsuit. She said that the attorney who was representing her in that suit was present in the courtroom. The trial court heard the testimony of the victim's attorney outside the presence of the jury, by way of a bill of exception. He testified that he had discussed with the victim the type of damages Texas law allows for her type of injury, including punitive damages and damages for pain and suffering but not the amount of damages. The trial court denied appellant's motion to place this testimony before the jury.

We see no meaningful discrepancy between the victim's written statement and her testimony at trial. She consistently maintained that appellant was armed with a knife which he pointed at her. Whether it was pointed at her throat, or some other part of her body is irrelevant. Appellant was allowed to place his theory of bias before the jury on cross examination. If the victim had denied filing a civil lawsuit arising out of the assault, it then might have been proper to allow the attorney to testify. We find that appellant was allowed to adequately attempt to prove bias, motive or prejudice. We hold that the trial court did not abuse its discretion in refusing to permit the tendered testimony. Appellant's sixth ground of error is overruled.

The judgment of conviction is affirmed.

STATE v. CHANCE

778 S.W.2d 457 (Tenn. Crim. App. 1989)

OPINION

BIRCH, Judge.

The defendant, Merle Chance, was convicted by a Stewart County jury of thirty-nine counts of fraud and false dealing. The trial judge sentenced defendant to two years on each forgery and fraudulent breach of trust count, and three years on each embezzlement and false bookkeeping entry count. Chance was ordered to serve the first four months of the sentence in the local jail and the remaining portion on probation. Since all sentences are concurrent, the defendant has an effective sentence of three years, with probation to follow the initial four-month confinement.

Chance appeals, insisting first that the evidence is insufficient to support the verdict. In other issues, he asserts that

STATE v. CHANCE   599

1) Certain testimony and other evidence was wrongly admitted in three specific instances;
2) Three of the supplemental instructions to the jury were erroneous;
3) The final argument on behalf of the state was improperly prejudicial; and
4) The trial court's approval of jurors taking notes during trial and carrying them into deliberations was reversible error.

We have thoroughly examined the record and carefully considered each of the defendant's contentions. The judgments are affirmed.

I

Merle Chance was for many years the principal of the Stewart County High School in Dover. He was responsible, of course, for the overall operation of the school. One of his specific jobs was to act as the school's treasurer, a role which required him to receive, safekeep, deposit, and disburse monies generated by the many and varied school activities. Chance handled the bookkeeping himself, and he invariably denied the teachers access to these financial records.

State auditors examined the school's financial condition. They inspected the financial records for the years 1984, 1985, 1986, and 1987, including journals, ledgers, cancelled checks, deposit slips, invoices, and bank statements. By their calculation, approximately $28,000 that Chance had received was missing and could not be accounted for.

The audit resulted in multiple charges, which have produced the convictions under review.

First, there are 22 counts of forgery. The proof shows that the defendant affixed the signature of almost every teacher in the school to ticket reconciliation forms. These forms were used to account for the monies generated by sales of tickets to athletic events in which the school's teams participated. Chance admitted having signed the names of the teachers without their knowledge or consent.

Second, there are five fraudulent breach of trust counts. These offenses involve Chance's use of school funds to purchase tires and insurance for his personal vehicles.

Third, Chance was convicted of eight counts of embezzlement. The state proved that Chance received funds on seven specific occasions. These funds, all generated by student activities, totaled approximately $4,000. The monies were not deposited in the school's bank account. The eighth count involves Chance's embezzlement of a 1972 Dodge truck, which had been donated to the school.

Finally, in four counts, the evidence indicates that Chance made false record entries.

Chance maintained his innocence. He blamed his inept bookkeeping practices for his plight. While we quickly agree that his bookkeeping records defy all understanding, there is abundant evidence from which the jury could conclude, as indeed they did, that Chance's bookkeeping was sloppy by design. Obviously, by "bookcooking" and account juggling, Chance muddled the financial status of the school's accounts, thereby concealing, at least for a long period, the true state of affairs.

We surmise from our review of the record that the presentation of the evidence in the trial court was tedious and mechanical. The jury was, nevertheless, able to thread its way through the evidentiary maze. In spite of testimony of his good character and reputation, the jury concluded, as they had a right to do, that Chance's conduct was, indeed, criminal.

Considering the entire proof, few, if any, of the facts are disputed. The aggregate of the evidence marshaled by the state is staggering—its effect unsurmountable.

The jury accredited the testimony of the state's witnesses and resolved all conflicts in the testimony in favor of the state. *State v. Hatchett*, 560 S.W.2d 627, 630 (Tenn. 1978). On appeal, the state is entitled to the strongest legitimate view of the evidence, together with all the reasonable and legitimate inferences which can be drawn from it. *State v. Cabbage*, 571 S.W.2d 832, 835 (Tenn. 1978).

Unquestionably, the evidence in this case is overwhelming to show the defendant's guilt beyond a reasonable doubt. The evidence clearly measures up to the required tests of *Jackson v. Virginia*, 443 U.S. 307, 99 S. Ct. 2781, 61 L. Ed. 2d 560 (1979), and

Rule 13(e), Tennessee Rules of Appellate Procedure.

II

For his next issue, defendant contends that the trial court erred in admitting photocopies of school records into evidence.

The transcript indicates that the pertinent records were sent to an out-of-county firm for audit, apparently upon the request of the Stewart County Board of Education. Unfortunately, a number of these records were not returned because the auditors misplaced them. Fortunately, however, Allen Tarpley, a district attorney's investigator, photocopied the documents before sending them to the auditors. The trial court permitted these photocopies to be admitted into evidence on several counts despite the defendant's objection and demand for production of the original documents.

The defendant's objection to the introduction of these photocopies, as we understand it, is that the photocopies were not made in compliance with the Uniform Photographic Copies of Business and Public Records as Evidence Act. Section 24-7-110(b)(1) of the act contains the following provisions:

If any business, institution, member of a profession or calling, or any department or agency of the government, in the regular course of business or activity has kept or recorded any memorandum, writing, entry, print, repre-

STATE V. CHANCE   601

sentation or combination thereof, of any act, transaction, occurrence or event, and in the regular course of the business has caused any or all of the same to be recorded, copied or reproduced by any photographic, photostatic, microfilm, microcard, miniature photographic, or other process which accurately reproduces or forms a durable medium for so reproducing the original, the original may be destroyed in the regular course of business unless its preservation is required by law.

He specifically contends that the records were not kept in the regular course of business, as the act requires, nor were they photocopies "in the regular course of business."

Clearly, this statute has no application to the instant case, since the original documents have been destroyed; but the photocopies are admissible nevertheless.

First, our cases have held that photocopies and copies produced by other similar processes are considered to be duplicate originals. As such, they can be admitted into evidence without explaining the reason for failure to produce the originals. See *Bolton v. State*, 617 S.W.2d 909 914 (Tenn. Crim. App. 1981), *p.t.a. denied* June 1, 1981; E. McCleary, *McCormick on Evidence* § 236 (3rd ed. 1984).

Moreover, the defendant had been, by his admission, not only the person who made the entries, but also the custodian of these records. He

made no suggestion of fraud or deception in the copying process and, indeed, authenticated many of the documents through his testimony. Additionally, he admitted affixing the names of other teachers to many of the documents.

An application of Federal Rules of Evidence, Rule 1003, which defines a photocopy as a "duplicate," would produce the same result, as would our own proposed Rules of Evidence, Rules 1003 and 1004, which are more liberal yet.

The defendant next narrows the focus of his general admissibility of photocopies to introduce a closely-related issue—whether forgery can be proved by a photocopy. He urges that the ancient Tennessee case of *Reeves v. State* supports his contention that a forgery conviction must be proved by the original writing.

Reeves was prosecuted for fraudulent breach of trust. In its opinion, the Court gratuitously allowed that were the charge forgery or perjury, the original would have to be produced. We feel no obligation to follow this dicta, especially since *Reeves* was decided long before the development of the technology to produce duplicate originals as we know them today.

We are of the opinion that the holding in the *Bolton* case, although involving grand larceny, applies with equal force to forgery prosecutions.

We find, therefore, that the photocopies were properly admitted into evidence on all counts; the defendant's contrary contentions are without merit.

III

In another issue, the defendant contests the trial judge's ruling with regard to certain testimony of Ms Norma Jean Dortch.

She testified that purported signatures of certain teachers appeared to have been in the defendant's handwriting. The defendant says that Ms Dortch should not have been permitted to give such testimony.

The witness, Ms Norma Dortch, had taught at the high school for 31 years, which included the defendant's tenure as principal. She said she was extremely familiar with Chance's signature and with the signatures of many other teachers.

The trial judge found that she was sufficiently familiar with Chance's signature to have an opinion, permitted the testimony, and admonished the jury that it was simply an opinion.

If a witness was familiar with the signature and handwriting of an individual by experience, the witness is competent to give opinion evidence as to the identity of the maker of the exhibited handwriting. *State v. Chestnut*, 643 S.W.2d 343, 347 (Tenn. Crim. App. 1982), *p.t.a. denied* October 4, 1982.

The trial judge has wide discretion in determining the admissibility of evidence. The trial judge's ruling in respect to Ms Dortch's testimony is within acceptable limits of discretion.

IV

The defendant next challenges three supplemental instructions to the jury.

Regarding the first, after having deliberated for almost two hours, the jury returned to open court and asked the following question:

> Does a printed name on a signature line constitute a signature by law?

The trial judge responded:

> It matters not what form the alleged forgery took if the defendant intended to defraud another. The writing may be cursive, printing, or any other method or writing if it was intended to defraud another. Does that answer your question?

A juror answered, "Yes, sir."

The defendant finds fault with this supplemental instruction not because of its content, but because, as he states, the trial judge should have admonished the jury "not to place undo [sic] emphasis upon those instructions and to consider them in conjunction with the entire charge." Defendant asserts that failure to accomplish this is reversible error, citing the case of *Burton v. State*, 217 Tenn. 62, 70-1, 394 S.W.2d 873, 876-77 (1965).

We conclude from *Burton* that admonition of the jury along the lines suggested is the far better practice, whether such failure amounts to reversible error must be determined from an examination of the entire record.

We do not reach that point in the case under review, for included in the trial judge's original charge is the following language:

> . . . [I]t is your duty to carefully consider all of them [instructions]. The order in which these instructions are given is no indication of their relative importance. You should not single out one or more of them to the exclusion of another or others but should consider each one in the light of and in harmony with the others.

In our opinion, the giving of the above instruction was sufficient to forestall the problem. See Leach v. State, 552 S.W.2d 407, 408 (Tenn. Crim. App. 1977) cert. denied May 2, 1977.

The trial judge responded the next day to additional questions asked by the jury. Those questions are not included in this record; however, the trial judge's responses appear of record:

> Ladies and gentleman of the jury, in answer to the questions which you have asked the Court:
> To defraud means to practice fraud, to cheat or trick, to deprive a person of property or any interest, estate, or right, by fraud, deceit, or artifice. Entries made into a ledger are not required to be made within a certain time. Funds received

by public officials are required to be deposited in the bank within three days. The defendant is not charged with violation of the three-day deposit law, but only with making false entries.

> Any person who is charged with the collection, safekeeping, transfer, or disbursement of money or property belonging to Stewart County, and who receives in the course of his employment money or property belonging to or for the benefit of his employer, and who embezzles or fraudulently converts to his own use such money or property is guilty of embezzlement.
> In the case of the two-court indictment, you may only find the defendant guilty, if at all, of one count of the indictment or the other, but not both.

> ******

> Ladies and gentleman of the jury, in answer to the question that you have asked concerning the date of the offense, the Court charges you as follows:
> The actual date of the commission of the offense may be different than that charged in the indictment so long as the proof established that the offense occurred prior to the finding and returning of the indictment which date was the the [sic] 18th day of November, 1986.

These are correct statements of the law regardless of the questions that produced them. Considered in the light of the entire charge, the quoted supplemental instructions provide no basis for reversal.

V

The defendant next asserts that "[t]he State's Attorney General erred in his argument to the jury." This bare assertion is unaccompanied by argument or citation to authority; therefore, it is waived. *See* Tennessee Rules of Appellate Procedure, Rule 27(a)(7); Rule 10(b), Rules of the Tennessee Court of Criminal Appeals; *State v. Galloway*, 696 S.W.2d 364, 368 (Tenn. Crim. App. 1985), *p.t.a., denied* August 12, 1985.

VI

Finally, we have examined the issue of juror note-taking. Although the defendant does not press this issue, were we to address it, we would find that juror note-taking rests in the discretion of the trial judge. Certainly we are unable to conclude from the record that the trial judge abused his discretion in this regard. *See Watkins v. State*, 216 Tenn. 545, 554-63, 393 S.W.2d 141, 145-49 (1965); *Brown v. State*, 3 Tenn. Crim. App. 678, 683-84, 466 S.W.2d 527, 529 (1971), *cert. denied* April 5, 1971.

The judgment is affirmed.

WADE and REID, JJ., concur.

Cases relating to Chapter 14
REAL EVIDENCE

SCHMERBER v. CALIFORNIA

384 U.S. 757, 86 S. Ct. 1826, 16 L. Ed 2d 908 (1966)

[Footnotes omitted]

Mr. Justice BRENNAN delivered the opinion of the Court.

Petitioner was convicted in Los Angeles Municipal Court of the criminal offense of driving an automobile while under the influence of intoxicating liquor. He had been arrested at a hospital while receiving treatment for injuries suffered in an accident involving the automobile that he had apparently been driving. At the direction of a police officer, a blood sample was then withdrawn from petitioner's body by a physician at the hospital. The chemical analysis of this sample revealed a percent by weight of alcohol in his blood at the time of the offense which indicated intoxication, and the report of this analysis was admitted in evidence at the trial. Petitioner objected to receipt of this evidence of the analysis on the ground that the blood had been withdrawn despite his refusal, on the advice of his counsel, to consent to the test. He contended that in that circumstance the withdrawal of the blood and the admission of the analysis in evidence denied him due process of law under the Four-teenth Amendment, as well as specific guarantees of the Bill of Rights secured against the States by that Amendment: his privilege against self-incrimination under the Fifth Amendment; his right to counsel under the Sixth Amendment; and his right not to be subjected to unreasonable searches and seizures in violation of the Fourth Amendment. The Appellate Department of the California Superior Court rejected these contentions and affirmed the conviction. In view of constitutional decisions since we last considered these issues in *Breithaupt* v. *Abram*, 352 U.S. 432, 77 S.Ct. 408, 1 L.Ed.2d 448—see *Escobedo* v. *State of Illinois*, 378 U.S. 478, 84 S.Ct. 1758, 12 L.Ed.2d 977; *Malloy* v. *Hogan*, 378 U.S. 1, 84 S.Ct. 1489, 12 L.Ed. 2d 653, and *Mapp* v. *State of Ohio*, 367 U.S. 643, 81 S.Ct. 1684, 6 L.Ed.2d 1081—we granted certiorari. 382 U.S. 971, 86 S.Ct. 542, 15 L.Ed.2d 464. We affirm.

I.
THE DUE PROCESS CLAUSE CLAIM

Breithaupt was also a case in

which police officers caused blood to be withdrawn from the driver of an automobile involved in an accident, and in which there was ample justification for the officer's conclusion that the driver was under the influence of alcohol. There, as here, the extraction was made by a physician in a simple, medically acceptable manner in a hospital environment. There, however, the driver was unconscious at the time the blood was withdrawn and hence had no opportunity to object to the procedure. We affirmed the conviction there resulting from the use of the test in evidence, holding that under such circumstances the withdrawal did not offend "that 'sense of justice' of which we spoke in *Rochin v. (People of) California,* 1952, 342 U.S. 165, 72 S.Ct. 205, 96 L.Ed. 183." 352 U.S., at 435, 77 S.Ct at 410 *Breithaupt* thus requires the rejection of petitioner's due process argument, and nothing in the circumstances of this case or in supervening events persuades us that this aspect of *Breithaupt* should be overruled.

II.
THE PRIVILEGE AGAINST SELF-INCRIMINATION CLAIM

Breithaupt summarily rejected an argument that the withdrawal of blood and the admission of the analysis report involved in that state case violated the Fifth Amendment privilege of any person not to "be compelled in any criminal case to be a witness against himself," citing *Twining* v. *State of New Jersey,* 211 U.S. 78, 29 S.Ct. 14, 53 L.Ed. 97. But that case, holding that the protections of the Fourteenth Amendment do not embrace this Fifth Amendment privilege, has been suc-

ceeded by *Malloy* v. *Hogan,* 378 U.S. 1, 8, 84 S.Ct. 1489, 1493, 12 L.Ed.2d 653. We there held that "(t)he Fourteenth Amendment secures against state invasion the same privilege that the Fifth Amendment guarantees against federal infringement—the right of a person to remain silent unless he chooses to speak in the unfettered exercise of his own will and to suffer no penalty * * * for such silence." We therefore must now decide whether the withdrawal of the blood and admission in evidence of the analysis involved in this case violated petitioner's privilege. We hold that the privilege protects an accused only from being compelled to testify against himself, or otherwise provide the State with evidence of a testimonial or communicative nature, and that the withdrawal of blood and use of the analysis in question in this case did not involve compulsion to these ends.

It could not be denied that in requiring petitioner to submit to the withdrawal and chemical analysis of his blood the State compelled him to submit to an attempt to discover evidence that might be used to prosecute him for a criminal offense. He submitted only after the police officer rejected his objection and directed the physician to proceed. The officer's direction to the physician to administer the test over petitioner's objection constituted compulsion for the purposes of the privilege. The critical question, then, is whether petitioner was thus compelled "to be a witness against himself."

If the scope of the privilege coincided with the complex of values it helps to protect, we might be obliged to conclude that the privilege was violated. In *Miranda* v. *Arizona*, 384 U.S. 436, at 460, 86 S.Ct. 1602, at 1620, 16 L.Ed.2d 694, at 715, the Court said of the interests protected by the privilege: "All these policies point to one overriding thought; the constitutional foundation underlying the privilege is the respect a government—state or federal—must accord to the dignity and integrity of its citizens. To maintain a 'fair state-individual balance,' to require the government 'to shoulder the entire load,' * * * to respect the inviolability of the human personality, our accusatory system of criminal justice demands that the government seeking to punish an individual produce the evidence against him by its own independent labors, rather than by the cruel, simple expedient of compelling it from his own mouth." The withdrawal of blood necessarily involves puncturing the skin for extraction, and the percent by weight of alcohol in that blood, as established by chemical analysis, is evidence of criminal guilt. Compelled submission fails on one view to respect the "inviolability of the human personality." Moreover, since it enables the State to rely on evidence forced from the accused, the compulsion violates at least one meaning of the requirement that the State procure the evidence against an accused "by its own independent labors."

As the passage in Miranda implicitly recognizes, however, the privilege has never been given the full scope which the values it helps to protect suggest. History and a long line of authorities in lower courts have consistently limited its protection to situations in which the State seeks to submerge those values by obtaining the evidence against an accused through "the cruel, simple expedient of compelling it from his own mouth. * * * In sum, the privilege is fulfilled only when the person is guaranteed the right 'to remain silent unless he chooses to speak in the unfettered exercise of his own will.'" Ibid. The leading case in this Court is *Holt* v. *United States*, 218 U.S. 245, 31 S.Ct. 2, 54 L.Ed. 1021.

There the question was whether evidence was admissible that the accused, prior to trial and over his protest, put on a blouse that fitted him. It was contended that compelling the accused to submit to the demand that he model the blouse violated the privilege. Mr. Justice Holmes, speaking for the Court, rejected the argument as "based upon an extravagant extension of the 5th Amendment," and went on to say: "(T)he prohibition of compelling a man in a criminal court to be a witness against himself is a prohibition of the use of physical or moral compulsion to extort communications from him, not an exclusion of his body as evidence when it may be material. The objection in principle would forbid a jury to look at a prisoner and compare his features with a photograph in proof." 218 U.S., at 252-253, 31 S.Ct., at 6.

It is clear that the protection of the privilege reaches an accused's communications, whatever form they might take, and the compulsion of responses which are also communications, for example, compliance with a subpoena to produce one's papers. *Boyd* v. *United States*, 116 U.S. 616, 6 S.Ct. 524, 29 L.Ed. 746. On the other hand, both federal and state courts have usually held that it offers no protection against compulsion to submit to fingerprinting, photographing, or measurements, to write or speak for identification, to appear in court, to stand, to assume a stance, to walk, or to make a particular gesture. The distinction which has emerged often expressed in different ways, is that the privilege is a bar against compelling "communications" or "testimony," but that compulsion which makes a suspect or accused the source of "real or physical evidence" does not violate it.

Although we agree that this distinction is a helpful framework for analysis, we are not to be understood to agree with past applications in all instances. There will be many cases in which such a distinction is not readily drawn. Some tests seemingly directed to obtain "physical evidence," for example, lie detector tests measuring changes in body function during interrogation, may actually be directed to eliciting responses which are essentially testimonial. To compel a person to submit to testing in which an effort will be made to determine his guilt or innocence on the basis of physiological responses, whether willed or not, is to evoke the spirit and history of the Fifth Amendment. Such situations call to mind the principle that the protection of the privilege "is as broad as the mischief against which it seeks to guard." *Counselman* v. *Hitchcock*, 142 U.S. 547, 562, 12 S.Ct. 195, 198.

In the present case, however, no such problem of application is presented. Not even a shadow of testimonial compulsion upon or enforced communication by the ac-

cused was involved either in the extraction or in the chemical analysis. Petitioner's testimonial capacities were in no way implicated; indeed, his participation except as a donor, was irrelevant to the results of the test which depend on chemical analysis and on that alone. Since the blood test evidence, although an incriminating product of compulsion, was neither petitioner's testimony nor evidence relating to some communicative act or writing by the petitioner, it was not inadmissible on privilege grounds.

Note: Parts of case relating to the right to counsel claim and search and seizure claim are not included. This case should be read in full for a more complete understanding of the rules concerning admissibility of the real evidence.

Affirmed.

Mr. Justice HARLAN, whom Mr. Justice STEWART joins, concurring.

In joining the Court's opinion I desire to add the following comment. While agreeing with the Court that the taking of this blood test involved no testimonial compulsion, I would go further and hold that apart from this consideration the case in no way implicates the Fifth Amendment. Cf. my dissenting opinion and that of Mr. Justice White in *Miranda* v. *Arizona*, 384 U.S. 436, 526, 86 S.Ct. 1643, 16 L.Ed. 2d. 694, 753.

Mr. Chief Justice WARREN dissenting.

While there are other important constitutional issues in this case, I believe it is sufficient for me to reiterate my dissenting opinion in *Breithaupt* v. *Abram*, 352 U.S. 432,

440, 77 S.Ct. 408, 412, as the basis on which to reverse this conviction.

Mr. Justice Black with whom Mr. Justice Douglas joins, dissenting.

I would reverse petitioner's conviction. I agree with the Court that the Fourteenth Amendment made applicable to the States the Fifth Amendment's provision that "No person * * * shall be compelled in any criminal case to be a witness against himself." But I disagree with the Court's holding that California did not violate petitioner's constitutional right against self-incrimination when it compelled him, against his will, to allow a doctor to puncture his blood vessels in order to extract a sample of blood and analyze it for alcoholic content, and then used that analysis as evidence to convict petitioner of a crime.

*   *   *

Mr. Justice DOUGLAS, dissenting.

I adhere to the views of the Chief Justice in his dissent in *Breithaupt* v. *Abram*, 352 U.S. 432, 440, 77 S.Ct. 408, 412, 1 L.Ed.2d 448, and to the views I stated in my dissent in that case (id., 442, 77 S.Ct. 413) and add only a word.

We are dealing with the right of privacy which, since the *Breithaupt* case, we have held to be within the penumbra of some specific guarantees of the Bill of Rights. *Griswold* v. *State of Connecticut*, 381 U.S. 479, 85 S.Ct. 1678, 14 L.Ed.2d 510. Thus the Fifth Amendment marks "a zone of privacy" which the Government may not force a person to surrender. Id., 484, 85 S.Ct. 1681. Likewise the Fourth Amendment recognizes that right of the people to be secure "in their persons." Ibid. No clearer invasion of this right of privacy can be imagined than forcible bloodletting of the kind involved here.

Mr. Justice FORTAS, dissenting.

I would reverse. In my view, petitioner's privilege against self-incrimination applies. I would add that, under the Due Process Clause, the State, in its role as prosecutor, has no right to extract blood from an accused or anyone else, over his protest. As prosecutor, the State has no right to commit any kind of violence upon the person, or to utilize the results of such a tort, and the extraction of blood, over protest, is an act of violence. Cf. Chief Justice Warren's dissenting opinion in *Breithaupt* v. *Abram*, 352 U.S. 432, 440, 77 S.Ct. 408, 412, 1 L.Ed.2d 448.

UNITED STATES v. OLSON

846 F.2d 1103 (7th Cir. 1988)

COFFEY, Circuit Judge.

Defendant-Appellant, Clifford Olson, appeals his conviction of first degree murder. We affirm.

I. Background

On Easter Sunday, April 10, 1977, the body of Clifford George

Albers was found in the Wolf River on the Menominee Indian Reservation in Menominee County, Wisconsin. Three years later an indictment was returned charging the defendant with first degree murder. On July 7, 1980, prior to the commencement of the trial, the government dismissed the original indictment without prejudice pursuant to Fed. R. Crim. P. 48(a). Olson was reindicted for the same offense in February, 1985 and went to trial in September of that year.

At trial, the government's case in chief consisted primarily of the testimony of three main witnesses, Wanda Dick, Brenda LaRock, and Ella Peters. Wanda Dick testified that on April 9, 1977, she lived with Clifford Olson on the Menominee Indian Reservation in an area known as "South Branch." On that date, Dick testified, she was with Olson, Ella Peters, Brenda LaRock, and Robert Kakwitch, riding in the defendant's car and drinking beer. At some point, the four left the reservation and turned onto a gravel road where they came upon a station wagon. Olson got out of their car and spoke to the man driving the station wagon; that man was later identified by Brenda LaRock as the victim, Clifford Albers. According to Dick, Olson grabbed Alber's arm and escorted him to Olson's car. Albers got into the back seat. Dick then drove Alber's station wagon to another location at Olson's request. When she returned to Olson's car, Albers was blindfolded. Olson, Dick, Peters, LaRock, Kakwitch and Albers then rode back to the South

Branch area of the Menominee Reservation, parked the car and walked into the woods. Dick testified that they built a fire and drank beer and brandy, the defendant pouring brandy into Albers' mouth. Later, Olson hit Albers in the leg or ankle with an ax. Shortly thereafter, Dick saw Olson shoot Albers in the face with a handgun. Olson handed her the gun and she shot Albers once. Dick did not recall who else shot the victim. The defendant asked her to get a blanket from the car. Dick did so, and they rolled Albers body into the blanket and placed it in the trunk of the car. Dick testified that they then drove to the Keshena Bridge and threw the body into the river.

Brenda LaRock's trial testimony substantially corroborated that of Wanda Dick. Her testimony differed only slightly from Dick's. LaRock stated that another individual, Charlie Peters, was also present during the events of April 9, that she was some distance away from the others in the woods when she heard gunshots, that when she walked back to the others she saw guns in the hands of Ella Peters, Bobby Kakwitch and Clifford Olson, and that after Wanda Dick shot the victim, Olson handed LaRock the gun, and she also shot him. Finally, LaRock identified a photograph of Clifford George Albers as that of the victim.

Ella Peters' trial testimony was also consistent with that of both Wanda Dick and Brenda LaRock. Peters' testimony differed from Dick's and LaRock's in that she did not, as

LaRock had, mention the involvement of Charlie Peters, and that she stated that when the group left the reservation, the defendant talked of burglarizing a house in the area of Lakewood. Peters also testified that all of the individuals involved shot at the victim, but she only saw one gun.

In addition to the testimony of the three main witnesses, the government introduced various physical evidence, including a number of .22 caliber and .32 caliber bullets, and a 9mm or .38 caliber bullet, all taken from the body, a number of cartridge cases taken from the scene of the crime in 1980, and a .22 caliber High Standard semiautomatic pistol that was seized in 1979 from the home of the defendant's mother pursuant to a search warrant. Special Agent Richard A. Crum of the Federal Bureau of Investigation (FBI) Laboratory in Washington, D.C. was qualified and testified as a firearms identification expert. In Agent Crum's opinion, several of the .22 caliber bullets found in the victim's body were fired from the pistol seized from the home of the defendant's mother, and three others could have been fired from that pistol. Agent Crum also testified that cartridge cases found at the scene of the crime in 1980 had been fired from the same pistol.

On September 13, 1985, the jury found the defendant guilty of first degree murder, and Olson appealed. On May 7, 1986, we granted his "Motion to Remand" to the district court for consideration of a claim of ineffective assistance of trial counsel. The trial

court held evidentiary hearing on June 23, 1986 and found that Olson had not received ineffective assistance. Defendant then filed a motion in this court requesting that we expand the remand to include consideration of a motion for a new trial based on newly discovered evidence; we granted that motion. On October 14, 1986, the trial court denied Olson's motion for a new trial.

Olson now appeals from his conviction and from the denial of his motion for a new trial. He alleges a variety of errors, namely: 1) he received ineffective assistance of trial counsel; 2) the trial court abused its discretion by refusing to order a new trial on the basis of newly discovered evidence; 3) the 1980 indictment should have been dismissed with prejudice; 4) the indictment was insufficient; 5) certain physical evidence was improperly admitted; and 6) the trial court erred by refusing to require the government to produce a statement regarding the purpose of a payment made to a witness' boyfriend. We find no merit in any of these contentions.

....

VI. Adequacy of chain of custody

Defendant next alleges that the trial court erroneously admitted certain physical evidence despite the government's failure to adequately establish a chain of custody for the items. "A trial court's decision to admit real evidence will not be reversed unless it has abused its discretion." *United States v. Wheeler*, 800 F.2d

100, 106 (7th Cir. 1986). We find no abuse of discretion in this case.

Briefly, the defendant argues that certain bullets and bullet fragments recovered from the victim's body during the autopsy were improperly admitted because the evidence at trial indicated that, after these items were brought to the Wisconsin State Crime Laboratory and sealed in containers, FBI Agent Gregory Hunter unsealed each container and wrapped the items in cotton for shipping to the FBI Laboratory in Washington, D.C. Defendant complains that, while the evidence at trial (in the form of the FBI Agent's "Report of Activity") indicated what the agent "did in terms of unsealing the package, [and] what he did in terms of wrapping [the items] . . . the report surely doesn't say anything about how they were replaced in the cartons or when they were replaced in the cartons or anything else."

The government concedes that because of the death of Agent Hunter prior to Olson's trial, there are unavoidable gaps in the chain of custody of the bullets and bullet fragments. An uninterrupted chain of custody, however, is not a prerequisite to admissibility. Gaps in the chain go to the weight of the evidence, not its admissibility. *Wheeler*, 800 F.2d at 106. "If the trial judge is satisfied that in reasonable probability the evidence has not been altered in any material respect, he may permit its introduction." *United States v. Aviles*, 623 F.2d 1192, 1198 (7th Cir. 1980).

In this case, the defendant presented no affirmative evidence of altering or tampering with the evidence. Additionally, the nature of the evidence—bullets and bullet fragments—makes alteration of the evidence unlikely. *See United States v. Brown*, 482 F.2d 1226, 1228 (8th Cir. 1973) (considering nature of the articles (packages of heroin) as factor in determining admissibility). Finally, where the items have been in official custody and there is no affirmative evidence of tampering, a "presumption of regularity attends official acts of public officers and the courts presume that their official duties have been discharged properly. *Aviles*, 623 F.2d at 1198; see also *United States v. Jefferson*, 714 F.2d 689, 696 (7th Cir. 1983). Given these factors, we find no abuse of discretion in the admission into evidence of the bullets and bullet fragments recovered from the victim's body during the autopsy.

Olson also objects to the admission of a lead fragment that allegedly fell out of the victim's arm when his body was taken from the Wolf River. There was testimony at trial that Alex Askanet, a Tribal Police Officer, picked up the piece of lead. There was also testimony that FBI Special Agent Robert Kleinschmidt gave FBI Special Agent Richard Prokop a piece of lead, allegedly the fragment retrieved by Officer Askanet, on the same day. The chain of custody of the lead fragment from that point on is not challenged; the defendant's argument is that there was no evidence connecting the lead fragment retrieved by Tribal Police Officer Askanet with that given by Kleinschmidt to Prokop. Neither Askanet nor Kleinschmidt testified at trial; Agent Kleinschmidt had retired and Officer Askanet was deceased. As the government points out, however, Agent Prokop did testify that he sent Agent Kleinschmidt to the scene with instructions to contact the tribal authorities. Moreover, Agent Prokop testified that he recognized Agent Kleinschmidt's initials as well as "Alex A," an abbreviation for "Alex Askanet," on the container that held the lead fragment. As stated above, "[t]he trial court's discretionary ruling on identification of evidence sufficient for its admissibility is subject to reversal only for an abuse of discretion," *United States v. Bridges*, 499 F.2d 179, 185 (7th Cir.), *cert. denied* 419 U.S. 1010, 95 S. Ct. 330, 42 L. Ed. 2d 284 (1974), and gaps in the chain of custody go to the weight of the evidence rather than its admissibility. We find no abuse of discretion in the trial court's determination that the testimony at trial established a chain of custody sufficient for admissibility; whatever deficiencies may have existed were properly a matter to be resolved by the jury in weighing the evidence.

VII. Failure to provide statement regarding payment of $400.00

Olson's final contention on appeal is that the trial court's refusal to require the government to provide a statement regarding the purpose of a payment of $400.00 to the boyfriend of prosecution witness Wanda Dick. constitutes reversible error. In 1980 Wanda Dick testified before a grand jury that she and Clifford Olson were responsible for the murder of Clifford Albers; in 1981 she testified that she, Clifford Olson, Ella Peters, Brenda LaRock, and Robert Kakwitch were involved in the murder. Prior to trial in 1985, the government disclosed to defendant's counsel that, in February or March of 1985, the FBI had paid Russell Biddle, Dick's boyfriend, an informant's fee of $400.00 At trial, outside the presence of the jury, Dick testified that she was not aware of any payment made to Biddle. The defense then requested that the government be required to provide a statement regarding the purpose of the payment. The court refused the request but did require that the U.S. Attorney disclose Russell Biddle's address to defendant's counsel. Following several unsuccessful attempts by the defense to contact Biddle, the court required the government to provide information regarding his place of employment. Attempts to contact Biddle there were similarly unavailing. The defense then renewed its motion for a statement by the government regarding the purpose of the payment to Biddle. The court denied this request. On appeal defendant contends that this denial constitutes reversible error.

Defendant cites no authority for the proposition that the prosecution can be compelled to assist the defendant's case by producing a potentially useful statement of the sort requested here. In its brief the government treats the contention as a due process claim under *Brady v. Maryland*, 373 U.S. 83, 83 S. Ct. 1194, 10 L. Ed. 2d 215 (1963), and *United States v. Bagley*, 473 U.S. 667, 105 S. Ct. 3375, 87 L. Ed. 2d 481 (1985). In *Brady* the Supreme Court held that the prosecution's failure to disclose evidence favorable to the defense denied the defendant due process. 373 U.S. at 87, 83 S. Ct. at 1196. More recently, in *Bagley*, the Court held that the holding in *Brady* applies to impeachment as well as exculpatory evidence. However, in *Bagley*, the Court also stated, "a constitutional error occurs, and the conviction must be reversed, only if the evidence is material in the sense that its suppression undermines confidence in the outcome of the trial." 105 S. Ct. at 3381. The Court further clarified the materiality standard: "The evidence is material only if there is a reasonable probability that, had the evidence been disclosed to the defense, the result would have been different. A 'reasonable probability' is a probability sufficient to undermine confidence in the outcome." *Id.* at 3384. This standard is not met here. The court's refusal to compel disclosure of the purpose of the payment, therefore, did not deny the defendant due process and does not require reversal of his conviction.

Wanda Dick had testified previously in the trial court, out of the presence of the jury, that she knew nothing of the payment to her boyfriend. While it is possible, as Olson argues on appeal, that Biddle somehow influenced her to testify against the defendant, this is mere speculation; no proof of Biddle's alleged influence was ever offered. Moreover, given the fact that she had testified against Olson before the grand jury as early as 1980, five years before the payment to Biddle was made, it is unlikely she testified as she did as a result of Biddle's influence. Further, Dick's credibility was impeached at trial by her prior convictions and by her admitted perjury before the grand jury and her lies to FBI agents. The incremental impeachment value of a statement by the government regarding the purpose of the payment to Biddle is therefore doubtful. Most importantly though, given the corroboration of Dick's testimony by that of Brenda LaRock and Ella Peters, it would be impossible for us to conceive, much less hold, that there is a "reasonable probability" that the disclosure of the requested information would have resulted in Olson's acquittal. The evidence of guilt was overwhelming. Our confidence in the outcome of the defendant's trial remains unshaken. The evidence requested was not material under the standard enunciated in *Bagley*, and the court's refusal to compel its disclosure does not require reversal.

VIII. Conclusion

Upon review of Olson's numerous allegations of reversible error, we hold each and every one to be without merit and accordingly affirm the defendant's conviction.

COMMONWEALTH v. ROGERS

401 A.2d 329 (Pa. 1979)

[Footnotes omitted]

EAGEN, Chief Justice.

On August 26, 1977, Richard Wayne Rogers was convicted by a jury in Cambria County of two separate counts of robbery and of murder of the first degree. Following denial of post-verdict motions, a sentence of life imprisonment was imposed on the murder conviction. A prison sentence of ten to twenty years was imposed on each robbery conviction, these prison sentences to run concurrently with the life imprisonment sentence. This appeal followed.

Several rulings of the trial court during the prosecution process are assigned as error. In view of our conclusion that the admission of certain photographic evidence was so prejudicial as to require a new trial, we need not reach or discuss every assignment of error.

At trial, the Commonwealth charged that, before leaving the scene of a coal weigh station where Rogers and two companions had committed a robbery, Rogers fatally shot the attendant of the station in the head with a shotgun as he sat injured and helpless on the snow-covered ground.

At trial, evidentiary use of four photographs, showing the dead body of the victim lying prostrate at the site of the fatal shooting, was permitted over objection. These photographs were also taken by the jury into the deliberation room and remained there throughout the jury's discussion of the case.

One of the challenged photo-graphs (Exhibit 20) depicted in close and graphic detail the victim's distorted face, head wounds, and blood, flesh and brains scattered in the snow alongside the head. The gruesomeness and inflammatory nature of this photograph is patently obvious. It is clear to us that the use of this photograph denied Rogers a constitutionally required fair and objective determination of his guilt of the crimes charged. We will, therefore, reverse and order a retrial.

We recently set forth in *Commonwealth* v. *Batty*, 482 Pa. 173, ___, 393 A.2d 435, 437 (1978), the considerations to be made by the trial judge if an inflammatory photograph is offered as evidence for consideration by the jury:

"If . . . [a] photograph is deemed to be inflammatory, the Court must then apply the balancing test . . . i.e., is the photograph of 'such essential evidentiary value that its need clearly outweighs the likelihood of inflaming the minds and passions of the jurors.'" [Emphasis, citations, and quotations omitted.]

The Commonwealth contends on appeal, as it did at trial, that the photograph in question was of such essential evidentiary value that its need clearly outweighed "the likelihood of inflaming the minds and passions of the jury." Specifically, the Commonwealth contends the photograph was necessary: (1) to establish "the head of the victim was parallel and in close proximity to the ground when he was shot"; and, (2) to support the Commonwealth's position that the shooting occurred after the robbery was accomplished and that, hence, its only purpose was the elimination of the victim as a possible witness against the robbers.

A study of the trial testimony readily demonstrates: (1) that use of the photograph was wholly unnecessary to establish where the victim's body was located at the moment of the fatal shot and that the shooting occurred after the robbery occurred; and, (2) that there was a clear likelihood it would inflame the minds and passions of the jury.

It is true that Pennsylvania State Police Officer McCommons viewed the photograph at trial and then expressed the opinion that the victim's head was parallel and in close proximity to the ground when he was shot. But the officer did not need the photograph to so testify because he observed the body and its condition as it lie on the ground after the shooting. In fact, Officer Mc-Commons, who took the challenged photograph, could have described what he saw without reference to the photograph and expressed his opinion on the basis of what he had observed. Additionally, one of Rogers' co-felons, Michael Noon, who testified as a Commonwealth witness, stated that the victim was seated on the ground, injured, and disabled immediately before he was fatally shot and that the shooting ensued after the robbery had succeeded.

Under the circumstances, the photograph was not of "essential evidentiary value."

Judgments reversed and a new trial is ordered.

ROBERTS and MANDERINO, JJ., filed concurring opinions.

LARSEN, J., filed a dissenting opinion.

ROBERTS, Justice, concurring.

I concur in the result for the reasons set forth in *Commonwealth* v. *Chacko*, 480 Pa. 304, 391 A.2d 999 (1978) (Roberts, J., concurring). See *Commonwealth* v. *Batty*, 482 Pa. 173, 393 A.2d 435 (1978) (Roberts, J., concurring).

MANDERINO, Justice, concurring.

I join the majority opinion but note that the test used by this Court for the admission of photographs should be changed. *Commonwealth* v. *Batty*, 482 Pa. 173, 393 A.2d 435 (1978).

If a picture is inflammatory it should never be admissible *because* I know of no situation nor can I conceive of one in which an inflammatory picture has *essential* evidentiary value.

LARSEN, Justice, dissenting.

I dissent. The evidence was so overwhelming that, with or without the photograph, the appellant would have been found guilty of murder of the first degree and robbery. Thus, any error was harmless beyond a reasonable doubt.

Additionally, an emotional response to pictures of violent death is natural. For some reason, however, the majority thinks that this emotional response is transferred into a negative reaction and then posited on the defendant. I do not think this psychological phenomena occurs.

The judgments of sentence should be affirmed.

BROWN v. STATE

550 So. 2d 527 (Fla. Dist. Ct. App. 1989)

WENTWORTH, Judge.

Appellant seeks review of a judgment of conviction and sentence for the offense of aggravated battery, arguing that the state was improperly allowed to use a knife and styrofoam head as demonstrative exhibits. We find that it was within the court's discretion to allow the use of these exhibits during the victim's testimony, and that appellant's counsel did not seek any curative instruction or clearly request a mistrial upon the further use of the exhibits during closing argument. The record fails to demonstrate such a prejudice as would constitute fundamental error, and we therefore affirm the appealed orders.

Appellant was tried on a charge of attempted murder. Various witnesses testified that appellant, after an argument with the alleged victim, obtained a knife and stabbed the victim three times in the head. The knife broke, the victim became unconscious, and when she awoke appellant struck her on the head with a fan. During the course of the trial the court allowed the state to use a knife and a styrofoam head as demonstrative exhibits. It was established that the knife was similar to the one used by appellant before it broke, and that the styrofoam head was approximately the

same size as the victim's head. These items were not received into evidence, but were used during the victim's testimony, over appellant's objection, for illustration and comparison. The victim was allowed to mark the styrofoam head so as to depict the three stab wounds which were inflicted by appellant.

At the commencement of the proceeding appellant's counsel asserted that while appellant may have been arguing with the victim and "cut" her, he did not intend to kill her. Appellant maintained this defense throughout the trial, asserting it again when unsuccessfully moving for a judgment of acquittal, and at closing argument.

During the state's closing argument the prosecutor directed the jury's attention to the styrofoam head where the victim's wounds were marked, and argued as to the intended effect of appellant's actions. Appellant's counsel's objection was overruled, and the prosecutor thereafter repeatedly inserted the demonstrative knife into the styrofoam while asking the jury to compare the diverse insertions when addressing appellant's intent. Appellant's counsel again objected, noting that no testimony had been presented as to the depth of the victim's wounds or the force used by appellant, and contending that the prosecutor was inserting the knife with more force and pressure than was necessary. Appellant's counsel suggested that "it's improper argument, and it's grounds for mistrial, I do believe." The court overruled the objection and did not grant a mistrial, allowing the prosecutor to continue with the demonstration and argument. The case was eventually submitted to the jury, and appellant was convicted of the lesser charge of aggravated battery.

Demonstrative exhibits to aid the jury's understanding may be utilized when relevant to the issues in the case, but only if the exhibits constitute an accurate and reasonable reproduction of the object involved. See Wade v. State, 204 So.2d 235 (Fla. 2d DCA 1967); Alston v. Shiver, 105 So.22d 785 (Fla. 1958). The determination as to whether to allow the use of a demonstrative exhibit is a matter within the trial court's discretion. See generally, First Federal Savings & Loan v. Wylie, 46 So.2d 396 (Fla. 1950). The demonstrative exhibits which the state used during the victim's testimony in the present case, in order to depict the knife before it was broken and the extent of the victim's stab wounds, were sufficiently accurate replicas to be allowable within the court's discretion.

As to the state's use of the demonstrative exhibits during closing argument, when the prosecutor inserted the knife into the styrofoam head, the record does not establish any alleged inaccuracy of this replication sufficient to demonstrate error. While appellant's counsel objected, and expressed a belief that the argument was grounds for a mistrial, counsel did not seek any curative instruction or state either in form or substance a motion for mistrial. Without such request, and absent any fundamental error, the challenged argument will not serve as a basis for reversal on appeal. See Clarke v. State, 363 So.2d 331 (Fla. 1978); Lynn v. State, 395 So.2d 621 (Fla. 1st DCA 1981).

Although appellant's counsel described the prosecutor as "inserting the knife . . . with some force and with some pressure, I think more than is required," the record does not otherwise delineate the severity or intensity of this demonstration. The case is thus unlike Spriggs v. State, 392 So.2d 9 (Fla. 4th DCA 1981), where the force required to stab a knife into the rail of the jury box was readily apparent. The record in the present case does not show an action of similar intensity, nor does it show the depth to which the prosecutor inserted the knife into the styrofoam head. The record is likewise inconclusive as to whether the victim's wounds were limited to lacerations and tissue damage, or also included damage to the skull. However, it was established that appellant inflicted multiple stab wounds requiring sutures in the victim's face and head, and that appellant used such force that the knife broke during the attack. The record does not indicate that during closing argument the prosecutor used excessive force or any other action beyond that consistent with the evidence as to the multiple stab wounds inflicted by appellant.

At the commencement of closing argument the court cautioned the jury that "what the attorneys say is not evidence," and that their "arguments are persuasive only, . . . for the purpose of helping you evaluate the evidence." The jury rejected the state's argument regarding appellant's intent, acquitting him of the attempted murder charge and convicting only of the lesser aggravated battery offense. The record contains overwhelming evidence as to appellant's commission of this lesser offense, and negates any reasonable possibility that appellant's conviction resulted from the challenged demonstration. No fundamental error or undue prejudice has been shown with regard to the prosecutor's use of the demonstrative exhibits during closing argument, and the decision to allow their use was otherwise within the trial court's discretion.

The judgment of conviction and sentence appealed are affirmed.

ERVIN, J., concurs.

ZEHMER, J., concurs and dissents with written opinion.

ZEHMER, Judge (dissenting and concurring).

I agree with the majority that the trial court acted within the scope of its discretion in permitting use of the knife and styrofoam head as demonstrative exhibits during the victim's testimony.

I vigorously disagree with the majority's treatment of the prosecutor's conduct during argument in stabbing the styrofoam head with the knife. The evidence from the victim and other witnesses established only that the victim's scalp was cut at three different places; there was no evidence of any penetration of the skull by the knife. Although the victim, while testifying, could have been permitted to demonstrate how the defendant stabbed her by using the knife and styrofoam head, she did not do so. The prosecutor was not a witness, and it was highly improper for him to reenact this demonstration. The evidence proved only cuts of the skin covering the skull. Despite the lack of evidence of penetration of the skull, the prosecutor stabbed the styrofoam head during argument in such a fashion as to insert the blade three times. The prosecutor's action did not accord with the evidence, but was highly misleading and prejudicial to the defendant's right to a fair trial. It was, in my view, the same kind of improper conduct condemned by the fourth district in *Spriggs v. State*, 392 So.2d 9 (Fla. 4th DCA 1981), where the prosecuting attorney stabbed a knife into the rail of a jury box.

The majority opinion approves the prosecutor's conduct in part on the premise that the record does not demonstrate the force with which he stabbed the styrofoam head during his final argument. Thus, the opinion states that the record is "inconclusive" both as to the "depth to which the prosecutor inserted the knife into the styrofoam head" and "as to whether the victim's wounds were limited to lacerations and tissue damage, or also included damage to the skull."[1] But why the inconclusiveness of the record to prove these facts should justify a demonstration during final argument that asserts the unproven facts as true defies logic. This record established only that the victim's face and scalp were lacerated, and the victim did not demonstrate the manner and force of the attack using a knife and the styrofoam head during her testimony. For the prosecutor, during argument, to perform such a demonstration by stabbing the knife into the "head" rather than lacerating it, thus going beyond the facts proven of record, was highly improper.

More importantly, however, the majority approves the prosecutor's conduct because the record does not demonstrate that the prosecutor used *excessive* force in stabbing the styrofoam head and concludes that the lack of proof of excessive force distinguishes *Spriggs v. State* from this case. In my view, this rationale completely misses the point of appellant's argument and the basis of the error committed. In *Spriggs* the prosecutor stabbed the jury rail during argument. Nothing in any of the three opinions filed in that case suggest that the error

stemmed from the excessiveness of the force used rather than the act of stabbing the jury rail. Clearly, it is not the excessiveness of the force used by the prosecutor in stabbing the head that was improper; rather, the error stems from the fact that the prosecutor engaged in an impermissible demonstration during argument that served only to inflame the jury and cause the verdict to rest upon emotional grounds rather than the truth of the facts proven by the evidence presented. *Spriggs v. State*, 392 So.2d 9. I cannot agree that the law should or does countenance such a practice.

While I would treat this misconduct as fundamental error, we need not do so in this case because defense counsel objected several times to this manner of argument, and at least once said this was grounds for a mistrial. Each time, the court overruled the objection. I am satisfied that these objections were sufficient to preserve the error for review on appeal.

The state's brief does not argue that the error complained of was harmless under the circumstances. Nevertheless, I am willing to agree with the majority's view that appellant suffered no prejudice as a result of this error because the jury acquitted him of attempted murder and found him guilty of the lesser included offense of aggravated battery, an offense clearly proved by the evidence. In so doing, the jury seemingly rejected the prosecutor's argument on intent so vigorously demonstrated with the knife and styrofoam exhibit. But treating the error as harmless un-

---

[1] Although the knife broke during the episode, the record is equally inconclusive as to the cause of the damage other than it occurred during the attack. Certainly this fact did not justify the prosecutor's demonstration during argument in this case.

der these circumstances is a far cry from giving approval to the prosecutor's blatant misconduct. I must, therefore, express in the strongest words possible my dissent to any suggestion supporting the propriety of this misconduct during final argument.

Cases relating to Chapter 15
RESULTS OF EXAMINATIONS AND TESTS

STATE v. WOODALL

385 S.E.2d 253 (W. Va. 1989)

NEELY, Justice:

On 22 January 1987, at about 1:15 p.m., a woman was abducted at knife point from the parking lot of the Huntington Mall in Barboursville, West Virginia by a man wearing a ski mask. The masked assailant forced the victim to shut her eyes throughout the attack. Repeatedly threatening to kill her, the assailant drove the victim in her own car around Cabell County. The victim could not identify the environs through which they drove.

While driving the car, the assailant had the victim raise her arms. He tore and cut her clothing and fondled her breasts. He ordered her to spread her legs. When she refused, he forced them apart, saying, "spread your legs, bitch, and do what I tell you and you won't get hurt. I'm only going to keep you a few minutes and then I'll let you go" He ordered her up and jerked her skirt aside. He hacked the victim's underwear with a knife and fingered her genitals. Holding his knife to her genitals, the assailant threatened to cut her up. "You don't think I'll do it, do you, bitch?' The victim pled for mercy. Driving on a

few minutes, the attacker then forced the victim to fellate him, again holding a knife to her throat. Angered at her attitude, he jerked her up in the seat. The victim sought solace in prayer. Her attacker accosted her, "What are you doing, bitch? You talk to me. What are you up to?" He again forced fellatio. While that continued he cut the victim's skirt and fingered her rectum, then her vagina. Claiming she didn't enjoy his attacks, he made her sit again with her head in her lap. Stopping the car, the attacker forced the victim to her knees. He threatened her again, "You better shut up, bitch, because I'll kill you. I've killed someone before and I'll do it to you." He sodomized her and then raped her. He then forced her into the back seat of the car, had her lie on her stomach, and sodomized her. He then raped her again. Biting the victim on the back, the attacker dismounted and had the victim get in the front seat and compose herself. He again threatened, "I'm going to have to kill you because I know you saw me."

The assailant searched the victim's purse, taking all her money ($5.00) and her watch. He again

623

forced fellatio. The victim briefly opened her eyes, noting that the attacker wore brown pants and that he was uncircumcised. Cursing her, the assailant then let her out of the car. He claimed a friend was following who would hurt her if she opened her eyes; he knew who she was, he said, and his friend would kill her if she called the police.

When she finally opened her eyes, the victim was alone on a roadside. She sought help from a woman nearby. It was then 2 p.m. Forty-five minutes had passed since the abduction began.

Another woman was held in the same terror a few weeks later, on 16 February 1987. At 3 p.m. she entered her car in the Huntington Mall parking lot and then got out to scrape ice from the windscreen. As she reentered the car, a man jumped her, struck her, and forced her into the passenger seat. He told her to shut up and close her eyes. "If you know who I am or if you see me, I'll kill you," he threatened. He rummaged through her pocketbook, accosted her by name, and asked her personal questions. He claimed to be acting for a friend revenging some slight by the victim.

The attacker bound the victim's eyes and hands with tape. He seized the gold wristwatch she wore. The victim was able to see slightly with her right eye, and observed that the assailant drove her car out of the parking lot and onto Interstate 64 East. On the way he pulled up the victim's clothing and fingered her vagina. He forced the victim to fellate

him, then he struck her and pushed her back to the passenger side of the car. As the car slowed to a stop at the Milton exit, the victim tried to unlock the door to escape. The attacker struck her to the floor, and yelled that he would kill her if she tried to escape.

The assailant drove to a secluded spot and parked to "wait" for his "buddy" in a van (he said). He took off the victim's clothes, climbed atop her and raped her. After a bit, he forced her to climb on top of him, maneuvering within the car, and raped her again. He turned the victim on her stomach and again raped her. He then flipped her over onto her back and again raped her.

The assailant had the victim put on her clothes, and began driving the car. He told her, "You'll not live to see another day. You won't see anything else." He stopped the car, claiming his "buddy's van" was there. He taped the victims hands to the gearshift, then took some time wiping the car interior and effects with paper towels he found there. He left her. She counted to sixty several times, then looked up to see that she had been returned to the Huntington Mall. About an hour had passed since she had first been abducted. She drove herself to a hospital.

Glen Dale Woodall stands convicted of nineteen criminal counts arising from these two attacks on women in the Huntington area. Counts one through seven charged first degree sexual assault as to the first victim, count eight charged first degree sexual abuse as to the first victim, count nine charged kidnapping of the first victim, and count ten charged aggravated robbery of the first victim. Counts eleven through fifteen charged first degree sexual assault of the second victim. Counts sixteen and seventeen charged first degree sexual abuse of the second victim, count eighteen charged kidnapping of the second victim, and count nineteen charged aggravated robbery of the second victim.

At trial, the victims' accounts of the crimes were largely undisputed, and the major issue was the identity of the assailant. The defendant's case consisted largely of alibi testimony, which the jury rejected. The prosecution's case consisted primarily of circumstantial evidence, which, taken together, the jury found convincing.

The evidence against Mr. Woodall included blood analysis of the defendant, compared to semen samples recovered from the victims; body hair and beard hair from the defendant compared to hair recovered from the car where victim one was attacked; an out-of-court voice identification of the defendant by victim two; a partial visual identification by victim two; a distinctive smell about the assailant noted by both victims, found also at the defendant's workplace; victim two's identification of the assailant's hair color, compared to the defendant's; victim one's identification of the pants worn by the assailant as similar to defendant's; both victims' testimony that the assailant was uncircumcised, as was the defendant; and, victim two's identification

of the defendant's boots and jacket as similar to the assailant's.

Mr. Woodall's case-in-chief asserted alibi. He offered several witnesses, generally family and friends, who stated that the defendant was otherwise occupied during the attacks. Mr. Woodall also testified for himself. Mr. Woodall was convicted of all nineteen counts, without mercy on the kidnapping counts. He was sentenced to two life terms without parole and 203 to 335 years, all to be served consecutively.

Before trial, the defendant sought to have the trial court order an experimental new blood test known as DNA print analysis. Because no expert testimony was offered by the defendant to show the validity or reliability of the DNA test, the trial court refused to order the test. After trial, the defense raised this issue again, and a DNA test was finally performed. The test compared DNA samples from the defendant's own blood with DNA samples recovered from semen of the assailant. The test proved inconclusive.

I.

The major point in this case is the admissibility of DNA print analysis tests. No state's high court has yet considered the use of DNA forensic tests; however, an intermediate court in Florida has held that these tests are admissible in criminal trials. *Andrews v. State*, 533 So.2d 841 (Fla. App. 1988).

The traditional test for admitting results of novel scientific techniques has been the *Frye* rule. *Frye v. United States*, 293 F. 1013 (D.C. Cir. 1923). *Frye* has been the rule in West Virginia. *State v. Clawson*, 165 W.Va. 588, 270 S.E.2d 659 (1980). The *Frye* rule is that evidence from new scientific tests will be admitted only on a showing that the tests are generally accepted by scientists in the field.

> Just when a scientific principle or discovery crosses the line between the experimental and demonstrable stages is difficult to define. Somewhere in the twilight zone the evidential force of the principle must be recognized, and while the courts will go a long way in admitting expert testimony deduced from a well-recognized scientific principle or discovery, the thing from which the deduction is made must be sufficiently established to have gained general acceptance in the particular field in which it belongs.

Under *Frye*, a hearing was required to determine scientific acceptance of new tests before the evidence could be admitted. There has been some confusion whether *Frye* has been implicitly superceded by the *Federal Rules of Evidence* and state rules that follow the federal pattern. See Gianelli, "The Admissibility of Novel Scientific Evidence: *Frye v. United States*, Half-Century Later," 80 *Colum. L. Rev.* 1197 (1980); *Reager v. Anderson*, ____ W.Va. ____, 371

S.E.2d 619, 628 n.4 (1988); *State v. Armstrong*, ____ W.Va. ____, 369 S.E.2d 870, 874, n. 4 (1988).

Under *W.Va. R. Evid.*, Rule 702, expert testimony is admissible when it "will assist the trier of fact to understand the evidence or to determine a fact in issue." This broad standard of admissibility seems to overrule *Frye* as the standard for admitting scientific evidence. Rule 702 is tempered, of course, by the broad limits on irrelevant, prejudicial, confusing, or misleading evidence. *W.Va. R. Evid.*, Rules 401 and 403 [1985].

Rules 702 and 403, taken together, preserve the policies underlying the *Frye* rule. But under *Frye* the burden was upon the proponent of the test to demonstrate its scientific reliability. Under the Rules, *W.Va. R. Evid.*, Rule 70 2, makes all expert testimony concerning generally recognized tests presumptively admissible and casts the burden of excluding such testimony upon the side seeking exclusion. Thus the side seeking exclusion must show that the test is substantially more prejudicial, misleading, or confusing than it is probative, under Rule 403.

However, when a test is not generally accepted, that circumstance alone meets the threshold requirement of rebutting any presumption of admissibility under Rule 702. Certainly a test clothed with all the trappings of science, but which is not scientifically accepted, is more misleading or prejudicial than it is probative. Pseudoscience is more dangerous than no science at all. Therefore, at the end of the day we are all brought back essentially to the *Frye* rule with regard to tests that are not generally accepted and the burden of proof that the test is reliable remains on the proponent.

The basic reliability of scientific tests is often at issue when such evidence is admitted. Judicial resources can be squandered attacking and supporting scientific tests that are, in fact, generally accepted by scientists in the field. "The tendency of the law must always be to narrow the field of uncertainty." O.W. Holmes, *The Common Law* 127 (1881). For reasons of judicial economy, at some point a trial court may take judicial notice of a test's general reliability. This point occurs when the issue of a test's reliability has been addressed authoritatively by senior appellate courts in a line of cases that determined that the test in question is generally accepted by scientists. This comports with provisions of *W.Va. R. Evid.*, Rule 201 [1985].

As to DNA typing analysis, we find that the reliability of these tests is now generally accepted by geneticists, biochemists, and the like. See Thompson and Ford, "DNA Typing: Acceptance and Weight of the New Genetic Identification Tests," 75 Va. L. Rev. 45 (1989). Thus, no *Frye* hearing will be required in the future for judicial notice of reliability.

This does not, however, mean that DNA tests should always be admitted. Expert testimony may be received to impeach the particular procedures employed in a specific test or the reliability of results obtained. For example, in the case at bar the laboratory wasn't able to isolate a DNA print from the semen. There being nothing to compare to the defendant's DNA print, such evidence would not meet the general relevance test for admission of evidence. Rule 401, *W.Va. R. Evid.* [1985]. In extreme cases, the evidence may properly be found admissible under Rules 401, 403 or 702 *W.Va. R. Evid.* [1985]. In other cases, expert testimony may go to the weight accorded the evidence, with the evidence admitted under Rule 702. *See, e.g., State v. Armstrong*, ____ W.Va. ____, 369 S.E.2d 870 (1988) and *State v. McCoy*, ____ W.Va. ____, 366 S.E.2d 731 (1988).

II.

The procedure to be followed in this case was established in *State v. Lawson*, 165 W.Va. 119, 267 S.E.2d 438 (1980). In *Lawson*, the defendant appealed a criminal conviction for statutory rape. The victim was pregnant at the time of trial. A blood test of the infant could show whether the defendant might have been the father. Because the victim claimed that she had not had sexual intercourse before, the test could have exculpated the defendant. The defendant sought a continuance until the birth of the child, so that a paternity test could be conducted. The trial court in *Lawson* refused the continuance and the defendant was convicted. This Court recognize the general validity of the blood test and its usefulness under the circumstances; accordingly we remanded the case to the trial court to conduct the test. "If the blood tests established lack of paternity, then the defendant's motion for a new trial should be granted; however, if they are merely inconclusive, the conviction should stand." 267 S.E.2d at 439.

Because the results of the DNA test that was done in the case before us are central to our holding, we quote from the laboratory report. As to the semen samples, "DNA banding patterns were not obtained . . . due to insufficient amounts of high molecular weight DNA." Defendant's Reply Brief, Exhibit 2. (March 27, 1989 letter from Cellmark Laboratories.) "No conclusion can be reached concerning the origin of the DNA" in the semen samples. *Id.*

This result is not exculpatory. If, for example, a print were obtained but couldn't be definitively linked to the defendant, that might meet the general test for relevant evidence. *W.Va. R. Evid.*, Rules 401 and 702 [1985]. When no print was obtained, any claim that the test tends to exculpate the defendant would only confuse the jury. *W.Va. R. Evid.*, Rule 403 [1985]. This doesn't go merely to the weight of the evidence, but to its relevancy: It does not tend to make more or less likely any factual issue in the case. *W.Va. R. Evid.*, Rule 401 [1985]. Similarly, the scientific testimony would not be helpful to the jury in determining the facts. *W.Va. R. Evid.*, Rule 702 [1985].

In the case before us, the disputed test has been conducted and has proved inconclusive. Therefore, a remand is inappropriate. If there was er-ror in not ordering the test initially, that error is now rendered harmless.

III.

The defendant challenges several forms of identification offered by the state: statistical evidence from blood-typing and enzyme tests, a voice identification, and a "one-on-one show up." We consider these in turn.

A. Statistical Blood Tests

The defendant claims that statistical interpretations of blood tests, presented at trial by the prosecution, were inherently misleading and should have been excluded under *W.Va. R. Evid.*, Rule 403 [1985]. We disagree.

The prosecution's expert compared the blood traits from Mr. Woodall's blood with semen recovered from the victims. He testified that the assailant's blood types were (1) ABO type O; (2) PGM type 2 +; (3) GLO type 2-1; and Lewis or secretor type a-b +. These traits were identical to Mr. Woodall's. The combination would statistically occur in 6 of every 10,000 males in West Virginia. The defendant's expert conducted his own test of blood and semen samples, and found the same blood types. The defendant's expert argued that the occurrence would be 12 in 10,000 males. On cross-examination, he conceded that the figure could be as small as 1 in 20,000 if independent factors such as age, hair color, and the like were considered.

There is no reason to believe that the jury here was unfairly swayed by the grandeur of science, and we find nothing inherently unreliable in statistical evidence based on blood-typing and enzyme tests. First, blood tests themselves are reliable when properly conducted, and these tests are valuable only when their results are placed in the context of statistical probability.

But statistics drawn from blood tests, or other evidence, can be unfairly prejudicial if the probabilities offered are too low or too high. Hypothetically, if 45 percent of people in one area have type O blood, as did assailant, and a defendant does, too, this standing alone proves so little that it borders on irrelevancy.

On the other extreme, very high probabilities may be misleading, because each factor considered multiplies the probabilities for each of the others, and unreliability in any one factor can substantially skew the overall figure given. In the celebrated case *People v. Collins*, 68 Cal.2d 319, 66 Cal. Rptr. 497, 438 P.2d 33 (1968), the defendants were an inter-racial couple. A witness described the robbers as a white woman and a black man who left the scene in a yellow car. The prosecution conjectured that 1 in 10 cars is yellow, and that 1 in 1,000 couples inter-racial. Thus the jury was given the figure of 10,000 to 1 odds the defendants were guilty.

In *Collins*, the underlying statistics were wholly conjectural. Moreover, they were based on one witness's possibly faulty observation or recall. Fearing the jury might have seized on the 1 in 10,000 figure to convict, the California Supreme Court reversed the trial court. *See generally* G. Lilly, *An Introduction to the Law of Evidence*, 496-99 (1987).

Although we recognize the dangers inherent in evidence of probabilities, we do not find them in this case. Blood type and enzyme tests have general scientific acceptance, and the distribution of particular blood traits in the population is ascertainable. The party seeking to impeach blood test evidence is free to cross-examine the proponent's experts and offer experts of his own to discredit the conduct of the tests and the underlying statistical probabilities. That was done in this case.

B. Voice Identification

The prosecution offered a voice identification of the defendant by the second victim, which the trial court admitted. Before he was charged, the defendant was answering polygraph questions inside a room at the police barracks. An officer led the second victim to the door, out of sight of the defendant, and asked if she recognized any voices. Of the two she heard, the victim identified one as the assailant's. It was Mr. Woodall's voice.

The factors we consider in admitting any out-of-court identification are outlined in *State v. Casdorph*, 159 W.Va. 909, 230 S.E.2d 476 (1976). The touchstone is the reliability of the identification, considering the length of time since the crime, the level of certainty given by the victim, the opportunity during the crime to observe the trait in question, and the degree of attention to the trait during the crime. Id. 230 S.E.2d 481; *Neil v. Biggers*, 409 U.S. 188, 93 S. Ct. 375, 34 L. Ed. 2d 401 (1972). Voice identifications as such are accepted in this jurisdiction. *State v. Hutchinson*, ___ W.Va. ___, 342 S.E.2d 138 (1986). In this case, the Casdorph factors suggest the identification's reliability, even if the procedure could be called "suggestive." The victim was quite certain of her identification, based on vivid memory of the assailant's voice, just nine days after the attack. The trial judge properly admitted the out-of-court voice identification.

C. Visual Identification

The second victim testified that after she made the voice identification, she made a partial visual identification of the defendant. The police sergeant had her observe while several men, Mr. Woodall among them, entered an adjoining room. Victim two was asked to watch for anything familiar about the man. Mr. Woodall entered and sat in the adjoining room. The victim had a clear view from behind him. She told the policeman that Mr. Woodall "fit the man perfect . . . from the shoulders down." She also said the boots Mr. Woodall wore resembled the assailant's. Defense counsel made no objection to this testimony when offered and did not ask about it on cross-examination.

After cross-examining the victim, the defense moved to strike the visual identification. Counsel agreed to accept a cautionary instruction. This was given. Whatever objection the defendant might have had to the out-of-court identification, if the objection had been voiced, was cured by the agreed-on cautionary instruction. We find no reversible error.

IV.

The defendant raises several constitutional claims, which we consider in turn.

A. Kidnapping and Rape

Mr. Woodall argues that separate convictions for kidnapping and rape arising out of the same incident violate his right not to be subjected to double jeopardy. As this Court held in *State v. Trail*, ___ W.Va. ___, 328 S.E.2d 671 (1985), abduction and sexual assault are separate and distinct offenses. *W.Va. Code*, 61-8B-3 [1984] and 61-2-14a [1965]. But, as this Court held in Syl. Pt. 2, *State v. Miller*, ___ W.Va. ___, 336 S.E.2d 910 (1985):

> The general rule is that a kidnapping has not been committed when incidental to another crime. In deciding whether the acts that technically constitute kidnapping were incidental to another crime, courts examine the length of time the victim was held or moved, the distance the victim was forced to move, the location and environment of the place the victim was detained, and the exposure of the victim to an increased risk of harm.

The kidnapping charges in this case were not merely incidental to the sexual assault charge. The abductions each lasted over half an hour; each victim was driven some miles from the place of abduction, to a more deserted place; and the victims' physical danger was substantially enhanced. These are harms to be protected against by the kidnapping statute, independent of the particular harm victims might suffer during the abduction.

B. *Multiple Courts*

Similarly, the defendant claims that his double jeopardy rights were violated by conviction of the separate counts of sexual assault based on repeated violations of the victims within a relatively short period. The *Code* defines sexual assault so that each violation of the victim is a separate criminal offense. *W.Va. Code*, 61-8B-1 [1986]; *State v. Carter*, 168 W.Va. 90, 282 S.E.2d 277 (1981). But as this Court held in *State v. Davis*, ____ W.Va. ____, 376 S.E.2d 563 (1988), there must be some evidence of the time that elapsed between separate violations charged as distinct counts of sexual assault. The victims' testimony made a sufficient showing of elapsed time between separate acts, and we find no error in allowing the several counts to go to the jury.

C. *Cruel and Unusual Punishment*

The defendant claims that the sentences imposed in this case—totalling two life sentences without parole and a maximum of 335 years, to be served consecutively—constitute cruel and unusual punishment under the Eighth Amendment to the *U.S. Constitution*. We do not agree. "The appellate court decides only whether the sentence under review is within constitutional limits." *Solem v. Helm*, 463 U.S. 277, 290 n. 16, 103 S. Ct. 3001, 3009 n. 16, 77 L. Ed. 2d 637 (1983). Although a death sentence for the crime of rape does violate the protection against cruel and unusual punishment, *Coker v. Georgia*, 433 U.S. 584, 97 S. Ct. 2861, 53 L. Ed. 2d 982 (1977), any sentences short of that, including life without parole, for serious crimes against the person, passes constitutional muster. See *Rummel v. Estelle*, 445 U.S. 263, 100 S. Ct. 1133, 63 L. Ed. 2d 382 (1980); cf. *Solem v. Helm*, 463 U.S. 277, 103 S. Ct. 3001, 77 L. Ed. 2d 637 (1983). Thus, the sentences the defendant received did not constitute cruel or unusual punishment.

D. *Unanimous Jury Verdict*

Appellant contends his right to a unanimous jury verdict was violated in this case. *W.Va. Const.*, art. III, §14 [1872]. Specifically, appellant claims there is no way to tell if the jury was unanimous in finding each element of each count charged, beyond reasonable doubt. See *In re Winship*, 397 U.S. 358, 90 S. Ct. 1068, 25 L. Ed. 2d 368 (1970); Jeffries and Stephan, "Defenses, Presumptions, and Burden of Proof in the Criminal Law," 88 *Yale L.J.* 1325 (1979).

The charges in the indictment went to the jury in general form. They were not directly linked to the victim's testimony. Counts I through VII, for example, read identically. The victims were not asked on the stand, for example, "So when he sodomized you in the back seat, after he had raped you twice, that would be Count 3 of the State's indictment?" (showing her the document). The jury had to recall the testimony of numerous violations, and itself connect the account of each assault with one of the numerous charges in the indictment. The defendant seems to argue here that the testimony had to come in the form we described hypothetically above. We find this claim without merit.

The usual instructions on the prosecution's burden of proof were given exhaustively. The defendant might have requested a more specific instruction that the state must meet its burden as to each specific element of each distinct count. Such a request was not made. For that reason, and not finding plain error, we reject the claim.

E. Jury Misconduct

At trial there was a charge of jury misconduct. The jury were taking lunch in a public restaurant, and were overheard discussing the case among themselves. The trial court had instructed them not to do so. The conversation had something to do with laughter during the trial. On hearing the charge, the trial judge interviewed the jurors involved, *in camera*, admonished them, and received their assurance they could and would determine the facts fairly, in accordance with the evidence and the law. This procedure has been held sufficient to meet the constitutional guarantee of a fair trial. *Smith v. Phillips*, 455 U.S. 209, 102 S. Ct. 940, 71 L. Ed. 2d 78 (1982) (defendant must show actual prejudice). The judge refused a mistrial. We find no prejudicial error in these events.

A perfect trial is a *rara avis*; accordingly, the law of prejudicial jury misconduct is amorphous. There are several policies to be protected: That the jury receives no evidence beyond the courtroom; that no jury member make up his mind before hearing all evidence and the law; and that the court and the jury system not appear unfair. The first is a right personal to the defendant, the second partially so, and the third not at all. *See generally Smith v. Phillips, supra*; Crump, "Jury Misconduct, Jury Interviews, and the Federal Rules of Evidence," 66 *N.C.L. Rev.* 509, 534 (1988); Comment, "Smith v. Phillips: Misconduct by or Affecting a Juror in a Criminal Prosecution," 62 *B.U.L. Rev.* 361 (1982).

When an outsider speaks to a juror, we are most concerned, because inadmissible testimony might be received. Jury discussion among themselves, however, are less troublesome, because they have heard the same evidence in court and remain free to weigh and argue when they later retire to reach a verdict. We find no reversible error.

V.

The defendant claims that he was entitled to a directed verdict on the ground that the circumstantial evidence against him was insufficient as a matter of law to support the charges against him. It is well settled in this State that circumstantial evidence fairly pointing to the defendant will support a conviction. If the evidence "concurs in pointing to the accused as the perpetrator of the crime, he may properly be convicted." Syl. Pt. 4, *State v. Phillips*, ____ W.Va. ____, 342 S.E.2d 210 (1986).

VI.

The defendant objected to the admission of evidence of flight. After a search of the defendant's house and work place in Huntington, the police told the defendant he was not yet under arrest. The police also told the defendant that a search warrant would soon issue to take samples of the defendant's hair. After speaking with his lawyer, the defendant left Huntington with his wife. On the road to nearby Ohio, police set up a roadblock to keep the defendant from leaving the state. Mr. Woodall was arrested at the bridge to Ohio.

At a pretrial hearing, the trial judge decided not to admit the evidence. During trial, the judge reconsidered and admitted the evidence. As this Court held in Syl. Pt. 6, *State v. Payne*, 167 W.Va. 252, 280 S.E.2d 72 (1981), "In certain circumstances evidence of the flight of the defendant will be admissible in a criminal trial as evidence of the defendant's guilty conscience or knowledge." The trial court gave a cautionary instruction to the jury about the possible prejudice in such testimony. We cannot say that the trial judge abused his discretion in finding that the evidence was more probative than prejudicial. *W.Va. R. Evid.*, Rule 403 [1985].

VII.

At trial, the court struck the testimony of three surrebuttal witnesses offered by the defense. Because beard hair had been found at the scene of the crime, in the first victim's car, the defense sought to prove that the defendant, usually bearded, was clean-shaven at the time of the crimes. Although fully aware that the state would present rebuttal testimony to show that the defendant did have a beard at the time in question, the defense rested without calling its witnesses. Because this opportunity had been refused by the defense in its case in chief, the trial court struck the surrebuttal testimony.

This Court stated in Syl. Pt. 4 of *State v. Massey*, ____ W.Va. ____, 359 S.E.2d 865 (1983). "The admissibility of evidence as rebuttal is within the sound discretion of the trial court, and the exercise of such discretion does not constitute ground for reversal unless it is prejudicial to the defendant." The point that the defendant did not have a beard at the time of the crime was covered in the defendant's case-in-chief, and because the defense had ample opportunity to call additional witnesses, we find no prejudice and no abuse of discretion here.

VIII.

We do find that conviction under five of the nineteen counts must be reversed. Counts XI and XV of the indictment charged the defendant with first-degree sexual assault of the second victim (on 14 February 1987). A conviction for first-degree sexual assault requires proof of non-consensual sexual intercourse when *serious bodily* injury is inflicted or when the defendant "employs a deadly weapon in the commission of the act." *W.Va. Code*, 61-8B-3 [1984]. The prosecution's theory was that the assailant used a knife in both attacks to threaten the victims. The charge was well supported in the case of the first victim. But for the second victim, there was no evidence that a knife was used to threaten the victim or evidence that the defendant had about his person a *deadly* weapon. Although there was some evidence that the victim's bra was cut, this was insufficient evidence from which the jury could have found that the defendant "employed" a deadly weapon. The jury thus should not, as to the second victim, have been instructed on sexual assault in the first degree. A charge of sexual assault in the *second* degree requires no showing of an injury or a weapon, and thus the jury could have convicted the defendant on five counts of that offense. The error was prejudicial, and requires reversal of those counts.

CONCLUSION

The defendant's convictions under Counts I through X and Counts XVI through XIX are affirmed; his convictions under Counts XI through XV are reversed. This case is remanded for a new order sentencing the defendant on the counts that have been affirmed and, in the discretion of the prosecution, for a new trial on Counts XI through XV for second degree sexual assault.

Affirmed in part; Reversed in part; and Remanded.

UNITED STATES v. PICCINONNA

885 F.2d 1529 (11th Cir. 1989)

FAY, Circuit Judge:

In this case, we revisit the issue of the admissibility at trial of polygraph expert testimony and examination evidence. Julio Piccinonna appeals his conviction on two counts of knowingly making false material statements to a Grand Jury in violation of Title IV of the Organized

Crime Control Act of 1970. 18 U.S.C. 1623 (1982). Piccinonna argues that the trial judge erred in refusing to admit the testimony of his polygraph expert and the examination results. Because of the significant progress made in the field of polygraph testing over the past forty years and its increasingly widespread use, we reexamine our per se rule of exclusion and fashion new principles to govern the admissibility of polygraph evidence. Accordingly, we remand the case to the trial court to reconsider the admissibility of the principles we espouse today.

I. Background

Julio Piccinonna has been in the waste disposal business in South Florida for over twenty-five years. In 1983, a Grand Jury conducted hearings to investigate antitrust violations in the garbage business. The government believed that South Florida firms in the waste disposal business had agreed not to compete for each other's accounts, and to compensate one another when one firm did not adhere to the agreement and took an account from another firm.

Piccinonna was compelled to testify before the Grand Jury pursuant to a grant of immunity. The immunity, however, did not protect Piccinonna from prosecution for perjury committed during his testimony. Piccinonna testified that he had not heard of the agreement between garbage companies to refrain from soliciting each other's accounts and to compensate each other for taking accounts. The Grand Jury, however, also heard testimony from several witnesses involved in the disposal industry who implicated Piccinonna in the garbage industry agreement. On August 1, 1985, Piccinonna was indicted on four counts of perjury.

Prior to trial, Piccinonna requested that the Government stipulate to the admission into evidence of the results of a polygraph test which would be administered subsequently. The Government refused to stipulate to the admission of any testimony regarding the polygraph test or its results. Despite the Government's refusal, George B. Slattery, a licensed polygraph examiner, tested Piccinonna on November 25, 1985. Piccinonna asserted that the expert's report left no doubt that he did not lie when he testified before the Grand Jury. (R1-38-2.) On November 27, 1985, Piccinonna filed a motion with the district court requesting a hearing on the admission of the polygraph testimony.1 On January 6, 1986, the district court held a hearing on the defendant's motions. Due to the per se rule, which holds polygraph evidence inadmissible in this circuit, the trial judge refused to admit the evidence. The judge noted, however, that the Eleventh Circuit may wish to reconsider the issue of the admissibility of polygraph evidence since these tests have become more widely used, particularly by the Government. Hence, the judge stated that if Piccinonna was convicted, the court would conduct a post-trial hearing to perfect the record for appeal.

Piccinonna was convicted on two counts of making false material declarations concerning a matter the Grand Jury was investigating. The court then conducted a hearing to perfect the record for appeal. At the hearing, the judge ordered the report of the polygraph examination and the complete transcript of the evidentiary hearing conducted in *United States v. Irwin Freedman*, No. 81-434-Cr-ARONOVOTZ to become part of the record. On appeal, Piccinonna urges us to modify our per se rule excluding polygraph evidence to permit its admission in certain circumstances.

II. The Per Se Rule

In federal courts, the admissibility of expert testimony concerning scientific tests or findings is governed by Rule 702 of the Federal Rules of Evidence. Rule 702 provides:

> If scientific, technical, or other specialized knowledge will assist the trier of fact to understand the evidence or to determine a fact in issue, a witness qualified as an expert by knowledge, skill, experience, training or education, may testify thereto in the form of an opinion or otherwise.

Under this rule, to admit expert testimony the trial judge must determine that the expert testimony will be relevant and will be helpful to the trier of fact. In addition, courts require the proponent of the testimony to show that the principle or technique is generally accepted in the scientific community. McCormick, *McCormick on Evidence* § 203 (3rd ed. 1984).

The general acceptance requirement originated in the 1923 case of *Frye v. United States*, 293 F. 1013 (D.C. Cir. 1923). *Frye* involved a murder prosecution in which the trial court refused to admit results from a systolic blood pressure test, the precursor of the polygraph. The defendant appealed, arguing that the admissibility of the scientific test results should turn only on the traditional rules of relevancy and helpfulness to the trier of fact. The court of appeals disagreed and imposed the requirement that the area of specialty in which the court receives evidence must have achieved general acceptance in the scientific community. *Id.* 293 F. at 1014. The court stated that "while courts will go a long way in admitting expert testimony deduced from a well-recognized scientific principle or discovery, the thing from which the deduction is made must be sufficiently established to have gained general acceptance in the particular field in which it belongs." *Id.* The court concluded that the systolic blood pressure test lacked the requisite "standing and scientific recognition among physiological and psychological authorities." *Id.*

Courts have applied the *Frye* standard to various types of scientific tests, including the polygraph. However, the *Frye* standard has historically been invoked only selectively to other types of expert testimony, and has been applied consistently only in cases where the admissibility of polygraph evidence was at issue. *See* Mc-Cormick, *Scientific Evidence: Defining a New Approach to Admissibility* 67 Iowa L. Rev. 879, 884 (1982). Most courts had little difficulty with the desirability of excluding polygraph evidence and thus, applied the *Frye* standard with little comment. *Id.* at 885. This circuit also has consistently reaffirmed, with little discussion, the inadmissibility of polygraph evidence. *United States v. Hilton*, 772 F.2d 783, 785 (11th Cir. 1985); *United States v. Rodriguez*, 765 F.2d 1546, 1558 (11th Cir. 1985); cf. *United States v. Beck*, 729 F.2d 1329, 1332 (11th Cir.) (court implied that polygraph evidence may be admissible when the parties stipulate to its admissibility), *cert. denied*, 469 U.S. 981, 105 S. Ct. 383, 83 L. Ed. 2d 318 (1984). Our position was derived from former Fifth Circuit precedent excluding polygraph evidence, which we adopted as law in this circuit. *Bonner v. City of Prichard*, 661 F.2d 1206, 1207 (11th Cir. 1981).

Recently, the application of the *Frye* standard to exclude polygraph evidence has been subject to growing criticism. Since the *Frye* decision, tremendous advances have been made in polygraph instrumentation and technique. Better equipment is being used by more adequately trained polygraph administrators. Further, polygraph tests are used extensively by government agencies. Field investigative agencies such as the FBI, the Secret Service, military intelligence and law enforcement agencies using the polygraph. Thus, even under a strict adherence to the traditional *Frye* standard, we believe it is no longer accurate to state categorically that polygraph testing lacks general acceptance for use in all circumstances. For this reason, we find it appropriate to reexamine the per se exclusionary rule and institute a rule more in keeping with the progress made in the polygraph field.

III. Differing Approaches to Polygraph Admissibility

Courts excluding polygraph evidence typically rely on three grounds: 1) the unreliability of the polygraph test, 2) the lack of standardization of polygraph procedure, and 3) undue impact on the jury. Proponents of admitting polygraph evidence have attempted to rebut these concerns. With regard to unreliability, proponents stress the significant advances made in the field of polygraphy. Professor McCormick argues that the fears of unreliability "are not sufficient to warrant a rigid exclusionary rule. A great deal of lay testimony routinely admitted is at least as unreliable and inaccurate, and other forms of scientific evidence involve risks of instrumental or judgmental error." McCormick, *supra*, § 206 at 629. Further, proponents argue that the lack of standardization is being addressed and will progressively be resolved as the polygraph establishes itself as a valid scientific test. Sevilla, *Polygraph 1984: Behind the Closed Door of Ad-*

missibility, 16 U. West L.A. L. Rev. 5, 19 (1984). Finally, proponents argue that there is no evidence that jurors are unduly influenced by polygraph evidence. In fact, several studies refute the proposition that jurors are likely to give disproportionate weight to polygraph evidence.

In the wake of new empirical evidence and scholarly opinion which have undercut many of the traditional arguments against admission of polygraph evidence, a substantial number of courts have revisited the admissibility question. Three roughly identifiable approaches to the problem have emerged. First, the traditional approach holds polygraph evidence inadmissible when offered by either party, either as substantive evidence or as relating to the credibility of a witness. McCormick, *supra*, section 206 at 628. Second, a significant number of jurisdictions permit the trial court, in its discretion, to receive polygraph evidence if the parties stipulate to the evidence's admissibility before the administration of the test and if certain other conditions are met. Finally, some courts permit the trial judge to admit polygraph evidence in the absence of a stipulation, but only when special circumstances exist. In these jurisdictions, the issue is within the sound discretion of the trial judge.

Relying on the typical grounds to exclude polygraph evidence, the Fourth, Fifth and District of Columbia Circuits historically have adhered to the traditional approach of per se inadmissibility. *United States v. Bre-*

vard, 739 F.2d 180 (4th Cir. 1984); *United States v. Clark*, 598 F.2d 994, 995 (5th Cir. 1979), vacated *en banc* 622 F.2d 917 (1980), *cert. denied*, 449 U.S. 1128, 101 S. Ct. 949, 67 L. Ed. 2d 116 (1981); *United States v. Skeens*, 494 F.2d 1050, 1053 (D.C. Cir. 1974). While these circuits have sometimes hinted at the possibility of adopting a more liberal approach, they have consistently returned to per se inadmissibility. *See e.g. United States v. Webster*, 639 F.2d 174, 186 (4th Cir.) (admissibility of polygraph evidence can be within the discretionary powers of trial judge), *cert. denied, Christian v. United States* (1981), *modified in other respects* 669 F.2d 185 (4th Cir.), *cert. denied*, 456 U.S. 935, 102 S. Ct. 1991, 72 L. Ed. 2d 455 (1982); *United States v. Brevard*, 739 F.2d 180 (4th Cir. 1984) (per se inadmissible); *United States v. Clark*, 622 F.2d 917, 917 (5th Cir. 1980) (twelve concurring judges agreed that the per se rule should be reconsidered), *cert. denied*, 449 U.S. 1128, 101 S. Ct. 949, 67 L. Ed. 2d 116 (1981); *Tyler v. United States*, 193 F.2d 24 (D.C. Cir. 1951), *cert. denied*, 343 U.S. 908, 72 S. Ct. 639, 96 L. Ed. 1326 (1952) (not error for trial court to admit polygrapher's testimony for purpose of deciding whether the defendant's confession was voluntary); *United States v. Skeens*, 494 F.2d at 1053 (D.C. Cir. 1974) (polygraph evidence per se inadmissible).

The Eighth Circuit has developed a more liberal approach which allows admission of polygraph evidence only when the parties stipulate. *Anderson v. United States*, 788 F.2d 517, 519 (8th Cir. 1986); *United States v. Alexander*, 526 f.2d 161, 166 (8th Cir. 1975). However, another line of Eighth Circuit cases appears to be more permissive in allowing the introduction of polygraph evidence. *United States v. Yeo*, 739 F.2d 385, 388 (8th Cir. 1984); *United States v. Oliver*, 525 F.2d 731, 736 (8th Cir. 1975) (a discretionary rather than a per se exclusionary rule is appropriate). Hence, while the Eighth Circuit falls within the second category, it appears to be leaning toward greater admissibility of polygraph evidence.

Finally, the Third, Sixth, Seventh, Ninth and Tenth Circuits, and the Court of Military Appeals permit admission of polygraph evidence even in the absence of a stipulation when special circumstances exist. The Third and Seventh Circuits permit polygraph evidence to be introduced for the purpose of rebutting a claim by the defendant that his confession was the result of coercion. *United States v. Johnson*, 816 F.2d 918, 923 (3rd Cir. 1987); *United States v. Kampiles*, 609 F.2d 1233, 1245 (7th Cir. 1979), *cert. denied*, 446 U.S. 954, 100 S. Ct. 2923, 64 L. Ed. 2d 812 (1980). The Tenth Circuit has permitted the government to introduce the fact that the defendant failed a polygraph test to explain why the police detective had not conducted a more thorough investigation. *United States v. Hall*, 805 F.2d 1410 (10th Cir. 1986). In its attempt to mitigate the potential problems with polygraph evidence, the Sixth Circuit

has promulgated a two-step approach to admission. *Wolfel v. Holbrook*, 823 F.2d 970 (6th Cir. 1987), *cert. denied*, ___ U.S. ___, 108 S. Ct. 1035, 98 L. Ed. 2d 999 (1988) "First, the trial court must determine if the proffered evidence is relevant. Second, if the court concludes that the proffered evidence is relevant, it must balance the probative value of the evidence against the hazard of unfair prejudice and/or confusion which could mislead the jury." Id. at 972. The Ninth Circuit holds polygraph evidence admissible only in instances narrowly tailored to limit the prejudicial impact of the evidence. *United States v. Miller*, 874 F.2d 1255, 1262 (9th Cir. 1989). The *Miller* court, in considering prior Ninth Circuit cases on this issue, noted that polygraph evidence might be admissible if it is "introduced for a limited purpose that is unrelated to the substantive correctness of the results of the polygraph examination." Id. at 1261. In *United States v. Bowen*, 857 F.2d 1337, 1341 (9th Cir. 1988), the court held that if "the polygraph evidence is being introduced because it is relevant that a polygraph examination was given, regardless of the result, then it may be admissible . . ."

The common thread running through the various approaches taken by courts which have modified the per se rule is a recognition that while wholesale exclusion under rule 702 is unwarranted, there must be carefully constructed limitations placed upon the use of polygraph evidence in court. Absent a stipulation by the parties, we are unable to locate any case in which a court has allowed polygraph expert testimony offered as substantive proof of the truth or falsity of the statements made during the polygraph examination. The myriad of "special circumstances" and conditions that have been held to constitute appropriate scenarios for use of polygraph evidence are necessarily rough estimates by the courts of when and where the danger of unfair prejudice due to the admission of the evidence is least significant.

IV. Principles for Admissibility

There is no question that in recent years polygraph testing has gained increasingly widespread acceptance as a useful and reliable scientific tool. Because of the advances that have been achieved in the field which have led to the greater use of polygraph examination, coupled with a lack of evidence that juries are unduly swayed by polygraph evidence, we agree with those courts which have found that a per se rule disallowing polygraph evidence is no longer warranted. Of course, polygraphy is a developing and inexact science, and we continue to believe it inappropriate to allow the admission of polygraph evidence in all situations in which more proven types of expert testimony are allowed. However, as Justice Potter Stewart wrote, "any rule that impedes the discovery of truth in a court of law impedes as well the doing of justice." *Hawkins v. United States*, 358 U.S. 74, 81, 79 S. Ct. 136, 140, 3 L. Ed. 2d 125 (1958)

(concurring). Thus, we believe the best approach in this area is one which balances the need to admit all relevant and reliable evidence against the danger that the admission of the evidence for a given purpose will be unfairly prejudicial. Accordingly we outline two instances where polygraph evidence may be admitted at trial, which we believe achieve the necessary balance.

A. Stipulation

The first rule governing admissibility of polygraph evidence is one easily applied. Polygraph expert testimony will be admissible in this circuit when both parties stipulate in advance as to the circumstances of the test and as to the scope of its admissibility. The stipulation as to circumstances must indicate that the parties agree on material matters such as the manner in which the test is conducted, the nature of the questions asked, and the identity of the examiner administering the test. The stipulation as to the scope of admissibility must indicate the purpose or purposes for which the evidence will be introduced. Where the parties agree to both of these conditions in advance of the polygraph test, evidence of the test results is admissible.

B. Impeachment or Corroboration

The second situation in which polygraph evidence may be admitted is when used to impeach or corroborate the testimony of a witness at trial. Admission of polygraph evidence for these purposes is subject to three preliminary conditions. First, the party planning to use the evidence at trial must provide adequate notice to the opposing party that the expert testimony will be admissible only if the opposing party was given reasonable opportunity to have its own polygraph expert administer a test covering substantially the same questions. Failure to provide adequate notice or reasonable opportunity for the opposing side to administer its own test is proper grounds for exclusion of the evidence.

Finally, whether used to corroborate or impeach the admissibility of the polygraph administrator's testimony will be governed by the Federal Rules of Evidence for the admissibility of corroboration or impeachment testimony. For example, Rule 608 limits the use of opinion or reputation evidence to establish the credibility of a witness in the following way: "[E]vidence of truthful character is admissible only after the character of the witness for truthfulness has been attacked by opinion or reputation evidence or otherwise." Thus, evidence that a witness passed a polygraph examination, used to corroborate that witness's in-court testimony, would not be admissible under Rule 608 unless or until the credibility of that witness were first attacked. Even where the above three conditions are met, admission of polygraph evidence for impeachment or corroboration purposes is left entirely to the discretion of the trial judge.

Neither of these two modifications to the per se exclusionary rule should be construed to preempt or limit in any way the trial court's discretion to exclude polygraph expert testimony on other grounds under the Federal Rules of Evidence. Our holding states merely that in the limited circumstances delineated above, the *Frye* general acceptance test does not act as a bar to admission of polygraph evidence as a matter of law. As we have stated, the chief criterion in determining whether expert testimony is appropriate is whether it will help the trier of fact to resolve the issues. Fed. R. Evid. 702; Worsham v. A.H. Robins Co., 734 F.2d 676, 685 (11th Cir. 1984). The expert testimony must also, of course, be relevant. Fed. R. Evid. 401; United States v. Roark, 753 F.2d 991, 994 (11th Cir. 1985). Rule 401 defines relevant evidence as evidence "having any tendency to make the existence of any fact that is of consequence to the determination of the action more probable or less probable than it would be without the evidence." Further, Rule 403 states that even though relevant, evidence may be excluded by the trial court "if its probative value is substantially outweighed by the danger of unfair prejudice, confusion of the issues, or misleading the jury, or by consideration of undue delay, waste of time, or needless presentation of cumulative evidence." Thus, we agree with the Ninth Circuit "that polygraph evidence should not be admitted, even for limited purposes, unless the trial court has determined that "the probative value of the polygraph evidence outweighs the potential prejudice and time consumption involved in presenting such evidence.' " *United States v. Miller*, 874 F.2d 1255 (95th Cir. 1989) (*quoting Brown v. Darcy*, 783 F.2d 1389, 1397 n. 14 (9th Cir. 1986)).

Thus under the Federal Rules of Evidence governing the admissibility of expert testimony, the trial court may exclude polygraph expert testimony because 1) the polygraph examiner's qualifications are unacceptable; 2) the test procedure was unfairly prejudicial or the test was poorly administered; or 3) the questions were irrelevant or improper. The trial judge has wide discretion in this area, and rulings on admissibility will not be reversed unless a clear abuse of discretion is shown. *Worsham*, 734 F.2d at 686.

V. Conclusion

We neither expect nor hope that today's holding will be the final word within our circuit on this increasingly important issue. The advent of new and developing technologies calls for flexibility within the legal system so that the ultimate ends of justice may be served. It is unwise to hold fast to a familiar rule when the basis for that rule ceases to be persuasive. We believe that the science of polygraphy has progressed to a level of acceptance sufficient to allow the use of polygraph evidence in limited circumstances where the danger of unfair prejudice is minimized. We proceed

with caution in this area because the reliability of polygraph testing remains a subject of intense scholarly debate. As the field of polygraph testing continues to progress, it may become necessary to reexamine the rules regarding the admissibility of polygraph evidence.

The judgment of conviction is VACATED and the case is REMANDED to the district court for further proceedings consistent with this opinion.

JOHNSON, Circuit Judge, concurring in part and dissenting in part, in which RONEY, Chief Judge, HILL and CLARK, Circuit Court Judges, join:

I concur with the Court's holding that polygraph evidence should be admissible in this Circuit when both parties stipulate in advance to the circumstances of the test and to the scope of its admissibility, subject to the understanding that such stipulations may be accepted or rejected by the trial judge at his discretion. I dissent, however, from the Court's finding that the polygraph has gained acceptance in the scientific community as a reliable instrument for detecting lies, and from the Court's holding that polygraph evidence is admissible under Fed. R. Evid. 608.

I. POLYGRAPH THEORY

A. *Introduction*

The Court's reasoning begins with the proposition that polygraph technology has reached the point where its accuracy is generally accepted by the scientific community. In fact, the scientific community remains sharply divided on the reliability of the polygraph. U.S. Congress, Office of Technology Assessment, *Scientific Validity of Polygraph Testing: A Research Review and Evaluation—A Technical Memorandum* 43 (1983) [herinafter *OTA Memorandum*] Many theorists question the basic assumptions underlying the polygraph: that telling lies is stressful, and that this stress manifests itself in physiological responses which can be recorded on a polygraph. *See* Ney, *Expressing Emotions and Controlling Feelings, in The Polygraph Test: Lies, Truth and Science* 65 (A. Gale ed. 1988) [hereinafter *The Polygraph Test*]; *Employee Polygraph Protection Act: Hearing on H.R. 208 Before the Education and Labor Comm.*, 100th Cong., 1st Sess. 51 (1987) (testimony of John F. Beary, III, M.D. on behalf of the American Medical Association) [hereinafter *H.R. Hearing*]. Moreover, Congress has sharply limited the use of the polygraph in the private sector. Employee Polygraph Protection Act of 1988, P.L. 100-347, 102 Stat. 646 (codified at 29 U.S.C.A. § 2001 (West. Supp. 1989)).

The polygraph records the subject's physiological activities (e.g., heart rate, blood pressure, respiration, and perspiration) as he is questioned by a polygraph examiner. Bull, *What is the Lie Detection Test? in The Polygraph Test* 11-12. There are two major types of polygraph examinations: the "control question test" and the "concealed information test." The control question test is used most frequently in investigating specific incidents. The examiner compares the data corresponding to (a) questions relevant to the crime (b) "control" questions designed to upset the subject but not directly relevant to the crime, and (c) neutral questions. If the subject reacts more strongly to the relevant questions than to the control and neutral questions, then the examiner infers that the subject is lying. *Id.* at 13-17. There is much debate about the accuracy of control question tests in specific-incident investigations. Raskin, *Does Science Support Polygraph Testing, in The Polygraph Test* 98-99.

The concealed information test focuses on the fact that only the person involved in the crime could know the answers to certain questions. The examiner presents a series of multiple choice questions concerning the crime while the polygraph machine records the subject's physiological activities. If the subject has relatively strong physiological reactions to the correct alternatives, then the examiner infers that the subject is attempting to conceal information about the crime. *Id.* at 102. The concealed information about the crime is protected, but in fact police inform all suspects and even the media about the crime. *Id.*

B. The Polygraph Is Based On Questionable Assumptions

Lie detection is based on four assumptions: (1) that individuals cannot control their physiologies and behavior, (2) that specific emotions can be triggered by specific stimuli, (3) that there are specific relationships between the different aspects of behavior (such as what people say, how they behave, and how they respond physiologically), and (4) that there are no differences among people, so that most people will respond similarly.

The assumption that individuals cannot control their physiologies is subject to serious debate. Some theorists argue that individuals can learn to control their physiological responses and that by producing physiological responses at opportune times during the polygraph test these people could portray themselves as truthful when they are not. Ney, *Expressing Emotions and Controlling Feelings* at 67 ("Jet-fighter pilots learn to control their emotions (and therefore their physiology) in order to operate with maximum efficiency under extreme physical and psychological stress.") These techniques for fooling the polygraph are called countermeasures. Gudjonsson, *How to Defeat the Polygraph Tests in The Polygraph Test* 126. Little research has been done on the effectiveness of countermeasures in reducing detection of lies, but the results of research that has been done, while conflicting, indicate that countermeasures can be effective. *OTA Memorandum* at 100-01; Gudjonsson, *How to Defeat the Polygraph Tests* at 135 (concluding that use of physical countermeasures (e.g., pressing toes to floor) is effective when the subject has been trained in countermeasures).

Another assumption underlying the polygraph is that specific emotions will be triggered by the act of lying. Some theorists, however, do not believe that emotions are automatically triggered by the presence of such specific stimuli. These theorists see a more direct causal chain between stimuli and emotion: a person is presented with stimuli, then appraises it, and only then reacts with an emotion, which is based on the person's cognitive appraisal of the stimuli. According to this theory, people can adjust their thinking to "reappraise" the stressful stimuli and create a different emotional reaction than one might expect. Ney, *Expressing Emotions and Controlling Feelings* 68 ("tell the truth and think of something painful and the truth may appear on the polygraph as a lie") Of course, there would be no way for an examiner to determine how the subject is appraising the stimuli in his mind.

The third assumption underlying the polygraph is that there are set patterns of physiological responses that reflect dishonesty: changed blood pressure, heart rate, respiration and perspiration. There is controversy over this proposition in the scientific community. *Id.* at 70; *H.R. Hearing* at 51 (statement of John F. Beary, III, M.D.) ("there is no Pinocchio response. If you lie your nose does not grow a half inch longer or some other unique bodily response.")

The fourth assumption underlying the lie detector is that people can be expected to respond to similar stimuli in similar ways. Some researchers maintain, however, that individuals do not respond to stress similarly and that no one index can be used to measure emotions in different individuals. Ney, *Expressing Emotions and Controlling Feelings* at 71-72; Gudjonsson, *How to Defeat the Polygraph Tests* 135.

C. Appellant's Statistics Are Misleading

Piccinonna claims that "the relevant scientific community" estimates the accuracy of the polygraph to be in the upper-eighty to mid-ninety percent range. *Appellant's En Banc Brief* at 9. This figure is misleading and subject to serious dispute. The polygraph must do two things: correctly identify liars and correctly identify those who are telling the truth. *Employee Polygraph Protection Act: Hearing on S. 185 Before the Senate Committee on Labor and Human Resources*, 100th Cong., 1st Sess. (Appendix to statement of John F. Beary, III, M.D.) (1988) [Hereinafter "*S. Hearing*"]. No single figure, therefore, can fully express the accuracy of the polygraph. The Office of Technology Assessment compiled the results of six prior reviews of polygraph research, ten field studies, and fourteen analog studies that the Office of Technology Assessment determined met minimum scientific standards. All of the studies used the control question technique in specific-incident criminal investigation settings. The results were as follows:

Six prior reviews of field studies:
-average accuracy ranged from 64 to 98 percent.

Ten individual field studies:
-correct guilty detections ranged from 70.6 percent to 98.6 percent and averaged 86.3 percent;

-correct innocent detections ranged from 12.5 to 94.1 percent and averaged 76 percent;

-false positive rate (innocent persons found deceptive) ranged from 0 to 75 percent and averaged 19.1 percent; and

-false negative rate (guilty persons found nondeceptive) ranged from 0 to 29.4 percent and averaged 10.2 percent.

Fourteen individual analog studies:
-correct guilty detections ranged from 35.4 to 100 percent and averaged 63.7 percent;

-correct innocent detections ranged from 32 to 91 percent and averaged 57.9 percent;

-false positives ranged from 2 to 50.7 percent and averaged 14.1 percent; and

-false negatives ranged from 0 to 28.7 percent and averaged 10.4 percent.

OTA Memorandum at 97.; Note that because the question "Is the subject lying?" is a yes or no question, a random method of answering the question (e.g., a coin toss) would be correct 50% of the time. The Memorandum concluded,

> The wide variability of results from both prior research reviews and [The Office of Technology Assessment's] own review of individual studies makes it impossible to determine a specific overall quantitative measure of polygraph validity. The preponderance of research evidence does indicate that, when the control question technique is used in specific-incident criminal investigation, the polygraph detects deception at a rate better than chance, but with error rates that could be considered significant.

Id.

D. Extrinsic Factors Affect Accuracy

A number of extrinsic factors affect polygraph validity. Most important, because the examiner must formulate the questions, supplement the data with his own impression of the subject during the exam, and infer lies from a combination of the data and his impressions, the level of skill and training of the examiner will affect the reliability of the results. S. Rep. No. 284, 100th Cong., 2d Sess. 42, *reprinted in* 1988 U.S. Code Cong. & Admin. News 726, 729 [hereinafter *Senate Report*]; Barland, *The Polygraph in the USA and Elsewhere* in the Polygraph Test 82. Un-

fortunately, there are no uniform standards for the training of polygraph examiners in this country. Senate Report at 43, U.S. Code Cong. & Admin. News at 731; S. Hearing at 27 (statement of Mr. William J. Scheve, Jr., American Polygraph Association); *see* Barland, *The Polygraph in the USA and Elsewhere* at 75 (the American Polygraph Association has accredited over 30 polygraph schools with courses ranging from seven to fourteen weeks).

A quality control system that reviews the examiners' conclusions also affects the validity of polygraph results. The results of most federally administered polygraph exams are checked by quality control officers, who call for reexaminations if the data does not indicate that the examiner's conclusion was correct. Barland, *The Polygraph in the USA and Elsewhere* 87. Few police examiners work within such a system, and almost no private examiners have quality control. *Id.* at 82.

The length of a polygraph exam will also affect the validity of the results. One advocate of the polygraph has stated that an expert polygraph exam would take a minimum of several hours to complete. *Senate Report* at 43, 1988 *U.S. Code Cong. and Admin. News* at 730-31.

II. POLYGRAPH TESTS SHOULD BE EXCLUDED UNDER THE FEDERAL RULES OF EVIDENCE

Under Federal Rule of Evidence 702, expert testimony is proper if the testimony would assist the trier of fact in analyzing the evidence. Fed R. Evid. 702 advisory committee's note (West 1989). Because the polygraph can predict whether a person is lying with accuracy that is only slightly greater than chance, it will be of little help to the trier of fact. Moreover, this slight helpfulness must be weighed against the dangers of unfair prejudice, confusion of the issues and waste of time. Fed. R. Evid. 403. The Ninth Circuit has found that polygraph evidence has an overwhelming potential for prejudicing the jury. *Brown v. Darcy*, 783 F.2d 1389, 1396 (9th Cir. 1986) (citing *United States v. Alexander*, 526 F.2d 161, 168 (8th Cir. 1975)); *see also* Gianelli, *The Admissibility of Novel Scientific Evidence: Frye v. United States, a Half-Century Later*, 80 Colum. L. Rev. 1197, 1237 (1980) ("The major danger of scientific evidence is its potential to mislead the jury; an aura of scientific infallibility may shroud the evidence and thus lead the jury to accept it without critical scrutiny.") The *Brown* court determined that unstipulated polygraph evidence is inadmissible under both Rule 702 and Rule 403. *Brown*, 783 F.2d at 1396 n. 13. The polygraph presents itself as being very scientific. For instance, it is said to measure "galvanic skin response," *Appellant's En Ban Brief* at 10, which merely means that it measure how much a person perspires. Bull, *What is the Lie-Detection Test?* at 11. This scientific aura tends to cloud the fact that the machine's accuracy at detecting lies is little better than chance.

Brown, 783 F.2d at 1396 (quoting *Alexander*, 526 F.2d at 168); *OTA Memorandum* at 97.

The Ninth Circuit also found that admission of polygraph evidence had the potential of confusing the issues and wasting time. *Id.* at 1397; see Fed. R. Evid. 403. In the *Brown* case, for instance, the polygraph evidence consumed one fourth of the entire trial. *Brown*, 783 F.2d at 1397 (two full days of an eight-day trial). Because polygraph evidence is of little help to the trier of fact, and has great potential for prejudicing the trier of fact, confusing the issues and wasting time, it should be excluded under Federal Rule of Evidence 403.

The danger of prejudice, confusion of the issues, and wasting time should also prevent courts from admitting polygraph evidence under Rule 608 for purposes of impeaching a witness. As the Court's opinion correctly states, all offers of polygraph evidence should be analyzed in light of Rule 403. *Cf. United States v. Miller*, 874 F.2d 1255, 1261 (9th Cir. 1989) (even when offered for a limited purpose, polygraph evidence must go through a Rule 403 analysis). To hold that polygraph evidence is admissible under Rule 608 would create too large an exception to the rule barring polygraph evidence generally, and polygraph test results would wind up being admitted into evidence in most cases. Moreover, there is nothing special about the Rule 608 impeachment procedure that lessens the dangers of prejudice and confusion of the issues. *Cf. United States v. Toney*,

615 F.2d 277 (5th Cir. 1980) ("Rule 403 is a general rule, 'designed as a guide for the handling of situations for which no specific rules have been formulated.' ")

III. CONCLUSION

The scientific community remains sharply divided over the issue of the validity of polygraph exams. Although presented as a rigorously "scientific" procedure, the polygraph test in fact relies upon a highly subjective, inexact correlation of physio logical factors having only a debatable relationship to dishonesty as such. The device detects lies at a rate only somewhat better than chance. Polygraph evidence, therefore, should not be admissible under Rule 702 or under Rule 608 to impeach a witness.

In this case, the government did not stipulate to the admissibility of the defendant's polygraph evidence and did not participate in selection of the examiner or the determination of the circumstances of the test. I would therefore AFFIRM the judgment below.

STATE v. TAILO

779 P.2d 11 (Hawaii 1989)

LUM, Chief Justice

Defendant-Appellant Peni Tailo, Jr. (Appellant) appeals from his conviction for driving a motor vehicle in excess of the legal speed limit in violation of Hawaii Revised Statutes (HRS) § 291C-102. The State's evidence consisted of the testimony of a single police officer who relied upon a reading from a K-15 radar speed detection device (K-15 gun) which clocked the speed of Appellant's vehicle at seventy miles per hour in a fifty-five mile per hour zone. The issue on appeal is whether the State must prove the accuracy of the K-15 gun before results of that device are admissible as evidence of a speeding violation. We hold that the officer's testimony at trial that he conducted a tuning fork test which indicated that the K-15 gun was accurately calibrated created a prima facie presumption that the tuning fork was itself accurately calibrated. Finding no merit to Appellant's other contention, we affirm the judgment of conviction.

I.

At trial, the police officer testified that prior to stopping Appellant for speeding he performed two tests to check the accuracy of the radar gun. The first test was an external test whereby the officer verified the K-15 gun's accuracy by striking a tuning fork, which was gauged so as to register a speed reading of 50 m.p.h. when held in front of the gun. The second test performed involved the utilization of an internal calibration unit within the radar device itself. Both tests indicated the K-15 gun was accurately calibrated.

On cross-examination, the officer testified that the K-15 gun was calibrated at the factory and that his methods for testing the gun were designed to determine "whether or not the unit was functioning properly"; "not [to] calibrate the gun" which "has to be done by a technician " Id. at 10. Further, he testified that he did not independently verify the accuracy of the tuning fork to test the accuracy of the K-15 gun.

At the close of the State's case, Appellant moved for a directed verdict on the ground that the State failed to prove that the K-15 gun was accurately calibrated, and hence accurate in determining the speed of his vehicle. The trial court denied the motion and found Appellant guilty as charged.

II.

Appellant contends that the trial court erred by denying his motion for directed verdict. He maintains that the State failed to prove that the K-15 gun accurately determined the speed of his vehicle since no evidence was introduced as to the accuracy of the tuning fork used to test the radar gun.

A.

Although the K-15 radar gun has been in use by the police in this jurisdiction for over a decade, this is the first occasion in which we have addressed the question of the admissibility of radar gun evidence as proof of a speeding violation.

The scientific principles upon which the radar gun is based are well established. The radar gun is a system which transmits a continuous flow of microwaves on a constant frequency which are reflected back whenever they strike a target. When the target is an approaching vehicle, the speed of the vehicle causes the deflected waves to return on a different and higher frequency than those sent out. A phenomena known as the Doppler effect posits that the faster the vehicle is moving into the radar transmissions, the higher the frequency of the reflected waves received by the radar gun. The radar gun measures the difference in the frequencies of the transmitted wave and the received wave, which enables it to use the Doppler effect to calculate the speed of the approaching vehicle. *See* Kopper, *The Scientific Reliability of Radar Speedmeters*, 16 Md. L. Rev. 1 (1956).

Because of the strength of the scientific principles on which the radar gun is based, every recent court which has dealt with the question has taken judicial notice of the scientific reliability of radar speedmeters as recorders of speed. *See State v. Gerdes*, 291 Minn. 353, 191 N.W.2d 428 (1971); *People v. MacLaird*, 264 Cal. App.2d 972, 71 Cal. Rptr. 191 (1968); *State v. Tomenelli*, 153 Con. 365, 216 A.2d 625 (1966); and Annotation, *Proof, by Radar or Other Mechanical or Electronic Devices, of*

Violation of Speed Regulations, 47 A.L.R.3d 822, 831-35 (1973). These courts have also consistently held that evidence of the particular radar unit is necessary to sustain a conviction for speeding obtained solely by radar. *State v. Primm*, 4 Kan. App. 2d 314, 606 P.2d 112 (1980); Annotation, *Proof by Radar or Other Mechanical or Electronic Devices of Violation of Speed Regulations*, 47 A.L.R.2d 822, 837-39 (1973). "The accuracy of a particular radar unit can be established by showing that the operator tested the device in accordance with accepted procedures to determine that the unit was functioning properly and that the operator was qualified by training and experience to operate the unit." *State. v. Spence*, 418 So.2d 583, 588 (La. 1982); *Gerdes*, *supra*; *Primm*, *supra*.

In the instant case, the officer testified that he was formally trained and certified to use the K-15 gun, and that prior to clocking Appellant's vehicle, he swept the target area for interference and received none. The office further testified that he performed an internal calibration test, and an external calibration test involving a tuning fork prior to clocking Appellant's vehicle. Courts have found both methods to be acceptable means of proving radar accuracy. See *People v. Lynch*, 61 Misc.2d 117, 304 N.Y.S.2d 985 (1969); *State v. Primm*, 4 Kan. App. 2d 314, 606 P.2d 112 (1980); *State v. Bechtel*, 24 Ohio App.3d 72, 24 Ohio B.R. 126, 493 N.E.2d 318 (1985); *State v. Shears*, 648 P.2d 841 (Okl. 1982); and *State v. Mills*, 99

Wis.2d 697, 299 N.W.2d 881 (1981). A special tuning fork can be used to check the calibration of the radar gun. The tuning fork is specially tuned to vibrate at a frequency equal to the Doppler frequency for some set speed stamped into the handle of the fork. To test the accuracy of the radar gun with the fork, the officer strikes the fork to get it vibrating and then holds the fork in front of the radar head. The radar unit will then read the fork's vibration and display the read Doppler frequency value for comparison by the officer with the imprinted value on the fork. *State v. Gerdes*, 291 Minn. 353, 191 N.W.2d 428, 432 (1971). No evidence was introduced by the State, however, establishing the accuracy of the tuning fork used in the test. Appellant maintains that the State's failure to do so rendered admission of the speeding obtained from the K-15 gun legal error.

The few courts which have considered the issue have split over requiring proof that the tuning fork used to test a radar device must itself be proven accurate. Those courts requiring such proof have done so by reasoning that the value of the tuning fork depends upon the accuracy of the particular tuning fork against which the radar gun is checked. See e.g. *St. Louis v. Boecker*, 370 S.W.2d 731, 736 (Mo. App. 1963). Other courts, however, have held that the government is not required to prove the accuracy of the tuning fork since requiring "[s]uch a chain of evidence might . . . [require the prosecution] to proceed ad infinitum." *State v. Sny-*

der, 184 Neb. 465, 466, 168 N.W.2d 530, 531 (1969). *Accord Shears v. State*, 648 P.2d 841 (Okl. 1982).

We are of the opinion that those cases holding that the government is not required to prove the accuracy of the tuning fork are of the better view. It is a daily occurrence in our district courts for police officers to rely upon the accuracy of testing devices used to vouch for the accuracy of their radar guns. Requiring proof of the accuracy of those testing devices in every case would impose an inordinate burden upon the State and a great waste of judicial time. Accordingly, we hold that once the State puts in evidence that the police conducted a tuning fork test indicating the K-15 gun was properly calibrated, this evidence creates a prima facie presumption that the tuning fork itself was accurately calibrated.

In the instant case, the citing officer testified that prior to clocking Appellant's vehicle, he "took a tuning fork . . . stamped 50 (fifty) MPH at the factory, . . . tapped . . . [and] held it in front of the [K-15] unit and got a reading of five zero . . . [which] indicated that the unit was functioning properly." The tuning fork used to test the K-15 gun was therefore entitled to a presumption of accuracy and the burden shifted to Appellant to prove otherwise. Appellant, having failed to introduce any evidence impeaching the accuracy of the tuning fork, failed to rebut this presumption. Accordingly, the trial court correctly concluded that there was sufficient evidence of the K-15 gun's accuracy to deny Appellant's motion for directed verdict.

Finding no merit to appellant's remaining contention, we affirm the judgment of conviction.

Cases relating to Chapter 16
EVIDENCE UNCONSTITUTIONALLY OBTAINED

UNITED STATES v. LEON

104 S.Ct. 3405 (1984)

Justice WHITE delivered the opinion of the Court.

This case presents the question whether the Fourth Amendment exclusionary rule should be modified so as not to bar the use in the prosecution's case-in-chief of evidence obtained by officers acting in reasonable reliance on a search warrant issued by a detached and neutral magistrate but ultimately found to be unsupported by probable cause. To resolve this question, we must consider once again the tension between the sometimes competing goals of, on the one hand, deterring official misconduct and removing inducements to unreasonable invasions of privacy and, on the other, establishing procedures under which criminal defendants are "acquitted or convicted on the basis of all the evidence which exposes the truth." *Alderman* v. *United States*, 394 U.S. 165, 175, 89 S.Ct. 961, 967, 22 L.Ed.2d 176 (1969).

In August 1981, a confidential informant of unproven reliability informed an officer of the Burbank Police Department that two persons known to him as "Armando" and "Patsy" were selling large quantities of cocaine and methaqualone from their residence at 620 Price Drive in Burbank, Cal. The informant also indicated that he had witnessed a sale of methaqualone by "Patsy" at the residence approximately five months earlier and had observed at that time a shoebox containing a large amount of cash that belonged to "Patsy." He further declared that "Armando" and "Patsy" generally kept only small quantities of drugs at their residence and stored the remainder at another location in Burbank.

On the basis of this information, the Burbank police initiated an extensive investigation focusing first on the Price Drive residence and later on two other residences as well. Cars parked at the Price Drive residence were determined to belong to respondents Armando Sanchez, who had previously been arrested for possession of marihuana, and Patsy Stewart, who had no criminal record. During the course of the investigation, officers observed an automobile belonging to respondent Ricardo Del Castillo,

653

who had previously been arrested for possession of 50 pounds of marihuana, arrive at the Price Drive resident. The driver of that car entered the house, exited shortly thereafter carrying a small paper sack, and drove away. A check of Del Castillo's probation records led the officers to respondent Alberto Leon, whose telephone number Del Castillo had listed as his employer's. Leon had been arrested in 1980 on drug charges, and a companion had informed the police at that time that Leon was heavily involved in the importation of drugs in this country. Before the current investigation began, the Burbank officers had learned that an informant had told a Glendale police officer that Leon stored a large quantity of methaqualone at his residence in Glendale. During the course of this investigation, the Burbank officers learned that Leon was living at 716 South Sunset Canyon in Burbank.

Subsequently, the officers observed several persons, at least one of whom had prior drug involvement, arriving at the Price Drive residence and leaving with small packages; observed a variety of other material activity at the two residences as well as at a condominium at 7902 Via Magadalena; and witnessed a variety of relevant activity involving respondents' automobiles. The officers also observed respondents Sanchez and Stewart board separate flights for Miami. The pair later returned to Los Angeles together, consented to a search of their luggage that revealed only a small amount of marihuana, and left the airport. Based on these and other observations summarized in the affidavit, App. 34, Officer Cyril Rombach of the Burbank Police Department, an experienced and well-trained narcotics investigator, prepared an application for a warrant to search 620 Price Drive, 716 South Sunset Canyon, 7902 Via Magdalena, and automobiles registered to each of the respondents for an extensive list of items believed to be related to respondents' drug-trafficking activities. Officer Rombach's extensive application was reviewed by several Deputy District Attorneys.

A facially valid search warrant was issued in September 1981 by a state superior court judge. The ensuing searches produced large quantities of drugs at the Via Magdalena and Sunset Canyon addresses and a small quantity at the Price Drive residence. Other evidence was discovered at each of the residences and in Stewart's and Del Castillo's automobiles. Respondents were indicted by a grand jury in the District Court for the Central District of California and charged with conspiracy to possess and distribute cocaine and a variety of substantive counts.

The respondents then filed motions to suppress the evidence seized pursuant to the warrant. The District Court held an evidentiary hearing and, while recognizing that the case was a close one, see App. 131, granted the motions to suppress in part. It concluded that the affidavit was insufficient to establish probable cause, but did not suppress all of the evidence as to all of the respondents because none of the respondents had standing to challenge all of the searches. In response to a request from the Government, the court made clear that Officer Rombach had acted in good faith, but it rejected the Government's suggestion that the Fourth Amendment exclusionary rule should not apply where evidence is seized in reasonable, good-faith reliance on a search warrant.

The District Court denied the Government's motion for reconsideration, App. 147, and a divided panel of the Court of Appeals for the Ninth Circuit affirmed. The Court of Appeals first concluded that Officer Rombach's affidavit could not establish probable cause to search the Price Drive residence. To the extent that the affidavit set forth facts demonstrating the basis of the informant's knowledge of criminal activity, the information included was fatally stale. The affidavit, moreover, failed to establish the informant's credibility. Accordingly, the Court of Appeals concluded that the information provided by the informant was inadequate under both prongs of the two-part test established in *Aguilar v. Texas*, 378 U.S. 108, 84 S.Ct. 1509, 12 L.Ed.2d 723 (1964), and *Spinelli v. United States*, 393 U.S. 410, 89 S.Ct. 584, 21 L.Ed.2d637 (1969). The officers' independent investigation neither cured the staleness nor corroborated the details of the informant's declarations. The Court of Appeals then considered whether the affidavit formed a proper basis for the search of the Sunset Canyon residence. In its view, the affidavit included no facts indicating the basis for the informants' statements concerning respondent Leon's criminal activities and was devoid of information establishing the informants' reliability. Because these deficiencies had not been cured by the police investigation, the District Court properly suppressed the fruits of the search. The Court of Appeals refused the Government's invitation to recog-

nize a good-faith exception to the Fourth Amendment exclusionary rule.

The Government's petition for certiorari expressly declined to seek review of the lower courts' determinations that the search warrant was unsupported by probable cause and presented only the question "(w)hether the Fourth Amendment exclusionary rule should be modified so as not to bar the admission of evidence seized in reasonable, good-faith reliance on a search warrant that is subsequently held to be defective." We granted certiorari to consider the propriety of such a modification. 463 U.S. ____, 103 S.Ct. 3535, 77 L.Ed.2d 1386 (1983). Although it undoubtedly is within our power to consider the question whether probable cause existed under the "totality of the circumstances" test announced last Term in *Illinois v. Gates*, 462 U.S. ____, 103 S.Ct. 2317, 76 L.Ed.2d 527 (1983), that question has not been briefed or argued; and it is also within our authority, which we choose to exercise, to take the case as it comes to us, accepting the Court of Appeals' conclusion that probable cause was lacking under the prevailing legal standards. See This Court's Rule 21.1(a).

We have concluded that, in the Fourth Amendment context, the exclusionary rule can be modified somewhat without jeopardizing its ability to perform its intended functions. Accordingly, we reverse the judgment of the Court of Appeals.

Language in opinions of this Court and of individual Justices has sometimes implied that the exclusionary rule is a necessary corollary of the Fourth Amendment, or that the rule is required by the conjunction of the Fourth and Fifth amendments. *Mapp* v. *Ohio*, supra, 367 U.S., at 661-662, 81 S.Ct., at 1694-1695 (Black, J., concurring); *Agnello* v. *United States*, 269 U.S.20, 33-34, 46 S.Ct. 4, 6-7, 70 L.Ed. 145 (1925). These implications need not detain us long. Fifth Amendment theory has not withstood critical analysis or the test of time, see *Andresen* v. *Maryland*, 427 U.S. 463, 96 S.Ct. 2737, 49 L.Ed.2d 627 (1976), and the Fourth Amendment "has never been interpreted to proscribe the introduction of illegally seized evidence in all proceedings or against all persons." *Stone* v. *Powell*, 428 U.S. 465, 486, 96 S.Ct. 3037, 3048, 49 L.Ed.2d 1067 (1976).

The Fourth Amendment contains no provision expressly precluding the use of evidence obtained in violation of its commands, and an examination of its origin and purposes makes clear that the use of fruits of a past unlawful search or seizure "work[s] no new Fourth Amendment wrong." *United States* v. *Calandra*, 414 U.S. 338, 354, 94 S.Ct. 613, 623, 38 L.Ed.2d 561 (1974). The wrong commended by the Amendment is "fully accomplished" by the unlawful search or seizure itself *ibid.*, and the exclusionary rule is neither intended nor able to "cure the invasion of the defendant's rights which he has already suffered." *Stone* v. *Powell*, supra, 428 U.S., at 540, 96 S.Ct., at 3073 (WHITE, J., dissenting). The rule thus operates as "a judicially created remedy designed to safeguard Fourth Amendment rights generally through its deterrent effect, rather than a personal constitutional right of the person aggrieved." *United States* v. *Cal-*

andra, supra, 414 U.S., at 348, 94 S.Ct., at 620.

Whether the exclusionary sanction is appropriately imposed in a particular case, our decisions make clear, is "an issue separate from the question whether the Fourth Amendment rights of the party seeking to invoke the rule were violated by police conduct." *Illinois* v. *Gates*, supra, 462 U.S., at ____, 103 S.Ct., at 2324. Only the former question is currently before us, and it must be resolved by weighing the costs and benefits of preventing the use in the prosecution's case-in-chief of inherently trustworthy tangible evidence obtained in reliance on a search warrant issued by a detached and neutral magistrate that ultimately is found to be defective.

The substantial social costs exacted by the exclusionary rule for the vindication of Fourth Amendment rights have long been a source of concern. "Our cases have consistently recognized that unbending application of the exclusionary sanction to enforce ideals of governmental rectitude would impede unacceptably the truth-finding functions of judge and jury." *United States* v. *Payner*, 447 U.S. 727, 734, 100 S.Ct. 2439, 2445, 65 L.Ed.2d 468 (1980). An objectionable collateral consequence of this interference with the criminal justice system's truth-finding function is that some guilty defendants may go free or receive reduced sentences as a result of favorable plea bargains. Particularly when law enforcement officers have acted in objective good faith or their transgressions have been minor, the magnitude of the benefit conferred on such guilty defendants offend basic concepts of the criminal justice system. *Stone* v. *Powell, supra*, 428

U.S., at 490, 96 S.Ct., at 3050. Indiscriminate application of the exclusionary rule, therefore, may well "generat[e] disrespect for the law and the administration of justice." *Id.*, at 491, 96 S.Ct., at 3051. Accordingly, "[a]s with any remedial device, the application of the rule has been restricted to those areas where its remedial objectives are thought most efficaciously served."

Close attention to those remedial objectives has characterized our recent decisions concerning the scope of the Fourth Amendment exclusionary rule. The Court has, to be sure, not seriously questioned, "in the absence of a more efficacious sanction, the continued application of the rule to suppress evidence from the [prosecution's] case where a Fourth Amendment violation has been substantial and deliberate..." Nevertheless, the balancing approach that has evolved in various contexts—including criminal trials—"forcefully suggest[s] that the exclusionary rule be more generally modified to permit the introduction of evidence obtained in the reasonable good-faith belief that a search or seizure was in accord with the Fourth Amendment."

In *Stone* v. *Powell, supra,* the Court emphasized the costs of the exclusionary rule, expressed its view that limiting the circumstances under which Fourth Amendment claims could be raised in federal habeas corpus proceedings would not reduce the rule's deterrent effect, *id.*, 428 U.S., at 489-495, 96 S.Ct., at 3050-3052, and held that a state prisoner who has been afforded a full and fair opprtunity to litigate a Fourth Amendment claim may not obtain federal habeas relief on the ground that unlawfully obtained evi-

dence had been introduced at his trial. Cf. *Rose* v. *Mitchell,* 443 U.S. 545, 560-563, 99 S.Ct. 2993, 3002-3004, 61 L.Ed.2d 739 (1979). Proposed extensions of the exclusionary rule to proceedings other than the criminal trial itself have been evaluated and rejected under the same analytic approach. In *United States* v. *Calandra, supra,* for example, we declined to allow grand jury witnesses to refuse to answer questions based on evidence obtained from an unlawful search or seizure since "[a]ny incremental deterrent effect which might be achieved by extending the rule to grand jury proceedings is uncertain at best." *Id.*, 414 U.S., at 348, 94 S.Ct., at 620. Similarly, in *United States* v. *Janis, supra,* we permitted the use in federal civil proceedings of evidence illegally seized by state officials since the likelihood of deterring police misconduct through such an extension of the exclusionary rule was insufficient to outweigh its substantial social costs. In so doing,we declared that, "[i]f...the exclusionary rule does not result in appreciable deterrence, then, clearly, its use in the instant situation is unwarranted." *Id.*, 428 U.S. at 454, 96 S.Ct., at 3032.

As cases considering the use of unlawfully obtained evidence in criminal trials themselves make clear, it does not follow from the emphasis on the exclusionary rule's deterrent value that "anything which deters illegal searches is thereby commanded by the Fourth Amendment." *Alderman* v. *United States,* 394 U.S., at 174, 89 S.Ct., at 967. In determining whether persons aggrieved solely by the introduction of damaging evidence unlawfully obtained from their co-

conspirators or co-defendants could seek suppressions, for example, we found that the additional benefits of such an extension of the exclusionary rule would not outweigh its costs. *Id.*, at 174-175, 89 S.Ct., at 967. Standing to invoke the rule has thus been limited to cases in which the prosecution seeks to use the fruits of an illegal search or seizure against the victim of police misconduct.

Even defendants with standing to challenge the introduction in their criminal trials of unlawfully obtained evidence cannot prevent every conceivable use of such evidence. Evidence obtained in violation of the Fourth Amendment and inadmissible in the prosecution's case-in-chief may be used to impeach a defendant's direct testimony. A similar assessment of the "incremental furthering" of the ends of the exclusionary rule led us to conclude in *United States* v. *Havens*, 446 U.S. 620, 627, 100 S.Ct. 1912, 1916, 64 L.Ed.2d 559 (1980), that evidence inadmissible in the prosecution's case-in-chief or otherwise as substantive evidence of guilt may be used to impeach statements made by a defendant in response to "proper cross-examination reasonably suggested by the defendant's direct examination." *Id.*, at 627-628, 100 S.Ct. at 1916-1917.

When considering the use of evidence obtained in violation of the Fourth Amendment in the prosecution's case-in-chief, moreover, we have declined to adopt a per se or but for rule that would render inadmissible any evidence that came to light through a chain of causation that began with an illegal arrest. *Brown* v. *Illinois*, 422 U.S. 590, 95 S.Ct. 2254, 45 L.Ed. 2d 416 (1975); *Wong Sun* v. *United States, supra,*

371 U.S., at 487-488, 83 S.Ct., at 417. We also have held that a witness' testimony may be admitted even when his identity was discovered in an unconstitutional search. *United States* v. *Ceccolini*, 435 U.S. 268, 98 S.Ct. 1054, 55 L.Ed.2d 268 (1978). The perception underlying these decisions—that the connection between police misconduct and evidence of crime may be sufficiently attenuated to permit the use of that evidence at trial—is a product of considerations relating to the exclusionary rule and the constitutional principles it is designed to protect. *Dunaway* v. *New York*, 442 U.S. 200, 217-218, 99 S.Ct. 2248, 2259-2260, 60 L.Ed.2d 824 (1979); *United States* v. *Ceccolini, supra,* 435 U.S., at 279, 98 S.Ct., at 1061. In short, the "dissipation of the taint" concept that the Court has applied in deciding whether exclusion is appropriate in a particular case "attempts to mark the point at which the detrimental consequences of illegal police action becomes so attenuated that the deterrent effect of the exclusionary rule no longer justifies its cost." Not surprisingly in view of this purpose, an assessment of the flagrancy of the police misconduct constitutes an important step in the calculus.

The same attention to the purposes underlying the exclusionary rule has also has characterized decisions not involving the scope of the rule itself. We have not required suppression of the fruits of a search incident to an arrest made in good-faith reliance on a substantive criminal statute that subsequently is declared unconstitutional. Similarly, although the Court has been unwilling to conclude that new Fourth Amendment principles are always to have only prospective effect, no Fourth Amendment decision marking a "clear break with the past" has been applied retroactively. The propriety of retroactive application of a newly announced Fourth Amendment principle, moreover, has been assessed largely in terms of the contribution retroactivity might make to the deterrence of police misconduct.

As yet, we have not recognized any form of good-faith exception to the Fourth Amendment exclusionary rule. But the balancing approach that has evolved during the years of experience with the rule provides strong support for the modification currently urged upon us. As we discuss below, our evaluation of the costs and benefits of suppressing reliable physical evidence seized by officers reasonably relying on a warrant issued by a detached and neutral magistrate leads to the conclusion that such evidence should be admissible in the prosecution's case-in-chief.

Because a search warrant "provides the detached scrutiny of a neutral magistrate, which is a more reliable safeguard against improper searches than the hurried judgment of a law enforcement officer 'engaged in the often competitive enterprise of ferretng out crime,'" we have expressed a strong preference for warrants and declared that "in a doubtful or marginal case a search under a warrant may be sustainable where without one it would fail." Reasonable minds frequently may differ on the question whether a particular affidavit establishes probable cause, and we have thus concluded that the preference for warrants is most appropriately effectuated by according "great deference" to a magistrate's determina-

tion.

Deference to the magistrate, however, is not boundless. It is clear, first, that the deference accorded to a magistrate's finding of probable cause does not preclude inquiry into the knowing or reckless falsity of the affidavit on which that determination was based. *Franks* v. *Delaware*, 438 U.S. 154, 98 S.Ct 2674, 57 L.Ed.2d 667 (1978). Second, the courts must also insist that the magistrate purport to "perform his 'neutral and detached,' function and not serve merely as a rubber stamp for the police." A magistrate failing to "manifest that neutrality and detachment demanded of a judicial officer when presented with a warrant application" and who acts instead as "an adjunct law enforcement officer" cannot provide valid authorization for an otherwise unconstitutional search.

Third, reviewing courts will not defer to a warrant based on an affidavit that does not "provide the magistrate with a substantial basis for determining the existence of probable cause." *Illinois* v. *Gates, supra*, 462 U.S., at ____ , 103 S.Ct., at 2332. "Sufficient information must be presented to the magistrate to allow that official to determine probable cause; his action cannot be a mere ratification of the bare conclusions of others." Even if the warrant application was supported by more than a "bare bones" affidavit, a reviewing court may properly conclude that, notwithstanding the deference that magistrates deserve, the warrant was invalid because the magistrate's probably-cause determination reflected an improper analysis of the totality of the circumstances, or because the form of the warrant was improper in some respect.

Only in the first of these three situations, however, has the Court set forth a rationale for suppressing evidence obtained pursuant to a search warrant; in the other areas, it has simply excluded such evidence without consdering whether evidence without considering whether Fourth Amendment interests will be advanced. To the extent that proponents of exclusion rely on its behavioral effects on judges and magistrates in these areas, their reliance is misplaced. First, the exclusionary is designed to deter police misconduct rather than to punish the errors of judges and magistrates. Second, there exists no evidence suggesting that judges and magistrates are inclined to ignore or subvert the Fourth Amendment or that lawlessness among these actors requires application of the extreme sanction of exclusion.

Third, and most important, we discern no basis, and are offered none, for believing that exclusion of evidence seized pursuant to a warrant will have a significant deterrent effect on the issuing judge or magistrate. Many of the factors that indicate that the exclusionary rule cannot provide an effective "special" or "general" deterrent for individual offending law enforcement officers apply as well to judges or magistrates. And, to the extent that the rule is thought to operate as a "systemic" deterrent on a wider audience, it clearly can have no such effect on individuals empowered to issue such warrants. Judges and magistrates are not adjuncts to the law enforcement team; as neutral judicial officers, they have no stake in the outcome of particular criminal prosecutions. The threat of exclusion thus cannot be expected significantly to deter them. Imposition of the exclusionary sanction is not necessary meaningfully to inform judicial officers of their errors, and we cannot conclude that admitting evidence obtained pursuant to a warrant while at the same time declaring that the warrant was somehow defective will in any way reduce judicial officers' professional incentives to comply with the Fourth Amendment, encourage them to repeat their mistakes, or lead to the granting of all colorable warrant requests.

If exclusion of evidence obtained pursuant to a subsequently invalidated warrant is to have any deterrent effect, therefore, it must alter the behavior of individual law enforcement officers or the policies of their departments. One could argue that applying the exclusionary rule in cases where the police failed to demonstrate probable cause in the warrant application deters future inadequate presentations or "magistrate shopping" and thus promotes the ends of the Fourth Amendment. Suppressing evidence obtained pursuant to a technically defective warrant supported by probable cause also might encourage officers to scrutinize more closely the form of the warrant and to point out suspected judicial errors. We find such arguments speculative and conclude that suppression of evidence obtained pursuant to a warrant should be ordered only on a case-by-case basis and only in those unusual cases in which exclusion will further the purposes of the exclusionary rule.

We have frequently questioned whether the exclusionary rule can have any deterrent effect when the offending officers acted in the objectively reasonable belief that their conduct did not violate the Fourth Amendment. "No empirical researcher, proponent or opponent of the rule, has yet been able to establish with any assurance whether the rule has a deterrent effect...." *United States* v. *Janis*, 428 U.S., at 452, n. 22, 96 S.Ct., at 3031, n. 22. But even assuming that the rule effectively deters some police misconduct and provides incentives for the law enforcement profession as a whole to conduct itself in accord with the Fourth Amendment, it cannot be expected, and should not be applied, to deter objectively reasonable law enforcement activity.

This is particularly true, we believe, when an officer acting with objective good faith has obtained a search warrant from a judge or magistrate and acted within its scope. In most such cases, there is no police illegality and thus nothing to deter. It is the magistrate's responsibility to determine whether the officers' allegations establish probable cause and, if so, to issue a warrant comporting in form with the requirements of the Fourth Amendment. In the ordinary case, an officer cannot be expected to question the magistrate's probable-cause determination or his judgment that the form of the warrant is technically sufficient. "[O]nce the warrant issues, there is literally nothing more the policeman can do in seeking to comply with the law." Penalizing the officer for the magistrate's error, rather than his own, cannot logically contribute to the deterrence of Fourth Amendment violations.

We conclude that the marginal or nonexistent benefits produced by suppressing evidence obtained in objectively reasonable reliance on a subsequently invalidated search warrant cannot justify the substantial costs of exclusion. We do not suggest, however, that exclusion is always inappropriate in cases where an officer has obtained a warrant and abided by its terms. "[S]earches pursuant to a warrant will rarely require any deep inquiry into reasonableness," for "a warrant issued by a magistrate normally suffices to establish" that a law enforcement officer has "acted in good faith in conducting the search." Nevertheless, the officer's reliance on the magistrate's probable cause determination and on the technical sufficiency of the warrant he issues must be objectively reasonable, and it is clear that in some circumstances the officer will have no reasonable grounds for believing that the warrant was properly issued.

Suppression therefore remains an appropriate remedy if the magistrate or judge in issuing a warrant was misled by information in an affidavit that the affiant knew was false or would have known was false except for his reckless disregard of the truth. *Franks* v. *Delaware*, 438 U.S. 154, 98 S.Ct. 2674, 57 L.Ed.2d 667 (1978). The exception we recognize today will also not apply in cases where the issuing magistrate wholly abandoned his judicial role in the manner condemned in *Lo-Ji Sales, Inc.* v. *New York*, 442 U.S. 319, 99 S.Ct. 2319, 60 L.Ed.2d 920 (1979); in such cicumstances, no reasonably well-trained officer should rely on the warrant. Nor would an officer manifest objective good faith in relying on a warrant based on an affidavit "so lacking in indicia of probably cause as to render official belief in its existence entirely unreasonable." Finally, depending on the circumstances of the particular case, a warrant may be so facially deficient—*i.e.*, in failing to particularize the place to be searched or the things to be seized—that the executing officers cannot reasonably presume it to be valid.

In so limiting the suppression remedy, we leave untouched the probable-cause standard and the various requirements for a valid warrant. Other objections to the modification of the Fourth Amendment exclusionary rule we consider to be insubstantial. The good-faith exception for searches conducted pursuant to warrants is not intended to signal our unwillingness strictly to enforce the requirements of the Fourth Amendment, and we do not believe that it will have this effect. As we have already suggested, the good-faith exception, turning as it does on objective reasonableness, should not be difficult to apply in practice. When officers have acted pursuant to a warrant, the prosecution should ordinarily be able to establish objective good faith without a substantial expenditure of judicial time.

Nor are we persuaded that application of a good-faith exception to searches conducted pursuant to warrants will preclude review of the constitutionality of search or seizure, deny needed guidance from the courts, or freeze Fourth Amendment law in present state. There is no need for courts to adopt the inflexible practice of always deciding whether the officers' conduct manifested objective good faith before turning to the question whether the Fourth Amendment has been vio-

lated. Defendants seeking suppression of the fruits of allegedly unconstitutional searches or seizures undoubtedly raise live controversies which Article III empowers federal courts to adjudicate. As cases addressing questions of good-faith immunity under 42 U.S.C. 1983, and cases involving the harmless error doctrine, make clear, courts have considerable discretion in conforming their decision-making processes to the exigencies of particular cases.

If the resolution of a particular Fourth Amendment question is necessary to guide future action by law enforcement officers and magistrates, nothing will prevent reviewing courts from deciding that question before turning to the good-faith issue. Indeed it frequently will be difficult to determine whether the officers acted reasonably without resolving the Fourth Amendment issue. Even if the Fourth Amendment question is not one of broad import, reviewing courts could decide in particular cases that magistrates under their supervision need to be informed of their errors and so evaluate the officers' good faith only after finding a violation. In other circumstances, those courts could reject suppression motions posing no important Fourth Amendment questions by turning immediately to a consideration of the officers' good faith. We have no reason to believe that our Fourth Amdendment jurisprudence would suffer by allowing reviewing courts to exercise an informed discretion in making this choice.

When the principles we have enunciated today are applied to the facts of this case, it is apparent that the judgment of the Court of

Appeals cannot stand. The Court of Appeals applied the prevailing legal standards to Officer Rombach's warrant application and concluded that the application could not support the magistrate's probable-cause determination. In so doing, the court clearly informed the magistrate that he had erred in issuing the challenged warrant. This aspect of the court's judgment is not under attack in this proceeding.

Having determined that the warrant should not have issued, the Court of Appeals understandably declined to adopt a modification of the Fourth Amendment exclusionary rule that this Court had not previously sanctioned. Although the modification finds strong support in our previous cases, the Court of Appeals' commendable self-restraint is not to be criticized. We have now re-examined the purposes of the exclusionary rule and the propriety of its application in cases where officers have relied on a subsequently invalidated search warrant. Our conclusion is that the rule's purposes will only rarely be served by applying it in such circumstances.

In the absence of an allegation that the magistrate abandoned his detached and neutral role, suppression is appropriate only if the officers were dishonest or reckless in preparing their affidavit or could not have harbored an objectively reasonable belief in the existence of probable cause. Only respondent Leon has contended that no reasonably well-trained police officer could have believed that there existed probable cause to search his house; significantly, the other respondents advance no comparable argument. Officer Rombach's application for a warrant clearly was supported by much more than a "bare bones" affidavit. The affidavit related the results of an extensive investigation and, as the opinions of the divided panel of the Court of Appeals make clear, provided evidence sufficient to create disagreement among thoughtful and competent judges as to the existence of probable cause. Under these circumstances, the officers' reliance on the magistrate's determination of probable cause was objectively reasonable, and application of the extreme sanction of exclusion is inappropriate.

Accordingly, the judgment of the Court of Appeals is

Reversed.

MIRANDA v. ARIZONA

384 U.S. 436, 86 S. Ct. 1062, 16 L. Ed. 2d 694, 36 Ohio Op.2d 237 (1966)

[Footnotes omitted]

Mr. Chief Justice WARREN delivered the opinion of the Court.

The cases before us raise questions which go to the roots of our concepts of American criminal jurisprudence: the restraints society must observe consistent with the Federal Constitution in prosecuting individuals for crime. More specifically, we deal with the admissibility of statements obtained from an individual who is subjected to custodial police interrogation and the necessity for procedures which assure that the individual is accorded his privilege under the Fifth Amendment to the Constitution not to be compelled to incriminate himself.

We dealt with certain phases of this problem recently in *Escobedo* v. *State of Illinois*, 378 U.S. 478, 32 O.O.(2d) 31, 84 S.Ct. 1758, 12 L.Ed.(2d) 977 (1964). There, as in the four cases before us, the law enforcement officials took the defendant into custody and interrogated him in a police station for the purpose of obtaining a confession. The police did not effectively advise him of his right to remain silent or of his right to consult with his attorney. Rather, they confronted him with an alleged accomplice who accused him of having perpetrated a murder. When the defendant denied the accusation and said "I didn't shoot Manuel, you did it," they handcuffed him and took him to an interrogation room. There, while handcuffed and standing, he was questioned for four hours until he confessed. During this interrogation, the police denied his request to speak to his attorney, and they prevented his retained attorney, who had come to the police station, from consulting with him. At his trial, the State, over his objection, introduced the confession against him. We held that the statements thus made were constitutionally inadmissible.

This case has been the subject of judicial interpretation and spirited legal debate since it was decided two years ago. Both state and federal courts, in assessing its implications, have arrived at varying conclusions. A wealth of scholarly material has been written tracing its ramifications and underpinnings. Police and prosecutor have speculated on its range and desirability. We granted certiorari in these cases, 382 U.S. 924, 925, 937, 86 S.Ct. 318, 320, 395, 15 L.Ed.(2d) 338, 339, 348, in order further to explore some facets of the problems, thus exposed, of applying the privilege against self-incrimination to in-custody interrogation, and to give concrete constitutional guidelines for law enforcement agencies and courts to follow.

We start here, as we did in *Escobedo*, with the premise that our holding is not an innovation in our jurisprudence, but is an application of principles long recognized and applied in other settings. We have undertaken a thorough re-examination of the *Escobedo* decision and the principles it announced, and we reaffirm it. That case was but an explication of basic rights that are enshrined in our Constitution—that "No person * * * shall be compelled in any criminal case to be a witness against himself," and that "the accused shall * * * have the Assistance of Counsel"—rights which were put in jeopardy in that case through official overbearing. These precious rights were fixed in our Constitution only after centuries of persecution and struggle. And in the words of Chief Justice Marshall, they were secured "for ages to come and * * * designed to approach immortality as nearly as human institutions can approach it," *Cohens* v. *Commonwealth of Virginia*, 6 Wheat. 264, 387, 5 L.Ed. 257 (1821).

Over 70 years ago, our predecessors on this Court eloquently stated:

"The maxim *'Nemo tenetur seip-sum accusare,'* had its origin in a protest against the inquisitorial and manifestly unjust methods of interrogating accused persons, which has long obtained in the continental system, and, until the expulsion of the Stuarts from the British throne in 1688, and the erection of additional barriers for the protection of the people against the exercise of arbitrary power, was not uncommon even in England. While the admissions or confessions of the prisoner, when voluntarily and freely made, have always ranked high in the scale of incriminating evidence, if an accused person be asked to explain his apparent connection with a crime under investigation, the ease with which the questions put to him may assume an inquisitorial character, the temptation to press the witness unduly, to browbeat him if he be timid or reluctant, to push him into a corner, and to entrap him into fatal contradictions, which is so painfully evidenced in many of these earlier state trials, notably in those of Sir Nicholas Throckmorton, and Udal, the Puritan minister, made the system so odious as to give rise to a demand for its total abolition. The change in the English criminal procedure in that particular seems to be founded upon no statute and no judicial opinion, but upon a general and silent acquiescence of the courts in a popular demand. But, however adopted, it has become firmly embedded in English, as well as in American jurisprudence. So deeply did the inequities of the ancient system impress them-selves upon the minds of the American colonists that the states, with one accord, made a denial of the right to question an accused person a part of their fundamental law, so that a maxim, which in England was a mere rule of evidence, became clothed in this country with the impregnability of a constitutional enactment." *Brown* v. *Walker,* 161 U.S. 591, 596-597, 16 S.Ct. 644, 646, 40 L.Ed. 819 (1896).

In stating the obligation of the judiciary to apply these constitutional rights, this Court declared in *Weems* v. *United States,* 217 U.S. 349, 373, 30 S.Ct. 544, 551, 54 L.Ed. 793 (1910):

"*º º º* our contemplation cannot be only of what has been, but of what may be. Under any other rule a constitution would indeed be as easy of application as it would be deficient in efficacy and power. Its general principles would have little value, and be converted by precedent into impotent and lifeless formulas. Rights declared in words might be lost in reality. And this has been recognized. The meaning and vitality of the Constitution have developed against narrow and restrictive construction."

This was the spirit in which we delineated, in meaningful language, the manner in which the constitutional rights of the individual could be enforced against overzealous police practices. It was necessary in *Escobedo,* as here, to insure that what was proclaimed in the Constitution had not become but a "form of words," *Silverthorne Lumber Co.* v. *United States,* 251 U.S. 385, 392,

40 S.Ct. 182, 64 L.Ed. 319 (1920), in the hands of government officials. And it is in this spirit, consistent with our role as judges, that we adhere to the principles of *Escobedo* today.

Our holding will be spelled out with some specificity in the pages which follow but briefly stated it is this: the prosecution may not use statements, whether exculpatory or inculpatory, stemming from custodial interrogation of the defendant unless it demonstrates the use of procedural safeguards effective to secure the privilege against self-incrimination. By custodial interrogation, we mean questioning initiated by law enforcement officers after a person has been taken into custody or otherwise deprived of his freedom of action in any significant way. As for the procedural safeguards to be employed, unless other fully effective means are devised to inform accused persons of their right of silence and to assure a continuous opportunity to exercise it, the following measures are required. Prior to any questioning, the person must be warned that he has a right to remain silent, that any statement he does make may be used as evidence against him, and that he has a right to the presence of an attorney, either retained or appointed. The defendant may waive effectuation of these rights, provided the waiver is made voluntarily, knowingly and intelligently. If, however, he indicates in any manner and at any stage of the process that he wishes to consult with an attorney before speaking there can be no questioning. Likewise, if the individual is alone and indicates in any manner that he does not wish

to be interrogated, the police may not question him. The mere fact that he may have answered some questions or volunteered some statements on his own does not deprive him of the right to refrain from answering any further inquiries until he has consulted with an attorney and thereafter consents to be questioned.

I.

The constitutional issue we decide in each of these cases is the admissibility of statements obtained from a defendant questioned while in custody and deprived of his freedom of action. In each, the defendant was questioned by police officers, detectives, or a prosecuting attorney in a room in which he was cut off from the outside world. In none of these cases was the defendant given a full and effective warning of his rights at the outset of the interrogation process. In all the cases, the questioning elicited oral admissions, and in three of them, signed statements as well which were admitted at their trials. They all thus share salient features—incommunicado interrogation of individuals in a police-dominated atmosphere, resulting in self-incriminating statements without full warnings of constitutional rights.

* * *

III.

Today, then, there can be no doubt that the Fifth Amendment privilege is available outside of criminal court proceedings and serves to protect persons in all settings in which their freedom of action is curtailed from being compelled to incriminate themselves.

We have concluded that without proper safeguards the process of in-custody interrogation of persons suspected or accused of crime contains inherently compelling pressures which work to undermine the individual's will to resist and to compel him to speak where he would not otherwise do so freely. In order to combat these pressures and to permit a full opportunity to exercise the privilege against self-incrimination, the accused must be adequately and effectively apprised of his rights and the exercise of those rights must be fully honored.

It is impossible for us to foresee the potential alternatives for protecting the privilege which might be devised by Congress or the States in the exercise of their creative rule-making capacities. Therefore we cannot say that the Constitution necessarily requires adherence to any particular solution for the inherent compulsions of the interrogation process as it is presently conducted. Our decision in no way creates a constitutional strait-jacket which will handicap sound efforts at reform, nor is it intended to have this effect. We encourage Congress and the States to continue their laudable search for increasingly effective ways of protecting the rights of the individual while promoting efficient enforcement of our criminal laws. However, unless we are shown other procedures which are at least as effective in apprising accused persons of their right of silence and in assuring a continuous opportunity to exercise it, the following safeguards must be observed.

At the outset, if a person in custody is to be subjected to interrogation, he must first be informed in clear and unequivocal terms that he has the right to remain silent. For those unaware of the privilege, the warning is needed simply to make them aware of it—the threshold requirement for an intelligent decision as to its exercise. More important, such a warning is an absolute prerequisite in overcoming the inherent pressures of the interrogation atmosphere. It is not just the subnormal or woefully ignorant who succumb to an interrogator's imprecations, whether implied or expressly stated, that the interrogation will continue until a confession is obtained or that silence in the face of accusation is itself damning and will bode ill when presented to a jury. Further, the warning will show the individual that his interrogators are prepared to recognize his privilege should he choose to exercise it.

The Fifth Amendment privilege is so fundamental to our system of constitutional rule and the expedient of giving an adequate warning as to the availability of the privilege so simple, we will not pause to inquire in individual cases whether the defendant was aware of his rights without a warning being given. Assessments of the knowledge the defendant possessed, based on information as to his age, education, intelligence, or prior contact with authorities, can never be more than speculative; a warning is a clearcut fact. More important, whatever the background of the person interrogated, a warning at the time of the interrogation is indispensable to overcome its pressures and to insure that the individual knows he is free to exercise the privilege at that point in time.

The warning of the right to remain silent must be accompanied by the explanation that anything said can and will be used against the individual in court. This warning is needed in order to make him aware not only of the privilege, but also of the consequences of forgoing it. It is only through an awareness of these consequences that there can be any assurance of real understanding and intelligent exercise of the privilege. Moreover, this warning may serve to make the individual more acutely aware that he is faced with a phase of the adversary system—that he is not in the presence of persons acting solely in his interest.

* * *

Accordingly we hold that an individual held for interrogation must be clearly informed that he has the right to consult with a lawyer and to have the lawyer with him during interrogation under the system for protecting the privilege we delineate today. As with the warnings of the right to remain silent and that anything stated can be used in evidence against him, this warning is an absolute prerequisite to interrogation. No amount of circumstantial evidence that the person may have been aware of this right will suffice to stand in its stead. Only through such a warning is there ascertainable assurance that the accused was aware of this right.

If an individual indicates that he wishes the assistance of counsel before any interrogation occurs, the authorities cannot rationally ignore or deny his request on the basis that the individual does not have or cannot afford a retained attorney. The financial ability of the individual

has no relationship to the scope of the rights involved here. The privilege against self-incrimination secured by the Constitution applies to all individuals. The need for counsel in order to protect the privilege exists for the indigent as well as the affluent. In fact, were we to limit these constitutional rights to those who can retain an attorney, our decisions today would be of little significance. The cases before us as well as the vast majority of confession cases with which we have dealt in the past involve those unable to retain counsel. While authorities are not required to relieve the accused of his poverty, they have the obligation not to take advantage of indigence in the administration of justice. Denial of counsel to the indigent at the time of interrogation while allowing an attorney to those who can afford one would be no more supportable by reason or logic than the similar situation at trial and on appeal struck down in *Gideon* v. *Wainwright*, 372 U.S. 335, 23 O.O.(2d) 258, 83 S.Ct. 792, 9 L.Ed.(2d) 799 (1963), and *Douglas* v. *People* of *State of California*, 372 U.S. 353, 83 S.Ct. 814, 9 L.Ed.(2d) 811 (1963).

In order fully to apprise a person interrogated of the extent of his rights under this system then, it is necessary to warn him not only that he has the right to consult with an attorney, but also that if he is indigent a lawyer will be appointed to represent him. Without this additional warning, the admonition of the right to consult with counsel would often be understood as meaning only that he can consult with a lawyer if he has one or has the funds to obtain one. The warning of a right to counsel would be hollow if not couched in terms that would convey to the indigent—the person most often subjected to interrogation—the knowledge that he too has a right to have counsel present. As with the warnings of the right to remain silent and of the general right to counsel, only by effective and express explanation to the indigent of this right can there be assurance that he was truly in a position to exercise it.

Once warnings have been given, the subsequent procedure is clear. If the individual indicates in any manner, at any time prior to or during questioning, that he wishes to remain silent, the interrogation must cease. At this point he has shown that he intends to exercise his Fifth Amendment privilege; any statement taken after the person invokes his privilege cannot be other than the product of compulsion, subtle or otherwise. Without the right to cut off questioning, the setting of in-custody interrogation operates on the individual to overcome free choice in producing a statement after the privilege has been once invoked. If the individual states that he wants an attorney, the interrogation must cease until an attorney is present. At that time, the individual must have an opportunity to confer with the attorney and to have him present during any subsequent questioning. If the individual cannot obtain an attorney and he indicates that he wants one before speaking to police, they must respect his decision to remain silent.

This does not mean, as some have suggested, that each police station must have a "station house lawyer" present at all times to advise prison-

ers. It does mean, however, that if police propose to interrogate a person they must make known to him that he is entitled to a lawyer and that if he cannot afford one, a lawyer will be provided for him prior to any interrogation. If authorities conclude that they will not provide counsel during a reasonable period of time in which investigation in the field is carried out, they may do so without violating the person's Fifth Amendment privilege so long as they do not question him during that time.

If the interrogation continues without the presence of an attorney and a statement is taken, a heavy burden rests on the Government to demonstrate that the defendant knowingly and intelligently waived his privilege against self-incrimination and his right to retained or appointed counsel. *Escobedo* v. *State of Illinois*, 378 U.S. 478, 490 n. 14, 32 O.O.(2d) 31, 36, 84 S.Ct. 1758, 1764, 12 L.Ed.(2d) 977. This Court has always set high standards of proof for the waiver of constitutional rights, *Johnson* v. *Zerbst*, 304 U.S. 458, 58 S.Ct. 1019, 82 L.Ed. 1461 (1938), and we reassert these standards as applied to in-custody interrogation. Since the State is responsible for establishing the isolated circumstances under which the interrogation takes place and has the only means of making available corroborated evidence of warnings given during incommunicado interrogation, the burden is rightly on its shoulders.

An express statement that the individual is willing to make a statement and does not want an attorney followed closely by a statement could constitute a waiver. But a valid waiver will not be presumed simply from the silence of the accused after warnings are given or simply from the fact that a confession was in fact eventually obtained. A statement we made in *Carnley* v. *Cochran*, 369 U.S. 506, 516, 82 S.Ct. 884, 890, 8 L.Ed.(2d) 70 (1962), is applicable here:

"Presuming waiver from a silent record is impermissible. The record must show, or there must be an allegation and evidence which show, that an accused was offered counsel but intelligently and understandingly rejected the offer. Anything less is not waiver."

❋   ❋   ❋

Our decision is not intended to hamper the traditional function of police officers in investigating crime. See *Escobedo* v. *State of Illinois*, 378 U.S. 478, 492, 32 O.O.(2d) 31, 37, 84 S.Ct. 1758, 1765. When an individual is in custody on probable cause, the police may, of course, seek out evidence in the field to be used at trial against him. Such investigation may include inquiry of persons not under restraint. General on-the-scene questioning as to facts surrounding a crime or other general questioning of citizens in the fact-finding process is not affected by our holding. It is an act of responsible citizenship for individuals to give whatever information they may have to aid in law enforcement. In such situations the compelling atmosphere inherent in the process of in-custody interrogation is not necessarily present.

In dealing with statements obtained through interrogation, we do not purport to find all confessions inadmissible. Confessions remain a proper element in law enforcement. Any statement given freely and voluntarily without any compelling influences is, of course, admissible in evidence. The fundamental import of the privilege while an individual is in custody is not whether he is allowed to talk to the police without the benefit of warnings and counsel, but whether he can be interrogated. There is no requirement that police stop a person who enters a police station and states that he wishes to confess to a crime, or a person who calls the police to offer a confession or any other statement he desires to make. Volunteered statements of any kind are not barred by the Fifth Amendment and their admissibility is not affected by our holding today.

To summarize, we hold that when an individual is taken into custody or otherwise deprived of his freedom by the authorities and is subjected to questioning, the privilege against self-incrimination is jeopardized. Procedural safeguards must be employed to protect the privilege, and unless other fully effective means are adopted to notify the person of his right of silence and to assure that the exercise of the right will be scrupulously honored, the following measures are required. He must be warned prior to any questioning that he has the right to remain silent, that anything he says can be used against him in a court of law, that he has the right to the presence of an attorney, and that if he cannot afford an attorney one will be appointed for him prior to any questioning if he so desires. Opportunity to exercise these rights must be afforded to him throughout the interrogation. After such warnings have been given, and such opportunity afforded him, the individual may knowingly and intelligently waive these rights and agree to answer questions or make a statement. But unless and until such warnings and waiver are demonstrated by the prosecution at trial, no evidence obtained as a result of interrogation can be used against him.

* * *

V.

Because of the nature of the problem and because of its recurrent significance in numerous cases, we have to this point discussed the relationship of the Fifth Amendment privilege to police interrogation without specific concentration on the facts of the cases before us. We turn now to these facts to consider the application to these cases of the constitutional principles discussed above. In each instance, we have concluded that statements were obtained from the defendant under circumstances that did not meet constitutional standards for protection of the privilege.

No. 759. *Miranda* v. *Arizona.*

On March 13, 1963, petitioner, Ernesto Miranda, was arrested at his home and taken in custody to a Phoenix police station. He was there identified by the complaining witness. The police then took him to "Interrogation Room No. 2" of the detective bureau. There he was questioned by two police officers. The officers admitted at trial that Miranda was not advised that he had a right to have an attorney present. Two hours later, the officers emerged from the interrogation room with a written confession signed by Miranda. At the top of the

statement was a typed paragraph stating that the confession was made voluntarily, without threats or promises of immunity and "with full knowledge of my legal rights, understanding any statement I make may be used against me."

At his trial before a jury, the written confession was admitted into evidence over the objection of defense counsel, and the officers testified to the prior oral confession made by Miranda during the interrogation. Miranda was found guilty of kidnapping and rape. He was sentenced to 20 to 30 years' imprisonment on each count, the sentences to run concurrently. On appeal, the Supreme Court of Arizona held that Miranda's constitutional rights were not violated in obtaining the confession and affirmed the conviction. 98 Ariz. 18, 401 P.(2d) 721. In reaching its decision, the court emphasized heavily the fact that Miranda did not specifically request counsel.

We reverse. From the testimony of the officers and by the admission of respondent, it is clear that Miranda was not in any way apprised of his right to consult with an attorney and to have one present during the interrogation, nor was his right not to be compelled to incriminate himself effectively protected in any other manner. Without these warnings the statements were inadmissible. The mere fact that he signed a statement which contained a typed-in clause stating that he had "full knowledge" of his "legal rights" does not approach the knowing and intelligent waiver required to relinquish constitutional rights. Cf. *Haynes* v. *State of Washington,* 373 U.S. 503, 512-513, 83 S.Ct. 1336, 1342, 10 L.Ed.(2d) 513 (1963);

Haley v. *State of Ohio*, 332 U.S. 596, 601, 36 O.O. 530, 68 S.Ct. 302, 304, 92 L.Ed. 224 (1948) (opinion of Mr. Justice DOUGLAS).

* * *

Mr. Justice CLARK, dissenting in Nos. 759, 760, and 761 and concurring in result in No. 584.

It is with regret that I find it necessary to write in these cases. However, I am unable to join the majority because its opinion goes too far on too little, while my dissenting brethren do not go quite far enough. Nor can I join in the Court's criticism of the present practices of police and investigatory agencies as to custodial interrogation. The materials it refers to as "police manuals" are, as I read them, merely writings in this field by professors and some police officers. Not one is shown by the record here to be the official manual of any police department, much less in universal use in crime detection. Moreover the examples of police brutality mentioned by the Court are rare exceptions to the thousands of cases that appear every year on the law reports. The police agencies—all the way from municipal and state forces to the federal bureaus—are responsible for law enforcement and public safety in this country. I am proud of their efforts, which in my view are not fairly characterized by the Court's opinion.

* * *

Mr. Justice HARLAN, whom Mr. Justice STEWART and Mr. Justice WHITE join, dissenting.

I believe the decision of the Court represents poor constitutional law and entails harmful consequences for the country at large. How serious these consequences may prove to be only time can tell. But the basic flaws in the Court's justification seem to me readily apparent now once all sides of the problem are considered.

* * *

IV. Conclusions.

All four of the cases involved here present express claims that confessions were inadmissible, not because of coercion in the traditional due process sense, but solely because of lack of counsel or lack of warnings concerning counsel and silence. For the reasons stated in this opinion, I would adhere to the due process test and reject the new requirements inaugurated by the Court. On this premise my disposition of each of these cases can be stated briefly.

In two of the three cases coming from state courts, *Miranda* v. *Arizona* (No. 759) and *Vignera* v. *New York* (No. 760), the confessions were held inadmissible and no other errors worth comment are alleged by petitioners. I would affirm in these two cases. The other state case is *California* v. *Stewart* (No. 584), where the state supreme court held the confession inadmissible and reversed the conviction. In that case I would dismiss the writ of certiorari on the ground that no final judgment is before us, 28 United States Code Section 1257 (1964 ed.); putting aside the new trial open to the State in any event, the confession itself has not even been finally excluded since the California Supreme Court left the State free to show proof of a waiver. If the merits of the decision in *Stewart* be reached, then I believe it should be reversed and the case remanded so the state supreme court may pass on the other claims available to respondent.

In the federal case, *Westover* v. *United States* (No. 761), a number of issues are raised by petitioner apart from the one already dealt with in this dissent. None of these other claims appears to me tenable, nor in this context to warrant extended discussion. It is urged that the confession was also inadmissible because not voluntary even measured by due process standards and because federal state cooperation brought the McNabb-Mallory rule into play under *Anderson* v. *United States*, 318 U.S. 350, 63 S.Ct. 599, 87 L.Ed. 829. However, the facts alleged fall well short of coercion in my view, and I believe the involvement of federal agents in petitioner's arrest and detention by the State too slight to invoke *Anderson*. I agree with the Government that the admission of the evidence now protested by petitioner was at most harmless error, and two final contentions—one involving weight of the evidence and another improper prosecutor comment—seem to me without merit. I would therefore affirm Westover's conviction.

In conclusion: Nothing in the letter or the spirit of the Constitution or in the precedents squares with the heavy handed and one-sided action that is so precipitously taken by the Court in the name of fulfilling its constitutional responsibilities. The foray which the Court takes today brings to mind the wise and farsighted words of Mr. Justice Jackson in *Douglas* v. *City of Jeannette*, 319 U.S. 157, 181, 63 S.Ct. 877, 889, 87 L.Ed. 1324 (separate opinion): "This Court is forever adding new stories to the temples of constitutional law, and the temples have a way of collapsing when one story too many is added."

[*Note. The dissenting opinion of* Mr. Justice WHITE, *with whom Mr.* Justice HARLAN *and* Mr. Justice STEWART *join, has been omitted.*]

MICHIGAN v. HARVEY

____ U.S. ____, 110 S. Ct. 1176 (1990)

Syllabus

Following respondent Harvey's arraignment on rape charges and the appointment of counsel for him, he told a police officer that he wanted to make a statement, but did not know whether he should talk to his lawyer. Although the record is unclear as to the entire context of the discussion, the officer told Harvey that he did not need to speak with his attorney, because "his lawyer was going to get a copy of the statement anyway." Harvey then signed a constitutional rights waiver form and made a statement detailing his version of the events on the night in question. When his testimony at his state-court bench trial conflicted with his statement to the police, the court allowed the State to use the statement to impeach his testimony. He was convicted of first-degree criminal sexual conduct, but the Michigan Court of Appeals reversed. That court ruled that the statement was inadmissible even for impeachment purposes, because it was taken in violation of Harvey's Sixth Amendment right to counsel, citing *Michigan v. Jackson*, 475 U.S. 625, 106 S. Ct. 1404, 89 L. Ed. 2d 631. The State concedes that the police transgressed the rule of *Jackson*, which held that once a defendant invokes his Sixth Amendment right to counsel, any waiver of that right—even if voluntary, knowing and intelligent under traditional standards—is presumed invalid if given in a police-initiated discussion, and that evidence obtained pursuant to that waiver is inadmissible in the prosecution's case-in-chief.

Held: A statement to police taken in violation of *Jackson* may be used to impeach a defendant's testimony. The Jackson rule is based on the identical "prophylactic rule" announced in *Edwards v. Arizona*, 451 U.S. 477, 101 S. Ct. 1880, 68 L. Ed. 2d 378, in the context of the Fifth Amendment privilege against self-incrimination during custodial interrogation. Moreover,

Harris v. New York, 401 U.S. 222, 91 S. Ct. 643, 28 L. Ed. 2d 1, and subsequent cases have held that voluntary statements taken in violation of Fifth Amendment prophylactic rules, while inadmissible in the prosecution's case-in-chief, may nevertheless be used to impeach the defendant's conflicting testimony. There is no reason for a different result in a *Jackson* case. Harvey's argument for distinguishing such cases—that because the adversial process is commenced at the time of a Jackson violation, postarraignment interrogations implicate the constitutional guarantee of the Sixth Amendment itself, whereas prearraignment Fifth Amendment violations relate only to procedural safeguards that are not themselves constitutionally protected rights—is without merit. Nothing in the Sixth Amendment prevents a suspect charged with a crime and represented by counsel from voluntarily choosing, on his own, to speak with police in the absence of an attorney. *Cf. Patterson v. Illinois*, 487 U.S. 285, 108 S. Ct. 2389, 101 L. Ed. 2d 261. Moreover, Harvey's view would render the *Jackson* rule wholly unnecessary, because even waivers given during *defendant-initiated* conversations would be *per se* involuntary or otherwise invalid, unless counsel were first notified. Harvey's alternative assertion—that the police officer who took his statement affirmatively mislead him as to the need for counsel and therefore violated the "core value" of the Sixth Amendment's constitutional guarantee, such that his purported waiver is invalid and the statement may not be used even for impeachment purposes—is also unavailing, since the present record is insufficient to determine whether there was a knowing and voluntary waiver of Sixth Amendment rights. Pp. 1179-82.

Reversed and remanded.

REHNQUIST, C.J., delivered the opinion of the Court, in which WHITE, O'CONNOR, SCALIA, and KENNEDY, JJ., joined. STEVENS, J., filed a dissenting opinion, in which BRENNAN, MARSHALL, and BLACKMUN, JJ. joined.

APPENDIX 1
FEDERAL RULES OF EVIDENCE

As amended through December 1, 1989

RULES OF EVIDENCE FOR
UNITED STATES COURTS AND MAGISTRATES

ARTICLE I: GENERAL PROVISIONS

RULE 101. Scope

These rules govern proceedings in the courts of the United States and before United States bankruptcy judges and United States magistrates, to the extent and with the exceptions stated in rule 1101.

(Amended, eff 10-1-87; 11-1-88).

RULE 102. Purpose and Construction

These rules shall be construed to secure fairness in administration, elimination of unjustifiable expense and delay, and promotion of growth and development of the law of evidence to the end that the truth may be ascertained and proceedings justly determined.

RULE 103. Rulings on Evidence

(a) Effect of erroneous ruling. Error may not be predicated upon a ruling which admits or excludes evidence unless a substantial right of the party is affected, and

(1) Objection. In case the ruling is one admitting evidence, a timely objection or motion to strike appears of record stating the specific ground of objection, if the specific ground was not apparent from the context; or

(2) Offer of proof. In case the ruling is one excluding evidence, the substance of the evidence was made known to the court by offer or was apparent from the context within which questions were asked.

(b) Record of offer and ruling. The court may add any other or further statement which shows the character of the evidence, the form in which it was offered, the objection made, and the ruling thereon. It may direct the making of an offer in question and answer form.

(c) Hearing of jury. In jury cases, proceedings shall be conducted, to the extent practicable, so as to prevent inadmissible evidence from being suggested to the jury by any means, such as making statements or offers of proof or asking questions in the hearing of the jury.

(d) Plain error. Nothing in this rule precludes taking notice of plain errors affecting substantial rights although they were not brought to the attention of the court.

RULE 104. Preliminary Questions

(a) Questions of admissibility generally. Preliminary questions concerning the qualification of a person to be a witness, the existence of a privilege, or the admissibility of evidence shall be determined by the court, subject to the provisions of subdivision (b). In making its determination it is not bound by the rules of evidence except those with respect to privileges.

(b) Relevancy conditioned on fact. When the relevancy evidence depends upon the fulfillment of a condition of fact, the court shall admit it upon, or subject to, the introduction of evidence sufficient to support a finding of the fulfillment of the condition.

(c) Hearing of the jury. Hearings on the admissibility of confessions shall in all cases be conducted out of the hearing of the jury. Hearings on other preliminary matters shall be so conducted when the interests of justice require, or when an accused is a witness and so requests.

(d) Testimony by accused. The accused does not, by testifying upon a preliminary matter, become subject to cross-examination as to other issues in the case.

(e) Weight and credibility. This rule does not limit the right of a party to introduce before the jury evidence relevant to weight or credibility.

(Amended, eff 10-1-87)

RULE 105. Limited Admissibility

When evidence which is admissible as to one party or for one purpose but not admissible as to another party or for another purpose is admitted, the court, upon request, shall restrict the evidence to its proper scope and instruct the jury accordingly.

RULE 106. Remainder of or Related Writings or Recorded Statements

When a writing or recorded statement or part thereof is introduced by a party, an adverse party may require the introduction at that time of any other party or any other writing or recorded statement which ought in fairness to be considered contemporaneously with it.

(Amended, eff 10-1-87)

ARTICLE II. JUDICIAL NOTICE

RULE 201. Judicial Notice of Adjudicative Facts

(a) Scope of rule. This rule governs only judicial notice of adjudicative facts.

(b) Kinds of facts. A judicially noticed fact must be one not subject to reasonable dispute in that it is either (1) generally known within the territorial jurisdiction of the trial court or (2) capable of accurate and ready determination by resort to sources whose accuracy cannot readily be questioned.

(c) When discretionary. A court may take judicial notice, whether requested or not.

(d) When mandatory. A court shall take judicial notice if requested by a party and supplied with the necessary information.

(e) Opportunity to be heard. A party is entitled upon timely request to an opportunity to be heard as to the propriety of taking judicial notice and the tenor of the matter noticed. In the absence of prior notification, the request may be made after judicial notice has been taken.

(f) Time of taking notice. Judicial notice may be taken at any stage of the proceeding.

(g) Instructing jury. In a civil action or proceeding, the court shall instruct the jury to accept as conclusive any fact judicially noticed. In a criminal case, the court shall instruct the jury that it may, but is not required to, accept as conclusive any fact judicially noticed.

ARTICLE III. PRESUMPTIONS IN CIVIL ACTIONS AND PROCEEDINGS

RULE 301. Presumptions in General in Civil Actions and Proceedings

In all civil actions and proceedings not otherwise provided for by Act of Congress or by these rules, a presumption imposes on the party against whom it is directed the burden of going forward with evidence to rebut or meet the presumption, but does not shift to such party the burden of proof in the sense of the risk of nonpersuasion, which remains throughout the trial upon the party on whom it was originally cast.

RULE 302. Applicability of State Law in Civil Actions and Proceedings

In civil actions and proceedings, the effect of a presumption respecting a fact which is an element of a claim or defense as to which State law supplies the rule of decision is determined in accordance with State law.

ARTICLE IV. RELEVANCY AND ITS LIMITS

RULE 401. Definition of "Relevant Evidence"

"Relevant evidence" means evidence having any tendency to make the existence of any fact that is of consequence to the determination of the action more probable or less probable than it would be without the evidence.

RULE 402. Relevant Evidence Generally Admissible; Irrelevant Evidence Inadmissible

All relevant evidence is admissible, except as otherwise provided by the Constitution of the United States, by Act of Congress, by these rules, or by other rules prescribed by the Supreme Court pursuant to statutory authority. Evidence which is not relevant is not admissible.

RULE 403. Exclusion of Relevant Evidence on Grounds of Prejudice, Confusion, or Waste of Time

Although relevant evidence may be excluded if its probative value is substantially outweighed by the danger of unfair prejudice, confusion of the issues, or misleading the jury, or by considerations of undue delay, waste of time, or needless presentation of cumulative service.

RULE 404. Character Evidence Not Admissible To Prove Conduct; Exceptions; Other Crimes

(a) **Character evidence generally.** Evidence of a person's character or trait of character is not admissible for the purpose of proving action in conforming therewith on a particular occasion, except:

(1) **Character of accused.** Evidence of a pertinent trait of character offered by an accused, or by the prosecution to rebut the same;

(2) **Character of victim.** Evidence of a pertinent trait of character of the victim of the crime offered by an accused, or by the prosecution to rebut the same, or evidence of a character trait of peacefulness of the victim offered by the prosecution in a homi-

cide case to rebut evidence that the victim was the first aggressor;

(3) Character of witness. Evidence of the character of witness, as provided in Rules 607, 608 and 609.

(b) Other crimes, wrongs, or acts. Evidence of other crimes, wrongs, or acts is not admissible to prove the character of a person in order to show action in conformity therewith. It may, however, be admissible for other purposes, such as proof of motive, opportunity, intent, preparation, plan, knowledge, identity, or absence of mistake or accident.

(Amended, eff 10-1-87)

RULE 405. Methods of Proving Character

(a) Reputation or opinion. In all cases in which evidence of character or trait of character of a person is admissible, proof may be made by testimony as to reputation or by testimony in the form of an opinion. On cross-examination, inquiry is allowable into relevant instances of conduct.

(b) Specific instances of conduct. In cases in which character or a trait of character of a person is an essential element of a charge, claim, or defense, proof may also be made of specific instances of that person's conduct.

(Amended, eff 10-1-87)

RULE 406. Habit; Routine Practice

Evidence of the habit of a person or of the routine practices of an organization, whether corroborated or not and regardless of the presence of eyewitnesses, is relevant to prove that the conduct of the person or organization on a particular occasion was in conformity with the habit or routine practice.

RULE 407. Subsequent Remedial Measures

When, after an event, measures are taken which, if taken previously, would have made the event less likely to occur, evidence of the subsequent measures is not admissible to prove negligence or culpable conduct in connection with the event. This rule does not require the exclusion of evidence of subsequent measures when offered for another purposes, such as proving ownership, control, or feasibility of precautionary measures, if controverted, or impeachment.

RULE 408. Compromise and Offers to Compromise

Evidence of (1) furnishing or offering or promising to furnish or (2) accepting or offering or promising to accept, a valuable consideration in compromising or attempting to compromise a claim which was disputed as to either validity or amount, is not admissible to prove liability for or invalidity of the claim or its amount. Evidence of conduct or statements made in compromise negotiations is likewise not admissible. This rule does not require the exclusion of any evidence otherwise discoverable merely because it is presented in the course of compromise negotiations. This rule does not require exclusion when the evidence is offered for another purpose, such as proving bias or prejudice of a witness, negativing a contention of undue delay, or proving an effort to obstruct a criminal investigation or prosecution.

RULE 409. Payment of Medical and Similar Expenses

Evidence of furnishing or offering or promising to pay medical, hospital, or similar expenses occasioned by an injury is not admissible to prove liability for the injury.

RULE 410. Inadmissibility of Pleas, Plea Discussions, and Related Statements

Except as otherwise provided in this rule, evidence of the following is not, in any civil or criminal proceeding, admissible against the defendant who made the plea or was a participant in the plea discussions:

(1) a plea of guilty which was later withdrawn;

(2) a plea of nolo contendere;

(3) any statement made in the course of any proceedings under Rule 11 of the Federal Rules of Criminal Procedure or comparable state procedure regarding either of the foregoing pleas; or

(4) any statement made in the course of plea discussions with an attorney for the prosecuting authority which do not result in a plea of guilty or which result in a plea of guilty later withdrawn.

However, such a statement is admissible (i) in any proceeding wherein another statement made in the course of the same plea or plea discussions has been introduced and the statement ought in fairness be considered contemporaneously with it, or (ii) in a criminal proceeding for perjury or false statement if the statement was made by the defendant under oath, on the record and in the presence of counsel.

(Amended, 12-12-75; 4-30-79, eff 12-1-80)

RULE 411. Liability Insurance

Evidence that a person was or was not insured against liability is not admissible upon the issue whether the person acted negligently or otherwise wrongfully. This rule does not require the exclusion of evidence of insurance against liability when offered for another purpose, such as proof of agency, ownership, or control, or bias or prejudice of a witness.

(Amended, eff 10-1-87)

RULE 412. Rape Cases; Relevance of Victim's Past Behavior

(a) Notwithstanding any other provision of law, in a criminal case in which a person is accused of rape or of assault with intent to commit rape, reputation or opinion evidence of the past sexual behavior of an alleged victim of such rape or assault is not admissible.

(b) Notwithstanding any other provision of law, in a criminal case in which a person is accused of rape or of assault with intent to commit rape, evidence of a victim's past sexual behavior other than reputation or opinion evidence is also not admissible, unless such evidence other than reputation or opinion evidence is—

(1) admitted in accordance with subdivisions (c)(1) and (c)(2) and is constitutionally required to be admitted; or

(2) admitted in accordance with subdivision (c) and is evidence of—

(A) past sexual behavior with persons other than accused, offered by the accused upon the issue of whether the accused was or was not, with respect to the alleged victim, the source of semen or injury; or

(B) past sexual behavior with the accused and is offered by the accused upon the issue of whether the alleged victim consented to the sexual behavior with respect to which rape or assault is alleged.

(c)(1) If the person accused of committing rape or assault with intent to commit rape intends to offer under subdivision (b) evidence of specific instances of the alleged victim's past sexual behavior, the accused shall make a written motion to offer such evidence not later than fifteen days before the date on which the trial in which such evidence is to be offered is scheduled to begin, except that the court may allow the motion to be made at a later date, including during trial, if the court determined either that the evidence is newly discovered and could not have been obtained earlier through the exercise of due diligence or that the issue to which such evidence relates has newly arisen in the case. Any motion made under this paragraph shall be served on all other parties and on the alleged victim.

(2) The motion described in paragraph (1) shall be accompanied by a written offer of proof. If the court determined that the offer of proof contains evidence described in subdivision (b), the court shall order a hearing in chambers to determine if such evidence is admissible. At such hearing the parties may call witnesses, including the alleged victim, and offer relevant evidence. Notwithstanding subdivision (b) of Rule 104, if the relevancy of the evidence which the accused seeks to offer in the trial depends upon the fulfillment of a condition of fact, the court, at the hearing in chambers or at a subsequent hearing in chambers scheduled for such purpose, shall accept evidence on the issue of whether such condition of fact is fulfilled and shall determine such issue.

(3) If the court determines on the basis of the hearing described in paragraph (2) that the evidence which the accused seeks to offer is relevant and that the probative value of such evidence outweighs the danger of unfair prejudice, such evidence shall be admissible in the trial to the extent an order made by the court specifies evidence which may be offered and areas with respect to which the alleged victim may be examined or cross-examined.

(d) For purposes of this rule, the term "past sexual behavior" means sexual behavior other than the sexual behavior with respect to which rape or assault with intent to commit rape is alleged.

(Effective 11-28-78)

ARTICLE V. PRIVILEGES

RULE 501. General Rule

Except as otherwise required by the Constitution of the United States or provided by Act of Congress or in rules prescribed by the Supreme Court pursuant to statutory authority, the privilege of a witness, person, government, State, or political subdivision thereof shall be governed by the principles of the common law as they may be interpreted by the courts of the United States in the light of reason and experience. However, in civil actions and proceedings, with respect to an element of a claim or defense as to which State law supplies the rule of decision, the privilege of a witness, person, government, State, or political subdivision thereof shall be determined in accordance with State law.

ARTICLE VI. WITNESSES

RULE 601. General Rule of Competency

Every person is competent to be a witness except as otherwise provided in these rules. However, in civil actions and proceedings, with respect to an element of a claim or defense as to which State law supplies the rule of decision, the competency of a witness shall be determined in accordance with State law.

RULE 602. Lack of Personal Knowledge

A witness may not testify to a matter unless evidence is introduced to support a finding that the witness has personal knowledge of the matter. Evidence to prove personal knowledge may, but need not, consist of the witness' own testimony. This rule is subject to the provisions of rule 703, relating to opinion testimony by expert witnesses.

(Amended, eff 10-1-87; 11-1-88)

RULE 603. Oath or Affirmation

Before testifying, every witness shall be required to declare that the witness will testify truthfully, by oath or affirmation administered in a form calculated to awaken the witness' conscience and impress the witness' mind with the duty to do so.

(Amended, eff 10-1-87)

RULE 604. Interpreters

An interpreter is subject to the provisions of these rules relating to qualification as an expert and the administration of an oath or affirmation to make a true translation.

(Amended, eff 10-1-87)

RULE 605. Competency of Judge as Witness

The judge presiding at the trial may not testify in that trial as a witness. No objection need be made in order to preserve the point.

RULE 606. Competency of Juror as Witness

(a) At the trial. A member of the jury may not testify as a witness before that jury in the trial of the case in which the juror is sitting. If the juror is called so to testify, the opposing party shall be afforded an opportunity to object out of the presence of the jury.

(b) Inquiry into validity of verdict or indictment. Upon an inquiry into the validity of a verdict or indictment, a juror may not testify as to any matter or statement occurring during the course of the jury's deliberations or the effect of anything upon that or any other juror's mind or emotions as influencing the juror to assent to or dissent from the verdict or indictment or concerning the juror's mental processes in connection therewith, except that a juror may testify on the question whether extraneous prejudicial information was improperly brought to the jury's attention or whether any outside influence was improperly brought to bear upon any juror. Nor may a juror's affidavit or evidence of any statement by the juror concerning a matter about which the juror would be precluded from testifying be received for these purposes.

(Amended, eff 12-12-75; 10-1-87)

RULE 607. Who May Impeach

The credibility of a witness may be attacked by any party, including the party calling the witness.

(Amended, eff 10-1-87)

RULE 608. Evidence of Character and Conduct of Witness

(a) Opinion and reputation evidence of character. The credibility of a witness may be attacked or supported by evidence in the form of opinion or reputation, but subject to these limitations: (1) the evidence may refer only to character for truthfulness or untruthfulness, and (2) evidence of truthful character is admissible only after the character of the witness for truthfulness has been attacked by opinion or reputation evidence or otherwise.

(b) Specific instances of conduct. Specific instances of the conduct of a witness, for the purpose of attacking or supporting the witness' credibility, other than conviction of crime as provided in rule 609, may not be proved by extrinsic evidence. They may, however, in the discretion of the court, if probative of truthfulness or untruthfulness, be inquired into on cross-examination of the witness (1) concerning the witness' character for truthfulness or untruthfulness, or (2) concerning the character for truthfulness or untruthfulness of another witness as to which character the witness being cross-examined has testified.

The giving of testimony, whether by an accused or by any other witness, does not operate as a waiver of the accused's or the witness' privilege against self-incrimination when examined with respect to matters which relate only to credibility.

(Amended, eff 10-1-87; 11-1-88)

RULE 609. Impeachment by Evidence of Conviction of Crime

(a) General rule. For the purpose of attacking the credibility of a witness, evidence that the witness has been convicted of a crime shall be admitted if elicited from the witness or established by public record during cross-examination but only if the crime (1) was punishable by death or imprisonment in excess of one year under the law under which the witness was convicted, and the court determines that the probative value of admitting this evidence outweighs its prejudicial effect to the defendant, or (2) involved dishonesty or false statement, regardless of the punishment.

(b) Time limit. Evidence of a conviction under this rule is not admissible if a period of more than ten years has elapsed since the date of the conviction or of the release of the witness from the confinement imposed for that conviction, whichever is the later date, unless the court determined, in the interests of justice, that the probative value of the conviction supported by specific facts and circumstances substantially outweighs its prejudicial effect. However, evidence of a conviction more than 10 years old as calculated herein, is not admissible unless the proponent gives to the adverse party sufficient advance written notice of intent to use such evidence to provide the adverse party with a fair opportunity to contest the use of such evidence.

(c) Effect of pardon, annulment, or certificate of rehabilitation. Evidence of a conviction is not admissible under this rule if (1) the conviction has been the subject of a pardon, annulment, certificate of rehabilitation, or other equivalent procedure based on a finding of the rehabilitation of the person convicted, and that person has not been convicted of a subsequent crime which was punishable by death or imprisonment in excess of one year, or (2) the conviction has been the subject of a pardon, annulment or other equivalent procedure based on a finding of innocence.

(d) Juvenile adjudications. Evidence of juvenile adjudications is generally not admissible under this rule. The court may, however, in a criminal case allow evidence of a juvenile adjudication of a witness other than the accused if conviction of the offense would be admissible to attack the credibility of an adult and the court is satisfied that admission in evidence is necessary for a fair determination of the issue of guilt or innocence.

(e) Pendency of appeal. The pendency of an appeal therefrom does not render evidence of a conviction inadmissible. Evidence of the pendency of an appeal is admissible.

(Amended, eff 10-1-87)

RULE 610. Religious Beliefs or Opinions

Evidence of the beliefs or opinions of a witness on matters of religion is not admissible for the purpose of showing that by reason of their nature the witness' credibility is impaired or enhanced.

(Amended, eff 10-1-87)

RULE 611. Mode and Order of Interrogation and Presentation

(a) Control by court. The Court shall exercise reasonable control over the mode and order of interrogating witnesses and presenting evidence so as to (1) make the interrogation and presentation effective for the ascertainment of the truth, (2) avoid needless consumption of time and, (3) protect witnesses from harassment or undue embarrassment.

(b) Scope of cross-examination. Cross-examination should be limited to the subject matter of the direct examination and matters affecting the credibility of the witness. The court may, in the exercise of discretion, permit inquiry into additional matters as if on direct examination.

(c) Leading questions. Leading questions should not be used on the direct examination of a witness except as may be necessary to develop the witness' testimony. Ordinarily leading questions should be permitted on cross-examination. When a party calls a hostile witness, an adverse party, or a witness identified with an adverse party, interrogation may be by leading questions.

(Amended, eff 10-1-87)

RULE 612. Writing Used To Refresh Memory

Except as otherwise provided in criminal proceedings by section 3500 of title 18, United States Code, if a witness uses a writing to refresh memory for the purpose of testifying, either—

(1) while testifying, or

(2) before testifying, if the court in its discretion determines it is necessary in the interests of justice,

an adverse party is entitled to have the writing produced at the hearing, to inspect it, to cross-examine the witness thereon, and to introduce in evidence those portions which relate to the testimony of the witness. If it is claimed that the writing contains matters not related to the subject matter of the testimony the court shall examine the writing in camera, excise any portions not so related, and order delivery of the remainder to the party entitled thereto. Any portion withheld over objections shall be preserved and made available to the appellate court in the event of an appeal. If a writing is not produced or delivered pursuant to order under this rule, the court shall make any order justice requires, except that in criminal cases when the prosecution elects not to comply, the order shall be one striking the testimony or, if the court in its discretion determines that the interests of justice so require, declaring a mistrial.

(Amended, eff 10-1-87)

RULE 613. Prior Statements of Witnesses

(a) Examining witness concerning prior statement. In examining a witness concerning a prior statement made by the witness, whether written or not, the statement need not be shown nor its contents disclosed to the witness at that time, but on request the same shall be shown or disclosed to opposing counsel.

(b) Extrinsic evidence of prior inconsistent statement of witness. Extrinsic evidence of a prior inconsistent statement by a witness is not admissible unless the witness is afforded an opportunity to explain or deny the same and the opposite party is afforded an opportunity to interrogate the witness thereon, or the interests of justice otherwise require. This provision does not apply to admissions of a party-opponent as defined in rule 801(d)(2).

(Amended, eff 10-1-87; 11-1-88)

RULE 614. Calling and Interrogation of Witnesses by Court

(a) Calling by court. The court may, on its own motion or at the suggestion of a party, call witnesses, and all parties are entitled to cross-examine witnesses thus called.

(b) Interrogation by court. The court may interrogate witnesses, whether called by itself or by a party.

(c) Objections. Objections to the calling of witnesses by the court or to interrogation by it may be made at the time or at the next available opportunity when the jury is not present.

RULE 615. Exclusion of Witnesses

At the request of a party the court shall order witnesses excluded so that they cannot hear the testimony of other witnesses, and it may make the order of its own motion. This rule does not authorize exclusion of (1) a party who is a natural person, or (2) an officer or employee of a party which is not a natural person designated as its representative by its attorney, or (3) a person whose presence is shown by a party to be essential to the presentation of the party's cause.

(Amended, eff 10-1-87; 11-1-88)

ARTICLE VII. OPINIONS AND EXPERT TESTIMONY

RULE 701. Opinion Testimony by Lay Witnesses

If the witness is not testifying as an expert, the witness' testimony in the form of opinions or inferences is limited to those opinions or inferences which are (a) rationally based on the perception of the witness and (b) helpful to a clear understanding of the witness' testimony or the determination of a fact in issue.

(Amended, eff 10-1-87)

RULE 702. Testimony by Experts

If scientific, technical, or other specialized knowledge can assist the trier of fact to understand the evidence or to determine a fact in issue, a witness qualified as an expert by knowledge, skill, experience, training, or education, may testify thereto in the form of an opinion or otherwise.

RULE 703. Bases of Opinion Testimony

The facts or data in the particular case upon which an expert bases an opinion or inference may be those perceived by or made known to the expert at or before the hearing. If of a type reasonably relied upon by experts in the particular

field in forming opinions or inferences upon the subject, the facts or data need not be admissible in evidence.
(Amended, eff 10-1-87)

RULE 704. Opinion on Ultimate Issue

(a) Except as provided in subdivision (b), testimony in the form of an opinion or inference otherwise admissible is not objectionable because it embraces an ultimate issue to be decided by the trier of fact.

(b) No expert witness testifying with respect to the mental state or condition of a defendant in a criminal case may state an opinion or inference as to whether the defendant did or did not have the mental state or condition constituting an element of the crime charged or of a defense thereto. Such ultimate issues are matters for the trier of fact alone.
(Amended, eff 10-12-84)

RULE 705. Disclosure of Facts or Data Underlying Expert Opinion

The expert may testify in terms of opinion or inference and give reasons therefor without prior disclosure of the underlying facts or data, unless the court requires otherwise. The expert may in any event be required to disclose the underlying facts or data on cross-examination.
(Amended, eff 10-1-87)

RULE 706. Court Appointed Experts

(a) **Appointment.** The court may on its own motion or on the motion of any party enter an order to show cause why expert witnesses should not be appointed, and may request the parties to submit nominations. The court may appoint any expert witnesses agreed upon by the parties, and may appoint expert witnesses of its own selection. An expert witness shall not be appointed by the court unless the witness consents to act. A witness so appointed shall be informed of the witness' duties by the court in writing, a copy of which shall be filed with the clerk, or at a conference in which the parties shall have opportunity to participate. A witness so appointed shall advise the parties of the witness' findings, if any; the witness' deposition may be taken by any party; and the witness may be called to testify by the court or any party. The witness shall be subject to cross-examination by each party, including a party calling the witness.

(b) **Compensation.** Expert witnesses so appointed are entitled to reasonable compensation in whatever sum the court may allow. The compensation thus fixed is payable from funds which may be provided by law in criminal cases and civil actions and proceedings involving just compensation under the fifth amendment. In other civil actions and proceedings the compensation shall be paid by the parties in such proportion and at such time as the court directs, and thereafter charged in like manner as other costs.

(c) **Disclosure of appointment.** In the exercise of its discretion, the court may authorize disclosure to the jury of the fact that the court appointed the expert witness.

(d) **Parties' experts of own selection.** Nothing in this rule limits the parties in calling expert witnesses of their own selection.
(Amended, eff 10-1-87)

ARTICLE VII. HEARSAY

RULE 801. Definitions

The following definitions apply under this article:

(a) Statement. A "statement" is (1) an oral or written assertion or (2) non-verbal conduct of a person, if it is intended by the person as an assertion.

(b) Declarant. A "declarant" is a person who makes a statement.

(c) Hearsay. "Hearsay" is a statement, other than one made by the declarant while testifying at the trial or hearing, offered in evidence to prove the truth of the matter asserted.

(d) Statements which are not hearsay. A statement is not hearsay if—

(1) Prior statement by witness. The declarant testifies at trial or hearing and is subject to cross-examination concerning the statement, and the statement is (A) inconsistent with the declarant's testimony, and was given under oath subject to the penalty of perjury at a trial hearing, or other proceeding, or in a deposition, or (B) consistent with the declarant's testimony and is offered to rebut an express or implied charge against the declarant of recent fabrication or improper influence or motive, or (C) one of identification of a person made after perceiving the person; or

(2) Admission by party-opponent. The statement is offered against a party and is (A) the party's own statement, in either an individual or a representative capacity or (B) a statement of which the party has manifested an adoption or belief in its truth, or (C) a statement made by a person authorized by the party to make a statement concerning the subject, or (D) a statement by the party's agent or servant concerning a matter within the scope of the agency or employment, made during the existence of the relationship, or (E) a statement by a coconspirator of a party during the course and in furtherance of the conspiracy.

(Amended, eff 10-31-75; 10-1-87)

RULE 802. Hearsay Rule

Hearsay is not admissible except as provided by these rules or by other rules prescribed by the Supreme Court pursuant to statutory authority or by Act of Congress.

RULE 803. Hearsay Exceptions; Availability of Declarant Immaterial

The following are not excluded by the hearsay rule, even though the declarant is available as a witness:

(1) Present sense impression. A statement describing or explaining an event or condition made while the declarant was perceiving the event.

(2) Excited utterance. A statement relating to a startling event or condition made while the declarant was under the stress of excitement caused by the event or condition.

(3) Then existing, mental, emotional, or physical condition. Statement of the declarant's then existing state of mind, emotion, sensation, or physical condition (such as intent, plan, motive, design, mental feeling, pain, and bodily health), but not including a statement of memory or belief to prove the fact remembered or believed unless it relates to the execution, revocation, identification, or terms of declarant's will.

(4) Statements for purposes of medical diagnosis or treatment. Statements made for purposes of medical diagnosis or treatment and describing medical history, or past or present symptoms, pain, or sensations, or the inception or general character of the cause or external source thereof insofar as reasonably pertinent to diagnosis or treatment.

(5) Recorded recollection. A memorandum or record concerning a matter about which a witness once had knowledge but now has insufficient recollection to enable the witness to testify fully and accurately, shown to have been made or adopted by the witness when the matter was fresh in the witness memory and to reflect that knowledge correctly. If admitted, the memorandum or record may be read into evidence but may not itself be received as an exhibit unless offered by an adverse party.

(6) Records of regularly conducted activity. A memorandum, report, record, or data compilation, in any form, of acts, events, conditions, opinions, or diagnoses, made at or near the time by, or from information transmitted by, a person with knowledge, if kept in the course of a regularly conducted business activity, and if it was the regular practice of that business activity to make the memorandum, report, record, or data compilation, all as shown by the testimony of the custodian or other qualified witness, unless the source of information or the method or circumstances of preparation indicate

lack of trustworthiness. The term "business" as used in this paragraph includes business, institution, association, profession, occupation, and calling of every kind, whether or not conducted for profit.

(7) Absence of entry in records kept in accordance with the provisions of paragraph (6). Evidence that a matter is not included in the memoranda, reports, records, or data compilations, in any form, kept in accordance with the provisions of paragraph (6) to prove nonoccurrence or nonexistence of the matter, if the matter was of a kind of which a memorandum, report, record, or data compilation was regularly made and preserved, unless the sources of information or other circumstances indicate lack of trustworthiness.

(8) Public records and reports. Records, reports, statements, or data compilations, in any form, of public offices or agencies, setting forth (A) the activities of the office or agency, or (B) matters observed pursuant to duty imposed by law as to which matters there was a duty to report, excluding, however, in criminal cases matters observed by police officers and other law enforcement personnel, or (C) in civil actions and proceedings and against the government in criminal cases, factual findings resulting from an investigation made pursuant to authority granted by law, unless the sources of information or other circumstances indicate lack of trustworthiness.

(9) Records of vital statistics. Records or data compilations, in any form, of births, fetal deaths, deaths, or marriages, if the report thereof was made to a public office pursuant to requirements of law.

(10) Absence of public record or entry. To prove the absence of a record, report, statement, or data compilation, in any form, or the nonoccurrence or nonexistence of a matter of which a record, report, statement, or data compilation, in any form, was regularly made and preserved by a public office or agency, evidence in the form of a certification in accordance with Rule 902, or testimony, that diligent search failed to disclose the record, report, statement, or data compilation, or entry.

(11) Records of religious organizations. Statements of births, marriages, divorces, deaths, legitimacy, ancestry, relationship by blood or marriage, or other similar facts of personal or family history, contained in a regularly kept record of a religious organization.

(12) Marriage, baptismal, and similar certificates. Statements of fact contained in a certificate that the maker performed a marriage or other ceremony or administered a sacrament, made by a clergyman, public official, or other person authorized by the rules or practices of a religious organization or by law to perform the act certified, and purporting to have been issued at the time of the act or within a reasonable time thereafter.

(13) Family records. Statements of fact concerning personal or family history contained in family Bibles, genealogies, charts, engravings on rings, inscriptions on family portraits, engravings on urns, crypts, or tombstones, or the like.

(14) Records of documents affecting an interest in property. The record of a document purporting to establish or affect an interest in property, as proof of the content of the original document and its execution and delivery by each person by whom it purports to have been executed, if the record is a record of a public office and an applicable statute authorizes the recording of documents of that kind in that office.

(15) Statements in documents affecting an interest in property. A statement contained in a document purporting to establish or affect an interest in property if the matter stated was relevant to the purpose of the document, unless dealings made with the property since the document was made have been inconsistent with the truth of the statement or the purport of the document.

(16) Statements in ancient documents. Statements in a document in existence twenty years or more the authenticity of which is established.

(17) Market reports, commercial publications. Market quotations, tabulations, lists, directories, or other published compilations, generally used and relied upon by the public or by persons in particular occupations.

(18) Learned Treatises. To the extent called to the attention of an expert witness upon cross-examination or relied upon by the expert witness in direct examination, statements contained in published treatises, periodicals, or pamphlets on a subject of history, medicine, or other science or art, established as a reliable authority by the testimony or admission of the witness or by other expert testimony or by judicial notice. If admitted, the statements may be read into evidence but may not be received as exhibits.

(19) Reputation concerning personal or family history. Reputation among members of a person's family by blood, adoption, or marriage or among a person's associates, or in the community, concerning a person's birth, adoption, marriage, divorce, death, legitimacy, relationship by blood, adoption, or marriage, ancestry, or other similar fact of personal or family history.

(20) Reputation concerning boundaries or general history. Reputation in a community, arising before the controversy, as to boundaries of or customs affecting lands in the community, and reputation as to events of general history important to the community or State or nation in which located.

(21) Reputation as to character. Reputation of a person's character among associates or in the community.

(22) Judgment of previous conviction. Evidence of a final judgment, entered after a trial or upon a plea of guilty (but not upon a plea of nolo contendere), adjudging a person guilty of a crime punishable by death or imprisonment in excess of one year, to prove any fact essential to sustain the judgment, but not including, when offered by the Government in a criminal prosecution for purposes other than impeachment, judgments against persons other than the accused. The pendency of an appeal may be shown but does not affect admissibility.

(23) Judgment as to personal, family, or general history, or boundaries. Judgments as proof of matters of family, or general history, or boundaries, essential to the judgment, if the same would be provable by evidence of reputation.

(24) Other exceptions. A statement not specifically covered by any of the foregoing exceptions but having equivalent circumstantial guarantees of trustworthiness, if the court determined that (A) the statement is offered as evidence of a material fact; (B) the statement is more probative on the point for which the proponent can procure through reasonable efforts; and (C) the general purposes of these rules and the interests of justice will be served by admission of the evidence. However, a statement may not be admitted under this exception unless the proponent of it makes known to the adverse party sufficiently in advance of the trial or hearing to provide the adverse party with a fair opportunity to prepare to meet it, the proponent's intention to offer the statement and the particulars of it, including the name and address of the declarant.

(Amended, eff 12-12-75; 10-1-87)

RULE 804. Hearsay Exceptions: Declarant Unavailable

(a) Definition of unavailability. "Unavailability as a witness" includes situations in which the declarant—

(1) is exempted by ruling of the court on the ground of privilege from testifying concerning the subject matter of the declarant's statement; or

(2) persists in refusing to testify concerning the subject matter of the declarant's statement; or

(3) testifies to a lack of memory of the subject matter of the declarant's statement; or

(4) is unable to be present or to testify at the hearing because of death or then existing physical or mental illness or infirmity; or

(5) is absent from the hearing and the proponent of a statement has been unable to procure the declarant's subdivisions (b)(2), (3), or (4) the declarant's attendance or testimony by process or other reasonable means.

A declarant is not unavailable as a witness if exemption, refusal, claim of lack of memory, inability, or absence due to the procurement or wrongdoing of the proponent of a statement for the purpose of preventing the witness from attending or testifying.

(b) Hearsay exceptions. The following are not excluded by the hearsay rule if the declarant is unavailable as a witness:

(1) Former testimony. Testimony given as a witness at another hearing of the same or a different proceeding, or in a deposition taken in compliance with law in the course of the same or another proceeding, if the party against whom the testimony is now offered, or, in a civil action or proceeding, a predecessor in interest, had an opportunity and similar motive to develop the testimony by direct, cross, or redirect examination.

(2) Statement under belief of impending death. In a prosecution for homicide or in a civil action or proceeding, a statement made by a declarant while believing that the declarant's death was imminent, concerning the cause or circumstances of what the declarant believed to be impending death.

(3) Statement against interest. A statement which was at the time of its making so far contrary to the declarant's pecuniary or proprietary interest, or so far tended to subject the declarant to civil or criminal liability, or to render invalid a claim by the declarant against another, that a reasonable person in the declarant's position would not have made the statement unless believing it to be true. A statement tending to expose the declarant to criminal liability and offered to exculpate the accused, is not admissible unless corroborating circumstances clearly indicate the trustworthiness of the statement.

(4) Statement of personal or family history. (A) A statement concerning the declarant's own birth, adoption, marriage, divorce, legitimacy, relationship by blood, adoption, or marriage, ancestry, or other similar fact of personal or family history, even though declarant had no means of acquiring personal knowledge of the matter stated; or (B) a statement concerning the foregoing matters, and death also, of another person, if the declarant was related to the other by blood, adoption, or marriage or was so intimately associated with the other's family as to be likely to have accurate information concerning the matter declared.

(5) Other exceptions. A statement not specifically covered by any of the foregoing exceptions but having equivalent circumstantial guarantees of trustworthiness, if the court determines that (A) the statement is offered as evidence of a material fact;

(B) the statement is more probative than any other evidence which the proponent can procure through reasonable efforts; and (C) the general purposes of these rules and the interest of justice will best be served by admission of the statement into evidence. However, a statement may not be admitted under this exception unless the proponent of it makes known to the adverse party sufficiently in advance of the trial or hearing to provide the adverse party with a fair opportunity to prepare to meet it, the proponent's intention to offer the statement and the particulars of it, including the name and address of the declarant.

(Amended, eff 12-12-75; 10-1-87)

RULE 805. Hearsay Within Hearsay

Hearsay included within hearsay is not excluded under the hearsay rule if each part of the combined statements conforms with an exception to the hearsay rule provided in these rules.

RULE 806. Attacking and Supporting Credibility of Declarant

When a hearsay statement, or a statement defined in Rule 801(d)(2), (C), (D), or (E), has been admitted in evidence, the credibility of the declarant may be attacked, and if attacked may be supported, by any evidence which would be admissible for those purposes if declarant had testified as a witness. Evidence of a statement or conduct by the declarant at any time, inconsistent with the declarant's hearsay statement, is not subject to any requirement that the declarant may have been afforded an opportunity to deny or explain. If the party against whom a hearsay statement has been admitted calls the declarant as a witness, the party is entitled to examine the declarant on the statement as if under cross-examination.

(Amended, eff 10-1-87)

ARTICLE IX. AUTHENTICATION AND IDENTIFICATION

RULE 901. Requirement of Authentication or Identification

(a) **General provision.** The requirement of authentication or identification as a condition precedent to admissibility is satisfied by evidence sufficient to support a finding that the matter in question is what its proponent claims.

(b) **Illustrations.** By way of illustration only, and not by way of limitation, the following are examples of authentication or identification conforming with the requirements of this rule:

(1) **Testimony of witness with knowledge.** Testimony that a matter is what it is claimed to be.

(2) **Nonexpert opinion on handwriting.** Nonexpert opinion as to the genuineness of handwriting, based upon familiarity not acquired for purposes of the litigation.

(3) **Comparison by trier or expert witness.** Comparison by the trier of fact or by expert witnesses with specimens which have been authenticated.

(4) **Distinctive characteristics and the like.** Appearance, contents, substance, internal patterns, or other distinctive characteristics, taken in conjunction with circumstances.

(5) Voice Identification. Identification of a voice, whether heard firsthand or through mechanical or electronic transmission or recording, by opinion based upon hearing the voice at any time under circumstances connecting it with the alleged speaker.

(6) Telephone conversations. Telephone conversations, by evidence that a call was made to the number assigned at the time by the telephone company to a particular person or business, if (A) in the case of a person, circumstances, including self-identification, show the person answering to be the one called, or (B) in the case of a business, the call was made to a place of business and the conversation related to business reasonably transacted over the telephone.

(7) Public records or reports. Evidence that a writing authorized by law to be recorded or filed and in fact recorded or filed in a public office, or a purported public record, report, statement, or data compilation, in any form, is from the public office where items of this nature are kept.

(8) Ancient documents or data compilation. Evidence that a document or data compilation, in any form, (A) is in such condition as to create no suspicion concerning its authenticity, (B) was in a place where it, if authentic, would likely be, and (C) has been in existence twenty years or more at the time it is offered.

(9) Process or system. Evidence describing a process or system used to produce a result and showing that the process or system produces an accurate result.

(10) Methods provided by statute or rule. Any method of authentication or identification provided by Act of Congress or by other rules prescribed by the Supreme Court pursuant to statutory authority.

RULE 902. Self-authentication

Extrinsic evidence of authenticity as a condition precedent to admissibility is not required with respect to the following:

(1) Domestic public documents under seal. A document bearing a seal purporting to be that of the United States, or of any State, district, Commonwealth, territory, or insular possession thereof, or the Panama Canal Zone, or the Trust Territory of the Pacific Islands, or of a political subdivision, department, officer or agency thereof, and a signature purporting to be an attestation or execution.

(2) Domestic public documents not under seal. A document purporting to bear the signature in the official capacity of an officer or employee of any entity included in paragraph (1) hereof, having no seal, if a public officer having a seal and having official duties in the district or political subdivision of the officer or employee certifies under seal that the signer has the official capacity and that the signature is genuine.

(3) Foreign public documents. A document purporting to be executed or attested in an official capacity by a person authorized by the laws of a foreign country to make the execution or attestation, and accompanied by a final certification as to the genuineness of the signature and official position (A) of the executing or attesting person, or (B) of any foreign official whose certificate of genuineness of signature and official position relates to the execution or attestation or is in a chain of certificates of genuineness of signature and official position relating to the execution or attestation. A final certification may be made by a secretary of an embassy or legation, consul general, consul, vice consul, or consular agent of the United States, or a diplomatic or consular official of the foreign country assigned or accredited to the United States. If reasonable opportunity has been given to all parties to investigate the authenticity and accuracy of official documents, the court may, for good cause shown, order that they be treated as presumptively authentic without final certification or permit them to be evidenced by an attested summary with or without final certification.

(4) Certified copies of public records. A copy of an official record or of a document authorized by law to be recorded or filed in a public office, including data compilations in any form, certified as correct by the custodian or other person authorized to make the certification, by certificate complying with paragraph (1), (2), or (3) of this rule or complying with any Act of Congress or rule prescribed by the Supreme Court pursuant to statutory authority.

(5) Official publications. Books, pamphlets, or other publications purporting to be issued by public authority.

(6) Newspapers and periodicals. Printed material purporting to be newspapers or periodicals.

(7) Trade inscriptions and the like. Inscriptions, signs, tags, or labels purporting to have been affixed the course of business and indicating ownership, control, or origin.

(8) Acknowledged documents. Documents accompanied by a certificate of acknowledgment executed in the manner provided by a law by a notary public or other officer authorized by law to take acknowledgments.

(9) Commercial paper and related documents. Commercial paper, signatures thereon, and documents relating thereto to the extent provided by general commercial law.

(10) Presumptions under Acts of Congress. Any signature, document, or other matter declared by Act of Congress to be presumptively or prima facie genuine or authentic.

(Amended, eff 10-1-87; 11-1-88)

RULE 903. Subscribing Witness' Testimony Unnecessary.

The testimony of a subscribing witness is not necessary to authenticate a writing unless required by the laws of the jurisdiction whose laws govern the validity of the writing.

ARTICLE X. CONTENTS OF WRITINGS, RECORDINGS, AND PHOTOGRAPHS

RULE 1001. Definitions

For purposes of this article the following definitions are applicable.

(1) Writings and recordings. "Writings" and "recordings" consist of letters, words, or numbers, or their equivalent, set down by handwriting, typewriting, printing, photostating, photographing, magnetic impulse, mechanical or electronic recording, or other forms of data compilation.

(2) Photographs. "Photographs" include still pictures, X-ray films, video tapes, and motion pictures.

(3) Original. An "original" of a writing or recording is the writing or recording itself or any counterpart intended to have the same effect by a person executing or issuing it. An "original" of a photograph included the negative or any print therefrom. If data are stored in a computer or similar device, any printout or other output readable by sight, shown to reflect the data accurately, is an "original."

(4) Duplicate. A "duplicate" is a counterpart produced by the same impression as the original, or from the same matrix, or by means of photography, including enlargements and miniatures, or by mechanical or electronic re-recording, or by chemical reproduction, or by other equivalent techniques which accurately reproduces the original.

RULE 1002. Requirement of Original

To prove the content of a writing, recording or photograph, the original writing, recording, or photograph is required, except as otherwise provided in these rules or by Act of Congress.

RULE 1003 Admissibility of Duplicates

A duplicate is admissible to the same extent as an original unless (1) a genuine question is raised as to the authenticity of the original or (2) in the circumstances it would be unfair to admit the duplicate in lieu of the original.

RULE 1004. Admissibility of Other Evidence of Contents

The original is not required, and other evidence of the contents of a writing, recording, or photograph is admissible if—

(1) Originals have been lost or destroyed. All originals are lost or have been destroyed, unless the proponent lost or destroyed them in bad faith; or

(2) Original not obtainable. No original can be obtained by any available judicial process or procedure; or

(3) Original in possession of opponent. At at time when an original was under the control of the party against whom offered, that party was put on notice, by the pleadings or otherwise, that the contents would be a subject of proof at the hearing, and that party does not produce the original at the hearing; or

(4) Collateral matters. The writing, recording, or photograph is not closely related to a controlling issue.

(Amended, eff 10-1-87)

RULE 1005. Public Records

The contents of an official record, or of a document authorized to be recorded or filed and actually recorded or filed, including data compilations in any form, if otherwise admissible, may be proved by copy, certified as correct in accordance with Rule 902 or testified to be correct by a witness who has compared it with the original. If a copy which complies with the foregoing cannot be obtained by the exercise of reasonable diligence, then other evidence of the contents may be given.

RULE 1006. Summaries

The contents of voluminous writings, recordings, or photographs which cannot conveniently be examined in court may be presented in the form of a chart, summary, or calculation. The originals, or duplicates, shall be made available for examination or copying, or both, by other parties at reasonable time and place. The court may order that they be produced in court.

RULE 1007. Testimony or Written Admission of a Party

Contents of writings, recordings, or photographs may be proved by the testimony or deposition of the party against whom offered or by that party's written admission, without accounting for the nonproduction of the original.
(Amended, eff 10-1-87)

RULE 1008. Functions of Court and Jury

When the admissibility of other evidence of contents of writings, recordings, or photographs under these rules depends upon the fulfillment of a condition of fact, the question whether the condition has been fulfilled is ordinarily for the court to determine in accordance with the provisions of Rule 104. However, when an issue is raised (a) whether the asserted writing ever existed, or (b) whether another writing, recording, or photograph produced at the trial is the original, or (c) whether other evidence of contents correctly reflects the contents, the issue is for trier of fact to determine as in the case of other issues of fact.

ARTICLE XI. MISCELLANEOUS RULES

RULE 1101. Applicability of Rules

(a) Courts and magistrates. These rules apply to the United States district courts, the District Court of Guam, the District Court of the Virgin Islands, the District Court for the Northern Mariana Islands, the United States Courts of Appeals, the United States Claims Court, and to United States bankruptcy judges and United States magistrates, in the actions, cases, and proceedings and to the extent hereinafter set forth. The terms "judge" and "court" in these rules include United States bankruptcy judges and United States magistrates.

(b) Proceedings generally. These rules apply generally to civil actions and proceedings, including admiralty and maritime cases, to criminal cases and proceedin8gs, to contempt proceedings except those in which the court may act similarly, and to proceedings and cases under title 11, United States Code.

(c) Rule of privilege. The rule with respect to privileges applies at all stages of all actions, cases, and proceedings.

(d) Rules inapplicable. The rules (other than with respect to privileges) do not apply in the following situations:

(1) Preliminary question of fact. The determination of questions of fact preliminary to admissibility of evidence when the issue is to be determined by the court under Rule 104.

(2) Grand jury. Proceedings before grand juries.

(3) Miscellaneous proceedings. Proceedings for extradition or rendition; preliminary examinations in criminal cases; sentencing, or granting or revoking probation; issuance of warrants for arrest, criminal summonses, and search warrants; and proceedings with respect to release on bail or otherwise.

(e) Rules applicable in part. In the following proceedings these rules apply to the extent that matters of evidence are not provided for in statutes which govern procedure therein or in other rules prescribed by the Supreme Court pursuant to statutory authority; the trial of minor and petty offenses by United States magistrates; review of agency actions when the facts are subject to trial de novo under section 706(2)(F) of title 5, United States Code; review of orders of the Secretary of Agriculture under section 2 of the Act entitled "An Act to authorize association of producers of agricultural products" approved February 18, 1922 (7 U.S.C. 292), and under sections 6 and 7(c) of the Perishable Agricultural Commodities Act, 1930 (7 U.S.C. 499f, 499g(c); naturalization and revocation of naturalization under section 310-318 of the Immigration and Nationality Act (8 U.S.C. 1421-1429); prize proceedings in admiralty under sections 7651-7681 of title 10, United States Code; review of orders of the Secretary of the Interior under section 2 of the Act entitled "An Act authorizing associations of producers of aquatic products" approved June 25, 1934 (15 U.S.C. 522); review of orders of petroleum control boards under section 5 of the Act entitled "An Act to regulate interstate and foreign commerce in petroleum and its products by prohibiting the shipment in such commerce of petroleum and its products produced in violation of State law, and for other purposes," approved February 22, 1935 (15 U.S.C. 715d); actions for fines, penalties, or forfeitures under part V of title IV of the Tariff Act of 1930 (19 U.S.C. 1581-1624), or under the Anti-Smuggling Act (19 U.S.C. 1701-1711); criminal libel for condemnation, exclusion of imports, or other proceedings under the Federal Food, Drug, and Cosmetic Act (21 U.S.C. 301-392); disputes between seamen under sections 4079, 4080, and 4081 of the Revised Statutes (22 U.S.C. 256-258); habeas corpus under sections 2241-2254 of title 28, United States Code; motions to vacate, set aside or correct sentence under section 2255 of title 28, United States Code; actions for penalties for refusal to transport seamen under section 4578 of the Revised Statutes (46 U.S.C. 679); actions against the United States under the Act entitled "An Act authorizing suits against the United States in admiralty for damage caused by and salvage service rendered to public vessels belonging to the United States, and for other purposes," approved March 3, 1925 (46 U.S.C. 781-790), as implemented by section 7730 of title 10, United States Code.
(Amended, eff 12-12-75; 10-1-79; 10-1-82; 10-1-87; 11-1-88)

RULE 1102. Amendments

Amendments to the Federal Rules of Evidence may be made as provided in section 2076 of title 28 of the United States Code.

RULE 1103. Title

These rules may be known and cited as the Federal Rules of Evidence.

APPENDIX 2
TABLE OF JURISDICTIONS WHEREIN UNIFORM RULES OF EVIDENCE HAVE BEEN ADOPTED—1986

Jurisdiction	Laws	Effective Date	Statutory Citation
Alaska	Supp.Ct.Order 364	8-1-1979	A.R.E. Rules 101 to 1101.
Arizona		9-1-1977	17A A.R.S. Rules of Evid., Rules 101 to 1103.
Arkansas	1975, No. 1143	7-1-1976	A.C.A. § 16-41-101
Colorado		1-1-1980	C.R.S., Vol. 7B, Colorado Rules of Evidence, Rules 101 to 1102.
Delaware		7-1-1980	D.R.E. 101 to 1103.
Florida	1976, c. 76-237	7-1-1977	West's F.S.A. §§ 90.101 to 90.958.
Guam	Pub.L. 16-78	7-5-1982	6 G.C.A. §§ 101 to 1102.
Hawaii	L.1980, C. 164	1-1-1981	HRS §§ 626-1 (Hawaii Rules of Evidence Rules 100 to 1102) to 626-3.
Idaho		7-1-1985	Rules of Evidence, Rules 101 to 1103.
Louisiana	1988 Act 515	1-1-1989	LSA-Evid.Code, arts. 101 to 1103.
Maine		2-2-1976	Rules of Evidence, Rules 101 to 1102.
Michigan		3-1-1978	Rules of Evidence, Rules 101 to 1102.
Minnesota		7-1-1977	50 M.S.A.Evid. Rules 101 to 1101.
Mississippi	Sup.Ct.Order 9-24-1985	1-1-1986	M.R.E. 101 to 1103.
Montana	1976, En. Sup.Ct. Ord. 12729	7-1-1977	Rules of Evidence, Rules 100 to 1008.
Nebraska	1975, L.B. 279	8-24-1975	R.R.S.1943, §§ 27-101 to 27-1103.
Nevada	L.1971, c. 775		N.R.S. § 47.929 et seq.
New Hampshire		7-1-1985	Rules of Evidence, Rules 100 to 1103.
New Mexico	1973, S.C.Order	7-1-1973	N.M.R.Evid. Rules 101 to 1103.
North Carolina	1983, c. 701	7-1-1984	G.S. § 8B-1, Rules 101 to 1102.
North Dakota		2-15-1977	NDR Evid.Rules 101 to 1103.
Ohio		7-1-1980	Rules of Evidence, Rules 101 to 1103.
Oklahoma	1978, c. 285	10-1-1978	12 Okl.St.Ann. §§ 2101 to 3103.
Oregon	1981, c. 892	1-1-1982	ORS 40.010 to 40.585.
Puerto Rico		10-1-1979	32 L.P.R.A.App. IV Rules 1 to 84.
Rhode Island		1986*	Rules of Evidence, Rules 100 to 1008.
South Dakota	SDCL 19-9-1 to 19-18-8.		
Texas1		9-1-1983	Rules of Civil Evidence, Rules 101 to 1008.
		9-1-1986	Rules of Criminal Evidence, Rules 101 to 1101.
Utah		9-1-1983	Rules of Evidence, Rules 101 to 1103.
Vermont		4-1-1983	Rules of Evidence, Rules 101 to 1103.
Washington		4-2-1979	Rules of Evidence, Rules 101 to 1103.
West Virginia		2-1-1985	W.V.R.E., Rules 101 to 1102.
Wisconsin	Sup.Ct.Order, 59 W.(2d), page R9	1-1-1974	W.S.A. 901.01 to 911.02.
Wyoming		1-1-1978	Rules of Evidence, Rules 101 to 1104.

TABLE OF CASES

This listing includes all cases cited in the textual material of Part I. Those cases that appear in **bold face type** are also reprinted in Part II. For those select cases, see the *Table of Cases in Part II*, which appears on page 423.

INDEX